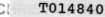
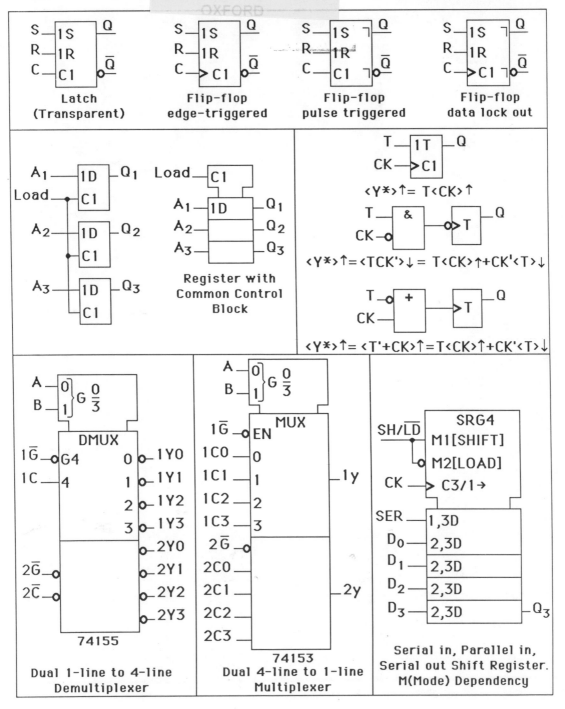

Latch
(Transparent)

Flip-flop
edge-triggered

Flip-flop
pulse triggered

Flip-flop
data lock out

Register with
Common Control
Block

$\langle Y*\rangle\uparrow = T\langle CK\rangle\uparrow$

$\langle Y*\rangle\uparrow = \langle TCK'\rangle\downarrow = T\langle CK\rangle\uparrow + CK'\langle T\rangle\downarrow$

$\langle Y*\rangle\uparrow = \langle T'+CK\rangle\uparrow = T\langle CK\rangle\uparrow + CK'\langle T\rangle\downarrow$

74155
Dual 1-line to 4-line
Demultiplexer

74153
Dual 4-line to 1-line
Multiplexer

Serial in, Parallel in,
Serial out Shift Register.
M(Mode) Dependency

XLV. 2. 740ᵇ

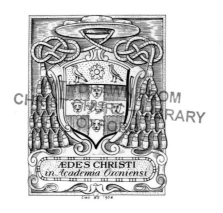

LOGIC
DESIGN
PRINCIPLES

LOGIC DESIGN PRINCIPLES

With Emphasis on Testable Semicustom Circuits

Edward J. McCluskey

Center for Reliable Computing
Stanford University

PRENTICE-HALL

Englewood Cliffs, New Jersey 07632

Library of Congress Cataloging-in-Publication Data

McCLUSKEY, EDWARD J. (date)
  Logic design principles.

  Includes bibliographies and index.
  1. Logic circuits. 2. Logic design. I. Title.
TK7868.L6M38 1986   621.395   85-28306
ISBN 0-13-539784-7

Editorial/production supervision and
  interior design: Reynold Rieger
Cover design: Photo Plus Art
Manufacturing buyer: Rhett Conklin

Printed in the United States of America

10 9 8 7 6 5 4 3 2 1

ISBN 0-13-539784-7 025

PRENTICE-HALL INTERNATIONAL (UK) LIMITED, *London*
PRENTICE-HALL OF AUSTRALIA PTY. LIMITED, *Sydney*
PRENTICE-HALL CANADA INC., *Toronto*
PRENTICE-HALL HISPANOAMERICANA, S.A., *Mexico*
PRENTICE-HALL OF INDIA PRIVATE LIMITED, *New Delhi*
PRENTICE-HALL OF JAPAN, INC., *Tokyo*
PRENTICE-HALL OF SOUTHEAST ASIA PTE. LTD., *Singapore*
EDITORA PRENTICE-HALL DO BRASIL, LTDA., *Rio de Janeiro*
WHITEHALL BOOKS LIMITED, *Wellington, New Zealand*

CONTENTS

4 INTEGRATED CIRCUITS 99

Contents

7 SEQUENTIAL CIRCUITS: FUNDAMENTAL-MODE ANALYSIS   273

Contents

Contents   **xi**

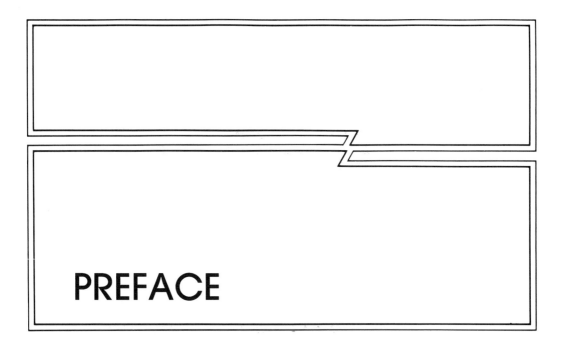

PREFACE

The purpose of this book is to teach the principles of good logic design. By a good logic design is meant one that not only meets its performance objectives in a cost effective manner, but one that can be tested economically as well. Another attribute that is emphasized is robustness, the ability to function correctly in spite of minor variations in component delays.

Those topics of switching theory that are relevant for practical design are covered; those topics that are of purely theoretical interest are omitted. This book is intended as a text for a lecture course or for individual study. Implementation details are omitted. They are better treated in a laboratory environment and in the appropriate laboratory manual; see for example J. F. Wakerly.[1]

Major features of this book are:

Design for Testability chapter
Use of new IEEE Standard for logic symbols
Thorough treatment of timing anomalies
Simplified but thorough coverage of synchronous logic
Careful complete presentation of latches and flip-flops

With the increased density of today's ICs, testing of these parts must be considered at the design stage and thus must be a concern of the logic designer. The Design for Testability chapter is included to permit this.

The IEEE standard symbols may appear strange at first glance, but in spite

[1] [Wakerly 76] Wakerly, J. F., *Logic Design Projects Using Standard Integrated Circuits*, John Wiley & Sons, New York, 1976.

of this initial negative reaction I have found them to be very effective in representing logic. Several manufacturers have already adopted them for their IC manuals and there is every indication that they will eventually become an industry as well as an IEEE standard. The best time to learn them is when learning logic design. They are introduced throughout the text along with the appropriate concept rather than as a separate topic, since learning symbols is not in itself a very interesting activity.

Timing anomalies such as hazards and metastability are being recognized as increasingly important for new designs. Accordingly they are treated very thoroughly in this book.

The treatment of synchronous logic has been simplified by eliminating purely theoretical topics. At the same time it has been made more useful by the inclusion of the structures such as two-phase and one-phase latch clocking systems. These structures are typically left out of textbooks, but are very common in actual systems.

The discussion of latches and flip-flops is very thorough and is integrated with the presentation of sequential circuits. A good understanding of the basic building blocks of sequential logic is increasingly important with the optimized designs now being produced.

USE OF THIS BOOK

This book was written for a one quarter course in logic design at Stanford University and has been used in this course for the past four years. This course is taken by entering Electrical Engineering or Computer Science students as well as by an occasional undergraduate (Stanford has many fewer EE undergraduates than graduates and no Computer Science undergraduates). The students in this course are expected to have had a previous course in computer hardware and thus the first three chapters are covered in one week with one week devoted to each of the remaining chapters. As with many one quarter courses there is little time left over, but it has been possible to cover the entire book in this fashion. In a semester course it should be feasible to cover all of the chapters in detail without any prerequisite.

The IEEE Computer Society 1983 Model Program in Computer Science and Engineering describes a set of topics in logic design as its Subject Area 6. All of the topics of this document are covered in this book with the exception of Module 5, Register Transfer Logic, of the Model Program. This module is replaced with the chapter on Design for Testability in this book. The feeling is that testability is a more direct concern for a logic designer than register transfer notation. Such notations are usually specific to a design environment (CAD system or workstation) and are more appropriately learned in such a situation.

This book should be a valuable reference for practicing logic designers and could be used for self study by a digital engineer wishing to become a logic designer or to learn about design for testability.

CHAPTER DESCRIPTIONS

Introductory or Review—Chapters 1, 2, 3, and 4

The first four chapters are introductory or review material. Many of the readers will already be familiar with much of the material presented in them. The purpose of including this material is to (1) establish a nomenclature that can be used in examples and problems in the rest of the book, (2) provide an easy source for the reader to refresh his understanding of this material, (3) set the background that is assumed in the remainder of the book, and (4) introduce a few topics that are often neglected in introductory treatments of digital logic.

The topics in this last category—those that are most likely to be unfamiliar—are:

1. **N-cubes and their symmetries.** (Chap. 1) This material is used in Chap. 5 when decomposition is presented, in Chap. 6 in connection with the discussion of Karnaugh maps, and in Chap. 9 for internal variable assignments.
2. **Error-detecting and error-correcting codes.** (Chap. 1) These topics are not explicitly used in the text, but are included for use in home problems and because of their increasing use in digital logic.
3. **Boolean rings.** (Chap. 2) The exclusive-or connective is very convenient to use in designing circuitry for error-detection or correction and for arithmetic circuitry. The object of the material in Chap. 2 is to develop some familiarity with handling the appropriate algebra for these applications.
4. **Multiple-valued logic.** (Chap. 2) Multiple-valued logic is not used for current commercial logic designs and it is discussed only in this one section of Chap. 2. The reasons for including a discussion of multiple-valued logic are that a great deal of both academic and industrial research has been devoted to it, and many designers are curious about how it is approached. There is always the possibility that it may become practical in some technology, in which case the discussion given here would provide a very good starting point for someone wishing to design with it.
5. **Combinational hazards.** (Chap. 3) The treatment of combinational hazards is more extensive then is typical in books on logic design or switching theory. The reason is the increasing importance of spurious delay effects in modern circuits. This is caused by the high performance requirements and, in semi-custom circuits, the lack of precise control over interconnect delays. Industrial reviewers have been particularly enthusiastic about this increased attention to timing anomalies.
6. **Gate symbols.** (Chaps. 3 and 4) A major feature of this book is its use of the new IEEE standard logic symbols. These are introduced throughout the book as appropriate, but the basic introduction to them is contained in these two chapters.

7. **Integrated circuits.** (Chap. 4) This chapter presents those features of modern integrated circuits most important for a logic designer. Logic design decisions are often dependent on aspects of the implementation technology. For readers who have already studied integrated circuits in detail, this chapter should be a review. For readers unfamiliar with integrated circuits, this chapter is a useful introduction to the subject. The experience in teaching this material has been that many of the students in electrical engineering know some, but far from all, of the subjects covered. The computer science students are usually not familiar with any of the topics, but seem to be quite successful in absorbing the subject at the level of this chapter.

Combinational Circuit Design—Chapters 5 and 6

These two chapters present the principles of combinational circuit design. Chapter 5 discusses special classes of combinational functions while the design of arbitrary combinational networks is presented in Chap. 6.

Chapter 5 is a bit specialized and could be omitted for a first reading. However, knowledge of the special classes of combinational functions allows easy design of very efficient circuits for some applications. The symmetric functions are very common in arithmetic and coding networks. Special design procedures are available in some technologies to produce efficient circuits without lengthy design procedures. The concept of unateness relates to interconnect issues such as double versus single rail routing. It is fundamental to threshold logic. While few implementations of threshold logic are used now, the potential of this type of logic is so attractive that efforts to produce practical implementations continue and may yet succeed.

The Boolean difference is not a special function class, but rather a Boolean operation. It is discussed in Chap. 5 because the concepts are closely related to those that arise in connection with unate and threshold functions. Boolean difference is used to introduce test pattern generation and path sensitization in Chap. 6. The techniques developed for function decomposition are used in Chap. 11 to produce efficient multiplexer networks.

Chapter 6 presents techniques for implementing arbitrary combinational functions. Various implementation procedures—using gates, ROMs, or PLAs (IFL, PAL, . . .)—are described. Minimization methods for multioutput two-stage networks are covered in detail, both Karnaugh map techniques as well as an introduction to tabular techniques (Quine-McCluskey Method). These are demonstrated in connection with both gate networks and PLAs. Input decoder and folding methods for PLAs are described. An introduction to multistage gate network design is presented.

Current industrial practice is evolving so that more and more responsibility for testing a design is being placed on the logic designer. It is thus appropriate that a discussion of test techniques is included along with the presentation of combinational design. The discussion of Design for Testability methods is deferred until after the sequential circuit chapters (Chap. 10) since many of these methods involve the sequential portions of the network.

Sequential Circuits—Chapters 7, 8, and 9

The first two of the sequential circuit chapters describe the different types of sequential circuit and the third chapter gives design procedures.

Chapter 7 introduces the various types of latches and flip-flops. It also describes analysis of fundamental mode circuits—circuits using feedback loops or latches as memory elements. The fundamental requirements for memory using feedback loops are discussed and the phenomenon of **metastability** is presented.

These topics are presented first, and in a separate chapter, because good design requires a thorough understanding of the basic sequential circuit building blocks—latches and flip-flops. Fundamental-mode circuit analysis offers a vehicle for precise description of flip-flops: modern flip-flops are all implemented as fundamental-mode circuits. Since most designs operate with pulses and pulse-mode circuits are easier to design, many designers are uncomfortable with fundamental-mode circuits. However many sequential functions are implemented more efficiently with fundamental- rather than pulse-mode designs. This is illustrated in Sec. 8.4, which shows various circuit implementations to produce an output square wave at one-third the frequency of an input square wave.

Essential hazards are described and their elimination using delays or two-phase nonoverlapping clocks is discussed.

Chapter 8 presents different implementations of finite-state machines, pulse-mode circuits with only one pulse (clock) input. The major distinction between a pulse-mode circuit and a fundamental-mode circuit is that in the pulse-mode circuit internal state transitions occur in response to only one edge (either the rising or the falling edge) of the input pulse; in a fundamental-mode circuit any input transition can cause an internal state transition.

There are three types of clocking structures used for synchronous logic: (1) edge-triggered flip-flops, (2) latches and a two-phase clock, and (3) latches and a one-phase clock. Each of these is described, and circuits using each method to realize the same sequential function example are shown.

Although much rarer than finite-state machines, circuits with more than one pulse input are often used. A counter with separate count-up and count-down pulse trains is a common example of such a circuit. The design of multipulse circuits, circuits having several pulse inputs, is not treated clearly in any of the standard texts now available. In this chapter a simple description is given of the three structures used to realize such circuits: (1) multiport flip-flops as used in design-for-testability scan structures, (2) non-gated T flip-flops as used in the SN54/74LS 192 and 193 up/down counters, and (3) use of a latch to derive a level mode signal as in the SN54/74ALS 192 and 193 up/down counters.

Most pulse-input circuits are designed so that all of the bistable elements change state on the same (leading or trailing) edge of the pulses and never change state in response to a state change in another bistable element. In very special situations, a circuit that violates one or both of these conditions may be useful (a ripple counter is one such example). The last part of Chap. 8 presents examples of various circuits that violate the pulse-mode conditions just stated.

Chapter 9 presents a design method for sequential circuits—either fundamental or pulse mode. State reduction and internal variable assignment techniques as actually used are discussed. The more abstruse switching theory aspects of these topics are deliberately omitted.

Design Structures—Chapters 10 and 11

Chapter 10 surveys the techniques and structures used to ensure that the final design can be tested economically. This material is increasingly important for new designs and cannot be found in any other existing text.

Chapter 11 discusses the structures used in semicustom or MSI design to permit designing at a higher level than with individual gates. The functions available as MSI parts or cell libraries are described and techniques for designing with them are presented.

ACKNOWLEDGMENTS

Lois Thornhill, my wife, was my most vital support in completing this book. She not only provided the happy environment that facilitated my often strange work habits, but pitched in with all kinds of direct help as needed. Her contributions ranged from entering text into the Apple II plus system on which the manuscript was prepared to the photography of the rear cover portrait.

Two of my sons, as in the age old tradition of the family business, did almost all of the nonwriting part of the manuscript preparation. Joseph did all of the text formatting as well as the major part of the proofreading. All the figures and many of the tables were done by David on an Apple Macintosh system. My secretary, Lydia Christopher, helped with the manuscript and kept the office from disaster.

Many of my professional colleagues contributed constructive criticism of technical details as well as writing style: Stu Daniels of Siemens, Rich Sedmak of Self-Test Services, Tom Williams and Paul Bardell of IBM, and Constantine Timoc of Spaceborne, Inc. Professors Sudhakar Reddy of The University of Iowa, Samiha Mourad of Fordham University (on leave at Stanford and San Jose State Universities), and Ravi Iyer of the University of Illinois taught from early versions of the manuscript and provided valuable comments.

Of the many editors I worked with on this book (several were promoted while I was writing) three deserve special mention: Frank Cerra, while he was at McGraw-Hill, convinced me to write a book and negotiated my first contract. At Prentice-Hall, Bernard Goodwin nurtured the delivery of the manuscript and Rennie Rieger has been an understanding and much appreciated production editor.

Many, many students helped in many, many ways: questioning the explanations that didn't explain and the justifications that didn't justify, suggesting better presentations, and identifying typographical errors. I can't mention all of them, but some students deserve to be singled out for the clarity and thoroughness of their comments. My current teaching assistant, Joshua Sakov, was particularly good at reporting typos. The Logic Design students that were most helpful include Brian Bray, Karen Huyser, Rick Wong, Gregory J. Cyr, Doris A. Stoessel, Pam Mayerfeld, David S. Rosenblum, and Soon Yau Kong.

E. J. McCLUSKEY
Palo Alto, California

1

NUMBER SYSTEMS
AND CODES

Arithmetic operations using decimal numbers are quite common. However, in logic design it is necessary to perform manipulations in the so-called binary system of numbers because of the on-off nature of the physical devices used. The present chapter is intended to acquaint the reader with the fundamental concepts involved in dealing with number systems other than decimal. In particular, the binary system is covered in considerable detail.

1.1 POSITIONAL NOTATION

An ordinary decimal number can be regarded as a polynomial in powers of 10. For example, 423.12 can be regarded as $4 \times 10^2 + 2 \times 10^1 + 3 \times 10^0 + 1 \times 10^{-1} + 2 \times 10^{-2}$. Decimal numbers like this are said to be expressed in a number system with **base**, or **radix**, 10 because there are 10 basic digits $(0, 1, 2, \ldots, 9)$ from which the number system is formulated. In a similar fashion we can express any number N in a system using any base b. We shall write such a number as $(N)_b$. Whenever $(N)_b$ is written, the convention of always expressing b in base 10 will be followed. Thus, $(N)_b = (p_n p_{n-1} \cdots p_1 p_0 \cdot p_{-1} p_{-2} \cdots p_{-m})_b$, where b is an integer greater than 1 and $0 \leq p_i \leq b - 1$. The value of a number represented in this fashion, which is called **positional notation**, is given by

$$(N)_b = p_n b^n + p_{n-1} b^{n-1} + \cdots + p_0 b^0 + p_{-1} b^{-1} \qquad (1.1\text{-}1)$$
$$+ p_{-2} b^{-2} + \cdots + p_{-m} b^{-m}$$

$$(N)_b = \sum_{i=-m}^{n} p_i b^i \qquad (1.1\text{-}2)$$

1

For decimal numbers, the symbol "." is called the **decimal point**; for more general base-b numbers, it is called the **radix point**. That portion of the number to the right of the radix point $(p_{-1}p_{-2} \cdots p_{-m})$ is called the **fractional part**, and the portion to the left of the radix point $(p_np_{n-1} \cdots p_0)$ is called the **integral part**.

Numbers expressed in base 2 are called **binary numbers**. They are often used in computers since they require only two coefficient values. The integers from 0 to 15 are given in Table 1.1-1 for several bases. Since there are no coefficient values for the range 10 to $b - 1$ when $b > 10$, the letters A, B, C, . . . are used. Base-8 numbers are called **octal numbers**, and base-16 numbers are called **hexadecimal numbers**. Octal and hexadecimal numbers are often used as a shorthand for binary numbers. An octal number can be converted into a binary number by converting each of the octal coefficients individually into its binary equivalent. The same is true for hexadecimal numbers. This property is true because 8 and 16 are both powers of 2. For numbers with bases that are not a power of 2, the conversion to binary is more complex.

1.1-1 Conversion of Base

To make use of nondecimal number systems, it is necessary to be able to convert a number expressed in one base into the correct representation of the number in another base. One way of doing this makes direct use of the polynomial expression (1.1-1). For example, consider the binary number $(1011.101)_2$. The corresponding polynomial expression is

$$1 \times 2^3 + 0 \times 2^2 + 1 \times 2^1 + 1 \times 2^0 + 1 \times 2^{-1} + 0 \times 2^{-2} + 1 \times 2^{-3}$$

or $8 + \quad\quad\quad\quad 2 + 1 + 1/2 + \quad\quad\quad\quad\quad 1/8$

or $11 + 5/8 = 11.625$

TABLE 1.1-1 Integers in various bases

	2	3	4	5	$\cdots$	8	$\cdots$	10	11	12	$\cdots$	16
	0000	000	00	00		00		00	00	00		0
	0001	001	01	01		01		01	01	01		1
	0010	002	02	02		02		02	02	02		2
	0011	010	03	03		03		03	03	03		3
	0100	011	10	04		04		04	04	04		4
	0101	012	11	10		05		05	05	05		5
	0110	020	12	11		06		06	06	06		6
$(N)_b$	0111	021	13	12		07		07	07	07		7
	1000	022	20	13		10		08	08	08		8
	1001	100	21	14		11		09	09	09		9
	1010	101	22	20		12		10	0A	0A		A
	1011	102	23	21		13		11	10	0B		B
	1100	110	30	22		14		12	11	10		C
	1101	111	31	23		15		13	12	11		D
	1110	112	32	24		16		14	13	12		E
	1111	120	33	30		17		15	14	13		F

This technique of directly evaluating the polynomial expression for a number is a general method for converting from an arbitrary base b_1 to another arbitrary base b_2. For convenience, it will be called the **polynomial method**. This method consists in:

1. Expressing the number $(N)_{b_1}$ as a polynomial, with base-b_2 numbers used in the polynomial
2. Evaluating the polynomial, base-b_2 arithmetic being used

This polynomial method is most often used by human beings whenever a number is to be converted to base 10, since it is then possible to utilize decimal arithmetic.

This method for converting numbers from one base to another is the first example of one of the major goals of this book: the development of algorithms. In general terms, an algorithm is a list of instructions specifying a sequence of operations that will give the answer to any problem of a given type. The important characteristics of an algorithm are: (1) that it is fully specified and does not rely on any skill or intuition on the part of the person applying it, and (2) that it always works (i.e., that a correct answer is always obtained). The notion of an algorithm is discussed in more detail in Sec. 1.1 of [Knuth 68].

It is not always convenient to use base-b_2 arithmetic in converting from base-b_1 to base-b_2. An algorithm for carrying out this conversion by using base-b_1 arithmetic will be discussed next. This discussion is specifically for the situation in which $b_1 = 10$, but it can be extended easily to the more general case. This will be called the **iterative method**, since it involves iterated multiplication or division.

In converting $(N)_{10}$ to $(N)_b$ the fraction and integer parts are converted separately. First, consider the integer part (portion to the left of the decimal point). The general conversion procedure is to divide $(N)_{10}$ by b, giving $(N)_{10}/b$ and a remainder. The remainder, call it p_0, is the least significant (rightmost) digit of $(N)_b$. The next least significant digit p_1 is the remainder of $(N)_{10}/b$ divided by b, and succeeding digits are obtained by continuing this process. A convenient form for carrying out this conversion is illustrated in the following example.

Example 1.1-1

(a) $(23)_{10} = (10111)_2$

2	23	(Remainder)
2	11	1
2	5	1
2	2	1
2	1	0
	0	1

(b) $(23)_{10} = (27)_8$

8	23	(Remainder)
8	2	7
	0	2

(c) $(410)_{10} = (3120)_5$

5	410	(Remainder)
5	82	0
5	16	2
5	3	1
	0	3

Now consider the portion of the number to the right of the decimal point (i.e., the fractional part). The procedure for converting this is to multiply $(N)_{10}$ (fractional) by b. If the resulting product is less than 1, then the most significant (leftmost) digit of the fractional part is 0. If the resulting product is greater than 1, the most significant digit of the fractional part is the integral part of the product. The next most significant digit is formed by multiplying the fractional part of this product by b and taking the integral part. The remaining digits are formed by repeating this process. The process may or may not terminate. A convenient form for carrying out this conversion is illustrated below.

Example 1.1-2

(a) $(0.625)_{10} = (0.5)_8$ $0.625 \times 8 = 5.000$ | 0.5

(b) $(0.23)_{10} = (0.001110 \ldots)_2$

$0.23 \times 2 = 0.46$	0.0
$0.46 \times 2 = 0.92$	0.00
$0.92 \times 2 = 1.84$	0.001
$0.84 \times 2 = 1.68$	0.0011
$0.68 \times 2 = 1.36$	0.00111
$0.36 \times 2 = 0.72$	$0.001110 \cdots$

(c) $(27.68)_{10} = (11011.101011 \ldots)_2 = (33.53 \ldots)_8$

2	27				
2	13	1	$0.68 \times 2 = 1.36$	0.1
2	6	1	$0.36 \times 2 = 0.72$	0.10
2	3	0	$0.72 \times 2 = 1.44$	0.101
2	1	1	$0.44 \times 2 = 0.88$	0.1010
	0	1	$0.88 \times 2 = 1.76$	0.10101
			$0.76 \times 2 = 1.52$	$0.101011 \cdots$
8	27		$0.68 \times 8 = 5.44$	0.5
8	3	3	$0.44 \times 8 = 3.52$	$0.53 \cdots$
	0	3		

This example illustrates the simple relationship between the base-2 (binary) system and the base-8 (octal) system. The binary digits, called **bits**, are taken three at a time in each direction from the binary point and are expressed as decimal digits to give the corresponding octal number. For example, 101 in binary is equivalent to 5 in decimal; so the octal number in Example 1.1-2(c) has a 5 for the most significant digit of the fractional part. The conversion between octal and binary is so simple that the octal expression is sometimes used as a convenient shorthand for the corresponding binary number.

When a fraction is converted from one base to another, the conversion may not terminate, since it may not be possible to represent the fraction exactly in the new base with a finite number of digits. For example, consider the conversion of $(0.1)_3$ to a base-10 fraction. The result is clearly $(0.333\ldots)_{10}$, which can be written as $(0.\overline{3})_{10}$ to indicate that the 3's are repeated indefinitely. It is always possible to represent the result of a conversion of base in this notation, since the nonterminating fraction must consist of a group of digits which are repeated indefinitely. For example, $(0.2)_{11} = 2 \times 11^{-1} = (0.1818\ldots)_{10} = (0.\overline{18})_{10}$.

It should be pointed out that by combining the two conversion methods it is possible to convert between any two arbitrary bases by using only arithmetic of a third base. For example, to convert $(16)_7$ to base 3, first convert to base 10,

$$(16)_7 = 1 \times 7^1 + 6 \times 7^0 = 7 + 6 = (13)_{10}$$

Then convert $(13)_{10}$ to base 3,

3	13	(Remainder)
3	4	1
3	1	1
3	0	1

$$(16)_7 = (13)_{10} = (111)_3$$

For more information about positional number systems, the following references are good sources: [Chrystal 61] and [Knuth 69].

1.2 BINARY ARITHMETIC

Many modern digital computers employ the binary (base-2) number system to represent numbers, and carry out the arithmetic operations using binary arithmetic. While a detailed treatment of computer arithmetic is not within the scope of this book, it will be useful to have the elementary techniques of binary arithmetic available. In performing decimal arithmetic it is necessary to memorize the tables giving the results of the elementary arithmetic operations for pairs of decimal digits. Similarly, for binary arithmetic the tables for the elementary operations for the binary digits are necessary.

1.2-1 Binary Addition

The binary addition table is as follows:

	Sum	Carry
$0 + 0 = 0$		0
$0 + 1 = 1$		0
$1 + 0 = 1$		0
$1 + 1 = 0$		1

Addition is performed by writing the numbers to be added in a column with the binary points aligned. The individual columns of binary digits, or **bits**, are added in the usual order according to the addition table above. Note that in adding a column of bits, there is a 1 carry for each pair of 1's in that column. These 1 carries are treated as bits to be added in the next column to the left. A general rule for addition of a column of numbers (using any base) is to add the column decimally and divide by the base. The remainder is entered as the sum for that column, and the quotient is carried to be added in the next column.

Example 1.2-1

$$Base\ 2$$

Carries: $10011\ 11$
$$1001.011 = (9.375)_{10}$$
$$+\ \ 1101.101 = (13.625)_{10}$$
$$10111.000 = (23)_{10} = Sum$$

1.2-2 Binary Subtraction

The binary subtraction table is as follows:

	Difference	Borrow
$0 - 0 = 0$		0
$0 - 1 = 1$		1
$1 - 0 = 1$		0
$1 - 1 = 0$		0

Subtraction is performed by writing the minuend over the subtrahend with the binary points aligned and carrying out the subtraction according to the table above. If a borrow occurs and the next leftmost digit of the minuend is a 1, it is changed to a 0 and the process of subtraction is then continued from right to left.

	Base 2	Base 10
Borrow:	1	
	0	
Minuend	1̶0	2
Subtrahend	-01	-1
Difference	01	1

If a borrow occurs and the next leftmost digit of the minuend is a 0, this 0 is changed to a 1, as is each successive minuend digit to the left that is equal to 0. The first minuend digit to the left that is equal to 1 is changed to 0, and then the subtraction process is resumed.

	Base 2	Base 10
Borrow:	1	
	011	
Minuend	1̶1̶0̶0̶0	24
Subtrahend	-10001	-17
Difference	00111	7

		Borrow:		1 1	

Borrow: 1   1

	01011	
	1̶0̶1̶0̶0̶0̶	
Minuend	1̶0̶1̶0̶0̶0̶	40
Subtrahend	−011001	−25
Difference	001111	15

1.2-3 Complements

It is possible to avoid this subtraction process by using a complement representation for negative numbers. This will be discussed specifically for binary **fractions**, although it is easy to extend the complement techniques to integers and mixed numbers. The **2's complement** (^2B) of a binary fraction B is defined as follows:

$$^2B = (2 - B)_{10} = (10 - B)_2$$

Thus, $^2(0.1101) = 10.0000 - 0.1101 = 1.0011$. A particularly simple means of carrying out the subtraction indicated in the expression for $^2(0.1101)$ is obtained by noting that $10.0000 = 1.1111 + 0.0001$. Thus, $10.0000 - 0.1101 = (1.1111 - 0.1101) + 0.0001$. The subtraction $1.1111 - 0.1101$ is particularly easy, since all that is necessary is to reverse each of the digits of 0.1101 to obtain 1.0010. Finally, the addition of 0.0001 is also relatively simple and yields 1.0011. In general, the process of forming ^2B involves reversing the digits of B and then adding $0.00 \cdots 01$.

The usefulness of the 2's complement stems from the fact that it is possible to obtain the difference $A - B$ by adding ^2B to A. Thus, $A + {}^2B = (A + 10 - B)_2 = (10 + (A - B))_2$. If $(A - B) > 0$, then $(10 + A - B)_2$ will be 10 plus the positive fraction $(A - B)$. It is thus possible to obtain $A - B$ by dropping the leftmost 1 in $A + {}^2B$. For example,

$A =$	0.1110	$A =$	0.1110
$-B =$	-0.1101	$+{}^2B =$	1.0011
	0.0001		10.0001

If $(A - B) < 0$, then $A + {}^2B = (10 - |A - B|)_2$, which is just equal to $^2(A - B)$, the 2's-complement representation of $A - B$. For example,

$A =$	0.1101	$A =$	0.1101	
$-B =$	-0.1110	$+{}^2B =$	1.0010	
	-0.0001		1.1111	$^2(0.0001) = 1.1111$

The 1's complement is also very commonly used. This is defined as

$$^1B = (10 - 0.000 \cdots 1 - B)_2$$

where the location of the 1 in $0.000 \cdots 1$ corresponds to the least significant digit of B. Since $(10 - 0.000 \cdots 1)_2$ is equal to $01.111 \cdots 1$, it is possible to form ^1B by reversing the digits of B and adding a 1 before the radix point. Thus, $^1(0.1101) = 1.0010$.

If $A + {}^1B$ is formed, the result is $(A - B + 10 - 0.000 \cdots 1)_2$. If $(A - B) > 0$, this can be converted to $A - B$ by removing the $(10)_2$ and adding a 1 to the least significant digit of $A + {}^1B$. This is called an **end-around carry**. For example:

$$
\begin{array}{rl}
A = & 0.1110 \\
-B = & -0.1101 \\
\hline
 & 0.0001
\end{array}
\qquad\qquad
\begin{array}{rl}
A = & 0.1110 \\
+{}^1B = & +1.0010 \\
\hline
A + {}^1B = & 10.0000
\end{array}
$$

End-around carry

$$+0.0001$$
$$\overline{0.0001}$$

so that $\qquad\qquad A - B = \quad 0.0001$

If $(A - B) < 0$, then $A + {}^1B$ will be the 1's complement of $|A - B|$. For example,

$$
\begin{array}{rl}
A = & 0.1101 \\
-B = & -0.1110 \\
\hline
 & -0.0001
\end{array}
\qquad\qquad
\begin{array}{rl}
A = & 0.1101 \\
{}^1B = & 1.0001 \\
\hline
A + {}^1B = & 1.1110 \qquad {}^1(0.0001) = 1.1110
\end{array}
$$

The **radix complement** of a base-b fraction F is defined as

$$ {}^bF = (10 - F)_b $$

and the **diminished radix complement** is defined as

$$ {}^{b-1}F = (10 - F - 0.000 \cdots 1)_b $$

Similar procedures hold for the formation of the complements and their use for subtraction.

When integers or mixed numbers are involved in the subtractions, the definitions of the complements must be generalized to

$$ {}^bN = (100 \cdots 0. - N)_b $$

and $\qquad\qquad {}^{b-1}N = (100 \cdots 0. - N - 0.00 \cdots 1)_b$

where $100 \cdots 0$ contains two more digits than any integer to be encountered in the subtractions. For example, if $(N)_2 = 11.01$, then

$$
\begin{aligned}
{}^2(N)_2 &= 1000.00 - 11.01 \\
&= 111.11 - 11.01 + 0.01 \\
&= 100.10 + 0.01 \\
&= 100.11
\end{aligned}
$$

$$
\begin{array}{rl}
M = & 11.10 \\
-N = & -11.01 \\
\hline
 & 0.01
\end{array}
\qquad\qquad
\begin{array}{rl}
M = & 11.10 \\
{}^2N = & 100.11 \\
\hline
 & 1000.01
\end{array}
$$

↑
Discard

1.2-4 Shifting

In carrying out multiplication or division there are intermediate steps which require that numbers be shifted to the right or the left. Shifting a base-b number k places to the right has the effect of multiplying the number by b^{-k}, and shifting k places to the left is equivalent to multiplication by b^{+k}. Thus, if

$$(N)_b = \sum_{i=-m}^{n} p_i b^i = (p_n p_{n-1} \cdots p_1 p_0 \cdot p_{-1} p_{-2} \cdots p_{-m})_b$$

shifting $(N)_b$ k places to the left yields

$$(p_n p_{n-1} \cdots p_1 p_0 p_{-1} \cdots p_{-k} \cdot p_{-k-1} \cdots p_{-m})_b = \sum_{i=-m}^{n} p_i b^{i+k}$$

and

$$\sum_{i=-m}^{n} p_i b^{i+k} = b^k \sum_{i=-m}^{n} p_i b^i = b^k (N)_b$$

A similar manipulation shows the corresponding situation for right shifts. Shifting the binary point k places (k positive for right shifts and negative for left shifts) in a binary number multiplies the value of the number by 2^k. For example,

$$(110.101)_2 = (6.625)_{10}$$

$$(1.10101)_2 = 2^{-2}(6.625)_{10} = \left(\frac{6.625}{4}\right)_{10} = (1.65625)_{10}$$

$$(11010.1)_2 = 2^{+2}(6.625)_{10} = (4 \times 6.625)_{10} = (26.5)_{10}$$

1.2-5 Binary Multiplication

The binary multiplication table is as follows:

$$0 \times 0 = 0$$
$$0 \times 1 = 0$$
$$1 \times 0 = 0$$
$$1 \times 1 = 1$$

The process of binary multiplication is illustrated by the following example:

110.10	Multiplicand
10.1	Multiplier
11010	Partial product
00000	Partial product
11010	Partial product
10000.010	

For every digit of the multiplier that is equal to 1, a partial product is formed consisting of the multiplicand shifted so that its least significant digit is aligned with the 1 of the multiplier. An all-zero partial product is formed for each 0 multiplier digit. Of course, the all-zero partial products can be omitted. The final product is formed by summing all the partial products. The binary point is placed in the product by using the same rule as for decimal multiplication: The number of digits to the right of the binary point of the product is equal to the sum of the numbers of digits to the right of the binary points of the multiplier and the multiplicand.

The simplest technique for handling the multiplication of negative numbers is to use the process just described to multiply the magnitudes of the numbers. The sign of the product is determined separately, and the product is made negative if either the multiplier or the multiplicand, but not both, are negative. It is possible to carry out multiplication directly with negative numbers represented in complement form. This is usually done using a recoding scheme called Booth's algorithm [Waser 82], which also speeds up the multiplication.

1.2-6 Binary Division

Division is the most complex of the four basic arithmetic operations. Decimal long division as taught in grade school is a trial-and-error process. For example, in dividing 362 by 46 one must first recognize that 46 is larger than 36 and then must guess how many times 46 will go into 362. If an initial guess of 8 is made and the multiplication 8 × 46 = 368 is carried out, the result is seen to be larger than 362 so that the 8 must be replaced by a 7. This process of trial and error is simpler for binary division because there are fewer possibilities in the binary case.

To implement binary division in a digital computer, a division algorithm must be specified. Two different algorithms, called restoring and nonrestoring division, are used.

Restoring division is carried out as follows. In the first step, the divisor is subtracted from the dividend with their leftmost digits aligned. If the result is positive, a 1 is entered as the quotient digit corresponding to the rightmost digit of the dividend from which a digit of the divisor was subtracted. The next rightmost digit of the dividend is appended to the result, which then becomes the next partial dividend. The divisor is then shifted one place to the right so that its least significant digit is aligned with the rightmost digit of the partial dividend, and the process just described is repeated.

If the result of subtracting the divisor from the dividend is negative, a 0 is entered in the quotient and the divisor is added back to the negative result so as to **restore** the original dividend. The divisor is then shifted one place to the right, and a subtraction is carried out again. The process of restoring division is illustrated in the example at top of next page.

```
Divisor = 1 1 1 1        Dividend =   1 1 0 0
                                  q₀   q₋₁  q₋₂  q₋₃  q₋₄  q₋₅
                                   0   .1   1    0    0    1
                         1 1 1 1√1 1 0 0   .0   0    0    0    0
Subtract                         1 1 1 1
Negative result   q₀  = 0       −0 0 1 1
Restore                         +1 1 1 1
                                 1 1 0 0 0
Subtract                         1 1 1 1
Positive result   q₋₁ = 1        1 0 0 1 0
Subtract                           1 1 1 1
Positive result   q₋₂ = 1        0 0 0 1 1 0
Subtract                             1 1 1 1
Negative result   q₋₃ = 0         −1 0 0 1
Restore                           +1 1 1 1
                                  0 1 1 0 0
Subtract                            1 1 1 1
Negative result   q₋₄ = 0         −0 0 1 1
Restore                           +1 1 1 1
                                  1 1 0 0 0
Subtract                            1 1 1 1
Positive result   q₋₅ = 1         1 0 0 1   (remainder)
```

In **nonrestoring division**, the step of adding the divisor to a negative partial dividend is omitted, and instead the shifted divisor is added to the negative partial dividend. This step of adding the shifted divisor replaces the two steps of adding the divisor and then subtracting the shifted divisor. This can be justified as follows. If X represents the negative partial dividend and Y the divisor, then $1/2Y$ represents the divisor shifted one place to the right. Adding the divisor and then subtracting the shifted divisor yields $X + Y - 1/2Y = X + 1/2Y$, while adding the shifted divisor yields the same result, $X + 1/2Y$. The steps that occur in using nonrestoring division to divide 1100 by 1111 are shown in the example at top of next page:

Divisor = 1 1 1 1   Dividend =   1 1 0 0

$$
\begin{array}{cccccc}
q_0 & q_{-1} & q_{-2} & q_{-3} & q_{-4} & q_{-5} \\
0 & .1 & 1 & 0 & 0 & 1
\end{array}
$$

1 1 1 1$\sqrt{}$1 1 0 0   .0   0   0   0   0

Subtract	1 1 1 1
Negative result $q_0 = 0$ Shift and add	$-$ 0 0 1 1 0 $+$ 1 1 1 1
Positive result $q_{-1} = 1$ Shift and subtract	$+$1 0 0 1 0 $-$ 1 1 1 1
Positive result $q_{-2} = 1$ Shift and subtract	$+$0 0 1 1 0 $-$ 1 1 1 1
Negative result $q_{-3} = 0$ Shift and add	$-$ 1 0 0 1 0 $+$ 1 1 1 1
Negative result $q_{-4} = 0$ Shift and add	$-$ 0 0 1 1 0 $+$ 1 1 1 1
Positive result $q_{-5} = 1$	$+$1 0 0 1 (remainder)

An important technique for improving the performance of digital arithmetic circuitry is the use of more sophisticated algorithms for the basic arithmetic operations. A discussion of these methods is beyond the scope of this book. The interested reader is referred to [Waser 82], [Hwang 78], or Chap. 2 and Sec. 8.1 in [Gschwind 75] for more details on arithmetic.

1.3 BINARY CODES

The binary number system has many advantages and is widely used in digital systems. However, there are times when binary numbers are not appropriate. Since we think much more readily in terms of decimal numbers than binary numbers, facilities are usually provided so that data can be entered into the system in decimal form, the conversion to binary being performed automatically inside the system. In fact, many computers have been designed which work entirely with decimal numbers. For this to be possible, a scheme for representing each of the 10 decimal digits as a sequence of binary digits must be used.

1.3-1 Binary-Coded-Decimal Numbers

To represent 10 decimal digits, it is necessary to use at least 4 binary digits, since there are 2^4, or 16, different combinations of 4 binary digits but only 2^3, or 8, different combinations of 3 binary digits. If 4 binary digits, or **bits**, are used and only one combination of bits is used to represent each decimal digit, there will be six unused or invalid code words. In general, any arbitrary assignment of combinations of bits to digits can be used so that there are 16!/6! or approximately

TABLE 1.3-1 Some common 4-bit decimal codes

Decimal digit	8 b_3	4 b_2	2 b_1	1 b_0	8	4	-2	-1	2	4	2	1	Excess-3			
0	0	0	0	0	0	0	0	0	0	0	0	0	0	0	1	1
1	0	0	0	1	0	1	1	1	0	0	0	1	0	1	0	0
2	0	0	1	0	0	1	1	0	0	0	1	0	0	1	0	1
3	0	0	1	1	0	1	0	1	0	0	1	1	0	1	1	0
4	0	1	0	0	0	1	0	0	0	1	0	0	0	1	1	1
5	0	1	0	1	1	0	1	1	1	0	1	1	1	0	0	0
6	0	1	1	0	1	0	1	0	1	1	0	0	1	0	0	1
7	0	1	1	1	1	0	0	1	1	1	0	1	1	0	1	0
8	1	0	0	0	1	0	0	0	1	1	1	0	1	0	1	1
9	1	0	0	1	1	1	1	1	1	1	1	1	1	1	0	0

2.9×10^{10} possible codes. Only a few of these codes have ever been used in any system, since the arithmetic operations are very difficult in almost all of the possible codes. Several of the more common 4-bit decimal codes are shown in Table 1.3-1.

The 8,4,2,1 code is obtained by taking the first 10 binary numbers and assigning them to the corresponding decimal digits. This code is an example of a **weighted code**, since the decimal digits can be determined from the binary digits by forming the sum $d = 8b_3 + 4b_2 + 2b_1 + b_0$. The coefficients 8, 4, 2, 1 are known as the **code weights**. The number 462 would be represented as 0100 0110 0010 in the 8,4,2,1 code. It has been shown in [White 53] that there are only 17 different sets of weights possible for a positively weighted code: (3, 3, 3, 1), (4, 2, 2, 1), (4, 3, 1, 1), (5, 2, 1, 1), (4, 3, 2, 1), (4, 4, 2, 1), (5, 2, 2, 1), (5, 3, 1, 1), (5, 3, 2, 1), (5, 4, 2, 1), (6, 2, 2, 1), (6, 3, 1, 1), (6, 3, 2, 1), (6, 4, 2, 1), (7, 3, 2, 1), (7, 4, 2, 1), (8, 4, 2, 1).

It is also possible to have a weighted code in which some of the weights are negative, as in the 8,4,-2,-1 code shown in Table 1.3-1. This code has the useful property of being **self-complementing**: if a code word is formed by complementing each bit individually (changing 1's to 0's and 0's to 1's), then this new code word represents the 9's complement of the digit to which the original code word corresponds. For example, 0101 represents 3 in the 8,4,-2,-1 code, and 1010 represents 6 in this code. In general, if b_i' denotes the complement of b_i, then a code is self-complementing if, for any code word $b_3 b_2 b_1 b_0$ representing a digit d_i, the code word $b_3' b_2' b_1' b_0'$ represents $9 - d_i$. The 2,4,2,1 code of Table 1.3-1 is an example of a self-complementing code having all positive weights, and the excess-3 code is an example of a code that is self-complementing but not weighted. The excess-3 code is obtained from the 8,4,2,1 code by adding (using binary arithmetic) 0011 (or 3) to each 8,4,2,1 code word to obtain the corresponding excess-3 code word.

Although 4 bits are sufficient for representing the decimal digits, it is sometimes expedient to use more than 4 bits in order to achieve arithmetic simplicity or ease in error detection. The 2-out-of-5 code shown in Table 1.3-2 has the property that each code word has exactly two 1's. A single error that complements

TABLE 1.3-2 Some decimal codes using more than 4 bits

Decimal digit	2-out-of-5	Biquinary 5043210
0	00011	0100001
1	00101	0100010
2	00110	0100100
3	01001	0101000
4	01010	0110000
5	01100	1000001
6	10001	1000010
7	10010	1000100
8	10100	1001000
9	11000	1010000

1 of the bits will always produce an invalid code word and is therefore easily detected. This is an unweighted code. The biquinary code shown in Table 1.3-2 is a weighted code in which 2 of the bits specify whether the digit is in the range 0 to 4 or the range 5 to 9 and the other 5 bits identify where in the range the digit occurs.

1.4 GEOMETRIC REPRESENTATION OF BINARY NUMBERS

An n-bit binary number can be represented by what is called a **point in n-space**. To see just what is meant by this, consider the set of 1-bit binary numbers, that is, 0 and 1. This set can be represented by two points in 1-space (i.e., by two points on a line). Such a presentation is called a **1-cube** and is shown in Fig. 1.4-1b. (A **0-cube** is a single point in 0-space.)

Now consider the set of 2-bit binary numbers, that is, 00, 01, 10, 11 (or, decimally, 0, 1, 2, 3). This set can be represented by four points (also called **vertices**, or **nodes**) in 2-space. This representation is called a **2-cube** and is shown in Fig. 1.4-1c. Note that this figure can be obtained by projecting the 1-cube (i.e., the horizontal line with two points) downward and by prefixing a 0 to 0 and 1 on the original 1-cube and a 1 to 0 and 1 on the projected 1-cube. A similar projection procedure can be followed in obtaining any next-higher-dimensional figure. For

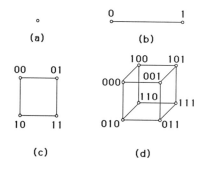

Figure 1.4-1 n-Cubes for $n = 0, 1, 2, 3$: (a) 0-cube; (b) 1-cube; (c) 2-cube; (d) 3-cube.

example, the representation for the set of 3-bit binary numbers is obtained by projecting the 2-cube representation of Fig. 1.4-1c. A 0 is prefixed to the bits on the original 2-cube, and a 1 is prefixed to the bits on the projection of the 2-cube. Thus, the 3-bit representation, or **3-cube**, is shown in Fig. 1.4-1d.

A more formal statement for the projection method of defining an n-cube is as follows:

1. A 0-cube is a single point with no designation.
2. An n-cube is formed by projecting an $(n-1)$-cube. A 0 is prefixed to the designations of the points of the original $(n-1)$-cube, and a 1 is prefixed to the designations of the points of the projected $(n-1)$-cube.

There are 2^n points in an n-cube. A **p-subcube** of an n-cube $(p \le n)$ is defined as a collection of any 2^p points that have exactly $(n-p)$ corresponding bits all the same. For example, the points 100, 101, 000, and 001 in the 3-cube (Fig. 1.4-1d) form a 2-subcube, since there are $2^2 = 4$ total points and $3 - 2 = 1$ of the bits (the second) is the same for all four points. In general, there are $(n!2^{n-p})/[(n-p)!p!]$ different p-subcubes in an n-cube, since there are $(C^n_{n-p}) = (n!/(n-p)!p!)$ (number of ways of selecting n things taken $n-p$ at a time) ways in which $n - p$ of the bits may be the same, and there are 2^{n-p} combinations which these bits may take on. For example, there are $(3!2^2)/(2!1!) = 12$ 1-subcubes (line segments) in a 3-cube, and there are $(3!2^1)/(1!2!) = 6$ 2-subcubes ("squares") in a 3-cube.

Besides the form shown in Fig. 1.4-1, there are two other methods of drawing an n-cube which are frequently used. The first of these is shown in Fig. 1.4-2 for the 3- and 4-cubes. It is seen that these still agree with the projection scheme and are merely a particular way of drawing the cubes. The dashed lines are usually omitted for convenience in drawing.

If in the representation of Fig. 1.4-2 we replace each dot by a square area, we have what is known as an **n-cube map**. This representation is shown for the 3- and 4-cubes in Fig. 1.4-3. Maps will be of considerable use to us later. Notice that the appropriate entry for each cell of the maps of Fig. 1.4-3 can be determined from the corresponding row and column labels.

It is sometimes convenient to represent the points of an n-cube by the decimal equivalents of their binary designations. For example, Fig. 1.4-4 shows the 3- and 4-cube maps represented this way. It is of interest to note that if a point has the decimal equivalent N_i in an n-cube, in an $(n+1)$-cube this point and its projection (as defined) become N_i and $N_i + 2^n$.

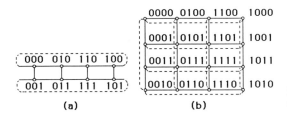

(a)　　　(b)

Figure 1.4-2 Alternative representations: (a) 3-cube; (b) 4-cube.

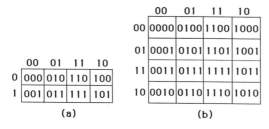

Figure 1.4-3 n-Cube maps: (a) $n = 3$; (b) $n = 4$.

1.4-1 Distance

A concept which will be of later use is that of the distance between two points on an n-cube. Briefly, the **distance** between two points on an n-cube is simply the number of coordinates (bit positions) in which the binary representations of the two points differ. This is also called the **Hamming distance**. For example, 10110 and 01101 differ in all but the third coordinate (from left or right). Since the points differ in four coordinates, the distance between them is 4. A more formal definition is as follows:

First, define the **modulo-2 sum** of two bits, $a \oplus b$, by

$$0 \oplus 0 = 0 \qquad 1 \oplus 0 = 1$$
$$0 \oplus 1 = 1 \qquad 1 \oplus 1 = 0$$

That is, the sum is 0 if the 2 bits are alike, and it is 1 if the 2 bits are different. Now consider the binary representations of two points, $P_i = (a_{n-1} a_{n-2} \cdots a_0)$ and $P_j = (b_{n-1} b_{n-2} \cdots b_0)$, on the n-cube. The modulo-2 sum of these two points is defined as

$$P_k = P_i \oplus P_j = (a_{n-1} \oplus b_{n-1}, a_{n-2} \oplus b_{n-2}, \ldots, a_0 \oplus b_0)$$

This sum P_k is the binary representation of another point on the n-cube. The number of 1's in the binary representation P_i is defined as the **weight** of P_i and is given the symbol $|P_i|$. Then the distance (or **metric**) between two points is defined as

$$D(P_i, P_j) = |P_i \oplus P_j|$$

The distance function satisfies the following three properties:

$$D(P_i, P_j) = 0 \qquad \text{if and only if } P_i = P_j$$
$$D(P_i, P_j) = D(P_j, P_i) > 0 \qquad \text{if } P_i \neq P_j$$
$$D(P_i, P_j) + D(P_j, P_k) \geq D(P_i, P_k) \qquad \text{Triangle inequality}$$

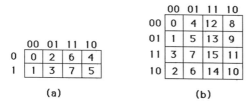

Figure 1.4-4 Decimal labels in n-cube maps: (a) 3-cube map; (b) 4-cube map.

To return to the more intuitive approach, since two adjacent points (connected by a single line segment) on an n-cube form a 1-subcube, they differ in exactly one coordinate and thus are distance 1 apart. We see then that to any two points that are distance D apart, there corresponds a **path** of D connected line segments on the n-cube joining the two points. Furthermore, there will be more than one path of length D connecting the two points (for $D > 1$ and $n \geq 2$), but there will be no path shorter than length D connecting the two points. A given shortest path connecting the two points, thus, cannot intersect itself, and $D + 1$ nodes (including the end points) will occur on the path.

1.4-2 Unit-Distance Codes

In terms of the geometric picture, a code is simply the association of the decimal integers (0, 1, 2, . . .) with the points on an n-cube. There are two types of codes, which are best described in terms of their geometric properties. These are the so-called **unit-distance codes** and **error-detecting** and **error-correcting codes**.

A unit-distance code is simply the association of the decimal integers (0, 1, 2, . . .) with the points on a connected path in the n-cube such that the distance is 1 between the point corresponding to any integer i and the point corresponding to integer $i + 1$ (see Fig. 1.4-5 and Table 1.4-1). That is, if P_i is the binary-code word for decimal integer i, then we must have

$$D(P_i, P_i + 1) = 1 \qquad i = 0, 1, 2, \ldots$$

Unit-distance codes are used in devices for converting analog or continuous signals such as voltages or shaft rotations into binary numbers that represent the magnitude of the signal. Such a device is called an **analog-digital converter**. In any such device there must be boundaries between successive digits, and it is always possible for there to be some misalignment among the different bit positions at such a boundary. For example, if the seventh position is represented by 0111 and the eighth position by 1000, misalignment could cause signals corresponding to 1111 to be generated at the boundary between 7 and 8. If binary numbers were used for such a device, large errors could thus occur. By using a unit-distance code in which adjacent positions differ only in 1 bit, the error due to misalignment can be eliminated.

The highest integer to be encoded may or may not be required to be distance 1 from the code word for 0. If it is distance 1, the path is closed. Of particular interest is the case of a closed nonintersecting path which goes through all 2^n points of the n-cube. In graph theory such a path is known as a (closed) **Hamilton line**. Any unit-distance code associated with such a path is sometimes called a **Gray code**, although this term is usually reserved for a particular one of these codes.

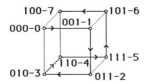

Figure 1.4-5 Path on a 3-cube corresponding to a unit-distance code.

TABLE 1.4-1 Unit-distance code of Fig. 1.4-5

0	000
1	001
2	011
3	010
4	110
5	111
6	101
7	100

To avoid confusing terminology, we shall refer to a unit-distance code that corresponds to a closed Hamilton line as a **closed *n* code**. This is a unit-distance code containing 2^n code words in which the code word for the largest integer ($2^n - 1$) is distance 1 from the code word for the least integer (0). An **open *n* code** is similar except that the code words for the least and largest integer, respectively, are not distance 1 apart.

The most useful unit distance code is the Gray code, which is shown in Table 1.4-2. The attractive feature of this code is the simplicity of the algorithm for translating from the binary number system into the Gray code. This algorithm is described by the expression

$$g_i = b_i \oplus b_{i+1}$$

TABLE 1.4-2 The Gray code

Decimal	Binary				Gray			
	b_3	b_2	b_1	b_0	g_3	g_2	g_1	g_0
0	0	0	0	0	0	0	0	0
1	0	0	0	1	0	0	0	1
2	0	0	1	0	0	0	1	1
3	0	0	1	1	0	0	1	0
4	0	1	0	0	0	1	1	0
5	0	1	0	1	0	1	1	1
6	0	1	1	0	0	1	0	1
7	0	1	1	1	0	1	0	0
8	1	0	0	0	1	1	0	0
9	1	0	0	1	1	1	0	1
10	1	0	1	0	1	1	1	1
11	1	0	1	1	1	1	1	0
12	1	1	0	0	1	0	1	0
13	1	1	0	1	1	0	1	1
14	1	1	1	0	1	0	0	1
15	1	1	1	1	1	0	0	0

Thus, the Gray code word corresponding to 1100 in binary is formed as follows:

$$g_0 = b_0 \oplus b_1 = 0 \oplus 0 = 0$$
$$g_1 = b_1 \oplus b_2 = 0 \oplus 1 = 1$$
$$g_2 = b_2 \oplus b_3 = 1 \oplus 1 = 0$$
$$g_3 = b_3 \oplus b_4 = b_3 = 1 \qquad b_4 \text{ understood to be } 0$$

1.4-3 Symmetries of the n-Cube

A **symmetry** of the n-cube is defined to be any one-to-one translation of the binary point representations on the n-cube which leaves all pairwise distances the same. If we consider the set of binary numbers, we see that there are only two basic translation schemes which leave pairwise distances the same. (1) The bits of one coordinate may be interchanged with the bits of another coordinate in all code words. (2) The bits of one coordinate may be complemented (i.e., change 1's to 0's and 0's to 1's) in all code words. Since there are $n!$ permutations of n coordinates, there are $n!$ translation schemes possible using scheme 1; and since there are 2^n ways in which coordinates may be complemented, there are 2^n translation schemes possible using scheme 2. Thus, in all there are $2^n(n!)$ symmetries of the n-cube. This means that for any n-bit code there are $2^n(n!) - 1$ rather trivial modifications of the original code (in fact, some of these may result in the original code) which can be obtained by interchanging and complementing coordinates. The pairwise distances are the same in all these codes.

It is sometimes desired to enumerate the different types of a class of codes. Two codes are said to be of the same **type** if a symmetry of the n-cube translates one code into the other (i.e., by interchanging and complementing coordinates). As an example, we might ask: What are the types of closed n codes? It turns out that for $n < 4$ there is just one type, and this is the type of the conventional Gray code. For $n = 4$, there are nine types. Rather than specify a particular code of each type, we can list these types by specifying the sequence of coordinate changes for a closed path of that type. On the assumption that the coordinates are numbered (3210), the nine types are shown in Table 1.4-3.

TABLE 1.4-3 Nine different types of unit-distance 4-bit code

Type																
1 (Gray)	0	1	0	2	0	1	0	3	0	1	0	2	0	1	0	3
2	1	0	1	3	1	0	1	2	0	1	0	3	0	1	0	2
3	1	0	1	3	0	1	0	2	1	0	1	3	0	1	0	2
4	1	0	1	3	2	3	1	0	1	3	1	0	2	0	1	3
5	1	0	1	3	2	0	1	3	1	0	1	3	2	0	1	3
6	1	0	1	3	2	3	1	3	2	0	1	2	1	3	1	2
7	1	0	1	3	2	0	2	1	0	2	0	3	0	1	0	2
8	1	0	1	3	2	1	2	0	1	2	1	3	0	1	0	2
9	1	0	1	3	2	3	1	0	3	0	2	0	1	2	3	2

1.5 ERROR-DETECTING AND ERROR-CORRECTING CODES

Special features are included in many digital systems for the purpose of increasing system reliability. In some cases circuits are included which indicate when an error has occurred—error detection—and perhaps provide some information as to where the error is—error diagnosis. Sometimes it is more appropriate to provide **error correction**: circuits not only detect a malfunction but act to automatically correct the erroneous indications caused by it. One technique used to improve reliability is to build two duplicate systems and then to run them in parallel, continually comparing the outputs of the two systems [Burks 62]. When a mismatch is detected, actions are initiated to determine the source of the error and to correct it [Keister 64]. Another approach uses three copies of each system module and relies on voter elements to select the correct output in case one of the three copies has a different output from the other two ([von Neumann 56], [Lyons 62]). This technique is called triple modular redundancy (TMR). Such costly designs are appropriate either when the components are not sufficiently reliable [Burks 62] or in systems where reliability is very important, as in real-time applications such as telephony [Keister 64], airline reservations [Perry 61], or space vehicles [Dickinson 64].

In many other applications where such massive redundancy is not justified it is still important to introduce some (less costly) techniques to obtain some improvement in reliability. A very basic and common practice is to introduce some redundancy in encoding the information manipulated in the system. For example, when the 2-out-of-5 code is used to represent the decimal digits, any error in only one bit is easily detected since if any single bit is changed, the resulting binary word no longer contains exactly two 1's. While it is true that there are many 2-bit errors which will not be detected by this code, it is possible to argue that in many situations multiple errors are so much less likely than single errors that it is reasonable to ignore all but single errors.

Suppose it is assumed that the probability of any single bit being in error is p and that this probability is independent of the condition of any other bits. Also suppose that p is very much less than 1 (i.e., that the components are very reliable). Then the probability of all 5 bits representing one digit being correct is $P_0 = (1 - p)^5$, the probability of exactly one error is $P_1 = 5(1 - p)^4 p$ and the probability of two errors is $P_2 = 10(1 - p)^3 p^2$. Taking the ratio $P_2/P_1 = 2p/(1 - p) \cong 2p(1 + p) << 1$, showing that the probability of a double error is much smaller than that of a single error. Arguments such as this are the basis for the very common emphasis on handling only single errors.

It is possible to easily convert any of the 4-bit decimal codes to single-error-detecting codes by the addition of a single bit—a parity bit, as illustrated for the 8421 code in Table 1.5-1. The **parity bit** p is added to each code word so as to make the total number of 1's in the resultant 5-bit word even (i.e., $p = b_0 \oplus b_1 \oplus b_2 \oplus b_3$). If any one bit is reversed, it will change the overall parity (number of 1's) from even to odd and thus provide an error indication.

This technique of adding a parity bit to a set of binary words is not peculiar

TABLE 1.5-1   8421 code with parity bit added

Decimal digit	8 b_3	4 b_2	2 b_1	1 b_0	Parity, p
0	0	0	0	0	0
1	0	0	0	1	1
2	0	0	1	0	1
3	0	0	1	1	0
4	0	1	0	0	1
5	0	1	0	1	0
6	0	1	1	0	0
7	0	1	1	1	1
8	1	0	0	0	1
9	1	0	0	1	0

to binary-coded-decimal schemes but is generally applicable. It is common practice to add a parity bit to all information recorded on magnetic tapes.

The 8421 code with a parity bit added is shown plotted on the 5-cube map of Fig. 1.5-1. Inspection of this figure shows that the minimum distance between any two words is two as must be true for any single-error-detecting code.

In summary, *any single-error-detecting code must have a minimum distance between any two code words of at least two,* and *any set of binary words with minimum distance between words of at least two can be used as a single-error-detecting code.* Also the addition of a parity bit to any set of binary words will guarantee that the minimum distance between any two words is at least two.

p=0
b_3b_2

b_1b_0	00	01	11	10
0 0	0			
0 1		5		9
1 1	3			
1 0		6		

p=0
b_3b_2

b_1b_0	00	01	11	10
0 0		4		8
0 1	1			
1 1		7		
1 0	2			

Figure 1.5-1   Five-cube map for the 8421 BCD code with parity bit p.

1.5-1 Single-Error-Correcting Codes

A parity check over all the bits of a binary word provides an indication if one of the bits is reversed; however, it provides no information about which bit was changed—all bits enter into the parity check in the same manner. If it is desired to use parity checks not only to detect an altered bit but also to identify the altered bit, it is necessary to resort to several parity checks—each checking a different set of bits in the word. For example, consider the situation in Table 1.5-2, in which there are three bits, M_1, M_2, and M_3, which are to be used to represent eight items of information; and there are two parity check bits, C_1 and C_2. The information

TABLE 1.5-2 Parity check table

M_1	M_2	M_3	C_1	C_2
×		×	×	
	×	×		×

$$C_1 = M_1 \oplus M_3, \; C_2 = M_2 \oplus M_3$$

bits, M_i, are often called **message bits** and the C_i bits **check bits**. As indicated in the table, C_1 is obtained as a parity check over bits M_1 and M_3, while C_2 checks bits M_2 and M_3.

At first glance it might seem that this scheme might result in a single-error-correcting code since an error in M_3 alters both parity checks, while an error in M_1 or M_2 each alters a distinct single parity check. This reasoning overlooks the fact that it is possible to have an error in a check bit as well as an error in a message bit. Parity check one could fail as a result of an error either in message bit M_1 or in check bit C_1. Thus in this situation it would not be clear whether M_1 should be changed or not. To obtain a true single-error-correcting code, it is necessary to add an additional check bit as in Table 1.5-3.

TABLE 1.5-3 Eight-word single-error-correcting code: (a) Parity check table; (b) Parity check equations; (c) Single-error-correcting code

(a)

M_1	M_2	M_3	C_1	C_2	C_3
×		×	×		
	×	×		×	
×	×				×

(b)

$$C_1 = M_1 \oplus M_3$$
$$C_2 = M_2 \oplus M_3$$
$$C_3 = M_1 \oplus M_2$$

(c)

	M_1	M_2	M_3	C_1	C_2	C_3
a	0	0	0	0	0	0
b	0	0	1	1	1	0
c	0	1	0	0	1	1
d	0	1	1	1	0	1
e	1	0	0	1	0	1
f	1	0	1	0	1	1
g	1	1	0	1	1	0
h	1	1	1	0	0	0

Inspection of the parity check table in Table 1.5-3a shows that an error in any one of the check bits will cause exactly one parity check violation, while an error in any one of the message bits will cause violations of a distinct pair of parity checks. Thus it is possible to uniquely identify any single error. The code words of Table 1.5-3c are shown plotted on the 6-cube map of Fig. 1.5-2. Each code word is indicated by the corresponding letter and all cells distance one away from a code word are marked with an ×. The fact that no cell has more than one × shows that no cell is distance one away from two code words. Since a single error changes a code word into a new word distance one away and each of such words is distance one away from only one code word, it is possible to correct all single errors. A necessary consequence of the fact that no word is distance one away from more than one code word is the fact that the minimum distance between any pair of code words is three. In fact, the *necessary and sufficient conditions for any set of binary words to be a single-error-correcting code is that the minimum distance between any pair of words be three.*

A single-error-correcting code can be obtained by any procedure that results in a set of words which are minimum distance three apart. The procedure illustrated in Table 1.5-3 is due to [Hamming 50] and, due to its systematic nature, is almost universally used for single-error-codes.

With three parity check bits it is possible to obtain a single-error-correcting code of more than eight code words. In fact, up to 16 code words can be obtained. The parity check table for a code with three check bits, C_1, C_2, and C_4, and four message bits, M_3, M_5, M_6, and M_7, is shown in Table 1.5-4. The peculiar numbering of the bits has been adopted to demonstrate the fact that it is possible to make a correspondence between the bit positions and the entries of the parity check table. If the blanks in the table are replaced by 0's and the ×'s by 1's, each column will be a binary number that is the equivalent of the subscript on the corresponding code bit. The check bits are placed in the bit positions corresponding to binary powers since they then enter into only one parity check, making the formation of the parity check equations very straightforward.

$M_1 M_2$

00
$M_3 C_1$

$C_2 C_3$	00	01	11	10
0 0	a	X	X	X
0 1	X	X	X	
1 1	X		X	X
1 0	X	X	b	X

01
$M_3 C_1$

$C_2 C_3$	00	01	11	10
0 0	X		X	X
0 1	X	X	d	X
1 1	c	X	X	X
1 0	X	X	X	

10
$M_3 C_1$

$C_2 C_3$	00	01	11	10
0 0	X	X		X
0 1	X	e	X	X
1 1	X	X	X	f
1 0		X	X	X

11
$M_3 C_1$

$C_2 C_3$	00	01	11	10
0 0	X	X	X	h
0 1		X	X	X
1 1	X	X		X
1 0	X	g	X	X

Figure 1.5-2 Six-cube map for the code of Table 1.5-3c.

TABLE 1.5-4 Parity check table for a single-error-correcting code with 3 check bits and 4 message bits

C_1	C_2	M_3	C_4	M_5	M_6	M_7
			×	×	×	×
	×	×			×	×
×		×		×		×

$$C_1 = M_3 \oplus M_5 \oplus M_7$$
$$C_2 = M_3 \oplus M_6 \oplus M_7$$
$$C_4 = M_5 \oplus M_6 \oplus M_7$$

The fact that Table 1.5-4 leads to a single-error-correcting code follows from the fact that each code bit enters into a unique set of parity checks. In fact, *the necessary and sufficient conditions for a parity check table to correspond to a single-error-correcting code are that each column of the table be distinct (no repeated columns) and that each column contain at least one entry.* It follows from this that with K check bits it is possible to obtain a single-error-correcting code having at most $2^K - 1$ total bits.[1] There are 2^K different columns possible, but the empty column must be excluded, leaving $2^K - 1$ columns.

1.5-2 Double-Error-Detecting Codes

If a code such as that generated by Table 1.5-4 is being used and a double error occurs, a correction will be carried out but the wrong code word will be produced. For example, suppose that bits C_1 and C_2 were in error; the first two parity checks would be violated and it would appear as if message bit M_3 had been in error. Similarly, errors in bits M_3 and M_6 would result in violations of the first and third parity checks,[2] and an indication of M_5 being in error would be produced. It is possible to add the ability to **detect** double errors as well as correct single errors by means of one addition parity check over all the bits. This is illustrated in Table 1.5-5. Any single error in the resulting code will result in the same parity check violations as without P and in addition will violate the P parity check. Any double error will **not** violate the P parity check but will violate some of the C parity checks, thus providing an indication of the double error.

A code that detects double errors as well as correcting single errors must consist of binary words having a minimum distance of four. This situation is illustrated by Fig. 1.5-3. Both the single-error codes and the double-error-detecting codes are in use in contemporary systems [Hsiao 70]. Many more sophisticated error-correcting codes have been studied ([Peterson 72], [Berlekamp 68]).

---

[1] In Table 1.5-4, $K = 3$, $2^K - 1 = 7$ and the table does indeed have a total of 7 bits.

[2] The two changes in parity check two would cancel.

TABLE 1.5-5 Parity check table for a code to detect all double errors and correct all single errors

C_1	C_2	M_3	C_4	M_5	M_6	M_7	P
			×	×	×	×	
	×	×			×	×	
×		×		×		×	
×	×	×	×	×	×	×	×

$$C_1 = M_3 \oplus M_5 \oplus M_7$$
$$C_2 = M_3 \oplus M_6 \oplus M_7$$
$$C_4 = M_5 \oplus M_6 \oplus M_7$$
$$P = C_1 \oplus C_2 \oplus M_3 \oplus C_4 \oplus M_5 \oplus M_6 \oplus M_7$$

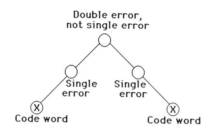

Figure 1.5-3 Fragment of an N-cube illustrating the distance between code words in a double-error-detecting, single-error-correcting code.

1.R REFERENCES

[BERLEKAMP 68] Berlekamp, E. R., *Algebraic Coding Theory*, McGraw-Hill Book Company, New York, 1968.

[BURKS 62] Burks, A. W., H. H. Goldstine, and J. von Neumann, "Preliminary Discussion of the Logical Design of an Electronic Computing Instrument," *Datamation*, Sec. 6.5, pp. 39–40, Oct. 1962.

[CHRYSTAL 61] Chrystal, G., *Textbook of Algebra*, Vol. I, Dover Publications, Inc., New York, 1961.

[DICKINSON 64] Dickinson, M. M., J. B. Jackson, and G. C. Randa, "Saturn V Launch Vehicle Digital Computer and Data Adapter," *Proc. AFIPS Fall Joint Comput. Conf.*, Vol. 26, Part 1, pp. 501–516, 1964.

[GSCHWIND 75] Gschwind, H. W., and E. J. McCluskey, *Design of Digital Computers*, Springer-Verlag, Inc., New York, 1975.

[HAMMING 50] Hamming, R. W., "Error Detecting and Error Correcting Codes," *Bell Syst. Tech. J.*, Vol. 29, pp. 147–160, Apr. 1950.

[HSIAO 70] Hsiao, M. Y., "A Class of Optimal Minimum Odd-Weight-Column SEC-DED Codes," *IBM J. Res. Dev.*, Vol. 14, No. 4, pp. 395–401, 1970.

[HWANG 78] Hwang, K., *Computer Arithmetic: Principles, Architecture, and Design*, John Wiley & Sons, Inc., New York, 1978.

[KEISTER 64] Keister, W., R. W. Ketchledge, and H. E. Vaughan, "No. 1 ESS: System Organization and Objectives," *Bell Syst. Tech. J.*, Vol. 43, No. 5, Sec. 4, pp. 1841–1842, 1964.

[KNUTH 68] Knuth, D. E., *Fundamental Algorithms*, Addison-Wesley Publishing Company, Inc., Reading, Mass., 1968.

[KNUTH 69] Knuth, D. E., *Seminumerical Algorithms*, Addison-Wesley Publishing Company, Inc., Reading, Mass., 1969.

[LYONS 62] Lyons, R. E., and W. Vanderkulk, "The Use of Triple-Modular Redundancy to Improve Computer Reliability," *IBM J. Res. Dev.*, Vol. 6, No. 2, pp. 200–209, 1962.

[PERRY 61] Perry, M. N., and W. R. Plugge, "American Airlines SABRE Electronics Reservations System," *Proc. 9th Western Joint Comput. Conf.*, Los Angeles, p. 593, May 1961.

[PETERSON 72] Peterson, W. W., and E. J. Weldon, Jr., *Error-Correcting Codes*, 2nd ed., John Wiley & Sons, Inc., New York, 1972.

[VON NEUMANN 56] von Neumann, J., "Probabilistic Logics and the Synthesis of Reliable Organisms from Unreliable Components," in *Automata Studies*, ed. C. E. Shannon and J. McCarthy, Annals of Mathematics Studies 34, pp. 43–98, Princeton University Press, Princeton, N.J., 1956.

[WASER 82] Waser, S., and M. J. Flynn, *Introduction to Arithmetic for Digital Systems Designers*, Holt, Rinehart and Winston, New York, 1982.

[WHITE 53] White, G. S., "Coded Decimal Number Systems for Digital Computers," *Proc. IRE*, Vol. 41, No. 10, pp. 1450–1452, 1953.

1.P PROBLEMS

1.1 Convert:
  (a) $(523.1)_{10}$ to base 8
  (b) $(523.1)_{10}$ to base 2
  (c) $(101.11)_2$ to base 8
  (d) $(101.11)_2$ to base 10
  (e) $(1100.11)_2$ to base 7
  (f) $(101.11)_2$ to base 4
  (g) $(321.40)_6$ to base 7
  (h) $(25/3)_{10}$ to base 2

1.2 In base 10 the highest number that can be obtained by multiplying together two single digits is $9 \times 9 = 81$, which can be expressed with two digits. What is the maximum number of digits required to express the product of two single digits in an arbitrary base-b system?

1.3 Given that $(79)_{10} = (142)_b$, determine the value of b.

1.4 Given that $(301)_b = (I^2)_b$, where I is an integer in base b and I^2 is its square, determine the value of b.

1.5 Let

$$N^* = (n_4 n_3 n_2 n_1 n_0)^* = 2 \cdot 3 \cdot 4 \cdot 5 \cdot n_4 + 3 \cdot 4 \cdot 5 \cdot n_3 + 4 \cdot 5 \cdot n_2 + 5 \cdot n_1 + n_0$$

$$= 120 n_4 + 60 n_3 + 20 n_2 + 5 n_1 + n_0$$

where

$$0 \le n_0 \le 4 \qquad 0 \le n_1 \le 3 \qquad 0 \le n_2 \le 2 \qquad 0 \le n_3 \le 1 \qquad 0 \le n_4 \le 1$$

with all the n_i positive integers.

(a) Convert $(11111)^*$ to base 10.

(b) Convert $(11234)^*$ to base 10.

(c) Convert $(97)_{10}$ to its equivalent $(n_4 n_3 n_2 n_1 n_0)^*$.

(d) Which decimal numbers can be expressed in the form $(n_4 n_3 n_2 n_1 n_0)^*$?

1.6 To write a number in base 16, the following symbols will be used for the numbers from 10 to 15:

10	t	12	w	14	u
11	e	13	h	15	f

(a) Convert $(4tu)_{16}$ to base 10.

(b) Convert $(2tfu)_{16}$ to base 2 directly (without first converting to base 10).

1.7 Convert $(1222)_3$ to base 5, $(N)_5$, using only binary arithmetic.

(a) Convert $(1222)_3$ to $(N)_2$.

(b) Convert $(N)_2$ to $(N)_5$.

1.8 Perform the following binary-arithmetic operations.

(a) $11.10 + 10.11 + 111.00 + 110.11 + 001.01 = ?$

(b) $111.00 - 011.11 = ?$

(c) $011.11 - 111.00 = ?$

(d) $111.001 \times 1001.1 = ?$

(e) $101011.1 + 1101.11 = ?$

1.9 Form the radix complement and the diminished radix complement for each of the following numbers.

(a) $(0.10111)_2$

(b) $(0.110011)_2$

(c) $(0.5231)_{10}$

(d) $(0.32499)_{10}$

(e) $(0.3214)_6$

(f) $(032456)_7$

1.10

(a) Write out the following weighted decimal codes.

(i) $7, 4, 2, -1$

(ii) $8, 4, -2, -1$

(iii) $4, 4, 1, -2$

(iv) $7, 5, 3, -6$

(v) $8, 7, -4, -2$

(b) Which codes of part (a) are self-complementing?

(c) If a weighted binary-coded-decimal code is self-complementing, what necessary condition is placed on the sum of the weights?

(d) Is the condition of part (c) sufficient to guarantee the self-complementing property? Give an example to justify your answer.

1.11 Write out the following weighted decimal codes: $(7, 3, 1, -2)$, $(8, 4, -3, -2)$, $(6, 2, 2, 1)$. Which of these, if any, are self-complementing?

1.12 Sketch a 4-cube and label the points. List the points in the p-subcubes for $p = 2, 3$.

1.13 Compute all the pairwise distances for the points in a 3-cube. Arrange these in a matrix form where the rows and columns are numbered 0, 1, . . ., 7, corresponding to the points of the 3-cube. The 0-, 1-, and 2-cube pairwise distances are given by submatrices of this matrix. By observing the relationship between these matrices, what is a scheme for going from the n-cube pairwise-distance matrix to the $(n + 1)$-cube pairwise-distance matrix?

1.14 What is a scheme for going from the Gray code to the ordinary binary code using addition modulo 2 only?

1.15 For the Gray code, a weighting scheme exists in which the weights associated with the bits are constant except for sign. The signs alternate with the occurrence of 1's, left to right. What is the weighting scheme?

1.16 List the symmetries of the 2-cube.

1.17 Write out a typical type-6 closed-unit-distance 4 code (Table 1.4-3).

1.18 Write out two open-unit-distance 4 codes of different type (i.e., one is not a symmetry of the other).

1.19 Write out a set of six code words that have a single-error-correcting property.

1.20 A closed error-detecting unit-distance code is defined as follows: There are k $(k < 2^n)$ ordered binary n-bit code words with the property that changing a single bit in any word will change the original word into either its predecessor or its successor in the list (the first word is considered the successor for the last word) or into some other n-bit word **not** in the code. Changing a single bit cannot transform a code word into any code word other than its predecessor or successor. List the code word for such a code with $k = 6$, $n = 3$. Is there more than one symmetry type of code for these specifications? Why?

2

SWITCHING ALGEBRA

2.1 INTRODUCTION

The distinguishing feature of the circuits to be discussed here is the use of two-valued, or binary, signals. There will be some deviation of the signals from their nominal values, but within certain limits this variation will not affect the performance of the circuit. If the variations exceed these limits, the circuit will not behave properly and steps must be taken to confine the signals to the proper ranges. When the statement is made that the signals are two-valued, what is really meant is that the value of each signal is within one of two (nonoverlapping) continuous ranges. Since the operation of the circuit does not depend on exactly which value within a given range the signal takes on, a particular value is chosen to represent the range and the signal is said to be equal to this value.

The exact numerical value of the signal is not important. It is possible to have two circuits perform the same function and have completely different values for their signals. To avoid any possible confusion that might arise because of this situation and to simplify the design procedures, it is customary to carry out the **logic design** without specifying the actual values of the signals. Once the logic design has been completed, actual values must be assigned to the signals in the course of designing the detailed electrical circuit. For the purposes of the logic design, *arbitrary* symbols are chosen to represent the two values to which the signals are to be restricted. An algebra using these symbols is then developed as the basis for formal design techniques. The development of such an algebra is the subject of this chapter. This algebra will be called **switching algebra**. It is identical with a Boolean algebra and was originally applied to switching circuits [Shannon 38] by reinterpreting Boolean algebra in terms of switching circuits rather than by developing a switching algebra directly, as will be done here.

2.2 POSTULATES

The two symbols most commonly chosen to represent the two logic values taken on by binary signals are 0 and 1. It should be emphasized that there is no numerical significance attached to these symbols. For an electronic circuit that has its signals equal to either 0 or 5 volts (V), it is possible to assign the symbol 1 to 0 V and the symbol 0 to 5 V. This choice for the correspondence between logic value and physical value in which 1 corresponds to the more negative physical value is called **negative logic**. More common is **positive logic**, in which the logic 1 is assigned to the more positive physical signal value. Negative logic is often used for technologies in which the active signal has the lower value, for example PMOS (described in Section 4.3). Unless stated otherwise, positive logic will be used here.

Some other set of symbols, such as T and F, H and L, or + and −, could be used instead of 1 and 0; but there is a strong tradition behind the use of 1 and 0. Furthermore, 1 and 0 are the symbols specified in the ANSI/IEEE Standard: "Graphic Symbols for Logic Functions (Std. 91-1984)" (described in [Mann 81]).

Switching variables are used in logic networks to represent the signals present at the network inputs and outputs as well as the signals on internal gate inputs and outputs. A switching variable is also useful in representing the state of a **switch**, shown in Fig. 2.2-1. A switch is a three-terminal device with a control input K and two symmetric data terminals, a and b. The use of switches to model single transistors and transmission gates is described in Chapter 4. An extensive discussion of switch models and their applications can be found in [Hayes 82]. Switches are also used to model (relay) contacts. For a description of relay contacts and their use in switching networks, see [McCluskey 65].

Positive switch operation (Fig. 2.2-1a) is defined as the two switch terminals (a and b) being connected together if and only if the control variable, K, equals 1. When $K = 0$, there is an open circuit between the two switch terminals. There is a variable T associated with the switch that equals 1 when the terminals are connected together and that equals 0 when there is an open circuit between the

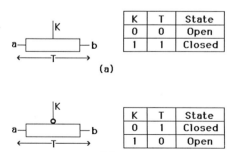

K	T	State
0	0	Open
1	1	Closed

(a)

K	T	State
0	1	Closed
1	0	Open

(b)

Figure 2.2-1 Transmission, T, of a switch: (a) positive switch; (b) negative switch.

terminals. The variable T is called the **transmission** of the switch. (It is also possible to associate with the switch a variable that equals 1 only when the switch is open. Such a variable is called the switch hindrance. This was used in the very early papers on switching theory in connection with contact networks. The transmission concept is the standard usage at present.)

A negative switch is shown in Fig. 2.2-1b. This has the same operation as the positive switch with the exception that a control value of 0 causes the switch to close and a 1 causes the switch to open. The small circle or "bubble" on the control input of the negative switch is an indication that the effect of the control signal is the reverse of the effect without the bubble. The use of this small circle as a negation indicator is part of the IEEE logic standard [Mann 81]. The negation bubble will be used throughout this book as a very useful aid in both analysis and design. It is particularly valuable in connection with NAND and NOR gate networks (Section 2.6).

The first postulate of the switching algebra can now be presented. This is merely a formal statement of the fact that switching variables are always equal to either 0 or 1. In the statements of postulates and theorems that follow, the symbols $X, Y, Z, X_1, X_2, \ldots, X_n$ will be used to represent switching variables.

$$(P1) \ X = 0 \quad \text{if } X \neq 1 \qquad (P1') \ X = 1 \quad \text{if } X \neq 0$$

To implement general switching networks it is necessary to be able to obtain, for any signal representing a switching variable, a signal that has the opposite value. A circuit for realizing this function is called an **inverter**. Inverter symbols are shown in Fig. 2.2-2. The symbol specified in the IEEE standard is shown in Fig. 2.2-2a. Use of the distinctive shape symbol of Fig. 2.2-2b is "not considered to be in contradiction" to the IEEE standard.

If X represents a switching variable, the symbol X' is used to represent the signal having the opposite value. This notation is specified formally in the second switching algebra postulate.

$$(P2) \text{ If } X = 0, \text{ then } X' = 1 \qquad (P2') \text{ If } X = 1, \text{ then } X' = 0$$

The two symbols X and X' are not two different variables, since they involve only X. In order to distinguish them the term *literal* is used, where a **literal** is defined as a variable with or without an associated prime and X and X' are different literals. The literal X' is called the complement[1] of X. 0 is called the complement of 1, and 1 is called the complement of 0. The logical operation of the inverter can now be described in terms of switching algebra. If X_1 represents the input signal and X_0 the output signal, then $X_0 = X_1'$, since X_0 is high when X_1 is low, and vice versa.

Figure 2.2-2 Symbol for inverter: (a) IEEE standard symbol; (b) distinctive shape symbol.

---

[1] The symbols $\overline{X}$ or $\sim X$ or $-X$ are also used for the complement of X.

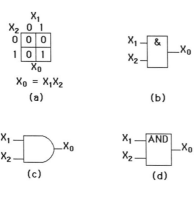

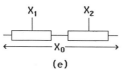

Figure 2.2-3 The AND function:
(a) table; (b) IEEE standard symbol;
(c) distinctive shape symbol; (d) common nonstandard symbol; (e) switches in series.

To represent the action of other switching devices, it is necessary to define additional algebraic operations. A two-input AND gate will be considered first. If the two inputs are represented by X_1 and X_2 and the output by X_0, the logical performance of the circuit is represented by the table of Fig. 2.2-3a. This table is also correct for the transmission X_0 of two switches X_1 and X_2 in series. (The series connection is closed only when both switches are closed.) The operation represented is identical with ordinary multiplication and will be defined as multiplication in the switching algebra developed here. Thus, the equation for an AND gate, or two switches in series, is $X_0 = X_1X_2$.[2] The IEEE Standard symbol is shown in Fig. 2.2-3b and the (discouraged) distinctive shape symbol in Fig. 2.2-3c. The symbol of Fig. 2.2-3d is also used sometimes.

The table for an OR gate, or two switches in parallel, is shown in Fig. 2.2-4a. This table will be taken as the definition of switching-algebra addition.[3] It is identical with ordinary addition except for the case $1 + 1 = 1$. Symbols for the OR gate are shown in Fig. 2.2-4b–e. The symbol shown in Fig. 2.2-4d will be used in this book whenever no confusion can arise. The IEEE standard symbol is not yet in common usage in the United States. The symbol of Fig. 2.2-4d is more familiar.

The remaining postulates are merely restatements of the definitions of multiplication and addition.

$$(P3) \quad 0 \cdot 0 = 0 \qquad\qquad (P3') \quad 1 + 1 = 1$$

$$(P4) \quad 1 \cdot 1 = 1 \qquad\qquad (P4') \quad 0 + 0 = 0$$

$$(P5) \quad 1 \cdot 0 = 0 \cdot 1 = 0 \qquad\qquad (P5') \quad 0 + 1 = 1 + 0 = 1$$

---

[2] The symbol $X_1 \wedge X_2$ is sometimes used to indicate logical multiplication.

[3] This operation is also called logical addition, and some writers use the symbol $X_1 \vee X_2$ rather than $X_1 + X_2$.

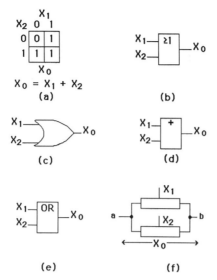

Figure 2.2-4 The OR function: (a) table;
(b) IEEE gate symbol; (c) distinctive
shape symbol; (d) symbol used in this
book; (e) common nonstandard symbol;
(f) parallel connection of switches.

All the postulates have been stated in pairs. These pairs have the property that when (0 and 1) and ($+$ and $\cdot$) are interchanged, one member of the pair is changed into the other. This is an example of the general **principle of duality**, which is true for all switching-algebra theorems since it is true for all the postulates. This algebraic duality arises from the fact that either 1 or 0 can be assigned to an open circuit. If 0 is chosen to represent a high voltage, the expression for an AND gate becomes $X_0 = X_1 + X_2$. Similarly, the transmission of two switches in series is equal to $X_1 + X_2$ if 0 is chosen to represent a closed circuit. Duality is discussed further in Sec. 2.8.

2.3 ANALYSIS

Analysis of a logic network consists of examining the network and somehow determining what its behavior will be for all possible inputs. The switching algebra of Sec. 2.2 is sufficient for analyzing those logic networks that have no memory and are constructed of only binary gates or only of switches.[4] A memoryless logic network is called a **combinational network**. A **combinational logic network** is defined as one for which the outputs depend only on the present inputs to the circuit.[5] The other type of network, called a **sequential logic network**, is one for which the outputs depend not only on the present inputs but also on the past history of inputs. Acyclic gate or switch networks (networks with no feedback loops) are always combinational. Sequential networks typically contain latches, flip-flops, or feedback loops. Chapters 7, 8, and 9 discuss sequential networks.

[4] It may be necessary to augment the switching algebra in order to handle networks containing both gates and switches.

[5] The term *combinatorial network* is sometimes used (incorrectly) as a synonym for *combinational network*.

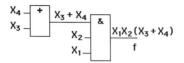

Figure 2.3-1 Very simple gate network analysis example.

The analysis of a combinational circuit consists in writing an algebraic function for each output. These are functions of the input variables from which the condition of each output can be determined for each combination of input conditions. For a switch network these output functions are the transmissions between each pair of external terminals. Only two-terminal networks will be considered for the present. In a gate network, an output function specifies those input conditions for which the output node will be at 1.

Network analysis is discussed in detail in Chap. 3. A very simple gate network analysis example is shown in Fig. 2.3-1 to serve as an introduction to the use of switching functions. In an acyclic network there will be at least one gate that has only network inputs connected to it. In Fig. 2.3-1 the OR gate is such a gate. The output of such gates can be written down directly. There will then be other gates that have either input variables or expressions on all their inputs—the AND gate in Fig. 2.3-1 is such a gate. It is then possible to write expressions for the output of all these gates. By repeating this procedure an expression will eventually be obtained for the network output.

The network behavior can be determined from these output functions. One procedure (which isn't very efficient but does demonstrate that it can be done) is to substitute a set of values for the input variables and then use the postulates to simplify the resulting expressions. A value will be obtained for the output variable that specifies the output for the particular input combination chosen. For example, if the input combination $X_1 = 0$, $X_2 = 1$, $X_3 = 0$, $X_4 = 1$ is chosen, the output of Fig. 2.3-1 becomes

$$f = X_1 X_2 (X_3 + X_4) = 0 \cdot 1(0 + 1) = 0(1) = 0$$

By carrying out this procedure for all possible 2^n input combinations it is possible to form a table that lists the output for each input combination. Such a table describes completely the circuit behavior and is called a **table of combinations**.[6] Table 2.3-1 is the table of combinations for the circuit of Fig. 2.3-1.

2.4 SYNTHESIS

In designing a combinational circuit it is necessary to carry out in reverse the procedure just described. The desired circuit performance is specified by means of a table of combinations. From this table an algebraic function is formed, and finally the circuit is derived from the function. A concise means of specifying the

---

[6] In logic, the table is called a **truth table**. Some writers use this term when discussing logic networks. Strictly speaking, only the steady-state behavior is described. This distinction is discussed in Chapter 3.

TABLE 2.3-1 Table of combinations
for $f = X_1 X_2 (X_3 + X_4)$

	X_1	X_2	X_3	X_4	f
0	0	0	0	0	0
1	0	0	0	1	0
2	0	0	1	0	0
3	0	0	1	1	0
4	0	1	0	0	0
5	0	1	0	1	0
6	0	1	1	0	0
7	0	1	1	1	0
8	1	0	0	0	0
9	1	0	0	1	0
10	1	0	1	0	0
11	1	0	1	1	0
12	1	1	0	0	0
13	1	1	0	1	1
14	1	1	1	0	1
15	1	1	1	1	1

table of combinations, called a **decimal specification**, is to list the numbers of the rows for which the output is to equal 1. For Table 2.3-1 this specification is

$$f(X_1, X_2, X_3, X_4) = \Sigma(13, 14, 15)$$

where the Σ signifies that the rows for which the function equals 1 are being listed. It is also possible to list the rows for which the function equals 0, such a list being preceded by the symbol Π to indicate that it is the zero rows which are listed. This specification for the preceding table is $f(X_1, X_2, X_3, X_4) = \Pi(0, 1, 2, 3, 4, 5, 6, 7, 8, 9, 10, 11, 12)$. To avoid any ambiguity in these specifications, it is necessary to adopt some rule for numbering the rows of the table of combinations. The usual procedure is to regard each row of the table as a binary number and then use the decimal equivalent of this binary number as the row number. The output-column entries are not included in forming the binary row numbers. There is nothing special about decimal numbers other than the fact that they are the most familiar—any other number base such as octal could be used. The reason for using a number system other than binary is simply that binary numbers take too much space to write down.

Another concise way to specify a switching function is to list just the output column of the table of combinations. This is called the **designation number** and is unambiguous if a fixed order is assumed for the rows of the table. Usually, the rows are arranged in arithmetic order as binary numbers. For the function of Table 2.3-1 the designation number is

$$\mathrm{DN}(f) = (0000000000000111)$$

In general, the designation number of a function $f(X_1, X_2, \ldots, X_n)$ is defined as

$$\mathrm{DN}(f) = (f_0, f_1, \ldots, f_{(2^n - 2)}, f_{(2^n - 1)})$$

Designation numbers are used much less frequently than the decimal specification described in the preceding paragraph. For an interesting application of designation numbers, see [McCluskey 78].

It has been pointed out that the table of combinations is a complete specification for a combinational circuit. The first step in designing a circuit is to formulate such a table. There are no general formal techniques for doing this. When a sequential circuit is being designed, it is customary to reduce the sequential-design problem to (several) combinational problems, and formal techniques exist for doing this. However, when a combinational circuit is being designed, no formal techniques are available and it is necessary to rely on common sense. This is not too surprising, since any formal technique must start with a formal statement of the problem, and this is precisely what the table of combinations is. As an example of how this is done, the table of combinations for a circuit to check binary-coded-decimal digits is shown in Table 2.4-1 for the 8,4,2,1 code. This circuit is to deliver a 1 output whenever a digit having an invalid combination of bits is received.

TABLE 2.4-1 Table of combinations for circuit to check binary-coded-decimal digits

	b_8	b_4	b_2	b_1	f	
0	0	0	0	0	0	
1	0	0	0	1	0	
2	0	0	1	0	0	
3	0	0	1	1	0	
4	0	1	0	0	0	
5	0	1	0	1	0	
6	0	1	1	0	0	
7	0	1	1	1	0	
8	1	0	0	0	0	
9	1	0	0	1	0	
10	1	0	1	0	1	
11	1	0	1	1	1	Invalid
12	1	1	0	0	1	code
13	1	1	0	1	1	words
14	1	1	1	0	1	
15	1	1	1	1	1	

In forming a table of combinations there very often are rows for which it is unimportant whether the function equals 0 or 1. The usual reason for this situation is that the combination of inputs corresponding to these rows can never occur (when the circuit is functioning properly). As an example of this, consider a circuit to translate from the 8,4,2,1 BCD code to a Gray (cyclic binary) code. When the circuit is working correctly, the input combinations represented by rows 10 through 15 of the table of combinations cannot occur. Therefore, the output need not be specified for these rows. The symbol d will be used to indicate the output condition for such a situation.[7] The output conditions so denoted are called don't-care

---

[7] In the literature, the symbols ϕ or $\times$ are also used.

conditions (see Table 2.4-2). It is possible to include the d rows in the decimal specification of a function by listing them after the symbol d. Thus, the decimal specification for g_1 of Table 2.4-2 would be

$$g_1(b_8, b_4, b_2, b_1) = \Sigma(1, 2, 5, 6, 9) + d(10, 11, 12, 13, 14, 15)$$

$$= \Pi(0, 3, 4, 7, 8) + d(10, 11, 12, 13, 14, 15)$$

TABLE 2.4-2 Table of combinations for circuit to translate from BCD 8,4,2,1 code to Gray code

	BCD-code input				Gray-code output			
	b_8	b_4	b_2	b_1	g_4	g_3	g_2	g_1
0	0	0	0	0	0	0	0	0
1	0	0	0	1	0	0	0	1
2	0	0	1	0	0	0	1	1
3	0	0	1	1	0	0	1	0
4	0	1	0	0	0	1	1	0
5	0	1	0	1	0	1	1	1
6	0	1	1	0	0	1	0	1
7	0	1	1	1	0	1	0	0
8	1	0	0	0	1	1	0	0
9	1	0	0	1	1	1	0	1
10	1	0	1	0	d	d	d	d
11	1	0	1	1	d	d	d	d
12	1	1	0	0	d	d	d	d
13	1	1	0	1	d	d	d	d
14	1	1	1	0	d	d	d	d
15	1	1	1	1	d	d	d	d

The handling of d rows will be discussed further in Chap. 6. For the present it will be assumed that the output specified for each row of the table of combinations is either 0 or 1.

2.4-1 Canonical Expressions

After forming the table of combinations, the next step in designing a circuit is to write an algebraic expression for the output function. The simplest output functions to write are those which equal 1 for only one row of the table of combinations or those which equal 0 for only one row. It is possible to associate with each row two functions—one that equals 1 only for the row and one that equals 0 only for the row (Table 2.4-3). These functions are called **fundamental products** or **min-terms** and **fundamental sums** or **maxterms**, respectively. Each fundamental product or sum contains all the input variables. The rule for forming the fundamental product for a given row is to prime any variables that equal 0 for the row and leave unprimed variables that equal 1 for the row. The fundamental product equals the product of the literals so formed. The fundamental sum is formed by a completely reverse or dual procedure. Each variable that equals 0 for the row is left unprimed, and each variable that equals 1 for the row is primed. The fundamental sum is the sum of the literals obtained by this process. The algebraic expression for any table for which the output is equal to 1 (or 0) for only one row can be written down directly by choosing the proper fundamental product (or sum). For example, the output function specified by $f(x_1, x_2, x_3) = \Sigma(6)$ is written algebraically as $f = x_1 x_2 x_3'$, and the output function $f(x_1, x_2, x_3) = \Pi(6)$ is written as $f = x_1' + x_2' + x_3$. The fundamental product corresponding to row i of the table of combinations will be denoted by p_i, and the fundamental sum corresponding to row i will be denoted by s_i.

TABLE 2.4-3 Table of combinations showing fundamental products and fundamental sums

	x_1	x_2	x_3	Fundamental product	Fundamental sum
0	0	0	0	$x_1' x_2' x_3'$	$x_1 + x_2 + x_3$
1	0	0	1	$x_1' x_2' x_3$	$x_1 + x_2 + x_3'$
2	0	1	0	$x_1' x_2 x_3'$	$x_1 + x_2' + x_3$
3	0	1	1	$x_1' x_2 x_3$	$x_1 + x_2' + x_3'$
4	1	0	0	$x_1 x_2' x_3'$	$x_1' + x_2 + x_3$
5	1	0	1	$x_1 x_2' x_3$	$x_1' + x_2 + x_3'$
6	1	1	0	$x_1 x_2 x_3'$	$x_1' + x_2' + x_3$
7	1	1	1	$x_1 x_2 x_3$	$x_1' + x_2' + x_3'$

The algebraic expression that equals 1 (or 0) for more than one row of the table of combinations can be written directly as a sum of fundamental products or as a product of fundamental sums. A function f that equals 1 for two rows, i and j, of the table of combinations can be expressed as a sum of the two fundamental products p_i and p_j: $f = p_i + p_j$. When the inputs correspond to row i, $p_i = 1$ and $p_j = 0$ so that $f = 1 + 0 = 1$. When the inputs correspond to row j, $p_i = 0$, $p_j = 1$, and $f = 0 + 1 = 1$. When the inputs correspond to any other row, $p_i = 0$, $p_j = 0$, $f = 0 + 0 = 0$. This shows that the function $f = p_i + p_j$ does equal 1 only for rows i and j. This argument can be extended to functions that equal 1 for any number of input combinations—they can be represented algebraically as a sum of the corresponding fundamental products (see Table 2.4-4). An algebraic expression that is a sum of fundamental products is called a **canonical sum**.

An arbitrary function can also be expressed as a product of fundamental sums. This form is called a **canonical product**. The canonical product for a function that is equal to 0 only for rows i and j of the table of combinations is given by $f = s_i \cdot s_j$. For row i, $s_i = 0$ so that $f = 0$. For row j, $s_j = 0$ so that $f = 0$, and for any other row $s_i = s_j = 1$ so that $f = 1$. In general, the canonical product is equal to the product of all fundamental sums that correspond to input conditions for which the function is to equal 0.

TABLE 2.4-4 $f(x_1, x_2, x_3) = \Sigma(1, 2, 3, 4)$: (a) Table of combinations; (b) Canonical sum; (c) Canonical product

(a)

	x_1	x_2	x_3	f
0	0	0	0	0
1	0	0	1	1
2	0	1	0	1
3	0	1	1	1
4	1	0	0	1
5	1	0	1	0
6	1	1	0	0
7	1	1	1	0

(b)

$$f = x_1'x_2'x_3 + x_1'x_2x_3' + x_1'x_2x_3 + x_1x_2'x_3'$$

(c)

$$f = (x_1 + x_2 + x_3)(x_1' + x_2 + x_3')$$
$$(x_1' + x_2' + x_3)(x_1' + x_2' + x_3')$$

It is possible to write a general expression for the canonical sum by making use of the following theorems:[8]

$$(T2')\ x \cdot 0 = 0$$

$$(T1)\ x + 0 = x \qquad (T1')\ x \cdot 1 = x$$

If the value of the function $f(x_1, x_2, \ldots, x_n)$ for the ith row of the table of combinations is f_i ($f_i = 0$ or 1), then the canonical sum is given by

$$f(x_1, x_2, \ldots, x_n) = f_0 p_0 + f_1 p_1 + \cdots + f_{(2^n-1)}p_{(2^n-1)}$$

$$= \sum_{i=0}^{2^n-1} f_i p_i$$

For the function $f(x_1, x_2) = \Sigma(0, 2)$ the values of the f_i are $f_0 = f_2 = 1$, $f_1 = f_3 = 0$ so that

$$f(x_1, x_2) = 1 \cdot p_0 + 0 \cdot p_1 + 1 \cdot p_2 + 0 \cdot p_3$$

$$= p_0 + 0 + p_2 + 0$$

$$= p_0 + p_2$$

$$= x_1'x_2' + x_1x_2'$$

In a similar fashion a general expression for the canonical product can be obtained by using the theorems

$$(T2)\ x + 1 = 1$$

$$(T1)\ x + 0 = x \qquad (T1')\ x \cdot 1 = x$$

[8] The theorems are presented in Sec. 2.5. The numbering of Sec. 2.5 is used here for consistency.

The resulting expression is

$$f(x_1, x_2, \ldots, x_n) = (f_0 + s_0)(f_1 + s_1) \cdots (f_{(2^n - 1)} + s_{(2^n - 1)})$$

$$= \prod_{i=0}^{2^n - 1} (f_i + s_i)$$

For $f(x_1, x_2) = \Sigma(0, 2) = \Pi(1, 3)$ this becomes

$$f(x_1, x_2) = (1 + s_0)(0 + s_1)(1 + s_2)(0 + s_3)$$

$$= 1 \cdot s_1 \cdot 1 \cdot s_3$$

$$= s_1 \cdot s_3$$

$$= (x_1 + x_2')(x_1' + x_2')$$

2.4-2 Networks

A technique for obtaining an algebraic expression from a table of combinations has just been described. A circuit can be drawn directly from this expression by reversing the procedures used to analyze series-parallel switch networks or gate networks. The circuit for a single fundamental product is just a series connection of switches or an AND gate with appropriate inputs. For a canonical sum involving more than one fundamental product, the circuit consists of a number of parallel subnetworks, each subnetwork corresponding to one fundamental product; or a number of AND gates with their outputs connected as inputs to an OR gate. This is shown in Figs. 2.4-1a and 2.4-2a. Similarly, the switch network corresponding to a canonical product consists of a number of subnetworks in series, each subnetwork corresponding to one fundamental sum and consisting of switches in parallel (see Fig. 2.4-1b). The gate network corresponding to a canonical product consists of a number of OR gates with their outputs connected as the inputs of

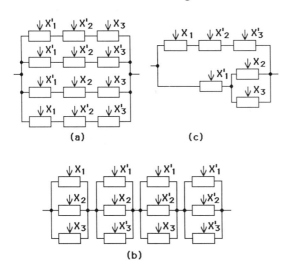

(a)   (c)

(b)

Figure 2.4-1 Switch networks for $\Sigma(1, 2, 3, 4)$: (a) network derived from canonical sum; (b) network derived from canonical product; (c) economical network.

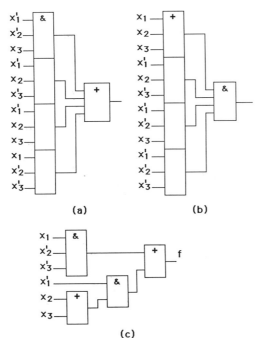

Figure 2.4-2 Gate networks for $\Sigma(1, 2, 3, 4)$: (a) network derived from canonical sums; (b) network derived from canonical product; (c) economical network.

an AND gate (Fig. 2.4-2b). These conclusions are summarized in the following theorem:

THEOREM 2.4-1. For any arbitrary table of combinations, a network whose behavior corresponds to the table of combinations can be constructed of:

1. **Switches**, or
2. **AND gates**, **OR gates**, and **inverters** if there are no restrictions on the number of components used.

In a certain sense our design procedure is now complete. A method has been presented for going from a table of combinations to a circuit diagram. However, the canonical circuits so designed are usually very uneconomical and therefore unsatisfactory. An example of this can be seen by comparing the circuits of Figs. 2.4-1a and b and 2.4-2a and b with those of Figs. 2.4-1c and 2.4-2c. To design satisfactory circuits, it is necessary to have procedures for simplifying them so that they correspond to simpler circuits. This is discussed in Chap. 6.

2.4-3 Number of Functions

An alternative practical approach to circuit design would be to make use of a table that listed economical circuits for all switching functions with fewer than some specified number of inputs. All circuits that did not have too many inputs could then be designed merely by looking them up in the table. Theoretically, there is no reason why this could not be done, since for any given number of input variables there are only a finite number of switching functions possible. In fact, the number of switching functions of n input variables is exactly 2^{2^n}. There are 2^n rows in an n-input table of combinations, and since the output for each row can be either 0 or 1, there are 2^{2^n} different output functions. Table 2.4-5 lists 2^{2^n} for values of n from 1 to 5. It is clear from this table that it would be impractical to list functions of more than three variables. The situation is not quite so bad as the listed values of 2^{2^n} would seem to indicate, since many of the functions counted differ only by an interchange of input variables. For example, the two functions $f_1 = x_1 + x_2 x_3$ and $f_2 = x_2 + x_1 x_3$ are different, but one can be converted into the other by interchanging the variables x_1 and x_2. Interchanging two variables corresponds to relabeling two leads, and therefore the same circuit can be used for both functions f_1 and f_2 by merely changing the labels on two leads. Similarly, the functions $f_1 = x_1 + x_2 x_3$ and $f_3 = x_1' + x_2 x_3$ can be interchanged by interchanging x_1 and x_1'.

TABLE 2.4-5 Numbers of switching functions

n	2^n	2^{2^n}	N_n*
1	2	4	3
2	4	16	6
3	8	256	22
4	16	65,536	402
5	32	4,294,967,296	1,228,158

* N_n = number of types of functions of n variables.

When one function can be changed into another by permuting and/or complementing input variables, the two functions are said to be of the same **type**. Clearly, a table of standard circuits need list circuits for only one function of each type. At first glance, it might seem that the number of types of n-input functions would be $2^{2^n} \div n!2^n$ since there are $n!$ permutations and 2^n different ways of complementing variables. This is not correct, for permuting and/or complementing variables does not necessarily convert a given function into a different function. For example, $f_1 = x_1 + x_2 x_3$ is left unchanged when the variables x_2 and x_3 are interchanged. The number of types of functions for n input variables have been computed [Slepian 54] and are listed as N_n in Table 2.4-5. If only types of functions are listed, it is practical to catalog circuits for functions of four variables. This has actually been done for contact networks [Grea 55] and for electronic tube circuits [Harvard 51]. Since circuits having more than five input variables are often required, it is necessary to develop a general design procedure. This will be the subject of Chap. 6.

2.5 THEOREMS

One use of switching algebra in logic design is to write an algebraic expression for the desired circuit performance and then to manipulate that expression into a form that represents a desirable network. The manipulations are carried out by means of the switching algebra theorems. They will be presented in this section.

The usual procedure for proving theorems is to prove some theorems by using only the postulates, then to prove further theorems by using both the theorems already proved and the postulates, and so on. When such a method of proof is used, it is customary to present the theorems in an order such that each theorem can be proved by using only the postulates and previous theorems. Since the algebra being developed here involves only the constants 0 and 1, it is possible to prove almost all theorems directly from the postulates using **perfect induction**. A proof by perfect induction involves substituting all possible combinations of values for the variables occurring in a theorem and then verifying that the theorem gives the correct result for all combinations. For example, the theorem $1 + X = 1$ is proved by first substituting 0 for X, which yields $1 + 0 = 1$, and then substituting 1 for X, obtaining $1 + 1 = 1$. The theorem is true since these results are precisely postulates P5′ and P3′. Because perfect induction is available as a method of proof, the theorems will be presented in an order designed to emphasize the structure of the algebra rather than to facilitate formal proofs. The presentation of the theorems will be in pairs, where one member of the pair is obtained from the other by interchanging (0 and 1) and (addition and multiplication). This is done for the same reason that it was done for the postulates. Strictly speaking, X and X' should also be interchanged. This is not done, for the variables appearing in the theorems are generic variables and a theorem such as $X' + 1 = 1$ is no different from the theorem $X + 1 = 1$. Actually, it is possible to substitute an entire expression for the variables appearing in a theorem. Thus, the theorem $X + XY = X$ implies that $ab + c + (ab + c)(de + fg) = ab + c$.

2.5-1 Single-Variable Theorems

The switching-algebra theorems that involve only a single variable are shown in Table 2.5-1. Three of these theorems, T2, T3, and T3′, are especially noteworthy since they are false for ordinary algebra. Theorems T3 and T3′ can be extended to $X + X + X + \cdots + X = nX = X$ and $X \cdot X \cdots X = X^n = X$.

TABLE 2.5-1 Switching-algebra theorems involving one variable

(T1) $X + 0 = X$	(T1′) $X \cdot 1 = X$	(Identities)
(T2) $X + 1 = 1$	(T2′) $X \cdot 0 = 0$	(Null elements)
(T3) $X + X = X$	(T3′) $X \cdot X = X$	(Idempotency)
(T4) $(X')' = X$		(Involution)
(T5) $X + X' = 1$	(T5′) $X \cdot X' = 0$	(Complements)

2.5-2 Two- and Three-Variable Theorems

Table 2.5-2 lists the switching-algebra theorems that involve two or three variables. Theorems T7 and T7′ are useful in eliminating terms from algebraic expressions and thereby eliminating elements from the corresponding networks. Theorem

T10′ is noteworthy in that it is not true for ordinary algebra even though its dual T10 is. Theorem T12 has no dual (T12′), for the dual would be identical with the original theorem.

TABLE 2.5-2 Switching-algebra theorems involving two or three variables

(T6)	$X + Y = Y + X$	(T6′) $XY = YX$	(Commutative)
(T7)	$X + XY = X$	(T7′) $X(X + Y) = X$	(Absorption)
(T8)	$(X + Y')Y = XY$	(T8′) $XY' + Y = X + Y$	
(T9)	$(X + Y) + Z = X + (Y + Z) = X + Y + Z$		
(T9′)	$(XY)Z = X(YZ) = XYZ$		(Associative)
(T10)	$XY + XZ = X(Y + Z)$		
(T10′)	$(X + Y)(X + Z) = X + YZ$		(Distributive)
(T11)	$(X + Y)(X' + Z)(Y + Z) = (X + Y)(X' + Z)$		
(T11′)	$XY + X'Z + YZ = XY + X'Z$		(Consensus)
(T12)	$(X + Y)(X' + Z) = XZ + X'Y$		

The following example shows how the theorems are used to manipulate a given algebraic expression into some other form. Very frequently the form desired is one which has as few literals occurring as possible. The number of literal occurrences corresponds directly to the number of switches in a switch network and roughly to the number of gate inputs in a gate network.

Example 2.5-1

By use of the theorems, the expression

$$(c' + abd + b'd + a'b)(c + ab + bd)$$

is to be shown equal to

$$b(a + c)(a' + c') + d(b + c)$$

	$(c' + abd + b'd + a'b)(c + ab + bd)$
(T12)	$c'(ab + bd) + c(abd + b'd + a'b)$
(T10)	$abc' + bc'd + abcd + b'cd + a'bc$
(T6)	$abc' + abcd + bc'd + a'bc + b'cd$
(T10)	$ab(c' + cd) + bc'd + a'bc + b'cd$
(T8′)	$ab(c' + d) + bc'd + a'bc + b'cd$
(T11′)	$ab(c' + d) + bc'd + a'bc + a'bd + b'cd$
(T10)	$abc' + abd + bc'd + a'bc + a'bd + b'cd$
(T6)	$(abd + a'bd) + abc' + bc'd + a'bc + b'cd$
(T10)	$bd(a + a') + abc' + bc'd + a'bc + b'cd$
(T5)	$bd(1) + abc' + bc'd + a'bc + b'cd$
(T1′)	$bd + abc' + bc'd + a'bc + b'cd$
(T6)	$bd + bc'd + abc' + a'bc + b'cd$
(T7)	$bd + abc' + a'bc + b'cd$
(T6),(T10)	$d(b + b'c) + abc' + a'bc$

(T8′)	$d(b + c) + abc' + a'bc$
(T10)	$d(b + c) + b(ac' + a'c)$
(T12)	$d(b + c) + b(a + c)(a' + c')$

2.5-3 n-*Variable Theorems*

The switching-variable theorems that involve an arbitrary number of variables are shown in Table 2.5-3. Three of these theorems (T13, T13′, and T14) cannot be proved by perfect induction. For these theorems, the proofs require the use of finite induction ([Birkhoff 77], [Prather 76], and [Stone 73]). Theorems T13 and T13′ are proved by first letting $n = 2$ and using perfect induction to prove their validity for this special case. It is then assumed that the theorems are true for $n = k$, and this is shown to imply that they must then be true for $n = k + 1$. This completes the proof. Theorem T14 is proved by using Theorems T13 and T13′ along with the fact that every function can be split into the sum of several functions or the product of several functions. By successively splitting the function into subfunctions and using T13 and T13′, it is possible to prove T14.

TABLE 2.5-3 Switching-variable theorems involving n variables

(DeMorgan's theorems)

(T13) $(X_1 + X_2 + \cdots + X_n)' = X_1'X_2' \cdots X_n'$

(T13′) $(X_1 X_2 \cdots X_n)' = X_1' + X_2' + \cdots + X_n'$

(Generalized DeMorgan's theorem)

(T14) $f(X_1, X_2, \ldots, X_n, +, \cdot)' = f(X_1', X_2', \ldots, X_n', \cdot, +)$

(Expansion theorem)

(T15) $f(X_1, X_2, \ldots, X_n) = X_1 f(1, X_2, \ldots, X_n) + X_1' f(0, X_2, \ldots, X_n)$

(T15′) $f(X_1, X_2, \ldots, X_n) = [X_1 + f(0, X_2, \ldots, X_n)][X_1' + f(1, X_2, \ldots, X_n)]$

Theorem T14, which is a generalization of T13, forms the basis of a method for constructing complementary networks. Two networks having outputs f_1 and f_2 are said to be **complementary** if $f_1 = f_2'$. The complementary network for any given network can be designed by writing the output f_1 for the first network, then forming f_1' by means of T14, and then designing a network having output f_1'. For example, if $f_1 = (x + y)[w(y' + z) + xy]$, then $f_1' = x'y' + (w' + yz')(x' + y')$.

It was pointed out in connection with Figs. 2.4-1 and 2.4-2 that the canonical networks are generally uneconomical. By manipulating the canonical sum or product with the aid of the theorems just presented, it is usually possible to obtain algebraic expressions that correspond to more economical networks than the canonical networks. The following example shows how this is done for the networks of Figs. 2.4-1 and 2.4-2. The final expressions correspond to the networks of Figs. 2.4-1c and 2.4-2c.

Example 2.5-2

$$f = X_1'X_2'X_3 \qquad + X_1'X_2X_3' \qquad\qquad + X_1'X_2X_3 + X_1X_2'X_3'$$

$$f = X_1'X_2'X_3 \qquad + X_1'X_2X_3 \qquad\qquad + X_1'X_2X_3' + X_1X_2'X_3'$$

$$f = X_1'X_2'X_3 \qquad + X_1'X_2X_3 + X_1'X_2X_3 \; + X_1'X_2X_3' + X_1X_2'X_3'$$

$$f = X_1'X_3(X_2' + X_2) \qquad\qquad + X_1'X_2(X_3 + X_3') \quad + X_1X_2'X_3'$$

$$f = X_1'X_3(1) \qquad\qquad + X_1'X_2(1) \qquad\qquad + X_1X_2'X_3'$$

$$f = X_1'X_3 \qquad\qquad\qquad + X_1'X_2 \qquad\qquad\qquad + X_1X_2'X_3'$$

$$f = X_1'(X_3 + X_2) \qquad\qquad\qquad\qquad\qquad\qquad + X_1X_2'X_3'$$

Many of the theorems of ordinary algebra are also valid for switching algebra. One that is not is the cancellation law. In ordinary algebra it follows that if $X + Y = X + Z$, then $Y = Z$. In switching algebra this is not true. For example, it is generally true that $X + XY = X = X + 0$, but it is not in general true that $XY = 0$. This can be easily verified by writing out the tables of combinations for $f_1(X, Y) = X + XY$, $f_2(X, Y) = X + 0$, and $f_3(X, Y) = XY$. Similar remarks apply to the situation in which $XY = XZ$ does not imply that $Y = Z$.

More precise techniques for simplifying algebraic expressions will be presented in Chap. 6.

2.6 COMPLEX GATES

The only types of gates yet considered have been AND gates and OR gates. These are the conceptually simplest gates and were the first types of gates used in electronic computers. Modern integrated circuit technologies use more complex gates. This section introduces the most important other gates: NAND gates, NOR gates, and EXCLUSIVE-OR gates. The less common and more complex THRESHOLD gate is discussed in Chapter 5.

2.6-1 Complete Sets

The discussion in connection with Theorem 2.4-1 showed that any arbitrary switching function could be realized by a network of AND gates, OR gates, and inverters. A natural question to ask in this connection is whether all three types of elements are necessary. To guarantee that any arbitrary switching function can be realized, inverters are required if the inputs to the network consist of signals representing the input variables but not of signals representing the complements of the input variables. The situation when signals representing the complements are available is called **double-rail logic**, and when the complements are not available, the term **single-rail logic** is used. Both techniques are employed, but for the purposes of the present discussion it will be assumed that complements are not directly available (single-rail logic).

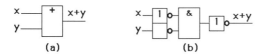

Figure 2.6-1 Realization of an OR gate by means of an AND gate and inverters: (a) OR gate; (b) AND gate with inverters realizing OR function.

Any function that can be realized by a network of AND gates and OR gates but no inverters must have a corresponding algebraic expression that does not contain any complemented variables or parentheses. It has been shown that only certain functions, called **frontal functions**, can be so expressed and that the majority of functions require complementation. Frontal functions are discussed in Chap. 5.

The function $f(x) = x'$ cannot be realized by a network of AND gates and OR gates only. In fact, a technique has been developed for calculating the minimum number of inverters required for a function [Markov 58]. In this development, it is shown that a network having three inputs, x_1, x_2, and x_3, and three outputs corresponding to the functions $f_1(x_1, x_2, x_3) = x_1'$, $f_2(x_1, x_2, x_3) = x_2'$, and $f_3(x_1, x_2, x_3) = x_3'$ can be realized with only two inverters and a quantity of AND gates and OR gates.

It is clear that inverters are required to realize arbitrary functions, but the possibility of using only AND gates and inverters still exists. That the OR gates are not necessary is easily demonstrated, for it is possible to construct a network having the function of an OR gate and using only AND gates and inverters. This is done by making use of DeMorgan's theorem—$X + Y = (X'Y')'$—as illustrated in Fig. 2.6-1. Thus, any network consisting of AND gates, OR gates, and inverters can be changed into a network containing only AND gates and inverters by using the replacement shown in Fig. 2.6-1 to remove the OR gates. By duality, a similar technique can be used to remove the AND gates instead.

Since it is not possible to use only inverters or only AND gates to realize arbitrary functions, a minimal set of elements has now been determined. Because it is possible to construct a network containing only AND gates and inverters for any arbitrary function, the AND gate and inverter are said to form a **complete gate set**. Similarly, the OR gate and inverter form a complete gate set.

2.6-2 NAND and NOR Gates

The two operations of the AND function and the complement can be combined in a single gate—the **NAND gate**—shown in Fig. 2.6-2. This is a very common integrated circuit gate. It comprises a complete gate set in one gate since (1) an inverter is obtained if all inputs are connected to the same input as in Fig. 2.6-2c, and (2) an AND gate is formed by combining two NAND gates as in Fig. 2.6-2d.

Two symbols for the NAND gate are shown in Fig. 2.6-2a. This is because the basic NAND gate function $(XY)'$ can also be written as $X' + Y'$ by using DeMorgan's theorem (T13). Use of the two symbols facilitates analysis and synthesis using these gates, as will be discussed in Chapters 3 and 6. The small circles ("bubbles") in Fig. 2.6-2 indicate inversion and from a logic standpoint each bubble can be replaced by an inverter.

Another very common integrated circuit gate is the **NOR gate** shown in

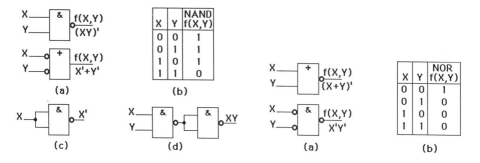

Figure 2.6-2 NAND gate: (a) NAND gate symbols; (b) NAND gate table of combinations; (c) inverter connection; (d) AND connection.

Figure 2.6-3 NOR gate: (a) NOR gate symbols; (b) NOR gate table of combinations.

Fig. 2.6-3. It is the dual of the NAND gate and is also a single gate that is sufficient to implement a network for any arbitrary switching function.

2.6-3 EXCLUSIVE-OR Gates

The other important IC gate type is the **SUM MODULO TWO**, or **EXCLUSIVE-OR (XOR)** gate, which is a two-input gate that has a 1 output when one, but not both, of its inputs is equal to 1.[9] The table of combinations for an XOR gate is given in Fig. 2.6-4a. This table shows that the output of an XOR gate with inputs x_1 and x_2 is given by $x_1 \oplus x_2 = x_1'x_2 + x_1x_2'$.

The XOR gate is usually more expensive to realize physically than either the AND gate or the OR gate. However, the XOR connective is very useful since it arises naturally in the design of arithmetic circuitry: S, the sum output of a binary adder with inputs X, Y and carry-in C, is given by $S = X \oplus Y \oplus C$. Error-detecting and error-correcting circuitry also often uses XOR gates. The **parity function**, the sum modulo 2 of a number of bits, is the most common type of function used in error control circuitry.

It is easily demonstrated that the XOR operation is both commutative and associative; that is,

$$x \oplus y = y \oplus x \qquad \text{and} \qquad (x \oplus y) \oplus z = x \oplus (y \oplus z)$$

Because of these properties, the two-input gate is easily generalized to a multi-input gate. The IEEE standard does not use the name EXCLUSIVE-OR for the multi-input gate. Rather, the terms "odd element," "odd-parity element," or "addition modulo 2 element" are used. Inspection of the table of combinations of Fig. 2.6-5a shows that the multi-input gate has a 1 output when an odd number of inputs equal 1. The IEEE standard symbol for this gate is shown in Fig. 2.6-5b for the particular case of a three-input gate. The multi-input gate symbol is often

---

[9] The OR gate (sometimes called INCLUSIVE-OR or IOR) has a 1 output if one or both inputs are equal to 1.

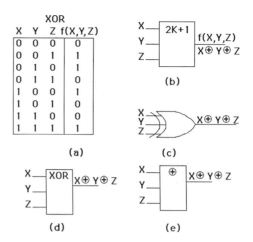

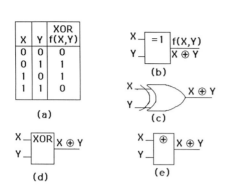

Figure 2.6-4 XOR gate: (a) table of combinations; (b) IEEE symbol; (c) distinctive shape symbol; (d) a popular nonstandard symbol; (e) another popular nonstandard symbol.

Figure 2.6-5 Three-input sum modulo-2 gate: (a) table of combinations; (b) IEEE symbol; (c) distinctive shape symbol; (d) a popular nonstandard symbol; (e) another popular nonstandard symbol.

used (and called an EXCLUSIVE-OR gate) even though most integrated-circuit EXCLUSIVE-OR gates can have only two inputs.

There are design situations in which it is very useful to be able to manipulate algebraic expressions involving the $\oplus$-connective; for example, when using a logic family that has XOR gates available or when designing arithmetic or error-control circuitry. Table 2.6-1 lists some algebraic identities that facilitate such manipulations.

TABLE 2.6-1 Some useful algebraic identities for the $\oplus$-connective

1. $X \oplus Y = XY' + X'Y = (X + Y)(X' + Y')$
2. $(X \oplus Y)' = X \oplus Y' = X' \oplus Y = XY + X'Y' = (X' + Y)(X + Y')$
3a. $X \oplus X = 0$ 3b. $X \oplus X' = 1$
4a. $X \oplus 1 = X'$ 4b. $X \oplus 0 = X$
5. $X(Y \oplus Z) = XY \oplus XZ$
6. $X + Y = X \oplus Y \oplus XY = X \oplus X'Y$
7. $X + Y = X \oplus Y$ if $XY = 0$
8. $X \oplus Y = Z \Rightarrow Z \oplus Y = X, Z \oplus X = Y, X \oplus Y \oplus Z = 0$
9. $X \oplus (X + Y) = X'Y$
10. $X \oplus XY = XY'$

Unlike the NAND gate, the XOR gate is not a complete gate set. Networks containing only XOR gates are limited to calculating the parity of the inputs. Such parity networks are very important constituents of error-control circuitry ([Khakbaz 82], and [Bossen 70]).

If a constant 1 signal is available to use as a gate input, it is possible to form

$$f = x \cdot 1' + x' \cdot 1 = x'$$

Figure 2.6-6 Use of a constant 1-signal to form an inverter from an XOR gate.

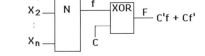

Figure 2.6-7 Use of an XOR gate as a "controlled inverter."

an inverter from an XOR gate as shown in Fig. 2.6-6. The XOR gate is sometimes used as a "controlled inverter" as shown in Fig. 2.6-7. When the control signal C is 0, the network output f appears at the final output F unchanged. When the control signal is 1, the final output F is the complement of the network output f. This connection is often provided at the outputs of a standard IC in order to increase its usefulness.

The AND gate and XOR gate together form a complete set (it has already been shown that AND gates and inverters are a complete set). In Sec. 2.4 canonical expressions were defined using AND, OR, and complement. It is possible to define a similar canonical expression using AND and XOR. To illustrate how this is done, the two-variable case will be considered. The canonical sum is given by

$$f(x, y) = f_0 x' y' + f_1 x' y + f_2 x y' + f_3 x y \tag{2.6-1}$$

Since the fundamental products (minterms) are pairwise disjoint ($p_i\, p_j = 0$ for $i \neq j$) the $+$ connectives can be replaced by $\oplus$ as shown in line 7 of Table 2.6-1.

$$f(x, y) = f_0 x' y' \oplus f_1 x' y \oplus f_2 x y' \oplus f_3 x y \tag{2.6-2}$$

Line 4 of Table 2.6-1 shows that the complemented variables can be replaced: $x' = x \oplus 1$, $y' = y \oplus 1$.

$$f(x, y) = f_0(x \oplus 1)(y \oplus 1) \oplus f_1(x \oplus 1)y \oplus f_2 x(y \oplus 1) \oplus f_3 xy \tag{2.6-3}$$

Using the distributive law (line 5 of the table) permits the factors to be "multiplied out":

$$f(x, y) = f_0(xy \oplus x \oplus y \oplus 1) \oplus f_1(xy \oplus y) \oplus f_2(xy \oplus x) \oplus f_3 xy \tag{2.6-4}$$

Multiplying out again and then collecting common terms yields

$$f(x, y) = f_0 \oplus (f_0 \oplus f_2)x \oplus (f_0 \oplus f_1)y \oplus (f_0 \oplus f_1 \oplus f_2 \oplus f_3)xy \tag{2.6-5}$$

This is the canonical XOR sum for two-variable functions. It is usually called the Reed-Muller canonical expansion and written as

$$f(x, y) = g_0 \oplus g_1 x \oplus g_2 y \oplus g_3 xy \tag{2.6-6}$$

where $g_0 = f_0$, $g_1 = f_0 \oplus f_2$, $g_2 = f_0 \oplus f_1$, $g_3 = f_0 \oplus f_1 \oplus f_2 \oplus f_3$.

This technique can be used to develop an expression for the Reed-Muller canonical expansion for any number of variables.

$$f(x_1, x_2, \ldots, x_n) = g_0 \oplus g_1 x_1 \oplus g_2 x_2 \oplus \cdots \oplus g_{(2^n - 1)} x_1 x_2 \ldots x_n \tag{2.6-7}$$

where g_j is equal to the sum of the f_i corresponding to all rows of the table of combinations for which all of the variables **not** multiplied by g_j have the value 0. Table 2.4-4 is repeated as Table 2.6-2 with the Reed-Muller canonical expansion included. The coefficient of the x_1 term is 1 since the sum of the f_i for the rows with $x_2 = x_3 = 0$ (rows 0, 4) is 1. The coefficient of the x_1x_2 term is 0 since the sum of the f_i for the rows with $x_3 = 0$, (0, 2, 4, 6), is 0.

TABLE 2.6-2 $f(x_1, x_2, x_3) = \Sigma(1, 2, 3, 4)$: (a) Table of combinations; (b) Canonical sum; (c) Canonical product; (d) Reed-Muller canonical expansion

(a)

	x_1	x_2	x_3	f
0	0	0	0	0
1	0	0	1	1
2	0	1	0	1
3	0	1	1	1
4	1	0	0	1
5	1	0	1	0
6	1	1	0	0
7	1	1	1	0

(b)

$$f = x_1'x_2'x_3 + x_1'x_2x_3' + x_1'x_2x_3 + x_1x_2'x_3'$$

(c)

$$f = (x_1 + x_2 + x_3)(x_1' + x_2 + x_3')$$
$$(x_1' + x_2' + x_3)(x_1' + x_2' + x_3')$$

(d)

$$f = x_1 \oplus x_2 \oplus x_3 \oplus x_2x_3$$

The Reed-Muller canonical expansion is the basis for a family of error-correcting codes called Reed-Muller codes. These are discussed in any of the standard coding theory books. The treatment in Chap. 13 of [MacWilliams 77] is recommended. The Reed-Muller canonical expansion is also used in a technique for designing combinational circuits so that they are easy to test. For a discussion of this application, see [Reddy 72] or [McCluskey 84].

The concept of a complete gate set is useful when the possibility of using some novel gate functions arises. It is necessary to establish that all switching functions can be implemented. For a more thorough discussion of complete gate sets, see [Friedman 75] and [Mukhopadhyay 71].

The design of efficient networks using XOR gates is discussed in [Robinson 82] and [Fleisher 83]. The mathematical structure corresponding to the use of EXCLUSIVE-OR and AND connectives is called a Boolean ring. This is discussed in Sec. 2.7-3.

2.7 BOOLEAN ALGEBRA

The switching algebra developed in the previous section is a particular example of a more general type of mathematical system called a **Boolean algebra**. Boolean algebras can be interpreted in terms of sets and logical propositions as well as switching variables. A general development of Boolean algebra will be presented next, and then the application to sets and logic will be discussed [Whitesitt 61].

A set is a collection of objects or elements. The members of a set can be specified by listing them explicitly or by specifying some property such that all elements satisfying this property are members of the set, while all other objects are not members of the set. For example, the set $X = \{a, b, c\}$, or the set $Y = \{$all the integers x such that x can be expressed as $2y$ for some integer $y\}$. Of course, the set Y consists of all the even integers. The notation $a \in X$ will be used to express the fact that the element a is a member of the set X. Two sets are said to be **equal**, written $X = Y$, if and only if they contain exactly the same elements.

To associate an algebraic structure with a set, it is necessary to specify one or more rules of combination or binary operations between the elements of the set. There are four such binary operations normally associated with the real numbers: addition, multiplication, subtraction, and division. Formally, a binary operation on a set is a rule that assigns to each ordered pair of elements of the set a unique element of the set. The fact that the element assigned to the ordered pair is also a member of the set is often called the **closure property**. The following formal definition of a Boolean algebra can now be stated:

DEFINITION. A set of elements $\{a, b, c, \ldots\}$ and two associated binary operations $+$ and $\cdot$ form a Boolean algebra if and only if the following postulates are satisfied:

(A1) The operations are commutative,

$$a + b = b + a \quad \text{and} \quad a \cdot b = b \cdot a$$

(A2) Each of the operations distributes over the other,

$$a(b + c) = a \cdot b + a \cdot c \quad \text{and} \quad a + b \cdot c = (a + b) \cdot (a + c)$$

(A3) There exist identity elements 0 and 1 for $+$ and $\cdot$, respectively,

$$0 + a = a \quad \text{and} \quad 1 \cdot a = a \quad \text{for all } a \in B$$

(A4) For each $a \in B$ there exists an $a' \in B$ such that

$$a + a' = 1 \quad \text{and} \quad a \cdot a' = 0$$

From this set of postulates it is possible to prove the following theorems:

$a + a = a$	$a \cdot a = a$	(Idempotent)
$a + 1 = 1$	$a \cdot 0 = 0$	(Null elements)
	$(a')' = a$	(Involution)
$a + ab = a$	$a(a + b) = a$	(Absorption)
$a + (b + c) = (a + b) + c$	$a \cdot (b \cdot c) = (a \cdot b) \cdot c$	(Associative)
$(a + b)' = a' \cdot b'$	$(a \cdot b)' = a' + b'$	(DeMorgan's laws)

These theorems are formally identical with the corresponding theorems proved for switching algebra. The remaining theorems of switching algebra can also be proved to follow from the postulates given above. It is not obvious that perfect induction can be used in proving these theorems, since the variables are not restricted to the two symbols 0 and 1.[10] In fact, nothing in the definition restricts the set B to containing only a finite number of elements, and it is possible to have a Boolean algebra with an infinite set B. The proofs of the theorems will not be discussed here since they can easily be found in the literature in Chap. 2 of [Whitesitt 61].

This discussion shows that the switching algebra developed earlier is simply a Boolean algebra for which the set B consists of only two elements, 0 and 1. An example of a Boolean algebra with more than two elements is given by $B = \{0, a, b, 1\}$, with $+$ and $\cdot$ defined by the accompanying tables.

+	0	a	b	1
0	0	a	b	1
a	a	a	1	1
b	b	1	b	1
1	1	1	1	1

·	0	a	b	1
0	0	0	0	0
a	0	a	0	a
b	0	0	b	b
1	0	a	b	1

2.7-1 Propositional Logic

Another interpretation of a Boolean algebra with two elements in the set B is in terms of propositional logic. This interpretation will be discussed next. A proposition in this context is the content or meaning of a declarative sentence for which it is possible to determine the truth or falsity. Thus, a sentence must be free of ambiguity and must not be self-contradictory in order to qualify as a proposition. The statements

"The sun is shining"

"All men have three heads"

are propositions. The first is sometimes true, while the second is always false. The statement "All men are tall" is not a proposition, since it is ambiguous, and the statement "The statement you are now reading is false" is not a proposition, since it is self-contradictory.

The lowercase letters $p, q, r, s, t, \ldots$ will be used to represent arbitrary or unspecified propositions (i.e., propositional variables). Two propositional constants are necessary also: one for a proposition that is always false, which will be represented by the symbol F, and one for a proposition that is always true, which will be represented by the symbol T. Two propositions p and q are said to be equal if whenever one is true the other is true, and vice versa. Thus, the expression $p = $ F represents a statement to the effect that the proposition p is always false.

---

[10] The fact that perfect induction is applicable in this general case is proved in [Whitesitt 61, p. 36].

If p represents the proposition "x is an even integer" and q represents the proposition "x can be expressed as $2y$, with y an integer," it follows that $p = q$.

Corresponding to any given proposition p, it is possible to form another proposition which asserts that p is false. This new proposition is called the **denial** (or complement, or negative) of p and is written as $\bar{p}$ (or p' or $\sim p$ or $-p$). It is clear that if p is true, $\bar{p}$ is false, and vice versa. This can be stated formally by means of the accompanying table. If p is the statement "It is raining," then $\bar{p}$ is the statement "It is false that it is raining" or "It is not raining."

p	$\bar{p}$
T	F
F	T

It is also possible to combine two propositions to form a new proposition. Thus, if p and q are two propositions, they can be combined to form a new proposition called the **conjunction** of p and q, written $p \wedge q$ (or p & q or $p \cdot q$). The conjunction of p and q is true only when both p and q are true and is false otherwise. The table expressing this relationship is shown herewith.

p	q	$p \wedge q$
F	F	F
F	T	F
T	F	F
T	T	T

A rule for combining two propositions to form a new proposition is called a **logical connective**. The logical-connective **conjunction** corresponds to the common usage of "and" to combine two statements. Thus, if p represents the proposition "It is raining" and q represents the proposition "The sun is shining," $p \wedge q$ represents the proposition "It is raining and the sun is shining."

Another common means for combining two statements involves the use of "or." The usage in this case is sometimes ambiguous. This is illustrated by the following two statements:

1. "To get a degree, a student must take an economics course or a history course."
2. "Each student is to leave the room by the front door or the side door."

The meaning of the first sentence is clearly economics or history or both, and thus the usage corresponds to an "inclusive or." In the second sentence it is presumably impossible to leave by more than one door; so an "exclusive or" is intended—one door or the other but **not** both. In propositional logic it is necessary to distinguish clearly between these two usages of "or."

The **disjunction** of two propositions p and q, written $p \vee q$, is defined as a proposition that is true when either p or q or **both** are true. Thus, disjunction corresponds to the inclusive or. The table for disjunction is shown herewith. Of course, it is also possible to define a logical connective that corresponds to the exclusive or.

p	q	$p \vee q$
F	F	F
F	T	T
T	F	T
T	T	T

The system of propositional logic that has just been described can be shown to be a Boolean algebra with a set B consisting of the propositional constants T and F. The two binary operations are: conjunction, corresponding to $\cdot$, and disjunction, corresponding to $+$. To show that propositional logic does form a Boolean algebra with this interpretation for B, $+$ and $\cdot$, it is necessary to verify that the four postulates are satisfied:

(P1) $\qquad\qquad p \vee q = q \vee p \qquad$ and $\qquad p \wedge q = q \wedge p$

(P2) $\qquad\qquad p \wedge (q \vee r) = (p \wedge q) \vee (p \wedge r)$

$\qquad\qquad\qquad p \vee (q \wedge r) = (p \vee q) \wedge (p \vee r)$

(P3) $\qquad\qquad F \vee p = p \qquad$ and $\qquad T \wedge p = p$

(P4) $\qquad\qquad p \vee \bar{p} = \text{T} \qquad$ and $\qquad p \wedge \bar{p} = \text{F}$

The correctness of postulate P1 follows directly from the definitions of conjunction and disjunction. The remaining three postulates can be verified by using truth tables, such as those used to define conjunction and disjunction, in much the same fashion as tables of combination were used to verify the theorems of switching algebra in Sec. 2.4 (perfect induction).

It follows from the fact that propositional logic is a Boolean algebra that no additional logical connectives are necessary in order to be able to express any arbitrary propositional function. In fact, because of DeMorgan's theorem, $p \vee q = (\overline{\bar{p} \wedge \bar{q}})$, so that only conjunction and negation are really necessary. It is convenient to have more than this absolute minimum set of connectives available. An additional logical connective, called **material implication**, is of considerable importance in propositional logic. This connective corresponds to the compound statements "p **implies** q" or "If p, then q" in everyday usage. The formal definition of **material implication**, written $p \rightarrow q$, is that $p \rightarrow q$ is false only when p is true and q is false.[11] This is shown in the accompanying table. For the proposition

---

[11] This is also sometimes written as $p \supset q$.

$p \rightarrow q$ to be true, it is necessary only that q be true whenever p is true. If p is false, the proposition $p \rightarrow q$ is true independent of the truth value of q. Thus, if p is the statement "The moon is a planet" and q is the statement "The moon is made of blue cheese," then $p \rightarrow q$ is true since p is false. It is possible to relate the material-implication connective to disjunction and negation: $p \rightarrow q = \bar{p} \vee q$.

p	q	$p \rightarrow q$
F	F	T
F	T	T
T	F	F
T	T	T

A switching algebra can be developed for gate networks and switch networks directly in terms of propositional logic. This is done by associating propositions with circuit elements, as shown in the following table. If leads i and j are inputs to an AND gate and lead k is the output lead of the AND gate, then it follows that $x_k = x_i \wedge x_j$ since the output will equal 1 only when both inputs are 1. For a negative switch X with control signal K, $X = K'$, since X is closed when K has a 0 signal.

Element	Proposition	Symbol
Lead i in a gate network	A 1 signal is present on lead i	x_i
Switch X	Switch X is closed	X

2.7-2 Algebra of Sets

Another system whose structure is formally identical with Boolean algebra is the algebra of sets. This algebra is concerned mainly with the ways in which sets can be combined. Thus, the **union** of two sets X and Y is written as $X \cup Y$ and is defined as the set containing all elements that are in either X or Y or both. If $X = \{0, 1, 2, 3\}$ and $Y = \{0, 2, 4\}$, then $X \cup Y = \{0, 1, 2, 3, 4\}$. The **intersection** of two sets X and Y is written as $X \cap Y$ and is defined as the set containing all elements that are in both X and Y. For the particular X and Y given above, $X \cap Y = \{0, 2\}$.

If two sets have exactly the same members, they are said to be equal. If a set X has only elements that are also elements of another set Y, X is said to be a **subset** of Y or X is said to be **included in** Y, written $X \subseteq Y$. If Y contains elements which are not also in X, then X is a **proper subset** of Y, written $X \subset Y$. This relation of inclusion has the following properties:

$$X \subseteq X \qquad \text{(Reflexive)}$$

$$\text{If} \quad X \subseteq Y \quad \text{and} \quad Y \subseteq X \quad \text{then} \quad X = Y \qquad \text{(Antisymmetric)}$$

If $X \subseteq Y$ and $Y \subseteq Z$ then $X \subseteq Z$ (Transitive)

A relation such as $\subseteq$ which has these three properties is said to be a **partial ordering**.

If the two sets X and Y happen to have no elements in common, their intersection $X \cap Y$ will be empty. It is customary to define a special set, the **null** (or **empty**) **set**, which contains no elements. The null set is represented by the symbol $\varnothing$ so that $X \cap Y = \varnothing$ if X and Y have no common elements. The other special set that is necessary is the **universal set**, written U, which by definition contains all elements under discussion. It is then possible to associate with each set X another set X', called the complement of X, which contains all members of U which are not in X. If only integers are being discussed so that U is the set of all integers, and X is the set of all even integers, it follows that X' is the set of all odd integers. The set inclusion property can be related to intersection and complementation since $X \subseteq Y$ if and only if $X \cap Y' = \varnothing$. There can be no elements of X that are not in Y.

From the definitions just given it can easily be shown that the following rules hold:

(S1) $X \cup Y = Y \cup X$ and $X \cap Y = Y \cap X$

(S2) $X \cap (Y \cup Z) = (X \cap Y) \cup (X \cap Z)$

  $X \cup (Y \cap Z) = (X \cup Y) \cap (X \cup Z)$

(S3) $\varnothing \cup X = X$ and $U \cap X = X$

(S4) $X \cup X' = U$ and $X \cap X' = \varnothing$

This shows that the algebra of sets is formally identical to Boolean algebra if the elements of B are chosen to be the subsets of some universal set U and the connectives $\cap$ and $\cup$ take the place of $\cdot$ and $+$. In fact, it has been shown on p. 42 in [Whitesitt 61] that for any abstract Boolean algebra there is a corresponding set U such that the algebra of the subsets of U has the same structure as that of the abstract Boolean algebra. In other words, there is no abstract Boolean algebra which cannot be interpreted as the algebra of subsets of some universal set U.

Visualization of the combination of sets is often possible by using a **Venn diagram** in which each set is represented by a certain area. Specifically, the universal set U is represented by the interior of a rectangle, and each other set is represented by the points inside a circle or closed region inside the rectangle. This is illustrated in Fig. 2.7-1.

2.7-3 Boolean Rings

Another important interpretation of a Boolean algebra is as a Boolean ring. The theory of rings is an important topic in abstract algebra.

DEFINITION. A set R of elements $\{a, b, c, \ldots\}$ and two associated binary operations $\oplus$ and $\cdot$ form a ring if and only if the following postulates are satisfied:

(R1) $a \oplus (b \oplus c) = (a \oplus b) \oplus c$ (Addition is associative)

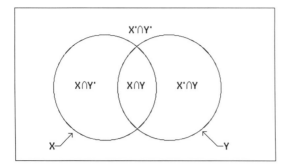

Figure 2.7-1 Venn diagram.

(R2) $a \oplus b = b \oplus a$ (Addition is commutative)

(R3) The equation $a \oplus x = b$ has a solution x in R

(R4) $a(bc) = (ab)c$ (Multiplication is associative)

(R5) $a(b \oplus c) = ab \oplus ac, (b \oplus c)a = ba \oplus ca$ (Distributivity)

If, in addition to these properties, it is also true that $a \cdot a = a$ for all elements of R (idempotent law), then the ring is said to be a **Boolean ring** [Bartee 62]. Any Boolean algebra forms a Boolean ring if the same operation is used for multiplication in both systems and if ring addition is defined by

$$a \oplus b = a'b + ab'$$

See also Sec. 2.6-3 for a discussion of the use of this connective in circuit design.

2.8 DUALITY

The principle of duality was mentioned briefly in Sec. 2.2. This section considers duality more thoroughly and presents some examples of its application in logic design.

A formal statement of the principle of duality is given in the following metatheorem:

METATHEOREM. Any true theorem about switching algebra whose statement involves only the three operations $+$, $\cdot$, and $'$ remains true if ($+$ and $\cdot$) and (0 and 1) are interchanged throughout.

This is called a metatheorem because it is a "theorem about theorems." It is proved just by noting that it is true for the postulates given in Sec. 2.2 and thus must be true for all theorems derived from these postulates. The statement of the metatheorem is based on the presentation in Chap. 5 of [Birkhoff 70].

One reason that duality is useful is because it permits results about dual situations to be obtained without detailed study. For example, the NOR gate is dual to the NAND gate. Thus, by duality, results that are obtained for networks of NAND gates can be used for NOR gate networks without detailed study. This will be done in Chap. 6 when two-stage networks are discussed. It will be shown that it is possible to obtain a two-stage NAND gate network from a sum-of-products expression. It follows from duality that a two-stage NOR gate network can be derived from a product-of-sums expression.

Another important application of duality is in converting expressions in sum-of-products form to product-of-sums form. One example of this is in connection with the discussion of hazards in Sec. 3.6. The following formal definition of a dual expression will facilitate the discussion of this technique.

DEFINITION. Given a Boolean expression $E(x_1, x_2, \ldots, x_n, \cdot, +, ')$, the **dual** of E is defined as

$$\text{dual of } E = D[E] = E(x_1, x_2, \ldots, x_n, +, \cdot, ')$$

For example, for an expression $E = xy' + z$, the dual expression is $D[E] = (x + y')z$. For $E = x + (y + pw')(a\{z' + yq\} + r)$, the dual expression is $D[E] = x(y\{p + w'\} + \{a + z'(y + q)\}r)$.

It is relatively easy to convert a product-of-sums (POS) expression to a sum-of-products expression by "multiplying out" the POS expression using the distributive property (Theorem T10). Thus, $(x + y)(w + v) = (x + y)w + (x + y)v = xw + yw + xv + yv$. A sum-of-products expression can be converted to a product-of-sums expression by the dual process of "adding out" using the dual distributive property (Theorem T10'). For example, $xy + wv = (xy + w)(xy + v) = (x + w)(y + w)(x + v)(y + v)$. Since the dual distributive property is not valid for ordinary algebra, many people have difficulty in using it for this conversion. This difficulty can be avoided by converting the sum-of-products expression to its dual, which is a POS form, multiplying out the dual expression to obtain a sum-of-products form, and then taking the dual of this form to obtain the desired product-of-sums form. For example, if $E = xy' + wv$, then $D[E] = (x + y')(w + v)$, which is $xw + y'w + xv + y'v$. $D[xw + y'w + xv + y'v]$ is $(x + w)(y' + w)(x + v)(y' + v)$, which is the desired form. The validity of this procedure depends on the following theorem stating that if two expressions are equal (represent the same function), their duals are also equal. The proof of the theorem follows directly from the duality metatheorem and the following lemma.

THEOREM 2.8-1. Let $E(x_1, x_2, \ldots, x_n, +, \cdot, ')$ and $G(x_1, x_2, \ldots, x_n, +, \cdot, ')$ be two expressions corresponding to function, $f(x_1, x_2, \ldots, x_n)$; then $D[E]$ and $D[G]$ both represent the same function, $h(x_1, x_2, \ldots, x_n)$ equal to $f'(x_1', x_2', \ldots, x_n')$

The generalized DeMorgan's theorem (T14) can be restated using the duality notation just presented. This form of the theorem shows the relationship between duals and complements.

LEMMA. $f'(x_1, x_2, \ldots, x_n) = D[f(x_1', x_2', \ldots, x_n')]$.

2.9 MULTIPLE-VALUED LOGIC

The circuits discussed in this book all operate with two (and only two) signal values.[12] This is because all digital products currently produced or planned use binary logic circuits exclusively. The monopoly position of binary logic does not result from a failure to consider nonbinary signals. There has been a continuing interest in the possibility of multivalued logic, MVL (using higher-radix signals). The two major advantages projected for MVL are:

1. **Reduced interconnect:** The information per package pin and interconnect line would be increased. Thus, fewer pins and interconnect lines could be used or more information could be transmitted.
2. **Increased packing density:** It should be possible to implement the same functional logic with fewer gates since fewer signals would need to be processed. Thus, less equipment would be needed to implement a given function.

These issues are also discussed in [Current 80c] and [Vranesic 81].

In spite of these advantages there have been no announcements of digital systems or circuits being produced which use multivalued logic. The only systems currently available that use multivalued digital signals are the Intel 43203 iAPX-432 and Intel 8087. These systems do not use multivalued logic circuits, but do use a ROM in which each cell stores one of four possible signal values [Stark 81].

There are a number of drawbacks to multivalued logic which may explain why they have not been used:

1. Tolerances in multivalued circuits are more critical than in binary circuits since multivalued circuits intrinsically have more threshold values than binary circuits. These tighter tolerances cause reduced noise immunity in the multivalued circuits.
2. There is some indication that multivalued circuits are slower than binary circuits. To cope with the tolerance problems, it may be necessary to increase the maximum signal values (voltage or current). Since it may not be practical to increase the circuit drive capability, this increase in signal swing can cause a decrease in operating speed.
3. There is a large capital investment—both in equipment and in human skill—in producing binary circuits. The cost of switching this investment to producing multivalued circuits may exceed the benefits to be obtained from multivalued techniques.

These drawbacks indicate that binary logic will probably not be replaced by multivalued logic circuits. However, the possibility still exists that multivalued circuits

---

[12] Even the tri-state gate discussed in Sec. 4.1 has only two information values represented by its output condition. The hi-Z condition represents the absence of any information rather than a third signal value.

will be used in specialized situations such as arithmetic processors ([Current 80a] and [Current 80b]) or in connection with testing.

One possible application for testing is the use of a third signal value on a pin to indicate a state that is used only for testing purposes. When a circuit has a built-in test mode it is undesirable to have to use a pin in order to place the circuit in this test mode. By using a signal value which is different from the values used for normal operation, one of the normal circuit pins could be used for this test signal. Similarly, a third signal value on an output pin could be used to send a signal indicating some internal test status. Another possibility might be the re-configuration of the circuit for testing purposes by changing the supply voltage.

Even though there have been no commercial multivalued circuits used, much effort has been devoted to such circuits. There has been an annual conference on multivalued logic held each year since 1971, there was a special MVL issue of *IEEE Computer* in 1974, and the *IEEE Transactions on Computers* had special sections of the December 1977 and September 1981 issues devoted to multivalued logic.

2.9-1 Design Techniques

The classic approach to designing MVL circuits has been to demonstrate, for a specific technology, circuits to realize a complete set of algebraic connectives [Vranesic 77]. The connectives have usually been chosen from:

Max and min functions: z = maximum (x, y) and w = minimum (x, y); these correspond to the binary AND and OR functions.

"T-gate": $T(x, y, z, q) = x$ if $q = 0$, y if $q = 1$, z if $q = 2$; this corresponds to a multiplexer and (MSI) multiplexer design techniques are applicable, but do not yield efficient designs.

Complement: $x' = M - x$ (M is equal to the radix minus 1).

Cycle gate: $x\{+y\} = (x + y)$ modulo R (R is equal to the radix).

J-functions: $J(k, x) = M$ for $x = k$ and 0 otherwise.

Literal gates: $x(a, b) = M$ if $a < x < b$ and 0 otherwise.

Since algebraic theories showing how to realize arbitrary functions using these connectives had been developed, for example see [Allen 77], such demonstrations were sufficient to show, in principle, that any multivalued function could be implemented. A drawback of this approach is that the efficiency (in terms of interconnect or packing density) is not evaluated since realizations for more complex functions such as adders or ALUs are not considered. In fact, it is questionable whether these techniques would lead to efficient designs since the circuits realizing the basic connectives are typically rather complex.

A quite different approach was taken in [McCluskey 79]. That paper presents a design technique for multivalued integrated injection logic circuits. The design technique was developed by studying a variety of actual circuit designs and then abstracting the connectives that produced efficient designs. A measure of the success of the technique is the fact that it results in circuits that are as efficient as those "invented" by an experienced designer. An efficient design for a base-4 full adder is demonstrated. Laboratory prototypes have been successfully constructed.

Another MVL implementation, using ECL circuitry, has been developed ([Current 80a] and [Current 80b]). This work has concentrated on developing base-4 circuits for use in signal processing applications. Experimental implementations that agree well with simulation results have been reported. The question of general design techniques for arbitrary functions has apparently not yet been studied.

Both the IIL and the ECL circuits just mentioned use the technique of adding currents that represent four-valued signals in order to implement logic operations. For the so-called voltage-mode technologies—TTL, NMOS, CMOS—there is no similar direct method for combining multilevel signals. The following section describes a design approach that can be used to design MVL circuits in any of the voltage-mode technologies. Only three-valued circuits are described since these are the most promising for actual production.

2.9-2 BITLON: Binary Implemented Ternary Logic Networks

Almost all realistic voltage-mode multivalued circuits which have been proposed seem to be feasible only for three-valued (ternary) logic. They also have in common the general structure shown in Fig. 2.9-1: the ternary input signals are decoded into binary signals which are combined using standard binary logic circuits and then the binary signals are reencoded into ternary output signals. This form of ternary logic can be implemented using any technology for which compatible decoder and encoder circuitry exists. Decoder and encoder circuits for MOS, CMOS, TTL, ECL, and ILL are shown in [McCluskey 82].

A ternary logic network that has the structure given in Fig. 2.9-1 will be called a binary implemented ternary logic network (BITLON). One significant advantage of BITLONs is that they can be designed using standard binary design techniques. The rules describing the operation of the decoder and encoder circuits are used to transform the ternary specifications into binary specifications, which are then realized using standard binary circuits. When these binary circuits are combined with decoders to transform the ternary inputs, and encoders to produce ternary outputs, the BITLON design is completed.

The observation that many of the proposals for implementing multivalued logic circuits could be represented by a network such as that of Fig. 2.9-1 was made previously in [Birk 75] and [Etiemble 77]. An algebraic technique for minimization is discussed in [Birk 75] in which it is assumed that MAX and MIN gates as well as "literal operators" are available. No circuit realizations are shown. Many circuit designs are shown in [Etiemble 77], but the most complex circuit shown is for a comparator. The algebraic treatment assumes the use of MAX and MIN

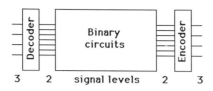

Figure 2.9-1 General structure for ternary logic.

functions as well as literal and complement functions. No well-specified design technique is given.

It is possible to design BITLON circuits in any suitable technology using only classical binary logic design methods. No ternary logic connective such as MAX or the successor function need be used. By a suitable technology is meant one for which ternary-to-binary and binary-to-ternary conversion circuits (as well as binary logic circuits) are available. Examples of conversion circuits for TTL, IIL, ECL, CMOS, and NMOS are given in [McCluskey 82]. It should be emphasized that only standard binary circuit logic design techniques are used. Thus, it is not necessary for a design engineer to learn a new design formalism in order to use this technique.

In [McCluskey 80] the design of ternary NMOS logic circuits in BITLON form is described. Detailed design examples of a ternary (base-3) half adder and full adder are included. Similar techniques can be used to design BITLON in any suitable technology.

A disadvantage of the BITLON structure is the use of binary circuits to implement the functional logic. In fact, it may seem a misnomer to call such a structure a ternary logic network since the functional logic is really binary. However, all of the realistic voltage-mode circuits seem to have this structure.

The BITLON structure could in theory be extended to more than three signal values. However, with present fabrication techniques it does not seem that tolerances can be controlled closely enough to make more than three signal values practical for other than IIL or ECL circuits. The circuit thresholds for IIL depend on injector current and for ECL on bias voltages. These are more easily controlled than the device thresholds that are used in the remaining technologies. Also, both ECL and IIL allow addition of currents representing variables, while the corresponding operation is not possible easily in the voltage-mode technologies. Thus, while BITLON can be designed for ECL and IIL using the technique described above, more promising designs are obtained for ECL using the circuits described in [Current 78] and for IIL with the circuits presented in [McCluskey 79]. Designs using CCDs or GaAs are also possible.

This discussion has been confined to combinational circuits. It is possible, in principle, to build multivalued flip-flops, but the circuits are typically very complex and thus of questionable practicality. A flip-flop for IIL is shown in [Dao 77]. Practical MVL sequential circuits may be possible in ECL since a simple latch is described in [Current 80b].

2.R REFERENCES

[ALLEN 77]   Allen, C. M., and D. D. Givone, "The Allen-Givone Implementation Oriented Algebra," in *Computer Science and Multiple-Valued Logic*, ed. D. C. Rine, North-Holland Publishing Company, New York, pp. 262–282, 1977.

[BARTEE 62]   Bartee, T., I. L. Lebow, and I. S. Reed, *Theory and Design of Digital Machines*, McGraw-Hill Book Company, New York, 1962.

[BIRK 75]   Birk, J. E., and D. E. Farmer, "An Algebraic Method for Designing Multivalued Logic Circuits Using Principally Binary Components," *IEEE Trans. Comput.*, C-24, No. 11, pp. 1101–1104, 1975.

[BIRKHOFF 77]   Birkhoff, G., and S. MacLane, *A Survey of Modern Algebra*, 4th ed., Macmillan Publishing Company, New York, 1977.

[BOSSEN 70]   Bossen, D. C., D. L. Ostapko, and A. M. Patel, "Optimum Test Patterns for Parity Networks," *Proc. AFIPS 1970 Joint Comput. Conf.*, Houston, Vol. 37, pp. 63–68, Nov. 17–19, 1970.

[CURRENT 78]   Current, K. W., and D. A. Mow, "Four-Value Threshold Logic Full Adder Circuit Implementations," *Proc. 8th Int. Symp. Multiple-Valued Logic*, Chicago, pp. 95–100, May 24–26, 1978.

[CURRENT 80a]   Current, K. W., "High Density Integrated Computing Circuitry with Multiple Valued Logic," *IEEE Trans. Comput.*, C-29, No. 2, pp. 191–195, 1980.

[CURRENT 80b]   Current, K. W., "Pipelined Binary Parallel Counters Employing Latched Quaternary Logic Full Adders," *IEEE Trans. Comput.*, C-29, No. 5, pp. 400–403, 1980.

[CURRENT 80c]   Current, K. W., and L. B. Wheaton, "Some Circuit Considerations for High Speed Computing with Multiple Valued Logic," *Proc. Symp. Very High Speed Comput. Technol.*, Georgia Institute of Technology, Atlanta, Ga., Sept. 9–10, 1980.

[DAO 77]   Dao, T. T., E. J. McCluskey, and L. K. Russell, "Multivalued Integrated Injection Logic," *IEEE Trans. Comput.*, C-26, No. 12, pp. 1233–1241, 1977.

[ETIEMBLE 77]   Etiemble, D., and M. Israel, "Implementation of Ternary Circuits with Binary Integrated Circuits," *IEEE Trans. Comput.*, C-26, No. 12, pp. 1222–1233, 1977.

[FLEISHER 83]   Fleisher, H., M. Tavel, and J. Yeager, "Exclusive-OR Representation of Boolean Functions," *IBM J. Res. Dev.*, Vol. 27, No.4, pp. 412–416, 1983.

[FRIEDMAN 75]   Friedman, A. D., and P. R. Menon, *Theory and Design of Switching Circuits*, Computer Science Press, Inc., Woodland Hills, Calif., 1975.

[GREA 55]   Grea, R., and R. Higonnet, *Études logiques des circuits électriques et des systèmes binaires*, Éditions Berger-Levrault, Paris, 1955.

[HARVARD 51]   Staff of the Harvard University Computation Laboratory, *Synthesis of Electronic Computing and Control Circuits*, Harvard University Press, Cambridge, Mass., 1951.

[HAYES 82]   Hayes, J. P., "A Unified Switching Theory with Applications to VLSI Design," *Proc. IEEE*, pp. 1140–1151, Oct. 1982.

[KHAKBAZ 82]   Khakbaz, J., "Self-Testing Embedded Parity Trees," *Dig. 12th Annu. Int. Symp. Fault-Tolerant Comput.* (FTCS-12), Santa Monica, Calif., pp. 109–116, June 22–24, 1982.

[MACWILLIAMS 77]   MacWilliams, F. J., and N. J. A. Sloan, *The Theory of Error-Correcting Codes*, North-Holland Publishing Company, New York, 1977.

[MANN 81] Mann, F. A., "Explanation of New Logic Symbols," Chap. 5 in *1981 Supplement to the TTL Data Book for Design Engineers*, 2nd ed., Texas Instruments, Inc., Dallas, 1981.

[MARKOV 58] Markov, A. A., "On the Inversion Complexity of a System of Functions," *J. ACM*, Vol. 5, No. 4, pp. 331–334, 1958.

[McCLUSKEY 65] McCluskey, E. J., *Introduction to the Theory of Switching Circuits*, McGraw-Hill Book Company, New York, 1965.

[McCLUSKEY 78] McCluskey, E. J., K. P. Parker, and J. J. Shedletsky, "Boolean Network Probabilities and Network Design," *IEEE Trans. Comput.*, C-27, No. 2, pp. 187–189, 1978.

[McCLUSKEY 79] McCluskey, E. J., "Logic Design of Multivalued IIL Logic Circuits," *IEEE Trans. Comput.*, C-28, No. 8, pp. 546–559, 1979.

[McCLUSKEY 80] McCluskey, E. J., "Logic Design of MOS Ternary Logic," *Proc. 10th Int. Symp. Multiple-Valued Logic*, Evanston, Ill., pp. 1–5, June 3–5, 1980.

[McCLUSKEY 82] McCluskey, E. J., "A Discussion of Multiple-Valued Logic C Circuits," *Proc. 12th Int. Symp. Mutiple-Valued Logic*, Paris, pp. 200–205, May 25–27, 1982.

[McCLUSKEY 84] McCluskey, E. J., "Design for Testability," in *Recent Developments in Fault-Tolerant Computing*, ed. D. K. Pradhan, Prentice-Hall, Inc., Englewood Cliffs, N.J., 1986.

[MUKHOPADHYAY 71] Mukhopadhyay, A., "Complete Sets of Logic Primitives," Chap. 1 in *Recent Developments in Switching Theory*, ed. A. Mukhopadhyay, Academic Press, Inc., New York, 1971.

[PRATHER 76] Prather, R. E., *Discrete Mathematical Structures for Computer Science*, Houghton Mifflin Company, Boston, 1976.

[REDDY 72] Reddy, S. M., "Easily Testable Realizations for Logic Functions," *IEEE Trans. Comput.*, C-21, No. 11, pp. 1183–1188, 1972.

[ROBINSON 82] Robinson, J. P., and C.-L. Yeh, "A Method for Modulo-2 Minimization," *IEEE Trans. Comput.*, C-31, No. 8, p. 800, 1982.

[SHANNON 38] Shannon, C. E., "A Symbolic Analysis of Relay and Switching Circuits," *Trans. Am. Inst. Electr. Eng.*, Vol. 57, pp. 713–723, 1938.

[SLEPIAN 54] Slepian, D., "On the Number of Symmetry Types of Boolean Functions of *n*-Variables," *Can. J. Math.*, Vol. 5, No. 2, pp. 185–193, 1954.

[STARK 81] Stark, M., "Two Bits per Cell ROM," *Dig. COMPCON Spring '81*, San Francisco, pp. 209–212, Feb. 23–26, 1981.

[STONE 73] Stone, H. S., *Discrete Mathematical Structures and Their Applications*, Science Research Associates, Inc., Chicago, 1973.

[VRANESIC 77] Vranesic, Z. G., and K. C. Smith, "Electronic Circuits for Multivalued Digital Systems," in *Computer Science and Multiple-Valued Logic*, ed. D. C. Rine, North-Holland Publishing Company, New York, pp. 397–419, 1977.

[VRANESIC 81] Vranesic, Z. G., "Applications and Scope of Multiple-Valued LSI Technology," *Dig. COMPCON Spring '81*, San Francisco, pp. 213–215, Feb. 23–26, 1981.

[WHITESITT 61] Whitesitt, J. E., *Boolean Algebra and Its Applications*, Addison-Wesley Publishing Company, Inc., Reading, Mass., 1961.

2.P PROBLEMS

2.1 A lock circuit is to be designed with 10 toggle switches, $x_0, x_1, \ldots, x_9$ as inputs. The lock is to be open only when the switches are alternately up and down. Write the decimal specification for the corresponding switching function.

2.2 An indicator circuit is to be designed for a room that has two swinging doors D_1 and D_2. Associated with each door there are two switches, e_1 and x_1 for D_1, e_2 and x_2 for D_2. The e_i switch is closed only when the corresponding D_i is open **in**, and the x_i switch is closed only when the corresponding D_i is open **out**. An indicator lamp is to be lit whenever there is a clear path through the room (one door opens in and the other door opens out). Fill out a table of combinations for the function corresponding to the indicator light.

2.3 Write the canonical sum and the canonical product for each of the following functions.
(a) $f(x, y, z) = \Sigma(0, 3, 6)$
(b) $f(x, y, z) = \Pi(1, 2, 7)$

2.4 You are to use the theorems of switching algebra to rewrite the following expression in a form that requires as few inversions as possible (complemented parentheses are allowed).
$$b'c + acd' + a'c + eb' + e(a + c)(a' + d')$$

2.5 Prepare a truth table for the following Boolean expressions.
(a) $xyz + xy'z'$
(b) $abc + ab'c' + a'b'c'$
(c) $a(bc' + b'c)$
(d) $(a + b)(a + c)(a' + b')$

2.6 Prove the following identities *without* using perfect induction.
(a) $ab' + bc' + ca' = a'b + b'c + c'a$
(b) $ab + a'c + bcd = ab + a'c$

2.7 Find the complements of the following functions.
(a) $f = a + bc$
(b) $f = (a + b)(a'c + d)$
(c) $f = ab + b'c + ca'd$

Prove that your answers are correct by showing that
$$f \cdot f' = 0 \quad \text{and} \quad f + f' = 1$$

2.8 Prove whether or not the following identities are valid. Do not use perfect induction.
(a) $ab + c'd' + a'bcd' + ab'c'd = (a + d')(b + c')$
(b) $(a + b')(b + c')(c + a') = (a' + b)(b' + c)(c' + a)$
(c) $(a + b)(b + c)(c + a) = (a' + b')(b' + c')(c' + a')$
(d) $ab + a'b'c = (c + a)(c + b)$

2.9 To increase the reliability of a combinational circuit constructed of AND and OR gates, three copies of the desired circuit are to be built. An additional circuit, whose inputs are the outputs of the three copies of the desired circuit and whose output signal agrees with the majority of the input signals, is to be constructed of very-high-reliability components. The overall circuit will thus have the correct output even though the output of one of the copies of the desired circuit is in error (see Fig. P2.9).
(a) Write the table of combinations for the majority circuit M.
(b) Write the equivalent decimal specification.
(c) Write a simplified algebraic expression for w as a function of z_1, z_2, z_3.

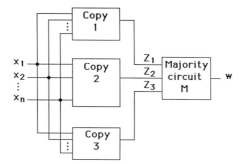

Figure P2.9

2.10 Prove or disprove the following propositions.
  (a) Let a and b be Boolean variables. Then $a \cdot b = 0$ and $a + b = 1$ implies that $a = b'$.
  (b) Let X and Y be Boolean **expressions**. Then $X \cdot Y = 0$ and $X + Y = 1$ implies $X = Y'$.

2.11 **(a)** If $f = x \oplus y$, express f in terms of x, x', y, y', $+$, and $\cdot$.
  (b) Prove that $(x \oplus y) \oplus z = x \oplus (y \oplus z)$.
  (c) Prove that if $x \oplus y = z$, then $x \oplus z = y$ and $x \oplus y \oplus z = 0$.
  (d) Prove that $x \oplus y = x + y$ if $xy = 0$.
  (e) Prove that $(a + b) \oplus (a + c) = a'(b \oplus c)$.
  (f) Prove that $x + y = x \oplus y \oplus xy$

$$x + y = x \oplus x'y.$$

2.12 Prove:
  (a) $x' \oplus y = x \oplus y'$
  (b) $x \oplus y = x' \oplus y'$
  (c) $x \cdot y' + x' \cdot y = (x \cdot y + x' \cdot y')'$

2.13 **(a)** Given $f(w, x, y, z) = w + (x + yz)(y' + xz)$, find a sum-of-products expression for f by "multiplying out" this expression.
  (b) Write the dual expression $D[f(w, x, y, z)]$ obtained from the expression given in part (a).
  (c) Find a product-of-sums expression for f by multiplying out the expression of part (b) and then taking the dual.

2.14 **(a)** Prove that $D[f(x_1, x_2, \ldots, x_n)] = f(x_1, x_2, \ldots, x_n)$ iff $f'(x_1, x_2, \ldots, x_n) = f(x_1', x_2', \ldots, x_n')$.
  (b) Find a function satisfying the conditions of part (a) having the smallest n ($n \geq 2$).
  (c) Prove that $D[f(x_1, x_2, \ldots, x_n)] = f'(x_1, x_2, \ldots, x_n)$ iff $f(x_1, x_2, \ldots, x_n) = f(x_1', x_2', \ldots, x_n')$.
  (d) Find a function satisfying the conditions of part (c) having the smallest n ($n \geq 2$).

3

ANALYSIS OF COMBINATIONAL CIRCUITS

3.1 INTRODUCTION

It is customary when studying logic networks to divide them into two broad classes: combinational networks and sequential networks. A **combinational network** is one in which the outputs at a particular time depend only on the inputs present at the same time. (More precisely, if inputs are applied to the network and held stable for long enough to allow all signal changes to propagate to the outputs, the values of the outputs will be determined only by the last set of input values.) This is a behavioral definition of combinational network. Some people prefer a structural definition in which a combinational network is one that contains no feedback loops or memory elements. While it is possible to design a network with feedback loops that satisfies the behavioral definition of a combinational network [Huffman 71], such networks are not used. In this book it will be assumed that both definitions are equivalent and they will be used interchangeably. The terms **memoryless** or **acyclic** are sometimes used as synonyms for combinational.[1]

A **sequential network** is one for which it is not always possible to predict the values of its outputs from a knowledge of its present inputs. In other words, a sequential network's outputs can depend on the past as well as present inputs.

The algebraic analysis techniques discussed in this chapter are limited to combinational networks. Formal methods for analyzing sequential networks are presented in Chaps. 7 and 8.

---

[1] The term **combinatorial** is also sometimes used, but this is to be discouraged. It is preferable to reserve the word *combinatorial* for its more customary mathematical meaning.

In designing a logic network, an appropriate structure must be determined. It is then necessary to check the structure to (1) verify both that its static functioning is correct and that it will still perform properly in the presence of circuit delays, and (2) determine a set of inputs which can be used to test physical implementations in order to establish that they are fault-free. Verification and test generation can be done algebraically, experimentally or by simulation.

Algebraic techniques are most suited for hand calculation. They are thus limited to small networks or to networks that can be partitioned into small subnetworks. (It's difficult to be precise about what is meant by small since whether or not a network can be analyzed by hand depends on its complexity as well as the ability and persistence of the person doing the analysis. As analysis techniques are discussed in detail this issue of size will become clearer.) Algebraic methods are of very little value in analyzing production networks. However, they are extremely important for the insight they give into network structures and in developing design methods. Since design is the main subject of this book, algebraic analysis techniques will be studied in detail.

Experimental techniques involve construction of a physical model of the network or system. Usually, some type of scaling is involved. Thus a chip may be modeled with a printed circuit board; a system that is to be realized using a high-speed technology may be modeled using standard TTL parts. This method is sometimes called **hardware simulation** or **emulation**. It is even possible to implement the model so that faults can be inserted in order to verify the effectiveness of the test patterns (inputs used to check for the presence of faults) [Timoc 79].

Hardware simulation may be quicker to implement and less expensive than programmed simulation if a good simulator is not available. However, software simulation is used much more commonly since it provides more flexibility in varying parameters and thus is more satisfactory for investigating the effects of parameter tolerances on system operation.

Most designers will have occasion to use simulation, so it is of interest to discuss its major features and limitations here. On the other hand, very few designers will be called on to implement their own simulator, so the discussion will be brief.

3.2 SIMULATION

A design is analyzed to determine the function that it realizes. When the specifications are known, this amounts to verifying that the design realizes these specifications. Otherwise, it is a question of determining the specifications that are realized.

Current industrial practice for verifying a design typically is to use a simulator. Most often this simulator is a program that models the network being studied. Time is quantized and a value for each signal in the network is calculated for each time period. The simulator derives the sequence of output signals caused by a particular sequence of input signals. Since for most practical designs it would be too time consuming to simulate all possible input sequences, the designer must specify a set of sequences that are considered sufficient to verify the correct functioning of the design. There is no technique known for discovering such a set of inputs. Thus it is possible for simulation to fail to discover an incorrect design due to an inadequate set of inputs. Simulation is an important practical tool. Its effectiveness is limited mainly by the expense caused by the large amount of computer time in order to carry out the calculations of all the signals in the network under study. A detailed discussion of simulation is outside the scope of this book. The interested reader is referred to [Chappell 74] and [Szygenda 76].

3.3 GATE SYMBOLS

The IEEE adopted a standard for Graphic Symbols for Logic Elements in 1973. In spite of this there continued to be a wide variation in the notation used by device and system manufacturers. One possible reason for this lack of acceptance of the standard was its incompleteness: the standard did not contain any symbol for transmission gates and fails to provide for distinguishing flip-flops from latches. However, a new standard that is much more complete was adopted in 1984. It is already in use by some manufacturers, notably Texas Instruments [Mann 81].

This new standard is ANSI/IEEE Std. 91-1984. It will be followed in this text with some minor exceptions. The standard will not be presented in its entirety in this section since standards are rather dull reading. Instead, the standard will be introduced here and additional symbols will be presented as they relate to the topics being discussed. The IEEE standard is based on an IEC (International Electrotechnical Commission) standard. The IEC standard is presented in [Kampel 85]. An early version of the IEEE standard is discussed in [Peatman 80].

The basic logic symbol is a rectangle with one or more qualifying symbols. The dimensions of the rectangle are not relevant to the logical operations represented by the symbol. The standard specifies only rectangular symbols, but there are also the "distinctive shape symbols" which the standard permits but does not recommend. Distinctive shape symbols exist for the AND gate, the OR gate, the XOR gate, and by extension, the NAND gate and the NOR gate. These distinctive shape symbols were shown in connection with the gate definitions in Chap. 2.

The structure of a logic symbol is shown in Fig. 3.3-1. The normal direction of signal flow is from left to right. When another direction must be used, the signal flow is indicated by an arrowhead on the corresponding signal line (Table

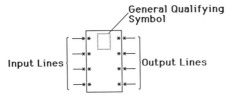

*Possible positions for qualifying symbols relating to inputs and outputs

Figure 3.3-1 Basic logic symbol structure.

TABLE 3.3-1 General qualifying symbols

Symbol	Description	Example
&	AND gate	5408
≥ 1	OR gate; at least one input must be active to activate output	5432
$+$	Nonstandard symbol used for OR gate in this text	
$= 1$	EXCLUSIVE-OR gate; one and only one input must be active to activate the output	5486
$\oplus$	Nonstandard symbol in common usage	
$=$	Logic identity; all inputs must stand at same state	54180
$2k$	An even number of inputs must be active	54180
$2k + 1$	An odd number of inputs must be active	54180
1	The one input must be active	5404

3.3-2e). All outputs of a single symbol have identical values except as modified by an associated qualifying symbol. Some of the general qualifying symbols are listed in Table 3.3-1. The last column of this table gives the number of a TTL part that illustrates the symbol described in the row. The qualifying symbols for inputs and outputs are shown in Table 3.3-2. The negation bubbles of Table 3.3-2a and b were introduced and used in previous sections. The "active-low" symbols of parts (c) and (d) are used to specify a relationship between the physical signal value and the corresponding logical signal value. In particular, the presence of one of these symbols indicates that a low physical signal value corresponds to a logical signal value of 1.

TABLE 3.3-2 Qualifying symbols for inputs and outputs

Symbol		Description
(a)	⊸○	Logical negation at input External 0 produces internal 1
(b)	○⊸	Logical negation at output Internal 1 produces external 0
(c)	—◺	Active-low input; equivalent to (a) in positive logic
(d)	◺—	Active-low output; equivalent to (b) in positive logic
(e)	——< ——	Signal flow from right to left
(f)	——< >——	Bidirectional signal flow

3.4 GATE NETWORKS

Analyzing a network amounts to transforming from one representation to another representation. It is possible to determine the response of a network to any particular input pattern by tracing paths through an electrical diagram or a gate diagram. This is a cumbersome procedure and it is usually preferable to have a representation of the network function in algebraic or tabular form. The variety of such forms and the methods for obtaining them from a gate diagram are the subject of this section.

The most common methods of hand analysis of combinational networks result in some algebraic representation of the network function. The algebraic expression is often converted to a tabular or graphic representation for final use. The variety of representations in use is partly a result of differing individual taste and partly of different intended use. The major distinction between different representations is in the amount of information that is retained concerning the network structure.

The simplest representations are those that retain information only about the steady-state function realized by the network. By **steady-state function** is meant the relationship between the network inputs and outputs when the outputs are observed only after they have become stable. In a combinational network, when the inputs are changed some of the outputs may change in response, perhaps more than once, but each output will finally stop changing and remain with one stable value. It is to this stable value that the steady-state function refers.

An algebraic expression for the steady-state function of a combinational network can, in principle, be easily obtained by a procedure of successively labeling each gate with an expression derived from the gate inputs and gate function. In a combinational network there will always be at least one gate whose inputs are all also circuit inputs. The first step in deriving output expressions is to label all such gates with expressions using the symbols for the circuit inputs and the function realized by the gate. This is shown in Fig. 3.4-1 by the leads labeled with (1). There will now be some gates whose inputs are all labeled either as a result of step 1 or because they are circuit inputs. Step 2 consists of labeling the outputs of all such gates—shown in Fig. 3.4-1 with (2) indications. This process of labeling leads is repeated until all the leads in the network have labels. The labels on the output leads are the desired expressions for the output functions. Figure 3.4-1 shows the application of this procedure to a network of AND and OR gates.

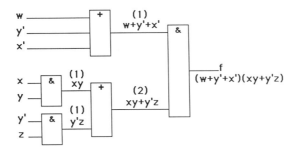

Figure 3.4-1 Algebraic analysis of combinational gate networks: AND and OR gates.

3.4-1 Tabular Representations

The most straightforward tabular representation of a switching function is the table of combinations or truth table, such as that shown in Table 3.4-1a for the function of Fig. 3.4-1. This representation is also easily extended to multi-output networks as shown in Table 3.4-1b for Fig. 3.4-2. It is often easier to use n-cube maps instead of tables of combinations. When n-cube maps are used for switching circuits they are usually called Karnaugh maps, after the man who pointed out their applicability to Boolean minimization. The Karnaugh map for Table 3.4-1a is shown in Table 3.4-2.

TABLE 3.4-1 Tables of combinations for: (a) Fig. 3.4-1; (b) Fig. 3.4-2

		(a)							(b)				
	w	x	y	z	f			w	x	y	z	f	g
0	0	0	0	0	0		0	0	0	0	0	1	1
1	0	0	0	1	1		1	0	0	0	1	0	0
2	0	0	1	0	0		2	0	0	1	0	0	0
3	0	0	1	1	0		3	0	0	1	1	0	1
4	0	1	0	0	0		4	0	1	0	0	1	1
5	0	1	0	1	1		5	0	1	0	1	0	0
6	0	1	1	0	0		6	0	1	1	0	0	0
7	0	1	1	1	0		7	0	1	1	1	0	1
8	1	0	0	0	0		8	1	0	0	0	0	0
9	1	0	0	1	1		9	1	0	0	1	0	0
10	1	0	1	0	0		10	1	0	1	0	0	0
11	1	0	1	1	0		11	1	0	1	1	0	1
12	1	1	0	0	0		12	1	1	0	0	1	0
13	1	1	0	1	1		13	1	1	0	1	1	0
14	1	1	1	0	1		14	1	1	1	0	1	0
15	1	1	1	1	1		15	1	1	1	1	1	1

TABLE 3.4-2 Karnaugh map for Table 3.4-1 function

y z \ wx	00	01	11	10
0 0	0	0	0	0
0 1	1	1	1	1
1 1	0	0	1	0
1 0	0	0	1	0

f

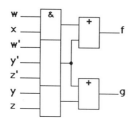

Figure 3.4-2 Multi-output network.

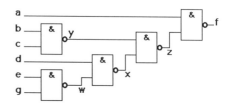

Figure 3.4-3 NAND gate network.

3.4-2 NAND and NOR Networks

The analysis technique illustrated in Fig. 3.4-1 is not limited to networks of AND and OR gates. The same technique is directly applicable to networks containing inverters and other types of multi-input gates. However, direct application of this technique to NAND or NOR gate networks can be cumbersome and inefficient. A modified technique for such networks will be presented next.

A network of NAND gates is shown in Fig. 3.4-3. The internal gate outputs are labeled with the variables w, x, y, and z to facilitate the following discussion. The steps in a straightforward analysis of this network are summarized in Table 3.4-3. Part (a) of this table shows the intermediate results when DeMorgan's theorem is used to remove complemented parentheses as soon as possible, and part (b) shows the results when no complements are removed until the output expression has been obtained. Both approaches have undesirable features. That of part (a) requires unnecessary effort in converting the same expression (for instance, eg) back and forth several times. That of part (b) requires that many levels of complemented parentheses be kept, with the consequent danger of error. These drawbacks can be eliminated by use of the modification to be described next.

TABLE 3.4-3 Intermediate steps in straightforward analysis of network of Fig. 3.4-3: (a) Complements on parentheses removed whenever possible; (b) Complements not removed until end

(a)

w	$x = (dw)'$	y	$z = (xy)'$	$f = (az)'$
$(eg)'$				
$e' + g'$				
	$[d(e' + g')]'$			
	$d' + eg$			
		$(bc)'$		
		$b' + c'$		
			$[(d' + eg)(b' + c')]'$	
			$d(e' + g') + bc$	
				$(a[d(e' + g') + bc])'$
				$a' + [d(e' + g') + bc]'$
				$a' + (d' + eg)(b' + c')$

w	$x = (dw)'$	y	$z = (xy)'$	$f = (az)'$
$(eg)'$				
	$[d(eg)']'$			
		$(bc)'$		
			$([d(eg)']'[bc]')'$	
				$[(a)([d(eg)']'[bc]')']'$
				$a' + ([d(eg)']'[bc]')$
				$a' + [d' + eg][b' + c']$

Figure 3.4-4 shows the network of Fig. 3.4-3 redrawn to make use of the gate symbol corresponding to the expression $x' + y'$ as well as that corresponding to the $(xy)'$ form. In Fig. 3.4-4b a fragment of this network is again redrawn, this time with detached inverters used rather than circles on gate inputs or gate outputs. This figure illustrates the fact that there are, in effect, two inverters in series between the output of the (eg) gate and the input of the (x) gate. Because of the involution theorem, $(X')' = X$, these inverters have no logical effect and can be ignored. This observation leads to the following conclusion: Whenever a lead has a circle output at one end and a circle input at the other end, *both* circles can be ignored. Thus the network of Fig. 3.4-4a can be transformed to the network of Fig. 3.4-5 *for the purposes of analysis*. The analysis of Fig. 3.4-5 is shown in Table 3.4-4. It should be emphasized that the technique just presented is merely a trick to avoid some unnecessary work in writing down an expression for the output of a NAND gate network. An exactly analogous technique can be used for networks of NOR gates.

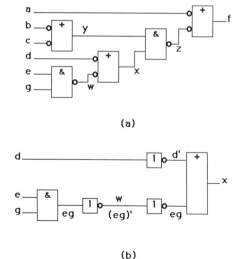

(a)

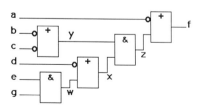

(b)

Figure 3.4-4 Network of Fig. 3.4-3 redrawn using two types of gate symbols: (a) network; (b) fragment.

Figure 3.4-5 Network of Fig. 3.4-4 redrawn to eliminate internal inversion symbols.

Sec. 3.4   Gate Networks

w	$x = d' + w$	y	$z = xy$	$f = a' + z$
eg				
	$d' + eg$			
		$b' + c'$		
			$(d' + eg)(b' + c')$	
				$a' + (d' + eg)(b' + c')$

Whenever a NAND or NOR gate network has no internal fanout (each gate output is connected to only one gate input), it is possible to transform the network diagram so that no internal inversion symbols remain. For networks with internal fanout (some gate output is connected to more than one gate input), it may not be possible to eliminate all of the internal inversion symbols. This is illustrated in Fig. 3.4-6.

The technique just described for analyzing NAND and NOR gate networks is also useful for designing such networks. If a network has been designed using OR and AND gates, it can be converted to NAND or NOR gates by inserting inversion circles in the appropriate places. This is illustrated in Fig. 3.4-7. In particular, a two-stage NAND network can be obtained directly from a two-stage network of AND gates connected to an output OR gate. A two-stage NOR network is obtained from a two-stage network in which the input gates are ORs and the output is derived from an AND gate. Thus while there are two types of two-stage networks using AND and OR gates, there is only one type of two-stage network when NAND or NOR gates are used.

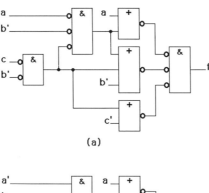

(a)

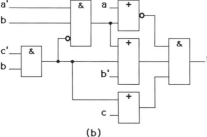

(b)

Figure 3.4-6 NOR gate network for which it is not possible to remove all inversion symbols: (a) before removal of inversion circles; (b) after removal of inversion circles.

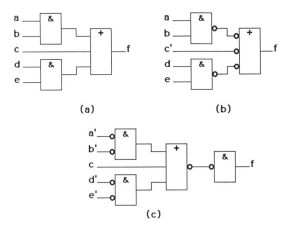

(a)   (b)

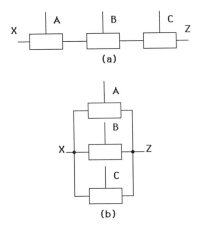

Figure 3.4-7 Transformation of AND and OR gate networks into NAND and NOR gate networks: (a) AND gates and OR gates; (b) NAND gates; (c) NOR gates.

(c)

3.5 SWITCH NETWORKS

Gate networks are composed of multi-input gates which realize Boolean functions of their input signals and possibly inverters which realize the complements of their inputs. The most common other class of logic network is made up of interconnected switches. Electronic realizations of switches, pass transistors, and transmission gates will be discussed in Chap. 4. Switch contacts and relay contacts are examples of electromechanical transmission gates. Since the emphasis in this book is on integrated circuits, contact networks will not be explicitly discussed. For more details on this topic, the reader is referred to [McCluskey 65] and [Caldwell 58].

When switches are used to realize logic functions, it is the interconnection pattern which determines the functional relationships. For example, in Fig. 3.5-1a a series connection of switches is shown. An AND function is realized by this connection since X and Z are equal only when all control inputs (A, B and C) are active. Similarly, Fig. 3.5-1b shows a parallel connection of switches realizing an OR function. By making use of the relationships illustrated in Fig. 3.5-1, it is

Figure 3.5-1 Analysis of simple switch networks: (a) series switches; (b) parallel switches.

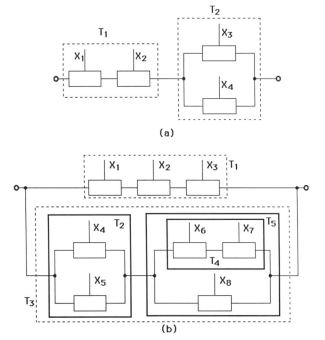

(a)

(b)

Figure 3.5-2 Analysis of series-parallel transmission networks: (a) network 1, $T = T_1T_2 = X_1X_2(X_3 + X_4)$; (b) network 2, $T = T_1 + T_3 = X_1X_2X_3 + (X_4 + X_5)(X_6X_7 + X_8)$.

easy to derive a function for any series-parallel network of switches. (A series-parallel network is one that is constructed only of series or parallel connections of subnetworks [McCluskey 65].)

Any series-parallel network can be split into either two subnetworks in series (Fig. 3.5-2a) or two subnetworks in parallel (Fig. 3.5-2b). If the transmissions of the two subnetworks are T_1 and T_2, the transmission of the original network is given by T_1T_2 or $T_1 + T_2$. Each of the subnetworks can again be split into two subnetworks, etc. This process of splitting into subnetworks is continued until each subnetwork consists only of switches in series or switches in parallel. The transmission of each subnetwork can be written directly, and the transmission of the original network obtained by combining the transmissions of the subnetworks. This procedure is illustrated in Fig. 3.5-2.

This method is not applicable to non-series-parallel networks. Another method which works for all networks consists of tracing all paths from input to output, writing for each path a transmission equal to the product of the controls of all gates in the path, and then forming the overall transmission as the sum of the individual path transmissions. This is illustrated in Fig. 3.5-3. The expression obtained by this method will be a sum of products of literals. The two terminals of the switch network will be connected only when all gates of at least one path through the network are activated. This corresponds to the fact that the transmission expression will equal 1 only when at least one of the product terms is equal to 1.

The network of Fig. 3.5-3b shows paths passing through the X_2 switch in both directions. It is true that switches are typically bilateral elements that allow signals

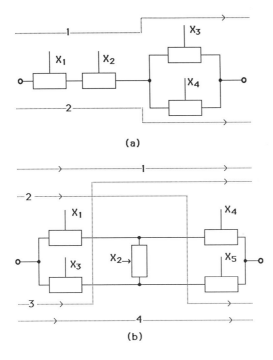

(a)

(b)

Figure 3.5-3 Analysis of transmission networks by path tracing: (a) series-parallel network, $T = X_1X_2X_3 + X_1X_2X_4$; (b) bridge network, $T = X_1X_4 + X_1X_2X_5 + X_3X_2X_4 + X_3X_5$.

to be propagated in either direction. Some contact networks make use of this property to minimize the number of contacts used.

Many integrated-circuit logic networks contain only multi-input gates. However, it is sometimes possible to obtain very efficient designs by combining multi-input gates and switches. The use of switch networks in NMOS designs is discussed in [Mead 80].

Techniques for analyzing networks of only multi-input gates or only switches have been presented. Networks that combine both classes of gates are simply analyzed by partitioning them into subnetworks containing only one class of gate. These subnetworks are analyzed using the previous techniques. The results are then combined to get the final network functions.

3.6 TRANSIENT ANALYSIS: HAZARDS

The previous sections have presented techniques for obtaining the steady-state functions for combinational networks. In many situations this is sufficient: for example, when the network outputs are strobed or clocked after an adequate settling time. However, there are also many situations in which it is necessary to discover whether temporary output changes can occur before the final stable values appear. A (simplified) example of such a situation is shown in Fig. 3.6-1a.

For this circuit when $w = x = 0$, a steady-state analysis predicts that the function S_2 will remain at 0 when the value of y_1 changes. When changing state

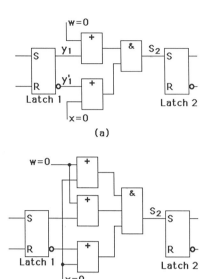

Figure 3.6-1 Simplified example of a circuit with a possible false output: (a) original circuit; (b) redesigned circuit.

a real (rather than an idealized) latch[2] can have both of its outputs momentarily equal to 1. Thus, it is possible in this situation to have a spurious 1 signal appear at S_2. If latch 2 was in the 0-state (reset) this could cause it to incorrectly enter the 1-state (set state). Whether the spurious pulse occurs and whether it affects latch 2 depends on the specific device parameters. In fact, it is possible for the circuit operation to vary according to its temperature or to be different for chips fabricated on different days.

Several possibilities exist for correcting a situation such as that illustrated in Fig. 3.6-1a.

1. The inputs to latch 2 can be **strobed** (enabled or clocked) by a pulse whose arrival is designed to occur only after the latch inputs have had adequate time to stabilize. This is an effective technique and is widely used. There are situations in which it is not desirable (such as internal to a latch). Strobing does tend to slow down the overall operation of a network since the strobe pulse must be delayed until the worst-case settling time for any output transition.

2. Latch 2 can be designed so that it does not respond to short input pulses. This can slow the response time of the latch and thus slow the network operation speed. Also, this makes the correct operation of the network depend on the latch parameters and can lead to unreliable operation. However, there are situations in which such an approach is warranted.

3. It may be possible to design one of the OR gates so that it has a longer

---

[2] An *SR* latch is a two-state element that retains its previous state when both inputs are 0. It enters the 1-state (set) when the *S* input is activated and the 0-state (reset) when the *R* input is activated. Latches are discussed in Sec. 7.2.

propagation delay than the other OR gate. This approach only works if a spurious pulse causing false setting of latch 2 can happen for only one of the two possible transitions of latch 1. This is illustrated in Fig. 3.6-2. Besides the limitation to unidirectional input changes, this technique has the disadvantage of relying on the relative delays in the two OR gates. Variation in these parameters could cause incorrect operation.

4. The combinational network interconnecting the latches can be redesigned so that the steady-state function is unchanged but no spurious output pulses are possible. The redesigned network is shown in Fig. 3.6-1b.

The various phenomena that can cause spurious transient outputs in combinational networks will be identified and classified in this section. Techniques will then be developed for analyzing a network to determine whether these spurious outputs can occur. These techniques lead directly to the design techniques to be presented in Chapter 6 for networks that cannot have such spurious outputs.

3.6-1 Types of Hazards

If the output signals for a combinational network depend on the internal circuit (element and interconnection) delays as well as the input signals, the network is said to contain a **hazard**. Only the transient part of the output can be affected by the delays. As discussed previously, the steady-state outputs depend only on the inputs. A large variety of transient waveforms are theoretically possible. In practice only two types of hazard waveforms are of interest. These are called static hazards and dynamic hazards.

A **static hazard** is present if it is possible for a momentary change of output to occur in response to an input change that does not cause the steady-state output to change. Static hazards are further classified as either **static 1-hazards** for which the steady-state output is 1 and **static 0-hazards** for which the steady-state output is 0. These are illustrated in Fig. 3.6-3.

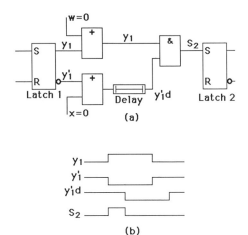

(a)

(b)

Figure 3.6-2 Redesign of Fig. 3.6-1a using gate delay: (a) circuit; (b) waveforms.

(a)   **(b)**   **(a)**   **(b)**

Figure 3.6-3 Static hazards: (a) static 1-hazard; (b) static 0-hazard.

Figure 3.6-4 Dynamic hazard: (a) steady-state output; (b) dynamic hazard waveform.

A **dynamic hazard** is present if when the output is supposed to change it is possible for the output to change several times before settling down to its steady-state value. A dynamic hazard is illustrated in Fig. 3.6-4.

The classification of hazards as static or dynamic is based on the output waveforms. It is also important to distinguish two specific causes of hazards. If the presence of a hazard is due to the function realized by an output, the hazard is called a **function hazard**. A hazard that is caused not by the output function but by the particular network used to implement the function is called a **logic hazard**. The circuit of Fig. 3.6-1 is clearly an example of a logic hazard since it was possible to eliminate the hazard by redesign of the circuit.

3.6-2 Function Hazards

Function hazards are present only for transitions in which more than one input variable is changed. Even as simple a function as a two-input AND can have a function hazard. The map for such a function is shown in Table 3.6-1. Consider the situation in which $A = 1$ and $CK = 0$. If A changes to 0 at the same time that CK changes to 1, the steady-state output will remain at 0. Depending on the circuit parameters and the precise timing of the changes a spurious 1-output can occur. A less-than-full-amplitude pulse, called a "runt pulse," can be generated. Thus, a two-input AND function contains a function static 0-hazard for the transition 01 to 10.

TABLE 3.6-1
Map for AND function

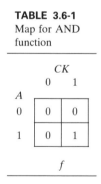

	CK	
	0	1
A		
0	0	0
1	0	1

f

The simplest technique for avoiding function hazards is to restrict all input transitions to single-variable changes. This is often done, but there is a very important situation in which such a restriction is not possible. This situation occurs when the value of an external signal must be sampled and recorded in a digital system or computer. The external signal changes are not synchronized by the system and thus there is no way to prevent the external signal from changing at the same time that the sampling signal changes. This situation is referred to in the literature as the synchronizer or asynchronous arbiter problem. It will be discussed in more detail in Chap. 7.

A less trivial example is given in Table 3.6-2, which shows a function containing several function hazards. (It is not necessary to show a circuit since these hazards will be present in any realization of this function.) In general, specific hazards correspond to specific input transitions.

A function static 0-hazard is present for the transition $\langle wxyz \rangle$: $\langle 0000 \rangle - \langle 0101 \rangle$. The output for both of these input states is 0. Unless x and z change exactly simultaneously, either state $\langle 0100 \rangle$ or state $\langle 0001 \rangle$ will occur as an intermediate input state.[3] Since the output for both of these states is 1, a spurious 1 output can be present even though the output is supposed to remain at 0. This situation is shown in the operating path diagram of Fig. 3.6-5a. A function static 1-hazard is present for the transition $\langle 0100 \rangle - \langle 0001 \rangle$ for similar reasons.

TABLE 3.6-2 Karnaugh map for function to illustrate function hazards

		00	01	11	10
y	z				
0	0	0	1	0	1
0	1	1	0	1	0
1	1	0	1	0	1
1	0	0	0	1	0

(column header group: wx)

f

The transition $\langle 0011 \rangle - \langle 0110 \rangle$ also corresponds to a function static 0-hazard. For this transition both stable states have 0 outputs. One of the intermediate unstable states $\langle 0111 \rangle$ has a 1 output while the other unstable state $\langle 0010 \rangle$ has a 0 output. Thus, if the transition is from $\langle 0011 \rangle$ to $\langle 0110 \rangle$ and if the z input is the first to change, there will be no spurious 1 output. If x changes first, there will be a transient 1 output. If the input transition is from $\langle 0110 \rangle$ to $\langle 0011 \rangle$, the situation is reversed. In any event the transition corresponds to a hazard since the output waveform depends on the circuit delays. This transition is shown in Fig. 3.6-5b.

A function dynamic hazard is present for the transition $\langle 1100 \rangle - \langle 1011 \rangle$. This situation is shown in the operating path diagram of Fig. 3.6-5c. For this transition three variables—x, y, z—are changing. After any one of the input variables has changed, the input state will correspond to a 1-output. After the second variable

[3] Even if the input changes are simultaneous, they will not propagate through the network simultaneously. The effect on the network will be the same as if the input changes had been skewed.

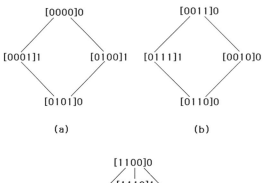

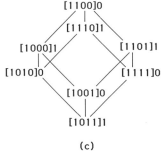

Figure 3.6-5 Operating path diagrams for function of Table 3.6-1 (notation is [*wxyz*]*f*): (a) *wxyz*: 0000-to-0101 transition; (b) *wxyz*: 0011-to-0110 transition; (c) *wxyz*: 1100-to-1011 transition.

change, the input state corresponds to a 0-output. When the third variable change happens, the final state corresponding to a 1-output is reached. The output waveform will be that shown in Fig. 3.6-4b. For this transition it is clear that a dynamic hazard output waveform is likely for any realization and any circuit delays. It is possible to have dynamic hazard transitions, for example ⟨0001⟩ − ⟨0110⟩, for which the output waveform depends on the order in which the inputs change. Such a transition also represents a dynamic hazard since spurious transient outputs are possible for some values of circuit delays.

3.6-3 Logic Hazards

If multiple-input changes are not allowed, there will be no function hazards present. It is still possible to have hazards for single input transitions. Such hazards depend on the particular realization of the function and are called **logic hazards**. An example of a circuit with such a hazard is given in Fig. 3.6-1.

For some design situations it is important to be able to analyze the network to determine whether any hazards are present. An algebraic analysis technique for detecting the existence of logic hazards will be presented next.

Static Logic Hazards. Static logic hazards are caused by the phenomenon whereby two signals (such as x and x') which always have opposite steady-state values take on the same value while the network signals are changing. An analysis technique for such hazards must therefore not use relations which assume that complementary variables have opposite values. In other words, literals such as x and x' must be taken as two different variables rather than complements of the same variable. The theorems $XX' = 0$ and $X + X' = 1$ must not be used to rewrite expressions. Neither must other theorems based on these two theorems be used:

$$(X + Y')Y = XY \qquad XY' + Y = X + Y$$

$$XY + X'Z + YZ = XY + X'Z \qquad (X + Y)(X' + Z)(Y + Z) = (X + Y)(X' + Z)$$

$$(X + Y)(X' + Z) = XZ + X'Y$$

The static logic hazard analysis procedure starts by forming *either* a sum-of-products or a product-of-sums expression for the network function. The theorems $X + XY = X$ and $X(X + Y) = X$ are used to eliminate redundant product terms or sum factors. The complement theorems discussed above **must not** be used. Each product term in a sum-of-products expression formed by this procedure corresponds to a "1-set" of the network. The sum factors in a product-of-sums expression obtained by this procedure correspond to "0-sets" of the network. Formal definitions of the 1-sets and 0-sets are:

DEFINITION. A set of literals is a **1-set** of a network N iff:
(a) Whenever all of the literals are equal to 1, the network output is equal to 1; and
(b) If any literal is removed, condition (a) no longer holds.

DEFINITION. A set of literals is a **0-set** of a network N iff:
(a) Whenever all of the literals are equal to 0, the network output is equal to 0; and
(b) If any literal is removed, condition (a) no longer holds.

Example 3.6-1

The network of Fig. 3.6-6 will be used to illustrate the calculation of 1- and 0-sets. Direct analysis of this network yields the expression

$$f = (xy + y'z)(x' + y' + w)$$

which is "multiplied out" to give the expression

$$f = x'xy + xyy' + xyw + y'zx' + y'z + y'zw$$

Elimination of the two redundant product terms results in the expression

$$f = x'xy + xyy' + xyw + y'z$$

The corresponding 1-sets are

$$[x, y, w] \; [y', z] \; [x, y, y'] \; [x, x', y]$$

The 0-sets can be found by taking the dual (Sec. 2.8) of the expression for f

$$f^D = (x + y)(y' + z) + x'y'w$$

Multiplying out this expression gives

$$f^D = xy' + zx + yy' + zy + x'y'w$$

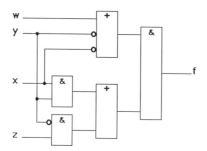

Figure 3.6-6 Network for logic hazard analysis examples.

Taking the dual again yields

$$f = (x + y')(x + z)(y + y')(y + z)(w + x' + y')$$

The corresponding 0-sets are

$$\text{0-sets:} \ [x, y'] \ [x, z] \ [y, y'] \ [y, z] \ [w, x', y']$$

In testing a network for static logic hazards it is only necessary to generate *either* the 1-sets or the 0-sets. Both types of sets are calculated in the example above solely to illustrate the procedure used to obtain them. For many networks it is much easier to calculate one type of set rather than the other type. Since either can be used for determining the hazards, the easier calculation is preferred. Note that the 1- and 0-sets depend on the network realization as well as the function. That is, different networks for the same function can have different 1-sets and 0-sets. For example, the 0-sets of the network of Fig. 3.6-1a are $[w, y_1] \ [x, y_1']$ while those of the Fig. 3.6-1b network are $[w, y_1] \ [x, y_1'] \ [w, x]$, even though both networks realize the same function.

It may seem odd to have product terms or sum factors such as xyy' or $(y + y')$ which contain both a variable and its complement. These must be kept since they are the key to the detection of static logic hazards. The corresponding sets, those containing both a variable and its complement, are called **unstable sets**.

DEFINITION. A 1-set or 0-set is called **unstable** if it contains at least one pair of complementary literals. Sets that do not contain any pairs of complementary literals are called **stable** sets.

Example. The set $[y, y', z]$ is unstable. The set $[w, x', y']$ is stable.

DEFINITION. The variables corresponding to the pairs of complemented literals are called **unstable variables**. The variables corresponding to the other literals of the set are called **stable variables**.

For each input state of the network the output is determined by one or more of **either** the 1-sets having all its literals equal to 1 **or** the 0-sets having all its literals equal to 0. The sets that determine the output value for a particular input state are called the active sets. It is not possible for an unstable set to be active for an

Analysis of Combinational Circuits   Chap. 3

input state. However, an unstable set can be active for a transition if its unstable variables change during the transition.

DEFINITION. A (stable) 1-set is said to be **active** for an input state iff all the literals of the 1-set are equal to 1 for that input state. A (stable) 0-set is said to be **active** for an input state iff all the literals of the 0-set are equal to 0 for that input state. An unstable 1-set (0-set) is active for a transition between a pair of input states iff all its stable literals are 1 (0) for both states of the transition and all its unstable variables have different values for the two states of the transition. Sets that are not active are called **inactive** sets.

Example. In the network of Fig. 3.6-6, when the input state is $w = x = y = z = 0$, all of the 1-sets are inactive and the active 0-sets are $[x, z]$ and $[y, z]$. The unstable 1-set $[x, x', y]$ is active for all transitions with $y = 1$ and x changing.

It is not possible to have both a (stable) 1-set and a (stable) 0-set active for the same input state since this would correspond to a conflict in the determination of the output value.

Static Logic Hazard Theorems. The theorems that relate the 1-sets (or 0-sets) to the presence of static logic hazards can now be stated. At first only the 1-sets will be considered. A static logic 1-hazard is present if there is a transition between two input states, both of which have 1-outputs, and there is no single 1-set that is active for both input states.

THEOREM 3.6-1. A static logic 1-hazard exists in a network iff:
(a) There is a pair of input states that both produce 1 outputs,
(b) There is no (stable) 1-set of the network that is active for input states of the pair.

Proof. Suppose that the variable that has different values for the two input states of the pair is v. Then either v or v' must appear in all 1-sets that are active for either state. If one of the active sets did not include a v or a v', it would be active for both states contrary to the hypothesis. Suppose now that both v and v' are equal to 0 during the transition between the two input states. All the 1-sets must become inactive since all the active sets for either input state have either a v or v'. When all 1-sets are inactive, the output must become equal to 0. A transition for which the output is 1 for both states and which has a 0 output during the transition corresponds to a static 1-hazard by definition.

Figure 3.6-7 shows a Karnaugh map for the function of the network of Fig. 3.6-6 with the 1-sets shown on the map. This map shows that there is one static logic 1-hazard corresponding to the transition $w = x = z = 1$, y changing. The 1-set $[w, x, y]$ is active for the input state $w = x = y = z = 1$. The 1-set $[y', z]$ is active for the input state $w = x = z = 1$ and $y = 0$. The fact that the unstable 1-set $[x, y, y']$ can become active during the transition is of no importance in this situation.

A static logic 0-hazard will be present in a network for a transition between a pair of input states that both have 0 outputs if there is an unstable 1-set that is active for the transition.

THEOREM 3.6-2. A static logic 0-hazard exists in a network iff:
(a) There is a pair of input states with the network output equal to 0 for both states,
(b) There is an (unstable) 1-set that is active for the transition between the pair of input states.

Proof. Since the unstable 1-set is active for the transition, a temporary 1 output can occur. This satisfies the definition of a static 0-hazard.

Inspection of Fig. 3.6-7 shows that there are three single-variable transitions which satisfy the conditions of this theorem:

$$w = 0, y = z = 1 \qquad w = 0, y = 1, z = 0 \qquad w = 0, x = 1, z = 0$$

Theorems 3.6-1 and 3.6-2 give conditions for determining both the static logic 1-hazards and 0-hazards from the network 1-sets. Both types of hazards can also be found from the 0-sets by using the dual theorems which will be stated next. Since they are derived and proved in the same fashion as the previous theorems they will be presented without further elaboration.

THEOREM 3.6-3. A static logic 0-hazard exists in a network iff:
(a) There is a pair of input states that both produce 0 outputs,
(b) There is no (stable) 0-set of the network that is active for input states of the pair.

THEOREM 3.6-4. A static logic 1-hazard exists in a network iff:
(a) There is a pair of input states with the network output equal to 1 for both states,
(b) There is an (unstable) 0-set that is active for the transition between the pair of input states.

Figure 3.6-8 shows a Karnaugh map for the network of Fig. 3.6-6 with the 0-sets and hazards indicated on it.

Dynamic Logic Hazards. Static logic hazards are caused by the phenomenon of two signals that have complementary steady-state values temporarily having the

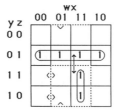

Figure 3.6-7 Karnaugh map plot of 1-sets of Fig. 3.6-6 network. Unstable 1-sets are shown with ------ lines; static 1-hazard is indicated by ⟷; static 0-hazards are indicated by ⟨ ⟩.

Analysis of Combinational Circuits   Chap. 3

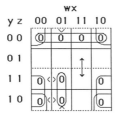

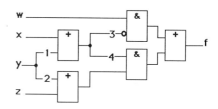

Figure 3.6-8 Karnaugh map plot of 0-sets for the network of Fig. 3.6-6. Unstable 0-sets are shown with ------- lines; static 1-hazard is indicated by $\longleftrightarrow$; static 0-hazards are indicated by $\langle\ \rangle$.

Figure 3.6-9 Network to illustrate fanout paths.

same value. If, *in addition*, two signals that always have the same steady-state value can temporarily have opposite values then a dynamic hazard is present. This situation occurs when some signal propagates to the network output via two (or more) different paths due to fanout. Figure 3.6-9 shows a simple network with fanout. The signal y can affect the output through two paths that originate with the leads marked 1 and 2 in the figure.

To detect dynamic hazards, it is necessary to modify the 1-sets and 0-sets to explicitly take fanout into account. Thus, for dynamic hazard analysis, 1-sets are replaced by P-sets and 0-sets are replaced by S-sets. In forming the P- and S-sets unique labels are associated with each fanout lead (e.g., leads 1 and 2 in Fig. 3.6-9). The 1- and 0-sets take into account the time skew between x and x' signals. The P- and S-sets in addition account for the time skew among different x signals in the network.

DEFINITION. A **marked logic diagram** is one in which each lead leaving a fanout node is labeled with a unique identifier (usually, a number).

Example. In Fig. 3.6-9 the input y is connected to a fanout point, and the two leads connected to this point are given numbers 1 and 2.

DEFINITION. A P-set (S-set) is defined and computed in the same fashion as a 1-set (0-set) with the additional specifications that:
(a) A marked logic diagram must be used,
(b) Whenever an input variable can propagate to the output along more than one path, each appearance of that variable must include a label identifying which path corresponds to that instance of the variable. This will be satisfied if whenever a variable is propagated through a marked lead, the lead mark is added as a subscript to the variable.

Example. The P-sets for Fig. 3.6-9 are formed as follows:

$$f = w(x_3'\, y_{1,3}') + (x_4 + y_{1,4})(y_2 + z)$$

To simplify the expressions it is possible to replace $y_{1,3}'$ by y_5' and $y_{1,4}$ by y_6 since it is only necessary to distinguish different paths. In fact, the subscripts can be dropped from the x literals since x and x' must refer to different paths. For the same reason the subscript can be dropped from y' since there is only one y' literal in the expression.

The simplified expression for f becomes

$$f = wx'y' + (x + y_6)(y_2 + z)$$

$$f = wx'y' + xy_2 + xz + y_6y_2 + y_6z$$

Example 3.6-2

Calculation of the P-sets and S-sets for Fig. 3.6-10

$$f = (w + y_1' + x_4')(x_5y_2 + y_3'z)$$

$$= wx_5y_2 + wy_3'z + y_1'x_5y_2 + y_1'y_3'z + x_4'x_5y_2 + x_4'y_3'z$$

$$f^D = wy_1'x_4' + (x_5 + y_2)(y_3' + z) = wy_1'x_4' + x_5y_3' + x_5z + y_2y_3' + y_2z$$

P-sets:

$$[w, x_5, y_2]\ [w, y_3', z]\ [y_1', x_5, y_2]\ [y_1', y_3', z]\ [x_4', x_5, y_2]\ [x_4', y_3', z]$$

S-sets:

$$[w, y_1', x_4']\ [x_5, y_3']\ [x_5, z]\ [y_2, y_3']\ [y_2, z]$$

THEOREM 3.6-5. A dynamic logic hazard exists in a network for a transition T between a pair of input states I and J iff:

(a) There is an unstable $P(S)$-set which is active for T. Denote this unstable set by U and the unstable variable by X.[4]

(b) There is a stable $P(S)$-set which is active for I and inactive for J. Denote this stable set by B. There is in B a literal X^* with a different subscript from any of the subscripts on X^* in U.

(c) All other $P(S)$-sets are inactive for J.

(d) All other $P(S)$-sets are either inactive for I or all $P(S)$-sets which are active for I have a literal X^* with a different subscript from any of the subscripts on X^* in U.

Proof. Suppose P-sets are used. For input state J, all P-sets are inactive, so the network output is 0. If the X^* literals of U change so they are all 1, the output will become 1. This can happen without the stable P-sets becoming active since each of the stable sets that are active for I have an X^* with a different subscript from those in U. Next let the X^* literals of U that have not yet changed to the appropriate value for I change. This will cause U to become inactive and the output to become 0. Finally, let the X^* literals in the P-sets which are active for I change. This causes the output to equal 1. Thus an output waveform of 0-1-0-1 has been produced.

---

[4] It is assumed that there is only one unstable variable. Unstable sets with more than one unstable variable can only cause hazards for multiple-input changes. For multiple-input transitions logic hazards are much less important than functional hazards. Thus only single-input transitions will be considered here.

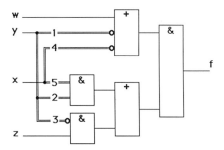

Figure 3.6-10 Marked logic diagram for Fig. 3.6-6.

Procedure to Determine Dynamic Hazards

1. Select an unstable P-set (S-set). Call this set U and its unstable variable X. If there are no unstable sets, no dynamic hazard is present.

2. Select a stable P-set (S-set) in which X appears with a different subscript from any of the subscripts on X in U. Call this set B. If no such set exists, a different choice must be made for U. If no suitable pair of U and B can be found, no dynamic hazard is present.

3. Assign to the input variables values that make all the non-X literals of U and B equal to 1 (0). If such values do not exist, U and B do not correspond to a dynamic hazard and another pair of P-sets must be chosen.

4. Assign values to the remaining input variables so that all of the other stable sets are either inactive or contain an X literal with a different subscript from the subscripts on X or X' in U. If such an assignment is not possible, U and B do not correspond to a dynamic hazard.

Example 3.6-3

For the network of Fig. 3.6-10 there is only one unstable S-set:

$$[y_2, y_3']$$

There is one stable S-set that contains y without either 2 or 3 as a subscript:

$$[w, y_1', x_4']$$

It is necessary to set $w = 0$ and $x = 1$ to have this set active. This makes all the other sets inactive except for $[y_2, z]$, which must be made inactive since it contains y_2. This is done by setting $z = 1$. This shows that there is one dynamic hazard in this network and it occurs for the transition with $w = 0$, $x = 1$, $z = 1$.

It is also possible to discover the same hazard information by using the P-sets. This will be done next, not because any new information about the network will be obtained, but rather because some different aspects of the procedure for determining dynamic hazards are illustrated.

There are two unstable P-sets for the Fig. 3.6-6 network:

$$[y_1', x_5, y_2] \ [x_4', x_5, y_2]$$

The set with x as its unstable variable does not correspond to a dynamic hazard. There is no stable set that has x in it with a subscript other than the subscripts 4 and 5 which occur in the unstable set.

For the unstable set with y unstable there are three stable sets with suitable subscripts on y:

$$[w, y'_3, z] \; [y'_1, y'_3, z] \; [x'_4, y'_3, z]$$

The last of these is not suitable since it is necessary to have $x = 0$ in order for it to be active, but this value of x makes the unstable set inactive since it contains x_5. The first of these sets turns out not to be suitable either. If w is set to 1 to make it active and x is set to 1 to make the unstable set active, there is no way to make the stable set $[w, x_5, y_2]$ inactive. This set contains y with the same subscript as the unstable set.

The remaining possibility is the set $[y'_1, y'_3, z]$. This is suitable because it has y with a 3 subscript and can be made active by setting $z = 1$. The unstable set can be activated by setting $x = 1$ and the stable set $[w, x_5, y_2]$ can be inactivated by setting $w = 0$. Thus the same transition with $w = 0$, $x = 1$, and $z = 1$ has been found to correspond to a dynamic hazard.

Theorem 3.6-5 on dynamic hazards has an important corollary which will be used in developing a procedure for the design of hazard-free networks. The corollary will be presented here, but the discussion of designing hazard-free networks will be deferred. It will be taken up in connection with the discussion of combinational circuit design in Chapter 6.

COROLLARY. If a network contains any dynamic hazards, it must contain at least one pair of unstable sets, one of which is a 1-set (P-set) and the other of which is a 0-set (S-set). The pair of unstable sets must share the same unstable variable, and any other variable that appears in both sets must be complemented in one of the sets and uncomplemented in the other.

Proof. The theorem requires that for any dynamic hazard transition there must be both an unstable P-set and an unstable S-set since the hazard can be found from either the P-sets or the S-sets.

Figure 3.6-11 shows the network of Fig. 3.6-6 reduced to show only the gates still active when all network inputs but y are fixed. The propagation of the changes

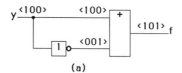

(a)

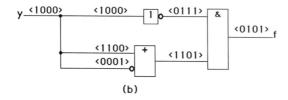

(b)

Figure 3.6-11 Network of Fig. 3.6-6 reduced for specific input values. Signal values at times t_1 t_2 t_3 t_4 are shown inside $\langle , \rangle$ symbols: (a) reduction for input state $(w, x, z) = (1, 1, 1)$; (b) reduction for input state $(w, x, z) = (0, 1, 1)$.

in the y signal throughout the network has been selected to make the hazards operational.

The presentation in this section is based on [McCluskey 62], [Eichelberger 64], and [David 69].

3.R REFERENCES

[CALDWELL 58] Caldwell, S. H., *Switching Circuits and Logical Design*, John Wiley & Sons, Inc., New York, 1958.

[CHAPPELL 74] Chappell, S. G., C. H. Elmendorf, and L. D. Schmidt, "LAMP: Logic-Circuit Simulators," *Bell Syst. Tech. J.*, Vol. 53, No. 8, pp. 1451–1476, 1974.

[DAVID 69] David, R., "Une méthode graphique pour déceler à la fois les aléas statiques et dynamiques dans les réseaux combinatoires," *Automatisme*, 14, No. 11, pp. 554–559, 1969.

[EICHELBERGER 65] Eichelberger, E. B., "Hazard Detection in Combinational and Sequential Switching Circuits," *IBM J. Res. Dev.*, pp. 90–99, Mar. 1965.

[HUFFMAN 71] Huffman, D. A., "Combinational Circuits with Feedback," Chap. 2 in *Recent Developments in Switching Theory*, ed. A. Mukhopadhyay, Academic Press, Inc., New York, pp. 27–55, 1971.

[KAMPEL 85] Kampel, I., *A Practical Introduction to the New Logic Symbols*, Butterworth, Stonham, MA., 1985.

[MANN 81] Mann, F. A., "Explanation of New Logic Symbols," Chap. 5 in *1981 Supplement to the TTL Data Book for Design Engineers*, 2nd ed., Texas Instruments, Inc., Dallas, 1981.

[McCLUSKEY 62] McCluskey, E. J., "Transients in Combinational Logic Circuits," in R. H. Wilcox and W. C. Mann (eds.), *Redundancy Techniques for Computing Systems*, Spartan Book, Washington, D.C. pp. 9–46, 1962.

[McCLUSKEY 65] McCluskey, E. J., *Introduction to the Theory of Switching Circuits*, McGraw-Hill Book Company, New York, 1965.

[MEAD 80] Mead, C., and L. Conway, "*Introduction to VLSI Systems*," Addison-Wesley Publishing Company, Inc., Reading, Mass., 1980.

[PEATMAN 80] Peatman, J. B., *Digital Hardware Design*, McGraw-Hill Book Company, New York, 1980.

[SZYGENDA 76] Szygenda, S. A., and E. W. Thompson, "Modeling and Digital Simulation for Design Verification and Diagnosis," *IEEE Trans. Comput.*, C-25, No. 12, pp. 1242–1253, Dec. 1976.

[TIMOC 79] Timoc, C. C., and L. M. Hess, "Fault Simulation: An Implementation into Hardware," *Proc. 1979 Test Conf.*, Cherry Hill, N.J., pp. 291–297, Oct. 23–25, 1979.

3.P PROBLEMS

3.1 Analyze the network shown in Fig. P3.1.
  (a) Find $f(x, c, y_1, y_2)$ without removing inversion bubbles; then use DeMorgan's theorem to eliminate any complemented terms or factors.

(b) Redraw network to remove as many inversion bubbles as possible.

(c) Find $f(x, c, y_1, y_2)$ from the redrawn network of part (b).

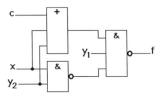

Figure P3.1

3.2 Analyze the circuit shown in Fig. P3.2.

   (a) Redraw with as few inverters as possible.

   (b) Write an algebraic expression for z.

   (c) Express z as a sum of products (this can be done with five products).

   (d) Write the dual of the expression of part (b).

   (e) Express z as a product of sums [multiply out the expression of part (d) and take the dual].

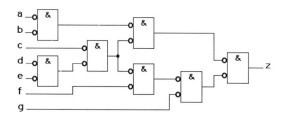

Figure P3.2

3.3 Analyze the NAND network shown in Fig. P3.3. Redraw the network to remove as many of the internal inverter bubbles as possible. Write a simple sum-of-products expression for Z.

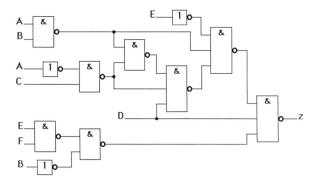

Figure P3.3

3.4 **(a)** Find $f(x_1, x_2, \ldots, x_{12})$ without removing inversion bubbles; then use DeMorgan's theorem to eliminate any complemented terms or factors.

   (b) Redraw network shown in Fig. P3.4 to remove as many inversion bubbles as possible.

   (c) Find $f(x_1, x_2, \ldots, x_{12})$ from the redrawn network of part (b).

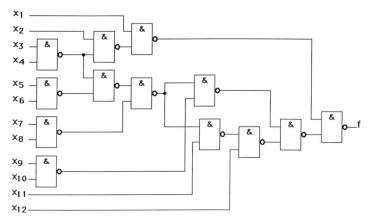

Figure P3.4

3.5 Analyze the network shown in Fig. P3.5 to obtain algebraic expressions for f_1, f_2. First redraw to eliminate all possible internal invertors.

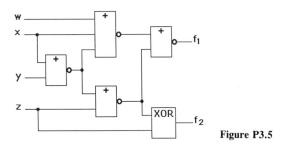

Figure P3.5

3.6 Analyze the network shown in Fig. P3.6, showing each step of your work clearly. (The box with ≥ 2 means that gate output $= 1$ iff 2 or more inputs are 1.)

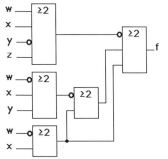

Figure P3.6

3.7 Analyze the switch network shown in Fig. P3.7.
    (a) Write an expression for the network transmission function.
    (b) Write this function as a simplified sum-of-products expression.

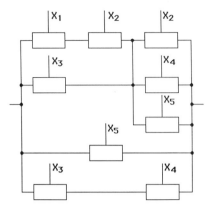

Figure P3.7

3.8 For the circuit shown in Fig. P3.8:
(a) Determine the 1-sets.
(b) Analyze the circuit for static hazards using only the 1-sets.
(c) Determine the 0-sets.
(d) Analyze the circuit for static hazards using only the 0-sets.

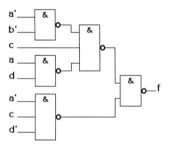

Figure P3.8

3.9

(a) Find P-sets or S-sets for the network shown in Fig. P3.9.
(b) Indicate P-sets or S-sets on map for f.
(c) Indicate static and dynamic hazards on map.
(d) If any type of hazard is not present, explain why not.

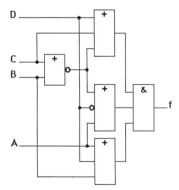

Figure P3.9

Analysis of Combinational Circuits   Chap. 3

3.10 For the circuit of Fig. P3.10:

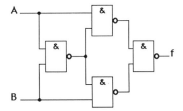

Figure P3.10

(a) Determine the P-sets. (Use as few and as simple subscripts as possible.)
(b) Plot f on a map.
(c) Plot and label P-sets on a map.
(d) Repeat the map from part (b) and mark all static hazards with the symbol <——>.
(e) Repeat the map from part (b) and mark all dynamic hazards with the symbol < >.
(f) Determine the S-sets. (Use as few and as simple subscripts as possible.)
(g) Plot f on a map.
(h) Plot and label S-sets on a map.
(i) Repeat the map from part (h) and mark all static hazards with the symbol <——>.
(j) Repeat the map from part (h) and mark all dynamic hazards with the symbol < >.

3.11 For each of the networks shown in Fig. P3.11:
(a) Redraw the network so as to minimize the number of internal inversions.
(b) Calculate the P-sets using as few subscripts as possible.
(c) Calculate the S-sets using as few subscripts as possible.
(d) Plot the 1-sets on a Karnaugh map and indicate all static logic hazards.
(e) Plot the 0-sets on a Karnaugh map and indicate all static logic hazards.
(f) Determine all dynamic hazards using the P-sets. Show the method used.
(g) Determine all dynamic hazards using the S-sets. Show the method used.
(h) Plot on a Karnaugh map the dynamic hazards and show on the same map all line segments corresponding to transitions with both an unstable 1-set and an unstable 0-set.
(i) Plot on a Karnaugh map the function realized by the network and show *one* transition corresponding to a static function hazard and *one* transition corresponding to a dynamic function hazard.

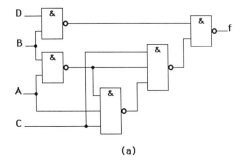

(a)

Figure P3.11

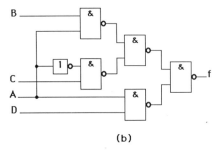

(b)   **Figure P3.11 (cont.)**

3.12 Consider the network shown in Fig. P3.12.

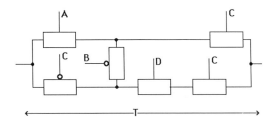

Figure P3.12

Note the bubbles on the control inputs of the negative switches.

(a) Write an expression for the transmission T.

(b) Label the diagram to prepare for dynamic logic hazard analysis.

(c) What are the P-sets? Underline the unstable P-sets.

(d) Plot f on a map—label all logic hazards ($<\!\!-\!\!-\!\!-\!\!>$ for static hazards, $<\ >$ for dynamic hazards).

4

INTEGRATED CIRCUITS

Logic design is not technology independent. Some minimum knowledge of integrated-circuit characteristics and limitations is essential for all logic design. The purpose of this chapter is to present the basic relevant aspects of digital electronics. No specific circuit background is assumed beyond that covered in high school physics (Kirchhoff's voltage and current laws). Most of the material of this chapter does not require even this knowledge of electricity. The student with no circuit background should still be able to learn enough to understand the remaining chapters of this book. Designing custom or semicustom chips requires a deeper understanding of microelectronics than is provided here. Students intending to do professional logic design are strongly encouraged to study at least one course devoted entirely to digital electronics.

The object of the following discussion is to study some of the most common families of digital integrated circuits. The approach taken will be to first discuss general properties and structures of integrated circuits. Then models for integrated diodes and transistors are presented. Finally, the models are used to analyze some of the basic properties of the common circuit families. Other components used in logic networks include electromechanical devices such as relays [McCluskey 65] and fluid logic elements [Wagner 69]. These will not be discussed here, but the interested reader is directed to the references.

Two properties are required of the elements used to construct logic networks. (1) They must be able to combine binary signals to obtain new binary signals. If inversion or complementation is not involved, this function can be achieved using only diodes and resistors; however, there are often technological advantages to using transistors rather than diodes. Inversion requires the use of an active element such as a transistor. (2) They must also be able to restore and maintain the signal levels, called quantization [Lo 67]. This requirement implies the ability to amplify, which in turn requires the use of active elements such as transistors.

4.1 INTRODUCTION

At present, the fastest commercially available ICs are built of gallium arsenide (GaAs). Such devices are used infrequently (only when ultrafast circuits are mandatory) since they are considerably more expensive than the standard silicon devices. Much of the material in this book applies to GaAs devices. However only silicon devices are discussed specifically since GaAs devices are still very rare. More details about GaAs devices are given in [Snyder 85].

There are two different types of (silicon) transistors used for digital logic: the bipolar transistor and the **MOS** (Metal Oxide Semiconductor) transistor. The logic portion of a digital system is typically constructed either of integrated circuits that contain only MOS transistors, (**MOS logic circuits**) or of **bipolar logic circuits**, containing only bipolar transistors. In the past, bipolar circuits were used in high-performance applications and MOS circuits for low-cost situations. It is still true that the highest-speed systems are based on bipolar circuits, but MOS circuits (in particular, CMOS circuits) are being used in the majority of new system designs (for high-performance as well as low-cost systems).

For each type of transistor there are a number of different basic gate circuits currently being manufactured. Each basic circuit along with the variations to implement different functions is called a **digital integrated-circuit family**. Examples of digital IC families are TTL (transistor-transistor logic), ECL (emitter-coupled logic), and CMOS (complementary MOS). The important feature of a logic family is that all of the circuits of one family have similar characteristics and can be freely interconnected without special interface circuitry. Most logic systems use only one family. Since the families have different characteristics, a choice of the family most suited to the application of the system must be made. The most important characteristics of integrated-circuit logic gates will be described next.

4.1-1 General Considerations

The circuits used to implement logic must have the ability to combine logic signals and to guarantee that the signals stay "quantized." As will be seen when the individual logic families are discussed, the techniques for combining signals do not vary greatly. The quantization requirement relates to ensuring that the signals remain within two nonoverlapping voltage (or current) ranges. This is necessary so that the logic value represented by a signal can be reliably determined. The circuit used to achieve quantization is the unique feature of a logic family. While it is not a fundamental requirement that quantization and inversion be implemented by the same circuit, it is true that all of the digital logic circuits currently used or contemplated combine these two functions in a single circuit. Thus, most of the discussion of IC logic characteristics will be carried out in terms of inverter elements.

The most important attributes of a logic circuit are its speed of operation, power consumption, and cost. The speed attribute is measured by the propagation delay time.

Propagation Delay Time. The propagation delay time is the key measure of the performance that can be obtained with a logic family. It measures the time required for an input change to be passed from a gate input to the corresponding gate output. The basic clock period is determined by adding up the propagation delays through the gates in the slowest chain of logic in the system. Thus the fundamental operating speed of a system is directly related to the gate propagation delay.

The propagation delay time is defined in terms of the input-output waveform of an inverter, such as is shown in Fig. 4.1-1. The formal definitions are:

DEFINITION. **Propagation delay time, low-to-high-level output, t_{PLH},** is the time between the specified reference points on the input and output voltage waveforms (usually 50% of the voltage change) with the output changing from the defined low level to the defined high level.

DEFINITION. **Propagation delay time, high-to-low-level output, t_{PHL},** is the time between the specified reference points on the input and output voltage waveforms (usually 50% of the voltage change) with the output changing from the defined high level to the defined low level.

DEFINITION. **Propagation delay time, t_{PD},** is the average delay time: $(t_{PLH} + t_{PHL})/2$.

Another important timing parameter is the gate transition time. This is a measure of the time required to change a signal from one value to the other value. Formal definitions are:

DEFINITION. The **transition time, low-to-high-level, t_{TLH},** is the time between a specified low-level voltage (usually 10% of the voltage signal range) and a specified high-level voltage (usually 90% of the voltage signal range) on a waveform that is changing from the defined low level to the defined high level.

DEFINITION. The **transition time, high-to-low-level, t_{THL},** is the time between a specified high-level voltage (usually 90% of the voltage signal range) and a specified low-level voltage (usually 10% of the voltage signal range) on a waveform that is changing from the defined high level to the defined low level.

Typical values of delay times are shown in Table 4.1-1.

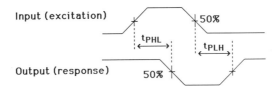

Figure 4.1-1 Input-output waveforms for a typical inverter.

TABLE 4.1-1 Typical delay times (ns)

Logic family	t_{PLH}	t_{PHL}	t_{PD}
ALS (advanced low-power Schottky)	4	5	4.5
AS (advanced Schottky)	2	2	2
MECL 10k	2	2	2
MECL 100k	0.75	0.75	0.75
CMOS (400B series)	105	105	105
CMOS 74 series	50	50	50
CMOS 74H series	10	10	10

Noise Margins. **Noise** is the generic term used to refer to the spurious voltages and currents that appear on the signal lines of an operating circuit. The noise signals can be introduced on a line by inductive, capacitive, or common impedance coupling. There are both external and internal causes for noise. These are listed in Table 4.1-2.

TABLE 4.1-2 Noise sources

External

Environmental noise: radiated into the system from circuit breaker arcing, motor brushes, relay contact arcing, etc.
Power-line noise: coupled through the ac or dc power distribution system

Internal

Crosstalk: induced into signal lines from adjacent signal lines
Transmission-line reflections: caused by ringing and overshoot on unterminated transmission lines
ICC current spikes: caused by switching of totem-pole output stages

When a logic signal has its value temporarily altered by a noise signal, the composite signal can be interpreted incorrectly by the rest of the system. This causes a **transient fault** to occur. Such a fault is extremely troublesome since it is very difficult to diagnose and correct. It is thus important to limit the noise effects so that transient faults don't occur. Two general approaches to limiting noise effects are used. One is to minimize noise generation. This involves the electrical and physical details of the system structure. Techniques for minimizing noise are discussed in [Morris 71], Chap. 5 and in [Allen 73]. The hazards discussed in Sec. 3.6 constitute another source of spurious signals. It can be very important to control the occurrence of hazards as well as to limit noise if transient faults are to be avoided. The other approach is to use basic circuits that are not sensitive to variations in signal values.

There are three basic noise immunity measures in use: (1) dc noise margin, (2) ac noise immunity, and (3) noise-energy immunity. The dc noise margin is the noise characteristic that is most often shown on the manufacturer's data sheets. It is the only measure that will be discussed here. The other measures provide additional accuracy. They are described in [Allen 73] and related to the dc margins.

The (dc) noise margin will be explained by means of the situation illustrated in Fig. 4.1-2. The existence of a noise margin depends on the fact that a correctly operating gate produces a smaller range of output voltages than it recognizes as correct input signals. A gate is designed to produce an output voltage greater than or equal to $V_{OH(min)}$, the minimum high-output voltage for worst-case output loading, when the correct output is a logical 1. Similarly, when the logical output is a 0, the gate is designed to produce no more than $V_{OL(max)}$, the maximum low-output voltage for worst-case output loading. When a gate-input voltage is at least $V_{IH(min)}$, the minimum high-input voltage to guarantee the appropriate output logic level, the gate output will correspond to a logic 1 signal present on that input. For a logic 0 input, the corresponding voltage must be no more than $V_{IL(max)}$, the maximum low-input voltage to guarantee the appropriate output logic level. Gates are designed so that the minimum high-level output voltage is greater than the minimum high-level input voltage. The difference is equal to the high-level signal-line noise margin, $V_{NSH(min)}$. Thus,

$$V_{NSH(min)} = V_{OH(min)} - V_{IH(min)}$$

The low-level signal noise margin, $V_{NSL(min)}$, is defined similarly:

$$V_{NSL(min)} = V_{IL(max)} - V_{OL(max)}$$

Some illustrative values of noise margin parameters are given in Table 4.1-3. As shown in this table, CMOS has a higher noise immunity than TTL.

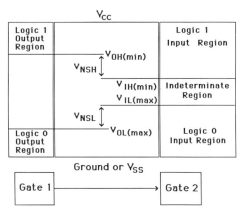

Figure 4.1-2 Dc noise margin.

TABLE 4.1-3 Illustrative noise margin parameters

	Logic family	
Parameter	54/74ALS TTL	B Series CMOS
$V_{OH(min)}$	2.5	4.95
$V_{IH(min)}$	2.0	3.5
$V_{OL(max)}$	0.4	0.05
$V_{IL(max)}$	0.8	1.0
$V_{NSH(min)}$	0.5	1.45
$V_{NSL(min)}$	0.4	0.95

Fanout. The term **fanout** is used in two somewhat different senses. Each gate in a logic network has its output connected to a network output or to one or more gate inputs. The number of gate inputs to which a gate output is connected is called the fanout of that particular gate. Thus, in Fig. 4.1-3 gates *B* and *C* have fanouts of 1, while gate *A* has a fanout of 2. The term *fanout* is also used to specify the maximum fanout allowed for gates of a particular logic family. In this sense the fanout is a measure of the drive capability of the gates of the logic family. The term **fanin** is sometimes used to describe the number of inputs of a gate.

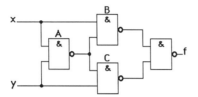

Figure 4.1-3 Network to illustrate fanout paths.

Wired Logic. Some logic families have gates with **wired logic** capability. When the outputs of such gates are connected together as in Fig. 4.1-4, the effect of an extra stage of logic is obtained without using an actual gate. For some gates tying together their outputs has the effect of producing the logical AND of the individual gate functions. This is the situation illustrated in Fig. 4.1-4a. Such an interconnection is called an **implied AND, dot AND,** or **wired AND.** The symbol for a wired AND is given in Fig. 4.1-4b. For other gates, connecting their outputs produces the effect of an OR function. This connection is called an **implied OR, dot OR,** or **wired OR.** The appropriate symbol is given in Fig. 4.1-4c. The IEEE standard symbols are shown in Fig. 4.1-4d and e. Not all gates can have their outputs tied directly together. Some will not produce a usable output or will cause the gates to be damaged electrically because of the connection. This will be discussed further in connection with the specific gate families. This discussion of gate families will also demonstrate the fact that some logic families permit easy realization of a rich variety of basic gates, such as gates with both the output and its complement available (NOR/OR gates).

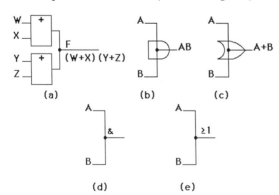

Figure 4.1-4 Wired logic connections: (a) wired-AND connection; (b) distinctive shape symbol for wired AND; (c) distinctive shape symbol for wired OR; (d) IEEE-preferred wired-AND symbol; (e) IEEE-preferred wired-OR symbol.

Buses. One application of wired logic is in connection with the routing of signals via a **bus.** Many situations arise in which it is necessary to select one of a number of locations and to transfer the information at that location to one of a number of possible destinations. Clearly, this could be done by providing a transfer path from each possible source location to each possible destination as in Fig. 4.1-5a. This technique, called **point-to-point**, is quite costly. A more usual approach is to provide a mechanism for transferring the chosen source information to a single path, called a **bus**, and another mechanism for transferring the information from the bus to the chosen destination (see Fig. 4.1-5b).

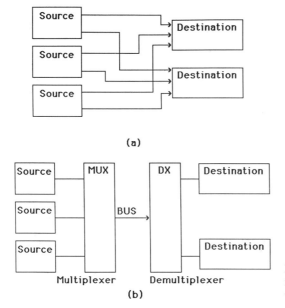

(a)

(b)

Multiplexer   Demultiplexer

Figure 4.1-5 Interconnection techniques: (a) point-to-point interconnections; (b) bus interconnection.

The circuit for selecting source information and placing it on the bus is called a **multiplexer**, and the term **demultiplexer** is used for the circuit that transfers information from the bus to the selected destination. The multiplexing operation can be accomplished using wired logic as shown in Fig. 4.1-6. When wired ORs are used, all enable signals are normally 0. To select a source the corresponding enable signal (E_i) is set equal to 1, causing the bus to equal S_i. With wired ANDs all inhibit signals are normally equal to 1. (With wired ORs the bus is normally equal to 0, while with wired ANDs the bus is normally at 1. This does not cause a problem since signals are only gated off the bus when some source is connected to it.) When one signal, I_i, is set equal to 0, the bus becomes equal to S_i.

Wired logic is useful, but it should not be used indiscriminately since it makes testing and servicing difficult; see [Writer 75] and Sec. 3.4 in [Turino 79]. Better techniques for bus connections are possible using tri-state logic or precharging techniques.

Tri-state Logic. A gate or buffer element with a tri-state output stage can have its output lead placed in a high-impedance state. Figure 4.1-7 shows the symbol used for a gate with a tri-state output and also the gate operation. When in the Hi-Z state, the output lead is, in effect, disconnected from the gate. Thus

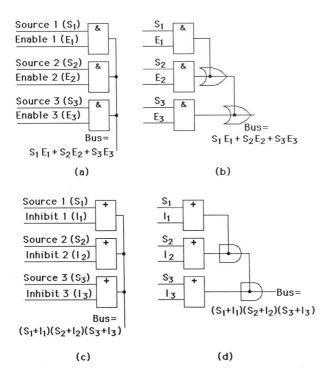

(a)   (b)

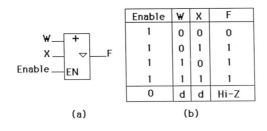

(c)   (d)

Figure 4.1-6 Multiplexing using wired logic: (a) physical connection using wired ORs; (b) logic equivalent of part (a); (c) physical connection using wired ANDs; (d) logic equivalent of part (c).

tri-state gates can be used to multiplex a number of signals. The gate outputs are connected together and the controls are arranged so that at most one gate is enabled at any given time. Figure 4.1-8 shows such an arrangement. The symbol "$\triangledown$" at the gate output indicates that it is a tri-state output. The symbol "EN" at the Enable input controls the tri-state nature of the output.

Another technique for driving a bus is used in MOS dynamic logic. The bus is always "precharged" to a high voltage during a fixed time period. Any of the

Enable	W	X	F
1	0	0	0
1	0	1	1
1	1	0	1
1	1	1	1
0	d	d	Hi-Z

(a)   (b)

Figure 4.1-7 Tri-state logic: (a) symbol for OR gate with tri-state output; (b) table of combinations for part (a).

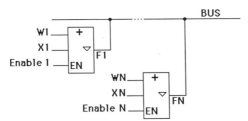

Figure 4.1-8 Tri-state logic used to connect to a bus.

possible sources can then discharge the bus during the succeeding time period. This technique will be discussed further in the section on MOS dynamic logic.

4.1-2 Types of Digital Integrated Circuits

The first transistorized digital circuits were constructed of discrete components; that is, each transistor, diode, and resistor was individually packaged and then interconnected with wires or by a printed circuit board. At the present time a circuit consisting of many interconnected devices is fabricated in a single chip of silicon and then packaged as a complete assembly. Strictly speaking, this is a **monolithic** integrated circuit since two or more silicon chips are sometimes interconnected in a single package. Multichip circuits in a single package are called **hybrid** integrated circuits and were used in the IBM 360 computers. It is possible to buy an integrated-circuit chip that is made up of four two-input NAND gates or a chip that contains an entire computer.

The advantages of packaging more complex circuits are that less interpackage wiring is required and fewer packages are necessary. A possible disadvantage is that some of the components might be unused (only three of the four two-input gates of a four-gate package might be required). Since the cost of intrapackage interconnections is much smaller than interpackage interconnections and the cost of the package is a major fraction of the entire integrated-circuit cost, it is economical to include many elements in a single package. Current practice is to produce an integrated circuit on a silicon chip which can be as small as 45×45 mils for very simple circuits to as large as 80×100 mils for more complex circuits. The chip is then encapsulated in a plastic or ceramic package, which typically has 14 or 16 leads but can have as many as several hundred leads.

The decision on which circuits to fabricate as single integrated circuits is influenced mainly by the generality of the function provided and by the limitation on the number of external connections that are possible due to the small number of pin leads available. The equivalent of more than 100,000 gates have been fabricated on a single chip. Several schemes for classifying chips are in use. One very important classification, called the level of integration, depends on the number of gates included on the chip. Table 4.1-4 shows this scheme.

TABLE 4.1-4 Classification based on level of integration

SSI	(small-scale integration) fewer than 10 gates/chip
	    available in ECL, CMOS, TTL
	    typical chips are up to four gates or two flip-flops

MSI	(medium-scale integration) 10 to 100 gates/chip
	    available in ECL, CMOS, TTL
	    typical chips are adders, multiplexers, and counters

LSI	(large-scale integration) 100 to 1000 gates/chip
	    most common in NMOS
	    typical chips are memories, microprocessors, and peripherals

VLSI	(very large scale integration) more than 1000 gates/chip
	    technologies used are NMOS, CMOS, STL, ISL, etc.
	    used for microcomputers, large computer parts, etc.

The collection of integrated circuits that are manufactured using one particular basic gate circuit is called an integrated-circuit **logic family**. The most common logic families are **TTL**, transistor-transistor logic; **ECL**, emitter-coupled logic; **NMOS**, *n*-channel MOS; and **CMOS**, complementary MOS. Typically, circuits from only one logic family are used in one design so that a logic family as well as the particular integrated circuits to be used must be chosen. The reason that several logic families are available is that no one basic gate circuit has been found to be superior for all applications. Each family has its strengths and weaknesses, as will be discussed subsequently. The families are manufactured in a variety of forms (subfamilies). Some of the subfamilies represent an evolution from early designs to improved designs. (Standard TTL has been replaced by Low Power Schottky TTL since the same speed is obtained with lower power consumption.) Other subfamilies are offered to permit matching the circuit characteristics to the application requirements. Table 4.1-5 lists the various logic families along with some of their major attributes.

TABLE 4.1-5 BIPOLAR logic families and attributes

Family	Speed-power (pJ)	t_{PD} (ns)	Power (mW)
Transistor-transistor logic (TTL)			
Low-power Schottky (LSTTL)	19	9.5	2
Lower power (LTTL)	33	33	1
Schottky (STTL)	57	3	19
Standard (TTL)	100	10	10
High speed (HTTL)	132	6	22
Advanced Schottky (ASTTL)	15	1.5	10
Advanced low-power Schottky (ALSTTL)	4	4	1
Emitter-coupled logic (ECL)			
10k	50	2	25
100k	32	0.8	40
CMOS logic			
74HC	15	10	1.5 at 1 mHz
400B	105	105	1 at 1 mHz

Catalog or Application Specific. A system designer has to choose between using standard ICs (catalog items) or using specially designed application specific (ASIC) ICs. The choice between the various options is based mainly on the projected number of units to be constructed.

Design using standard circuits is done by consulting manufacturers' catalogs to determine which integrated circuits—separately packaged circuits—are available, then choosing those appropriate for the system being designed, and finally by specifying the required interconnections among the microcircuits. Thus the design process often involves more complex building blocks than individual gates.

The next few chapters will present the general design topics applicable to both catalog and application specific parts. Chapter 11 discusses the use of complex building blocks.

A classification based on the technique used for completing the chip design is given in Table 4.1-6. The catalog items and the full custom chips have their design completed before any processing takes place. They are typically used when large production runs are anticipated. Every effort is made to optimize their design. The programmable logic devices are arrays that have the final interconnections determined for a particular application. The basic cell design is fully optimized since many chips with this design are produced. The chip is "personalized" for a particular application either by the final level of metalization or by electrically "programming" the chips to be used in a specific system.

TABLE 4.1-6   Classification based on chip design

Catalog items: SSI, MSI, LSI (general purpose)

Programmable items: ROM, PROM, EPROM, PLA, PAL, HAL

Semicustom: gate array or master slice, prediffused-custom logic transistor array, macrocell array, uncommitted logic array (ULA)

Full custom: logic specific to one system

The semicustom items have a standard, optimized array of transistors, gates, or macrocells that are common to all versions of the chip. Each chip produced has the final interconnections designed specifically for a particular application. The manufacturer stocks a supply of prediffused wafers that have the final processing carried out to produce a specific design. The advantages of semicustom products are:

1. Basic array design cost is amortized over many uses.
2. Device electrical and manufacturing parameters are set and controlled by the silicon manufacturer.
3. Conversion from system logic to placed and routed chip logic is a specifiable process which can be performed very well by CAD (Computer-Aided Design).
4. Design cost to the user for a specific custom array is minimized.
5. Elapsed times from design release to part availability are reasonable and short (1 to 2 weeks).
6. Arrays are available and they work.

The disadvantages to this approach are:

1. Not the smallest possible die for the function.
2. Not the highest possible performance or lowest power.
3. Available array cell types and I/O circuits are not ideal for the application.

The advantages of full custom designs are:

1. Smallest die giving highest yields (lowest processing cost)
2. Best performance—tailored logic devices and shortest interconnect—and lowest power.

The disadvantages of full custom designs are:

1. Much more time-consuming and demanding design requirements.
2. All development cost goes against the one design.
3. Design errors are more likely—more costly in time and dollars to correct.
4. Longer and possibly more complex fabrication processing.

For more details, see [Bond 84].

4.2 GATE STRUCTURES

The study of gate structures will begin with a survey of the different forms of output stages in use. The primary function of the output stage is to connect a quantized signal to the output lead.

4.2-1 Pullup and Pulldown Both Active

A very straightforward output structure is shown in Fig. 4.2-1a. In this structure, a switch is connected between the output lead and a source of high voltage; and a similar device is connected between the output and a low-voltage source. By properly controlling when each of these switches is closed, it is possible to ensure that a correct output signal is generated. (v and vbar must have opposite voltages present.) This is the standard structure used in **TTL**. (In TTL it is called a totem-pole output structure. TTL is described in Sec. 4.4-5.) It is used in NMOS when extra drive capacity is required. The NMOS circuit is called a pushpull or a super buffer and is used for driving large capacitive loads. (NMOS is discussed in Secs. 4.3-3 and 4.3-4.)

One feature of this circuit that can be a drawback is the requirement to have both the input signal voltage and the complementary voltage available. This can be avoided if two types of switch are used, as in Fig. 4.2-1b. This is the standard CMOS structure, to be described in Sec. 4.3-2.

In CMOS two kinds of switch are obtained by using two types of transistor, a P-channel device and an N-channel device, in the same circuit. The necessity of including both device types on a single chip makes the manufacture of the chip more complex and expensive than designs (such as NMOS or PMOS) that use only one transistor type. The CMOS design has the advantages of providing a simple inverter gate since the output stage itself has an inherent inversion, and high noise immunity because of the stability of the output signal values. Also, the CMOS

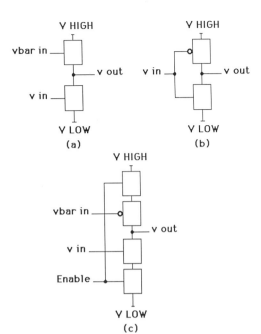

Figure 4.2-1 Inverter output stages with two active devices: (a) active pullup and pulldown with complementary inputs; (b) active pullup and pulldown with two switch types; (c) tri-state configuration.

structure has very low power dissipation since there is no resistive path between the voltage supplies.

Wired logic is not practical with both pullup and pulldown active. With two outputs connected directly together, there can be a conducting path between the two voltage sources through an active pullup device from one gate and an active pulldown device from another gate. This will happen whenever one gate has a 0-output and the other gate has a 1-output. The resulting voltage on the common node will be an intermediate value that will most likely lie in the indeterminate region (Fig. 4.1-2) of the driven gate input. Thus a predictable logic value does not result from the wired connection.

In spite of the lack of wired logic, bus-oriented designs are easy with this type of output stage through the use of tri-state logic. The high-impedance state is obtained by disconnecting both the pullup and the pulldown gates from the power supply. Figure 4.2-1c shows one structure for implementing a tri-state design in NMOS. When the Enable signal is high, the topmost and lowest switches both conduct and the circuit functions as in part (a). When Enable is low, both the topmost and lowest switches are nonconducting: the output is in the high-impedance state, disconnected from the supply voltages.

4.2-2 Passive Pullup or Pulldown

It is possible to replace one of the switches by a resistor as in Fig. 4.2-2. When the active device is conducting, its resistance is much smaller than the load resistor and the output voltage will be very close to the supply voltage connected to the transmission gate. When the active device is off, the output is connected to the

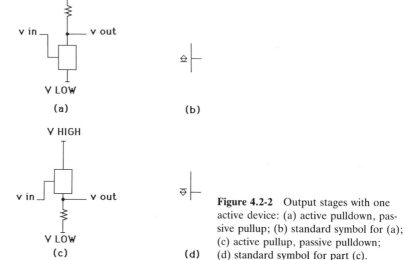

Figure 4.2-2 Output stages with one active device: (a) active pulldown, passive pullup; (b) standard symbol for (a); (c) active pullup, passive pulldown; (d) standard symbol for part (c).

voltage source through the resistor. This output stage design is very common—use of one active device rather than two can result in a cheaper circuit. Also, wired logic is possible. The active pulldown structure is the more common. It is used in TTL (called **open-collector**). When two or more active pulldown structures are connected together, a **wired-AND** results. All of the gate outputs must be in the 1-state for the common output to be a 1. The active pullup structure is used in ECL. A **wired-OR** is realized by connecting such output structures together.

4.2-3 Binary Logic Functions

The output structures just described provide the inversion function. In addition, at least one binary connective—AND, OR, NAND, or NOR—is necessary to realize arbitrary combinational circuits. Two general techniques are used for the binary connectives: switch networks or "diode logic." The discussion of the diode logic approach will be deferred until after the section on diodes. As described in Section 3.5, a series connection of switches yields the AND function and a parallel connection produces the OR function. N-input gates can be obtained by replacing the switches of Figs. 4.2-1 and 4.2-2 by series or parallel connections of switches. Figure 4.2-3 shows the structures that result from carrying out these replacements on the structure of Fig. 4.2-2a. These are the gate structures used in NMOS.

Figure 4.2-4 shows the structure of a two-input NOR gate derived from the structure of Fig. 4.2-1b. When either X or Y are 1, the corresponding lower switch will be on, and the output will be 0 as required. The upper two gates connected in series ensure that when both inputs are 0, the output will be 1. These two gates realize the desired function, $X'Y'$, and control the conditions when the output is 1. The lower two gates realize the complement of the desired function, $X + Y$, and control when the output is 0. If the upper gates are connected in parallel and

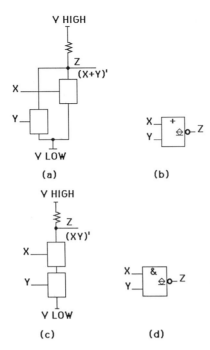

(a)

(b)

(c)

(d)

Figure 4.2-3 Passive pullup gates:
(a) NOR gate; (b) standard symbol for
part (a); (c) NAND gate; (d) standard
symbol for part (c).

the lower gates in series, a NAND gate results. The extensions to gates with more than two inputs are direct. These are the gate structures that are standard in CMOS.

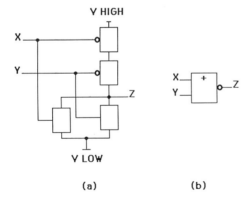

(a)

(b)

Figure 4.2-4 NOR gate with active pull-up and pulldown: (a) switch diagram; (b) standard symbol.

4.3 MOS LOGIC

4.3-1 MOS Transistors

The metal-oxide semiconductor or MOS transistor (this device is actually a form of **field-effect transistor** and is sometimes called an **insulated-gate field-effect transistor** or **IGFET**) is a three-terminal semiconductor device which is the basis for a large variety of digital integrated circuits. At the present time all digital integrated circuits make use of either junction or MOS transistors and there are no indications that this will change in the near future. There is research on other technologies, but their practical application is still in question. In recent years MOS circuits have accounted for an ever-increasing fraction of the total production of ICs. MOS circuits have been most successful in the LSI and VLSI areas, particularly for memories and microcomputers. The MOS transistor differs from the junction transistor in the following ways:

1. The current flow through an MOS transistor is controlled by an electric field rather than by a (base) current as in the junction transistor.

2. Because of (1) the MOS transistor has a very high input resistance (10^{10} to 10^{15} ohms) and thus draws negligible input current.

3. The junction transistor depends on current flow across both forward- and reverse-biased junctions (both majority and minority carrier current) and is thus called a bipolar transistor. The MOS transistor relies on only one type of current flow (only majority carrier current) and is thus a unipolar transistor.

4. The MOS transistor is simpler to fabricate as an integrated circuit and requires very little space, about 5 square mils. A junction transistor takes about 100 square mils.

5. The MOS transistor has a lower gain (transconductance) than the junction transistor. This limits the speed at which the MOS transistor can charge stray capacitance. MOS circuits are inherently slower than bipolar circuits ([Crawford 67], Sec. 1-4); bipolar circuits can operate at frequencies well beyond the 100-megahertz range, while MOS has an upper frequency limit around 15 to 25 MHz [Galloway 71].

A drawing of an MOS transistor is shown in Fig. 4.3-1a and circuit symbols are given in Fig. 4.3-1b. The MOS transistor is a four-terminal device, but it is often used as a three-terminal device with the substrate connected internally to the source. The MOS transistor is an almost ideal voltage-controlled switch. When the gate is connected to the source or is negative with respect to the source ($V_{GS} \leq 0$) as in Fig. 4.3-2a, the drain and source are in effect open circuited (only a few nanoamperes flow in this path) since the resistance of this path is of the order of 10^{10} ohms. When the gate-to-source voltage, V_{GS}, is raised to a critical level—the **threshold voltage** V_t—the transistor turns "on" and current can flow between source and drain. The "on resistance" of the drain-source path is of the order of 10 to 10,000 ohms. The MOS transistor acts like a variable resistor modulated by the gate voltage. For the type of transistor shown in Fig. 4.3-1 the value of the threshold voltage, V_t, is typically 1 to 2 volts.

There are two types of MOS devices: the **n-channel** or **NMOS transistor** and the **p-channel** or **PMOS transistor**. The n-channel transistor was shown in Fig. 4.3-1. A p-channel transistor is shown in Fig. 4.3-3. The PMOS transistor is the complement of the NMOS transistor. Its operation is the same as was described for the n-channel device with the polarity of the voltage V_{GS} reversed. Thus in the p-channel device the source-drain connection acts like an open circuit for $V_{GS} \geq 0$ and conducts when V_{GS} is more negative than the threshold voltage ($V_{GS} < V_t$).

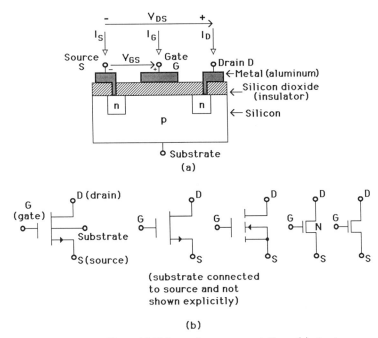

Figure 4.3-1 *n*-Channel MOS transistor representations: (a) structure;
(b) symbols.

The *p*-channel threshold voltage V_t typically varies from -1.5 to -5 volts. The basic PMOS structure shown in Fig. 4.3-3a leads to a typical threshold voltage of -4 volts. MOS logic circuits using this device are called **high-threshold** MOS

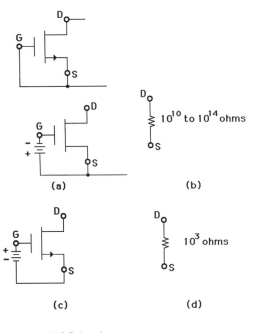

Figure 4.3-2 Operation of an NMOS transistor: (a) negative or zero gate voltage; (b) equivalent circuit for part (a); (c) gate voltage more positive than threshold; (d) equivalent circuit for part (c).

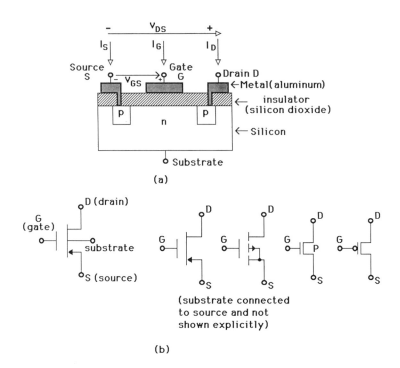

Figure 4.3-3 *p*-Channel MOS transistor representations: (a) structure; (b) symbols.

circuits. They have good noise immunity but have the serious disadvantage of not being compatible with TTL, which has signal levels of 0.2 and 3.5 volts. Several techniques are used to produce PMOS devices with lower values of V_t. They are:

1. Using a different type of silicon, $\langle 100 \rangle$silicon, for the basic device material.
2. Using (heavily doped) silicon instead of aluminum for the gate element. Such devices are called **silicon-gate MOS devices**.
3. Using silicon nitride instead of silicon dioxide for the insulator. Such devices are called **NMOS devices**.

All three of these techniques are in use and lead to values of V_t in the range -1.5 to -2.5 volts. The NMOS transistor inherently has a low V_t. NMOS devices also are basically faster and more compact (require less area) than PMOS devices. MOS logic circuits use NMOS devices almost exclusively. PMOS devices are used only for applications where cost dominates other considerations. Also, PMOS devices are used in combination with NMOS devices in CMOS logic.

When it is desired to indicate the presence of an MOS device without specifying whether it is a *p*-channel or an *n*-channel device, the symbol of Fig. 4.3-4 is used. The MOS devices which have been just described all have the property that no current flows between source and drain when there is no gate voltage applied. Devices with this property are called **enhancement** devices and are those most common in logic circuits. It is also possible to fabricate MOS devices in which

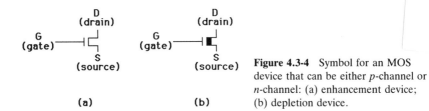

the source-drain connection is normally conducting and which require the application of a gate voltage to prevent conduction. Such devices are called **depletion** devices. They are used in place of the load resistor in passive pullup MOS circuits.

4.3-2 Complementary MOS Logic (CMOS)

A logic family that does not require dc power and which performs static logic with a single dc power source is **complementary MOS logic (CMOS)**. This logic family uses for its basic building block a pair of transistors in series, one *p*-channel and the other *n*-channel. The CMOS inverter circuit is shown in Fig. 4.3-5. When the input voltage v_x is 0 volts, the gate-to-source voltage (V_{GS}) for the *p*-channel device is $-V_{DD}$ and this device is on. V_{GS} for the lower transistor, the *n*-channel device, is 0 volts, so this device is off. Thus the output voltage v_z is $+V_{DD}$. When v_x is $+V_{DD}$, the upper transistor has a V_{GS} of 0 volts and is off. The lower transistor has a V_{GS} of $+V_{DD}$ volts and since it is an *n*-channel device it is on, making v_z equal to 0 volts.

This inverter circuit has active devices for both pullup and pulldown. It is an implementation of the structure of Fig. 4.2-1b. The MOS transistors are used as switches with the *p*-channel device functioning as the device with an inverted input.

One of the two series transistors is off in either stable state, so dc power is not consumed (except for a small power consumption due to the leakage current through the off device). Power is consumed when switching from one state to the other since both devices are partially on during this time.

CMOS NOR and NAND gates are shown in Figs. 4.3-6 and 4.3-7. Each input is connected to one *p*-channel device and one *n*-channel device. In the NOR circuit the *n*-channel devices are connected in parallel and the *p*-channel devices are connected in series. If either input voltage is at V_{DD}, the corresponding *n*-channel device is on, connecting the output to ground; and the corresponding *p*-channel device is off, disconnecting V_{DD} from the output. When both input

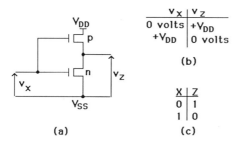

v_x	v_z
0 volts	$+V_{DD}$
$+V_{DD}$	0 volts

(b)

X	Z
0	1
1	0

(c)

Figure 4.3-5 Basic CMOS inverter: (a) circuit diagram; (b) voltages; (c) truth table.

(a)

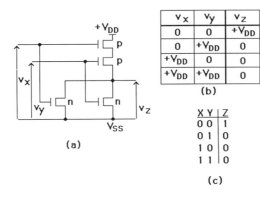

v_x	v_y	v_z
0	0	$+V_{DD}$
0	$+V_{DD}$	0
$+V_{DD}$	0	0
$+V_{DD}$	$+V_{DD}$	0

(b)

```
X Y | Z
0 0 | 1
0 1 | 0
1 0 | 0
1 1 | 0
```

(c)

Figure 4.3-6 Two-input CMOS NOR gate: (a) circuit; (b) voltages; (c) truth table.

voltages are at 0, both n-channel transistors are off and both p-channel devices are on, connecting the output to V_{DD}. The NOR gate circuit corresponds directly to the structure of Fig. 4.2-4.

Transmission Gates. While it would be possible to use a single PMOS or NMOS transistor as a switch to interconnect CMOS gates, this is typically not done. Instead, the more complex CMOS transmission gate (also called **transfer gate**) shown in Fig. 4.3-8 is used. This gate results in much better performance than a single transistor gate. Specifically, higher-speed operation and better drive capability are obtained with the CMOS transmission gate. A thorough discussion of the performance issues involved can be found in Sec. 8.6 of [Holt 78] and in [RCA 72].

The circuit for the CMOS transmission gate is shown in Fig. 4.3-8a and the equivalent switch circuit in Fig. 4.3-8b. Part (c) shows the IEEE standard symbol, which uses "X" to denote transmission dependency. Various other symbols in common use are given in part (d). A 0 value at E causes a very large resistance (10^9 ohms) between input and output. When the enable input E is at 1 there is a very low resistance between the input and output terminals. This conductive path is bilateral—signals pass in either direction. This property is not used in digital logic circuits and can cause problems. In general, the transmission gate must be used with great care. Its main application is in forming feedback loops in latches and flip-flops. A disadvantage of the CMOS transmission gate is the

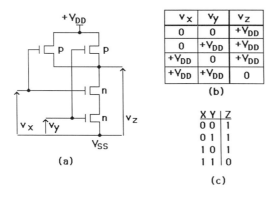

v_x	v_y	v_z
0	0	$+V_{DD}$
0	$+V_{DD}$	$+V_{DD}$
$+V_{DD}$	0	$+V_{DD}$
$+V_{DD}$	$+V_{DD}$	0

(b)

```
X Y | Z
0 0 | 1
0 1 | 1
1 0 | 1
1 1 | 0
```

(c)

Figure 4.3-7 Two-input CMOS NAND gate: (a) circuit; (b) voltages; (c) truth table.

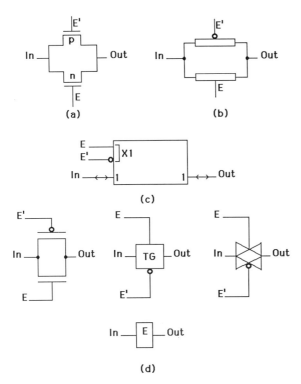

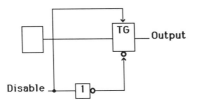

Figure 4.3-8 CMOS transmission gate: (a) gate circuit; (b) switch circuit; (c) IEEE standard symbol; (d) various commonly used symbols.

requirement for a two-rail enable signal. Because of this it is often necessary to use an inverter circuit to derive the enable signal if it is not already available in both complemented and uncomplemented forms.

Tri-state Outputs. Another important application of transmission gates is in tri-state (three-state) logic. By placing a transmission gate in series with an output lead it is possible to ensure that the output is held in a high-impedance state. This is shown in Fig. 4.3-9. When the disable input is 1, the transmission gate is in its high-impedance state and the output lead is, in effect, disconnected from the driving circuit.

Other CMOS tri-state circuits are shown in Fig. 4.3-10. In the circuit of part (a), when the disable input is high, there is a high signal at the gate of the PMOS device, which is thus off. The gate of the NMOS device has a low signal, so it is also off. Thus with disable = 1, the output is disconnected from both supply voltages. When disable = 0, the circuit functions as a normal inverter.

Figure 4.3-9 CMOS transmission gate used to provide a tri-state output.

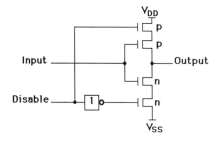

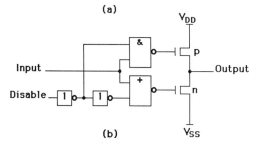

Figure 4.3-10 CMOS Tri-state outputs not using transmission gates: (a) inverter circuit with series devices to provide tri-state [Motorola 75]; (b) circuit using NAND and NOR gates to provide tri-state output [National 81].

In the circuit of Fig. 4.3-10b when the disable input is high, the NAND gate output is 1, forcing the PMOS device off. With disable high, the NOR output is 0 and the NMOS device is also off. Thus, the output is disconnected from both supplies with disable = 1. When the disable input is low, it has no effect on the circuit and the output is equal to the input.

4.3-3 NMOS Static Logic

The simplest form of NMOS logic circuit is the static inverter shown in Fig. 4.3-11. This circuit is a realization of the active pulldown, passive pullup structure of Fig. 4.2-2. When the input voltage, v_x, is at ground, the transistor will not conduct, so the output voltage, v_z, will be at V_{DD} volts. Since only n-channel devices are used in NMOS, when v_x is higher than the threshold voltage, V_t, the transistor will conduct and v_z will be 0 volts. It clearly acts as an inverter if $V_{DD} > V_t$. In actual NMOS circuits the load resistor R_L is replaced by an NMOS depletion-mode transistor. Since this device has its gate connected to its source, it is always turned on. Such a circuit is shown in Fig. 4.3-11b. The reason for using a load transistor rather than a resistor is that substantially less area is required for the transistor

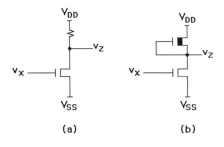

Figure 4.3-11 Static NMOS inverter (all transistors are n-channel): (a) load resistor; (b) depletion transistor load device.

than for the resistor [Mead 80]. Even though the load device is a transistor, it acts as a passive rather than an active pullup since it does not have its state controlled by the input signal (it is always turned on).

Logic gates based on this inverter circuit are easily formed by connecting additional transistors in series or parallel with the input transistor. The techniques described in connection with Fig. 4.2-3 are directly applicable. Figure 4.3-12 shows a circuit with two parallel transistors replacing the input transistor. When either input voltage, v_x or v_y is high, the corresponding transistor will conduct and bring the output, v_z, low (V_{SS}). Thus, the NOR function is realized. The corresponding

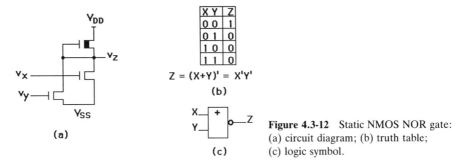

$$Z = (X+Y)' = X'Y'$$

(b)

(a)

(c)

Figure 4.3-12 Static NMOS NOR gate: (a) circuit diagram; (b) truth table; (c) logic symbol.

circuit with series-connected input transistors is a NAND gate. It is shown in Fig. 4.3-13. Since the on-resistances of the series devices must add, these devices must be fabricated to have lower on-resistances than those of parallel-connected input devices. This requires the series-connected devices to be larger than parallel-connected devices. Clearly, gates with parallel-connected input devices are to be preferred over those with series-connected inputs. Gates with both series- and parallel-connected devices are also possible.

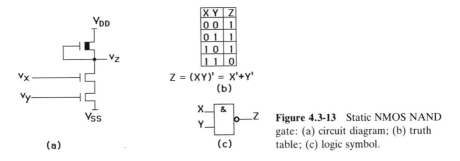

$$Z = (XY)' = X'+Y'$$

(b)

(a)

(c)

Figure 4.3-13 Static NMOS NAND gate: (a) circuit diagram; (b) truth table; (c) logic symbol.

4.3-4 NMOS Dynamic Logic

One very important characteristic of a logic gate is its power consumption. Two approaches are used to develop MOS logic families having low power consumption. One of these approaches makes use of both p-channel and n-channel devices. It is called complementary MOS logic or CMOS logic and was described in Sec. 4.3-2. The other approach reduces the power by periodically connecting and disconnecting the power supply by means of clocked load devices. Power is not used continuously but only when needed. It is possible to do this because MOS devices have parasitic capacitance associated with their terminals. This capacitance is used to store voltages temporarily while the power is switched off.

Since logic is performed and signals propagated only when the power supplies are on, the flow of information through a pulsed power network is synchronized with the clock pulses. A logic network in which the flow of information is not continuous but is synchronized with an external signal is called a **dynamic logic** network. Logic that is not synchronized with an external signal is called **static logic**. *It is possible to mix both static and dynamic logic within the same network.* As will be explained below, there are four possible benefits to be derived from using dynamic logic. These are (1) reduced power consumption, (2) smaller area, (3) faster operation, and (4) very economical dynamic registers. Static logic has the advantage of simplicity and the ability to operate over wide ranges of clock frequency.

Dynamic Ratioed Logic. The simplest form of MOS dynamic logic is two-phase ratioed logic. It is illustrated in Fig. 4.3-14a, which shows two inverters connected in series. These dynamic inverter circuits differ from the static inverter circuits in two ways:

1. The load transistors (Q_2 and Q_5) are enhancement rather than depletion transistors. The gates of the load transistors (Q_2 and Q_5) are connected to $CK1$ and $CK2$, respectively, rather than directly to their sources. These load transistors will conduct only when the corresponding clock signal is at V_{DD}. The waveforms for the clock signals are shown in Fig. 4.3-14b. These are a pair of two-phase nonoverlapping clocks. They are never both equal to V_{DD}.

2. The output of each inverter is not connected to the next inverter directly but is connected through a switch called a pass transistor (Q_3 or Q_6). These coupling transistors have their gate inputs connected to $CK1$ and $CK2$ and thus conduct only when these signals are at V_{DD}. The action of this circuit is as follows:

   (a) When $CK1$ and $CK2$ are both 0, no current flows and no action takes place in the circuit.

   (b) When $CK1$ becomes equal to 1, Q_2 will conduct. Current will flow in Q_1 if $v_{in} > V_t$ ($v_{in} = V_{DD}$) and will not flow if $v_{in} < V_t$ ($v_{in} = V_{SS}$). If current flows in Q_1 ($v_{in} = V_{DD}$), point A will be at a voltage close to V_{SS}. Since the pass transistor Q_3 is conducting, the gate of transistor Q_4 will also be at a voltage close to V_{SS}. If $v_{in} = V_{SS}$ so that current does not flow in Q_1, point A will be at V_{DD}, which will cause Q_4's gate to be at V_{DD}. The capacitance associated with this gate will be charged to V_{DD} and will remain at this voltage after $CK1$ returns to 0.

   (c) When $CK2$ becomes equal to V_{DD}, similar actions will take place in the portion of the circuit involving transistors Q_4, Q_5, and Q_6. The condition

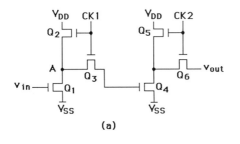

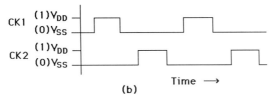

Figure 4.3-14 Series connection of two-phase ratioed inverters: (a) circuit diagram; (b) clock waveforms.

of transistor Q_4 will depend on the voltage placed on its gate during the time when $CK1$ was equal to V_{DD}.

The principal advantage of this circuit is its reduced power consumption. If the inverter made up of Q_1 and Q_2 is considered, it is seen that power is consumed only when $CK1$ is at V_{DD} and v_{in} causes Q_1 to conduct. In the corresponding static inverter circuit power is consumed whenever v_{in} causes Q_1 to conduct. The waveforms of Fig. 4.3-14b show that $CK1$ is equal to V_{DD} for less than half the time, resulting in a substantial saving in power.

In Fig. 4.3-14 inverters were shown for the sake of simplicity. More complex functions can be realized by connecting additional transistors in series or parallel with Q_1 or Q_2 just as in the static case. Several stages of gates can be included in a cell clocked by the same clock phase so that propagation of signals within the cell is static rather than dynamic. This allows more logic to be carried out during one of the clock phases, but increases the logic propagation delay that limits the clock frequency. A coupling device (pass transistor) must be placed between cells that are clocked with different phases. Figure 4.3-15 illustrates the use of complex cells in ratioed dynamic logic.

One of the disadvantages of the circuit of Fig. 4.3-14 is that its successful operation depends on the inverter transistor Q_1 and Q_2 (also Q_4 and Q_5) having the proper ratio of on-resistance ($R_{Q_2} >> R_{Q_1}$). This **aspect ratio** is necessary to ensure that the voltage at point A is below V_t when both Q_1 and Q_2 are conducting. (This requirement also holds for the static inverter.) For this reason the circuit is called a **ratioed circuit**. By redesigning the circuit so that this constraint on the ratio of transistor resistances is not present, it is possible to obtain circuits which permit the use of smaller transistors. Such circuits are called **ratioless circuits**.

Dynamic Ratioless Logic. The basic principle of dynamic ratioless logic is illustrated in Fig. 4.3-16. Two phases are used in order to establish the correct

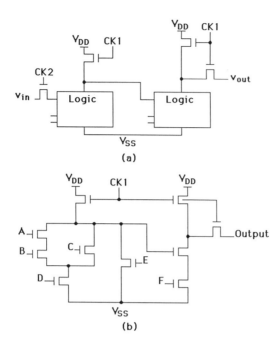

(a)

(b)

Figure 4.3-15 Use of complex cells in ratioed dynamic logic—one cell with two stages of logic: (a) general form; (b) specific example cell circuit.

signal at a logic node (represented by line A in Fig. 4.3-16). During phase 1, the node is **precharged** (perhaps conditionally) to the high voltage. The final correct value on the node is established during phase 2 when the node is discharged if the correct value is 0. For the circuit of Fig. 4.3-16, node A will always be precharged during phase 1 and will be discharged during phase 2 only if $x = 1$. Thus, the final value on node A will represent X' since this node will be high only if $x = 0$.

The most valuable characteristic of this scheme is that there is no requirement on the ratio of the on-resistances of the two transistors. They are never both conducting at the same time and therefore no voltage-divider action takes place. The area required can be less than with ratioed circuits since minimum-geometry devices can be used. Alternatively, high-speed operation can be obtained by using larger devices with low resistance to permit fast discharge of the node capacitances.

Correct operation depends on the ability of the node capacitance to retain a voltage (by stored charge) until the signals controlled by the voltage have been evaluated. It is usually not necessary to introduce explicit capacitance to satisfy this requirement. The clock cycle is chosen to be compatible with the inherent total nodal capacitance. This includes intrinsic device capacitance as well as the capacitance associated with the interconnections.

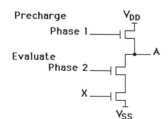

Figure 4.3-16 Basic ratioless dynamic logic technique.

4.4 BIPOLAR LOGIC

4.4-1 Ideal Diodes

An ideal diode is an abstract device that embodies the most important property of a physical diode: **rectification** or the ability to pass current in one direction only. (Since rectification is the significant characteristic of a diode some physical realizations are actually called rectifiers.) Figure 4.4-1 shows the schematic symbol for an ideal diode and the voltage-current characteristic is shown in Fig. 4.4-2. When a voltage is applied which tends to produce current in the positive direction of current flow, the diode is said to be **forward biased** and acts as a short circuit. This is illustrated in Fig. 4.4-3a. A voltage applied tending to produce current in the reverse direction is said to **reverse bias** the diode. A **reverse-biased** diode does not permit any current flow and thus acts like an open circuit, as in Fig. 4.4-3b.

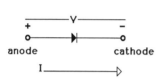

Figure 4.4-1 Schematic symbol for an ideal diode.

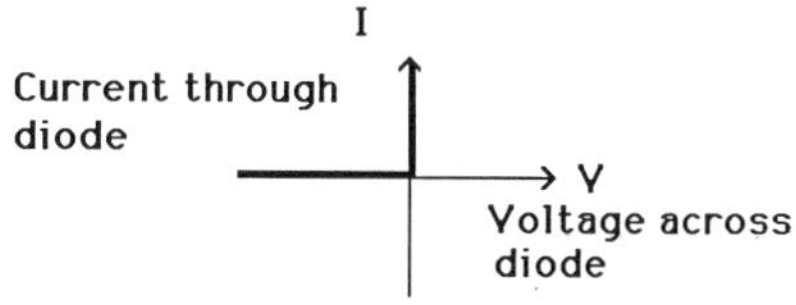

Figure 4.4-2 Voltage–current characteristics of an ideal diode.

Diode Gates. Before the use of integrated circuits, gates were commonly constructed of discrete diodes (the earliest diodes used were actually vacuum tubes, then crystal diodes, and finally semiconductor diodes) and resistors. Diode gates have now been displaced by integrated-circuit gates, which are not merely integrated versions of diode gates but use different circuit configurations. However, it is still instructive to examine the operation of diode gates as an introduction to the more complex integrated-circuit gates.

Figure 4.4-4a shows the circuit diagram for a two-input diode AND gate. The relation between the output voltage e_z and the input voltages e_x and e_y is summarized in Table 4.4-1a. If the voltages e_x, e_y, and e_z are represented by the

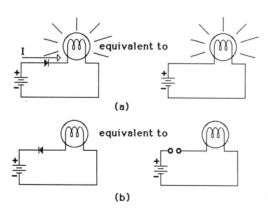

Figure 4.4-3 Forward- and reverse-biased diodes: (a) forward-biased diode—conducts current and lights bulb; (b) reverse-biased diode—no current flows and bulb remains unlit.

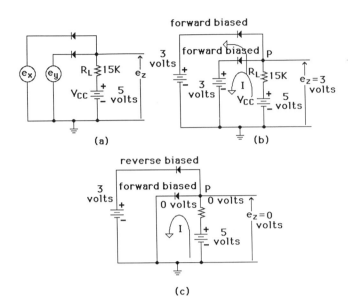

Figure 4.4-4 Diode AND gate (Ideal diodes assumed): (a) a two-input diode AND gate; (b) circuit conditions with $e_x = e_y = 3$; (c) circuit conditions with $e_x = 3$ volts and $e_y = 0$ volts.

logic variables X, Y, and Z, then the circuit can be described by the truth table of Table 4.4-1b.

TABLE 4.4-1 Input-output relationships for two-input AND gate of Fig. 4.4-4: (a) Voltages; (b) Table of combinations

(a)				(b)
e_x	e_y	e_z		1 corresponds to 3 V
				0 corresponds to 0 V
0	0	0		X to e_x, Y to e_y, Z to e_z
0	3	0		
3	0	0		
3	3	3		

XY	Z
00	0
01	0
10	0
11	1

The operation of this circuit can be understood by referring to Figs. 4.4-4b and c. The condition of the circuit with e_x and e_y both equal to 3 volts is shown in Fig. 4.4-4b. The voltage shown for point P is 3 volts. To see that this must be the voltage of P, assume first that it is larger than 3 volts, say 4 volts. In this case the diodes would still be forward biased but each would have a voltage drop of 1 volt across it. However, this is not possible since a forward-biased diode acts like a short circuit and cannot have any voltage drop across it (Fig. 4.4-2). On the other hand, if the voltage of P were less than 3 volts, each of the diodes would be reverse-biased and thus open circuits. In this case no current could flow, so that there could be no voltage drop across R_L and the voltage of P could not differ from V_{CC}. (It is assumed that there is no load connected to the circuit. If the circuit is used to drive another circuit, the input characteristics of the driven circuit must be such as not to alter the basic operation of the driving circuit.)

The situation in the circuit with e_x equal to 3 volts and e_y equal to 0 volts is shown in Fig. 4.4-4c. The analysis of this and of the remaining case with both inputs at 0 volts parallels that just given for Fig. 4.4-4b.

This gate is called an AND gate because the output is 1 (high) only if inputs X and Y are both 1 (high). The symbol for an AND gate is shown in Fig. 4.4-5. An AND gate with more than two inputs is easily constructed by connecting additional diodes to point P as shown in Fig. 4.4-6.

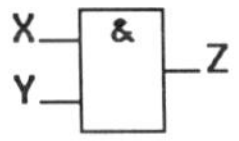

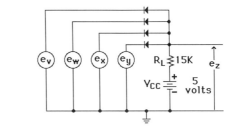

Figure 4.4-5 AND gate symbol.

Figure 4.4-6 Four-input diode AND gate.

TABLE 4.4-2 Input-output relationships for two-input OR gate of Fig. 4.4-7: (a) Voltages; (b) Truth table

(a)				(b)		
e_x	e_y	e_z		X	Y	Z
0	0	0		0	0	0
0	3	3		0	1	1
3	0	3		1	0	1
3	3	3		1	1	1

The other type of diode gate is an OR gate for which the output is 1 (high) if input X **or** input Y (or both) is 1 (high). The circuit for such a gate is shown in Fig. 4.4-7, and the tables describing its operation are given in Table 4.4-2.

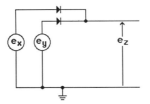

Figure 4.4-7 Two-input diode OR gate.

The symbol for the OR gate is shown in Fig. 4.4-8. This gate is sometimes called an **INCLUSIVE-OR gate** (IOR gate) to distinguish it from the **EXCLUSIVE-OR gate** (XOR gate), which has an output of 1 only when one but not both of the inputs are equal to 1.

This discussion of diode gates has neglected both the effects due to the fact that physical diodes differ from ideal diodes and the effects that occur when gates are interconnected. Although interconnected diode gates have been thoroughly analyzed in the past [Richards 57], the questions involved are not particularly relevant for integrated circuits and thus will not be discussed here. The effects due to the nonideal characteristics of semiconductor diodes are relevant and will be studied next.

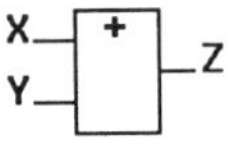

Figure 4.4-8 OR gate symbol.

4.4-2 Semiconductor Diodes

A semiconductor diode is made by joining together two different types of semiconductor material. One type of material is called *p*-type and contains an excess of positive current carriers (holes), while the other is called *n*-type and contains an excess of negative current carriers (electrons). When two dissimilar semiconductors are joined, a **semiconductor junction** is formed. Semiconductor junctions have rectifying properties and are thus suitable for use as diodes. The two materials that have been used most for semiconductor devices are germanium and silicon. The discussion here will concentrate on silicon devices since most current integrated circuits use silicon as the basic semiconductor material. Silicon is called a semiconductor since its conductivity properties are intermediate between those of a conductor (a material such as a metal, having high conductivity) and those of an insulator (a very poor conductor, such as glass). *P*-type and *n*-type silicon are obtained by the precise introduction of impurities such as indium or boron into pure silicon. The particular impurity used determines whether a *p*-type or an *n*-type silicon results. A discussion of the physics or technology of integrated circuits is beyond the scope of this book. Those interested in learning about these topics should consult the following references: [Colclaser 80], [Glaser 77], [Hamilton 75], [Muller 77], [Oldham 77], and [Sze 83].

The voltage-current characteristic for a silicon diode (silicon pn junction) is shown in Fig. 4.4-9. Examination of this figure shows that the silicon diode differs from an ideal diode in two major respects:

1. For positive currents there is a voltage drop across the diode.
2. This voltage drop is not constant but increases when the current increases.

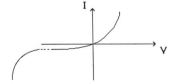

Figure 4.4-9 Voltage–current characteristic of a silicon diode.

Two other differences between ideal and silicon diodes are also exhibited by this curve:

3. Since the curve is not a straight line, there is a nonlinear relationship between the voltage and the current. This nonlinearity is not significant in the circuits to be studied here and will not be included in the model to be used for the silicon diode.

4. For large negative voltages, reverse current begins to flow. Usually, such negative voltages are not present in digital integrated circuits and thus this aspect of the characteristic does not present a problem. As will be seen later, this negative breakdown can be used to advantage, but further discussion of it will be deferred until zener diodes are considered.

If the actual diode characteristic of Fig. 4.4-9 is represented by the linear approximation of Fig. 4.4-10, a simple equivalent circuit for the silicon diode can be developed. This equivalent circuit is shown in Fig. 4.4-11. It incorporates a battery, $V_d = 0.6$ volts, to account for the voltage drop across a conducting diode and a resistance, $R_f = 20 \, \Omega$, to account for the changes in voltage caused by changes in forward diode current. Often, the resistance R_f can be neglected since it is small compared to the other resistances in the circuit. The voltage V_d is called the **offset** or **threshold** voltage since the diode will not begin to conduct until the applied forward voltage exceeds V_d. The resistance R_f is called the **forward resistance** of the diode. An outlined symbol, as in Fig. 4.4-11a, will be used to distinguish it from an ideal diode, which will be represented by a filled-in symbol as in Fig. 4.4-1. Note that the equivalent circuit for a semiconductor diode incorporates an ideal diode in it.

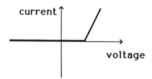

Figure 4.4-10   Linear approximation to the silicon diode characteristic of Fig. 4.4-9.

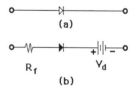

Figure 4.4-11   Diode symbol and equivalent circuit; (a) symbol for semiconductor diode; (b) equivalent circuit for silicon semiconductor diode $V_d = 0.6$ volt and $R_f = 20 \, \Omega$.

Semiconductor Diode Gates.   A two-input semiconductor diode AND gate is shown in Fig. 4.4-12a. The situation with $e_x = 3$ volts, $e_y = 0$ volts, and the semiconductor gates replaced by equivalent circuits is shown in Fig. 4.4-12b. The forward resistance, R_f, is omitted from the equivalent circuit since it is very small compared to R_L ($20 << 15,000$). The output voltage is seen to be 0.6 volt rather than 0 volts because of the offset voltage of the diode. The operation of this equivalent circuit model of the AND gate is summarized in Table 4.4-3. This table shows that the output voltage levels differ from the input voltage levels. If the

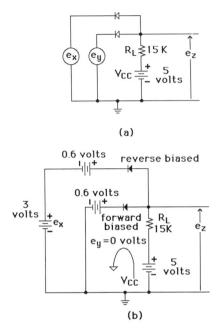

Figure 4.4-12 Semiconductor AND gate: (a) a two-input semiconductor diode AND gate; (b) circuit conditions with $e_x = 3$ volts, $e_y = 0$ volts and semiconductor diodes replaced by equivalent circuits. R_f is omitted since it is very small in comparison with R_L.

gate is followed by an active element that can restore (requantize) the voltage levels no serious problem arises since the two output levels are well separated. Attempts to cascade several gates before restoring the signal levels can lead to problems, but since such designs are no longer used this situation will not be discussed further.

TABLE 4.4-3 Voltages for the equivalent circuit model of a two-input semiconductor diode AND gate with R_f neglected

e_x	e_y	e_z
0	0	0.6
0	3	0.6
3	0	0.6
3	3	3.6

4.4-3 Bipolar Transistors

A **transistor** is a three-terminal semiconductor device that is capable of power amplification. (Actually, transistors having more than three elements and thus more than two *pn* junctions are also used.) A **bipolar** or **junction transistor** is a transistor that consists of two *pn* junctions. Thus a junction transistor exhibits some similarity to a semiconductor diode. Since there can be interactions between the two junctions of a transistor, it is a more complex (and powerful) device than two interconnected diodes. The purpose of the following material is to develop a model of a junction transistor. The model developed will be adequate for a simple analysis of the basic integrated-circuit gates. However, it is admittedly an oversimplified transistor model. More precise transistor models are presented in [Colclaser 80], [Glaser 77], [Hamilton 75], [Muller 77], [Oldham 77], and [Sze 83]. A junction transistor is composed of a region of *n*-type material between two regions of *p*-type material—a ***pnp* transistor**—or of a region of *p*-type material between two regions of *n*-type material—an ***npn* transistor**. The following discussion will be carried out in terms of *npn* transistors but the operation of *pnp* transistors does not differ except for the polarities of voltages and directions of current flow. The three regions are called the **emitter**, the **base**, and the **collector**. The base region separates the emitter from the collector. The emitter and collector regions are very similar, but their specific geometries differ so that their characteristics are not quite identical. The junctions between these regions are called the collector-base junction and the base-emitter junction.

Schematic representations of transistors are given in Fig. 4.4-13a and the commonly used circuit symbols are shown in Fig. 4.4-13b. A transistor is usually operated with the collector-base junction reverse biased as in Fig. 4.4-14. This figure shows three situations in which not only is the collector-base junction reverse biased, but the emitter-base junction is not forward biased. With the base-emitter junction nonconducting, the collector-base junction behaves like a semiconductor diode and no current flows in the collector circuit. When the transistor is in this situation it is said to be **cut off** or to be in its **cutoff region**.

The other situation of interest is illustrated in Fig. 4.4-15, in which a reverse voltage is still applied to the collector-base junction but the base-emitter junction is forward biased. Since the base-emitter junction is forward biased, current will flow across it—electrons will be supplied from the voltage source V_e and will be swept across the base-emitter junction. However, because of the voltage across the base-collector junction, most of these electrons will proceed on across the base-

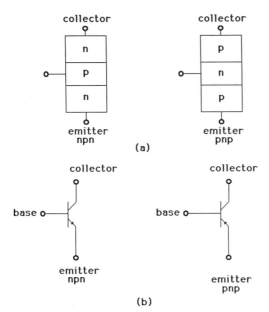

Figure 4.4-13 Representations for transistors: (a) schematic representations; (b) circuit symbols.

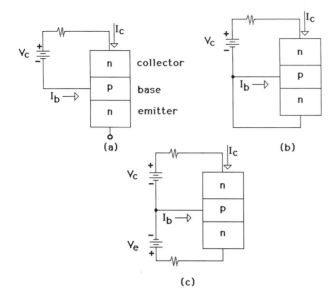

(a)

(b)

(c)

Figure 4.4-14 Situations with collector–emitter junction reverse biased, $I_b = 0$ and $I_c = 0$. Transistor is cut off: (a) base–emitter junction open circuited; (b) base–emitter junction short circuited; (c) base–emitter junction reverse biased.

collector junction and will actually flow out of the collector lead. Thus the current flow across the forward-biased emitter-base junction actually causes a current flow across the reverse-biased base-collector junction.

The proportion of electrons that flow on to the collector after entering the base region rather than flowing out of the base depends critically on the specific geometry of the device and directly on the fact that the base region is small compared to the other two regions. The ratio of collector current divided by emitter current is called the **current transfer ratio** α. It is given by $\alpha = I_c/I_e$. Typical values of α lie in the range from 0.9 to 0.995, indicating that most of the emitter current is going to the collector circuit. Another important transistor parameter is the ratio between the base and collector currents. This ratio is given by $\beta = I_c/I_b$, the **dc current gain**. It is equal to $\alpha/(1 - \alpha)$ and ranges from 10 to 150.

These ratios among currents vary somewhat with the magnitudes of the currents and also with temperature, but these effects will not be important for the phenomena to be considered here. However, these current ratios hold true only as long as the collector-base junction is reverse biased, a situation that may be

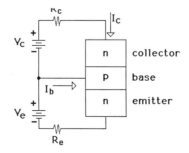

Figure 4.4-15 *Npn* transistor with reverse bias on its collector–base junction and forward bias on its emitter–base junction.

changed by the flow of collector current. This effect is important for integrated-circuit gates and will be considered in detail later. When the transistor is operated with the collector-base junction reverse biased and the emitter-base junction forward biased, it is said to be operating in the **active** region and its currents are related by the α and β parameters.

Transistor Inverter. The most common circuit for a bipolar transistor inverter is shown in Fig. 4.4-16a. Suppose that the input voltage v_x is equal to 0 volts. In this case the voltage across the base-emitter junction, v_{be}, is equal to zero and the transistor is cut off. In the cutoff region no collector current flows so there is no current through R_L and the output voltage, e_z, is equal to the supply voltage, V_{CC}.

In order to have this circuit perform as an inverter, a low input voltage should cause a high output—it has already been shown that a zero input leads to an output equal to V_{CC}—and a high input voltage should cause a low output. Thus, it would appear that circuit parameters should be chosen such that an input voltage equal to V_{CC} leads to a base current which makes v_z equal to zero. Actually, it is not possible to lower the output voltage completely to zero, although a sufficiently low voltage of approximately 0.2 volt can be obtained. As the output voltage is lowered (by increasing I_c) a point is reached where the transistor is no longer in its active region since the collector-base junction is no longer reverse biased. If the voltages between the transistor terminals are defined as in Fig. 4.4-17, then Kirchhoff's voltage law requires that they satisfy the relation

$$V_{BC} - V_{BE} + V_{CE} = 0$$

Since the collector-emitter voltage V_{CE} is equal to the output voltage $v_z = V_{CC} - I_c R_L$, and the base-emitter voltage V_{BE} is equal to the offset voltage, $V_t = 0.6$ volt, this can be written as

$$V_{BC} = V_{BE} - V_{CE} = 0.6 - v_z = 0.6 - V_{CC} + I_c R_L$$

The collector-base junction is reverse biased when V_{BC} is negative. Thus, when the transistor is in its active region, $V_{BC} < 0$ and $I_c = \beta I_b$, which implies that

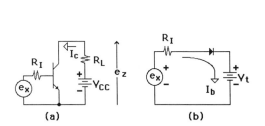

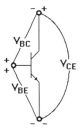

Figure 4.4-16 Transistor inverter circuit: (a) transistor inverter circuit; (b) equivalent circuit for base circuit with forward-biased base–emitter junction.

Figure 4.4-17 Transistor terminal voltages.

$0.6 - V_{CC} + \beta I_b R_L < 0$ or that $\beta I_b R_L < V_{CC} - 0.6$. If I_b is increased so that $\beta I_b R_L > V_{CC} - 0.6$, the collector-base junction becomes forward biased and the transistor is said to become **saturated** or be in its **saturation region**. When $\beta I_b R_L = V_{CC} - 0.6$, the voltage V_{CE} is equal to 0.6 volt. As I_b is increased to make $\beta I_b R_L > V_{CC} - 0.6$, the value of V_{CE} decreases until it reaches the collector-emitter voltage of saturation, $V_{CE,Sat}$ which is approximately 0.2 volt. Further increases in I_b will not cause further changes in V_{BC} since the collector-emitter voltage of a saturated transistor remains about 0.2 volt and is independent of the base current as long as the base current is large enough to keep the transistor saturated. Thus, for values of base current such that $\beta I_b R_L > V_{CC} - 0.2$, the transistor is fully saturated so that $V_{CE} = 0.2$ volt and $I_c = (V_{CC} - 0.2)/R_L$. It is not customary to operate the transistor with values of base current which partially saturate it $(V_{CC} - 0.2 > \beta I_b R_L > V_{CC} - 0.6)$. This discussion is summarized in Table 4.4-4.

TABLE 4.4-4 Active and saturation region characteristics

Base current	V_{CE}	I_c	Operating region
$V_{CC} - \beta I_b R_L > 0.6$	$V_{CE} = V_{CC} - \beta I_b R_L$	$I_c = \beta I_b$	Active
$V_{CC} - \beta I_b R_L < 0.2$	$V_{CE} = 0.2$ V	$I_c = (V_{CC} - 0.2)/R_L$ or $I_c \approx V_{CC}/R_L$ for $V_{CC} \gg 0.2$	Saturation

If a positive voltage, v_x, is applied, the base-emitter junction will be forward biased and the base current I_b can be calculated from the equivalent circuit of Fig. 4.4-16b, in which the base-emitter junction has been replaced by a voltage source equal to the offset voltage for a forward-biased junction. The base current, I_b, can be calculated by applying Kirchhoff's voltage law (voltage around a loop must sum to zero) to this circuit:

$$v_x - R_I I_b - V_t = 0$$

or

$$I_b = (v_x - V_t)/R_I \qquad (4.4-1)$$

The current can be calculated from (4.4-1) independent of whether the transistor is in its active or saturated region.

Representative values for the parameters in this circuit might be: $V_{CC} = 3$ volts, $R_I = 1.2$ KΩ, $R_L = 640$ Ω, and $\beta = 50$. If v_x is assumed to equal 3 volts, the base current derived from (4.4-1) is $I_b = (v_x - V_t)/R_I = (3.0 - 0.6)/1200 = 2$ mA. Table 4.4-4 shows that the region of operation of the transistor can be determined by calculating $V_{CC} - \beta R_L I_b$, which is equal to $3 - (50)(640)(2 \times 10^{-3}) = 3 - 64 = -61$. Since this is far less than 0.2, the transistor is fully saturated and the output voltage v_z is equal to 0.2 volt. The operation of this circuit is summarized in Table 4.4-5, which clearly shows that it does perform inversion.

The fact that the output voltage is 0.2 volt rather than 0 volts does not present a serious problem. If the low value for input voltage v_x had been taken to be

TABLE 4.4-5 Operation of the circuit
of Fig. 4.4-16a

Input voltage, e_x (V)	Output voltage, e_z (V)
0	3
3	0.2

0.2 volt instead of 0 volts, the output would have been 3 volts. A value of 0.2 volt for V_{BE} is too small to overcome the base-emitter offset voltage and the transistor thus remains cut off. The values for V_t and $V_{CE,Sat}$ may vary somewhat from transistor to transistor and with the transistor operating conditions. This variation is usually not important since the circuits must be designed so that they work in spite of small variations in the transistor parameters. The values used here are representative of typical values. The calculations given are useful to indicate the mode of operation rather than for obtaining precise values of voltage or current.

Saturated Switching.   The preceding discussion has described how the circuit of Fig. 4.4-16 can be operated as an inverter by having the input voltage switch the transistor between its cutoff and saturation regions. The speed at which these transitions can be made to occur is important and will be considered next. Representative waveforms for the output voltage and current when a square pulse is applied to the input of the inverter circuit are shown in Fig. 4.4-18. There are three phenomena which are the most important factors in causing the output response to lag behind the input voltage changes:

1. When the input voltage changes from 0 to a positive voltage, the base-emitter junction does not change immediately since a finite time is required to charge up the capacitance associated with this junction. The transistor current will not start to rise until this junction voltage reaches the offset voltage. The time from when the input voltage goes positive until the base and collector currents start to flow is called the **turn-on time delay, t_d.**

2. A finite time is required for the collector current to change between its cutoff value of zero and its saturation value of approximately V_{CC}/R_L. When the

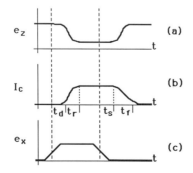

Figure 4.4-18 Transient response of the transistor inverter circuit: (a) output voltage; (b) collector current; (c) input voltage.

current is changing from 0 to V_{CC}/R_L the associated time delay is called the **rise time, t_r.** The delay for the current to fall from V_{CC}/R_L to 0 is called the **fall time, t_f.**

3. Circuits such as the transistor inverter are usually operated with a much larger base current than the minimum value required to saturate the transistor. This larger current is necessary to ensure that the transistor will saturate even when the transistor parameters and supply voltages depart from their nominal values in directions that reduce the base current. The time that it takes to reduce the base current from its full saturation value to its value when the transistor is at the edge of saturation is called the **storage time, t_s.** Note that this delay only occurs when the collector current is being turned off. Thus the total **turn-off time, t_{OFF},** will be longer than the **turn-on time, t_{ON}.** Various techniques have been used to decrease gate delay by reducing the storage time. In particular, two gate families—Schottky TTL and ECL—achieve high speeds by not driving the transistors into saturation.

A more detailed discussion of saturated switching can be found in [Hodges 83], Chap. 6; [Holt 78], section 2.5; [Millman 72], section 6-5; [Stern 68], section 9-3; [Lo 67], section 2.2.2.

4.4-4 Diode-Transistor Logic

One of the first techniques used to obtain transistor gates was to use a diode AND gate connected to a transistor inverter. The circuit for the basic integrated-circuit diode-transistor logic (DTL) gate developed using this approach is shown in Fig. 4.4-19a. If one of the input voltages, say v_w, is at a low voltage (0.2 volt), the situation shown in the equivalent circuit of Fig. 4.4-19b occurs. Fig. 4.4-19c shows that the voltage across the series diodes D_4 and D_5 is 0.8 volt. A voltage of $2V_d = 1.2$ volts is required to sustain current flow through two diodes in series, so no current will flow and point B will be at zero volts. Since V_{BE} for the transistor T is equal to the voltage at point B (0 volts) the transistor will be cut off. With no current flowing in R_2 the output voltage, v_z, will be equal to V_{CC} or 4 volts.

When all the input voltages are high (4 volts) the input diodes, D_1, D_2, and D_3 are reverse biased and thus do not conduct. The situation is as shown in Fig. 4.4-19d. If no current flowed in the base-emitter junction of the transistor, the voltage at point B would be $(20,000)(4 - 1.2)/(22,000) = 2.5$ volts. Since this is greater than the base-emitter offset voltage the transistor does conduct, it goes into saturation. The voltage at point B drops to 0.6 volt and the output voltage drops to $V_{CE,Sat}$ or 0.2 volt. This shows that the output voltage will be high if any one or more of the input voltages are low, thus realizing the NAND function, $Z = (WXY)' = W' + X' + Y'$.

This discussion of the circuit operation does not explain why one diode would not be used instead of the series connection of D_4 and D_5. If only one diode is used, then when at least one input voltage is low, the voltages at points A and B are as in Fig. 4.4-19f. The voltage across $D_{4,5}$ (0.8 volt) is greater than V_d, the

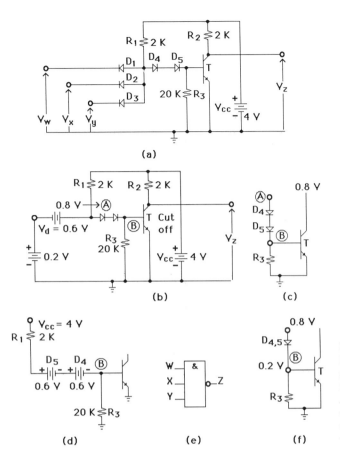

Figure 4.4-19 DTL (diode-transistor logic) gate: (a) basic DTL gate; (b) DTL gate with at least one input voltage low (0.2 volt); (c) voltage relations of points *A* and *B* of part (b); (d) DTL gate with all input voltages high (4 volts); (e) logic symbol; (f) situation of part (c) with D_4 and D_5 combined.

diode will conduct, and the voltage at point *B* will be $0.8 - V_d$ or 0.2 volt. This voltage is less than the base-emitter offset voltage, so the transistor will not conduct. However, this would not be a particularly good design since a small noise voltage $(0.6 - 0.2) = 0.4$ volt could switch the transistor on. In fact, the use of three series diodes has been considered to increase the noise immunity.

The effect of driving other DTL gate inputs from a DTL gate output must be considered. When the output voltage is high, no current flows between the driving and driven gates. In this situation the loading effects of the driven gates are not significant. On the other hand, when the driving gate output is low, current flows from the driven gates input diodes through the output transistor. Thus the load gates are "sink loads" since the driving gate is required to act as a current sink for them. This increase in collector current produces little change in the output voltage, $V_{CE,\text{Sat}}$, as long as sufficient base current flows to keep the transistor in saturation. Since the available collector current depends directly on the base current and the dc current gain of the transistor, β, it is these parameters that determine the allowable fanout. The fanout can be increased by increasing the beta of the transistor or by modifying the circuit to increase the base current. If the diode D_4 of the basic gate is replaced by a transistor as in Fig. 4.4-20, the

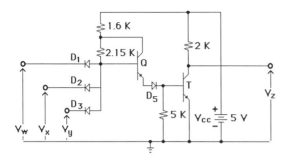

Figure 4.4-20 Modified DTL circuit for increased fanout.

current gain of this transistor can be used to increase the base current to the output transistor and thus the fanout of the gate circuit. [A further modification of this circuit consists in replacing the diode D_5 with a 6.9-volt zener diode and increasing V_{CC} to 15 volts. This results in a gate with much higher noise immunity (a noise margin of 7 volts). This form of DTL is called **HTL, high threshold logic.**]

A useful feature of DTL is its wired logic capability. Fig. 4.4-21a shows the output circuits of two DTL gates with their output points connected together. Fig. 4.4-21b is the same circuit redrawn to make its operation more obvious. This figure shows that tying the outputs together places the output transistors directly in parallel: the output from these interconnected gates can be high only when both transistors are cut off. Thus the composite output will be high only when both of the individual gate outputs are high. Connecting the two gate outputs directly together produces the effect of an AND gate—a wired AND. This is shown in Fig. 4.4-21c.

Diode-transistor logic is no longer used in new designs. Instead, an improved design—TTL or transistor-transistor logic—is used. The DTL input circuit is, however, found in many of the low-power Schottky (LSTTL and ALSTTL) TTL gates.

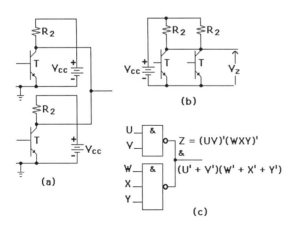

Figure 4.4-21 Wired logic with DTL: (a) two DTL gate outputs connected together; (b) part (a) redrawn; (c) logic symbol for wired AND.

4.4-5 Transistor-Transistor Logic

The logic family used most often for designs based on catalog parts is called transistor-transistor logic or TTL. The TTL logic family is, in fact, made up of a number of subfamilies such as low-power TTL, Schottky TTL, etc. They differ in their parameter values and in the use of Schottky diodes. Some small differences in circuit configuration are also present. There are two reasons for the existence of TTL subfamilies: (1) Some subfamilies are improvements over earlier designs and have replaced the earlier parts for new designs. (2) The differences in subfamily characteristics (power, speed, noise margin, etc.) permit a designer to better match the IC characteristics to the requirements of the system being designed. The original TTL circuits will be presented first. Then the newer subfamilies will be discussed.

TTL can be considered a modification of DTL in which the input diodes are replaced by base-emitter transistor junctions. The level-shifting diodes, D_4 and D_5 (Fig. 4.4-19a), are also replaced by transistor junctions in the TTL circuit shown in Fig. 4.4-22a. In this circuit the base-emitter junctions of transistors T_1, T_2, and T_3 replace the input diodes D_1, D_2, and D_3. The base-collector junctions of T_1, T_2, and T_3 collectively replace the level-shifting diode D_4 and the base-emitter junction of T_5 replaces the other level-shifting diode D_5. In this circuit the three transistors T_1, T_2, and T_3 have all of their collectors connected together. This permits these three transistors to be fabricated by a single device having three emitters and a single base and collector as shown in Fig. 4.4-22b. The operation of this circuit is described next.

First assume that one of the input voltages is low, say $v_w = 0.2$ volt. Then the corresponding emitter junction of Q_1 is forward biased, emitter current flows, and the base voltage of Q_1 (point A) is $0.2 + V_d = 0.2 + 0.6 = 0.8$ volt. In this situation the transistors Q_2 and Q_3 must be cut off. This will be shown by demonstrating that the assumption that they are conducting leads to a contradiction. If base-emitter current flows in Q_3, its base must be at 0.6 volt. To raise the Q_3 base to this voltage, there must be base-emitter current in Q_2 and Q_2's base must be 0.6 volt higher than its emitter, which is at the same voltage as Q_3's base, namely 0.6 volt. Thus, Q_2's base must be at 1.2 volts. But in order for base current to flow in Q_2, there must be base-collector current in Q_1 requiring Q_1's base to be at a higher voltage than Q_1's collector. Since the Q_1 base voltage is 0.8 volt and the required collector voltage to turn on Q_2 and Q_3 is 1.2 volts, the transistor Q_1 cannot have collector current flowing (which would require a base voltage of 1.8 volts) and Q_2 and Q_3 must be cut off. With Q_3 cut off the open-circuit output voltage, v_z, will be equal to V_{CC} or 5 volts.

If all the input voltages are high, say $v_w = v_x = v_y = 5$ volts, transistors Q_2 and Q_3 will be turned on. The voltage at point A will be equal to the sum of the offset voltages of three forward-biased junctions or 1.8 volts. The emitters of Q_1 are all reverse biased. The output voltage, v_z, is $V_{CE,Sat}$ or 0.2 volt. This discussion shows that, as expected, the TTL gate realizes the same logic function as a DTL gate—the NAND function, $Z = (WXY)' = W' + X' + Y'$.

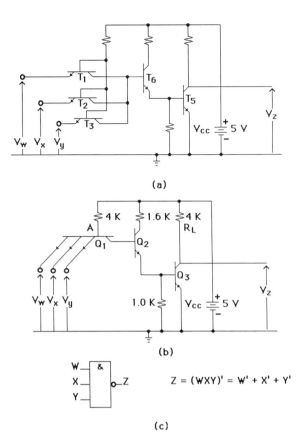

(a)

(b)

W —[&]— Z
X
Y

$$Z = (WXY)' = W' + X' + Y'$$

(c)

Figure 4.4-22 Basic TTL gate circuit: (a) modification of DTL gate with diodes replaced by transistors; (b) TTL gate; (c) logic symbol.

Actual TTL gates have diodes connected to the input transistor, as shown in Fig. 4.4-23. These diodes have no effect on the normal operation of the circuit and are included to protect against problems created by an input voltage going negative momentarily due to noise. They also damp oscillations called "ringing" caused by switching transients.

Totem-Pole Output Stage. Speed of operation is affected by the spurious capacitance present in the circuit. When the gate output voltage is switched from a low to a high value, these spurious capacitances associated with the leads and the input diodes of the driven circuits must be charged up. The time constant for this charging is determined by the value of these parasitic capacitances and the value of the output load resistance, R_L. One way to reduce this time constant is

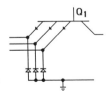

Figure 4.4-23 Input transistor of TTL gate showing clamping diodes.

to lower the value of R_L. However, this is undesirable since a smaller R_L increases the power consumption of the circuit. In particular, when the output is low, 0.2 volt, the power dissipation in R_L is $(V_{CC} - V_{CE,Sat})^2/R_L$. Clearly, decreasing R_L will increase this power. Thus, a large R_L is good when the output is low, but a small R_L is desirable when switching the output to a high value. By adding a transistor and a diode in series with R_L and decreasing R_L to 100 Ω, as shown in Fig. 4.4-24, it is possible to obtain an effective resistance satisfying these criteria. The circuit that results from the addition of these two devices is called a **totem-pole** output stage. It is said to be an active pullup circuit in contrast to the output configuration of Fig. 4.4-22b, which is a passive pullup output.

The action of the circuit of Fig. 4.4-24 will be considered next. First the situation when the output v_z is low will be examined. In this case all the inputs must be high and transistors Q_2 and Q_3 are saturated. The voltage at the base of Q_4 is equal to the collector voltage of Q_2, which is equal to $V_{CE,Sat} + V_{BE,Sat} = 0.2 + 0.6 = 0.8$ volt. The voltage at the cathode of the diode is $V_{CE,Sat} = 0.2$ volt. Thus, $0.8 - 0.2 = 0.6$ volt is the voltage across the series connection of the diode and the base-emitter junction of Q_4. This voltage is insufficient to maintain current flow through these devices so that they are cut off. With transistor Q_4 cut off, current will not flow through its 100-Ω collector resistor. The objective of avoiding the power dissipation in this resistor when the output is low has thus been achieved.

If one of the input voltages is now changed to a low value, transistors Q_1 and Q_2 will be cut off and the base voltage of Q_4 will rise. The output voltage, v_z, will rise until it reaches a value of V_{CC} minus the voltages necessary to sustain

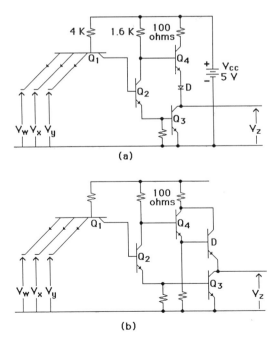

(a)

(b)

Figure 4.4-24 TTL NAND gates with totem-pole output stages: (a) basic totem-pole output gate; (b) gate with Darlington totem-pole output stage.

current flow through Q_4 and D, or approximately $5 - (0.6 + 0.6) = 3.8$ volts. While the output is rising from 0.2 volt to 3.8 volts, current will flow to charge the spurious capacitance through the 100-Ω resistance in series with the forward resistance of the diode and the saturation resistance of Q_4. Since these device resistances are very small, the effective resistance has been decreased from the 4000 Ω of the Fig. 4.4-22 circuit to almost 100 Ω. The objective of decreasing the charging time constant is thus also met.

A circuit with even greater drive capability can be obtained by replacing the diode D in Fig. 4.4-24a with a transistor to obtain the circuit of Fig. 4.4-24b. In this circuit the emitter current of Q_4 is amplified by transistor D to provide the final output current. This form of circuit in which two transistors are directly connected with the emitter of the first driving the base of the second transistor is called a **Darlington stage**.

From the foregoing discussion it is not clear why it is necessary to include the 100-Ω output resistor. With this resistor eliminated, the charging time constant would be even smaller without altering the situation when the output is low. However, the 100-Ω resistor is necessary because of the situation that occurs when switching from one state to another. If, as is very possible, transistor Q_4 turns on before Q_3 turns off, there will be a time when the power supply is in effect, short circuited through the series combination of Q_4, Q_3, and the diode. The resulting current spike generates noise in the power distribution system and increases power consumption at high frequencies. The 100-Ω resistor is used to limit the size of these current spikes. One of the disadvantages of the totem-pole circuit is that it inherently generates noise because of these current pulses.

Another disadvantage of the totem-pole configuration is that it does not permit wired logic. Since it is an output structure with both pullup and pulldown active, the reasons given in Section 4.2 for not using wired logic apply.

Wired Logic. Two special forms of TTL gates that permit wired logic are produced: open-collector gates and tri-state gates. The first special type of TTL gate is the so-called **open-collector** form shown in Fig. 4.4-25a. The output collector resistor is omitted from the "open-collector" gates since its value depends on which gates are interconnected. A circuit with two open-collector gates used in a wired-logic connection is shown in Fig. 4.4-25b. The Standard symbol for an open-collector output is shown in part (c) of the figure. This is the same as the passive pullup symbol (Fig. 4.2-2b) except that the horizontal line inside the diamond is omitted to indicate that an external resistor is required. The external resistor must be included to perform the function of the output collector resistance. A discussion of choosing the value of this resistance is given on pp. 47–51 of [Morris 71]. Just as for DTL, the output of two gate outputs tied together can be high only when both individual gate outputs are high. Thus, a wired-AND function is realized as shown in Fig. 4.4-25c. The disadvantages of open-collector TTL gates is that they lose the speed improvement of the totem-pole output stage.

Tri-state Logic. As discussed previously, one of the most important applications of wired logic is for multiplexing onto a bus. It is possible to retain both

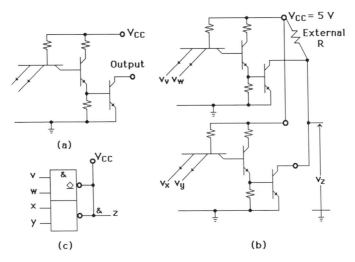

Figure 4.4-25 Open-collector TTL gates: (a) open collector TTL gate; (b) two open collector gates connected for wired logic; (c) wired AND. $Z = (WV)'(XY)' = (V' + W')(X' + Y')$

the totem-pole output speed and the ability to make wired bus connections by use of a **tri-state logic** (also called *bus-organized TTL*, *wired-OR'able TTL*, or *bus OR'able TTL*) technique. A circuit designed using this technique is shown in Fig. 4.4-26.

When the Disable signal in Fig. 4.4-26b is set to 1, it has the same effect as closing the switch in Fig. 4.4-26a. The base of Q_4 is grounded, causing Q_4 to be cut off. Ground is also applied to one of the emitters of the input transistor Q_1. This removes base drive from transistors Q_2 and Q_3, causing them to be cut off. With the Disable input equal to 1, both output transistors Q_3 and Q_4 are cut off and no current can flow in the output line in either direction. Thus the circuit of Fig. 4.4-26 can have its output stage in one of three possible states:

1. Hi-Z with both output transistors cut off. This state occurs when Disable = 1 independent of the other inputs to the gate.
2. 0 with Q_3 on and Q_4 off. This occurs when Disable = 0 and all of the other inputs are equal to 1.
3. 1 with Q_3 off and Q_4 on. This occurs when Disable = 0 and any one or more of the other inputs are equal to 0.

Suppose that a number of such gates have their outputs connected together and no more than one of the gates has its Disable input equal to 0. The common output lead will then be in the hi-Z state when all Disable inputs are equal to 1. When one Disable input is equal to 0, the state of the common output lead will be determined by the logic value of the corresponding gate. Thus, a wired connection is obtained.

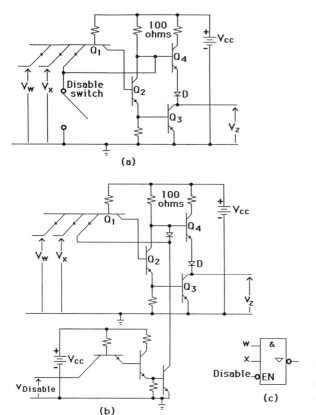

Figure 4.4-26 Tri-state NAND gate:
(a) functional form of disable input;
(b) actual circuit for disable input;
(c) logic symbol.

Complex Gates. The provision of "open-collector" gates and tri-state gates are ways in which logic flexibility is provided in TTL. Another way is by making available gates that realize logic functions other than the basic NAND. Figure 4.4-27a shows the circuit for a TTL NOR gate. If either input v_w or v_x, is high, the corresponding transistors, Q_{1w} and Q_{2w} or Q_{1x}, and Q_{2x}, will conduct, causing Q_3 to conduct and the output to be low. When both inputs are low, transistors Q_{2w}, Q_{2x}, and Q_3 are cut off, making the output high. Thus $Z = W'X' = (W + X)'$ and the NOR function is realized. If the input transistors of Fig. 4.4-20a are replaced by multiemitter transistors, the circuit of Fig. 4.4-20b results. This circuit realizes the function $Z = (UW)'(XY)' = (UW + XY)'$ since the output will be low if either both v_u and v_w or both v_x and v_y are high. The function realized is the AND-OR-INVERT, as shown in the logic diagrams of Fig. 4.4-27c.

TTL is produced in a variety of forms to accommodate different applications. Table 4.4-6 lists the power and delay parameters for many TTL subfamilies. By increasing the resistor values in the basic TTL circuit, a design with substantially lower power consumption is obtained at the cost of slower performance. The family based on this modification is called low-power TTL.

TABLE 4.4-6   TTL power and speed characteristics

	Logic family	Power (mW per gate)	t_{PD} (ns)
74	Standard TTL	10	9
74L	Low-power TTL	1	33
74H	High-speed TTL	22	6
74S	Schottky TTL	20	3
74LS	Low-power Schottky TTL	2	9
74AS	Advanced Schottky TTL	20	1.6
74ALS	Advanced low-power Schottky	1.3	5
74F	FAST	5	3

A design having lower propagation delay but larger power consumption than standard TTL is obtained by decreasing the resistor values and using the Darlington output stage.   This is called high-speed TTL.

As discussed previously, speed in digital gates is limited by two main factors: the time required to charge and discharge capacitances—the RC time constants, and by the time required to turn off saturated transistors—storage time.   Some

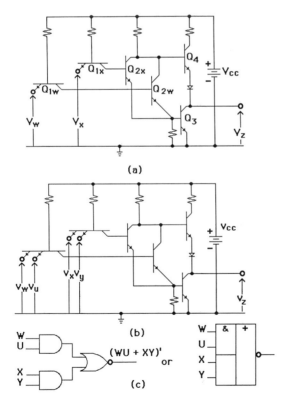

(a)

(b)

(c)

(WU + XY)'
or

Figure 4.4-27   NAND and AOI TTL gates: (a) a TTL NOR gate; (b) AND-OR-INVERT (AOI) gate; (c) logic diagram for part (b).

of the approaches used to reduce the *RC* time constants have already been discussed. Two techniques are used to reduce storage time. One uses circuits that do not permit saturation. This approach results in what is called current-mode or emitter-coupled logic and will be presented in the following section. The other approach uses TTL circuits but makes use of Schottky devices to limit the degree of saturation of the transistors by limiting the base-collector voltage.

A Schottky diode is a surface barrier diode which has a very low forward voltage drop (0.3 volt). (It is made of a contact between a suitable metal and an *N*-type semiconductor.) A Schottky-clamped transistor, usually just called a Schottky transistor, is formed by connecting a Schottky diode as a bypass between the base and collector (Fig. 4.4-28). When the transistor starts conducting and is about to saturate, the excess base current is diverted to the collector through the Schottky diode. The transistor is never fully saturated and recovers quickly when the base current is interrupted.

The use of Schottky transistors permitted the development of Schottky TTL with half the delay of high-speed TTL and approximately the same power consumption. This series, STTL, displaced HTTL for high-speed applications.

By combining Schottky transistors with low-power TTL, a gate is obtained with the delay of standard TTL and only one-fifth the required power. This family, LSTTL, is currently the most popular of the TTL series.

Improvements in processing have resulted in TTL designs having reduced capacitances and decreased transistor switching times. This has permitted the introduction of advanced Schottky TTL series. One of these, advanced low-power Schottky TTL, has both less power and smaller delays compared to LSTTL. The other, advanced Schottky TTL—ASTTL—is almost twice as fast as STTL with the same power consumption.

4.4-6 Current-Mode Logic

The fastest form of integrated-circuit logic currently available uses **current-mode logic** gates. This is also called **emitter-coupled logic**, **current-steering logic**, or **nonsaturating logic**. The basic circuit used for this logic family is radically different from the circuits of any of the logic circuits previously discussed. Transistor saturation is prevented by the basic circuit operation. Special devices such as Schottky transistors are not required. The principle of operation of this circuit is illustrated in Fig. 4.4-29a. Two transistors share a common-emitter resistor as in a differential amplifier. When the input voltage v_x is low (Fig. 4.4-29a) transistor T is cut off, transistor Q conducts, and the output voltage v_y is low. If v_x is made high (Fig. 4.4-29b), transistor T will conduct, transistor Q will be cut off, and $v_{y'}$ will be low.

Figure 4.4-28 Schottky transistor.

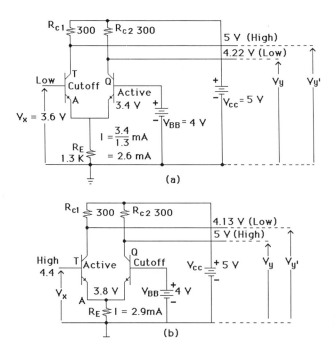

Figure 4.4-29 CML gate circuit: (a) with low input; (b) with high input.

Changing the input voltage causes the R_E current to switch from Q to T, hence the name current-switching logic. Figure 4.4-29a shows that inversion is obtained by this circuit. If more transistors are connected in parallel with T as in Fig. 4.4-30b, a NOR function is obtained. The signal $v_{y'}$ is the complement of the v_y signal so that "double-rail" outputs are available from this ECL gate, a substantial advantage since the need to include separate inverter stages is drastically reduced.

One difficulty with the circuit of Fig. 4.4-29a is that the output voltage levels differ from the input voltage levels, so that it would not be possible to directly interconnect such gates. This problem can be corrected by careful redesign of the circuit with different component parameters. The circuit has another weakness: poor output drive capability (small output fanout limitation). Both the problems of output drive and signal level can be corrected by adding circuits (called emitter followers) to the outputs as shown in Fig. 4.4-30.

In the 10k ECL logic family the 1.5-kΩ output load resistors shown in Fig. 4.4-30 are omitted. Instead, resistors are provided at each gate input so that the driven gate provides the load resistance.[1]

The terms "ECL, emitter-coupled logic" and "CML, current-mode logic" are used inconsistently. Sometimes they are treated as synonyms, as in [Holt 78]. Other writers restrict the ECL designation to circuits with emitter-follower output stages as in Fig. 4.4-30 and use CML for circuits such as shown in Fig. 4.4-29.

---

[1] This is done because 10k ECL is designed for use with transmission lines. Since the line termination provides an output load, internal load resistors would be a waste of power. This is discussed in [Blood 72].

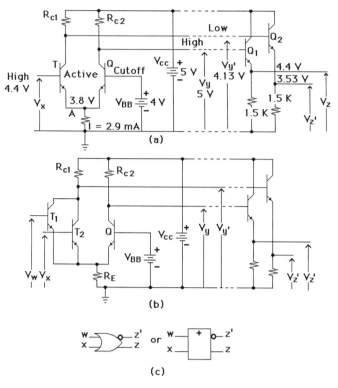

Figure 4.4-30 (a) Circuit with level-shifting output stage; (b) NOR-OR circuit; (c) logic symbol.

Circuit Operation. A more quantitative discussion of the operation of the basic ECL circuit follows. Assume that the voltage v_x is 3.6 volts as in Fig. 4.4-29a. Then transistor Q will be conducting, the voltage at point A will be $4 - V_t = 3.4$ volts, and transistor T must be cut off ($V_{BE} = 3.6 - 3.4 = 0.2$ volt, which is too small to cause conduction in the emitter circuit of T). The collector voltage of transistor T, $v_{y'}$, will thus be 5 volts. To calculate the collector voltage of Q, the collector current must be determined. First, the emitter current is calculated as the current through R_E which is 3.4/1.3k = 2.6 mA. Then, if it is assumed that the alpha, (I_c/I_e), of transistor Q is very close to unity, the collector current will be very close to 2.6 mA. The collector voltage of Q, v_y, is thus approximately $5 - (2.6)(300)10^{-3} = 4.22$ volts.

If the input voltage v_x is raised, say to 4.4 volts as in Fig. 4.4-29b, transistor T will conduct and the voltage at point A will also be raised to $4.4 - 0.6 = 3.8$ volts. The base-emitter voltage of transistor Q is now $4.0 - 3.8 = 0.2$ volt, which is insufficient to maintain conduction and Q will become cut off. Similar calculations to those used for Fig. 4.4-29a show that for Fig. 4.4-29b the values of $v_{y'}$ and v_y are 4.13 and 5 volts, respectively.

Figure 4.4-30a shows the output stage (emitter followers) used to restore the output voltage levels to the same values as the inputs. The voltages v_z and $v_{z'}$ will

TABLE 4.4-7 Operation of Fig. 4.4-30b circuit

v_w	v_x	T_1	T_2	Q	$v_{y'}$	v_y	$V_{z'}$	V_z
Low	Low	Off	Off	On	High	Low	High	Low
Low	High	Off	On	Off	Low	High	Low	High
High	Low	On	Off	Off	Low	High	Low	High
High	High	On	On	Off	Low	High	Low	High

be approximately one diode drop (V_d) less than the v_y and $v_{y'}$ voltages. (This neglects the drop in the 300-Ω R_{c1} and R_{c2} resistors due to the Q_1 and Q_2 base currents, but these base currents are very small.)

The fact that the transistors do not saturate can be seen by examining Fig. 4.4-29. In Fig. 4.4-29a the base-collector voltage of transistor Q is $4.0 - 4.29 = -0.29$ volt. Thus, the transistor is reverse biased and is operating in its active region. Transistor T in Fig. 4.4-29b has a base-collector voltage of $4.4 - 4.13 = 0.27$ volt. While this is a forward bias, it is too small to cause saturation (less than V_d), and thus this transistor is also operating in its active region.

If the input transistor T is replaced by the parallel combination of two transistors, T_1 and T_2, the circuit of Fig. 4.4-30b results. If both input voltages v_w and v_x are low, transistor Q will conduct, T_1 and T_2 will be cut off, $v_{y'}$ will be high, and v_y will be low. If v_w or v_x (or both) are high, the corresponding transistor(s) T_1 or T_2 (or both) will conduct, Q will be cut off, $v_{y'}$ will be low, and v_y will be high. This behavior is summarized in Table 4.4-7 and corresponds to the logic functions $Z' = W'X' = (W + X)'$, $Z = W + X$. Thus, the output Z' realizes the NOR function of the inputs while Z realizes the OR function.

The versatility of CML is enhanced because of the fact that wired logic is possible. The direct connection of two output stages is shown in Fig. 4.4-31a, and the corresponding equivalent circuit is shown in Fig. 4.4-31b. When both voltages v_{y_1} and $v_{y_2'}$ are at the same level, it is clear that no logic is performed and v_F is at the appropriate shifted level. When v_{y_1} and v_{y_2} have different values, the voltage v_F must be at a level corresponding to the higher value. (If it were at a lower value, one of the transistors would have a voltage greater than V_t across its emitter

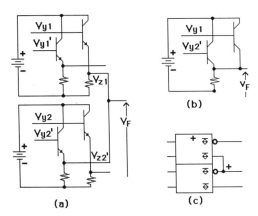

Figure 4.4-31 Wired-OR connection: (a) wired-OR circuit; (b) equivalent circuit for part (a); (c) logic diagram.

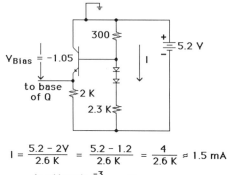

$$I = \frac{5.2 - 2V}{2.6\ K} = \frac{5.2 - 1.2}{2.6\ K} = \frac{4}{2.6\ K} \cong 1.5\ mA$$

$V_{Base} = -(1.5)(300)10^3 = -.45$

$V_{Bias} = -.45 - V = -.45 - .6 = -1.05$

Figure 4.4-32 Bias voltage network (to supply V_{BB}).

junction and this is not possible.) Thus, an OR function—a wired-OR—is obtained: $F = Z_1 + Z'_2$.

Actual CML integrated circuits differ somewhat from the circuit shown in Fig. 4.4-29. Better noise immunity is obtained by grounding the common terminal of the collector resistors R_{c1} and R_{c2}. The bottom terminal of R_E is held at -5.2 volts and V_{BB} is held at -1.15 or -1.3 volts with respect to ground. Early forms of CML used two voltage supplies to provide the -5.2 and -1.15 voltages. More current circuits include a bias network such as that shown in Fig. 4.4-32 in order to derive V_{BB} on the chip, thus avoiding the necessity for the V_{BB} pin and external connections.

Noise margins can be determined easily from Fig. 4.4-29. With the input low as in Fig. 4.4-29a, the V_{BE} of transistor T is $3.6 - 3.4 = 0.2$ volt; an input noise signal of 0.4 volt would bring this voltage to V_t and cause T to conduct. A high input as in Fig. 4.4-29b produces a V_{BE} for transistor Q of $4 - 3.8 = 0.2$ volt; an input noise signal of -0.4 volt will reduce the voltage at point A to 3.4 volts and make V_{BE} of Q equal to $4 - 3.4 = 0.6$ volt, causing Q to conduct. Thus, the noise margins are $+$ or $-$ 0.4 volt, which are quite small. However, since the current drawn from the power supply changes very little as the gate changes state, less noise is created by the circuit (the large current pulses of TTL do not occur in CML).

ECL is one of the logic families used for gate arrays (semicustom VLSI).

4.4-7 Resistor-Transistor Logic (RTL), Integrated Injection Logic (I²L), ISL, and STL

One of the first bipolar logic families, resistor-transistor logic, is a direct implementation of the passive pullup gate shown in Fig. 4.2-3a. *Npn* transistors are used as switches. The resulting circuit is shown in Fig. 4.4-33.

If all three input voltages—v_w, v_x, v_y—are less than 0.6 volt, the emitter junction threshold voltage, none of the transistors will conduct and the output voltage, v_z, will be equal to V_{CC} or 3 volts (Fig. 4.4-5b). If one input voltage is raised to a value that is sufficiently high to cause the corresponding transistor to

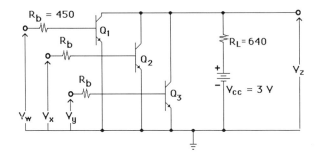

Figure 4.4-33 Three-input RTL NOR gate.

become saturated, the output voltage, v_z, will decrease to $V_{CE,\text{Sat}}$ or 0.2 volt. The output remains at 0.2 volt if more than one input is high, causing several transistors to saturate. Thus, the output is high only if all inputs are low and the NOR function $Z = W'X'Y' = (W + X + Y)'$ is realized.

A number of variations on the basic *RTL* circuit discussed here have been developed. In one of these, called DCTL for direct-coupled transistor logic, the base input resistors, R_b, are omitted entirely. While this reduces the component count, it introduces a number of difficulties. Perhaps the most serious of these difficulties is called **current hogging**. This occurs when one gate drives several other gates (fanout is greater than 1). Since there are no base resistors, the driven transistors are directly in parallel and the current from the driving gate will divide among these transistors according to their input characteristics. Since these characteristics are never identical, the current will divide unequally and some transistors may not receive sufficient current to cause proper operation.

Resistor-transistor logic is no longer an important logic family. It is presented here to show the use of bipolar transistors in passive pullup circuits and to serve as an introduction to integrated injection logic, a very important bipolar LSI and VLSI logic family.

Integrated Injection Logic (I²L). Figure 4.4-34a shows one DCTL gate with its output connected to the inputs of two other gates. Since the two transistors Q_1 and Q_2 have their bases connected together and their emitters connected together, they can be replaced by a single multicollector transistor, Q, as shown in Fig. 4.4-34b. This use of a single transistor eliminates the DCTL problem of current hogging since there no longer are parallel bases among which the drive current is divided.

In Figure 4.4-34b the load resistor, R_L, and voltage source, V_{CC}, are shown associated with the base of transistor Q rather than with the output of the gate driving Q. This is merely a redrawing of the circuit rather than any change in the circuit itself. However, with the circuit drawn in this form it is clear that the function of the $V_{CC}-R_L$ combination is to supply base current to turn Q on. Q will be on when the transistors driving Q are off and allow base current to flow in Q. If either of the transistors T_A or T_B (or both) are on, the $V_{CC}-R_L$ current will be diverted to the collector of the on transistor. No Q base current will flow and Q will be off.

Sec. 4.4   Bipolar Logic

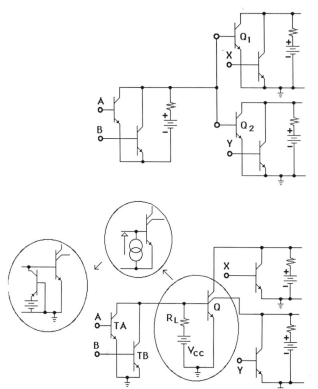

Figure 4.4-34 Derivation of I^2L gate from DCTL gate.

It is not necessary to use a resistor-voltage source to supply the Q base current—any current source will permit the circuit to function correctly. The transistor Q with $R_L - V_{CC}$ replaced by a current source is shown in Fig. 4.4-34c. This circuit is the basic structure for a very important bipolar VLSI logic family—integrated injection logic, I^2L. In I^2L the current source is implemented by means of a *pnp* transistor and a voltage source connected as in Fig. 4.4-34d. The use of this circuit structure results in a gate structure that is very compact and which has a very low speed-power product.

Two I^2L gates with their outputs connected together at the base of a third gate are shown in Fig. 4.4-35a. When either Q_1 or Q_2 (or both) are conducting, T will be off ($Z = 1$) since it will receive no base current. T will be on only when

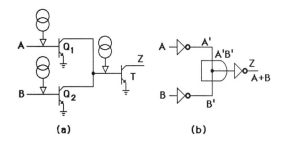

(a)   **(b)**

Figure 4.4-35 Wired-AND connection of I^2L gates: (a) electrical circuit; (b) logic circuit.

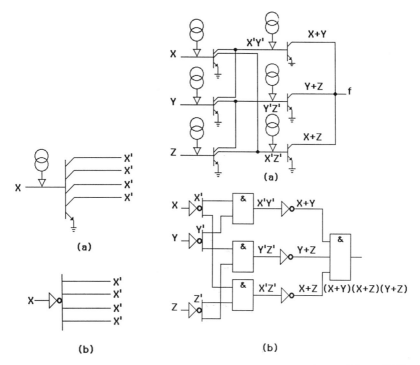

Figure 4.4-36 I^2L logic symbol: (a) circuit; (b) symbol.

Figure 4.4-37 I^2L circuit for $(X + Y)(X + Z)(Y + Z)$: (a) electrical circuit; (b) logic circuit.

both Q_1 and Q_2 are off and thus have high outputs. Since A must be low (0) for Q_1 to be off, T will be on for $A'B' = 1$. Z is 0 when T conducts, so the logic function realized is $Z' = A'B'$ or $Z = A + B$. A wired-AND is formed where the two I^2L transistors have their outputs connected together. The equivalent logic diagram is shown in Fig. 4.4-35b.

An I^2L gate implements an inversion with a fixed number of fanout connections. A typical fanout for such a gate is 4. The symbol that will be used for an I^2L gate is shown in Fig. 4.4-36. It consists of an inverter with specific fanout leads shown. Logic is carried out by connecting gate outputs together to obtain the wired-AND function. This is illustrated in Fig. 4.4-37, which shows an I^2L circuit to realize the function $(X + Y)(X + Z)(Y + Z)$.

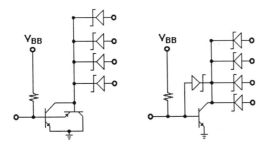

Figure 4.4-38 ISL and STL circuits.

Integrated injection logic is a very important logic family for VLSI designs. Several variations have been developed to obtain higher speed. The most important of these are integrated Schottky logic (ISL) and Schottky transistor logic (STL), shown in Fig. 4.4-38. They both use Schottky diodes as outputs rather than multicollectors. ISL is more complex to process than I^2L, but is faster. STL is faster than ISL, but its process complexity is greater. The logic design with these three families is essentially the same.

4.R REFERENCES

[ALLEN 73] Allen, A., *Noise Immunity Comparison of CMOS versus Popular Bipolar Logic Families*, Application Note AN-707, Motorola Semiconductor Products, Inc., Mesa, Ariz., 1973.

[BLOOD 72] Blood, W. R., *MECL System Design Handbook*, 2nd ed., Motorola Semiconductor Products, Inc., Mesa, Ariz., 1972.

[BOND 84] Bond, J., "Semicustom Circuits Arrive," *Computer Design*, Vol. 23, No. 3, pp. 159–169, Mar. 1984.

[COLCLASER 80] Colclaser, R. A., *Microelectronics: Processing and Device Design*, John Wiley & Sons, Inc., New York, 1980.

[GLASER 77] Glaser, A. B., and G. E. Subak-Sharpe, *Integrated Circuit Engineering*, Addison-Wesley Publishing Company, Inc., Reading, Mass., 1977.

[HAMILTON 75] Hamilton, D. J., and W. G. Howard, *Basic Integrated Circuit Engineering*, McGraw-Hill Book Company, New York, 1975.

[HODGES 83] Hodges, D. A., and H. G. Jackson, *Analysis and Design of Digital Integrated Circuits*, McGraw-Hill Book Company, New York, 1983.

[HOLT 78] Holt, C. A., *Electronic Circuits Digital and Analog*, John Wiley & Sons, Inc., New York, 1978.

[LO 67] Lo, A. W., *Introduction to Digital Electronics*, Addison-Wesley Publishing Company, Inc., Reading, Mass., 1967.

[McCLUSKEY 65] McCluskey, E. J., *Introduction to the Theory of Switching Circuits*, McGraw-Hill Book Company, New York, 1965.

[MAVOR 83] Mavor, J., M. A. Jack and P. B. Denyer, *Introduction to MOS LSI Design*, Addison-Wesley Publishing Co., Reading, Mass., 1983.

[MEAD 80] Mead, C., and L. Conway, *Introduction to VLSI Systems*, Addison-Wesley Publishing Company, Inc., Reading, Mass., 1980.

[MILLMAN 72] Millman, J., and D. Halkias, *Integrated Electronics: Analog and Digital Circuits and Systems*, McGraw-Hill Book Company, New York, 1972.

[MORRIS 71] Morris, R. L., and J. R. Miller, eds., *Designing with TTL Integrated Circuits*, Texas Instruments Electronics Series, McGraw-Hill Book Company, New York, 1971.

[MOTOROLA 75] Motorola, *Motorola MEGALOGIC—The Modular Approach to Bipolar LSI*, Motorola Semiconductors, Inc., Mesa, Ariz., 1975.

[MULLER 77] Muller, R. S., and T. I. Kamins, *Device Electronics for Integrated Circuits*, John Wiley & Sons, Inc., New York, 1977.

[NATIONAL 81] *CMOS Data Book*, National Semiconductor Corporation, Santa Clara, Calif., 1981.

[OLDHAM 77]   Oldham, W. G., "The Fabrication of Microelectronic Circuits," *Sci. Am.*, Vol. 237, No. 3, pp. 111–128, Sept. 1977.

[RCA 72]   *COS/MOS Integrated Circuits Manual*, Tech. Series CMS-271, RCA Solid State Division, Somerville, N.J., 1972.

[RICHARDS 57]   Richards, R. K., *Digital Computer Components and Circuits*, D. Van Nostrand Company, New York, 1957.

[SNYDER 85]   Snyder, D. R., "Gallium Arsonide Technology Widens its Niche," *Integrated Circuits Magazine*, Vol. 3, No. 5, pp. 23–28, May 1985.

[STERN 68]   Stern, L., *Fundamentals of Integrated Circuits*, Hayden Book Company, Inc., New York, 1968.

[SZE 83]   Sze, S. M., *VLSI Technology*, McGraw-Hill Book Company, New York, 1983.

[TURINO 79]   Turino, J., "Testability Guidelines," *Electron. Test*, pp. 18–20, Apr. 1979.

[WAGNER 69]   Wagner, R. E., "Fluidics—A New Control Tool," *IEEE Spectrum*, Vol. 6, No. 11, pp. 58–68, 1969.

[WRITER 75]   Writer, P. L., "Design for Testability," *'75 ASSC Conf. Rec.* (Automatic Support Systems Symposium for Advanced Maintainability), pp. 84–87, Oct. 1975.

4.P PROBLEMS

4.1 For the logic diagram shown in Fig. P4.1 write an expression for the function $Z(A, B, C, D, E)$.

4.2 Analyze Fig. P4.2. Write an algebraic expression for f as a function of A, B, and C.

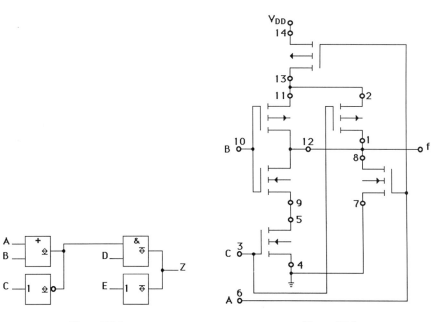

Figure P4.1   **Figure P4.2**

4.3 Analyze Fig. P4.3.
 (a) What logic family is being used?
 (b) Write an expression for $g(A, B, C, D, E)$.
 (c) Write an expression for $A(g, W)$.

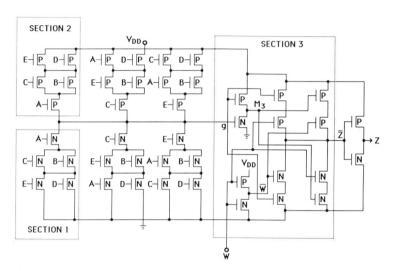

Figure P4.3

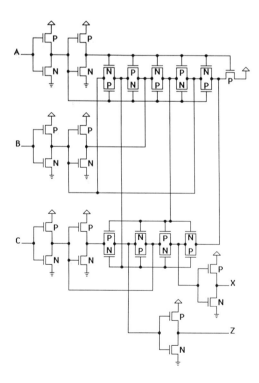

Figure P4.4

4.4 **(a)** Draw a logic diagram for the circuit shown in Fig. P4.4. (It is okay to use transmission gates).

(b) Determine functions $X(A, B, C)$ and $Z(A, B, C)$.

4.5 Write expressions for $Y(A, B)$ and $W(A, B)$ for the circuits shown in Fig. P4.5.

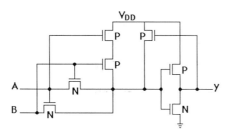

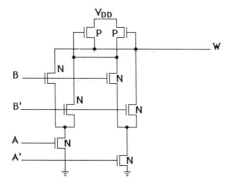

Figure P4.5

4.6 For the MOS circuit shown in Fig. P4.6:

(a) Draw an equivalent gate-level logic diagram.

(b) Write an expression for the function $Z(A, B)$.

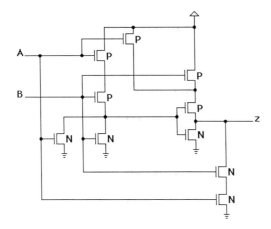

Figure P4.6

4.7 For each MOS network in Fig. P4.7:
   (a) Convert it into a NAND/NOR gate representation.
   (b) Write a simplified switching expression for the outputs f and g.

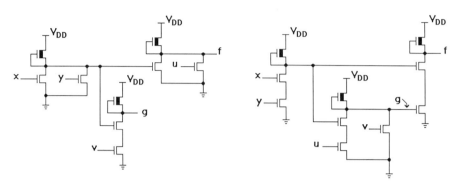

Figure P4.7

4.8 Given the logic diagram (Fig. P4.8) for a "Tally circuit" $[Z_i = 1$ iff i of (ABC) are 1$]$, draw a NMOS transistor diagram for the circuit.

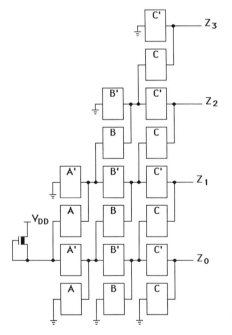

Figure P4.8

4.9 For the MOS circuits shown in Fig. P4.9:
   (a) Draw equivalent circuits using switches, gates, resistors, etc.
   (b) Write an expression for $Z(X, Y)$.

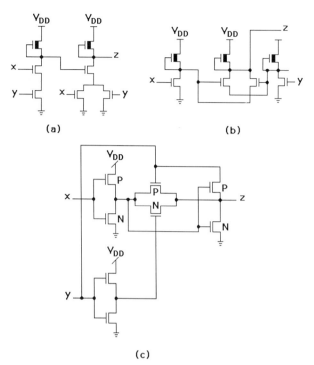

(a)

(b)

(c)

Figure P4.9

4.10 **(a)** For Fig. P4.10a, find $Z = f(X, Y)$.
   (b) For the circuit of Fig. P4.10b, fill in Table P4.10.

TABLE P4.10

X	Y	Z
0	0	
0	1	
1	1	
1	0	

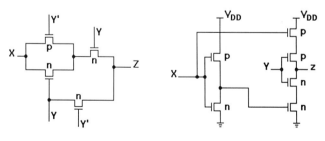

Figure P4.10a

Figure P4.10b

4.11 **(a)** Two DTL gates are wired together as shown in Fig. P4.11a. Obtain the output function F realized by this composite circuit.

(b) Obtain the output function produced by the TTL gate circuit shown in Fig. P4.11b.

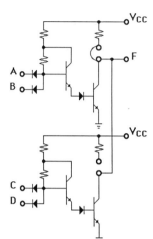

Figure P4.11a

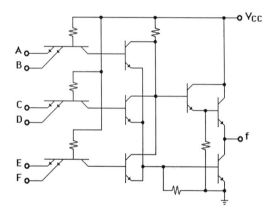

Figure P4.11b

4.12 Design an I^2L circuit to implement the NAND network of Fig. P4.12.

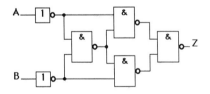

Figure P4.12

4.13 **(a)** For each of the blocks of the circuit in Fig. P4.13, specify the "logic" technology used: RTL, DTL, TTL, I^2L, or ECL.

(b) Write a Boolean expression for the output function $[y = f(a, b, c, d), z = g(a, b, c, d)]$.

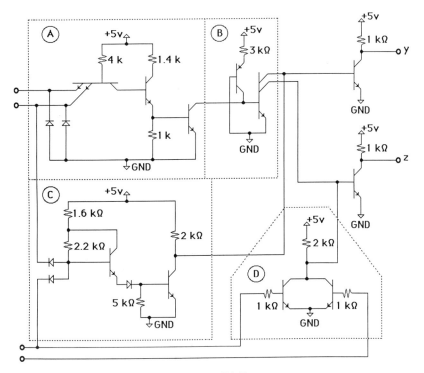

Figure P4.13

4.14 For each network shown in Fig. P4.14, specify the logic family and give an expression for the output z in terms of the inputs A, B, C, and D.

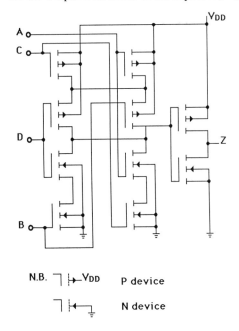

N.B. ⊐|–V_{DD} P device

⊐|←   N device

Figure P4.14a

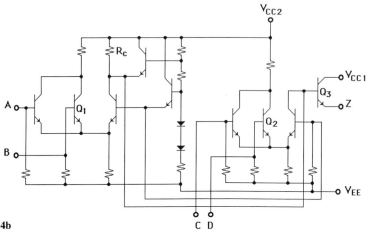

Figure P4.14b

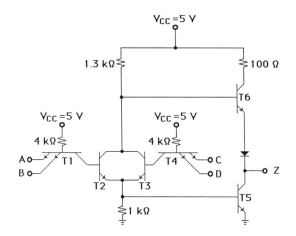

Figure P4.14c

4.15 Analyze Fig. P4.15. Write an algebraic expression for Y as a function of A and B.

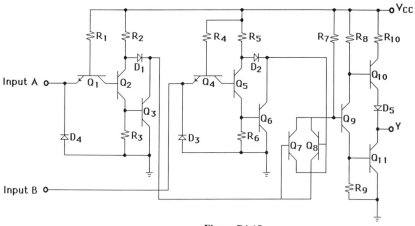

Figure P4.15

4.16 For the I²L circuit shown in Fig. P4.16:
(a) Draw the equivalent circuit using standard gate symbols.

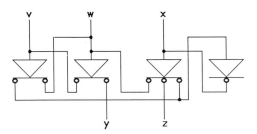

Figure P4.16

(b) Draw an equivalent transistor-level circuit.

4.17 For Fig. P4.17 (assume that A voltage is compatible with V_{bb1}, B voltage is compatible with V_{bb2}):
(a) What is the logic family?
(b) Write expressions for f_1 and f_2.

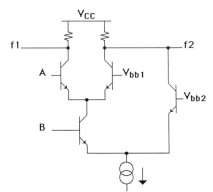

Figure P4.17

SWITCHING ALGEBRA: SPECIAL PROPERTIES

5.1 INTRODUCTION

Some switching functions have very special properties. For example, if a function is totally symmetric, any network realization can have its inputs unlabeled since they all interchangeable. If a function is frontal, it can be realized with AND and OR gates without any inverters. Functions with special properties can be represented, and often realized, more easily than arbitrary general functions. Because of these benefits, a number of classes of special switching functions have been identified and their properties studied. One of the aims of this chapter is to introduce the basic concepts of special functions. To maintain perspective it should be mentioned that while most switching functions do not have any of the special properties discussed [Shannon 49], many of the functions actually used in practical systems do have some special property.

The other aim of this chapter is to investigate a special property of all networks: the Boolean difference of a function f with respect to one of its independent variables x. The Boolean difference gives those values of the other (non-x) independent variables for which the function value will be determined by x. The reason for studying the Boolean difference is its importance in deriving tests to determine whether any faults are present in a network. Testing networks for faults is a very important topic, which will be discussed in Chap. 6.

5.2 SYMMETRIC FUNCTIONS

A **symmetric function** is one in which each of the input variables plays the same role in determining the value of the function. The majority function and the parity function are important symmetric functions. The **majority function** is defined by requiring that it be 1 only when more than half of the input variables are 1. (It is most often used for odd numbers of input variables.) This is a very important function since it is the function for the carry in binary addition and the "voter" function used in fault-tolerant computers.

The (odd) **parity function** is 1 only if an odd number of the inputs are 1. It is the sum function for binary addition and is used in the most important error detecting or correcting code circuits.

Many functions are not symmetric: $f = x + y'z$ is not. In fact, if a function were chosen at random from all possible switching functions, it is extremely likely that it would not be symmetric. Of course, the functions used in realizing computers and other digital systems are not randomly chosen. Many important functions used in real systems are symmetric. A formal definition of a symmetric function is:

DEFINITION. A function $f(x_1, x_2, \ldots, x_n)$ is **totally symmetric** iff it is unchanged by any permutation of its variables.

Examples. The three-variable majority function: $f = xy + xz + yz$. The two-variable parity function: $f = xy' + x'y$.

One of the benefits of dealing with symmetric functions as such rather than treating them as arbitrary functions is that it is much simpler to specify a symmetric function than an arbitrary function. For symmetric functions it is sufficient to specify how many of the inputs must be 1 for the function to be 1. This is stated formally as the following theorem.

THEOREM 5.2-1. $f(x_1, x_2, \ldots, x_n)$ is totally symmetric iff it can be specified by stating a list of integers $A = \{a_1, a_2, \ldots, a_m\}$, $0 \le a_j \le n$ so that $f = 1$ iff exactly a_j of the variables are 1.

Examples. For the three-variable majority function, $f = xy + xz + yz$, $A = \{2, 3\}$; for the two-variable parity function, $f = xy' + x'y$, $A = \{1\}$.

The customary notation for symmetric functions uses the symbol S to indicate a symmetric function and adds the list A as subscripts to S to indicate the specific function described.

DEFINITION. The symbol S_A is used to indicate a symmetric function. Thus $S_1(x, y) = xy' + x'y$ (sum modulo 2, exclusive or), and $S_{2,3}(x, y, z) = xy + xz + yz$ (carry out, majority function).

It is possible to extend the concept of symmetric function to include those functions that have symmetries involving some complemented as well as uncomplemented variables. Such functions are called mixed symmetric and are defined formally by:

DEFINITION. A function $f(x_1, x_2, \ldots, x_n)$ is **mixed symmetric** iff it is not totally symmetric, but it can be changed into a totally symmetric function by replacing some of its variables by their complements.

Example. $f = xy'z'$ is not totally symmetric, but the function—xyz—obtained by replacing y' by y and z' by z is totally symmetric. Thus, $xy'z'$ is mixed symmetric.

Notation. The symbol $S_A(x, y', z')$ is used to indicate a mixed symmetric function that becomes totally symmetric when y and z are replaced by their complements.

In many situations it isn't important to distinguish between mixed and totally symmetric functions. It is thus convenient to use the term **symmetric function** to refer to a function that is either totally or mixed symmetric.

DEFINITION. A function $f(x_1, x_2, \ldots, x_n)$ will be called **symmetric** if it is either totally or mixed symmetric.

The symmetric functions are not particularly easy to realize with multi-input gates [Epstein 58]. However, switch networks do have very efficient forms for implementing symmetric functions. Figure 5.2-1 shows a switch network for all elementary symmetric functions of two variables. An **elementary symmetric function** is a symmetric function that has only one number in the A list. That is, there is only one number of variables equal to 1 that can make the function equal to 1. This same structure can be extended directly to realize elementary symmetric functions of more variables. More general symmetric functions are realized by connecting together the network outputs that correspond to numbers in the A list, and removing those portions of the network that do not appear in any path to an

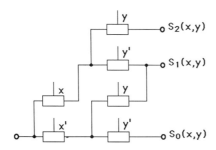

Figure 5.2-1 Switch network for all elementary symmetric functions of two variables.

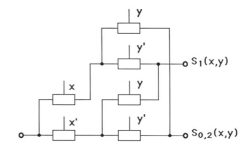

Figure 5.2-2 Switch network for even and odd parity functions of two variables.

output. Figure 5.2-2 shows the result of modifying the circuit of Fig. 5.2-1 to realize the even and odd parity functions of two variables.

Examples of the realization of these symmetric function networks using NMOS pass transistor logic are given in Sec. 3.9 of [Mead 80]. (A network that realizes all the elementary symmetric functions is called a "Tally function network" in the Mead book.)

There are many functions that are unchanged when some, but not all, of their variables are permuted. Examples of such functions are $f = x + yz$, which is unchanged by a permutation of y and z, and $f = wx + yz$, which is unchanged by an interchange of w and x or an interchange of y and z. Such functions are called partially symmetric. The function $x + yz$ is said to be partially symmetric in yz, and the function $wx + yz$ is partially symmetric in wx and in yz.

DEFINITION. A function $f(x_1, x_2, \ldots, x_n)$ is **partially symmetric** in $x_{i1}, x_{i2}, \ldots, x_{im}$ iff it is unchanged by any permutation of the variables $x_{i1}, x_{i2}, \ldots, x_{im}$.

Techniques for discovering partial symmetries have been published [McCluskey 56], but they are not of sufficiently general usefulness to be presented here. The concept of partial symmetry is of some value and will be used in later sections.

5.3 UNATE FUNCTIONS

The fact that any arbitrary switching function could be realized by a network of either gates or switches was demonstrated in Chap. 2. However, this demonstration assumed double-rail logic: for each variable two signals were assumed to be available: one for the uncomplemented variable and one for the complement of the variable. The present section concerns the use of single-rail logic and, in particular, the identification of those functions that can be implemented with single-rail inputs using only AND gates and OR gates. This is a special situation since any complete gate set can realize inversion and can thus obtain the complementary signals from single-rail inputs. However, there do exist applications in which inversion is very expensive to implement; for example, in the internal decoding circuitry of a RAM.[1] The use of single-rail rather than double-rail signals is very common: Single-rail signals require fewer chip pins and less interconnect.

5.3-1 Classification of Variables

Figure 5.3-1 shows a circuit to convert from the 8421 binary-coded-decimal code to the 242*1 binary-coded-decimal code. (These codes are discussed in Sec. 1.3.)

---

[1] A RAM is a random-access memory. It will be discussed in Chap. 6.

The functions realized by this circuit are

$$C_2 = (b_8 + b_4)(b_8 + b_2 + b_1) = b_8 + b_4b_2 + b_4b_1$$

$$C_4 = (b_8 + b_4)(b_8 + b_2 + b_1') = b_8 + b_4b_2 + b_4b_1'$$

$$C_2^* = (b_4' + b_2')(b_8 + b_4 + b_2)(b_8 + b_2 + b_1)$$

$$= b_8b_4' + b_8b_2' + b_4'b_2 + b_4b_2'b_1$$

$$C_1 = b_1$$

Consider the function C_4. Whenever b_8 or b_4 or b_2 change from 0 to 1, the C_4 output must either change from 0 to 1 or else remain unchanged. This relationship is described by saying that the function C_4 is **positive** in b_8, positive in b_4, and positive in b_2. When b_1 changes from 0 to 1, the C_4 output must either change in the opposite sense (from 1 to 0) or else remain unchanged. Because of this relation the function C_4 is said to be **negative** in b_1. These terms are defined formally as follows:

DEFINITION. A function $f(x_1, x_2, \ldots, x_n)$ is **positive** in x_i iff it is possible to write a sum-of-products expression for f in which x_i' does not appear.

DEFINITION. A function $f(x_1, x_2, \ldots, x_n)$ is **negative** in x_i iff it is possible to write a sum-of-products expression for f in which x_i does not appear.

The function C_2 is positive in all of the variables b_8, b_4, b_2, b_1. The function C_2^* is positive in b_8 and b_1, and the function C_1 is positive in b_1.

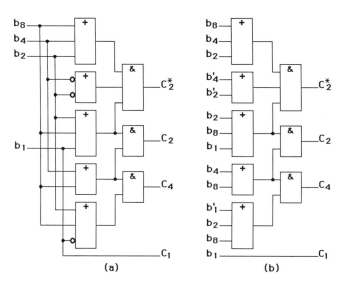

Figure 5.3-1 Circuit to convert 8421 binary-coded decimal to 242*1 binary-coded decimal: (a) single-rail inputs; (b) double-rail inputs.

Switching Algebra: Special Properties   Chap. 5

The C_1 output will never change in response to a change in b_8 or b_4 or b_2 since none of these inputs are connected to C_1. This situation is described formally by saying that C_1 is vacuous in b_8 and b_4 and b_2 (or independent of b_8 and b_4 and b_2).

DEFINITION. A function $f(x_1, x_2, \ldots, x_n)$ is **vacuous** in x_i iff it is possible to write a sum-of-products expression for f in which neither x_i nor x_i' appear.

Note that if a function is vacuous in x_i, it is (trivially) both positive and negative in x_i. A function can't be vacuous in all of its variables unless it is one of the constant functions: $f = 0$ or $f = 1$. Those variables that do determine the value of f are called essential for f.

DEFINITION. If a function $f(x_1, x_2, \ldots, x_n)$ is not vacuous in x_i, then x_i is said to be **essential** for f.

If a function depends on both x_i and x_i', it is mixed in x_i. C_2^* is mixed in b_2 and in b_4.

DEFINITION. A function $f(x_1, x_2, \ldots, x_n)$ is **mixed** in x_i iff it is not possible to write a sum-of-products expression for f in which x_i and x_i' do not both appear.

Table 5.3-1 gives an example of how this variable classification scheme applies to the function $f(w, x, y, z) = wx + w'z'$. Figure 5.3-2 shows a network for this function with particular attention to the variable x. Since f is positive in x, when x changes from 0 to 1 the network output can either remain unchanged (the case when $w = 0$) or can change from 0 to 1 (as happens when $w = 1$).

TABLE 5.3-1 Example
of variable classification
for $f(w, x, y, z) =$
$wx + w'z'$

Essential	w, x, z
Vacuous	y
Positive	x, y
Negative	z, y
Mixed	w

Residues. The function that is obtained from setting one of the variables, say x_i, equal to 1 is called the x_i-residue. If x_i is set equal to 0, the resulting function is called the x_i'-residue. This is illustrated in Fig. 5.3-3. A formal definition follows.

DEFINITION. For a function $f(x_1, x_2, \ldots, x_n)$ define the x_i-residue as

$$f_{x_i}(x_1, x_2, \ldots, x_n) = f(x_1, x_2, \ldots, x_i = 1, \ldots, x_n)$$

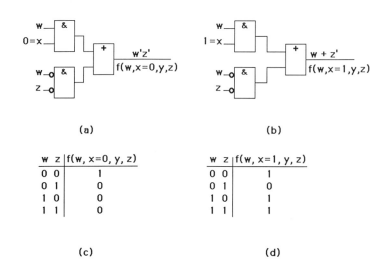

Figure 5.3-2 Network for $f(w, x, y, z) = wx + w'z'$: (a) input x set to 0; (b) input x set to 1; (c) table of combinations for $f(w, x = 0, y, z)$; (d) table of combinations for $f(w, x = 1, y, z)$.

and the x_i'-**residue** as

$$f_{x_i'}(x_1, x_2, \ldots, x_n) = f(x_1, x_2, \ldots, x_i = 0, \ldots, x_n)$$

The residue notation will be used in the following sections when the Boolean difference and threshold functions are considered. The expansion theorems T15 and T15′ shown in Table 2.5-3 can be restated using the residue notation as

$$(\text{T15}) \; f(X_1, X_2, \ldots, X_i, \ldots, X_n) = X_i f_{X_i} + X_i' f_{X_i'}$$

$$(\text{T15}') \; f(X_1, X_2, \ldots, X_i, \ldots, X_n) = [X_i + f_{X_i'}][X_i' + f_{X_i}]$$

Example 5.3-1

Let $f(w, x, y, z) = (w' + x)(w + y')(w + z')$; then

$f_w(w, x, y, z) = x$	$f_{w'}(w, x, y, z) = y'z'$
$f_x(w, x, y, z) = (w + y')(w + z')$	$f_{x'}(w, x, y, z) = w'y'z'$
$f_y(w, x, y, z) = wx$	$f_{y'}(w, x, y, z) = (w' + x)(w + z')$
$f_z(w, x, y, z) = wx$	$f_{z'}(w, x, y, z) = (w' + x)(w + y')$

Since $f = wf_w + w'f_{w'}$, $f(w, x, y, z)$ can be written as $wx + w'y'z'$.

As discussed above, if a function $f(X_1, X_2, \ldots, X_n)$ is positive in X_i, the function value cannot change from 0 to 1 in response to a change in X_i from 1 to 0. This relation can be stated in terms of the residues by saying that the X_i'-residue cannot be 1 for a set of input values for which the X_i-residue is 0. This is illustrated in Fig. 5.3-2 by the fact that the only row of Fig. 5.3-2c with a 1-output also has a 1-output in the corresponding row of Fig. 5.3-2d.

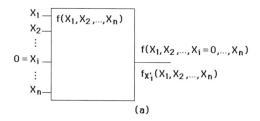

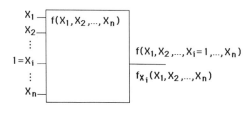

(a)

(b)

Figure 5.3-3 Illustration of residues:
(a) X_i'-residue; (b) X_i-residue.

DEFINITION. Suppose that there are two functions, say $f(X_1, X_2, \ldots, X_n)$ and $g(X_1, X_2, \ldots, X_n)$, for which it is true that whenever $f(X_1, X_2, \ldots, X_n) = 1$, $g(X_1, X_2, \ldots, X_n)$ is also 1. This relation between the pair of functions is expressed by saying that f **implies** g (written $f \Rightarrow g$) or that g **includes** f (written $g \supset f$) or that f is included in g (written $f \subset g$).

Thus $xy \Rightarrow x + y$, since xy is 1 when x and y are both 1; and for these values of x and y, the function $x + y$ is 1. If two functions are equal (they are both 0 or both 1 for all possible input values), either one of the functions can be said to imply the other.

THEOREM 5.3-1. $f(X_1, X_2, \ldots, X_n) = g(X_1, X_2, \ldots, X_n)$ iff $f(X_1, X_2, \ldots, X_n) \Rightarrow g(X_1, X_2, \ldots, X_n)$ and $g(X_1, X_2, \ldots, X_n) \Rightarrow f(X_1, X_2, \ldots, X_n)$.

Testing a pair of functions to determine whether either implies the other can, in principle, be done by comparing their tables of combinations. This is often a tedious technique that is better replaced by tests based on the following theorem.

THEOREM 5.3-2. $f(X_1, X_2, \ldots, X_n) \Rightarrow g(X_1, X_2, \ldots, X_n)$ iff

$$f(X_1, X_2, \ldots, X_n) + g(X_1, X_2, \ldots, X_n) = g(X_1, X_2, \ldots, X_n)$$

and

$$f(X_1, X_2, \ldots, X_n)g(X_1, X_2, \ldots, X_n) = f(X_1, X_2, \ldots, X_n)$$

Example
(a) $f(w, x, y, z) = x$, $g(w, x, y, z) = y'z'$. Since $fg = xy'z' \neq f$ or g, neither f nor g implies the other.

(b) $g(w, x, y, z) = (w + y')(w + z')$, $f(w, x, y, z) = w'y'z'$. $fg = f$, so $f \Rightarrow g$.

(c) $g(w, x, y, z) = wx$, $f(w, x, y, z) = (w' + x)(w + z')$. $fg = g$, so $g \Rightarrow f$.

This relation is directly analogous to the concepts of material implication and set inclusion as presented in Sec. 2.7. The relation of implication forms the basis for a method for testing a function to determine the classification of its variables.

THEOREM 5.3-3

(a) $f_{x_i} = f_{x_i'}$ iff f is vacuous in x_i.

(b) $f_{x_i} \Rightarrow f_{x_i'}$ iff f is negative in x_i.

(c) $f_{x_i'} \Rightarrow f_{x_i}$ iff f is positive in x_i.

(d) f_{x_i} and $f_{x_i'}$ not compatible ($f_{x_i} \not\Rightarrow f_{x_i'}$ and $f_{x_i'} \not\Rightarrow f_{x_i}$) iff f is mixed in x_i.

Example. Let $f(w, x, y, z) = (w' + x)(w + y')(w + z')$; then

$$f_w(w, x, y, z) = x \qquad\qquad f_{w'}(w, x, y, z) = y'z'$$

$$f_x(w, x, y, z) = (w + y')(w + z') \qquad f_{x'}(w, x, y, z) = w'y'z'$$

$$f_y(w, x, y, z) = wx \qquad\qquad f_{y'}(w, x, y, z) = (w' + x)(w + z')$$

$$f_z(w, x, y, z) = wx \qquad\qquad f_{z'}(w, x, y, z) = (w' + x)(w + y')$$

f_w and $f_{w'}$ not compatible $\qquad$ f is mixed in w

$f_{x'} \Rightarrow f_x$ $\qquad$ f is positive in x

$f_y \Rightarrow f_{y'}$ $\qquad$ f is negative in y

$f_z \Rightarrow f_{z'}$ $\qquad$ f is negative in z

5.3-2 Classification of Functions

A function such as C_2 (Fig. 5.3-1) can be realized with single-rail inputs using only AND gates and OR gates since it is positive in all its variables. Such a function is called frontal.[2]

DEFINITION. A function $f(x_1, x_2, \ldots, x_n)$ is a **frontal** function iff it is positive in all its variables.

---

[2] The term *frontal* was used to describe this class of function when it was first studied to determine the value of a relay invented at Bell Telephone Laboratories. The relay could be built very inexpensively, but it had only contacts that closed when the relay operated. Such contacts are called "front" contacts, hence the term *frontal* [Gilbert 54].

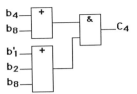

Figure 5.3-4 Inverter-free network for $C_4 = (b_8 + b_4)(b_8 + b_2 + b_1')$.

Some writers use **monotone increasing** as a synonym for frontal. The carry function for a binary full adder, $ab + ac + bc$, is an example of a very common and useful frontal function.

The C_4 function is not frontal since it depends on b_1'. Figure 5.3-4 shows that it is still possible to realize C_4 with an inverter-free network using only one signal per input variable. Any function that can be realized with this type of network is called a unate function.

DEFINITION. A function $f(x_1, x_2, \ldots, x_n)$ is a **unate function** iff it is positive or negative in each of its variables.

All frontal functions are automatically unate. It is also possible to have a function that is negative in all its variables. Such functions are called backal.

DEFINITION. A function $f(x_1, x_2, \ldots, x_n)$ is a **backal function** iff it is negative in each of its variables.

Any unate function can be represented by an expression in which no variable appears both primed and unprimed. (Of course, other expressions are also possible; for example, $f = x + y = x + x'y$.)

DEFINITION. A Boolean expression is unate iff each variable appears only primed or unprimed but not both.

Unate functions are of most interest in connection with the study of threshold functions, which are the subject of Sec. 5.4.

Frontal functions were first discussed in [Gilbert 54]. The earliest survey of the properties of unate functions appears in [McNaughton 61]. Other text presentations of unate functions can be found in Sec. 6.6 of [Harrison 65], Sec. 7.2 of [Kohavi 70], and Sec. 16.9 of [Hill 81].

5.4 THRESHOLD FUNCTIONS

The majority function is an example of a "threshold function," a function whose value depends on whether the (arithmetic) sum of the values of its inputs exceeds a "threshold." The 3-variable majority function is given by $f(x, y, z) = xy + xz + yz$. It is equal to 1 iff a majority (2 or more) of the inputs are equal to 1. The class of threshold functions can be considered a generalization of the usual AND, NAND,

OR, and NOR gate functions. These gates realize threshold functions with the threshold equal to either 1 or n (number of input variables). Threshold functions are formally defined as follows.

DEFINITION. A **threshold function** is one that can be defined by a system of inequalities:

$$f(X) = 1 \text{ iff } a_1 x_1 + a_2 x_2 + \cdots + a_n x_n \geq T$$

The a_i are the weights, T is the threshold value, and the $+$ is an arithmetic sum rather than a Boolean OR. Because the definition is in terms of linear inequalities, threshold functions are often called **linearly separable functions**.

Example

$a_1 = a_2 = 1, T = 2; f = 1 \text{ iff } x_1 + x_2 \geq 2; f = x_1 x_2$

$a_1 = a_2 = 1, T = 1; f = 1 \text{ iff } x_1 + x_2 \geq 1; f = x_1 + x_2$

$a_1 = a_2 = a_3 = 1, T = 2; f = 1 \text{ iff } x_1 + x_2 + x_3 \geq 2; f = x_1 x_2 + x_1 x_3 + x_2 x_3$

$a_1 = 2, a_2 = a_3 = 1, T = \frac{3}{2}; f = 1 \text{ iff } 2x_1 + x_2 + x_3 \geq \frac{3}{2}; f = x_1 + x_2 x_3$

Figure 5.4-1a shows the IEEE standard symbol for a threshold gate with all input weights equal to 1. The standard does not have any symbol for a threshold gate with weights other than 1. It is possible to construct a symbol for a threshold function with more general weights by tying together several inputs.[3] Using several gate inputs for a single variable can result in a cumbersome symbol, so the non-standard symbol of Fig. 5.4-1b will be used as a "shorthand" for a threshold gate with weights not equal to 1.

Since threshold functions realize more complex functions than the standard integrated circuit gate functions, systems could be implemented with fewer threshold gates than with standard gates. Designs for integrated-circuit threshold gates have been proposed, but none has yet been a commercial success [Dao 77]. It has not been possible to produce sufficiently reliable gates with thresholds other than 1 or n. The difficulty is in controlling the variations in the parameters that determine the weights and threshold values.

Another use of threshold functions has been for modeling nerve nets and brain organization [Glorioso 80]. Because of the possibility of varying the threshold values, they have been used in connection with models for learning systems, adaptive systems, self-repairing systems, pattern recognition systems, etc.

In spite of the lack of practical realizations of threshold gates, their properties have been studied extensively. There are many publications about threshold func-

---

[3] To obtain a weight of 2 for the X_1 input, it would be required to connect X_1 to two gate inputs. A weight of 3 would be obtained by connecting X_1 to three gate inputs, etc. Any threshold function can be represented in this way because it can be proved that any threshold function can be obtained with integer weights.

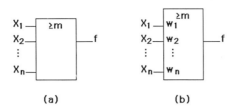

Figure 5.4-1 Threshold gate symbols: (a) all weights equal to 1; (b) weights not equal to 1.

tions, including [Dertouzos 65], [Lewis 67], and [Muroga 71]. The problem that has received most attention is that of determining whether an arbitrary switching function can be realized by a single threshold gate (i.e., determining whether a given switching function is a threshold function). In a sense this is a trivial problem: It is always possible to write the inequalities corresponding to a switching function, and then to determine the solution or the fact that no solution exists. This technique is illustrated in the following examples.

Example 5.4-1

A threshold gate realization is to be found for the function $f(x, y, z) = x(y + z)$. The table of combinations and the corresponding inequalities are:

	x	y	z	f			x	y	z	f	
(0)	0	0	0	0		(4)	1	0	0	0	$a_x < T$
(1)	0	0	1	0	$a_z < T$	(5)	1	0	1	1	$a_x + a_z \geq T$
(2)	0	1	0	0	$a_y < T$	(6)	1	1	0	1	$a_x + a_y \geq T$
(3)	0	1	1	0	$a_y + a_z < T$	(7)	1	1	1	1	$a_x + a_y + a_z \geq T$

By combining inequalities it can be shown that all coefficients must be positive:

From (5) and (4): $a_x + a_z \geq T > a_x \Rightarrow a_x + a_z > a_x \Rightarrow a_z > 0$

From (5) and (1): $a_x + a_z \geq T > a_z \Rightarrow a_x + a_z > a_z \Rightarrow a_x > 0$

From (6) and (4): $a_x + a_y \geq T > a_x \Rightarrow a_x + a_y > a_x \Rightarrow a_y > 0$

For positive coefficients, inequalities (1) and (2) are redundant since they are implied by (3). Similarly, (7) is implied by (6). The remaining inequalities are

$$a_x + a_y \geq T > a_y + a_z$$

$$a_x + a_z \geq T > a_x$$

Formal linear programming techniques exist for solving such inequalities, but these are so simple that a solution can be easily guessed: $a_x = 2$, $a_y = a_z = 1$, $T = 2.5$.

Example 5.4-2

A threshold gate realization is to be found for the function $f(x, y) = xy' + x'y$. The table of combinations and the corresponding inequalities are:

x	y	f	
0	0	0	
0	1	1	$a_y \geq T$
1	0	1	$a_x \geq T$
1	1	0	$a_x + a_y < T$

Clearly, there is no solution to this set of inequalities, so the function is not a threshold function.

While this procedure is straightforward, it is not very practical for functions with many input variables. For 8 inputs, 256 inequalities follow from the table of combinations. In general, n variables require 2^n inequalities. The solution of such large set of inequalities is a challenging computation. Also, this approach does not give any insight into the properties of threshold functions that might be useful for designers. As a result, a lot of research has been aimed at finding a simple design technique for threshold functions. This search has not been successful, but a number of very useful properties of threshold functions have been discovered. The most important of these are that all threshold functions are unate, but not all unate functions are threshold functions [Paull 60].

Since there are as yet no practical threshold gates, the discussion of threshold function properties will not be extensive. However, it does seem worthwhile to discuss some of the most basic of these properties. The search for practical threshold devices still continues and may yet be successful.

PROPERTY 1. All threshold functions are unate.

Consider an n-input threshold gate and assume that values are assigned to each of the n inputs. Suppose further than a_1 is positive and that X_1 is 0. If X_1 is changed to 1, the value of the sum

$$\sum_{i=1}^{n} a_i X_i$$

must increase. Thus if the sum was greater than T with $X_1 = 0$, it will remain greater than T for $X_1 = 1$ and f will be 1 for both values of X_1. If the sum was less than T for $X_1 = 0$, it will either remain less than T for $X_1 = 1$ or will become greater than T for $X_1 = 1$. Thus f will either be 0 for both values of X_1 or will change from 0 to 1 as X_1 changes from 0 to 1. In summary, as X_1 changes from 0 to 1, f will either remain unchanged or will change from 0 to 1 also. This is precisely the condition for f to be positive in X_1, as described in Sec. 5.3.

If a_1 is negative, a similar experiment will demonstrate that f must be negative in X_1. The same conditions apply to all the other variables so that f must be either positive or negative in all its variables and hence must be unate.

PROPERTY 2. Some unate functions are not threshold functions.

Consider the function $f = uv + yz$. For this function to be a threshold function, the following inequalities must be satisfied by the weights:

$$a_u + a_v \geq T \qquad a_y + a_z \geq T$$

$$a_u + a_y < T \qquad a_v + a_z < T$$

These can be rewritten as follows:

$$a_u + a_v \geq T, a_u + a_y < T \Rightarrow a_u + a_v > a_u + a_y \Rightarrow a_v > a_y$$

$$a_y + a_z \geq T, a_v + a_z < T \Rightarrow a_y + a_z > a_v + a_z \Rightarrow a_y > a_v$$

Since a_v cannot be both greater than and less than a_y, there are no values of the weights that satisfy the inequalities and thus no threshold function realization of $f = uv + yz$. This is one example of a unate function that is not a threshold function. For n less than 4, all unate functions are threshold functions. There are many unate functions that are not threshold functions for $n \geq 4$.

The following properties will be stated without proof. The proofs are rather straightforward and will be left to the problems.

PROPERTY 3. Threshold functions don't have unique weights. In fact, any threshold function can be expressed with integer weights and threshold.

PROPERTY 4. All members of the same symmetry class as a threshold function are threshold functions. Both the complement and the dual of a threshold function are threshold functions.

PROPERTY 5. If $a_i = a_j$, then f is partially symmetric in x_i and x_j.

5.5 BOOLEAN DIFFERENCE

The Boolean difference is not another special property of switching functions. Rather, it is a technique that is used in connection with testing logic networks. It is appropriate to consider the Boolean difference here because it is based on the residues that were discussed in the previous sections of this chapter. The Boolean difference of a function $f(X_1, X_2, \ldots, X_n)$ with respect to one of the independent variables, X_i, is written as $df(X_1, X_2, \ldots, X_n)/dX_i$, and is defined as the EXCLUSIVE OR of f_{X_i} and $f_{X'_i}$. The motivation for this definition will be explained by referring to Fig. 5.3-2, which is repeated here as Fig. 5.5-1.

Suppose that the x input is suspected of being faulty. (Perhaps the bonding wire between the x pin and the IC bonding pad is broken.) A reasonable test for this condition would be to change the signal on x and observe the f output to see

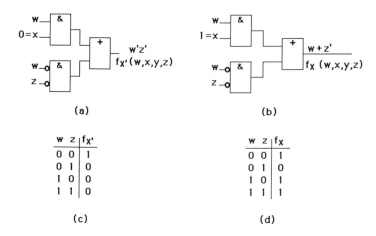

Figure 5.5-1 Network for $f(w, x, y, z) = wx + w'z'$: (a) input x set to 0; (b) input x set to 1; (c) table of combinations for $f_{x'}(w, z)$; (d) table of combinations for $f_x(w, z)$.

whether f changes in response to the x change. Of course, the other input signals must be held fixed at values that make f dependent on x. If f is not vacuous in x, such values must exist. Comparison of Fig. 5.5-1a and b shows that with w fixed at 1, the output f will have the same value as the x input. For a general network it is necessary to find those values of the non-x variables for which the output f is different when $x = 0$ from the output with $x = 1$. The function realized by a network with $x = 0$ is given by $f_{x'}$, and by f_x when $x = 1$. The EXCLUSIVE-OR of these two residues will be 1 when the two residues have different values. The values of the non-x inputs that make $f_x \oplus f_{x'} = 1$ are the values that must be used for testing x. For the network of Fig. 5.5-1, this is: $w'z' \oplus (w + z') = w$. This algebraic calculation confirms the result obtained by inspection of the figure.

The usefulness of the EXCLUSIVE-OR of the residues leads to the following formal definition of the Boolean difference.

DEFINITION. The Boolean difference of a function f with respect to the independent variable x_i is defined as

$df(x_1, x_2, \ldots, x_n)/dx_i$

$$= f(x_1, x_2, \ldots, x_i = 0, \ldots, x_n) \oplus f(x_1, x_2, \ldots, x_i = 1, \ldots, x_n)$$

Example. For the function, $f = yz + y'(w + x)$, the residues and Boolean differences for each of the independent variables are

$$f_{w'} = yz + xy' \qquad f_w = y' + z \qquad df/dw = x'y'$$

$$f_{x'} = wy' + yz \qquad f_x = y' + z \qquad df/dx = w'y'$$

$$f_{y'} = w + x \qquad f_y = z \qquad df/dy = w'x'z + (w + x)z'$$

$$f_{z'} = (w + x)y' \qquad f_z = w + x + y \qquad df/dz = y$$

As an example of the calculation of the Boolean differences, the derivation of df/dw is given next.

$$df/dw = (yz + xy') \oplus (y' + z) = (y + x)(y' + z) \oplus (y' + z)$$

$$= (y' + z)x'y' \quad \text{by identity 10 of Table 2.6-1}$$

$$= x'y'$$

The Boolean difference is not used directly for practical test pattern generation. (The subject of testing will be discussed in greater detail in Chap. 6.) The usefulness of the Boolean difference is as a tool for theoretical studies of testing and checking methods [Sellers 68]. Even for these applications the algebraic manipulations required for the Boolean difference can be very tedious and error prone. Two approaches have been tried for making the Boolean difference easier to use: the development of algebraic properties of the Boolean difference that permit "shortcuts" in its use, and the use of tabular methods that are more suitable for computer implementation. The algebraic properties are listed in Table 5.5-1. They will not be discussed further since skill in using the Boolean difference is not one of the objectives of this text.

TABLE 5.5-1 Properties of the Boolean difference

1. If $df/dx_i = 0$, f is independent of x_i
   If $df/dx_i = 1$, f depends on x_i for all values of the other x_j
2. Complements: $df/dx_i = df'/dx_i$; $df/dx_i = df/dx_i'$
3. Two independent variables: $d(df/dx_j)/dx_i = d(df/dx_i)/dx_j$
4. Products: $d[f(X)g(X)]/dx_i = f(X)[dg(X)/dx_i] \oplus g(X)[df(X)/dx_i] \oplus [df(X)/dx_i \, dg(X)/dx_i]$
5. Sums: $d[f(X) + g(X)]/dx_i = f'(X)[dg(X)/dx_i] \oplus g'(X)[df(X)/dx_i] \oplus [df(X)/dx_i \, dg(X)/dx_i]$

5.6 DECOMPOSITION

A common and often very effective approach to design is to decompose a large problem into a number of smaller problems. This process is repeated until the small problems are easily solved. The original design is obtained by combining the small designs. This technique is frequently used in designing computers and other digital systems. For example, the design of a computer is typically done by designing an arithmetic-logic unit, a control unit, etc., and then combining the individual units into the complete system. This is not a formal process, but rather a design approach on the system level.

There have been attempts to develop synthesis techniques for combinational and sequential circuits based on this same general approach of decomposing the design problem into a number of smaller design problems. The general problem of combinational circuit synthesis will be discussed in Chap. 6. The decomposition theory for such circuits is presented here since this approach requires that the function being designed have special properties. The tests for these properties are based on the function residues used in connection with the tests for unateness and threshold functions.

During the fifties there was a substantial research effort to find synthesis techniques for combinational circuits. This research was only partially successful. Techniques were found for designing minimal two-stage networks (these are presented in Chap. 6), but the general problem of designing the "best" circuit automatically remains unsolved. With the increasing emphasis on automated design and the availability of much greater computer power, attention is again being directed to this synthesis problem. One of the approaches studied in the fifties for combinational circuit synthesis is based on decomposition. While this did not produce the hoped-for general design technique, decomposition theory is of some use for MSI or standard-cell design using multiplexers (described in Chap. 10). The basic ideas of decomposition theory will be presented here. The best source for the full details of this theory is [Curtis 62].

As an example of combinational circuit decomposition, consider the situation shown in Fig. 5.6-1. Part (a) shows a network for realizing $f(w, x, y, z) = \Sigma(0, 5, 7, 9, 11, 12) = w'xz + w'x'y'z' + wx'z + wxy'z'$ by interconnecting two subnetworks in the general structure of Fig. 5.6-1b. The basic question addressed by decomposition theory is that of determining whether a given function can be realized by a circuit having the type of structure shown in Fig. 5.6-1b.

Before developing the general theory, the specific circuit of Fig. 5.6-1 will be studied to develop some insight into the techniques involved. Figure 5.6-2 shows the circuit of Fig. 5.6-1b with the inputs y and z both equal to 0. The network structure constrains the circuit output to equal 0, 1, $g(w, x)$, or $g'(w, x)$. This restriction on the circuit output is true for any pair of values applied to y and z. An arbitrary function can be tested to see whether it can be implemented by a structure such as Fig. 5.6-1b by checking the functions realized when y and z are fixed.

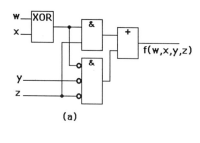

(a)

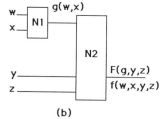

(b)

Figure 5.6-1 Example of combinational circuit decomposition: (a) circuit for $f(w, x, y, z) = \Sigma(0, 5, 7, 9, 11, 12) = w'xz + w'x'y'z' + wx'z + wxy'z'$; (b) circuit structure.

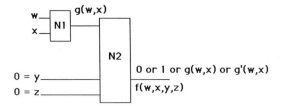

Figure 5.6-2 Network of Fig. 5.6-1b with 0's applied to the y and z inputs.

For example, the function of Fig. 5.6-1a is $f(w, x, y, z) = w'xz + w'x'y'z' + wx'z + wxy'z'$. This function takes on the following forms when the inputs y and z have fixed values:

$$f(w, x, 0, 0) = w'x' + wx = g(w, x) \qquad f(w, x, 0, 1) = w'x + wx' = g'(w, x)$$

$$f(w, x, 1, 0) = 0 \qquad\qquad\qquad f(w, x, 1, 1) = w'x + wx' = g'(w, x)$$

Since only 0, g, and g' occur, this verifies that f can be realized with the structure of Fig. 5.6-1b.

It is possible to use this same technique to determine whether the same general structure is possible for this function with a different pair of variables connected to the N2 network. If w and x were connected to N2 instead of y and z, the corresponding expressions are

$$f(0, 0, y, z) = y'z' \qquad f(0, 1, y, z) = z$$

$$f(1, 0, y, z) = z \qquad f(1, 1, y, z) = y'z'$$

Since z and $y'z'$ are not complements, this shows that it is not possible to realize the function of Fig. 5.6-1a with the structure of Fig. 5.6-1b if w and x are connected to N2 instead of y and z.

Residues. The expressions such as $f(0, 0, y, z)$ that occur in the previous example are generalizations of the residues introduced in Sec. 5.3. The results of decomposition theory are most conveniently presented in terms of these generalized residues. To simplify the statement of the following definitions and theorems, capital letters will be used to represent sets of variables and lowercase letters for individual variables. For example, X will be used to represent the set of variables $x_1, x_2, \ldots, x_n$. X^* will be used for the corresponding set of literals.

DEFINITION. Let $X = x_1, x_2, \ldots, x_n$ and $Y = y_1, y_2, \ldots, y_m$ be a subset of X. The residue $f_{Y^*}(X)$ is defined as the function obtained from $f(X)$ by setting to 1 those variables that correspond to unprimed variables in Y^* and to 0 those variables that correspond to primed variables in Y^*.

For example, if $f(u, v, w, x, y, z) = uvw + x'y'z'$, then $f_{ux'z} = f(u = 1, v, w, x = 0, y, z = 1) = vw$ and $f_{vy'z'} = f(u, v = 1, w, x, y = 0, z = 0) = uw + x'$.

Simple Disjoint Decompositions. Fig. 5.6-3 shows the result of generalizing the network structure of Fig. 5.6-1b to n input variables. Any function that can be realized by a network such as this is said to have a **simple disjoint decomposition**. It must be possible to write an expression of the form $F(g[Y], Z)$ for any such function. This decomposition is called simple because there is only one g sub-network and is called disjoint because none of the inputs are connected to both the g and the F subnetworks.

THEOREM 5.6-1. A function $f(X)$ has a simple disjoint decomposition $F(g[Y], Z)$ iff each residue f_{Z^*} equals either 0, 1, $g[Y]$, or $g'[Y]$.

This theorem is the basis for testing a function for a simple disjoint decomposition. To determine whether a decomposition corresponding to $F(g[Y], Z)$ is possible, all the residues f_{Z^*} must be examined. To determine whether *any* decomposition exists, *all* the residues for all the $(2^n - n - 2)$ nontrivial decompositions must be tested. There are $2^n - 2$ ways to separate n variables into two nonempty sets. Of these, n corresponds to trivial partitions which have a single Y variable. [If $g(Y) = y$ or y', there is no difference between the structure of Fig. 5.6-3 and a completely general network.] This can be a prohibitive calculation for functions with many input variables. The usefulness of this theory has been mainly in connection with functions of few variables such as occur in standard cells or MSI functions.

There have been special charts, called decomposition charts, developed to make hand calculation easier [Curtis 62]. These will not be presented here since they provide little improvement over the Karnaugh map technique to be discussed next. Karnaugh maps are also used for minimization, so they are necessary for the actual design of the decomposed network. Thus by using maps for decomposition the introduction of an additional type of chart is avoided.

The Karnaugh map for $f(w, x, y, z) = \Sigma(0, 5, 7, 9, 11, 12)$ is shown in Table 5.6-1a. (This is the same function as in Fig. 5.6-1.) Table 5.6-1b shows the maps for $f_{y'}$ and f_y. The map for $f_{y'}$ is just the top two rows of the map for f. The map for f_y is the bottom two rows of the f map, but these rows have been interchanged so that the row for $z = 0$ is in the same top position as in the map for $f_{y'}$. Inspection of the f_y and $f_{y'}$ maps shows that neither function is a constant (1 or 0) and that $f_{y'} \neq f_y$ or $(f_y)'$. Thus, f cannot be written as $F(g[w, x, z], y)$.

The maps for $f_{w'}$ and f_w are shown in Table 5.6-1c. The $f_{w'}$ map consists of the first two columns of the f map. The f_w map is the two rightmost columns of

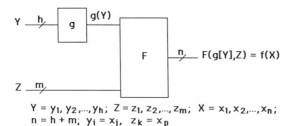

$Y = y_1, y_2,...,y_h; \quad Z = z_1, z_2,..., z_m; \quad X = x_1, x_2,...,x_n;$
$n = h + m; \quad y_i = x_j, \quad z_k = x_p$

Figure 5.6-3 Simple disjoint decomposition network.

TABLE 5.6-1 Karnaugh maps for $f(w, x, y, z) = \Sigma(0, 5, 7, 9, 11, 12)$: (a) Map for f; (b) Maps for $f_{y'}$ and f_y residues; (c) Maps for $f_{w'}$ and f_w residues; (d) Maps for $f_{x'}$ and f_x residues

(a)

wx

y	z	00	01	11	10
0	0	1	0	1	0
0	1	0	1	0	1
1	1	0	1	0	1
1	0	0	0	0	0

(b)

wx

	y	z	00	01	11	10
$f_{y'}$	0	0	1	0	1	0
		1	0	1	0	1
f_y	1	0	0	0	0	0
		1	0	1	0	1

(c)

$f_{w'}$ ($w = 0$) $\qquad$ f_w ($w = 1$)

y	z	x: 0	1	x: 0	1
0	0	1	0	0	1
0	1	0	1	1	0
1	1	0	1	1	0
1	0	0	0	0	0

(d)

$f_{x'}$ ($x = 0$) $\qquad$ f_x ($x = 1$)

y	z	w: 0	1	w: 0	1
0	0	1	0	0	1
0	1	0	1	1	0
1	1	0	1	1	0
1	0	0	0	0	0

the f map. In forming the f_w map the order of the columns has been reversed from their order in the f map. This is done to make the column for $x = 0$ the leftmost column as in the $f_{w'}$ map, for ease of comparing the two maps. Table 5.6-1c shows that f cannot be written as $F(g[x, y, z], w)$ since $f_{w'} \neq 0, 1, f_w$, or $(f_w)'$.

Table 5.6-1d shows the maps for $f_{x'}$ and f_x. They are formed from the f map analogously to the way that the $f_{w'}$ and f_w maps are formed. The $f_{x'}$ and f_x maps show that f cannot be written in the form $F(g[w, y, z], x)$. The maps for $f_{z'}$ and f_z are not shown, but they are formed the same way that the $f_{y'}$ and f_y maps are formed. As an exercise it is suggested that the reader form the $f_{z'}$ and f_z maps, and verify that $f_{z'} = y'(w \oplus x'), f_z = w \oplus x$, so that no $F(g[w, x, y], z)$ expression is possible. This concludes the demonstration that it is not possible to express f in the form $f(g[A], B)$ with B equal to a single variable. Having B consist of three variables is a trivial case since A is then a single variable. Thus, the only case remaining to be considered is when B contains two variables.

The maps for $f_{y'z'}, f_{y'z}, f_{yz'}, f_{yz}$ are shown in Table 5.6-2b. Since $(f_{y'z'})' = f_{y'z} = f_{yz} = w \oplus x$ and $f_{yz'} = 0$, f can be written as $F(w \oplus x, y, z)$ and realized as shown in Fig. 5.6-1a. Table 5.6-2c shows the maps for $f_{w'x'}, f_{w'x}, f_{wx'}, f_{wx}$. These

TABLE 5.6-2 Karnaugh maps for $f(w, x, y, z) = \Sigma(0, 5, 7, 9, 11, 12)$: (a) Map for f; (b) Maps for $f_{y \cdot z \cdot}$ residues; (c) Maps for $f_{w \cdot x \cdot}$ residues

<table>
<tr><td colspan="5" align="center">(a)
wx</td><td></td><td colspan="5" align="center">(b)
wx</td></tr>
<tr><td></td><td></td><td>00</td><td>01</td><td>11</td><td>10</td><td></td><td>00</td><td>01</td><td>11</td><td>10</td></tr>
<tr><td>y</td><td>z</td><td></td><td></td><td></td><td></td><td></td><td></td><td></td><td></td><td></td></tr>
<tr><td>0</td><td>0</td><td>1</td><td>0</td><td>1</td><td>0</td><td>$f_{y'z'}$</td><td>1</td><td>0</td><td>1</td><td>0</td></tr>
<tr><td>0</td><td>1</td><td>0</td><td>1</td><td>0</td><td>1</td><td>$f_{y'z}$</td><td>0</td><td>1</td><td>0</td><td>1</td></tr>
<tr><td>1</td><td>1</td><td>0</td><td>1</td><td>0</td><td>1</td><td>f_{yz}</td><td>0</td><td>1</td><td>0</td><td>1</td></tr>
<tr><td>1</td><td>0</td><td>0</td><td>0</td><td>0</td><td>0</td><td>$f_{yz'}$</td><td>0</td><td>0</td><td>0</td><td>0</td></tr>
</table>

<table>
<tr><td colspan="6" align="center">(c)</td></tr>
<tr><td></td><td></td><td>$f_{w'x'}$</td><td>$f_{w'x}$</td><td>f_{wx}</td><td>$f_{wx'}$</td></tr>
<tr><td>y</td><td>z</td><td></td><td></td><td></td><td></td></tr>
<tr><td>0</td><td>0</td><td>1</td><td>0</td><td>1</td><td>0</td></tr>
<tr><td>0</td><td>1</td><td>0</td><td>1</td><td>0</td><td>1</td></tr>
<tr><td>1</td><td>1</td><td>0</td><td>1</td><td>0</td><td>1</td></tr>
<tr><td>1</td><td>0</td><td>0</td><td>0</td><td>0</td><td>0</td></tr>
</table>

maps show that $f_{w'x'} = f_{wx} = y'z'$ and $f_{w'x} = f_{wx'} = z$. From this it follows that f cannot be expressed as $F(g[y, z], w, x)$. Thus far the only decomposition that has been found possible is $F(g[w, x], y, z)$. There are four decompositions that remain to be checked: $F(g[x, z], w, y)$, $F(g[w, y], x, z)$, $F(g[x, y], w, z)$, $F(g[w, z], x, y)$. The first two of these will be checked by means of Table 5.6-3b.

TABLE 5.6-3 Karnaugh maps for $f(w, x, y, z) = \Sigma(0, 5, 7, 9, 11, 12)$: (a) Map with wx columns; (b) Map with wy columns; (c) Map with wz columns

<table>
<tr><td colspan="5" align="center">(a)
w x</td><td colspan="5" align="center">(b)
w y</td><td colspan="5" align="center">(c)
w z</td></tr>
<tr><td></td><td>00</td><td>01</td><td>11</td><td>10</td><td></td><td>00</td><td>01</td><td>11</td><td>10</td><td></td><td>00</td><td>01</td><td>11</td><td>10</td></tr>
<tr><td>y z</td><td></td><td></td><td></td><td></td><td>x z</td><td></td><td></td><td></td><td></td><td>x y</td><td></td><td></td><td></td><td></td></tr>
<tr><td>0 0</td><td>1</td><td>0</td><td>1</td><td>0</td><td>0 0</td><td>1</td><td>0</td><td>0</td><td>0</td><td>0 0</td><td>1</td><td>0</td><td>1</td><td>0</td></tr>
<tr><td>0 1</td><td>0</td><td>1</td><td>0</td><td>1</td><td>0 1</td><td>0</td><td>0</td><td>1</td><td>1</td><td>0 1</td><td>0</td><td>0</td><td>1</td><td>0</td></tr>
<tr><td>1 1</td><td>0</td><td>1</td><td>0</td><td>1</td><td>1 1</td><td>1</td><td>1</td><td>0</td><td>0</td><td>1 1</td><td>0</td><td>1</td><td>0</td><td>0</td></tr>
<tr><td>1 0</td><td>0</td><td>0</td><td>0</td><td>0</td><td>1 0</td><td>0</td><td>0</td><td>0</td><td>1</td><td>1 0</td><td>0</td><td>1</td><td>0</td><td>1</td></tr>
</table>

In Table 5.6-3b, f is represented by a map in which the columns correspond to wy and the rows correspond to xz. Since each row represents one of the four xz-residues, inspection of the rows shows that no $F(g[w, y], x, z)$ decomposition exists. Similarly, a check of the columns shows that it is not possible to write f as $F(g[x, z], w, y)$.

The impossibility of the decompositions $F(g[x, y], w, z)$, $F(g[w, z], x, y)$ is shown by Table 5.6-3c, in which the columns represent wz and the rows xy. Study of Tables 5.6-1, 2, and 3 has thus demonstrated that the function $f(w, x, y, z) = \Sigma(0, 5, 7, 9, 11, 12)$ has only one nontrivial simple disjoint decomposition, the one shown in Fig. 5.6-1.

It is usually not necessary to explicitly draw out the residue maps such as shown in Tables 5.6-1b–d and 5.6-2b and c. They are so simply related to the Karnaugh map for f (Table 5.6-1a) that the information necessary to determine the decompositions can typically be derived from the basic map for f. The maps such as Table 5.6-3b and c representing permutations of the independent variables do need to be explicitly drawn.[4] Table 5.6-4 shows 4-variable Karnaugh maps for the three important permutations of the input variables. The entries in these maps are the decimal numbers identifying the corresponding rows of the table of combinations. These entries provide a simple mechanism for deriving the maps for permuted inputs from the basic map for the function since they show the correspondence among the cells of the different maps. It is straightforward to derive similar 5- and 6-variable Karnaugh maps for permuted inputs. By using these, functions of 5- and 6-variables can be tested for decompositions.

TABLE 5.6-4 Karnaugh maps for $f(w, x, y, z)$: (a) Map with wx columns; (b) Map with wy columns; (c) Map with wz columns

	(a) w x					(b) w y					(c) w z			
	00	01	11	10		00	01	11	10		00	01	11	10
y z					x z					x y				
0 0	0	4	12	8	0 0	0	2	10	8	0 0	0	1	9	8
0 1	1	5	13	9	0 1	1	3	11	9	0 1	2	3	11	10
1 1	3	7	15	11	1 1	5	7	15	13	1 1	6	7	15	14
1 0	2	6	14	10	1 0	4	6	14	12	1 0	4	5	13	12

More Complicated Decompositions. It is possible to have decompositions other than the simple disjunctive decomposition. A direct generalization leads to the **multiple disjunctive decomposition** that is characterized by having more than one subfunction: $F(g1[X], \ldots, gs[Y], Z)$, where $X, \ldots, Y, Z$ have no common

---

[4] It is possible to identify on the f-map the subcubes corresponding to the two-variable residues. However, there is more chance for error in doing this and it is probably simpler to fill in the maps for the permuted variables.

variables. Another generalization results in the **iterative disjunctive decomposition**, in which the subfunction itself has a decomposition: $F(g[h(X), Y], Z)$, with no common variables among X, Y, Z. A function for which a combination of these decompositions is possible is said to have a **complex disjunctive decomposition**: $F(g[h(X), Y], k[Z], W)$. The relationships among these decompositions are studied in [Curtis 62]. Any function that cannot be expressed with a simple disjunctive decomposition will not possess any of these more involved decompositions.

One drawback to using decompositions as a general design method is the fact that most switching functions can't have any disjunctive decomposition [Shannon 49]. In spite of this general result, it does turn out that many of the functions used for computer design can be decomposed. Also, it is possible to define more general decompositions which are possible for more functions than the disjunctive decompositions discussed thus far. An example of a less restrictive decomposition is the **simple nondisjunctive decomposition**, $F(g[X], Y)$, in which it is not required that X and Y have no variables in common. Since there are more possibilities for such decompositions, it takes longer to test for them. At present there doesn't seem to be any promise for practical application of any but the simplest decompositions. The interested reader is referred to [Curtis 62] for a more complete discussion of decomposition theory.

5.R REFERENCES

[CURTIS 62] Curtis, H. A., *A New Approach to the Design of Switching Circuits*, D. Van Nostrand Company, Princeton, N.J., 1962.

[DAO 77] Dao, T., "Threshold I²L and Its Application to Binary Symmetric Functions and Multi-valued Logic," *IEEE J. Solid-State Circuits*, pp. 463–475, Oct. 1977.

[DERTOUZOS 65] Dertouzos, M. L., *Threshold Logic: A Synthesis Approach*, The MIT Press, Cambridge, Mass., 1965.

[EPSTEIN 58] Epstein, G., "Synthesis of Electronic Circuits for Symmetric Functions," *IRE Trans. Electron. Comput.*, EC-7, No. 1, pp. 57–60, 1958.

[GILBERT 54] Gilbert, E. N., "Lattice-Theoretic Properties of Frontal Switching Functions," *J. Math. Phys.*, Vol. 33, pp. 57–67, 1954.

[GLORIOSO 80] Glorioso, R. M., and F. C. Colon Osorio, *Engineering Intelligent Systems*, Digital Press, Bedford, Mass., 1980.

[HARRISON 65] Harrison, M. A., *Introduction to Switching and Automata Theory*, McGraw-Hill Book Company, New York, 1965.

[HILL 81] Hill, F. J., and G. R. Peterson, *Introduction to Switching and Logical Design*, 3rd ed., John Wiley & Sons, Inc., New York, 1981.

[KOHAVI 70] Kohavi, Z., *Switching and Finite Automata Theory*, McGraw-Hill Book Company, New York, 1970.

[LEWIS 67] Lewis, P. M., and C. L. Coates, *Threshold Logic*, John Wiley & Sons, Inc., New York, 1967.

[MCCLUSKEY 56] McCluskey, E. J., "Detection of Group Invariance or Total Symmetry of a Boolean Function," *Bell Syst. Tech. J.*, Vol. 35, pp. 1445–1453, November 1956.

[McNaughton 61]   McNaughton, R., "Unate Truth Functions," *IRE Trans. Electron. Comput.*, EC-10, No. 1, pp. 1–6, 1961.

[Mead 80]   Mead, J. D., and L. Conway, *Introduction to VLSI Systems*, Addison-Wesley Publishing Company, Inc., Reading, Mass., 1980.

[Muroga 71]   Muroga, S., *Threshold Logic and Its Applications*, Wiley-Interscience, New York, 1971.

[Paull 60]   Paull, M. C., and E. J. McCluskey, "Boolean Functions Realizable with Single Threshold Devices," *Proc. IRE*, Vol. 48, pp. 1335–1337, July 1960.

[Sellers 68]   Sellers, F. F., M.-Y. Hsiao, and L. W. Bearnson, *Error Detecting Logic for Digital Computers*, McGraw-Hill Book Company, New York, 1968.

[Shannon 49]   Shannon, C. E., "The Synthesis of Two-Terminal Switching Circuits," *Bell Syst. Tech. J.*, Vol. 28, pp. 59–98, 1949.

5.P PROBLEMS

5.1 Let $f_1(x_1, x_2, \ldots, x_n)$ and $f_2(x_1, x_2, \ldots, x_n)$ both be symmetric functions.
   (a) Which, if any, of the following functions are guaranteed to be symmetric functions? Why?
       (i) $f_1 + f_2$
       (ii) $f_1 \cdot f_2$
       (iii) $f_1 \oplus f_2$
   (b) Under what conditions, if any, will the functions of part (a) be symmetric if f_1 is symmetric but f_2 is not?

5.2 **(a)** Prove that

$$S_{a_1, a_2, \ldots, a_k}(x_1, x_2, \ldots, x_n) = S_{b_1, b_2, \ldots, b_k}(x_1', x_2', \ldots, x_n')$$

   (b) Rewrite $S_{0,3,4}(w', x', y', z')$ as a symmetric function.

5.3 Write each of the following as symmetric functions.
   (a) $f_1(A, B, C, D, E) = A'S_{0,1,4}(B, C, D, E) + AS_{0,3,4}(B, C, D, E)$
   (b) $f_3(A, B, C, D, E) = A'S_{0,1,2}(B, C, D, E) + AS_{0,3,4}(B', C', D', E')$

5.4 How many symmetric functions of n variables are possible?

5.5 If $f(x_1, x_2, \ldots, x_n)$ is a symmetric function, S_A, for which A is a single integer ($f = 1$ iff exactly a of its variables equal 1, $0 \le a$, $a \le n$), it is called an **elementary symmetric function**. Such a function will be represented as $E_a(x_1, x_2, \ldots, x_n)$.
   (a) Prove that $E_a(x_1, x_2, \ldots, x_n)E_b(x_1, x_2, \ldots, x_n) = 0$ if $a \ne b$.
   (b) Prove that $\displaystyle\sum_{i=0}^{n} E_i(x_1, x_2, \ldots, x_n) = 1$.

5.6 For the following expressions, find an expression for each function as a single symmetric function.
   (a) $S_{1,3,5,7}(x_1, \ldots, x_7)S_{4,5,6,7}(x_1, \ldots, x_7)$
   (b) $S_{2,3,5}(x_1, \ldots, x_5) + S_3(x_1, \ldots, x_5)$
   (c) $S_{1,3,4}(x_1', x_2', \ldots, x_5')S_{2,3,4,5}(x_1, x_2, \ldots, x_5)$
   (d) $x_1'S_{0,1,2}(x_2, x_3, x_4) + x_1S_{2,3}(x_2', x_3', x_4')$
   (e) $[S_{2,3}(x_1, x_2, x_3, x_4)]'[S_{1,2,3,4}(x_1, x_2, x_3, x_4)]$

(f) $wxy + wx'y' + w'xy' + w'x'y$

(g) $w'x' + x'y' + wx + xy$

5.7 Determine whether each of the following functions is frontal, backal, unate, or not unate. For those functions that are not unate, determine in which variables the function is positive, negative, mixed, or vacuous.

(a) $S(x, y, c)$, the sum function for a full adder

(b) $C(x, y, c)$, the carry function for a full adder

(c) $B(x, y, b)$, the borrow function for a full subtracter

(d) $f(w, x, y, z) = \Sigma(2, 3, 5, 6, 7, 9, 11, 13)$

(e) $f(w, x, y, z) = \Sigma(0, 1, 2, 3, 4, 5, 8, 9)$

(f) $f(w, x, y, z) = \Sigma(0, 1, 2, 3, 4, 5)$

5.8 Determine which of the literals of $f(X) = \Sigma(0, 8, 17, 25, 76, 156, 158, 218)$ are essential.

5.9 Prove that if $f_{x_i} \cdot f_{x_i'} = f_{x_i'}$, then f is positive in x_i.

5.10 Write expressions for three-variable functions, $f(x, y, z)$, satisfying each of the given specifications. The functions in your answers should not be vacuous in any variable.

(a) A function that is both a totally symmetric function and a threshold function (use S notation).

(b) A function that is a threshold function but which is not totally symmetric.

(c) A function that is totally symmetric but not a threshold function (use S notation).

(d) A function that is totally symmetric and not unate (use S notation).

(e) A function that is backal (negative in all three variables) and also a threshold function.

5.11 This question involves designing with the MC14530 chip. The chip realizes the function $M + w'$, where w is one of the inputs and M is the majority function of the five inputs A, B, C, D, E. (A majority function is one for which the output has the same value as the majority of its inputs.)

(a) Write an expression for M using the S notation.

(b) Write an expression for M using switching-algebra notation.

5.12 Given $f = wx + xyz$, find:

(a) a_w, a_x, a_y, a_z, and T for a threshold gate realization of f.

(b) a_w, a_x, a_y, a_z, and T for a threshold gate realization of $f(w, x, z, y)$.

(c) a_w, a_x, a_y, a_z, and T for a threshold gate realization of $f(x, w, y, z)$.

(d) a_w, a_x, a_y, a_z, and T for a threshold gate realization of $f(w', x, y, z)$.

(e) a_w, a_x, a_y, a_z, and T for a threshold gate realization of $f'(w, x, y, z)$.

(f) a_w, a_x, a_y, a_z, and T for a threshold gate realization of $D[f(w, x, y, z)]$.

5.13 **(a)** You are to design a full-adder circuit using NAND gates and threshold gates. Use as few gates as possible.

(b) Repeat part (a) using NOR gates and threshold gates.

N.B. For a full adder: $\text{Sum} = x \oplus y \oplus \text{CIN}$

$$\text{COUT} = xy + x\,\text{CIN} + y\,\text{CIN}$$

5.14 Prove that the definition

$$df/dx_i = f(x_1, x_2, \ldots, x_i, \ldots, x_n) \oplus f(x_1, x_2, \ldots, \bar{x}_i, \ldots, x_n)$$

is equivalent to the definition

$$df/dx_i = f(x_1, x_2, \ldots, x_i = 1, \ldots, x_n) \oplus f(x_1, x_2, \ldots, x_i = 0, \ldots, x_n)$$

5.15 Find dF/dx, dF/dy, and dF/dz for each of the following functions.

(a) $F(x, y, z) = x(y + z')$

(b) $F(x, y, z) = (x' + y)(x + z)$

(c) $F(x, y, z) = x'y'(x' + y'z)$

5.16 For each of the following functions, determine all simple disjoint decompositions (if any).

(a) $f(w, x, y, z) = \Sigma(0, 4, 5, 7, 9, 10, 15)$

(b) $f(w, x, y, z) = \Sigma(0, 3, 4, 11, 12, 15)$

(c) $f(v, w, x, y, z) = \Sigma(3, 10, 14, 17, 18, 22, 23, 24, 27, 28, 31)$

5.17 Given $f(w, x, y, z) = \Sigma(1, 3, 5, 7, 8, 11, 13, 15)$:

(a) Find all simple disjoint decompositions.

(b) At least one of the answers to part (a) will yield a functional form $f = F[a, b, g(c, d)]$. Choose one such form and then test $F(a, b, g)$ for simple disjoint decomposition to determine an expression of the form $G(t, h[v, g(c, d)])$ (iterative disjunctive decomposition).

(c) Draw a circuit diagram for your answer to part (b).

5.18 Given $f(v, w, x, y, z) = \Sigma(0, 2, 3, 12, 14, 15, 17, 20, 21, 22, 23, 24, 25, 26, 27, 29)$:

(a) Find all simple disjoint decompositions of the form $F[a, b, c, g(d, e)]$.

(b) Find one decomposition of the form $G[r, h(s, t), k(q, u)]$ (multiple disjunctive decomposition).

5.19 Figure P5.19 shows an nMOS pass transistor network for $S_3(W, X, Y)$, $S_2(W, X, Y)$, $S_1(W, X, Y)$, and $S_0(W, X, Y)$. You are to modify this network to realize the two functions $S_{1,3}(W, X, Y)$ and $S_{0,2}(W, X, Y)$ with as few transistors as possible.

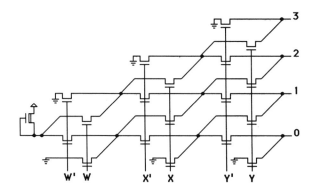

Figure P5.19

5.20 Let $ST_A(X_1, X_2, \ldots, X_n)$ represent a **symmetric threshold** function for n variables with threshold A, which is defined as

$$ST_A(X_1, X_2, \ldots, X_n) = \begin{cases} 1 & \text{iff } A \text{ or more of the } X_i \text{ equal 1} \\ 0 & \text{iff fewer than } A \text{ of the } X_i \text{ equal 1} \end{cases}$$

(a) Design a two-stage, AND-OR network for $ST_2(X_1, X_2, X_3, X_4)$.

(b) Design a two-stage, OR-AND network for $ST_2(X_1, X_2, X_3, X_4)$.

(c) Give a formula for the number of gates in a two-stage OR-AND network to realize $ST_A(X_1, X_2, \ldots, X_n)$.

5.21 Let $ST_A(X_1, X_2, \ldots, X_n) = ST_A^n$ be a symmetric threshold function as defined in Problem 5.20. Then if $n = p + q$,

$$ST_A^n = ST_0^p ST_A^q + ST_1^p ST_{A-1}^q + \cdots + ST_A^p ST_0^q$$

where some terms may be 0 since $ST_j^i = 0$ for $j > i$; for example, $ST_2^4 = ST_0^2 ST_2^2 = ST_1^2 ST_1^2 + ST_2^2 ST_0^2$.

$$ST_2(W, X, Y, Z) = (1)YZ + (W + X)(Y + Z) + WX(1)$$

(a) Design a four-stage network for $ST_4(X_1, X_2, \ldots, X_8)$.

(b) Repeat procedure to get networks with more stages until no more repetitions are possible.

(c) Write a table showing the number of gates required for the networks of parts (a) and (b) as well as a two-stage network for ST_4^8.

6

COMBINATIONAL CIRCUIT DESIGN

6.1 INTRODUCTION

This chapter describes how to design efficient combinational logic networks. It will be necessary to discuss a number of design approaches since the design methodology depends heavily on the technology and the type of implementation chosen. The various logic families and their attributes were presented in Chap. 4. As discussed in Sec. 4.1-5, there are a variety of implementation types possible: catalog items, programmable items, and semicustom and full custom designs. Some issues relating to the choice of an implementation type are given in Sec. 4.1-5. Other characteristics will become clear as the design methods are described.

Two very important topics in combinational design will not be covered in this chapter because it is inconvenient to cover them without also discussing sequential circuits at the same time. These topics are: design using larger building blocks than individual gates (MSI or custom cell design) and design for testability. These topics will be covered in Chaps. 10 and 11, after sequential circuits have been studied.

The first technique discussed is a type of "table lookup." The table of combinations is stored in a memory that is read out when the function value is desired.

Several sections follow which present techniques for obtaining minimal two-stage expressions: either a sum-of-products expression or a product-of-sums expression. There are two reasons for this emphasis on two-stage expressions. First, important methods for deriving such expressions are known and the two-stage expression is a good starting point for other forms. Second, the two-stage expression is the appropriate form for programmable logic array realizations, a very important current implementation technique.

A separate section follows in which the use of programmable logic arrays, PLAs, is presented. The design of hazard-free networks is then described. The final sections introduce the subject of testing combinational networks.

The ultimate design methodology would be one in which the desired output functions as well as implementation-dependent attributes such as cost specifications and constraints are specified. The design method would then produce a minimum-cost design satisfying the implementation constraints. Such a general design methodology is not available at the present time. Instead, there are a variety of design approaches that depend on the implementation constraints. Some of these design approaches are presented in this chapter. At one extreme are the table-lookup and PLA techniques, in which the form of the final network is very severely constrained. At the other extreme is the so-called "random logic" design, in which the basic elements are gates and the only constraints are fanin, fanout, and delay specifications. Random logic design is suitable for SSI-based or full custom design. Design in which the basic elements are more complex than gates is discussed in Chap. 11. This design style is appropriate for MSI design and for VLSI design using standard cells.

6.2 ROM-BASED DESIGN

The problem considered in this chapter is that of designing a multioutput combinational network. It will be assumed that the network is specified by listing the value (perhaps undefined) of each of the outputs for each combination of values of the input variables.

Conceptually, the simplest design procedure is one in which a signal corresponding to each row of the table of combinations (each fundamental product or minterm) is generated and then each output is derived by connecting the appropriate fundamental products to the output via an OR gate. Figure 6.2-1 shows such a structure for a circuit to convert from a 3-bit binary code to a 3-bit Gray code. The table of combinations for this network is shown in Table 6.2-1. In Fig. 6.2-1 the circuit that generates the signals corresponding to fundamental products is

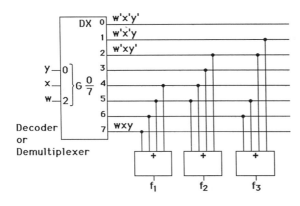

Figure 6.2-1 ROM implementation of binary-Gray code conversion shown in Table 6.2-1.

called a decoder. Such a circuit produces "one-hot" output signals with only one signal equal to 1 for each pattern of values on the inputs. This class of circuit will be discussed in Chap. 11 since it is an important MSI element. The decoder of Fig. 6.2-1 can be realized by using one AND gate for each output and connecting signals representing the appropriate w, x, and z literals to each gate.

There are standard catalog parts that provide the logical structure shown in Fig. 6.2-1. Such a part is called a Read Only Memory or ROM. In a ROM, the specific functions realized are determined either by the final masking step in the fabrication of the device (which is then called a mask-programmed device) or by the user. Particularizing the device to a specific application is called "programming." The term programmable read-only memory or PROM is used to describe a ROM that can have its interconnection pattern fixed after processing. Such devices are available in either bipolar or MOS versions and differ in their propagation delays and in the means for implementing the interconnections.

TABLE 6.2-1 Binary-to-Gray code conversion

w	x	y	f_1	f_2	f_3
0	0	0	0	0	0
0	0	1	0	0	1
0	1	0	0	1	1
0	1	1	0	1	0
1	0	0	1	1	0
1	0	1	1	1	1
1	1	0	1	0	1
1	1	1	1	0	0

ROMs are often used to implement code conversion, character generation, arithmetic functions, or encryption. In fact, standard mask-programmed ROMs are available for some of the standard code conversions, character generation, and arithmetic functions. A very common use of a ROM is to realize the combinational portion of a sequential circuit. The control portion of a computer is very often realized by means of a ROM (a technique called microprogramming).

A drawback of the use of a ROM to generate arbitrary logic functions is that the size of a ROM is proportional to 2^n, where n is the number of input variables. Thus adding one additional input variable requires doubling the size of the ROM. This area penalty can be avoided by using a PLA rather than a ROM. PLA design will be discussed in Sec. 6.9. For simple logic functions it is much more efficient to use gate or switch structures rather than a ROM. Also, the highest speed of operation is obtained by optimizing the logic network rather than using a standard structure such as a ROM. Because of their structure, ROMs have hazards on their outputs and are not suitable for use when the effects of the hazard pulses cannot be controlled externally.

The electrical structures used in ROMs and examples of specific applications are discussed in Chap. 4 of [Hnatek 77] and in Sec. 7.2 of [Carr 72]. Applications are considered in [Kvamme 70].

6.3 THE MAP METHOD

The simplest sum-of-product-terms form of a function will be called a **minimal sum**.[1] The precise definition will be discussed later, but for the present the sum-of-products form that has the fewest terms will be taken as the minimal sum. If there is more than one sum-of-products form having the minimum number of terms, and if these forms do not all contain the same total number of literals, then only the form(s) with the fewest literals will be called the minimal sum(s). For example, the function $f = x'yz + xyz + xyz'$ can be written as $f = yz + xyz'$, $f = x'yz + xy$, and $f = yz + xy$. Each of these forms contains two terms, but only the third form is a minimal sum, since it contains four literals, while the other two forms contain five literals each.

The minimal sum corresponds to a gate circuit in which the circuit inputs are connected to AND gates and the outputs of the AND gates form the inputs to an OR gate whose output is the circuit output. Such a circuit is called a **two-stage circuit**, since there are two gates connected in series between the circuit inputs and output. It is also possible to have two-stage circuits in which the circuit inputs are connected to OR gates and the circuit output is obtained from an AND gate. The minimal sum just defined corresponds to the two-stage circuit in which the output is derived from an OR gate and which contains the minimum number of gates. The basic method for obtaining the minimal sum is to apply the theorem $XY + X'Y = Y$ to as many terms as possible and then to use the theorem $XY + X'Z + YZ = XY + X'Z$ to eliminate as many terms as possible.

Example 6.3-1

$$f = x'y'z' + x'y'z + xy'z + xyz$$

$$x'y'z' + x'y'z = x'y'$$

$$xy'z + xyz = xz$$

$$f = x'y' + xz \qquad \text{minimal sum}[2]$$

Example 6.3-2

$$f = w'x'y'z + w'x'yz + w'xy'z + w'xyz + wxy'z' + wxy'z + wx'y'z' + wx'y'z$$

$$f = \qquad w'x'z \qquad + \qquad w'xz \qquad + \qquad wxy' \qquad + \qquad wx'y'$$

$$f = \qquad\qquad w'z \qquad\qquad\qquad + \qquad\qquad wy'$$

$$f = w'z + wy' \qquad \text{minimal sum}[2]$$

Example 6.3-3

$$f = xyz + x'yz + xy'z$$

$$xyz = xyz + xyz$$

$$f = (xyz + x'yz) + (xyz + xy'z)$$

$$f = yz + xz \qquad \text{minimal sum}[2]$$

[1] This is called minimal rather than minimum, since there may be more than one such form.

[2] It is possible to prove that this is a minimal sum. This will be discussed subsequently.

Example 6.3-2 illustrates the fact that it may be necessary to apply the theorem $XY + X'Y = Y$ several times, the number of literals in the terms being reduced each time. A single term may be paired with more than one other term, as shown in Example 6.3-3.

The process of comparing pairs of terms to determine whether or not the theorem $XY + X'Y = Y$ applies can become very tedious for large functions. This comparison process can be simplified by using an n-cube map.

6.3-1 Maps for Two, Three, and Four Variables

A map for a function of two variables, as shown in Fig. 6.3-1, is a square of four cells or a 2-cube map. The value 0 or 1 which the function is to equal when $x = 1$, $y = 0$ (the entry in the 10 location or 2 row of the table of combinations) is placed in the cell having coordinates $x = 1$, $y = 0$. In general, the scheme for filling in the map is to place a 1 in all cells whose coordinates form a binary number that corresponds to one of the fundamental products included in the function and to place a 0 in all cells whose binary numbers correspond to fundamental products not included in the function. This is done very simply by writing a 1 in each cell whose decimal designation (decimal equivalent of the binary number formed by the coordinates) occurs in the decimal specification of the function and writing 0's in the remaining cells.

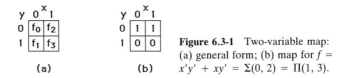

Figure 6.3-1 Two-variable map: (a) general form; (b) map for $f = x'y' + xy' = \Sigma(0, 2) = \Pi(1, 3)$.

The maps for functions of three and four variables are direct extensions of the two-variable map and are shown in Figs. 6.3-2 and 6.3-3. Discussion of maps for more than four variables will be postponed temporarily, since such maps are more complex.

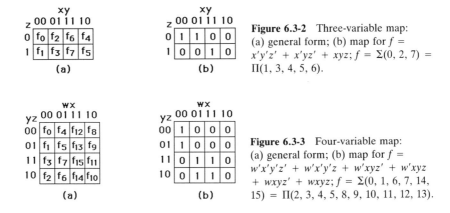

Figure 6.3-2 Three-variable map: (a) general form; (b) map for $f = x'y'z' + x'yz' + xyz; f = \Sigma(0, 2, 7) = \Pi(1, 3, 4, 5, 6)$.

Figure 6.3-3 Four-variable map: (a) general form; (b) map for $f = w'x'y'z' + w'x'y'z + w'xyz' + w'xyz + wxyz' + wxyz; f = \Sigma(0, 1, 6, 7, 14, 15) = \Pi(2, 3, 4, 5, 8, 9, 10, 11, 12, 13)$.

6.3-2 Prime Implicants

Two fundamental products can be "combined" by means of the theorem $XY + XY' = X$ if their corresponding binary numbers differ in only 1 bit. For the fundamental products $wxyz$ and $wxyz'$,

$$wxyz + wxyz' = wxy$$

The corresponding binary numbers are 1111 and 1110, which differ only in the lowest-order bit position. The fundamental products $wxyz$ and $w'xyz'$ cannot combine, and their corresponding numbers, 1111 and 0110, differ in the first and last bit positions.

In terms of the distance concept introduced in Chap. 1, two fundamental products combine only if the corresponding points on an n-cube or n-cube map are distance 1 apart. Points distance 1 apart on an n-cube become adjacent cells on a map, so that cells that represent fundamental products that can be combined can be determined very quickly by inspection. In carrying out this inspection process it must be remembered that cells such as f_4 and f_6 or f_1 and f_9 in Fig. 6.3-3 must be considered to be adjacent.

In a four-variable map each cell is adjacent to four other cells corresponding to the four bit positions in which two binary numbers can differ. In inspecting a map to determine which fundamental products can be combined, only cells with 1 entries (1-cells) need be considered, since these correspond to the fundamental products included in the function. Figure 6.3-4 shows a four-variable map with adjacent 1-cells encircled. Notice that the 0111-cell is adjacent to two 1-cells. The rule for writing down the algebraic expression corresponding to a map is that there will be one product term for each pair of adjacent 1-cells and a fundamental product for each 1-cell which is not adjacent to any other 1-cell. The fundamental products are written down according to the rule given in Chap. 3: Any variable corresponding to a 0 in the binary number formed by the coordinates of the corresponding 1-cell is primed; the variables corresponding to 1's are left unprimed. The product terms corresponding to pairs of adjacent 1-cells are obtained by the same rule, with the exception that one variable is not included in the product. The variable excluded is that corresponding to the bit position in which the coordinates of the two 1-cells differ (see Fig. 6.3-4).

Figure 6.3-4 Four-variable map with adjacent 1-cells encircled. $f = \Sigma(0, 5, 7, 8, 15) = x'y'z' + w'xz + xyz$.

The situation where it is possible to combine two of the terms obtained from pairs of the fundamental terms as in Example 6.3-2 must be considered next. In such a situation four of the fundamental products can be combined into a single product term by successive applications of the $XY + XY' = X$ theorem. A function that is the sum of four such fundamental products is $f = wxyz + wxyz' +$

$wxy'z + wxy'z'$. Application of the theorem to this function yields

$$f = (wxyz + wxyz') + (wxy'z + wxy'z') = wxy + wxy' = wx$$

The characteristic property of four fundamental products which can be combined in this fashion is that all but two of the variables are the same (either primed or unprimed) in all four terms. The corresponding four binary numbers are identical in all but two bit positions. The corresponding cells on a map form "squares" (Fig. 6.3-5a) or "lines" (Fig. 6.3-5b) of four adjacent cells.

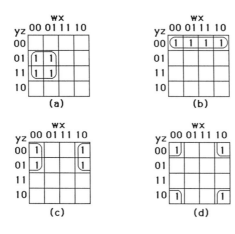

Figure 6.3-5 Four-variable maps showing sets of cells corresponding to four fundamental products that can be combined: (a) $f = w'z$; (b) $f = y'z'$; (c) $f = x'y'$; (d) $f = x'z'$.

For such a group of four cells on the map of a function the corresponding product term is written just as for two adjacent cells, except that two variables corresponding to the two bit positions for which the cell coordinates change must be omitted.

It is also possible that eight of the fundamental products can be combined. In this case all but three of the variables are identical (either primed or unprimed) in all eight terms. Figure 6.3-6 shows some sets of eight cells on a map which have all but three coordinates fixed. The general rule is that if in 2^i fundamental products all but i of the variables are identical (primed or unprimed), then the 2^i products can be combined and the i variables that change can be dropped.

In searching for a minimal sum for a function by means of a map the first step is to encircle all sets of cells corresponding to fundamental products that can be combined (see Fig. 6.3-7). If one such set is contained in a larger set, only the larger set is encircled.[3] In Fig. 6.3-7 the set (0101, 0111) is not encircled. The

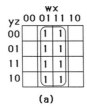

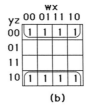

Figure 6.3-6 Four-variable maps showing sets of cells corresponding to eight fundamental products that can be combined: (a) $f = x$; (b) $f = z'$.

[3] This corresponds to using the theorem $X + XY = X$.

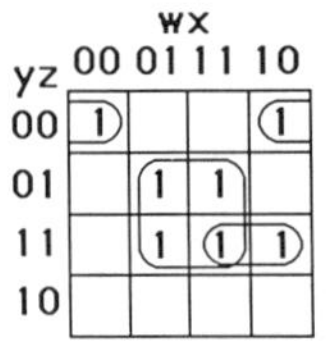

$$f = \Sigma(0,5,7,8,11,13,15) = xz + x'y'z' + wyz.$$

Figure 6.3-7 Map showing prime implicants.

encircled sets and the corresponding product terms will be called **prime implicants**.[4] These are exactly the terms that would result from repeated applications of the theorem $XY + XY' = X$. The terms appearing in the minimal sum will be some or all of the prime implicants.

6.3-3 Maps for Five and Six Variables

While the map is most useful for functions of four variables, it is also helpful for five- and six-variable functions. A five-variable map is formed by using two four-variable maps (Fig. 6.3-8), and a six-variable map is composed of four four-variable maps (Fig. 6.3-9).

Figure 6.3-8 Five-variable map.

In the five-variable map, one of the four-variable maps represents all rows of the table of combinations for which $v = 0$, and the other four-variable map represents all rows for which $v = 1$. Similarly, one of the four-variable maps making up the six-variable map represents all rows of the table of combinations for which $u = 0$ and $v = 0$, and another four-variable map represents all rows for which $u = 0$, $v = 1$, etc.

The basic rule for combining cells for five- or six-variable maps is the same as for four-variable maps: It is possible to combine any set of 1-cells for which some of the coordinates remain fixed while the remaining coordinates take on all possible combinations of values. For cells on the same four-variable map, the patterns of sets of cells that can be combined are the same patterns discussed in connection with four-variable maps. Two cells that are on different four-variable maps can be combined only if they occupy the same relative position on their respective four-variable maps. In Fig. 6.3-8 the cells containing f_4 and f_{20} can be combined, but it is not permissible to combine the cells containing f_4 and f_{16}. For the six-variable map, only cells from two maps that are horizontally or vertically adjacent can be combined—a cell from the map labeled $u = 0$, $v = 0$ cannot be

---

[4] This term was introduced by W. V. Quine [Quine 52]. It is derived from the terminology of mathematical logic, but it has received widespread use in connection with switching theory.

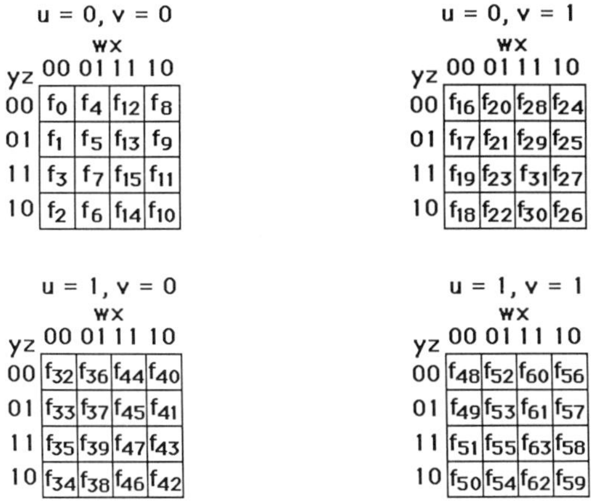

u = 0, v = 0

wx

yz	00	01	11	10
00	f_0	f_4	f_{12}	f_8
01	f_1	f_5	f_{13}	f_9
11	f_3	f_7	f_{15}	f_{11}
10	f_2	f_6	f_{14}	f_{10}

u = 0, v = 1

wx

yz	00	01	11	10
00	f_{16}	f_{20}	f_{28}	f_{24}
01	f_{17}	f_{21}	f_{29}	f_{25}
11	f_{19}	f_{23}	f_{31}	f_{27}
10	f_{18}	f_{22}	f_{30}	f_{26}

u = 1, v = 0

wx

yz	00	01	11	10
00	f_{32}	f_{36}	f_{44}	f_{40}
01	f_{33}	f_{37}	f_{45}	f_{41}
11	f_{35}	f_{39}	f_{47}	f_{43}
10	f_{34}	f_{38}	f_{46}	f_{42}

u = 1, v = 1

wx

yz	00	01	11	10
00	f_{48}	f_{52}	f_{60}	f_{56}
01	f_{49}	f_{53}	f_{61}	f_{57}
11	f_{51}	f_{55}	f_{63}	f_{58}
10	f_{50}	f_{54}	f_{62}	f_{59}

Figure 6.3-9 Six-variable map.

combined with a cell from the map labeled $u = 1$, $v = 1$, since the two cells differ in two coordinates rather than in one, as required. Four cells, such as those labeled f_5, f_{21}, f_{37}, and f_{53} (in Fig. 6.3-9), that all occupy the same position in their individual four-variable maps can all be combined.

The first step in the procedure for picking the minimal sets on a five- or six-variable map is to determine the prime implicants for each of the individual four-variable maps (Fig. 6.3-10).

Each prime implicant must now be compared with the prime implicants of the (horizontally and vertically) adjacent maps. If there is an identical prime implicant in an adjacent map, the two prime implicants are combined into one prime implicant (Fig. 6.3-10).

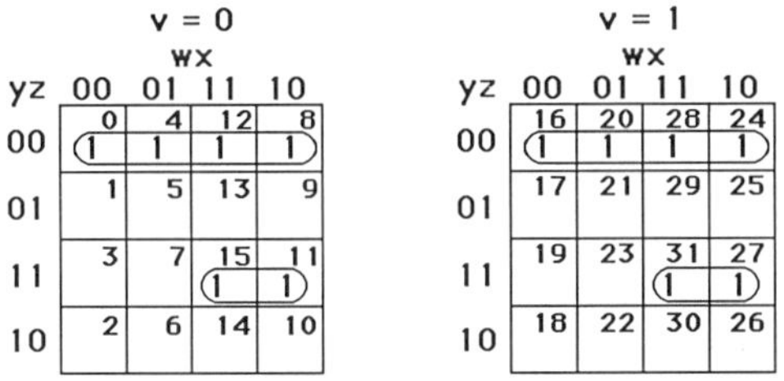

v = 0

wx

yz	00	01	11	10
00	0 [1]	4 [1]	12 [1]	8 [1]
01	1	5	13	9
11	3	7	15 [1]	11 [1]
10	2	6	14	10

v = 1

wx

yz	00	01	11	10
00	16 [1]	20 [1]	28 [1]	24 [1]
01	17	21	29	25
11	19	23	31 [1]	27 [1]
10	18	22	30	26

Figure 6.3-10 Five-variable map for $f = \Sigma(0, 4, 8, 11, 12, 15, 16, 20, 24, 27, 28, 31) = y'z' + wyz$.

Prime Implicants: (0,4,8,12,16,20,24,28); (11,15,27,31)

If, in one four-variable map, there is a prime implicant (such as A in Fig. 6.3-11) which is identical with a subset (B, Fig. 6.3-11) of a prime implicant (C, Fig. 6.3-11) in an adjacent map, a new prime implicant is formed from the original prime implicant A and the subset B. In such a case, the original prime implicant A is no longer a prime implicant, since it is included in the larger prime implicant A, B. The set C which included B is still a prime implicant. One further situation must be considered: There may be two prime implicants D, E (Fig. 6.3-12) in two different four-variable maps which are not identical and for which neither is identical to a subset of the other, but which both have identical subsets F, G (Fig. 6.3-12). The two identical subsets can be combined to form a

Sec. 6.3 The Map Method

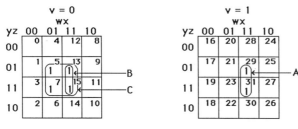

Prime Implicants: (5,7,13,15); (13,15,29,31)

Figure 6.3-11 Five-variable map for $f = \Sigma(5, 7, 13, 15, 29, 31) = wxz + v'xz$.

new prime implicant. Both the original prime implicants remain as prime implicants. For a six-variable map, it is also necessary to consider prime implicants made up of a four-variable prime implicant that is identical with prime implicants or subsets of prime implicants in all the three remaining four-variable maps (see Fig. 6.3-13).

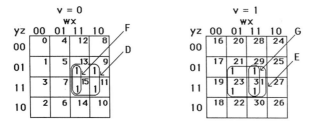

Prime Implicants: (9,11,13,15); (21,23,29,31); (13,15,29,31)

Figure 6.3-12 Five-variable map for $f = \Sigma(9, 11, 13, 15, 21, 23, 29, 31) = v'wz + vxz$.

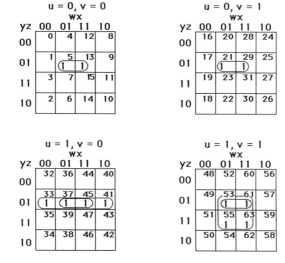

Prime implicants: (5,13,21,29,37,45,53,61); (33,37,41,45); (53,55,61,63)

Figure 6.3-13 Six-variable map for $f = \Sigma(5, 13, 21, 29, 33, 37, 41, 45, 53, 55, 61, 63) = xy'z + uv'y'z + uvxz$.

Combinational Circuit Design   Chap. 6

6.3-4 Formation of Minimal Sums

As was shown in Chap. 3, it is possible to express a function as a sum of the fundamental products that correspond to rows of the table of combinations for which the function is to equal 1 (the canonical sum). It is also possible to express any function as the sum of all its prime implicants. This form of the function will be called a **complete sum**. This is a correct representation for the function, since it is possible to derive the complete sum from the canonical sum by use of the theorems $XY + XY' = X$ and $X = X + X$. Moreover, just as there is only one canonical sum for any function and only one function corresponding to a given canonical sum, there is only one complete sum for each function, and vice versa.

Usually, it is a minimal sum rather than the complete sum that is desired. As will be shown in the following section, the minimal sum always consists of a sum of the prime implicants. For some functions all the prime implicants must be included, and for these functions the minimal sum and the complete sum are identical. For most functions it is not necessary to include all the prime implicants, since some of them can be removed by use of the theorem $XY + X'Z + YZ = XY + X'Z$. The minimal sum can be obtained from the complete sum by using this theorem to remove as many prime implicants as possible. There usually are several orders in which prime implicants can be eliminated, and some of these orders of elimination will result in minimal sums and others may not.

Example 6.3-4

For the function $f(w, x, y, z) = \Sigma(2, 3, 5, 6, 7, 9, 11, 13)$ the order in which terms are eliminated from the complete sum determines whether or not the minimal sum is obtained.

Complete sum:

$$f = w'y + xy'z + w'xz + wy'z + x'yz + wx'z$$

First order of elimination:

$$xy'z + w'xz + wy'z = wy'z + w'xz$$

$$wy'z + x'yz + wx'z = wy'z + x'yz$$

$$f = w'y + w'xz + wy'z + x'yz$$

No further eliminations are possible.

Second order of elimination:

$$w'xz + w'y + xy'z = w'y + xy'z$$

$$wy'z + xy'z + wx'z = xy'z + wx'z$$

$$x'yz + w'y + wx'z = w'y + wx'z$$

$$f = w'y + xy'z + wx'z \qquad \textbf{Minimal sum}$$

The maps corresponding to these two simplified forms of f are shown in Fig. 6.3-14.

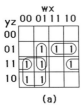
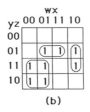

Figure 6.3-14 Maps for $f = \Sigma(2, 3, 5, 6, 7, 9, 11, 13)$ showing two simplified forms of f: (a) $f = w'y + w'xz + wy'z + x'yz$; (b) $f = w'y + xy'z + wx'z$.

A sum-of-products form from which no term or variable(s) can be deleted without changing the value of the expression is called an **irredundant sum**. Both the simplified expressions of Example 6.3-4 are irredundant sums.

Once the prime implicants have been formed, the minimal sum can be determined directly from the map. The rule that must be followed in choosing the prime implicants which are to correspond to terms of the minimal sum is that each 1-cell must be included in at least one of the chosen prime implicants. The problem of obtaining a minimal sum is equivalent to that of selecting the fewest prime implicants. This rule is based on the fact that for each combination of values of the input variables for which the function is to equal 1, the minimal sum must equal 1 and therefore at least one of its terms must equal 1. More simply, the map corresponding to the minimal sum must have the same 1 cells as the map of the original function.

A procedure for determining the minimal sum is first to determine whether any 1 cells are included in only one prime implicant. In Fig. 6.3-15 an asterisk has been placed in each 1-cell that is included in only one prime implicant. A 1-cell that is included in only one prime implicant is called a **distinguished 1-cell**.

A prime implicant which includes a 1-cell that is not included in any other prime implicant is called an **essential prime implicant** *and must be included in the corresponding minimal sum.*[5] In Fig. 6.3-15a both the prime implicants are essential and must be included in the minimal sum. A minimal sum does not always consist only of essential prime implicants. In Fig. 6.3-15b, only the essential prime

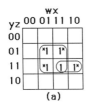
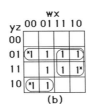

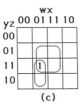
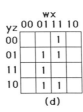

Figure 6.3-15 Determination of minimal sums: (a) $f = \Sigma(5, 7, 11, 13, 15)$, minimal sum: $f = xz + wyz$; (b) $f = \Sigma(1, 2, 5, 6, 7, 9, 11, 13, 15)$, essential prime implicants; (c) Figure 6.3-15b after removal of the essential prime implicants; (d) $f = \Sigma(5, 6, 7, 12, 13, 14)$, no essential prime implicants present.

[5] Actually, an essential prime implicant must be included in all irredundant sums.

implicants are shown. Cell 7 is not included in any of these; so another prime implicant that includes cell 7 must be present in the minimal sum. Figure 6.3-15c shows the function of Fig. 6.3-15b after removal of the essential prime implicants. One of the two prime implicants shown must be included in the minimal sum, and the larger is chosen because the corresponding term contains fewer literals. The final minimal sum is $f = y'z + wz + w'yz' + xz$.

There are some functions, such as that shown in Fig. 6.3-15d, which do not contain any essential prime implicants. For such functions the minimum number of prime implicants required in the minimal sum can be determined by trial and error.[6] The function of Fig. 6.3-15d has two minimal sums,

$$f = wxy' + w'xz + xyz'$$

and

$$f = wxz' + xy'z + w'xy$$

6.3-5 Incompletely Specified Functions

The addition of d terms does not introduce any extra complexity into the procedure for determining minimal sums. Any d terms that are present are treated as 1-terms in forming the prime implicants, *with the exception that no prime implicants containing only d terms are formed. The d terms are disregarded in choosing terms of the minimal sum.* No prime implicants are included in order to ensure that each d term is contained in at least one prime implicant of the minimal sum. The explanation of this procedure is that d terms are used to make the prime implicants as large as possible so as to include the maximum number of 1-cells and to contain as few literals as possible. No prime implicants need be included in the minimal sum because of the d terms, for it is not required that the function equal 1 for the d terms. An example of a function with d terms is given in Fig. 6.3-16.

It is often convenient to avoid determining all the prime implicants. This can sometimes be done by searching for 1-cells that are contained in only one prime implicant and thus determining the essential prime implicants. A 1-cell is selected, and the prime implicant or prime implicants that include the 1-cell are determined. If there is only one prime implicant, it is essential and must be included in the minimal sum. This procedure is continued until all the 1-cells are included in prime implicants of the minimal sum.

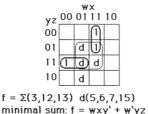

$f = \Sigma(3,12,13) \ d(5,6,7,15)$
minimal sum: $f = wxy' + w'yz$

Figure 6.3-16 Determination of minimal sum for a function with d terms. Prime implicants used in minimal sums are shown darkened.

---

[6] Systematic procedures for such functions will be discussed in connection with tabular methods.

6.3-6 Minimal Products

It is also possible to express a function as a product of factors. The simplest such form will be called a **minimal product**. The definition of minimal product is analogous to the definition of minimal sum: The minimal product is the product-of-factors form that contains the fewest factors. If there is more than one such form, only the form or forms also containing the fewest literals are minimal products. Minimal products are obtained by using the theorems $(X + Y)(X + Y') = X$ and $(X + Y)(X' + Z)(Y + Z) = (X + Y)(X' + Z)$ to simplify the canonical product.

Example 6.3-5

$$f = (x + y' + z')(x + y' + z)(x + y' + z)(x' + y' + z)$$

$$(x + y' + z')(x + y' + z) = (x + y')$$

$$(x + y' + z)(x' + y' + z) = (y' + z)$$

$$f = (x + y')(y' + z) \qquad \text{minimal product}$$

By combining 0 cells rather than 1 cells, a map can be used for minimal products in exactly the same way as it is used for minimal sums. The encircled sets and the corresponding sum factors will be called prime implicates. The algebraic expressions are obtained from the map in the same way as the fundamental sums are obtained from the table of combinations. A variable corresponding to a 1 is primed. The rule for omitting variables is the same for prime implicates as for prime implicants. An example of the formation of a minimal product by means of a map is given in Fig. 6.3-17a.

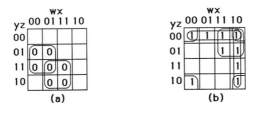

$$f = (w + z')(x' + y') \qquad f = wx' + wy' + x'z' + y'z'$$

Figure 6.3-17 Derivation of minimal product and minimal sum for $f = \Sigma(0, 2, 4, 8, 9, 10, 11, 12, 13)$: (a) minimal product; (b) minimal sum.

The minimal product corresponds to the two-stage gate circuit in which the output is derived from an AND gate and which contains the minimum number of gates. For some functions the minimal sum leads to a more economical circuit, and for other functions the converse is true. For the function of Fig. 6.3-17 the minimal product requires fewer gates (three) than the minimal sum (five). There is no known method for determining which form will lead to a more economical circuit without actually obtaining both the minimal sum and product.

In obtaining a minimal product, d terms are handled in exactly the same fashion as in obtaining a minimal sum. The process of forming a minimal product for a function f is exactly equivalent to that of writing a minimal sum for the complementary function f'. If a minimal sum is written for f' and then Theorem 14 is used[7] to obtain f, the result will be the minimal product for f.

6.4 GENERAL PROPERTIES OF MINIMAL SUMS AND PRODUCTS

There are several other definitions of minimal sum and minimal product besides the definitions given in the preceding section. Two factors affect the definition chosen: (1) the devices and circuits to be used, and (2) the difficulty of obtaining an expression satisfying the definition. The definitions for minimal sums and minimal products used in the preceding section correspond to a two-stage gate circuit which contains the minimum number of gates. This is appropriate for networks constructed out of standard gate circuits for which the implementation cost is determined by the number of gates (TTL NAND gates, for example). When the implementation cost depends on the number of gate inputs as well as the number of gates, the desired expression is one in which the sum of the number of literals plus the number of terms (or factors) containing more than a single literal is a minimum. CMOS gates might be an example of this situation. The number of terms (or factors) that contain more than a single literal is equal to the number of gates whose outputs are connected as inputs to the output gate. The number of literals is equal to the number of gate inputs which are connected to circuit inputs. These remarks apply only to two-stage circuits. Other types of circuits will be discussed in a later section. Another possible definition of the minimal sum would involve obtaining the expression containing the fewest literals.

For the vast majority of functions, these three definitions of the minimal sum all result in the same final expression. Because of this the exact definition used is relatively unimportant. Since the definition of the minimal sum given in Sec. 6.3 is ordinarily easier to use than the other definitions, this is the one that will be used here.

In general, a rule is given for associating a number called the **cost** with each sum-of-products expression, and the minimal sum is defined as an expression for which this cost takes on its minimum value. The three definitions of the minimal sum given previously can all be restated in terms of this cost function. If the total number of literals is to be minimized, the cost is just equal to the number of literal appearances in an expression. When the number of gate inputs is to be minimized, the cost is defined as the number of literals plus the number of terms (or factors) containing more than one literal. If the definition of Sec. 6.3 is used, the appropriate cost is equal to the number of literals plus a large multiple of the number of terms containing more than one literal. This is necessary so that the cost will always be lower for an expression containing more literals but fewer terms than some other expression.

---

[7] Theorem 14: $f(X_1, X_2, \ldots, X_n, +, \cdot)' = f(X_1', X_2', \ldots, X_n', \cdot, +)$.

Example 6.4-1

$$f = w'y + xy'z + wx'y$$

$$N_l = \text{number of literals} = 8$$

$$N_t = \text{number of terms containing more than 1 literal} = 3$$

$$(\text{cost})_A = N_l = 8$$

$$(\text{cost})_B = N_l + N_t = 8 + 3 = 11$$

$$(\text{cost})_C = N_l + 10^6 N_t = 8 + 3 \times 10^6$$

These three definitions of cost all have the property that the cost increases if a literal is added to any expression. The following theorem shows that the corresponding minimal sums must always contain only prime implicants.

It is usually true that the total number of inputs that any single gate can have is restricted. To be strictly accurate, this restriction should be taken into account in the cost function. Since there has been only limited success in including such considerations in the theory of combinational-circuit design [Lawler 60], no further attention will be devoted to them here.

6.4-1 Prime Implicant Theorem

THEOREM 6.4-1. A minimal sum must always consist of a sum of prime implicants if any definition of cost is used in which the addition of a single literal to any expression increases the cost of the expression [Quine 52].

To prove this theorem, a more formal definition of prime implicant is required. It is convenient first to give the following preliminary definition:

DEFINITION. One function $f(x_1, x_2, \ldots, x_n)$ is said to **include** another function $g(x_1, x_2, \ldots, x_n)$ if for each combination of values of the variables for which $g = 1$, it is also true that $f = 1$. This does not exclude the case where $f = g$. In this case f **includes** g and g **includes** f. This is the same relation defined in Sec. 5.3. Another way to say that g includes f is to say that f implies g.

Thus, if f **includes** g, then f has a 1 in every row of the table of combinations in which g has a 1. In terms of the decimal specification, f **includes** g if every number that appears in the decimal specification of g as a canonical sum also appears in the decimal specification of f as a canonical sum. It follows from this definition that if

$$f(x_1, x_2, \ldots, x_n) = f_1(x_1, x_2, \ldots, x_n) + f_2(x_1, x_2, \ldots, x_n)$$

then f includes f_1 and f includes f_2, since $f = 1$ whenever f_1 or f_2 equals 1.

DEFINITION. A prime implicant of a function $f(x_1, x_2, \ldots, x_n)$ is a product of literals $x_{i_1}^* x_{i_2}^* \cdots x_{i_m}^*$, $m \leq n$, which is included in f (f includes $x_{i_1}^* x_{i_2}^* \cdots x_{i_m}^*$) and which has the property that if any literal is removed from the product, the remaining product is not included in f.

The prime implicants which were discussed in connection with n-cube maps (Sec. 6.3) satisfy this definition. The product terms derived from the map equal 1 only for combinations of values of the variables that correspond to 1-cells of the map. Removing a literal from a product term corresponds to picking a larger set of 1-cells on the map, but this contradicts the rule of Sec. 6.3 that prime implicants correspond to sets of 1-cells which are not included in any larger set of 1-cells.

Proof of Prime Implicant Theorem. Suppose that for some function f, a minimal sum exists in which at least one of the product terms is not a prime implicant. Let $f = P + R$, where P is a term that is not a prime implicant and R is equal to the remaining terms of f. Then f includes P, as discussed previously. Since P is not a prime implicant, it must be possible to remove a literal from P, forming $Q (P = x_i^* Q)$, and have f include Q. Since Q equals 1 whenever $P = 1$, $f = Q + R$. This is a sum-of-products expression that contains the same number of terms but one fewer literal than the given minimal sum, $f = P + R$. For any definition of cost that decreases with the removal of a literal, this proves that the original expression could not be a minimal sum and that any minimal sum must contain only prime implicants.

This theorem does not apply to a situation in which only the gate cost is important and the number of gate inputs has no effect on the cost of the circuit. It is possible to prove a more general theorem which does apply to this situation and which shows it is always possible to obtain a minimal sum by considering only sums of prime implicants.

6.4-2 Generalized Prime Implicant Theorem

THEOREM 6.4-2. When a definition of circuit cost is used such that the cost does not increase when a literal is removed from the corresponding sum-of-products expression, there is at least one minimal sum that is a sum of prime implicants.

Proof. Suppose that a minimal sum exists which is not a sum of prime implicants. This means that there must be some product terms that are not prime implicants, because some of their literals can be removed without changing the fact that they are included in the original function. Consider the expression that results from removing all such literals. It must be a sum of prime implicants. Further it must be a minimal sum, since the removal of the literals does not increase the cost associated with the expression.

6.5 MULTIPLE-OUTPUT NETWORKS

Very often combinational circuits are desired which have several outputs rather than just one. The design specifications for such a multiple-output network typically consist of several functions—$f_1(w, x, y, z), f_2(w, x, y, z), \ldots, f_m(w, x, y, z)$—

of input variables. Each function refers to one of the output leads and specifies the relationship between the condition on this output lead and the conditions of the input leads. The methods described in the preceding sections for single-output networks can be extended to the multiple-output case, but certain modifications will be required [Bartee 61], [McCluskey 62].

Perhaps the most obvious technique to try for the multiple-output case is to find minimal sums for each of the output functions separately and then to construct a separate network for each output function. While this technique has the advantage of simplicity, it unfortunately does not lead to the most economical (two-stage) multiple-output network. The truth of this statement can be demonstrated by means of some simple examples. If the functions $f_1(x, y, z) = \Sigma(1, 3, 7)$ and $f_2(x, y, z) = \Sigma(3, 6, 7)$ are minimized separately, the network of Fig. 6.5-1b results. A more economical two-stage network is shown in Fig. 6.5-1c. For this circuit it is fairly obvious that it is not necessary to include AND gates to form the yz term appearing in both outputs. A less obvious example is shown in Fig. 6.5-2 for the functions $f_1(x, y, z) = \Sigma(1, 3, 7)$ and $f_2(x, y, z) = \Sigma(2, 6, 7)$. In the most economical circuit for these functions, use is made of the term xyz, which is not a prime implicant of either of the output functions. For a single-output circuit, only the prime implicants need be considered in determining the minimal two-stage circuit. This example shows that it is not sufficient to consider only the prime implicants of the output functions in designing multiple-output networks. A more general study of the multiple-output problem will be necessary before a synthesis technique can be arrived at.

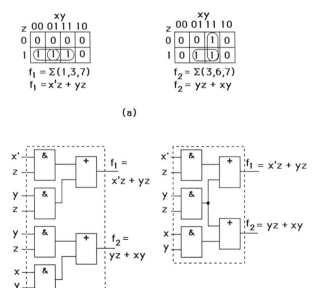

(a)

(b)   (c)

Figure 6.5-1 Example of a multiple-output circuit: (a) output functions; (b) circuit obtained from minimal sums for f_1 and f_2; (c) minimal two-stage circuit for f_1 and f_2.

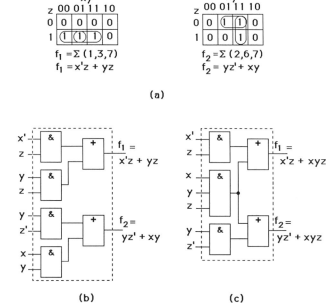

Figure 6.5-2 Example of a multiple-output circuit: (a) output functions; (b) circuit obtained from minimal sums for f_1 and f_2; (c) minimal two-stage circuit for f_1 and f_2.

6.5-1 Multiple-Output Prime Implicants

The general form of a two-stage three-output circuit is shown in Fig. 6.5-3. Each of the input gates must directly drive output gates because of the two-stage requirement. The only freedom that exists is in the number of output gates which are directly driven by a given input gate. The numbers inside the AND gates indicate to which outputs they are connected. Thus, the AND gates labeled 1 are connected only to output f_1, those labeled 23 are connected only to outputs f_2 and f_3, etc. The AND gates that "drive" a single output will be considered first. Whenever all the inputs to one of these gates are equal to 1, the output of the AND gate will be equal to 1 and the output of the OR gate to which it is connected will also be equal to 1. Thus the product $x_{i_1}^* x_{i_2}^* \cdots x_{i_p}^*$ realized by an AND gate labeled j must be included in the function f_j. (Whenever this product is 1, the function is 1.) The products realized by the gates labeled j therefore satisfy the first requirement on the prime implicants of the function f_j. For the usual definitions of circuit cost it would be uneconomical to include any more inputs to these gates than necessary. Under these conditions, the AND gates with single labels must also satisfy the second prime-implicant requirement—none of the inputs to the gate labeled j can be removed without changing the function f_j. Throughout the remainder of this section it will be assumed that *the cost criterion used is one for which the addition of an input to any gate increases the circuit cost.* It follows from this that *the AND gates which are connected only to output* f_j *must correspond*

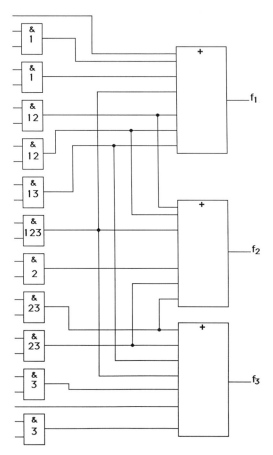

Figure 6.5-3 General form of two-stage three-output circuit.

to prime implicants of f_j. Input variables that are connected directly to output gates can be thought of as input AND gates with only one input.

The situation for input gates which are connected to two outputs is more complicated. Whenever all the inputs to one of these gates are equal to 1, the gate output will be equal to 1 and *both* the circuit outputs to which this input gate is connected will be equal to 1. Thus the product $x_{i_1}^* x_{i_2}^* \cdots x_{i_p}^*$ realized by a gate labeled *jk* is included not only in f_j and in f_k but also in the function $f_j \cdot f_k$, which is 1 only when both f_j and f_k are equal to 1.[8] If the circuit is minimal, removing one of the inputs to a gate labeled *jk* must change either f_j or f_k or both. Thus the product realized by this gate satisfies both the requirements for prime implicants for the function $f_j \cdot f_k$. From this it follows that *the AND gates which are connected to both outputs* f_j *and* f_k *must correspond to prime implicants of the function* $f_j \cdot f_k$. These AND gates need not correspond to prime implicants of f_j for example, since removing one of the input leads need not change f_j if f_k is changed. Thus the

---

[8] If $f_j(x, y, z) = \Sigma(1, 3, 7) = x'z + yz$ and $f_k(x, y, z) = \Sigma(2, 6, 7) = yz' + xy$, then $f_j \cdot f_k = \Sigma(7) = (x'z + yz)(yz' + xy) = xyz$.

second requirement for prime implicants of f_j need not be satisfied. Removal of a different input lead might change f_j but not f_k so that the product would be a prime implicant of $f_j \cdot f_k$ but not a prime implicant of f_j or f_k. This situation is illustrated by the functions of f_1 and f_2 of Fig. 6.5-2. The product xyz is a prime implicant of $f_1 \cdot f_2 = \Sigma(7)$ but is not a prime implicant of either f_1 (because, for f_1, the x can be removed, leaving yz) or f_2 (because, for f_2, the z can be removed, leaving xy).

The situation for gates that are connected to more than two outputs is a direct extension of the two-output case. The entire situation can be summarized as follows: *An AND gate that is connected to all the outputs* $f_1, f_2, \ldots, f_r$ *must correspond to a prime implicant of the function* $f_1 \cdot f_2 \cdots f_r$.

In the technique that was developed for single-output networks all the prime implicants were determined, and then a selection was made of those prime implicants that would appear in the minimal circuit. In this case the set of prime implicants corresponds to all the input gates that could possibly appear in a minimal circuit. For the multiple-output problem, the set of possible input gates corresponds to all the prime implicants of $f_1 \cdot f_2, f_1 \cdot f_3, f_2 \cdot f_3, \ldots,$ $f_1 \cdot f_2 \cdot f_3, f_1 \cdot f_2 \cdot f_4, \ldots$ In designing a multiple-output network it is necessary to generate the prime implicants of each of the individual output functions plus the prime implicants of the functions that are equal to all possible products of two output functions, of three output functions, etc. This collection of prime implicants will be called the **multiple-output prime implicants**. The algebraic expressions corresponding to the minimal multiple-output circuits will be called **multiple-output minimal sums**.

The selection of those prime implicants to be used in the minimal circuit is similar to the single-output technique. Naturally, all these remarks about multiple-output networks with OR gates as output gates apply equally well to networks using AND gates as output gates, provided that the obvious changes in terminology are made. The preceding discussion of multiple-output minimal sums can be summarized formally as follows:

DEFINITION. A **multiple-output prime implicant** of a set of functions $\{f_1(x_1, x_2, \ldots, x_n), f_2(x_1, x_2, \ldots, x_n), \ldots, f_m(x_1, x_2, \ldots, x_n)\}$ is a product of literals $x_{i_1}^* x_{i_2}^* \cdots x_{i_h}^*$ ($h \le n, 1 \le i_j \le n$), which is:

1. Either a prime implicant of one of the functions

$$f_k(x_1, x_2, \ldots, x_n), \quad \text{or}$$

2. A prime implicant of one of the product functions

$$f_{j_1}(x_1, x_2, \ldots, x_n) \cdot f_{j_2}(x_1, x_2, \ldots, x_n) \cdots f_{j_k}(x_1, x_2, \ldots, x_n)$$

The fact that the multiple-output prime implicants are the only product terms that need be considered in designing a minimum-cost two-stage multiple-output network is demonstrated by the following theorem.

THEOREM 6.5-1. For any definition of network cost such that the cost does not increase when a gate or gate input is removed, there exists at least one minimum-cost two-stage network in which the corresponding expressions for the output functions f_j are all sums of multiple-output prime implicants. All the product terms that occur only in the expression for f_j are prime implicants of f_j; all the product terms that occur in both the expression for f_j and f_k but in no other expressions are prime implicants of $f_j \cdot f_k$, etc.

6.5-2 Essential Multiple-Output Prime Implicants and Maps

The first step in obtaining a multiple-output minimal sum is to determine the multiple-output prime implicants. One technique for doing this is to form all the appropriate product functions and then for each of these to obtain the prime implicants. This procedure is illustrated for a three-output example in Fig. 6.5-4.

Once the multiple-output prime implicants have been determined, a selection must be made of the prime implicants to be used in constructing the minimal circuit. Just as in the case of single-output circuits, these are essential prime implicants which must be included in any minimal multiple-output circuit. For example, in the map of Fig. 6.5-4, for f_1 the essential prime implicant A ($w'yz'$) is shown

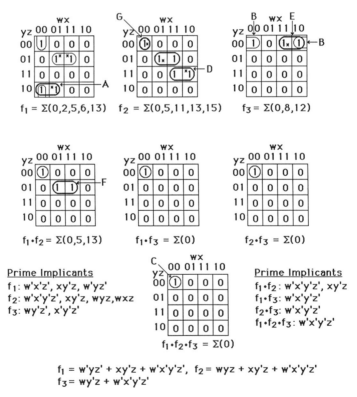

Figure 6.5-4 Determination of multiple-output prime implicants for $f_1 = \Sigma(0, 2, 5, 6, 13)$, $f_2 = \Sigma(0, 5, 11, 13, 15)$, and $f_3 = \Sigma(0, 8, 12)$.

darkened, since it is the only prime implicant that includes the distinguished fundamental product $w'xyz'$. On the other hand, the prime implicant B $(x'y'z')$ of f_3 is **not** essential even though it is the only prime implicant of f_3 that includes the fundamental product $w'x'y'z'$. The reason why this prime implicant is **not** essential is that the fundamental product $w'x'y'z'$ is also included in the prime implicant C $(w'x'y'z')$ of $f_1 \cdot f_2 \cdot f_3$. Basically, the reason B is not essential is that there is a choice possible between using B or using C to ensure that f_3 will be equal to 1 when $w = x = y = z = 0$ $(w'x'y'z' = 1)$. In general, a multiple-output prime implicant is essential for a function f_i if there is a fundamental product of f_i that is included in only the one multiple-output prime implicant.

DEFINITION. Let $\{f_1(x_1, x_2, \ldots, x_n), f_2(x_1, x_2, \ldots, x_n), \ldots, f_m(x_1, x_2, \ldots, x_n)\}$ be a set of output functions and let $\{P_1, P_2, \ldots, P_t\}$ be the corresponding set of multiple-output prime implicants. Then a fundamental product of one of the output functions of the set, f_i, is a **distinguished fundamental product** if and only if the fundamental product is included in only one product of literals which is a multiple-output prime implicant of f_i or of any of the product functions involving f_i $(f_i \cdot f_j, f_i \cdot f_j \cdot f_k, \text{etc.})$.

DEFINITION. A multiple-output prime implicant of a set $\{f(x_1, x_2, \ldots, x_n), f_2(x_1, x_2, \ldots, x_n), \ldots, f_m(x_1, x_2, \ldots, x_n)\}$ is essential for an **output function** f_i if and only if it includes a distinguished fundamental product of f_i.

THEOREM 6.5-2. Let $\{f_1(x_1, x_2, \ldots, x_n), f_2(x_1, x_2, \ldots, x_n), \ldots, f_m(x_1, x_2, \ldots, x_n)\}$ be a set of output functions, and let $\{E_1(x_1, x_2, \ldots, x_n), E_2(x_1, x_2, \ldots, x_n), \ldots, E_m(x_1, x_2, \ldots, x_n)\}$ be a set of multiple-output minimal sums corresponding to these functions. Then a multiple-output prime implicant which is essential for function f_i must appear in the corresponding minimal-sum expression E_i.

In Fig. 6.5-4 the distinguished fundamental products are marked with an asterisk, and the corresponding essential prime implicants are shown darkened. The prime implicant G is a little different from the others. It is an essential prime implicant of f_2 but it is also a prime implicant of $f_1 \cdot f_2 \cdot f_3$. What this means is that it is necessary that G be used for f_2 and that it may also be used for f_1 and f_3. For example, it is possible to use B rather than G for f_3. It is not possible to reduce the total number of gates by not using G for f_1 and f_3 as well as f_2; the only possibility is that some inputs can be saved on the f_1 or f_3 OR gates. This will be illustrated in a later example. G is an example of a prime implicant of $f_1 \cdot f_2 \cdot f_3$ which is essential only for f_2; F is an example of a prime implicant of $f_1 \cdot f_2$ which is essential for both f_1 and f_2.

The prime implicants A, D, E, G, and F of Fig. 6.5-4 have been determined as essential. Only two fundamental products which have not been included in prime implicants remain: $w'x'y'z'$ of f_1 and $w'x'y'z'$ of f_3. The obvious solution is to connect G to f_1 and f_3 as well as to f_2, since this requires no additional gates. The resulting circuit is shown in Fig. 6.5-5.

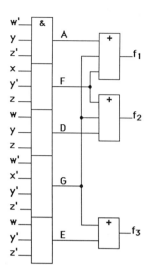

Figure 6.5-5 Minimal circuit for the functions of Fig. 6.5-4.

Figure 6.5-6 shows a three-output problem in which there is a prime implicant $w'x'y'z'$ of $f_1 \cdot f_2 \cdot f_3$ which is used only for f_1 and f_2 in the minimal circuit. The fundamental product $w'x'y'z'$ is included in f_3, but it is not necessary to connect the $w'x'y'z'$ gate output to f_3, since this fundamental product is included in the $w'y'z'$ prime implicant that is essential for f_3. By not using the $w'x'y'z'$ gate output it is possible to avoid using any OR gate in forming f_3. The circuit corresponding to Fig. 6.5-6 is shown in Fig. 6.5-7.

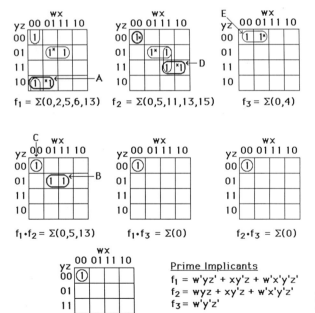

$f_1 = \Sigma(0,2,5,6,13)$ $f_2 = \Sigma(0,5,11,13,15)$ $f_3 = \Sigma(0,4)$

$f_1 \cdot f_2 = \Sigma(0,5,13)$ $f_1 \cdot f_3 = \Sigma(0)$ $f_2 \cdot f_3 = \Sigma(0)$

$f_1 \cdot f_2 \cdot f_3 = \Sigma(0)$

Prime Implicants
$f_1 = w'yz' + xy'z + w'x'y'z'$
$f_2 = wyz + xy'z + w'x'y'z'$
$f_3 = w'y'z'$

Figure 6.5-6 Determination of multiple-output minimal sums for $f_1 = \Sigma(0, 2, 5, 6, 13)$, $f_2 = \Sigma(0, 5, 11, 13, 15)$, and $f_3 = \Sigma(0, 4)$.

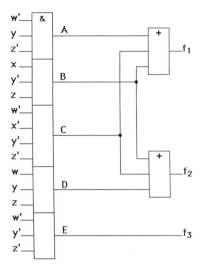

Figure 6.5-7 Minimal circuit for the functions of Fig. 6.5-6.

If a realization is desired in which the outputs are derived from AND gates rather than OR gates (minimal products rather than minimal sums), the easiest procedure is to work with $f'_1, f'_2, \ldots, f'_m$ to get minimal sums and then obtain minimal products by using DeMorgan's theorem to obtain f_i from f'_i.

Unspecified output conditions are treated in exactly the same fashion as for single-output problems—the d entries are treated as 1's in forming the minimal sums.

6.6 TABULAR DETERMINATION OF PRIME IMPLICANTS

The map techniques described in the preceding sections are usually quite satisfactory for functions of four or fewer variables and are useful for some functions of five or six variables. To handle functions of larger numbers of variables, different techniques must be developed. What would be most desirable would be an algorithm for obtaining minimal sums which could be used for hand calculation and also could be programmed on a digital computer. An algorithm satisfying these criteria will be described first for single-output functions [McCluskey 56] and will then be extended to multiple-output functions.

6.6-1 Binary-Character Method

To avoid any limitation as to the number of variables that can be handled, it will be necessary to avoid any attempt to rely on geometric intuition and to work directly with the fundamental products. Actually, it will be more convenient to work with binary characters corresponding to algebraic product terms than to work with the algebraic expressions themselves. Thus each fundamental product will be represented by the corresponding row of the table of combinations; for example, the fundamental product $w'xy'z$ will be represented by the binary character 0101. The first step in this minimization procedure is to list in a column the binary characters corresponding to the fundamental products of the function for which the minimal sum is desired. This amounts to listing the rows of the table of combinations for which the function is to equal 1. Each row is labeled with its decimal equivalent. Such a list is shown in Table 6.6-1a. Each pair of these binary characters is then compared to see whether they differ in only one coordinate (corresponding to being distance 1 apart on the n-cube). The fundamental products corresponding to two characters differing in only one coordinate could be combined by means of the theorem $XY + XY' = X$. Thus, for each pair of binary characters that differ in only one position, a new character is formed which has the same value as both the original characters in each position in which they agree and has a dash in the position in which they disagree. The label of the new row is made up of the labels of the two rows from which it is formed. These new characters are listed in Table 6.6-1b. They correspond to product terms that have one variable (the one corresponding to the dash) missing. A check is placed next to each character of the first column which is used in forming a character of the second column, since a character that can be combined with another cannot correspond to a prime implicant.

The characters in Table 6.6-1a have been arranged in a particular format in order to facilitate the comparison process. They have been arranged in groups so that all the characters in one group contain the same number of 1 entries. Since two characters that differ in only one position must also differ by exactly 1 in the number of 1's which they contain, it is necessary only to compare each character with each of the characters in the next lower group. Comparison with the next upper group is not necessary, since this would cause each comparison to be carried out twice. A simple rule is that a new character is formed when a character has 1's wherever the character (from the next upper group) with which it is being compared has 1's.

The characters in the second column are now compared in the same fashion, and a new character is formed whenever two characters are found that differ in only one position and which both have their dashes in the same position. Again the characters that are used in forming a new character have check marks placed next to them. This procedure corresponds to combining two product terms which both have the same variable missing and which are identical in all the other variables except one. This procedure will result in a new column such as Table 6.6-1c. The same procedure is repeated for each of the new columns (always requiring that the dashes "line up" in two characters which can combine) until no further combinations are possible. Of course, one character can combine with several other characters to form new characters. The unchecked characters that remain after no further combinations are possible correspond to the prime implicants.

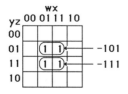 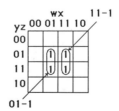

Figure 6.6-1 Maps for Table 6.6-2.

TABLE 6.6-1 Determination of prime implicants for
$f = \Sigma(0, 2, 4, 6, 7, 8, 10, 11, 12, 13, 14, 16, 18, 19, 29, 30)$

(a)

	v	w	x	y	z	
(0)	0	0	0	0	0	✓
(2)	0	0	0	1	0	✓
(4)	0	0	1	0	0	✓
(8)	0	1	0	0	0	✓
(16)	1	0	0	0	0	✓
(6)	0	0	1	1	0	✓
(10)	0	1	0	1	0	✓
(12)	0	1	1	0	0	✓
(18)	1	0	0	1	0	✓
(7)	0	0	1	1	1	✓
(11)	0	1	0	1	1	✓
(13)	0	1	1	0	1	✓
(14)	0	1	1	1	0	✓
(19)	1	0	0	1	1	✓
(29)	1	1	1	0	1	✓
(30)	1	1	1	1	0	✓

(b)

	v	w	x	y	z	
(0, 2)	0	0	0	—	0	✓
(0, 4)	0	0	—	0	0	✓
(0, 8)	0	—	0	0	0	✓
(0, 16)	—	0	0	0	0	✓
(2, 6)	0	0	—	1	0	✓
(2, 10)	0	—	0	1	0	✓
(2, 18)	—	0	0	1	0	✓
(4, 6)	0	0	1	—	0	✓
(4, 12)	0	—	1	0	0	✓
(8, 10)	0	1	0	—	0	✓
(8, 12)	0	1	—	0	0	✓
(16, 18)	1	0	0	—	0	✓
(6, 7)	0	0	1	1	—	
(6, 14)	0	—	1	1	0	✓
(10, 11)	0	1	0	1	—	
(10, 14)	0	1	—	1	0	✓
(12, 13)	0	1	1	0	—	
(12, 14)	0	1	1	—	0	✓
(18, 19)	1	0	0	1	—	
(13, 29)	—	1	1	0	1	
(14, 30)	—	1	1	1	0	

(c)

	v	w	x	y	z	
(0, 2, 4, 6)	0	0	—	—	0	✓
(0, 2, 8, 10)	0	—	0	—	0	✓
(0, 2, 16, 18)	—	0	0	—	0	
(0, 4, 8, 12)	0	—	—	0	0	✓
(2, 6, 10, 14)	0	—	—	1	0	✓
(4, 6, 12, 14)	0	—	1	—	0	✓
(8, 10, 12, 14)	0	1	—	—	0	✓

(d)

	v	w	x	y	z
(0, 2, 4, 6, 8, 10, 12, 14)	0	—	—	—	0

One phenomenon should be pointed out in connection with this process. Each of the characters with more than one dash will be formed in more than one way. This is illustrated in Table 6.6-2, and the corresponding map is shown in Fig. 6.6-1. One way to avoid this repetition is to compare only pairs of characters whose labels form an increasing sequence of decimal numbers. If this is done, care must be taken to place check marks not only next to all characters used in forming new characters but also next to each character that has all the numbers of its label occurring in another character's label. Thus in Table 6.6-2 the characters

(5, 13) and (7, 15) would not be compared, since their labels do not form an increasing sequence, but they would both receive check marks because their labels are included in the (5, 7, 13, 15) label. The other possibility is to ignore the labels and form each character several times as a check on the calculations but not to write down the repetitions of the characters.

TABLE 6.6-2 Example of the two ways of forming a character with two dashes

	w	x	y	z			w	x	y	z			w	x	y	z
(5)	0	1	0	1		(5, 7)	0	1	—	1		(5, 7, 13, 15)	—	1	—	1
						(5, 13)	—	1	0	1		[(5, 13, 7, 15)	—	1	—	1]
(7)	0	1	1	1												
(13)	1	1	0	1		(7, 15)	—	1	1	1						
						(13, 15)	1	1	—	1						
(15)	1	1	1	1												

6.6-2 Use of Octal Numbers

For hand calculation it is usually easier to work with octal numbers rather than the binary characters [Beatson 58]. This can be done by making use of the fact that if two binary numbers differ in only 1 bit, the two corresponding octal numbers must differ in only one octal digit (since each octal digit corresponds directly to 3 binary digits) and that the difference in the single octal digit must be a power of 2 (1, 2, or 4). This is illustrated in Table 6.6-3, which lists all the combinations possible for 3 binary digits, along with the corresponding differences in the octal

TABLE 6.6-3 Example showing that octal equivalents of two binary numbers which combine always differ by a power of 2

	x	y	z			x	y	z
0	0	0	0	0, 1	(1)	0	0	—
				0, 2	(2)	0	—	0
1	0	0	1	0, 4	(4)	—	0	0
2	0	1	0					
4	1	0	0	1, 3	(2)	0	—	1
				1, 5	(4)	—	0	1
3	0	1	1	2, 3	(1)	0	1	—
5	1	0	1	2, 6	(4)	—	1	0
6	1	1	0	4, 5	(1)	1	0	—
				4, 6	(2)	1	1	— · · 0
7	1	1	1					
				3, 7	(4)	—	1	1
				5, 7	(2)	1	—	1
				6, 7	(1)	1	1	—

difference in octal labels

equivalents. Table 6.6-4 shows the use of octal numbers to determine the prime implicants for the function of Table 6.6-1.

The octal equivalents of the binary numbers corresponding to the fundamental products are listed in a column according to the number of 1's in the binary numbers (Table 6.6-4a). Each number of this column is then compared with each number of the next lower group; if two numbers differ in only one of their octal digits, the difference being a power of 2, an entry is made in the next column (Table 6.6-4b). This entry is a double entry consisting of the smaller of the pair of octal numbers that differ by a power of 2 and also the power of 2 by which they differ. Thus, the two octal numbers 15 and 35 would give rise to a new entry 15, 20. The smaller octal number is called the **base label** (15), and the power of 2 is called the **difference label** (20). These entries are partitioned into groups according to the number of 1's in their base labels.[9] Each entry of the second column (Table 6.6-4b) is then compared with each entry of the next lower group having the **same difference label**. A new entry in the third column is formed whenever two entries of the second column are found which have the same difference label and which differ by a power of 2 in their base labels. The new entry has the same

TABLE 6.6-4 Determination of prime implicants for the function of Table 6.6-1 by use of octal numbers

(a)		(b)				(c)			
00	✔	Base	Difference			Base	Difference		
02	✔	00	02	✔		00	02, 04	✔	
04	✔	00	04	✔		00	02, 10	✔	
10	✔	00	10	✔		00	02, 20		G
20	✔	00	20	✔		00	04, 10	✔	
06	✔	02	04	✔		02	04, 10	✔	
12	✔	02	10	✔		04	02, 10	✔	
14	✔	02	20	✔		10	02, 04	✔	
22	✔	04	02	✔					
		04	10	✔		(d)			
07	✔	10	02	✔					
13	✔	10	04	✔		00	02, 04, 10	H	
15	✔	20	02	✔					
16	✔								
23	✔	06	01		A				
		06	10	✔					
35	✔	12	01		B				
36	✔	12	04	✔					
		14	01		C				
		14	02	✔					
		22	01		D				
		15	20		E				
		16	20		F				

[9] The easiest way to do this is to note that two entries will have the same number of 1's in their base labels only if they were formed from entries from the same pair of groups of the preceding column.

TABLE 6.6-5 Formation of the prime implicants from the unchecked entries of Table 6.6-4

	(a)			(b)						(c)		
				v	w	x	y	z				
A	06	01		0	0	1	1	—	v'	w'	x	y
B	12	01		0	1	0	1	—	v'	w	x'	y
C	14	01		0	1	1	0	—	v'	w	x	y'
D	22	01		1	0	0	1	—	v	w'	x'	y
E	15	20		—	1	1	0	1	w	x	y'	z
F	16	20		—	1	1	1	0	w	x	y	z'
G	00	02, 20		—	0	0	—	0	w'	x'	z'	
H	00	02, 04, 10		0	—	—	—	0	v'	z'		

base label as the smaller of the two octal numbers from which it is formed and has a difference label made up of the difference label of the original pair of entries and also of the power of 2 by which the base labels of the two entries differ. Thus, the two second-column entries 02; 04 and 12; 04 will produce the third-column entry 02; 04, 10.

This process is repeated, the rule always being continued that entries can be combined only if their difference labels are identical, until no further combinations are possible. The rule about the difference labels arises from the fact that they specify the locations of the dashes in the corresponding binary characters. The rule for assigning check marks is the same as in using binary characters, and the same remarks about the formation of an entry in more than one way also still apply.

Table 6.6-5 illustrates the procedure for converting from the octal entries representing the prime implicants to the corresponding prime implicants. This is done by converting the base label to the equivalent binary number and then replacing by dashes the binary digits corresponding to the powers of 2 appearing in the difference labels. The binary numbers corresponding to the fundamental products included in a given prime implicant are obtained by replacing the dashes in the binary character representing the prime implicant by all possible combinations of 0's and 1's. For example, the binary numbers corresponding to $-$ 0 1 $-$ are 0 0 1 0, 0 0 1 1, 1 0 1 0, 1 0 1 1. Schemes have also been devised for working directly with the decimal equivalents [Mueller 56] rather than the octal equivalents, but these decimal techniques are more involved than the octal method and are less generally useful.

The techniques just described will result in a list of all the prime implicants. Additional techniques are required for selecting the prime implicants to be used in the minimal sum.

6.7 PRIME IMPLICANT TABLES

The basic requirement which the terms of the minimal sum must satisfy is that each fundamental product of the function must be included in at least one of the terms of the minimal sum. The relation between the fundamental products and the prime implicants can be specified most conveniently by means of a **prime implicant table** [McCluskey 56] such as Table 6.7-1. Each row of this table corresponds to a prime implicant, and each column corresponds to a fundamental product. An × is placed at the intersection of a row and column if the corresponding prime implicant includes the corresponding fundamental product. In terms of the table the basic requirement on the minimal-sum terms becomes that *each column must have an × in at least one of the rows which correspond to minimal sum terms.*

TABLE 6.7-1   Prime implicant table for the function of Table 6.6-1

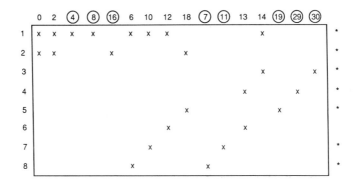

Minimal sum: $f = (0,2,4,6,8,10,12,14) + (0,2,16,18) + (14,30) + (13,29)$
$+ (18,19) + (10,11) + (6,7)$

$f = v'z' + w'x'z' + wxyz' + wxy'z + vw'x'y' + v'wx'y + v'w'xy$

6.7-1 Essential Rows

If any column contains only a single ×, the column corresponds to a distinguished fundamental product (it is included in only one prime implicant) and the row in which the × occurs corresponds to an essential prime implicant. Rows and columns corresponding to essential prime implicants and distinguished fundamental products will be called **essential rows** and **distinguished columns**, respectively.

The first step in obtaining a minimal sum from a prime implicant table is to determine the distinguished columns and essential rows (if any exist). In Table 6.7-1 the essential rows are marked with an asterisk, and the labels of the distinguished columns are encircled. The next step is to draw a line through each column which contains an × in any of the essential rows, since inclusion of the essential rows in the solution will guarantee that these columns contain at least one ×. The result of doing this for Table 6.7-1 would be a table in which all the columns were "lined out." Thus, for this table, the essential prime implicants include all the fundamental products, and the minimal sum is just the sum of all the essential prime implicants. This function represents a special case, since for most functions the essential prime implicants do not cover all the fundamental products. Usually, after the essential rows have been discovered and the corresponding columns have been lined out, a reduced table in which each column has at least two ×'s will result.

6.7-2 Dominance

A prime implicant table for which the essential prime implicants do not include all the fundamental products is shown in Table 6.7-2. The essential rows are marked with an asterisk, and the labels of the distinguished columns are encircled. The reduced table that results when the essential rows and the columns in which they have ×'s are removed is shown in Table 6.7-3 (row *L* has also been removed, since it has no ×'s in the remaining columns). Each of the columns of this reduced table contains at least two ×'s. It is not possible to select any more rows that *must* be included in the minimal sum. However, certain rows can be eliminated, since it can be shown that at least one minimal sum exists which does not include the prime implicants corresponding to these rows.

For example, in Table 6.7-3, row *F* is identical with row *I*, and row *K* is identical with row *M*. Also, the gates corresponding to the rows *F, I, K, M* all have the same number of gate inputs. (This can be seen in Table 6.7-2 by noting that each of these rows contains four ×'s.) Thus, these four rows correspond to gates that all have the same cost regardless of whether gates or gate inputs are

TABLE 6.7-2 Prime implicant table for
$f = \Sigma(1, 4, 5, 7, 8, 9, 11, 13, 14, 15, 18, 19, 20, 21, 23, 24, 25, 26, 27, 28, 29, 30)$

	(1)	(4)	(8)	5	9	(18)	20	24	7	11	13	14	19	21	25	26	28	15	23	27	29	30
*A	x			x	x						x											
*B		x		x			x							x								
*C			x		x			x							x							
D				x					x		x							x				
E				x					x					x					x			
F				x							x			x							x	
G					x					x	x							x				
H					x					x					x					x		
I					x						x				x						x	
*J						x							x			x				x		
K							x							x			x				x	
L								x							x	x				x		
M								x							x		x				x	
N								x								x	x					x
O													x						x			
P												x										x
Q												x						x				

222 Combinational Circuit Design Chap. 6

TABLE 6.7-3 Table that results after removal of essential rows and corresponding columns from Table 6.7-2

	7	11	14	28	15	23	29	30
D	X				X			
E	X					X		
F							X	
G		X			X			
H		X						
I							X	
K				X			X	
M				X			X	
N				X				X
O				X	X			
P				X				X
Q						X		

F = I , K = M remove I and M

being minimized. It follows from this that the cost will be the same for two circuits which are identical, except that one circuit contains a gate corresponding to row *F* and the other contains instead a gate corresponding to row *I*. Since rows *I* and *F* include the same set of fundamental products, it makes no difference if one of these rows is chosen rather than the other. A decision to exclude one of these rows from the minimal sum being sought cannot prevent the discovery of at least *one* minimal sum. If a minimal sum exists that contains row *F*, then another minimal sum containing *I* instead of *F must* exist. Thus, it is possible to remove rows *I* and *M* from Table 6.7-3 and work with the reduced table shown in Table 6.7-4. This table still contains at least two ×'s in each column, so that further reduction must be attempted before any rows can be chosen for inclusion in the minimal sum.

Rows *K* and *F* of Table 6.7-4 both correspond to gates having the same cost, and row *F* has an × in column 29, while row *K* has ×'s in column 29 and also in column 28. Thus, any minimal sum that contains row *F* will also be a minimal sum if row *F* is replaced by row *K*. The converse is not true, since replacing row *K* by row *F* could cause column 28 to be left without any × in a row of the "minimal sum." From this it follows that row *F* can be removed from Table 6.7-4 without preventing the obtaining of a minimal sum. The reason is analogous to that used for equal rows. In Table 6.7-4, row *G* contains ×'s in all the columns where row *H* has ×'s. Since rows *G* and *H* do not differ in their corresponding costs, row *H* can be removed from the table. Row *Q* has an × only in column 23, while row *E* has ×'s in columns 23 and 7. These two rows do not necessarily correspond to gates of equal cost. From Table 6.7-2 it can be seen that row *Q* corresponds

TABLE 6.7-4 Table that results from Table 6.7-3 after removal of rows *I* and *M*

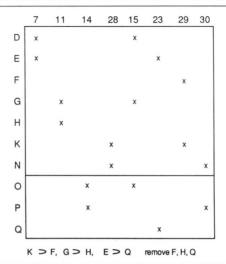

	7	11	14	28	15	23	29	30
D	x				x			
E	x					x		
F							x	
G		x			x			
H		x						
K				x			x	
N				x				x
O			x		x			
P			x					x
Q						x		

K ⊃ F, G ⊃ H, E ⊃ Q   remove F, H, Q

to a gate with four inputs, while row *E* corresponds to a gate with three inputs.[10] In Table 6.7-4 row *E* includes all the fundamental products that row *Q* includes and also corresponds to a gate of equal (if gates are being minimized) or smaller (if gate inputs are being minimized) cost than row *Q*. Row *Q* can be removed from the table, since replacement of *Q* by *E* in a minimal sum cannot increase (and may actually decrease) the corresponding circuit cost. The table that results from removal of rows *F*, *H*, and *Q* from Table 6.7-4 is shown in Table 6.7-5. Before proceeding with Table 6.7-5, the reductions discussed in connection with Table 6.7-4 will be summarized in general terms.

DEFINITION. Two rows *I* and *J* of a prime implicant table which have ×'s in exactly the same columns are said to be equal (written *I* = *J*).

DEFINITION. A row *K* of a prime implicant table is said to **dominate** another row *L* of the same table (written *K* ⊃ *L*) if row *K* has ×'s in all the columns in which row *L* has ×'s and if, in addition, row *K* has at least one × in a column in which row *L* does not have an ×.

THEOREM 6.7-1. A row *I* of a prime implicant table can be removed and at least one minimal sum can still be obtained from the reduced table (with row *I* missing) if (1) there is another row *J* of the table which is equal to row *I* and which does not have a higher cost than row *I*[11] or (2) there is another row *K* of the table which dominates row *I* and which does not have a higher cost than row *I*.

---

[10] Row *Q* contains two (2^1) ×'s, indicating that it corresponds to the combination of two fundamental products and therefore to a product having one fewer variable than a fundamental product. Row *E* contains four (2^2) ×'s. It corresponds to the combination of four fundamental products and thus to a product term containing two fewer variables than a fundamental product.

[11] Of course, only one of a pair of equal rows can be removed, and the row of higher cost is the one that should be removed. Since the theorem applies to the removal of rows one at a time, this is automatically taken into account.

TABLE 6.7-5 Table that results from Table 6.7-4 after removal of dominated rows

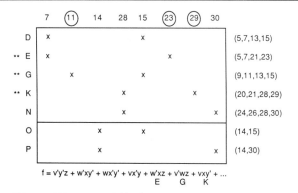

	7	⑪	14	28	15	㉓	㉙	30	
D	x				x				(5,7,13,15)
** E	x					x			(5,7,21,23)
** G		x			x				(9,11,13,15)
** K				x			x		(20,21,28,29)
N				x				x	(24,26,28,30)
O			x	x					(14,15)
P			x					x	(14,30)

$$f = v'y'z + w'xy' + wx'y' + vx'y + w'xz + v'wz + vxy' + ...$$
$$\quad\quad\quad\quad\quad\quad\quad\quad E \quad G \quad K$$

Table 6.7-5 contains three columns that have only a single ×. The corresponding rows must therefore be chosen. These rows are marked with a double asterisk on the figure and are called **secondary essential rows**. The reason for the qualifier "secondary" is that an essential row is one that must appear in **all** minimal sums (in fact, it must appear in all irredundant sums), while a secondary essential row may not appear in some of the minimal sums. For example, if the secondary essential row was one of a pair of equal rows (for example, K and M) another minimal sum will exist which includes the other member of the pair. After removal of the secondary essential rows and corresponding columns from Table 6.7-5, Table 6.7-6 is obtained. In this table row P dominates rows N and O. Row O can be removed, since it has the same cost as row P. With row O removed, row P is secondary essential. Selection of row P completes the process of obtaining the minimal sum, since row P has ×'s in both columns of Table 6.7-6.

The relation of dominance between rows has been presented and shown to be useful for "solving" prime implicant tables. There is a similar relation between columns of a prime implicant table which is also useful.

DEFINITION. Two columns i and j of a prime implicant table which have ×'s in exactly the same rows are said to be equal (written $i = j$).

TABLE 6.7-6 Table that results from Table 6.7-5 after removal of essential rows and corresponding columns

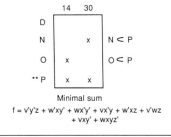

	14	30	
D			
N		x	N ⊂ P
O	x		O ⊂ P
** P	x	x	

Minimal sum
$$f = v'y'z + w'xy' + wx'y' + vx'y + w'xz + v'wz$$
$$+ vxy' + wxyz'$$

TABLE 6.7-7 A table to illustrate column dominance

	1	2	3	4
A	x	x	x	
B	x	x		x
C		x	x	x

DEFINITION. A column i of a prime implicant table is said to **dominate** another column j of the same table (written $i \supset j$) if column i has $\times$'s in all the rows in which column j has $\times$'s and if, in addition, column i has at least one $\times$ in a row in which column j does not have an $\times$.

In Table 6.7-7, column 2 dominates column 1. Column 1 requires that either row A or row B must be selected, while column 2 requires that row A or row B or row C must be selected. If the requirement of column 1 is satisfied, that of column 2 will automatically be satisfied (column 1 will cause row A or row B to be selected and this selection will satisfy the column 2 requirement). Removal of column 2 from this table will thus have no influence on the final minimal sum. It is sometimes possible first to use column dominance to eliminate some columns, and then eliminate rows by row dominance, and then have some additional column dominance develop so that more columns can be eliminated, etc. This will be illustrated in an example in the section on multiple-output prime implicant tables.

THEOREM 6.7-2. A column i of a prime implicant table can be removed without affecting the minimal sum being sought if (1) there is another column j of the table which is equal to column i, or (2) there is another column h of the table that is dominated by column i.

Note that, for rows, the **dominated row** is removed and that, for columns, the **dominating column** is removed. It is not always true that removing essential rows, dominated rows, and dominating columns will suffice for the "solution" of a prime implicant table. It can happen that a table results in which each column contains at least two $\times$'s and no rows or columns can be removed. Such a table is called a **cyclic** table.

6.7-3 Cyclic Prime Implicant Tables

Table 6.7-8 shows a prime implicant table that contains one essential row and one secondary essential row. When these and the dominated rows (there are no dominating columns) are removed, the cyclic table of Table 6.7-9 results. This table cannot have any rows or columns removed from it so that a new technique is required for selecting the remaining terms of the minimal sum.

One method for "solving" cyclic tables consists in arbitrarily selecting one row for inclusion in the minimal sum and then using the reduction techniques to

TABLE 6.7-8   Prime implicant tables for $f = \Sigma(0, 4, 12, 16, 19, 24, 27, 28, 29, 31)$: (a) Removal of essential row G and dominated row I; (b) Removal of secondary essential row J and dominated row H

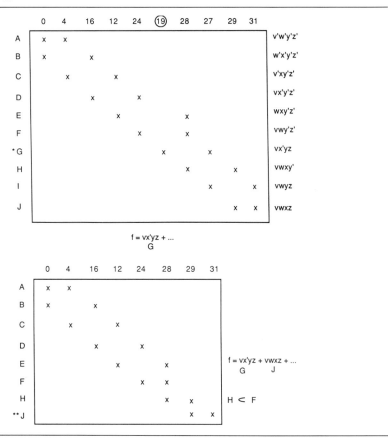

remove rows and columns from the table that results after removal of this row. This entire process must then be repeated for each row that could replace the original selected row, and the final minimal sum is obtained by comparing the costs of the expressions that result from each arbitrary choice of a selected row.

This process is commonly called the **branching method** [McCluskey 56], Sec. 6. In Table 6.7-9 column 0 requires that either row A or row B must appear in the minimal sum. If row A is arbitrarily chosen, Table 6.7-10a results. In this table row B is dominated by row D. After removal of row B, row D is secondary essential, and after selection of row D, rows C and F are dominated by row E and row E must be selected. There is no guarantee that the rows selected from Table 6.7-10a actually correspond to a minimal sum. It is necessary to determine also the result of arbitrarily selecting row B instead of row A (column 0 ensures that either A or B must be in the minimal sum). If row B is selected, Table 6.7-10b results, and the corresponding sum turns out to be of the same cost as the sum for Table 6.7-10a. For this particular function, there happen to be two minimal sums.

TABLE 6.7-9 Cyclic prime implicant table that results from Table 6.7-8

	0	4	16	12	24	28
A	x	x				
B	x		x			
C		x		x		
D			x		x	
E					x	x
F					x	x

This is *not* true in general, and, for this reason, all alternative arbitrary selections must be checked in detail.

The choice of column 0 in this example is purely arbitrary. Any other column could equally well have been used. If column 12 was chosen, first row *C* and then row *E* would have to be selected and the resulting "minimal" sums determined. Usually, it is convenient to choose a column with only two ×'s. If a column with more than two ×'s is chosen, more than two alternative solutions will have to be determined.

It is possible for another cyclic table to result after the arbitrary selection of

TABLE 6.7-10 Branching method applied to Table 6.7-9: (a) After selection of row *A*; (b) After selection of row *B*

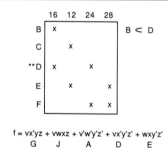

	16	12	24	28
B	x			
C		x		
**D	x		x	
E		x		x
F			x	x

B ⊂ D

$$f = vx'yz + vwxz + v'w'y'z' + vx'y'z' + wxy'z'$$

G   J   A   D   E

(b) After selection of row B

	4	12	24	28
A	x			
** C	x	x		
D			x	
E		x		
F			x	x

A ⊂ C

$$f = vx'yz + vwxz + w'x'y'z' + v'xy'z' + vwy'z'$$

G   J   B   C   F

a row and the resulting reduction of the table. If this happens, another arbitrary selection must be made and all alternative "minimal" sums determined.

Cyclic tables can be "solved" by means of another method which produces all the irredundant sums [McCluskey 56], Sec. 9.[12] The costs of the irredundant sums are then compared in order to choose the minimal sum. In this method a binary variable is associated with each row of the prime implicant table. This variable is set equal to 1 if the corresponding row is selected and is set equal to 0 if the row is not selected. Since these are binary variables, it is possible to interpret them as switching variables and to specify a new switching function which is equal to 1 only when each column has an $\times$ in at least one of the selected rows. This function will be called a **prime implicant function**,[13] or **p function**, and will be represented by p. A p function could be specified by a table of combinations, but this would not usually be satisfactory because of the large number of variables involved. Another possibility is to write an algebraic expression for p directly from the prime implicant table. This can be done for Table 6.7-9 by observing that the p function for this table must be equal to 0. This must be true because if A and B are both 0, neither of these rows is selected and no selected row can have an $\times$ in column 0. If the p function has the form $p = (A + B)q$, where q is a function of A, B, C, D, E, F, which is as yet undetermined, p will be 0 when both A and B are 0. In a similar fashion, column 4 requires that $p = 0$ when $A = 0$ and $C = 0$. This means that p must also have $(A + C)$ as a factor and must be of the form

$$p = (A + B)(A + C)r$$

Either the condition $A = B = 0$ or $A = C = 0$ will thus make p equal to 0. By similar reasoning, each column will contribute a factor to p which contains those variables that correspond to rows in which the column has $\times$'s. It is also true that this product of factors completes the specification of p. The p function should equal 0 if and only if there is some column of the prime implicant table which does not have an $\times$ in any selected row. The product factors corresponding to the columns will equal 0 only when some factor is equal to 0, and a factor can equal 0 only if there are no selected rows having $\times$'s in the corresponding column. The p function for Table 6.7-9 is

$$p = (A + B)(A + C)(B + D)(C + E)(D + F)(E + F)$$

The preceding remarks will be summarized before the procedure for determining the irredundant sums is presented.

DEFINITION. The **prime implicant function**, or **p function**, corresponding to a given prime implicant table is a switching function that is equal to 1 only when each column of the table has an $\times$ in at least one row for which the corresponding switching variable is equal to 1 (selected rows).

---

[12] This technique is sometimes called **Petrick's method**.

[13] It should be remembered that this is a new function in which each variable corresponds to a prime implicant of the original function.

THEOREM 6.7-3. The p function for a prime implicant table can be expressed as a product of factors. Each factor corresponds to one column in the table and is equal to the sum of the variables that correspond to rows in which the column has $\times$'s.

If the total number of gates is to be minimized, the minimal sum corresponds to the fewest variables that when set equal to 1 will cause p to equal 1. It is difficult to discover these variables when p is expressed as a product of factors. If the factors are "multiplied out" by using the theorems of switching algebra, a sum-of-products terms expression will result. When all the variables of any of these product terms are equal to 1, the function will equal 1. Thus, the product terms involving the smallest number of variables correspond to the minimal sums. The p function for Table 6.7-9 is multiplied as follows:

$$p = (A + B)(A + C)(B + D)(C + E)(D + F)(E + F)$$

$$p = (A + BC)(D + BF)(E + CF)$$

$$p = (AD + ABF + BCD + BCF)(E + CF)$$

$$p = ADE + ACDF + ABEF + ABCF + BCDE + BCDF + BCEF + BCF$$

$$p = ADE + ACDF + ABEF + BCDE + BCF$$

This shows that the minimal sums contain the prime implicants corresponding either to rows A, D, and E or to rows B, C, and F. This agrees with the results of Table 6.7-10. The other product terms of p correspond to other irredundant sums.

If a different cost criterion is used, the procedure is to associate a cost with each of the rows of the prime implicant table. The cost corresponding to each term of the associated p function is found by adding the costs of each of the variables in the product term. The minimal sum then corresponds to the term with lowest cost. This will be illustrated by an example in connection with multiple-output minimal sums.

6.8 TABULAR METHODS FOR MULTIPLE-OUTPUT CIRCUITS

For multiple-output problems that are too large or complicated to be solved by map techniques, it is necessary to turn to a tabular method for either hand computation or digital-computer usage [Bartee 61], [McCluskey 62]. The most obvious way to extend the single-output technique would be to form each of the product functions—$f_1 \cdot f_2 \cdot f_3 \cdots$—and then to determine the prime implicants for all the original functions and all the product functions. Although this approach is straightforward, it is unnecessarily lengthy. All the required prime implicants can be obtained without ever forming the product functions explicitly. This is done by forming a binary character for each fundamental product that appears in any of the output functions. This binary character is made up of two parts: the **identifier**, which is the same as the single-output binary character and identifies the corresponding fundamental product, and the **tag**, which specifies which of the output functions include the fundamental product specified by the identifier portion of the character. Each symbol of the identifier corresponds to one of the variables and is 0, 1, or − depending on whether the variable is primed, unprimed, or missing. Each symbol of the tag corresponds to one of the output functions and is either 0 or 1 depending on whether the corresponding fundamental product is not included in the output function or is included in the output function. These multiple-output characters are shown in Table 6.8-1a. They have been ordered according to the number of 1's in their identifiers.

TABLE 6.8-1 Determination of multiple-output prime implicants for
$f_1(w, x, y, z) = \Sigma(2, 3, 5, 7, 8, 9, 10, 11, 13, 15)$,
$f_2(w, x, y, z) = \Sigma(2, 3, 5, 6, 7, 10, 11, 14, 15)$, and
$f_3(w, x, y, z) = \Sigma(6, 7, 8, 9, 13, 14, 15)$

(a)

	w	x	y	z	f_1	f_2	f_3	
2	0	0	1	0	1	1	0	✓
8	1	0	0	0	1	0	1	✓
3	0	0	1	1	1	1	0	✓
5	0	1	0	1	1	1	0	✓
6	0	1	1	0	0	1	1	✓
9	1	0	0	1	1	0	1	✓
10	1	0	1	0	1	1	0	✓
7	0	1	1	1	1	1	1	✓
11	1	0	1	1	1	1	0	✓
13	1	1	0	1	1	0	1	✓
14	1	1	1	0	0	1	1	✓
15	1	1	1	1	1	1	1	✓
	Identifier				Tag			

(b)

	w	x	y	z	f_1	f_2	f_3	
(2, 3)	0	0	1	—	1	1	0	✓
(2, 6)	0	—	1	0	0	1	0	✓
(2, 10)	—	0	1	0	1	1	0	✓
(8, 9)	1	0	0	—	1	0	1	
(8, 10)	1	0	—	0	1	0	0	✓
(3, 7)	0	—	1	1	1	1	0	✓
(3, 11)	—	0	1	1	1	1	0	✓
(5, 7)	0	1	—	1	1	1	0	
(5, 13)	—	1	0	1	1	0	0	✓
(6, 7)	0	1	1	—	0	1	1	✓
(6, 14)	—	1	1	0	0	1	1	✓
(9, 11)	1	0	—	1	1	0	0	✓
(9, 13)	1	—	0	1	1	0	1	
(10, 11)	1	0	1	—	1	1	0	✓
(10, 14)	1	—	1	0	0	1	0	✓
(7, 15)	—	1	1	1	1	1	1	
(11, 15)	1	—	1	1	1	1	0	✓
(13, 15)	1	1	—	1	1	0	1	
(14, 15)	1	1	1	—	0	1	1	✓

(c)

	w	x	y	z	f_1	f_2	f_3	
(2, 3, 6, 7)	0	—	1	—	0	1	0	✓
(2, 3, 10, 11)	—	0	1	—	1	1	0	
(2, 6, 10, 14)	—	—	1	0	0	1	0	✓
(8, 9, 10, 11)	1	0	—	—	1	0	0	
(3, 7, 11, 15)	—	—	1	1	1	1	0	
(5, 7, 13, 15)	—	1	—	1	1	0	0	
(6, 7, 14, 15)	—	1	1	—	0	1	1	
(9, 11, 13, 15)	1	—	—	1	1	0	0	
(10, 11, 14, 15)	1	—	1	—	0	1	0	✓

TABLE 6.8-1 Continued

(d)

	w	x	y	z	f_1	f_2	f_3
(2, 3, 6, 7, 10, 11, 14, 15)	—	—	1	—	0	1	0

(e)

	w	x	y	z	f_1	f_2	f_3	$(\text{Cost})_d$
(2, 3, 6, 7, 10, 11, 14, 15)	—	—	1	—	0	1	0	1
(9, 11, 13, 15)	1	—	—	1	1	0	0	3
(6, 7, 14, 15)	—	1	1	—	0	1	1	3
(5, 7, 13, 15)	—	1	—	1	1	0	0	3
(3, 7, 11, 15)	—	—	1	1	1	1	0	3
(8, 9, 10, 11)	1	0	—	—	1	0	0	3
(2, 3, 10, 11)	—	0	1	—	1	1	0	3
(13, 15)	1	1	—	1	1	0	1	4
(7, 15)	—	1	1	1	1	1	1	4
(9, 13)	1	—	0	1	1	0	1	4
(5, 7)	0	1	—	1	1	1	0	4
(8, 9)	1	0	0	—	1	0	1	4

The first step in forming the multiple-output prime implicants is to compare each pair of characters to determine whether or not the identifier portions differ in only one coordinate.[14] If two characters whose identifiers satisfy this condition are found, a new character is formed. The identifier of the new character is formed in the same way as in the single-output technique. *The tag portion of the new character will have 0's in all coordinates in which either of the original characters has 0's and 1's in the remaining coordinates* (Table 6.8-1b).

The reasoning behind this tag-formation rule is as follows: The new character corresponds to a product term which is included in those functions that include *both* the fundamental products used in forming the product term. This is why there are ones in the new tag only where there are ones in *both* the original characters. This is illustrated in Fig. 6.8-1, in which three maps are shown corresponding to the three functions of Table 6.8-1. Only the entries corresponding to the 2, 3 and 6 fundamental products are shown. The (2, 3) character of Table 6.8-1b has ones corresponding to f_1 and f_2, since both the 2-character and the 3-character of Table 6.8-1a have ones for f_1 and f_2. In Fig. 6.8-1 it is evident that the 2-cell and the 3-cell can be combined on both the f_1 and f_2 maps. On the other hand, the (2, 6) character of Table 6.8-1b has a 1 only for f_2. In Table 6.8-1a, the 2-character has 1's for f_1 and f_2, while the 6-character has 1's for

---

[14] The rules for this comparison are the same as in the single-output case. Only characters that differ by 1 in their total number of 1's need be compared.

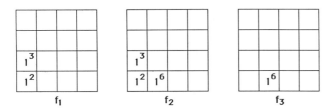

Figure 6.8-1 Illustration of the rule for formation of binary character tags.

f_2 and f_3. The only function for which *both* these characters have 1's is f_2. In Fig. 6.8-1, the 2- and 6-cells can be combined only on the f_2 map.

Just as in the single-output technique, it is necessary to check off some of the characters, since they do not all correspond to prime implicants. The rule for this is as follows. A binary character is checked when (1) it is used in the formation of a new binary character, and (2) the new character has 1's in the same positions as the character to be checked. Thus, in Table 6.8-1, when the (2, 3) character is formed, both the 2-character and the 3-character are checked. However, when the (2, 6) character is formed, neither the 2- nor the 6-character should be checked. The reasoning behind this rule can be seen by considering Fig. 6.8-1. Even though the 6-cell is combined with the 2-cell for f_2, the 6-cell itself is still a prime implicant of $f_2 \cdot f_3$.

The multiple-output prime implicants are obtained by continuing the process of comparing binary characters, using the single-output rule for forming new iden-tifiers, and using the rule just stated for forming new tag portions. The characters that remain unchecked after the completion of this process correspond to the multiple-output prime implicants. Of course, a binary character with an all-0 tag portion need not be written down, since it corresponds to a product which is not included in any of the output functions. Octal numbers can also be used for the identifiers, but the details of this technique will not be described, since they are so similar to the octal technique for single-output prime implicants.

6.8-1 Multiple-Output Prime Implicant Tables

The process of selecting those prime implicants which are used in forming the multiple-output minimal sums is carried out by means of a prime implicant table which is quite similar to the one used in the single-output case, [McCluskey 62]. There must be a column of this table for each fundamental product of each of the output functions. The table is partitioned into sets of columns so that all the fundamental products corresponding to one of the output functions are represented by a set of adjacent columns as in Table 6.8-2. If a fundamental product occurs in more than one of the functions, it will be represented by more than one column of the table. (In Table 6.8-2, there are two columns labeled 2, one for f_1 and one for f_2.) Each row of the table corresponds to one of the multiple-output prime implicants. These are also partitioned into sets of rows by listing first the rows that correspond to prime implicants of f_1, then those for f_2, . . . , those for $f_1 \cdot f_2$, etc.

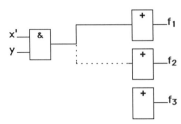

Figure 6.8-2 Illustration of the fact that $x'y$ is a prime implicant of $f_1 \cdot f_2$ but is essential only for f_1.

Just as in the single-output case enough rows must be selected so that there is at least one $\times$ in each column. Again, a column that contains only one $\times$ is a distinguished column, and the corresponding row represents an essential prime implicant. In Table 6.8-2 there are five distinguished columns—those with their labels encircled. The fact that the 2 column of f_1 is distinguished shows that the (2, 3, 10, 11) prime implicant (row F) is essential for f_1. This prime implicant is a prime implicant of both f_1 and f_2; however, it is essential only for f_1. This is illustrated in Fig. 6.8-2.

It has been determined that the solid connection from the $x'y$ gate to the f_2 gate (shown dotted) is also **possible**, but it has not yet been determined whether or not it should be present in the minimal circuit. Thus, the fact that the 2 column of f_1 is distinguished shows that the f_1 **portion** of the F row must be selected. This has been indicated on the table by darkening the $\times$'s in the f_1 portion of row F. The 2, 3, 10, and 11 columns of f_1 can now be removed from the table, since they will have $\times$'s in the selected portion of a selected row. The 2, 3, 10, and 11 columns of f_2 *cannot* be removed, since this portion of row F has not been selected. Similar remarks apply to column 5 of f_2 and columns 6, 8, and 14 of f_3. The corresponding rows F, G, J, K have been marked with an asterisk to indicate that they are essential and have been selected. The table that results after removal of the appropriate columns is shown in Table 6.8-3.

TABLE 6.8-2 Multiple-output prime implicant table for the functions of Table 6.8-1

Column groups: f1 columns = ②, 3, 5, 7, 8, 9, 10, 11, 13, 15 ; f2 columns = 2, 3, ⑤, 6, 7, 10, 11, 14, 15 ; f3 columns = ⑥, 7, ⑧, 9, 13, ⑭, 15

Term	Row	②	3	5	7	8	9	10	11	13	15	2	3	⑤	6	7	10	11	14	15	⑥	7	⑧	9	13	⑭	15	Functions
(9,11,13,15)	A						x		x	x	x																	
(5,7,13,15)	B			x	x					x	x																	f1
(8,9,10,11)	C					x	x	x	x																			
(2,3,6,7,10,1,14,15)	D											x	x		x	x	x	x	x	x								f2
(3,7,11,15)	E		x		x				x		x		x			x		x		x								
* (2,3,10,11)	F	**x**	**x**					**x**	**x**			x	x				x	x										f1 f2
* (5,7)	G			x	x									x		x												
(13,15)	H									x	x														x		x	
(9,13)	I						x			x														x	x			f1 f3
* (8,9)	J					x	x																x	x				
* (6,7,14,15)	K														x	x			x	x	x	x				x	x	f2 f3
(7,15)	L				x						x					x				x		x					x	f1 f2 f3

$$f_1 = (2,3,10,11) +$$
$$f_2 = (5,7) +$$
$$f_3 = (8,9) + (6,7,14,15) +$$

	f₁						f₂							f₃			
	5	7	8	9	13	15	2	3	6	10	11	14	15	13		C_g	C_d
(9,11,13,15)				x	x	x									A	1	3
(5,7,13,15)	x	x			x	x									B$>$G	1	3
(8,9,10,11)			x	x											C $=$ J	1	3
(2,3,6,7,10,11,14,15)							x	x	x	x	x	x	x		D$>$F,K	0	1
(3,7,11,15)		x				x		x			x		x		E$>$L	1	3,4
*(2,3,10,11)							x	x		x	x				F$\subset$D	0	1
*(5,7)	x	x													G$\subset$B	0	1
(13,15)					x	x								x	H	1	4,5
(9,13)				x	x									x	I	1	4,5
*(8,9)			x	x											J $=$ C	0	1
*(6,7,14,15)									x			x	x		K$\subset$D	0	1
(7,15)		x				x							x		L$\subset$E	1	4,5

```
              7        9           2    3     6    10   11   14   15
              V        V           ||   V     ||   V    V    ||   V
              5        8           10   2     14   2    2    6    6
```

f₁ = (2,3,10,11) +
f₂ = (5,7) +
f₃ = (8,9) + (6,7,14,15)

Remove:
rows C,F,K,L
columns 7,9 of f₁
10,14,3,11,15 of f₂

Dominance can be used to remove rows and columns from Table 6.8-3. The same basic dominance rules apply as in the single-output case, but column dominance rules apply only to two columns from the same function. A dominating column can be removed only if the column it dominates refers to the same function. Since these rules depend on the costs corresponding to the rows, these costs have been listed in Table 6.8-3. Both the gate cost C_g and the gate-input cost C_d have been listed. The C_g for row A is 1, since one gate will have to be added if row A is selected. The C_d for row A is 3, since the prime implicant corresponding to row A contains two literals: Two inputs will be required on the corresponding AND gate plus one input on the f_1 OR gate. The C_g for row D is 0, since the corresponding prime implicant has only one literal, and the C_d is 1, since only one input on the output f_2 gate would be required for row D. Row F also has a C_g equal to 0 and a C_d equal to 1, but for a different reason from row D. A gate is already necessary for row F, since it has already been determined that the corresponding prime implicant is essential for f_1. If row F is selected for f_2, it is not necessary to form an additional gate—just one additional gate input is required on the f_2 output gate. (In a sense, the costs listed are incremental costs.) Rows J and K have the same costs as row F for the same reasons. Rows E, H, I, and L have two values listed for C_d. This is because these rows can be used for either one or two functions. If they are used for two functions, one more output-gate input is required than if they are used for only one function.

Examination of Table 6.8-3 shows that row C is equal to row J ($C = J$). Since the costs for C are greater than the costs of J, row C is removed. Rows F, K, and L can also be removed, for they are dominated by lower-cost rows D and E. Row G is dominated by row B, but row G cannot be removed, since it has lower costs than row B. Columns 7 and 9 of f_1 can be removed since they dominate columns 5 and 8 of f_1. In f_2, column 2 equals column 10, and column 6 equals

Sec. 6.8   Tabular Methods for Multiple-Output Circuits

column 14, so that columns 10 and 14 can be removed. Also in f_2, columns 3, 11, and 15 can be removed because they dominate columns 2 and 6. The table that results after the removal of these rows and columns is shown in Table 6.8-4.

In Table 6.8-4a there are three distinguished columns (shown encircled) and two essential rows D and J. Selection of row D completes the formation of the minimal sum for f_2. Also, rows, A, E, and I can be removed, for they are dominated by rows of equal cost, B and H. Row G is dominated by row B, but it cannot be removed, for row B is of higher cost than row G. Column 13 of f_1 dominates column 13 of f_3, but it cannot be removed, since the two columns refer to different functions. The table that results after the removal of these rows and columns is shown in Table 6.8-4b. In this table, column 13 of f_3 is distinguished, and row H must be selected for f_3. This completes the formation of the minimal sum for f_3. The table that results after removal of column 13 of f_3 is shown in Table 6.8-4c. Rows G and H of this table are dominated by row B, but since row B has higher cost than rows G and H, no rows can be removed from the table, which is thus cyclic. The p function is shown in Table 6.8-4c. This p function has two product terms B and GH after it has been multiplied out. The costs for row B are $(1, 3)$, and the sums of the costs for rows G and H are $(0, 2)$. The minimal sum is thus obtained by choosing rows G and H since they are of lower cost. The multiple-output minimal sums are shown in Table 6.8-4d.

6.9 PROGRAMMABLE ARRAYS

The programmable logic array or PLA is a structure that is similar to a ROM but which does not have the disadvantage of doubling in size for each additional input variable. Rather than using a complete decoder to develop one signal for each fundamental product as in the ROM, the PLA implements one signal for each product term in the minimal sums for the functions to be realized. This is illustrated in Fig. 6.9-1, which shows ROM and PLA designs for the 4-bit binary incrementer circuit whose Table of Combinations is given in Table 6.9-1. The ROM circuit requires 16 lines for the fundamental products, while the PLA circuit needs only 10 lines for the product terms of the minimal sums (the maps for the minimal sums are shown in Fig. 6.9-2). Since the cost of implementing a ROM or PLA is proportional to the area and similar technologies are used, the cost for the PLA of Fig. 6.9-1 should be about 5/8 of the ROM cost.

Programmable Logic Arrays are a very popular structure for realizing arbitrary combinational networks. Compared to "random logic" the PLA has the advantage of ease of design. In fact, programs exist for deriving the PLA design directly from the specifications of the functions. Random or custom logic design techniques are used when it is necessary to obtain the minimum area or highest performance. PLAs are available as catalog parts and are used in custom and semicustom designs.

TABLE 6.8-4 Tables that result after removal of dominated rows and dominating columns of Table 6.8-3: (a) Result of removing rows C, F, K, L and columns 7, 9 of f_1 and 10, 14, 3, 11, 15 of f_2 from Table 6.8-3; (b) Table that results after removal of rows and columns from part (a); (c) Table that results from part (b) after removal of column 13 of f_3; (d) Minimal sums

(a)

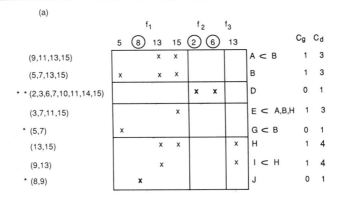

Remove rows A, E, I, D, J
columns 8 of f_1
2,6 of f_2

$f_1 = (2,3,10,11) + (8,9) +$
$f_2 = (5,7) + (2,3,6,7,10,11,14,15)$
$f_3 = (8,9) + (6,7,14,15) +$

(b) Table which results after removal of rows and columns from (a)

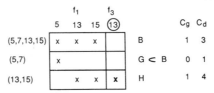

Remove column 13

$f = (8,9) + (6,7,14,15) + (13,15)$

(c) Table which results from (b) after removal of column 13 of f_3.

f_1

	5	13	15		C_g	C_d
(5,7,13,15)	x	x	x	B	1	3
(5,7)	x			G $\subset$ B	0	1
(13,15)		x	x	H $\subset$ B	0	1

$p = (B + G)(B + H) = B + GH$
$\qquad\qquad\qquad\quad (1,3)\quad (0,2)$

(d) Minimal sums

$f_1 = (2,3,10,11) + (8,9) + (5,7) + (13,15) = x'y + wx'y' + w'xz + wxz$
$f_2 = (5,7) + (2,3,6,7,10,11,14,15) \qquad\qquad = w'xz + y$
$f_3 = (8,9) + (6,7,14,15) + (13,15) \qquad\quad = wx'y' + xy + wxz$

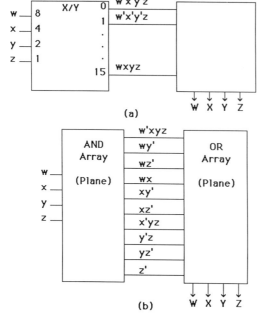

(a)

(b)

Figure 6.9-1 ROM and PLA structures for 4-bit incrementer defined in Table 6.9-1: (a) ROM structure; (b) PLA structure.

6.9-1 PLA Circuits

The electrical structure of a bipolar PLA is shown in Fig. 6.9-3a. This PLA implements the functions of Fig. 6.5-2. The left-hand portion of the circuit consists of a number of diode AND gates that realize the required product terms. The gate outputs are called **product** or **word lines** and the gate inputs representing the

TABLE 6.9-1 Table of Combinations for incrementer network

	w	x	y	z	W	X	Y	Z
0	0	0	0	0	0	0	0	1
1	0	0	0	1	0	0	1	0
2	0	0	1	0	0	0	1	1
3	0	0	1	1	0	1	0	0
4	0	1	0	0	0	1	0	1
5	0	1	0	1	0	1	1	0
6	0	1	1	0	0	1	1	1
7	0	1	1	1	1	0	0	0
8	1	0	0	0	1	0	0	1
9	1	0	0	1	1	0	1	0
10	1	0	1	0	1	0	1	1
11	1	0	1	1	1	1	0	0
12	1	1	0	0	1	1	0	1
13	1	1	0	1	1	1	1	0
14	1	1	1	0	1	1	1	1
15	1	1	1	1	0	0	0	0

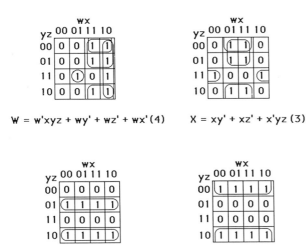

$$W = w'xyz + wy' + wz' + wx' \quad (4)$$

$$X = xy' + xz' + x'yz \quad (3)$$

$$Y = y'z + yz' \quad (2)$$

$$Z = z'$$

Figure 6.9-2 Derivation of minimal sums for functions of Table 6.9-1.

input variable literals are called **bit lines**. The part of a PLA that develops the product terms is called the **AND array** or **AND plane**. The right-hand portion of the circuit has passive pulldown (emitter follower) OR gates to realize the output functions. The circuitry that develops the output functions is called the **OR array** or **OR plane**. The outputs of the OR array are the **output lines** which drive the circuit outputs, and the inputs are the product lines. The intersection of a product line with either a bit line or an output line is called a **crosspoint**. If a circuit is

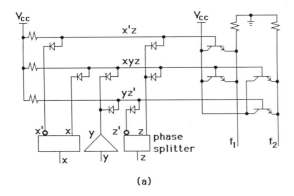

(a)

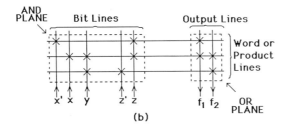

(b)

Figure 6.9-3 Bipolar PLA implementing the functions of Fig. 6.5-2: $f_1 = x'z + xyz$, $f_2 = yz' + xyz$: (a) electrical circuit; (b) symbolic representation.

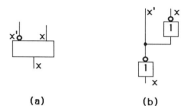

Figure 6.9-4 Structure of a phase splitter: (a) symbol; (b) circuit.

(a)   (b)

present connecting the two intersecting lines, the intersection is called a **used crosspoint**; otherwise, it is called an **unused crosspoint**.

The x and z inputs are connected to circuits, called **phase splitters**, that generate the signals for the bit lines. The phase splitters have two purposes: They derive signals representing the complements of the inputs and are buffers to provide fanout capability to drive the AND gates. Since neither of the outputs depends on y', a simple buffer is connected to the y input. The circuit for a phase splitter is shown in Fig. 6.9-4.

A symbolic representation of the PLA is shown in Fig. 6.9-3b. Design and analysis of PLAs is usually carried out in terms of the symbolic representation rather than the electrical diagram.

An MOS PLA corresponding to the same symbolic representation as Fig. 6.9-3b is shown in Fig. 6.9-5a. The equivalent gate representation is shown in Fig. 6.9-5b. Both the AND plane and the OR plane are realized by means of static NMOS NOR gates (see Fig. 4.3-12). Inverters are used on the outputs to convert from the product-of-sums form that results from the NOR gates to the more familiar

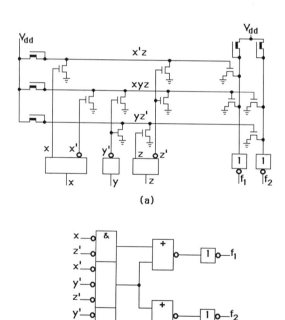

Figure 6.9-5 MOS PLA implementing the functions of Fig. 6.5-2: $f_1 = x'z + xyz$, $f_2 = yz' + xyz$: (a) electrical circuit; (b) gate-level representation.

sum-of-products form. (This does not really add to the cost since some form of output buffer is usually required anyway.) Due to the use of NOR gates, the AND array inputs have logical inversion present. Because of this it is necessary to use x to obtain x' in a product term, x' to obtain x, etc. This has been taken care of in Fig. 6.9-5a by reversing the outputs of the phase splitters from the arrangement in Fig. 6.9-3a. For a discussion of the use of NAND implementations in an MOS PLA, see [Lin 81].

6.9-2 Catalog PLAs

A number of PLAs and related structures are available as standard catalog parts. Two types of devices are available: field or mask programmable. The field-programmable devices contain nichrome (Ni-Cr) or titanium-tungsten (Ti-W) fusible links which can be "blown" to disconnect the corresponding lead. Blowing the appropriate links to cause the device to carry out the desired function is called "programming" the device. A circuit that has the structure of Fig. 6.9-3 with a circuit and fusible link at every crosspoint is called a **field-programmable logic array** or **FPLA**.

Figure 6.9-6 shows a schematic for the Signetics 82S100/82S101 field-programmable PLA [Cavlan 79]. This device has 16 inputs, 8 outputs, and 48

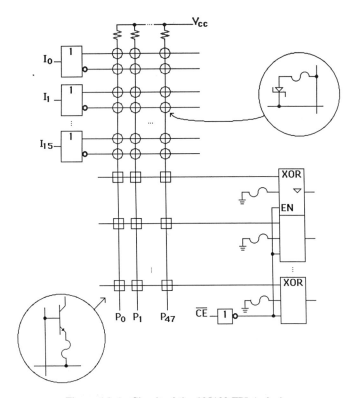

Figure 6.9-6 Circuit of the 82S100 FPLA device.

AND gates. Any set of eight Boolean functions which can be realized using not more than 48 AND gates connected to eight OR gates in a two-stage logic circuit can be realized by programming this chip appropriately. The access time for this device is 50 ns and it is available with either tri-state or open-collector outputs. Each output gate can be programmed to be either an OR or a NOR gate. Note that every crosspoint has a device and a fusible link present. The function realized by the device is determined by which fuses are removed (blown).

The field-programmable devices are typically programmed by the user. They are particularly useful for constructing prototype systems or parts for low-volume products. These single-chip PLAs are typically a bipolar technology. (The 82S100 and 82S201 devices use Schottky diodes for the AND gates and emitter followers for the OR gates.)

A number of variations of the basic FPLA are available as catalog parts. One of these, the Programmable Array Logic family or PAL of Monolithic Memories [MMI 83], has fewer fusible crosspoints than the FPLA and is thus less expensive. In the PAL, the connections to the AND gate inputs are fused (programmable) and the connections to the OR gates are fixed. The structure of the PAL 10H8 device is shown in Fig. 6.9-7. Typical propagation delays are 25 ns for the standard parts and 15 ns for the high-speed version. Corresponding to each PAL device there is typically a mask programmed version called a HAL (Hard Array Logic) device. The HAL is identical to the PAL except that the connections are not programmable but rather are done by a custom metal mask. The HAL is less expensive than the corresponding PAL and is thus suitable for larger-volume applications.

Another important structure is obtained by adding a register to the field-programmable array circuitry. The register is set by some of the OR gate outputs and the register outputs can be connected as inputs to the array of AND gates. It is thus possible to realize an entire sequential circuit with one programmable chip. An FPLA with an added register is called a **field-programmable logic sequencer**, **FPLS**. PAL devices with added registers are also available.

For an interesting story of using PALs in a minicomputer read Chap. 6 of [Kidder 81].

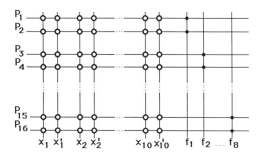

Crosspoints: ⟡fusible link, ╋fixed connection

Figure 6.9-7 Structure of the PAL 10H8 device.

6.9-3 PLA Structures

Two modifications to the basic PLA structure are described in this section. The first of these replaces the input phase splitters by decoders. This technique is used to increase the complexity of the functions that can be realized by a fixed-size catalog part. It is also used to reduce the area required for a custom PLA design. The second technique, called folding, is used only for custom PLAs since it involves rearranging the bit and work lines according to the functions being realized. Its objective is also to reduce the area required by the PLA.

Input Decoders. The most common input arrangement for a PLA has each input connected to a phase splitter, a buffer that provides both true and complement signals as outputs. Thus each input has two lines connected to the AND array. By replacing these two-output input buffers with decoders, it is often possible to reduce substantially the area required to realize a given set of functions. If two inputs are decoded to realize signals corresponding to $x + y$, $x + y'$, $x' + y$, and $x' + y'$, the same number of lines (four) are used to connect the two inputs to the AND array as when phase splitters are used. However, it now becomes possible to realize products with factors such as $x + y$ or even $x \oplus y$ with single product lines [Fleisher 75]. This is illustrated in Fig. 6.9-8. Part (a) shows a PLA realizing

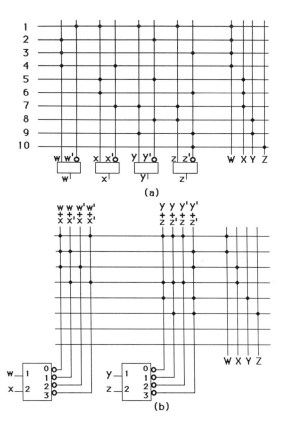

(a)

(b)

Figure 6.9-8 PLAs for the incrementer network of Table 6.9-1: (a) using phase splitters; (b) using two-variable input decoders.

the incrementer network functions (Table 6.9-1) according to the minimum sums derived in Fig. 6.9-2. Part (b) shows the same functions realized by a PLA having two-variable decoders on its inputs. Use of the two-variable decoders requires only six product lines, a reduction of four from the design using input phase splitters.

Design of an optimum PLA using phase splitters can be done directly from the minimum multiple-output sums. Derivation of the optimum PLA using two-variable input decoders is not straightforward. In fact, there is no simple way to tell the best pairs of inputs to decode together. For the incrementer network, the Y output is equal to $y \oplus z = (y + z)(y' + z')$. The EXCLUSIVE-OR function of two variables connected to the same two-variable decoder can always be realized with a single product line. Thus, a design with a y, z decoder and a w, x decoder was considered first. The Z output is equal to $z' = (y + z')(y' + z')$, which requires one product line. The X output is equal to $xy' + xz' + x'yz$, which can be rewritten as $x(y' + z') + x'yz$. Since $x = (w + x)(w' + x)$, $x' = (w + x')(w' + x')$, this can be realized with two product lines. The derivation of the W output is more difficult and is best done on a map as illustrated in Fig. 6.9-9.

Designing PLAs with 2-bit input decoders is a more difficult task than design with phase splitters. Attempts have been made to write programs to do the design automatically, but information on their effectiveness is not yet available. Also, the 2-bit decoders are more complex than phase splitters so that the saving in word lines must be sufficient to offset the increased decoder cost. The circuitry of a PLA with 2-bit decoders is presented in [Wood 79].

Folding a PLA. Another variation in the basic PLA structure involves using one row of the array for two product lines or having two bit lines share the same column of the AND array. In Fig. 6.9-10c, bit lines (b, c) and (b', c') each share a single column. Figure 6.9-10e shows a structure in which the product line for ab and the cd product line share a single row. This technique permits a more compact design to be achieved by sharing the column and row space between two interconnections [Wood 79]. A property of a PLA that permits this modification is the fact that the relative order of the product lines doesn't affect the functions realized. Neither is the order of the product lines critical to the logic realized. The output lines can be arranged on either side of the AND array. Figure 6.9-10a shows a PLA to realize the functions $f = a'c'd' + ab$ and $g = a'b'd' + cd$. Part (b) shows the same PLA with row 1 moved from the top to the bottom. The b bit lines only intersect the two topmost rows (2 and 3) and the c bit lines intersect only the two bottom rows (4 and 1). It is thus possible to combine the b and c

$$W = (w \oplus x)yz + w(y' + z')$$

Figure 6.9-9 Use of a map to derive the W output function for a PLA using two-variable input decoders.

Combinational Circuit Design   Chap. 6

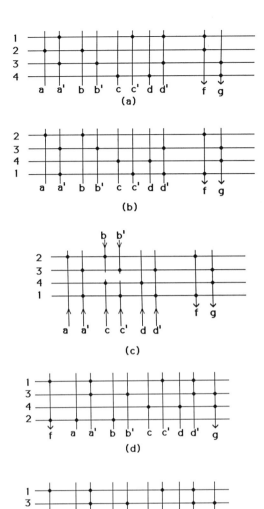

Figure 6.9-10 Example of folding: (a) unfolded PLA; (b) row 1 moved to bottom; (c) splitting of b and c columns; (d) original PLA with row 2 moved to bottom; (e) splitting of rows 2 and 4.

lines in the same columns as shown in Fig. 6.9-10c. This technique is called **column splitting**. Figure 6.9-10d shows the PLA of part (a) modified by moving row 2 to the bottom and moving output line f to the left of the AND array. Row 2 connects to bit lines a and b, and row 4 connects to c and d. It is thus possible to combine rows 2 and 4 as shown in Fig. 6.9-10e. This technique is called **row splitting**.

In the PLA of Fig. 6.9-8a row splitting leads to the design of Fig. 6.9-11a in which rows (5, 10) and (4, 8) have been combined. If the shared row (5, 10) is moved to the bottom of the array, folding of the output columns is possible, leading to the structure of Fig. 6.9-8b. The straightforward design of Fig. 6.9-8a is a PLA of dimension 10 by 12. This can be reduced to 6 by 12 with 2-bit input decoders (Fig. 6.9-8b). Folding produces the Fig. 6.9-11b structure of dimension 8 by 10. Folding is an important technique for reducing the area required to realize a custom

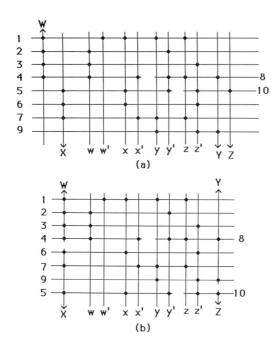

Figure 6.9-11 Folding of incrementer PLA of Fig. 6.9-8: (a) row splitting of rows (4, 8) and (5, 10); (b) column splitting of columns (W, X) and (Y, Z).

PLA. Design automation techniques for PLA folding have been developed; for example, see [Hachtel 82].

6.9-4 PLA Minimization

It is often advantageous to minimize a PLA design either to reduce the required silicon area for an embedded array or to fit the design on as few chips as possible. This minimization problem is very similar to the classic two-stage minimization of switching theory. In the case of the PLA it can be argued that minimizing the number of gates is important, but that it is not necessary to minimize the number of gate inputs. It is possible to have a design which does not have the minimum number of gate inputs, but which does not contain any redundant connections. More likely a nonoptimum design will contain redundant connections which may not contribute directly to the cost, but do make testing more difficult and to that extent may cause the design to be more expensive than a minimum structure.

Minimizing PLA designs is a very difficult problem because large numbers of inputs and multiple outputs are involved. An exact minimum is usually not possible to obtain because of the amount of computation involved (the problem is np complete). Many programs involving heuristics have been written to handle this problem [Soong 77], [Kambayashi 79], and [Brayton 84]. Two programs are reported to be in use for actual designs: one at IBM [Hong 74] and one at Signetics [Bricaud 78].

There are situations in which a network having no logic hazards is needed. Such a network can be obtained by a straightforward extension of the techniques presented in Secs. 6.3 to 6.8. This is based on the following theorem.

THEOREM 6.10-1. A network whose 1-sets satisfy the following conditions will not contain any static or dynamic logic hazards.

1. For each pair of adjacent input states that both produce a 1 output, there is at least one 1-set that includes both input states of the pair.
2. There are no 1-sets that contain exactly one pair of complementary literals.

Proof. Condition 1 guarantees that there will be no static logic 1-hazards by the first theorem of Sec. 3.6-3. The second theorem of Sec. 3.6-3 shows that there will be no static logic 0-hazards if condition 2 is satisfied. The corollary to Theorem 3.6-5 demonstrates that there will be no dynamic logic hazards if condition 2 holds since there will be no unstable sets satisfying the premise of the corollary.

The procedure described in this section leads to a two-stage sum-of-products network satisfying the conditions of this theorem. The second condition is easily satisfied by not including any AND gates having both a variable and its complement as inputs. The first condition can be met by modifying the procedure for obtaining a minimal sum so that it is met. It is still possible to use only prime implicants as 1-sets, but it may be necessary to include some prime implicants in addition to those in the minimal sum. All pairs of adjacent input states that both have a 1 output must be checked to see that they are both included in a single prime implicant included in the sum-of-products expression.

The Karnaugh map for the function $\Sigma(0, 3, 7, 11, 12, 13, 15)$ is shown in Fig. 6.10-1. The minimal sum for this function is $w'x'yz + wxy' + yz$. This leaves the pair of adjacent input states 1101 and 1111 included only in different prime implicants. Thus the minimal sum is not hazard-free since condition 1 of the theorem is not satisfied. A hazard-free expression can be obtained by adding the prime implicant wxz to the minimal sum.

A modification of the tabular method for minimal sums is illustrated in Table 6.10-1. Parts (a), (b), and (c) of this table are no different from the basic minimal sum method. Part (d) shows the hazard-free prime implicant table. This

Figure 6.10-1 Karnaugh map for $f(w, x, y, z) = \Sigma(0, 3, 7, 11, 12, 13, 15)$.

TABLE 6.10-1   Derivation of hazard-free minimal sum for $f(w, x, y, z) = \Sigma(0, 3, 7, 11, 12, 13, 15)$ using a modified tabular method

(a)

	w	x	y	z
0	0	0	0	0
3	0	0	1	1
12	1	1	0	0
7	0	1	1	1
11	1	0	1	1
13	1	1	0	1
15	1	1	1	1

(b)

	w	x	y	z
3, 7	0	—	1	1
3, 11	—	0	1	1
12, 13	1	1	0	—
7, 15	—	1	1	1
11, 15	1	—	1	1
13, 15	1	1	—	1

(c)

	w	x	y	z
3, 7, 11, 15	—	—	1	1

(d)

	3 / 0	3 / 7	12 / 11	7 / 13	11 / 15	13 / 15	
0	×						*
12, 13				×			*
13, 15						×	*
3, 7, 11, 15		×	×		×	×	*

table has all of the prime implicants as rows. However, the columns correspond to pairs of adjacent input states. These are obtained as all of the entries of Table 6.10-1b since this part of the formation of the prime implicants derives exactly all of the adjacent inputs having 1 outputs. Since the 0 input state is not included in any of the pairs, it corresponds to an essential prime implicant and must be included in the sum-of-products expression. Selection of rows from the prime implicant table is done in exactly the same way as presented in Sec. 6.7. For Table 6.10-1 all prime implicants are essential for a hazard-free minimal sum.

The fact that it is not always necessary to use all of a function's prime implicants in forming a hazard-free minimal sum is demonstrated by the function $f(w, x, y, z) = \Sigma(3, 4, 5, 6, 7, 10, 11, 12, 14, 15)$. Figure 6.10-2 shows the map for this function and Table 6.10-2 shows the steps of the tabular method for the function.

Figure 6.10-2   Karnaugh map for $\Sigma(3, 4, 5, 6, 7, 10, 11, 12, 14, 15)$.

TABLE 6.10-2 Tabular derivation of hazard-free minimal sum for
$f(w, x, y, z) = \Sigma(3, 4, 5, 6, 7, 10, 11, 12, 14, 15)$

	4 / 5	4 / 6	4 / 12	3 / 7	3 / 11	5 / 7	6 / 7	6 / 14	10 / 11	10 / 14	12 / 14	7 / 15	11 / 15	14 / 15	
4 5 6 7	⊗	×				⊗	×								*
4 6 12 14		×	⊗					×			⊗				*
3 7 11 15				⊗	⊗							×		×	*
6 7 14 15							×	×				×		×	
10 11 14 15									⊗	⊗			⊗	×	*

	w	x	y	z
4	0	1	0	0
3	0	0	1	1
5	0	1	0	1
6	0	1	1	0
10	1	0	1	0
12	1	1	0	0
7	0	1	1	1
11	1	0	1	1
14	1	1	1	0
15	1	1	1	1

	w	x	y	z
4, 5	0	1	0	—
4, 6	0	1	—	0
4, 12	—	1	0	0
3, 7	0	—	1	1
3, 11	—	0	1	1
5, 7	0	1	—	1
6, 7	0	1	1	—
6, 14	—	1	1	0
10, 11	1	0	1	—
10, 14	1	—	1	0
12, 14	1	1	—	0
7, 15	—	1	1	1
11, 15	1	—	1	1
14, 15	1	1	1	—

	w	x	y	z
4, 5, 6, 7	0	1	—	—
4, 6, 12, 14	—	1	—	0
3 7 11 15	—	—	1	1
6 7 14 15	—	1	1	—
10 11 14 15	1	—	1	—

A two-stage network can be realized directly from the hazard-free minimal sum. It is also possible to use the switching algebra theorems to obtain expressions representing multistage networks. The hazard-free nature of the network is preserved if no theorems are used that alter the 1-sets. For a more detailed discussion of which theorems cannot be used, see Sec. 3.6-3. Hazards can also be controlled by the use of delay elements as in Fig. 3.6-2.

6.11 FAULT MODELS

Production and usage of digital integrated circuits involves a variety of testing problems: wafer probe, wafer sort, pre-ship screen, incoming test of chips and boards, test of assembled boards, system test, periodic maintenance, repair testing, etc. The discussion in this book is aimed specifically at those testing problems that involve packaged chips. The first step in developing a testing strategy involves identifying the malfunctions to be tested for and deriving models for the logical effects of these faults. This section discusses these topics.

6.11-1 Malfunctions

The underlying cause of a malfunction is always some type of failure. These failures can be due to a physical component functioning incorrectly, an improper design, or an erroneous human interaction.

Physical failures can be either permanent or temporary. A **permanent failure** is caused by a component that breaks due to a mechanical rupture or some wear-out phenomenon, such as metal migration, purple plague, oxide defects, etc., [Camenzind 72]. Usually, permanent failures are localized. The occurrence of permanent failures can be minimized by careful processing and initial screening tests. They can never be eliminated completely.

Temporary failures can be either transient or intermittent. A **transient failure** is caused by some externally induced signal perturbation usually due to electro-magnetic or alpha-particle radiation, or power supply fluctuation [Deavenport 80]. Transient failures can be controlled by careful attention to shielding and decoupling in the design of the equipment [Morrison 77].

An **intermittent failure** often occurs when a component is in the process of developing a permanent failure. Some parameter may degrade so that signal level separation is lessened. Noise margins decrease and false signal values appear in an apparently random fashion. The occurrence of intermittent failures is minimized in the same way that permanent failures are controlled. Since it is not possible to guarantee devices free of permanent failures, intermittent failures will always be present. Accurate data on the relative frequency of permanent and temporary failures are not available. There does seem to be general agreement that temporary failures occur at least 10 times more often than permanent failures. Permanent failures are sometimes referred to as **hard failures** and temporary failures as **soft failures**.

Improper design of the hardware or software can result in a system that does not function at all. Such mistakes are, of course, quickly discovered. Determining the cause of the problem and fixing it can be difficult. Other, less obvious design defects usually remain in any system even after it has been in service for a long time. These are usually mistakes that affect the system only when rare combinations of signal values occur or for unusual signal timing relationships. Design mistakes can produce symptoms which are very similar to those caused by temporary physical failures. Careful design discipline with specific attention to avoiding hazards, races, deadlocks, etc. can reduce design mistakes of this nature. As a system is used, design defects are discovered and corrected. Eventually, a system results in which most, if not all, of these problems have been corrected.

Whenever a human being interacts with a computer system there is the possibility that the human being will do the wrong thing. Incorrect data or control information can be entered. Improper repair actions can be taken. While little can be done to improve the basic reliability of human beings, it is possible to reduce incorrect actions by careful training. Also, interlocks can be provided so that another person checks an operator's actions or so that dangerous actions are automatically inactivated. Deliberately malicious operations by a knowledgeable human being are even harder to prevent. It appears that the most reliable computer systems will be those in which any human interaction is reduced to near zero.

6.11-2 Faults

Some failures will cause the system to stop functioning. Those failures that are most difficult to deal with are those that cause some signals to have incorrect values. When a system is designed to minimize or control the impact of failures, it is these changes in signal values which are dealt with rather than their underlying failure causes. The effects of failures are thus modeled in terms of the incorrect signal values which they produce. A **fault model** is the representation of the effect of a failure by means of the change that is produced in the system signals. The usefulness of a fault model is determined by the accuracy with which it represents the effects of failures as well as by its tractability as a design tool.

Fault models often represent compromises between these frequently conflicting objectives of accuracy and tractability. A large variety of models are used. The choice of a model or models depends on the failures expected for the particular technology and system being designed as well as on the design tools available for the various models.

The most common fault model in use is the **single stuck-at fault**: Exactly one of the signal lines in a circuit is assumed to have its value fixed at either a logical 1 or a logical 0, rather than having its value determined by a gate output or circuit input. More complex fault models are the multiple stuck-at fault and the bridging fault. In the **multiple stuck-at fault** it is assumed that one or more signal lines can have values that are fixed and independent of the other signals in the network. The **bridging fault** assumes that two signal lines are connected together so that wired logic occurs. A particularly troublesome aspect of the bridging fault is the fact that it can convert a combinational circuit into a sequential circuit. This can make test generation difficult.

The single stuck-at fault has gained wide acceptance in connection with testing. It is the simplest model to use. Also, it has been shown both theoretically and empirically to result in tests that detect very many multiple stuck-at faults and bridging faults without the necessity to explicitly consider these more complex faults.

Another variation of the stuck-at fault model is the **unidirectional fault**, in which it is assumed that one or more stuck-at faults may be present, but all the stuck signals have the same logical value, either all 0 or all 1. This model is used in connection with storage media whose faults are appropriately represented by such a fault. Special error-correcting codes are used in such situations.

Bridging faults and stuck-at faults have the convenient property that their effects are independent of the signals present in the circuit. However, it is well known that there are failure modes in RAMs which cannot be adequately modeled by such faults. In order to develop tests for RAMs it is necessary to consider **pattern-sensitive faults** in which the effect of the fault is dependent on the particular input applied to the device. There is presently concern that for the newer, high-density dynamic MOS circuits it may also be necessary to consider pattern-sensitive faults.

It has been shown [Wadsack 78] that a somewhat similar situation can arise in CMOS logic. A failed connection in the output stage of a CMOS gate causes a failure mode whose effects can depend on the *rate* at which signals are applied. This is modeled as a **stuck-open fault**.

The previous fault models all involve signals having incorrect values. A different class of fault occurs when a signal does not assume an incorrect value, but instead fails to change value soon enough. More specifically, a **delay fault** occurs when a gate has a propagation delay exceeding the specified worst case [Shedletsky 78].

Many situations occur in which a less detailed fault model is the most effective choice. In designing a fault-tolerant or gracefully degrading system the most useful fault model may be one in which it is assumed that any single module can fail in an arbitrary fashion. This is called a **single module fault**. The only restriction placed on the fault is the assumption that at most one module will be bad at any given time.

6.12 TEST SETS

Efficient techniques for testing and diagnosis of digital systems and modules are becoming of critical importance. Current trends for increased density of devices on integrated circuits are creating a situation in which:

1. System hardware costs are being significantly decreased due to this increased density,
2. Testing is becoming more difficult since the number of pins per IC is not increasing in proportion to the number of gates per IC, thus reducing the observability and controllability of the logic on the chip, and
3. Due to the combination of these two effects, the percentage of the system cost due to testing is increasing drastically.

As a result of this situation attention is being focused on using some of the devices on a chip for circuits whose sole purpose is to reduce the cost of obtaining good system testability.

This section presents a discussion of test set generation. Techniques for designing circuits so that they are easily testable—**design for testability** or **DFT**— are discussed in Chap. 10.

Perhaps the most important feature of a testability technique is its coverage: the fraction of the possible failures that the test technique can detect. Also important is the ability of a technique to identify which unit has the fault. When a failure cannot be detected or located to a particular unit, either false results can be produced or a great deal of time consumed in repair. The other important parameter is the cost of the testability technique. Cost depends on the tester equipment cost, the time taken by the test, and the expense due to extra components added to the system to facilitate testing.

6.12-1 Exhaustive Testing

Perhaps the most obvious testing technique for combinational circuits consists of applying all possible input patterns (2^n of them for an n-input circuit) and comparing the output responses with the specifications for the circuit. This is, in effect, verifying the table of combinations for the circuit and requires that this table be stored in the testing device. The coverage is excellent since any failure that changes the static functions realized by the circuit is guaranteed to be detected. Delay faults are not discovered, but this is a complexity whose discussion is best postponed. The cost is very high since the entire table of combinations must be stored and the time of test is long. The cost of test generation is low since the table of combinations is either known or can be easily generated. The analogous technique for sequential circuits is the use of a checking experiment which verifies that the circuit realizes the flow table specification of the desired sequential functions. This technique has all the disadvantages that the table of combinations verification does for combinational circuits and, in addition, is much longer than the combinational test and is quite difficult to generate. These verification techniques have not been considered practical because of the long test times that they required. However, current research has shown that if the circuit is first partitioned into subcircuits with a sufficiently small number of inputs, exhaustive testing of combinational circuits is feasible [McCluskey 81].

6.12-2 Minimum-Length Tests

One approach to reducing testing cost is to reduce the number of test patterns that must be applied. If the circuit layout is known and it is possible to identify the set of failures that must be tested for, it is not necessary to verify that the circuit specification is implemented by the tested circuit. All that is required is to establish that none of the circuits that can be produced by the occurrence of a failure are present. Useful but not wholly satisfactory programs exist for generating efficient tests for combinational circuits; but the generation of reasonable tests for sequential circuits is often impossible. The cost of running the test generation program can be quite high and is very dependent on the circuit configuration. Usually, less than 100% fault coverage is obtained and it becomes increasingly expensive to generate tests for the last untested faults.

The first step in using this testing technique is to decide on the set of faults for which test patterns are to be generated. The standard practice is to use the single stuck-at faults. This choice is justified by assuming that most of the multiple stuck-at faults as well as many of the bridging faults will automatically be detected by the set of tests generated for single stuck-at faults. Both empirical and theoretical results exist which support this assumption (e.g., [Kodandapani 80], [Mei 74], [Smith 79], and [Agarwal 81]).

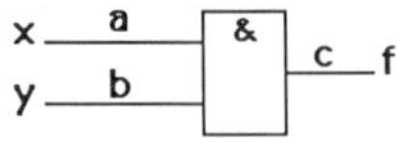

Figure 6.12-1 AND gate with inputs x and y, output f and leads a, b, and c.

Figure 6.12-1 shows an extremely simple circuit, a two-input AND gate, which will be used to illustrate the approach used. Table 6.12-1 shows the table of combinations for this circuit when no faults are present and also when each single stuck-at fault is present. The notation $a/1$ is used to indicate lead a stuck at 1. The notation f represents the fault-free function and $f_{a/1}$ represents the function realized by the circuit when lead a is stuck at 1.

Inspection of this table shows that the columns corresponding to $f_{a/0}$, $f_{b/0}$, and $f_{c/0}$ are identical. Since these three faults have the same effect on the function realized by the network they are said to be **equivalent**. It is possible to derive test sets by considering only the equivalence classes of single stuck-at faults rather than the individual faults themselves. Thus, for the AND gate of Fig. 6.12-1 there are only four different fault classes that need be considered in generating tests. Input faults such as $a/0$ and $b/0$ are called **dominant** since they force the output to a fixed value that is independent of all other inputs. The other input faults, such as $a/1$ and $b/1$, are **nondominant** since they do not force the output value independent of other inputs. In general, for AND, OR, NAND, and NOR gates with n inputs, there are $n + 2$ single stuck-at fault classes: two output fault classes, one of which is equivalent to all of the dominant input faults; n nondominant input faults, which are each alone in a fault class. The technique of dealing with fault classes rather than individual faults is called **fault collapsing**.

To test a circuit for the presence of a fault it is necessary to apply an input combination for which the circuit output with the fault present is different from the circuit output of the fault-free circuit. To test for all stuck-at faults, enough input patterns must be applied so that at least one pattern tests for each fault. Inspection of Table 6.12-1 shows that the input pattern $xy = 11$ must be applied to test for the fault class, including $a/0$. To test for $a/1$ the input $xy = 01$ is needed, and $xy = 10$ is necessary to test for $b/1$. The only remaining fault class is $c/1$, but this is tested by both inputs $xy = 01$ and 10. Thus, three inputs are sufficient to test the circuit of Fig. 6.12-1 for all single stuck-at faults. The set of all input patterns, sometimes called **test vectors** in this context, which tests for the faults specified is called a **test set**. The test set for single stuck-at faults in the Fig. 6.12-1 circuit has just been shown to be $xy = 01, 10, 11$.

TABLE 6.12-1 Table of Combinations for circuit of Fig. 6.12-1

x	y	f	$f_{a/0}$	$f_{b/0}$	$f_{c/0}$	$f_{a/1}$	$f_{b/1}$	$f_{c/1}$
0	0	0	0	0	0	0	0	1
0	1	0	0	0	0	1	0	1
1	0	0	0	0	0	0	1	1
1	1	1	0	0	0	1	1	1

It is, in principle, possible to derive test sets by a procedure such as that illustrated by Table 6.12-1. However, such an approach is completely impractical for all but the simplest circuits because of the calculation time and storage requirements. The Boolean difference can be used to determine test patterns. This technique is useful for small circuits, but fails for large networks. It is difficult to be precise about the size circuit for which the Boolean Difference is useful since it depends on the skill of the user. It is a manual technique at present since no programs implementing it have been announced. Test set generation techniques for large networks are derived from the concept of **path sensitization**.

6.12-3 Boolean Difference Test Generation

The circuit of Fig. 6.12-2 will be used to illustrate test generation with the Boolean difference. First a test input will be generated to detect the fault $a/1$. The Boolean difference can be used to discover the values of the variables that will cause the output to depend on the value on lead a. This is done by calculating df/dx since x is the signal on lead a. The function realized by the circuit is $f = xy + yz$. Thus

$$df/dx = f_{x'} \oplus f_x = yz \oplus y = yz'$$

This shows that it is necessary to have $yz = 10$ in order to have the output depend on the value of lead a. Since a stuck-at-1 fault is being tested for the opposite value (0) must be applied to the tested lead. The only test input for $a/1$ is thus $xyz = 010$.

A similar procedure can be used to determine the test inputs for a stuck-at fault on one of the internal leads of a circuit. This will be illustrated by finding the test set for a stuck-at-0 fault on lead g of Fig. 6.12-2. Let G represent the value of the signal on lead g and $G(y, z)$ be the functional relationship between this signal and the circuit inputs y and z. Similarly, let F represent the value of the signal on lead h and $F(x, y, G)$ be the function giving the dependence of this signal on signals x, y, and G. Then $dF(x, y, G)/dG$ gives the values of x and y for which F depends on the value of G. Since $F(x, y, G) = xy + G$, dF/dG is $xy \oplus 1 = (xy)'$. This shows that F will depend on G if either x or y is equal to 0.

To test for g stuck-at-0, a 1-signal must be placed on g. The values of y and z that correspond to g being 1 are found by finding when $G(y, z)$ is equal to 1. Since $G(y, z) = yz$, y and z must be equal to 1 in order for G to equal 1. The

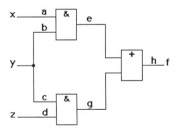

Figure 6.12-2 Circuit to illustrate Boolean difference test generation.

test input for lead g stuck-at-0 is thus $xyz = 011$. This could have been obtained by evaluating the expression $G \, dF/dG = yz(xy)' = yz(x' + y') = x'yz$.

In a similar fashion the test inputs for the fault $g/1$ are obtained by evaluating $G' \, dF/dG = (yz)'(xy)' = (y' + z')(x' + y') = y' + x'z'$. G' gives the conditions for having a 0-signal on lead g. This means that any input that has $y = 0$ or $xz = 00$ will test for $g/1$. Any one of the input combinations $xyz = 000, 001, 010, 100, 101$ will test for this fault.

This discussion can be summarized in the following theorem.

THEOREM 6.12-1.   Let g be a lead in a combinational circuit and G be the function giving the dependence of the value on g to the values of the circuit inputs. Let F be a function giving the dependence of the circuit output on the circuit inputs and also on the value of g. Then the tests for the fault $g/0$ are given by $G \, dF/dG$ and the tests for the fault $g/1$ are given by $G' \, dF/dG$.

6.12-4 Path Sensitization

Fixing some of the inputs to a network so that the network output depends on the signal on a particular lead is called **sensitizing** the output to the particular lead. The Boolean difference of a network output with respect to the signal on a specific lead represents all input patterns that will sensitize the output to the specific lead. For all but very simple networks the calculation of the Boolean difference is not practical. Moreover, it is not vital to know all the ways in which to achieve the sensitization. Just one sensitization pattern is usually satisfactory. It is possible to find a sensitization pattern by tracing a **sensitized path** through the network. All of the standard automatic test pattern generation programs are based on tracing sensitized paths through a network.

Figure 6.12-3 shows the circuit of Fig. 6.12-2 when the output is sensitized to input x (inputs $yz = 10$). There is a sensitized path from the x input to the output via leads a, e, and h. The output of an AND gate is sensitized to one of its inputs by placing 1-signals on all of the other gate inputs. The output of an OR gate is sensitized to one of its inputs by placing 0-signals on all its other inputs. Because of these rules it is necessary to make $b = 1$ in order to sensitize e to x. It is necessary to make $g = 0$ in order to sensitize h to e. Since y must be set equal to 1 in order to make $b = 1$, the only way that g can be forced to 0 is by setting $z = 0$ so that the d-input of the bottom AND gate is 0.

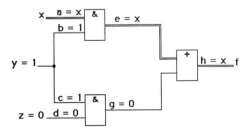

Figure 6.12-3 Sensitized-path example.

A test input for a fault on any lead, say lead k, of a circuit can be found by (1) finding a path from k to the output, (2) finding the signals that must be present on the other inputs to the gates of the path to cause the output to be sensitized to k, (3) finding the input signals necessary to produce these signals at the gate inputs, and (4) determining the input signals necessary to produce the appropriate signal on lead k (opposite to the fault value).

6.12-5 Compact Tests

A quite different approach, called compact testing, reduces the storage requirements of test patterns and test results almost to zero, but uses a large number of test patterns. A pseudo-random-number generation circuit (linear feedback shift register) is used to produce a long sequence of input patterns. Thus, a small circuit is used instead of a large memory for obtaining the input test patterns. Instead of storing the circuit's response to each test pattern input, some simple function of all the responses is retained. Typical functions that have been used to reduce the circuit output are the total number of 1's that occur at each output, the total number of 0-to-1 or 1-to-0 transitions at each output, and the output of a linear feedback shift register that has the circuit output as its input.

Compact testing has the advantages of very low storage and test generation costs. Its disadvantages are imperfect coverage, since there is always the possibility that a faulty circuit may produce the same output function as a good circuit, and lengthy test sequences. The test sequence length is not necessarily a problem since the actual time taken by high-speed logic can be short enough to not cause a problem. However, the imperfect coverage can cause difficulties since it can be very expensive to simulate the long test sequences to determine which faults are detected. Sequential as well as combinational circuits can be handled with the compact testing technique.

6.13 MULTISTAGE NETWORKS

The techniques discussed in Secs. 6.3 to 6.9 are directly applicable only to two-stage networks. There have been attempts to extend the two-stage minimization methods to more stages [Lawler 62], but this approach has not produced useful techniques. The methods developed are too computationally expensive to be practical. In fact, no multistage network design methods that are both computationally feasible and sufficiently systematic to be programmed effectively are known. The problem is important enough that research aimed at developing such methods continues [Darringer 81].

Multistage networks can be designed by hand with the help of the switching algebra theorems. This technique is usually called "factoring." As an example, consider the function whose minimum sum is

$$f = stv + stwx + styz + uv + uwx + uyz$$

By factoring out st and u from common terms this can be rewritten as

$$f = st(v + wx + yz) + u(v + wx + yz)$$

The factor $(v + wx + yz)$ is common to both terms and can be factored out, leading to the expression

$$f = (st + u)(v + wx + yz)$$

This expression can be realized with six gates while the minimum sum requires seven gates. The minimum product can be obtained by "adding out" the factored expression or by multiplying out its dual. Since there are six prime implicates in the minimum product, it leads to a seven-gate network.

The optimization criterion is not always that of using the minimum number of gates. There may be restrictions on the gate fanin or fanout, or it may be desirable to reduce the amount of interconnect. In the previous example, the minimum sum and product both require an output gate with a fanin of 6 while the factored network has a maximum fanin requirement of 3.

Factoring can be a very useful method for NAND design, but its success is directly dependent on the skill of the designer. The expressions that result correspond directly to networks of AND and OR gates. Often other types of gates are preferable. To convert from an AND-OR network to a NAND gate network is a reasonably straightforward procedure. The method described in Sec. 3.4-2, in which inversion bubbles are removed from a NAND gate network to obtain a network of AND and OR gates, can be reversed to go from an AND-OR gate network to a NAND network.

The previous discussions have all assumed the availability of double-rail inputs. There are many situations such as when pins or interconnect are to be minimized when only single-rail inputs are available. There are techniques for designing three-stage NAND networks so that only single-rail inputs are required.

6.13-1 TANT Networks

If only single-rail inputs are available, a NAND network realization will require three stages of gates for any function that depends on an input variable both complemented and uncomplemented. A direct method for finding such a network is to get a two-stage network and then add inverter gates to form the required complements. It is often possible to reduce the number of gates by combining several of these third-stage inverter gates so that complements of more than one variable are derived from one gate. As an example of this technique consider the function

$$f = wz + wy' + wx' + x'yz$$

Figure 6.13-1a shows a direct realization requiring seven gates, two of them being used to produce x' and y'. The expression can be factored by combining the wy' and wx' terms to obtain an expression corresponding to a six-gate network (Fig. 6.13-1b):

$$f = wz + w(y' + x') + x'yz$$

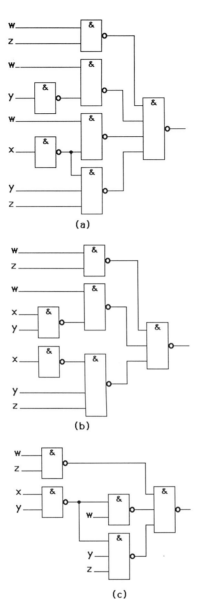

Figure 6.13-1 TANT networks for $f = wz + wy' + wx' + xyz$: (a) minimal sum network; (b) factored minimal sum network; (c) minimum gate network.

A useful "trick" in designing this class of networks comes from realizing that the term $x'yz$ can be rewritten as $(y' + x')yz$ since $y'y = 0$. This leads to the following expression which corresponds to a five-gate network (Fig. 6.13-1c):

$$f = wz + w(y' + x') + (y' + x')yz$$

This technique must be used with extreme care if hazards are of concern since it results in the introduction of unstable 1-sets. Systematic procedures using this approach are described in [McCluskey 63] and [Gimpel 67]. The name TANT networks was coined in [McCluskey 63] to specify this class of network. It is an acronym for "*t*hree-stage *A*ND-*N*OT gate network with *t*rue or uncomplemented inputs."

6.13-2 Transformation Techniques

Another approach to finding a method for designing efficient NAND networks is based on the application of local transformations to change an existing design to a more desirable design. This approach is presented in [Lee 72] and [Darringer 81].

Other interesting discussions of NAND network design can be found in [Davidson 69], [Dietmeyer 69], [Ellis 65], [Hellerman 63], [Muroga 79], and [Maley 63].

6.R REFERENCES

[AGARWAL 81] Agarwal, V. K., and A. S. F. Fung, "Multiple Fault Testing of Large Circuits by Single Fault Test Sets," *IEEE Trans. Comput.*, C-30, No. 11, pp. 855–865, 1981.

[BARTEE 61] Bartee, T. C., "Computer Design of Multiple-Output Logical Networks," *IRE Trans. Electron. Comput.*, EC-10, No. 2, pp. 21–30, 1961.

[BEATSON 58] Beatson, T. J., "Minimization of Components in Electronic Switching Circuits," *Trans. Am. Inst. Electr. Eng.* Part I, Communications and Electronics, Vol. 77, pp. 283–291, July 1958.

[BRAYTON 84] Brayton, R. K., G. D. Hachtel, C. T. McMullen, A. L. Sangiovanni-Vincentelli, *Logic Minimization Algorithms for VLSI Synthesis*, Kluwer Academic Publishers, Boston, MA., 1984.

[BRICAUD 78] Bricaud, P., and J. Campbell, "Multiple Output PLA Minimization: EMIN," *Proc. 1978 WESCON Prof. Program*, Los Angeles, Sept. 12–14, 1978.

[CAMENZIND 72] Camenzind, H. R., *Electronic Integrated Systems Design*, Van Nostrand Reinhold Company, Inc., New York, 1972.

[CARR 72] Carr, W. N., and J. P. Mize, *MOS/LSI Design and Application*, McGraw-Hill Book Company, New York, 1972.

[CAVLAN 79] Cavlan, N., and S. J. Durham, "Field-Programmable Arrays," *Electronics*, Part 1: "Powerful Alternatives to Random Logic," pp. 109–114, July 5, 1979; Part 2: "Sequencers and Arrays Transform Truth Tables into Working Systems," pp. 132–139, July 19, 1979.

[DARRINGER 81] Darringer, J. A., W. H. Joyner, C. L. Berman, and L. Trevillyan, "Logic Synthesis through Local Transformations," *IBM J. Res. Dev.*, Vol. 25, No. 4, pp. 272–280, 1981.

[DAVIDSON 69] Davidson, E. S., "An Algorithm for NAND Decomposition under Network Constraints," *IEEE Trans. Electron. Comput.*, C-18, No. 12, pp. 1098–1109, 1969.

[DEAVENPORT 80] Deavenport, J. E., "EMI Susceptibility Testing of Computer Systems," *Comput. Des.*, pp. 145–149, Mar. 1980.

[DIETMEYER 69]   Dietmeyer, E. L., and Y. H. Su, "Logic Design of Fan-In Limited NAND Networks," *IEEE Trans. Electron. Comput.*, C-18, No. 1, pp. 11–22, 1969.

[ELLIS 65]   Ellis, D. T., "A Synthesis of Combinational Logic with NAND or NOR Elements," *IEEE Trans. Electron. Comput.*, EC-14, No. 5, pp. 701–705, 1965.

[FLEISHER 75]   Fleisher, H., and L. I. Maissel, "An Introduction to Array Logic," *IBM J. Res., Dev.*, pp. 98–109, Mar. 1975.

[GIMPEL 67]   Gimpel, J. F., "The Minimization of TANT Networks," *IEEE Trans. Electron. Comput.*, EC-16, pp. 18–38, Feb. 1967.

[HACHTEL 82]   Hachtel, G. D., et al., "An Algorithm for Optimal PLA Folding," *IEEE Trans. CAD*, CAD-1, No. 2, pp. 63–77, 1982.

[HELLERMAN 63]   Hellerman, L., "A Catalogue of Three-Variable OR-Invert and AND-Invert Logical Circuits," *IEEE Trans. Electron. Comput.*, EC-12, pp. 198–223, June 1963.

[HNATEK 77]   Hnatek, E. R., *A User's Handbook of Semiconductor Memories*, John Wiley & Sons, Inc., New York, 1977.

[HONG 74]   Hong, S. J., R. G. Cain, and D. L. Ostapko, "MINI: A Heuristic Approach for Logic Minimization," *IBM J. Res. Dev.*, pp. 443–458, Sept. 1974.

[KAMBAYASHI 79]   Kambayashi Y., "Logic Design of Programmable Logic Arrays," *IEEE Trans. Comput.*, C-28, No. 9, pp. 609–617, 1979.

[KIDDER 81]   Kidder, T., *The Soul of a New Machine*, Avon Books, New York, N.Y., 1981.

[KODANDAPANI 80]   Kodandapani, K. L., and D. K. Pradhan, "Undetectability of Bridging Faults and Validity of Stuck-At Fault Test Sets," *IEEE Trans. Comput.*, C-29, No. 1, pp. 55–59, 1980.

[KVAMME 70]   Kvamme, F., "Standard Read-Only Memories Simplify Complex Logic Design," *Electronics*, pp. 88–95, Jan. 5, 1970.

[LAWLER 60]   Lawler, E. L., and G. A. Salton, "The Use of Parenthesis-Free Notation for the Automatic Design of Switching Circuits," *IRE Trans. Electron. Comput.*, EC-9, No. 3, pp. 342–352, 1960.

[LAWLER 62]   Lawler, E. L., "Minimal Boolean Expression with More Than Two Levels of Sums and Products," *Proc. 3rd Annu. Symp. Switching Circuit Theory Logical Des.*, pp. 50–59, 1962.

[LEE 72]   Lee, H.-P., and E. S. Davidson, "A Transform for NAND Network Design," *IEEE Trans. Comput.*, C-21, No. 1, pp. 12–20, 1972.

[LIN 81]   Lin, C. M., "A 4-μm NMOS NAND Structure PLA," *IEEE J. Solid-State Circuits*, SC-16, No. 2, pp. 103–107, 1981.

[MALEY 63]   Maley, G. A., and J. Earle, *The Logic Design of Transistor Digital Computers*, Prentice-Hall, Inc., Englewood Cliffs, N.J., 1963.

[MCCLUSKEY 56]   McCluskey, E. J., "Minimization of Boolean Functions," *Bell Syst. Tech. J.*, Vol. 35, No. 5, pp. 1417–1444, 1956.

[MCCLUSKEY 62]   McCluskey, E. J., and H. Schorr, "Essential Multiple-Output Prime Implicants, Mathematical Theory of Automata," *Proc. Polytechnic Inst. Brooklyn Symp.*, Vol. 12, pp. 437–457, Apr. 1962.

[MCCLUSKEY 63]   McCluskey, E. J., "Logical Design Theory of NOR Gate Networks with No Complemented Inputs," *Proc. 4th Annu. Symp. Switching-Circuit Theory Logic Des.*, Chicago, Oct. 28–30, 1963.

[McCluskey 81] McCluskey, E. J., and S. Bozorgui-Nesbat, "Design for Autonomous Test," *IEEE Trans. Comput.*, C-30, No. 11, pp. 1070–1078, 1981.

[Mei 74] Mei, K. C. Y., "Bridging and Stuck-at-Faults," *IEEE Trans. Comput.*, C-23, No. 7, pp. 720–727, 1974.

[MMI 83] Monolithic Memories, PAL Programmable Array Logic Handbook, 3rd Ed., 1983.

[Morrison 77] Morrison, R., *Grounding and Shielding Techniques in Instrumentation*, John Wiley & Sons, Inc., New York, 1977.

[Mueller 56] Mueller, R. K., and R. H. Urbano, "A Topological Method for the Determination of the Minimal Forms of a Boolean Function," *IRE Trans. Electron. Comput.*, EC-5, No. 3, pp. 126–132, 1956.

[Muroga 79] Muroga, S., *Logic Design and Switching Theory*, John Wiley & Sons, Inc., New York, 1979.

[Quine 52] Quine, W. V., "The Problem of Simplifying Truth Functions," *Am. Math. Monthly*, Vol. 59, No. 8, pp. 521–531, 1952.

[Shedletsky 78] Shedletsky, J. J., "Delay Testing LSI Logic," *Dig. 8th Annu. Int. Symp. Fault-Tolerant Comput. (FTCS-8)*, Toulouse, France, pp. 159–164, June 21–23, 1978.

[Signetics 76] Signetics, *Signetics Field Programmable Logic Arrays*, Signetics Corporation, Sunnyvale, Calif., Feb. 1976.

[Smith 79] Smith, J. E., "On Necessary and Sufficient Conditions for Multiple Fault Undetectability," *IEEE Trans. Comput.*, C-28, No. 10, pp. 801–802, 1979.

[Soong 77] Soong, G., "An Algorithm for Minimizing Programmable Logic Array Realization," Rep. R-766, University of Illinois, Urbana, Ill., Apr. 1977.

[Wadsack 1978] Wadsack, R. L., "Fault Modeling and Logic Simulation of CMOS and MOS Integrated Circuits," *Bell Syst. Tech. J.*, Vol. 57, No. 5, pp. 1449–1474, 1978.

[Wood 79] Wood R., "A High Density Programmable Logic Array Chip," *IEEE Trans. Comput.*, C-28, pp. 602–608, Sept. 1979.

6.P PROBLEMS

6.1 Find minimal sums and minimal products for each of the following functions:
   (a) $\Sigma(0, 2, 4, 8, 10, 12)$
   (b) $\Sigma(2, 3, 6, 7, 8, 9, 12, 13)$
   (c) $\Sigma(0, 2, 3, 4, 6, 7, 8, 9, 10, 12, 13, 14)$
   (d) $\Sigma(1, 4, 6, 7, 13)$
   (e) $\Sigma(1, 3, 7, 13, 15)$
   (f) $\Sigma(9, 11, 12, 13, 14, 15, 16, 18, 24, 25, 26, 27)$
   (g) $\Sigma(8, 9, 13, 14, 15, 24, 26, 30)$
   (h) $\Sigma(8, 9, 10, 11, 17, 19, 21, 23, 25, 27, 41, 43, 44, 45, 46, 47, 56, 57, 58, 59)$
   (i) $\Sigma(3, 5, 7, 11) + d(6, 15)$
   (j) $\Sigma(3, 5, 7, 11, 12, 29, 31) + d(1, 2, 6, 10, 28)$
   (k) $\Sigma(2, 7, 9, 10, 11, 12, 14, 15)$

6.2 For each of the functions listed below.
   (a) Determine the complete sum.
   (b) Underline the essential prime implicants.

(c) Show (on a map) one minimal sum.
(d) Determine the number of different minimal sums.
(e) If there are any irredundant sums that are not minimal sums, display one of these irredundant sums on a map.

$$f_1(w, x, y, z) = \Sigma(1, 5, 6, 7, 11, 12, 13, 15)$$

$$f_2(w, x, y, z) = \Sigma(2, 3, 5, 7, 8, 9, 12, 13)$$

$$f_3(w, x, y, z) = \Sigma(0, 2, 5, 6, 7, 8, 9, 12, 13, 15)$$

$$f_4(w, x, y, z) = \Sigma(0, 1, 4, 5, 6, 7, 9, 10, 13, 14, 15)$$

$$f_5(w, x, y, z) = \Sigma(3, 5, 6, 7, 9, 11, 12, 13, 14, 15)$$

$$f_6(w, x, y, z) = \Sigma(0, 1, 2, 3, 5, 6, 7, 8, 9, 10, 12, 13, 14, 15)$$

6.3 For the function $f(v, w, x, y, z) = \Sigma(4, 5, 8, 9, 12, 13, 14, 15, 16, 17, 20, 21, 22, 23, 24, 25, 26, 28, 29, 30, 31)$:
(a) Plot the function on a map, encircling the prime implicants.
(b) How many prime implicants does the function have?
(c) How many essential prime implicants does the function have?

6.4 For the function $f(w, x, y, z) = \Sigma(1, 4, 5) + d(2, 3, 6, 7, 8, 9, 12, 13)$:
(a) Determine a minimal sum.
(b) Determine a minimal product.

6.5 For the circuit of Fig. P6.5:
(a) Write an algebraic expression for f.
(b) Write the decimal specification for f.
(c) Design the analogous circuit for f, using NOR gates with maximum fanin of 3 (nine gates are sufficient, no inverters).

6.6 For the circuit of Fig. P6.6:
(a) What must g be in order that $f(w, x, y, z) = \Sigma(0, 1, 2, 3, 4, 7, 8, 11)$?
(b) Draw a map for g.
(c) Draw a two-stage gate circuit for g. Use the minimum number of gates. (Four gates are sufficient.)

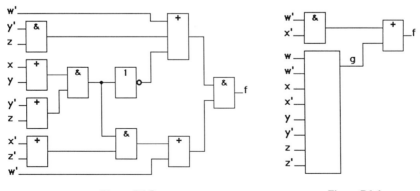

Figure P6.5   **Figure P6.6**

6.7 Given that $x \oplus y = xy' + x'y$ and that $x \oplus (y \oplus z) = (x \oplus y) \oplus z$:

(a) Prove that $x + y = x \oplus y \oplus xy$.

(b) If the canonical sum for a function f is given by $f = p_{i1} + p_{i2} + \cdots + p_{ir}$, where the p_i are fundamental products, prove that $f = p_{i1} \oplus p_{i2} \oplus \cdots \oplus p_{ir}$.

(c) Given that $x \oplus x = 0$ and that $f = \Sigma(5, 7, 8, 9, 12, 13, 14, 15)$, design a circuit in which the output is derived from an $\oplus$ gate and the inputs are connected to AND gates. (Use the minimum number of gates.)

6.8 A circuit is to be constructed for the function $f(v, w, x, y, z) = \Sigma(0, 3, 5, 7, 8, 11, 13, 15, 20, 21, 22, 23, 28, 29, 30, 31)$. The gates which are to be used are OR gates and AND gates. Each gate has either two or four inputs, and gates with one, three, or five inputs are not available and cannot be used. Design a two-stage circuit for this function, using the minimum number of gates.

(a) With an OR gate as the output gate.

(b) With an AND gate as the output gate.

6.9 For the function $f(w, x, y, z) = \Sigma(0, 1, 2, 3, 4, 5, 7, 10)$:

(a) Write a minimal sum for f.

(b) Multiply this out, using the theorems $(X + Y)(W + Z) = WX + WY + XZ + YZ$ and $XX = X, XX' = 0, X + XY = X$. Your result should be a sum-of-products expression.

(c) Write a minimal sum for f.

(d) Compare the results of parts (b) and (c)—can you make any general statement as a result of this comparison?

6.10 A function $f(x_1, x_2, \ldots, x_{17})$, is to equal 1 only when exactly one of the variables $(x_1, x_2, \ldots, x_{17})$ is equal to 1.

(a) How many prime implicants does this function have?

(b) If a circuit for this function was constructed and then the input leads were relabeled

$$x_1 \text{ lead changed to } x_2 \text{ lead}$$

$$x_2 \text{ lead changed to } x_3 \text{ lead}$$

.

.

.

$$x_{16} \text{ lead changed to } x_{17} \text{ lead}$$

$$x_{17} \text{ lead changed to } x_1 \text{ lead}$$

what function would the circuit with new labels realize?

6.11 (a) Write an expression for the output of the circuit shown in Fig. P6.11.

(b) Design a minimal two-stage circuit using only OR-NOT gates which realizes the same function as the circuit of Fig. P6.11.

6.12 Design a minimal multiple-output two-stage (AND-OR or OR-AND) circuit for the following functions.

$$f_1 = \Sigma(0, 4, 5)$$

$$f_2 = \Sigma(0, 2, 3, 4, 5)$$

$$f_3 = \Sigma(0, 1, 2)$$

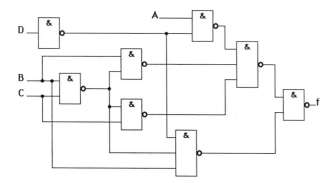

Figure P6.11

6.13 Determine the multiple-output minimal sums for each of the following sets of functions.

(a)

$$f_1 = wxy + w'y'z$$

$$f_2 = x'z' + wxz + xy'z$$

$$f_3 = x'z' + wxyz + w'x'y'$$

(b)

$$f_1 = yz + wz$$

$$f_2 = yz + wz + wxy$$

$$f_3 = wy'z + w'xyz'$$

(c)

$$f_1 = wx' + x'z + xy'z'$$

$$f_2 = wz + xz' + xy + w'x'z$$

(d)

$$f_1 = y'z + w'z$$

$$f_2 = w'xy' + wy'z + wx'y + x'yz'$$

$$f_3 = xyz' + wx'z$$

6.14 Design a minimal-gate multiple-output two-stage network (using AND gates, OR gates) for the following functions.

$$f_1(w, x, y, z) = \Sigma(1, 4, 5, 7, 13) + d(3, 6)$$

$$f_2(w, x, y, z) = \Sigma(3, 5, 7) + d(6)$$

$$f_3(w, x, y, z) = \Sigma(3, 4, 11, 13, 15) + d(9, 14)$$

6.15 For each of the following specifications, plot functions satisfying these specifications on n-cube maps. (Use variables v, w, x, y, z.)
(a) A five-variable function containing no essential prime implicants.
(b) A five-variable function for which all the prime implicants are essential.
(c) A four-variable function that is unchanged when the variables y and z are interchanged.
(d) Two four-variable functions for which the multiple-output minimal sums contain none of the prime implicants of the product function.

(e) A four-variable function having at least two terms in its minimal sum and having no variables primed in the minimal sum.

(f) A function having at least two different irredundant sums.

6.16 For the function $f(x_1, x_2, x_3, x_4, x_5, x_6, x_7) = \Sigma(0, 5, 16, 21, 32, 37, 45, 48, 53, 61, 64, 69, 80, 96, 112, 117, 125)$, use a tabular method to find:

(a) All prime implicants.

(b) A minimal sum.

6.17 Use a tabular method to determine a minimal multiple-output two-stage circuit (AND-OR) for the following functions.

$$f_1(w, x, y, z) = \Sigma(1, 5, 7, 8, 12, 13, 14, 15)$$

$$f_2(w, x, y, z) = \Sigma(0, 1, 5, 8, 14)$$

$$f_3(w, x, y, z) = \Sigma(0, 2, 3, 6, 8, 9, 10, 11, 14)$$

6.18 A circuit receives two 3-bit binary numbers $A = A_2 A_1 A_0$, and $B = B_2 B_1 B_0$. Design a minimal sum-of-products circuit to produce an output whenever A is greater than B.

6.19 In certain memory applications it has been found useful to implement the complete decoding of a 4-bit address by first converting to another code and then decoding this intermediate code (Fig. P6.19). If this intermediate code consists of 6 bits, 3 of which equal 1 (3-out-of-6 code), it is possible to design a final decoding network that requires no inversion. Thus, the final decoding network has six inputs, 16 one-hot outputs, and no internal inverters. If the intermediate code were not used, the final decoding network would require eight inputs (double-rail) in order to eliminate the need for inversion.

You are to specify the 3-out-of-6 code and design both the code converter and the decoding network. Choose a code that leads to economical networks for the converter and decoder.

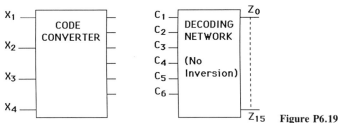

Figure P6.19

6.20 A modulo-10 incrementer is to be designed. For inputs from 0000 to 1000 the outputs are to be the next higher binary number. For all other inputs the outputs are to be all zeros.

(a) Design a minimal PLA for this circuit using phase-splitter (true-complement) inputs.

(b) Design a minimal PLA using 2-bit decoders.

6.21 For the circuit of Fig. P6.21 list all input combinations that will produce an incorrect output value when the v-input lead is stuck at 1.

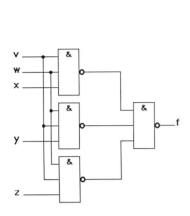

Figure P6.21

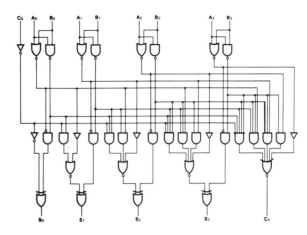

Figure P6.22

6.22 Assume that the darkened lead on Fig. P6.22 has a stuck-at-0 fault on it. You are to specify a test input that will detect this fault.

6.23 Given four functions:

$$f_1(x_1, x_2, x_3, x_4) = x_1 x_3 + x_4$$

$$f_2(x_1, x_2, x_3, x_4) = x_1' x_3' + x_4$$

$$f_3(x_1, x_2, x_3, x_4) = x_2 x_3 + x_4'$$

$$f_4(x_1, x_2, x_3, x_4) = x_2'$$

(a) Draw a standard PLA structure to implement these functions.
(b) Draw a minimum-area folded PLA to realize the same functions.

6.24 For the circuit of Fig. P6.24, determine all the test sets to detect:
(a) Lead h stuck at 0: $\langle a, b, c \rangle = \langle \quad \rangle, \langle \quad \rangle, \ldots$
(b) Lead g stuck at 1: $\langle a, b, c \rangle = \langle \quad \rangle, \langle \quad \rangle, \ldots$

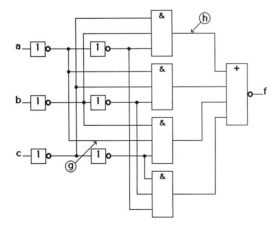

Figure P6.24

6.25 Design minimum-area PLA implementations for the three functions $f_1(w, x, y) = \Sigma(0, 3, 4, 5, 7)$, $f_2(w, x, y) = \Sigma(0, 2, 3)$, and $f_3(w, x, y) = \Sigma(0, 1, 3, 6, 7)$.
  (a) Using phase splitters, no folding.
  (b) Using two-variable decoders.
  (c) Using folding.

6.26 Design minimum-gate TANT networks for:
  (a) $f(w, x, y, z) = \Sigma(4, 5, 9, 11, 12)$
  (b) $f(a, b) = \Sigma(1, 2)$
  (c) $f(A, B, C, D) = \Sigma(0, 1, 2, 5, 6, 9, 10, 15)$

6.27 Design minimum-gate TANT networks for:
  (a) $f(w, x, y, z) = \Sigma(2, 3, 4, 5, 8, 9, 10)$ [7 gates]
  (b) $f(w, x, y, z) = \Sigma(1, 3, 4, 5, 6, 8, 10)$ [7 gates]
  (c) $f(w, x, y, z) = \Sigma(0, 2, 3, 4, 6, 7, 8, 9, 10, 12, 13, 14)$ [four gates]

6.28 Design a combinational circuit (using two-input EXCLUSIVE-OR gates, two-input NAND gate, and inverters) which has as inputs $X_0, X_1, \ldots, X_n$ and M; and as outputs $Y_0, Y_1, \ldots, Y_n$. When $M = 0$, the circuit is to accept a binary number at $X_0, X_1, \ldots, X_n$ and put out the corresponding Gray number at $Y_0, Y_1, \ldots, Y_n$. When $M = 1$, the circuit is to accept a Gray number and convert it to the corresponding binary number.

6.29 Assume that you are the quality engineer in a company that manufactures transistors. A quality test is devised so that a random sample made of three transistors is tested at periodic intervals of time. Four tests, A, B, C, and D, are performed simultaneously on each transistor in the sample. If three or more test failures are found in any one transistor, the unit is rejected. If two or more defective units are found in any one sample, the production line becomes suspected and it is to be stopped until a larger sample is tested and the production faults are located. You are asked to automate the quality test by designing the appropriate logical circuits. It is assumed that all tests are made simultaneously. Let x, y, z, and w represent the binary electrical signals, which are generated, respectively, by the tests A, B, C, and D. A test failure is signified by a 1, so that if $x = 1$ appears at the output of the A test, it will signify a test failure in A.
  (a) Design a circuit with input x, y, z, w and output f_i for which $f_i = 1$ iff the transistor tested is to be rejected.
  (b) Design a circuit with inputs f_1, f_2, f_3 and output F such that $F = 1$ iff the production line is to be stopped (f_1, f_2, f_3 represent the test results for the three sample transistors).

6.30 A 4-bit register has been built to store one decimal digit according to the code shown in Table P6.30. No other combination except the ones shown in the code below may be contained in the register. Design a minimal logical circuit which, when inputed by the register's cells, will recognize and put out a 1 if the register contains a 0, 2, 6, 7, or 8.
  (a) Use only AND gates, OR gates, and inverters.
  (b) Use only NAND gates.
  (c) Use only NOR gates.

6.31 A number represented in the (8421) BCD code can be converted to a binary representation by repeated right shifts provided that whenever a 1 bit is shifted into the 8-position of any of the digit groups, the constant number N is subtracted from that digit.
  (a) Determine the value of the constant number N.

TABLE P6.30

Decimal digit	x_1	x_2	x_3	x_4	Decimal digit	x_1	x_2	x_3	x_4
0	0	0	1	1	5	1	0	0	1
1	0	1	0	0	6	1	0	1	1
2	0	1	0	1	7	1	1	0	0
3	0	1	1	1	8	1	1	0	1
4	1	0	0	0	9	1	1	1	1

(b) Design a circuit to carry out the subtraction of the constant N for one digit group. (Use AND, OR, or XOR gates; use as few as possible.)

6.32 Design a network to convert five bits—g_4, g_3, g_2, g_1, g_0—representing a number in the Gray code into five bits—b_4, b_3, b_2, b_1, b_0—which represent the same number in binary. Recall that the conversion from binary to Gray is given by $g_i = b_i \oplus b_{i+1}$. You use AND gates, OR gates, inverters, and XOR gates.

6.33 For the NAND gate network shown in Fig. P6.33:
(a) Write an algebraic expression for the output function F.
(b) Draw a network realizing the same function F using AND gates, OR gates, and inverters (use as few gates as possible).
(c) Draw a network realizing the same function F using NOR gates.
(d) Transform the NAND network into another NAND network which contains no gates having more than three inputs. This can be done with no increase in the total number of gates in the network by removing one of the inputs to the final gate and connecting this input elsewhere in the network.

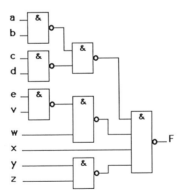

Figure P6.33

6.34 Design a four-input circuit whose output is some encoding of the number of inputs which are 1. Note that there are five outputs, 0 through 4, so at least three lines must be used to encode the outputs. State the coding scheme being used.

6.35 Using only NOR gates, show circuits for:
(a) EXCLUSIVE-OR
(b) NAND
(c) $a \cdot b'$

6.36 Suppose that you have two functions to implement:

$$f = a'c'd' + abcd' + ab'cd + abc'd$$

$$g = ac'd' + ab'd' + abcd + ab'c'$$

How can you achieve some saving by using the complement of one function as part of the other?

6.37 Simplify the following expressions algebraically and draw a block diagram of the circuit for each simplified expression using AND and OR gates. Assume that the inputs are from flip-flops.

(a) $ab'c' + a'b'c' + a'bc' + a'b'c$

(b) $abc + a'bc + ab'c + abc' + ab'c' + a'bc' + a'bc'$

(c) $a(a + b + c)(a' + b + c)(a + b' + c)(a + b + c')$

(d) $(a + b + c)(a + b' + c')(a + b + c')(a + b' + c)$

6.38 A very frequently used circuit is one that converts from n fully encoded input variables to 2^n "one-hot" outputs. Each output lead corresponds to exactly one of the 2^n possible input combinations and has a 1 signal only when that input combination is present. Such a circuit is called a complete decoding network. A circuit for two single-rail inputs using AND gates and inverters is shown in Fig. P6.38. You are to design a complete decoding network for single-rail inputs using only NOR gates. Use as few gates as possible (can be done with four gates).

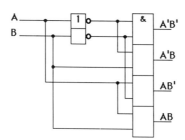

Figure P6.38

6.39 A shaft-position encoder provides a 4-bit signal indicating the position of a shaft in steps of 30°, using a reflected (Gray) code as listed in Table P6.39. It may be assumed that the four possible combinations of four bits not listed in the table will never occur. Design a minimal circuit to produce an output whenever the shaft is in the first quadrant (0 to 90°). Assume that double-rail inputs are available.

(a) Use AND gates and OR gates.

(b) Use NOR gates.

6.40 In digital computers, letters of the alphabet are coded in the form of unique combinations of 5 or more bits. One of the most common codes is the 6-bit Flexowriter code, which is used for punched paper tape. This code is shown in Table P6.40, in terms of the octal equivalents. For example,

$$C = (16)_8 = \underbrace{0\ 0\ 1}_{1}\ \underbrace{1\ 1\ 0}_{6}$$

TABLE P6.39

Shaft position	Encoder output			
	E_1	E_2	E_3	E_4
0–30°	0	0	1	1
30–60°	0	0	1	0
60–90°	0	1	1	0
90–120°	0	1	1	1
120–150°	0	1	0	1
150–180°	0	1	0	0
180–210°	1	1	0	0
210–240°	1	1	0	1
240–270°	1	1	1	1
270–300°	1	1	1	0
300–330°	1	0	1	0
330–360°	1	0	1	1

Design a minimal AND-OR circuit that will receive this code as an input and produce an output whenever the letter is a vowel. The alphabet uses only 26 of the possible codes, and the others are used for numerals and punctuation marks. However, you may assume that the data are pure alphabetic, so that only the codes listed will occur. Assume also that Y is a consonant.

TABLE P6.40

A	30	N	06
B	23	O	03
C	16	P	15
D	22	Q	35
E	20	R	12
F	26	S	24
G	13	T	01
H	05	U	34
I	14	V	17
J	32	W	31
K	36	X	27
L	11	Y	25
M	07	Z	21

6.41 Table P6.41 shows the Flexowriter codes for the 10 decimal numerals. Assume that a device receives alphanumeric data in this code (i.e., either these codes for numerals or the codes for letters as listed in Problem 6.40). Design a minimal AND-OR circuit that will develop a 1 out when the data are numeric, a 0 out when they are alphabetic. You may assume that any possible 6-bit codes not used for either letters or numerals will not occur.

6.42 Referring again to the Flexowriter code listed in Problems 6.41 and 6.42, design an "error circuit," a circuit that will put out a signal if a code other than one of the 36 "legal" alphanumeric codes is received.

TABLE P6.41

0	77
1	37
2	74
3	70
4	64
5	62
6	66
7	72
8	60
9	33

7

SEQUENTIAL CIRCUITS: FUNDAMENTAL-MODE ANALYSIS

7.1 INTRODUCTION

The methods developed in the preceding chapters are for combinational circuits—circuits whose outputs are determined completely by their present inputs. While many circuits have this property, there are also many circuits whose outputs depend on past as well as present inputs. This past dependence is achieved by "storing" signals in feedback loops and deriving the circuit outputs from the stored signals as well as the circuit inputs. A circuit whose output is a function of past as well as present inputs is called a **sequential circuit**.

Figure 7.1-1 illustrates the difference between a combinational and a sequential circuit. Whether the lock of Fig. 7.1-1a is open or closed depends only on the present setting of its dials; past settings are unimportant, just as, in a combinational circuit, past inputs don't affect the present circuit outputs. The condition of the Fig. 7.1-1b lock is determined by the numbers stopped at previously in addition to the current pointer position. Similarly, the output of a sequential circuit depends on previous as well as present inputs.[1]

There are two major classes of sequential circuits: pulse-mode circuits and fundamental-mode circuits. Pulse-mode operation is the subject of the following chapter and is defined precisely there; its most obvious attribute is that the circuit responds only to pulses[2] on particular inputs. Pulse-mode circuits are often called

---

[1] This analogy is taken from Chap. 5 of [McCluskey 65]. It is used here with the permission of the author. It appears also in [Hill 68].

[2] Pulses are discussed thoroughly in Sec. 8.1-1. A pulse is defined in the 1984 IEEE Dictionary as "a wave that departs from an initial level for a limited duration of time and ultimately returns to the original level [IEEE 84].

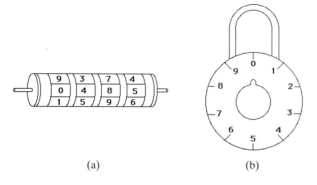

(a)   (b)

Figure 7.1-1 Two types of combination lock: (a) combinational; (b) sequential.

synchronous circuits since their action is "synchronized" with the pulse input. Terminology relating to such circuits is discussed in more detail in Chap. 8.

Fundamental-mode operation can be characterized by (1) not having any special kinds of inputs such as pulses—all inputs can affect the circuit in the same way, and (2) the need to keep track of all changes in internal stored signals. Fundamental-mode analysis is more complex than pulse-mode analysis; consequently, many texts discuss pulse-mode first. Here the choice has been made to treat fundamental-mode first. This approach has the following advantages:

1. The simplest way to introduce pulse-mode circuits is in terms of those circuits that store information in flip-flops. All modern flip-flops are fundamental-mode circuits; thus it is natural to learn about flip-flop operation in connection with fundamental-mode analysis. A thorough understanding of the differences between flip-flop-based pulse-mode circuits and those that use latches to store information depends on a good appreciation of the properties of flip-flops and latches. This is best obtained via fundamental-mode analysis techniques.

2. Correct operation of sequential circuits depends critically on proper timing. The timing issues are understood best in the context of fundamental-mode analysis. It is important that these timing considerations be introduced as early as possible so that a good understanding of them can be obtained. This cannot be overemphasized since with the move toward semicustom and custom implementations the logic designer must pay careful attention to timing to avoid inconsistent circuit operation and major testing difficulties.

3. By presenting both fundamental-mode and pulse-mode analysis before synthesis, it is possible to have a unified design methodology. This avoids unnecessary duplication of similar topics and confusion as to the basic design issues involved.

Fundamental-mode circuits are often called **asynchronous** circuits when the term *synchronous* is used to describe pulse-mode circuits. This is somewhat misleading since it is possible for a fundamental-mode circuit to have a synchronizing input and, in fact, to have the same external behavior as a pulse-mode circuit.

To guarantee proper operation of a fundamental-mode sequential circuit, it is necessary to restrict the way in which the inputs are changed: *Only one input is allowed to change at any given time.* Not only are simultaneous changes of more than one input forbidden but also changes that occur before the circuit has had a chance to settle down from the last input change.

More precisely, an input change is permitted only after any internal changes caused by previous input transitions have completed. In other words, an input can be changed only when the circuit is stable internally, the **stable input transition** property. If this property is violated, the action of the circuit will depend critically on the internal delays and can change if the delays change. This is a very undesirable situation since the aim is to have the circuit operation as independent as possible of internal analog parameters. It is because of the stable input transition property that flip-flops have restrictions on when their inputs may be changed. These restrictions are given as pulse-width, setup, and hold-time parameters.

This chapter begins with a discussion of the most basic electronic sequential circuit—the **latch**. A general method for analyzing fundamental-mode sequential circuits is then given. The electrical properties needed to store signals in a feedback loop are considered. Three sources of incorrect operation of sequential circuits are identified and discussed: the critical race, the essential hazard, and metastability. The different types of flip-flops are explained. Pulse-mode analysis is given in the next chapter, which is followed by a chapter on design of both pulse- and fundamental-mode circuits.

7.2 LATCHES

In order for the output of a sequential circuit to depend on past inputs, the circuit must have some mechanism to retain information about previous inputs. This mechanism is some type of memory element. The memory element used in the first electronic logic circuits is now called a latch. A latch constructed of NOR gates is shown in Fig. 7.2-1. This circuit is called a **set-reset latch** or *S-R* **latch**. (*S* represents the set input and *R* represents the reset input.)

7.2-1 The Set-Reset Latch

The operation of the *S-R* latch is illustrated in the Fig. 7.2-1. When $S = 1$ and $R = 0$ as in Fig. 7.2-1a, the circuit is "set" and the output values are $Q = 1$, $\overline{Q} = 0$. The shading of the top NOR gate of this figure indicates that the output of that gate is "forced" by an external signal (*S* in this case). If *S* is then changed to 0, the circuit remains in the set condition as shown in Fig. 7.2-1b. Changing *S* back to 1 returns the circuit to the situation of Fig. 7.2-1a. If, instead, *R* becomes 1, the circuit becomes "reset" and the conditions of Fig. 7.2-1c are present. The circuit remains in the reset state if *R* is returned to 0 as in Fig. 7.2-1d. Thus, when *S* and *R* are both 0, the output indicates which of *S* or *R* was last equal to 1—the circuit "remembers" the last nonzero input condition. Figure 7.2-1 includes tables showing the circuit conditions and the logic symbol for a set-reset latch with the appropriate signal values. Waveforms illustrating the latch operation are shown in Fig. 7.2-2. Note that when both *S* and *R* equal 1, both of the latch outputs are

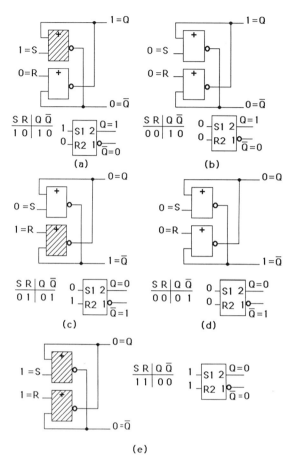

Figure 7.2-1 Set-reset latch constructed of NOR gates.

held at 0. This circuit condition is shown in Fig. 7.2-1e. As shown in Fig. 7.2-2, if both S and R are changed from 1 to 0 simultaneously, the latch state is not controlled. Either of the stable states with both S and R equal to 0 is possible. Because of this unspecified state, the usual practice is to design circuits with S-R latches so that the S and R inputs are never both equal to 1 simultaneously. In fact, earlier graphic symbol standards did not have any notation to indicate the latch state with both inputs at 1. There are situations in which it is useful to allow the $S = R = 1$ state, and the new IEEE standard does provide symbols to specify the latch condition for this state.

The numerals included within the latch symbols in Fig. 7.2-1 are used to indicate the output state when both inputs equal 1. This is called "set and reset dependencies" in the IEEE standard. The rule is that when an input labeled Sm is at 1, any outputs labeled with m will have the same value that they would have for $S = 1$, $R = 0$ irrespective of the actual value on the R input. When $R_h = 1$, all outputs labeled with h have the value they have for $S = 0$, $R = 1$ irrespective of the value on the S input. If no numerals indicating S and R dependencies are

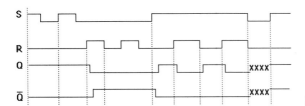

Figure 7.2-2 *S-R* latch waveforms.

present, the outputs are undefined when $S = R = 1$. This notation is illustrated in Fig. 7.2-3.

The outputs of the latch are labeled with Q and $\overline{Q}$. In this book the notation Q' is used to indicate the complement. $\overline{Q}$ is used for the second latch output to provide for those situations when this output is not the complement of the Q latch output. $\overline{Q}$ can be used as the complement of Q except when set and reset dependencies are specifically shown. In this case care must be taken in using $\overline{Q}$ for Q'. This convention is not widespread and should be used with caution.

A very important characteristic of the latch is that when an input value is changed, any effect on the output appears right after the new input appears. The new output is delayed only by the propagation times of the devices in the circuit. All latches have this property, but it is sometimes emphasized by calling them **transparent latches** [TI 81, p. 338].

A word of warning is appropriate here. The terminology used in connection with bistable circuits such as the set-reset latch can be very confusing since there is a lack of consistency and care in naming such circuits. The biggest problem with naming bistable circuits is the failure to identify carefully those circuits with

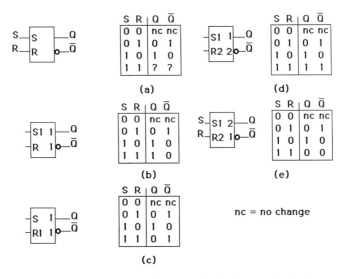

Figure 7.2-3 Illustration of set and reset dependencies notation: (a) operation with $S = R = 1$ undefined; (b) set-dominant latch; (c) reset-dominant latch; (d) $Q = \overline{Q} = 1$ when $S = R = 1$; (e) $Q = \overline{Q} = 0$ when $S = R = 1$.

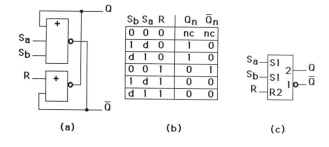

S_b	S_a	R	Q_n	$\bar{Q}_n$
0	0	0	nc	nc
1	d	0	1	0
d	1	0	1	0
0	0	1	0	1
1	d	1	0	0
d	1	1	0	0

(a)   (b)   (c)

Figure 7.2-4 NOR gate set-reset latch with two set inputs: (a) gate-level circuit; (b) table; (c) IEEE symbol.

the transparency property. Often the term *flip-flop* is used indiscriminately for bistable circuits. In this book, the term *latch* will be used for bistable circuits with the transparency property and the term *flip-flop* will be reserved for circuits without this property.

It is possible to have *S-R* latches with more than two inputs. Figure 7.2-4 shows an *S-R* latch with two set inputs. The operation is the same as would be obtained by connecting *Sa* and *Sb* to an OR gate that is connected to the usual *S* input. Of course, extra *R* inputs are also possible, and there can be more than two of a given type of input.

The IEEE standard also permits more complex input dependencies to be shown within the basic latch symbol. Figure 7.2-5a shows the symbol for a latch with a set function equal to the AND of two signals. The equivalent circuit using detached gate symbols is shown in Fig. 7.2-5b. Either representation is acceptable. An even more complex set function is shown in Fig. 7.2-6. The symbol of Fig. 7.2-6a represents a latch with the set input equal to *UV* + *WX*. The detached gate circuit is shown in Fig. 7.2-6b.

The form of logic diagram used for the latches in the previous figures is very common and emphasizes the "cross-coupled" nature of the circuit. Figure 7.2-7 is an example of another diagram that is also used often to represent the logic structure of the *S-R* latch.

Synchronous Latch Inputs. In very many applications of latches the new data are entered into the latch only when another signal—a control signal—becomes active. A straightforward modification of the circuit of Fig. 7.2-1 to add

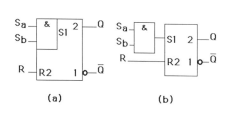

(a)   (b)

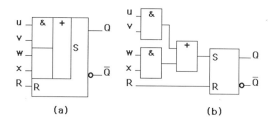

(a)   (b)

Figure 7.2-5 Set-reset latch with AND function of set inputs: (a) IEEE standard symbol; (b) equivalent circuit using detached gates.

Figure 7.2-6 Set-reset latch with set function equal to *UV* + *WX*: (a) IEEE standard symbol; (b) equivalent circuit using detached gates.

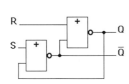

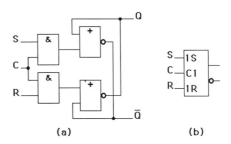

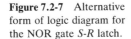

Figure 7.2-7 Alternative form of logic diagram for the NOR gate *S-R* latch.

Figure 7.2-8 NOR gate *S-R* latch with synchronous inputs: (a) logic diagram; (b) logic symbol.

the control (*C*) input is shown in Fig. 7.2-8a. In this circuit the *S* and *R* latch inputs are replaced by signals equal to *CS* and *CR* which cannot equal 1 unless *C* is 1 (as well as *S* or *R*). Thus, the *S* and *R* inputs have no effect on the latch state until *C* becomes equal to 1. The waveforms for the operation of this circuit are shown in Fig. 7.2-9. The transitions at times t_a and t_b demonstrate the transparency property of this latch. If the *S* or *R* inputs change while the control input is active, any effects caused by the change have an immediate effect on the latch state. Any change in the latch outputs appears after only the propagation delay of the circuit gates. The logic symbol is shown in Fig. 7.2-8b. The *C*1 symbol represents a **control dependency**. The rule is that when *C*1 = 1, all 1*S* and 1*R* inputs have their normal effect; when *C*1 = 0, the 1*S* and 1*R* inputs have no effect.

Inputs affected by a control dependency are often called **synchronous inputs**. A latch that has such inputs is sometimes called a **gated latch**. Inputs such as those of Fig. 7.2-1 which are not affected by a control dependency are sometimes called **asynchronous inputs**. The basis for this terminology is that synchronous inputs have their effect on the latch "synchronized" to the activity of the control input. It is possible for a latch to have both synchronous and asynchronous inputs. Many catalog parts provide this type of input structure. The terms "preset input" and "clear input" were used previously to specify asynchronous set and reset inputs. Figure 7.2-10 shows a latch with both kinds of inputs. A very detailed discussion of asynchronous inputs can be found on p. 286 of [Taub 77].

The input state with *S* = *R* = 1 is not allowed in a gated *S-R* latch. In the designs used for these latches, the state reached after *C* is changed from 1 to 0 with both *S* and *R* equal to 1 is not well defined. Thus set and reset dependencies do not apply for gated *S-R* latches.

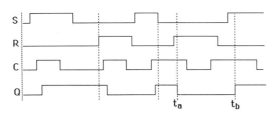

Figure 7.2-9 Waveforms for latch of Fig. 7.2-8.

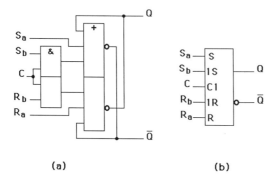

Figure 7.2-10 Latch with both synchronous and asynchronous inputs: (a) logic diagram; (b) logic symbol.

7.2-2 The D Latch

Figure 7.2-11 shows the logic diagram and logic symbol for the other type of gated latch: the D latch. This latch has two advantages over the S-R latch—it requires only a single-rail data input, and there is no input state that either has to be avoided or which leads to noncomplementary outputs. Waveforms illustrating the D latch operation are shown in Fig. 7.2-11d. The transparency property is illustrated by the transitions that occur at times t_a, t_b, and t_c in response to changes in the D input while the control input is active.

The structure of Fig. 7.2-11 is often used for TTL latches. Structures used in some other technologies are shown in Fig. 7.2-12.

It is possible to combine both D, S, and R inputs in a single latch. Figure 7.2-13 shows such an element. It is also possible to have a latch that has more than one D input, as shown in Fig. 7.2-14. Latches with more than one D input are called **multiple-port latches**. The most common type of such latches have two D inputs and are called **dual-port latches**. When $C1 = 1$ the signal present at $1D$ is entered into the latch, and when $C2 = 1$ the signal present at $2D$ is entered into the latch. Correct operation assumes that $C1$ and $C2$ are never both equal to 1. Multiple-port latches are discussed further in Chap. 8.

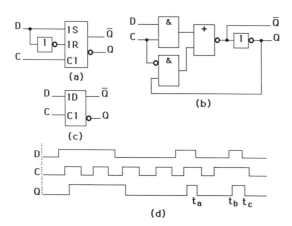

Figure 7.2-11 The D latch: (a) D latch formed from S-R latch; (b) gate-level logic diagram (74LS75); (c) logic symbol; (d) waveforms.

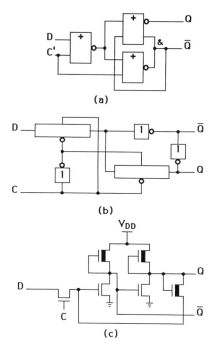

Figure 7.2-12 Latch structures for various technologies: (a) ECL; (b) CMOS; (c) NMOS.

7.2-3 Latch Timing Conditions

To ensure correct operation of a gated latch it is necessary to control the relative timing of the latch inputs as well as the signal durations. The important time intervals are illustrated in Fig. 7.2-15 and are defined as:

Setup time, t_{su}: the time interval immediately preceding the transition of the control input to its latching level, during which the data to be recognized must be maintained at the input to ensure their recognition

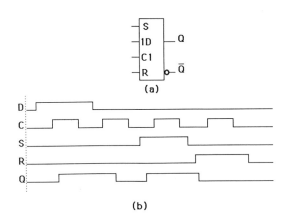

Figure 7.2-13 Latch with D, S, and R inputs: (a) logic symbol; (b) waveforms.

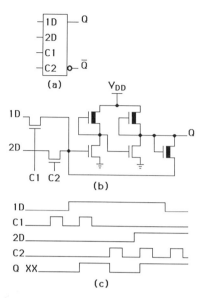

(a)

(b)

(c)

Figure 7.2-14 Multiple-port latches:
(a) symbol for dual-port latch;
(b) NMOS circuit for dual-port latch;
(c) waveforms.

Hold time, t_h: the time interval immediately following the transition of the control input to its latching level, during which the data to be recognized must be maintained at the input to ensure their continued recognition

Control pulse width, t_w: the time interval during which the control signal must remain in the active state

The setup time requirement is necessary to ensure that any changes in the data inputs have propagated throughout the input circuitry before the control input arrives to activate the new data input values. The hold-time and control pulse-width requirements guarantee that a new latch state has propagated throughout the latch circuitry before the input signals producing the state are removed. These requirements come about because latches are designed to be operated in **fundamental-mode**, a mode of operation in which time is allowed for any effects of an input change to become stable before any other input changes occur. Fundamental-mode operation will be discussed more fully in the following sections. If the signals at a latch input violate these timing parameters, the result is uncertain. The data input could have no effect on the latch state, a temporary output pulse

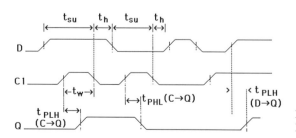

Figure 7.2-15 Waveforms illustrating latch timing.

could be generated, or the latch could enter a metastable state. Metastability is discussed in Sec. 7.5.

The other important timing characteristics of a latch have to do with the time taken for changes in the inputs to affect the outputs of the latch. These times are called **propagation delay times** and are defined as the time from when an input (D or C) changes until the corresponding change appears on the outputs (Q or $\overline{Q}$). The propagation delay times are usually stated both for the output changing from a high to a low level t_{PHL} and for the output changing from a low level to a high level, t_{PLH}, since these two delays don't necessarily have the same value. Some of the propagation delay times for latches are labeled on Fig. 7.2-15. Table 7.2-1 lists timing parameter values for various latches available as standard catalog parts.

TABLE 7.2-1 Some typical latch timing parameters (ns)

	From:	To:	TTL 'LS75		TTL 'ALS373		ECL F100130		CMOS MM54/74	CMOS HC75
									Typ.	Max.
Setup time, t_{su}			20		10		0.70		12	20
Hold time, t_h			5		7		0.60		−2	0
Control pulse width, t_w			20		10		2.00		10	16
			Typ.	Max.	Typ.		Min.	Max.		
t_{PLH}	D	Q	15	27	8		0.50	1.70	10	25
	D	$\overline{Q}$	12	20			0.50	1.70	12	22
	C	Q	15	27	13		0.75	2.00	18	29
	C	$\overline{Q}$	16	30	13		0.75	2.00	13	25
t_{PHL}	D	Q	9	17	Same		Same		14	23
	D	$\overline{Q}$	7	15	as		as		10	20
	C	Q	14	25	t_{PLH}		t_{PLH}		16	27
	C	$\overline{Q}$	7	15					11	23

Static Hazards in D Latch.   There is a static hazard present in the latch circuit of Fig. 7.2-11b. The expression for the input to the inverter is $(DC + C'Q)'$. Since the two 1-sets are adjacent but are not linked, a static 1-hazard exists in the circuit. Waveforms illustrating the action of this hazard are shown in Fig. 7.2-16a. On the falling $(1 \rightarrow 0)$ transition of the control input there is not only the possibility of a spurious 0 pulse, but the latch can incorrectly go from the 1 state to the 0 state due to the hazard. The rising $(0 \rightarrow 1)$ transition of the control input can cause a temporary false 0 output, but in this case the latch is held in the correct 1 state by the presence of the D input. The hazard can be removed by the addition of another gate with D and Q as inputs. This is shown in Fig. 7.2-16b. This technique is now standard practice at IBM ([Eichelberger 77] and [Eichelberger 83]) and is also used in catalog latch elements [Fairchild 73]. It is also possible to eliminate the hazard effects by controlling the relative timing of the C and C' signals. Figure 7.2-16c shows the use of a circuit called a "clock skew driver" to

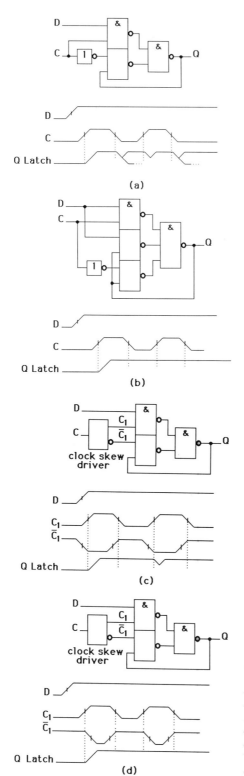

Figure 7.2-16 Hazards in the *D* latch: (a) illustration of hazard pulses in basic circuit; (b) elimination of hazard by addition of a gate; (c) elimination of hazard effect on falling edge of *C* by means of a clock skew driver; (d) elimination of the hazard effects on both edges of *C* by using a more complex clock skew driver.

ensure that the C' signal always changes before the C signal. This eliminates the hazard pulse from the falling edge of the control signal, thus removing the possibility of the latch going into an incorrect state. The occurrence of a faulty output pulse at the rising edge of the control signal is made more likely by this circuit, but this is more tolerable than the incorrect latch state. This circuit is discussed in [Wagner 83]. Both hazard pulses can be removed by using a more complex clock skew driver circuit as shown in Fig. 7.2-16d. In this circuit C' rises before C falls and C rises before C' falls eliminating both hazard possibilities.

This discussion relates directly to TTL latches. [Eichelberger 83] has a good discussion of latches in other technologies. Books on electronic circuits such as [Holt 78] are also good sources for latch circuitry.

7.3 INFORMAL ANALYSIS

To gain some insight into the performance of sequential circuits, the circuit of Fig. 7.3-1 will be analyzed intuitively before any formal methods are developed. The outputs of this circuit (z_1 and z_2) depend not only on the circuit inputs (x_1 and x_2) but also on the outputs of the two latches (y_1 and y_2). The latch outputs in turn depend on the past and present circuit inputs. If $x_1 = x_2 = 1$, then latch 1 must be set and y_1 must equal 1; and if $x_1 = x_2 = 0$, then latch 1 must be reset and y_1 must equal 0. However, if $x_1 = 0$ and $x_2 = 1$ or $x_1 = 1$ and $x_2 = 0$, neither input to latch 1 is energized and this latch remains in the state (set or reset) caused by previous inputs. It is customary to make the assumption that only one of the inputs to a circuit changes at a time. This is a very reasonable assumption, since physically it is, in effect, impossible to have simultaneous changes. Also, the effects of the input changes will propagate through the circuit at different speeds so that the effects of the input changes will not be simultaneous throughout the

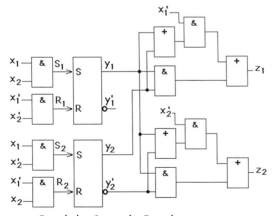

$S_1 = x_1 x_2, \ R_1 = x_1' x_2', \ S_2 = x_1 x_2', \ R_2 = x_1' x_2$

$z_1 = x_1' (y_1 + y_2) + y_1 y_2$
$z_2 = x_2' (y_1 + y_2') + y_1 y_2'$

Figure 7.3-1 Illustrative circuit.

circuit. This discrepancy in propagation of signals can lead to unreliable operation, and thus simultaneous changes are usually forbidden. Throughout this book single changes will be assumed unless a different assumption is stated specifically. With x_1 and x_2 restricted to changing one at a time, the state of latch 1 is determined either by the present values of x_1 and x_2 or by their values before the last input change. Thus, if $x_1 = 0$ and $x_2 = 1$ or $x_1 = 1$ and $x_2 = 0$, $y_1 = 1$ if the previous values of x_1 and x_2 were $x_1 = 1$ and $x_2 = 1$, and $y_1 = 0$ if the previous values of x_1 and x_2 were $x_1 = 0$ and $x_2 = 0$. Another way of stating this same conclusion is that when $x_1 = 0$ and $x_2 = 1$ or $x_1 = 1$ and $x_2 = 0$, $y_1 = 1$ if the previous value of y_1 was 1 and $y_1 = 0$ if the previous value of y_1 was 0. A similar statement can be made for y_2. These conclusions are summarized in Table 7.3-1.

TABLE 7.3-1 Latch conditions for Fig. 7.3-1

Previous value		Present value		Previous value		Present value	
x_1	x_2	x_1	x_2	y_1	y_2	y_1	y_2
1	0	1	1	d	1	1	1
0	1	1	1	d	0	1	0
1	0	0	0	d	1	0	1
0	1	0	0	d	0	0	0
1	1	1	0	1	d	1	1
0	0	1	0	0	d	0	1
1	1	0	1	1	d	1	0
0	0	0	1	0	d	0	0

When $x_1 = x_2$, $y_2 = $ previous value of x_1.

When $x_1 = x_2'$, $y_1 = $ previous value of x_1.

In analyzing a sequential circuit, what is desired is some scheme for determining what sequence of outputs will be produced by any sequence of inputs. Since the outputs are just switching functions of the circuit inputs and latch outputs, the output sequences can be determined directly once the sequences of latches are known. For any given sequence of inputs, the latch outputs can be determined by using Table 7.3-1. The switching functions can then be used to determine the output sequence. Table 7.3-2 shows the sequences that result from a typical input sequence.

For the sequence in this table, the values of z_1 and z_2 are equal to the values of x_1 and x_2 before the last input change. It can be shown that this relationship is true not only for the particular sequence of this table, but for any input sequence. Thus, this circuit performs like an asynchronous one-unit delay line. To establish that this circuit does have this same performance for any input sequence, a more general analysis technique is required. Such a technique will be described in the following section. It should be pointed out that the ultimate objective of this investigation is not really an analysis technique but a synthesis technique. The analysis technique to be developed will therefore be one that can be "turned inside out" and used for synthesis.

TABLE 7.3-2 Input–output sequences for Fig. 7.3-1

	a	b	c	d	e	f	g	h
x_1	0	0	1	0	1	1	0	0
x_2	0	1	1	1	1	0	0	1
y_1	0	0	1	1	1	1	0	0
y_2	?	0	0	0	0	1	1	0
z_1	?	0	0	1	0	1	1	0
z_2	?	0	1	1	1	1	0	0

Time ⟶

An assumption about the way in which the circuit inputs are changed is implicit in the preceding discussion. Specifically, it has been assumed that the inputs are never changed unless the circuit is in a stable condition (i.e., unless none of the internal signals are changing). Whenever a sequential circuit's inputs are controlled so that this assumption is valid, the circuit is said to be operating in fundamental-mode [McCluskey 63]. This chapter deals with fundamental-mode operation. In Chap. 8, the analysis of circuits not operating in fundamental-mode is considered. Much of the theory of fundamental-mode operation was developed by [Huffman 54].

7.4 FORMAL ANALYSIS OF SEQUENTIAL CIRCUITS WITH LATCHES

As was pointed out previously, in a sequential circuit such as that of Fig. 7.3-1, the outputs are switching functions of the circuit inputs and the latch outputs. The determination of the circuit outputs from the circuit inputs and latch outputs is a straightforward combinational-circuit problem, and the techniques of Chap. 3 can be used. The novel aspect of sequential circuits is the relationship between the circuit inputs and the latch outputs. The latch inputs are switching functions of the circuit inputs,[3] but the latch outputs are not switching functions of the circuit inputs, so the basic problem in analyzing sequential circuits is that of determining the relationship between the circuit inputs and the latch outputs.

Since the relationships between the circuit inputs and the latch outputs are not characterized by switching functions, some new representation of this relationship will have to be developed. This development is one of the major objectives of this section.

To investigate the relation between the circuit inputs and latch outputs, let us consider a specific situation in the circuit of Fig. 7.3-1. Let the circuit inputs x_1 and x_2 both be equal to 0 and the latch outputs y_1 and y_2 also both be equal to 0. Now let x_1 change to become equal to 1. Since S_2 is equal to $x_1 x_2'$, S_2 now becomes equal to 1 and latch 2 must change state so that y_2 becomes equal to 1. From this little "experiment" it is clear that the circuit is unstable when $x_1 = 1$,

---

[3] The latch inputs will, in general, depend also on latch outputs. The method to be developed here will be applicable to circuits in which this dependency is present.

$x_2 = 0$, $y_2 = 0$ and the y_2 latch must change so that the stable state with $x_1 = 1$, $x_2 = 0$, $y_2 = 1$ is reached. This transition from an unstable situation to a stable situation by a latch changing is the key to sequential-circuit behavior.

In Table 7.4-1, all possible combinations of values of x_1, x_2, y_1, and y_2 are listed. Each combination of values of the circuit inputs and latch outputs is called a total state of the sequential circuit, since all signals in the circuit (including the circuit outputs) can be determined from the circuit inputs and latch outputs. Each stable total state in Table 7.4-1 is encircled, and an arrow is drawn from each unstable state to the stable state to which the circuit goes from the unstable state. The stable states and unstable-state behavior can be determined directly from the circuit or from Table 7.4-1. For example, row 1 of the table corresponds to the stable state with $x_1 = x_2 = y_1 = y_2 = 0$. Since the state is stable, the circuit will remain in this state until some input is changed. If x_1 is changed to 1, the circuit is then in the total state represented by row 13. This row represents an unstable state, and the table shows that a latch change must take place so that the circuit enters the stable state represented by row 14.

By means of a table such as Table 7.4-1, the output sequence corresponding to any input sequence can easily be obtained. In a very real sense, the derivation of Table 7.4-1 completes the analysis of the circuit in that it permits the determination of the output sequence corresponding to any input sequence. On the other hand, it could be argued that the analysis is still incomplete because the word statement "The outputs are equal to the previous values of the inputs" has not been obtained. The analysis techniques to be developed here will *not* result in such word statements for several reasons. First, many circuits do not have any simple word statement, since they are part of a larger system and their operation

TABLE 7.4-1 Table showing stable and unstable states for the circuit of Fig. 7.3-1

Row	x_1	x_2	y_1	y_2	z_1	z_2
1	0	0	0	0	0	1
2	0	0	0	1	1	0
3	0	0	1	1	1	1
4	0	0	1	0	1	1
5	0	1	0	0	0	0
6	0	1	0	1	1	0
7	0	1	1	1	1	0
8	0	1	1	0	1	1
9	1	1	0	0	0	0
10	1	1	0	1	0	0
11	1	1	1	1	1	0
12	1	1	1	0	0	1
13	1	0	0	0	0	1
14	1	0	0	1	0	0
15	1	0	1	1	1	1
16	1	0	1	0	0	1

specifications are determined by the system. Second, since English is not a formal language in a mathematical sense, it is not really possible to have a *formal* procedure for obtaining word statements. This does not change the fact that some presentations of the circuit operation are more easily understood than others. The presentation in Table 7.4-1 is not the most acceptable for ease of understanding, and hence a variation of this table is in common use.

7.4-1 Transition Table

In Table 7.4-1, the transitions between unstable and stable states are shown by means of arrows. Another method of describing these transitions is to list, for each total state, the *next* values of the y_1 and y_2 variables. In fundamental-mode operation the inputs do not change until the latches have reached their state values, so that only the next values of the **latch variables** need be listed. In Table 7.4-2, the *next* values of y_1 and y_2 symbolized by Y_1 and Y_2, are listed for each total state of the circuit of Fig. 7.3-1. The variables $y_1, y_2, \ldots$ will be called **internal variables**, or present-state variables, and $Y_1, Y_2, \ldots$ will be called **next-state variables**. Values of Y_1 and Y_2 which are the same as the corresponding values of y_1 and y_2 are encircled, since they represent stable states.

It is customary to draw Table 7.4-2 in a slightly different form which distinguishes more strongly between the circuit inputs and the latch outputs. This form, called a **transition table**, is shown in Table 7.4-3a. Each column of this table corresponds to a specific assignment of values to the circuit-input variables or to an **input state**. Each row of the table corresponds to a specific assignment of values to the latch output variables, or to an **internal state**. Each cell of the table corresponds to an assignment of values to the circuit inputs and the latch outputs, or

TABLE 7.4-2 Table showing Y_1 and Y_2 (next states of y_1 and y_2) for each total state in the circuit of Fig. 7.3-1

Row	x_1	x_2	y_1	y_2	Y_1	Y_2	z_1	z_2
1	0	0	0	0	(0)	(0)	0	1
2	0	0	0	1	(0	1)	1	0
3	0	0	1	1	0	1	1	1
4	0	0	1	0	0	0	1	1
5	0	1	0	0	(0	0)	0	0
6	0	1	0	1	0	0	1	0
7	0	1	1	1	1	0	1	0
8	0	1	1	0	(1	0)	1	1
9	1	1	0	0	1	0	0	0
10	1	1	0	1	1	1	0	0
11	1	1	1	1	(1	1)	1	0
12	1	1	1	0	(1	0)	0	1
13	1	0	0	0	0	1	0	1
14	1	0	0	1	(0	1)	0	0
15	1	0	1	1	(1	1)	1	1
16	1	0	1	0	1	1	0	1

TABLE 7.4-3 Tables for the circuit of Fig. 7.3-1: (a) Transition table; (b) Output table; (c) Table 7.3-2

(a)

x_1x_2

y_1y_2	00	01	11	10
00	⓪⓪ (h)	⓪⓪ (b)	10	01
01	⓪1 (g)	00	11	⓪1
11	01	10	⑪	⑪ (f)
10	00	⑩ (d) (c)	⑩ (e)	11

Y_1Y_2

(b)

x_1x_2

y_1y_2	00	01	11	10
00	01	00	00	01
01	10	10	00	00
11	11	10	10	11
10	11	11	01	01

Z_1Z_2

(c)

	a	b	c	d	e	f	g	h
x_1	0	0	1	0	1	1	0	0
x_2	0	1	1	1	1	0	0	1
y_1	0	0	1	1	1	1	0	0
y_2	?	0	0	0	0	1	1	0
z_1	?	0	0	1	0	1	1	0
z_2	?	0	1	1	1	1	0	0

to a **total state**. The entries of the table are the appropriate **next internal states** for each total state. Thus a change of input variable causes a change from one column of the table to another column without any row change. If, in the new column, the Y_1Y_2 values disagree with the y_1y_2 values for the row, a row change must take place to a new row whose y_1y_2 values are the same as the Y_1Y_2 values of the original row. It is sometimes helpful to think of an "operating point" that represents the total state of the circuit and which moves around on the transition table in accordance with the changes in the total state of the circuit. The operating points that correspond to the sequence of Table 7.3-2 have been plotted on Table 7.4-3a. Table 7.3-2 is repeated as Table 7.4-3c for the sake of convenience. The corresponding output states are shown in the output table of Table 7.4-3b.

7.4-2 The Transition Diagram and State Table

A more pictorial representation of the transition table is sometimes used in which each stable total state is represented by a small circle and each total state is represented by a dot. Arrows are drawn showing the transitions between

TABLE 7.4-4 Tables for the circuit of Fig. 7.3-1: (a) Transition table; (b) Output table; (c) Transition diagram; (d) State table; (e) State table

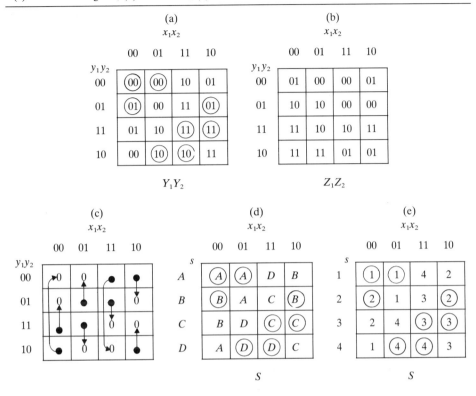

(a)

x_1x_2

y_1y_2	00	01	11	10
00	⟨00⟩	⟨00⟩	10	01
01	⟨01⟩	00	11	⟨01⟩
11	01	10	⟨11⟩	⟨11⟩
10	00	⟨10⟩	⟨10⟩	11

Y_1Y_2

(b)

x_1x_2

y_1y_2	00	01	11	10
00	01	00	00	01
01	10	10	00	00
11	11	10	10	11
10	11	11	01	01

Z_1Z_2

(c)

x_1x_2

y_1y_2	00	01	11	10
00				
01				
11				
10				

(d)

x_1x_2

s	00	01	11	10
A	⟨A⟩	⟨A⟩	D	B
B	⟨B⟩	A	C	⟨B⟩
C	B	D	⟨C⟩	⟨C⟩
D	A	⟨D⟩	⟨D⟩	C

S

(e)

x_1x_2

s	00	01	11	10
1	⟨1⟩	⟨1⟩	4	2
2	⟨2⟩	1	3	⟨2⟩
3	2	4	⟨3⟩	⟨3⟩
4	1	⟨4⟩	⟨4⟩	3

S

unstable and stable states. This is called a **transition diagram** and is illustrated in Table 7.4-4c.

Another form of the transition table is often used in which each internal state is replaced by an arbitrary letter or decimal number. This form of table is called a **state table** and is illustrated in Table 7.4-4d and e. By using a state table and an output table, it is possible to determine the output sequence produced by any input sequence. It is not possible to determine the sequence of states of the circuit latches, but this information is not important to the **external** performance of the circuit. The state table is important because it will form the starting point for the **synthesis** of sequential circuits.

7.4-3 The Excitation Table

In discussing the transition and state tables and showing that they are reasonable forms in which to present the operation of a sequential circuit, the question of how these tables are obtained from the circuit diagram has not been discussed. To complete the formal analysis procedure, a formal technique must be determined for going from a circuit diagram to a transition table. The first step in this technique

TABLE 7.4-5 Excitation table for the circuit of Fig. 7.3-1: (a) Excitation functions; (b) Excitation table

(a)

$$S_1 = x_1 x_2 \qquad R_1 = x_1' x_2' \qquad S_2 = x_1 x_2' \qquad R_2 = x_1' x_2$$

(b)

$y_1 y_2$	$x_1 x_2$			
	00	01	11	10
00	01, 00	00, 01	10, 00	00, 10
01	01, 00	00, 01	10, 00	00, 10
11	01, 00	00, 01	10, 00	00, 10
10	01, 00	00, 01	10, 00	00, 10

$$S_1 R_1, \; S_2 R_2$$

is to obtain, from the circuit diagram, the switching functions that describe the effect of the circuit inputs and latch inputs. These switching functions are called **excitation functions**. The excitation functions for the circuit of Fig. 7.3-1 are shown in Table 7.4-5a. The excitation functions are then used to fill in an excitation table. The **excitation table** is the same as the transition table, except that its entries are the values of the latch inputs $(S_1, R_1, \ldots)$ rather than the next states $(Y_1, Y_2, \ldots)$ of the latch outputs. An excitation table is shown in Table 7.4-5b.

The crucial step in analyzing a sequential circuit is that of going from an excitation table to the corresponding transition table. One method of doing this is to note that whenever S and R are both equal to 0, the value of Y will be the same as the value of y; whenever $S = 1$ and $R = 0$, Y will be equal to 1; and whenever $S = 0$ and $R = 1$, Y will be equal to 0. In the following it will be assumed that the circuit is designed so that the state $S = R = 1$ never occurs at any latch input. If this is not the case, straightforward modifications to the procedure described below are necessary to take into account the set and reset dependencies of the latches. By using these simple rules the transition table can readily be written down from the excitation table. This procedure can also be formalized by writing these rules down in a table of combinations and obtaining a function giving the dependence of Y on S, R, and y. This is done in Table 7.4-6, and the function is shown to be $Y = S + R'y$. This function is called the **characteristic function** for set-reset latches.

It is perhaps well to point out now that the variable Y is quite different from the other variables, such as S, R, y, and Z, in that Y does *not* correspond to any *physical signal* in the circuit. The variable Y is in some sense a fictitious variable representing the *next* condition of the y variable.

A formal technique for analyzing sequential circuits has been presented. The steps in this procedure are illustrated in Fig. 7.4-1. The following sections will show how this technique is applied to sequential circuits using devices other than set-reset latches and to circuits operating in different modes.

TABLE 7.4-6 Relationship between S, R, y, and Y: (a) Table of Combinations; (b) Map; (c) Characteristic function for set-reset latches with no set and reset dependencies

(a)			
S	R	y	Y
0	0	0	0
0	0	1	1
0	1	0	0
0	1	1	0
1	1	0	d
1	1	1	d
1	0	0	1
1	0	1	1

(b)

S-R

y	00	01	11	10
0	0	0	d	1
1	1	0	d	1

(c)

$$Y = S + R'y$$

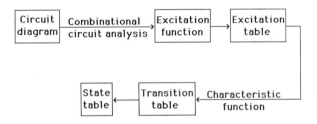

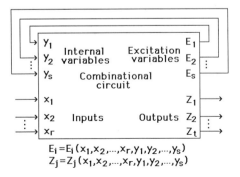

Figure 7.4-1 Sequential-circuit analysis.

7.5 VARIOUS "MEMORY" DEVICES FOR SEQUENTIAL CIRCUITS

The preceding discussion has been concerned with sequential circuits containing *S-R* latches. There are, of course, many other devices that can be used to construct sequential circuits. The analysis technique that was presented for *S-R* latches will still be valid with minor modifications for circuits containing other devices. Specifically, different devices will require changes in the rules used for obtaining the transition table from the excitation table, but the rest of the technique will remain unchanged. Before considering some different devices in detail, it seems appropriate to consider the question of what physical properties the devices used to construct sequential circuits must have.

$$E_i = E_i(x_1, x_2, \ldots, x_r, y_1, y_2, \ldots, y_s)$$
$$Z_j = Z_j(x_1, x_2, \ldots, x_r, y_1, y_2, \ldots, y_s)$$

Figure 7.5-1 General form of a sequential circuit.

One essential feature of a sequential circuit is that there must be some signal or signals in the circuit whose value is determined not only by the present circuit inputs but by past circuit inputs as well. The devices controlling these signals are usually called **memory devices**, **internal devices**, or **secondary devices**. In the circuit analyzed previously, the latches were the internal devices. The mechanism by which these devices operate usually involves some sort of feedback to provide the memory, and it is customary to represent a generalized sequential circuit as a combinational circuit with some feedback loops (Fig. 7.5-1). In a latch these feedback loops are contained within the latch circuit, but they are present nevertheless.

7.5-1 Physical Requirements

As an introduction to different types of memory devices, the requirements on the electrical properties of the feedback loops will be considered [Unger 57]. Suppose that one of the feedback loops has been broken, as in Fig. 7.5-2, and a terminating impedance added to simulate the impedance presented by the rest of the loop. There must be some set of values for the inputs (x_i) and the internal variables (y_j) such that either a 1 or a 0 can be present in this feedback loop. (If this is not true, it is not possible to store two memory states in the loop. Such a loop would not really represent an internal variable and it would be possible to redesign the circuit without this loop.) Assume that this set of values is present and that the loop characteristic is measured (e_o versus e_i). When the loop is closed, $e_o = e_i$; therefore, there must be two intersections of the open-loop characteristic with the $e_o = e_i$ line. One of these intersections corresponds to a 1 stored in the loop and therefore occurs with $e_o = e_i = E_H$ and the other intersection occurs with $e_o = e_i = E_L$ and corresponds to a stored 0. These intersections are labeled A and B in Fig. 7.5-3. For these intersections to correspond to stable operating points, the slope of the open-loop characteristic must be less than the slope of the closed-loop characteristic. (If the open-loop slope were greater than the closed-loop slope, any small change in e_i, perhaps due to noise, would cause a larger change in e_o. This change in e_o would produce a change in e_i which would again produce a larger change in e_o and the values of e_i and e_o would continue to change away from the original operating point until a stable operating point is reached.)

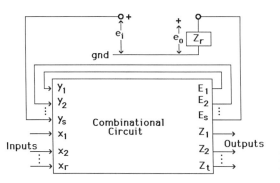

Figure 7.5-2 General sequential circuit with feedback loop broken.

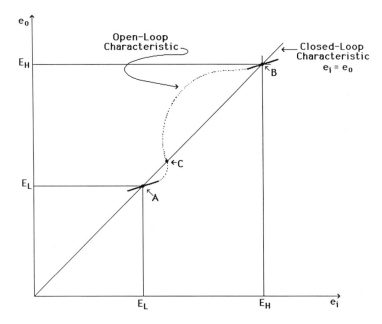

Figure 7.5-3 Feedback-loop characteristics.

This is indicated by the heavy portion of the open-loop characteristic. The rest of the open-loop characteristic has to be a continuous curve connecting the two heavy portions.

Any curve connecting the two stable operating points where the characteristic has slope less than one must pass through a region where the slope is greater than one. In this region a change in e_i will result in a larger change in e_o. Clearly, some sort of active device providing amplification must be present in the loop. Since integrated-circuit gates are designed to provide a noise margin (Sec. 4.1-1), this amplification function is present in each gate.

Metastability. In addition to points A and B in which the open-loop and closed-loop characteristics intersect, there must be another intersection at a point such as point C in Fig. 7.5-3. (It's not possible to draw a curve between two stable points such as A and B without having an intersection such as C.) Since the closed-loop characteristic has a slope greater than 1 at point C, this represents a **metastable** situation. Any change in the value of e_i will produce a larger change in e_o. If the loop ever enters a metastable state such as represented by point C, it will eventually leave that state and go to either point A or point B. Metastability can be a very severe problem because:

1. While the loop is in the metastable state the voltage stored in the loop (and used as the value of the state variable) will not be equal to either of the normal signal values. This intermediate voltage can be outside the noise margins of the other gates in the system and can thus produce unpredictable actions in the rest of the circuit.

2. The loop will leave the metastable state after a delay that *cannot be predicted deterministically*.

The obvious conclusion to be drawn from these observations is that metastable states should be avoided. Unfortunately, this is not always possible. Whenever an external signal must be used in a system, it is not possible to guarantee the timing relations between the external signal and the internal system signals. The external signal is asynchronous with respect to the system signals. For the external signal to be usable by the system its value must be stored in an internal memory device such as a latch. This means that the external signal must be used as a "synchronous latch input" controlled by an internal signal. It is not possible to guarantee that the timing requirements (setup and hold time) are satisfied. The effect is that two inputs to an AND gate are possibly changed simultaneously. A function hazard is present and a small pulse, called a "runt pulse," may be generated at the gate output. This is illustrated in Fig. 7.5-4a. This runt pulse may not have sufficient energy to switch the latch from one stable state to the other and instead may place the latch in a metastable state.

An approach to avoiding the effects of metastability is illustrated in Fig. 7.5-4b. A second latch is connected to the output of the latch having the asynchronous signal as an input. The second latch is controlled by a delayed version of the signal used to control the first latch. Thus the value of the first latch is not read into the second latch until after a time interval to allow the first latch to leave the metastable state. A circuit such as this will decrease the number of times that metastable signals enter the system, but will not eliminate them entirely. It is not possible to bound the length of time that the first latch will remain in the metastable state. Thus it is not possible to choose a value for the delay such that all metastable signals will be eliminated. No method of eliminating all metastability is known. The first latch that receives the asynchronous input is sometimes called a synchronizer or arbiter.

An interesting discussion of how to calculate the probability of metastability in a system is given in [Stoll 82]. A number of experimental and theoretical studies of metastability have been reported in the literature: [Chaney 72], [Chaney 73], [Chaney 79], [Couranz 75], [Kinniment 76], [Lacroix 82], [Marino 81], [Pearce 75], [Pechoucek 76], [Plummer 72], [Rosenberger 82], [Strom 78], and [Veendrick 80].

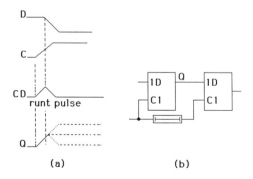

Figure 7.5-4 Phenomenon of metastability: (a) runt pulse production; (b) a circuit to reduce the effect of metastability.

7.5-2 Analysis of Sequential Circuits with Feedback Loops

Figure 7.5-5 shows a sequential circuit constructed of NAND gates. In this circuit there are two feedback loops (indicated by the heavy lines) each of which can contain either a 1 signal or a 0 signal. To analyze the circuit it is necessary to "break" these feedback loops and write switching functions for the signals present in them. One way to do this is to imagine that there are amplifiers present in the loops. It is then possible to write expressions for the amplifier inputs in terms of the circuit inputs and the amplifier outputs. For the Fig. 7.5-5 circuit with amplifiers as shown, these expressions are

$$E_1 = x_1 x_2 + y_1(x_1 + x_2)$$

$$E_2 = x_1 x_2' + y_2(x_1 + x_2')$$

It is not always immediately obvious where to place the amplifiers to break the feedback loops in a circuit. One approach would be to use graph theory to identify the leads that allow a minimum number of amplifiers to be used. For hand calculation it is typically not necessary to take such a formal approach. It is not possible to use too few amplifiers since it would not be possible to write the equations in this case. If too many amplifiers are used, the tables will be larger, but the correct analysis is still possible. Care should be taken in the placement of the amplifiers; their location in the circuit can have a large impact on the complexity of the circuit analysis.

The first step in analyzing a feedback-loop circuit is to write down the excitation functions; in this case, the switching functions for the signals at the inputs to the feedback-loop amplifiers, E_1 and E_2. The next step is to form an excitation table such as that shown in Table 7.5-1a. To obtain the transition table, the effect of E_1 on y_1 must be determined, or, equivalently, the characteristic function must be obtained. In the case of an ordinary amplifier it is clear that the amplifier

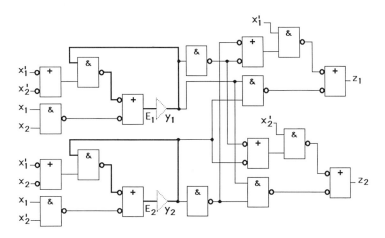

Figure 7.5-5 Sequential circuit constructed of NAND gates.

output y will change to become equal to the amplifier input E. Because of this, the characteristic function is particularly simple, $Y = E$; and *the transition table is identical with the excitation table*. Passing from the transition table to the state table and the output table completes the analysis (Table 7.5-1b and c). Since these are the same as Table 7.4-4e and b, it can be concluded that the circuits of Figs. 7.3-1 and 7.5-5 have the same external performance.

It is an interesting thing to compare the results of this analysis with the analysis obtained by "breaking" the feedback loops in different places. Since this operation of inserting fictional amplifiers is merely a convenience for analysis and does not affect the circuit performance, the same results should be obtained for different locations of the fictional amplifiers. This question will be studied further in the problems at the end of the chapter.

Figure 7.5-6 shows the analysis of a D latch by breaking its feedback loop. The circuit is shown in Fig. 7.5-6a and the corresponding transition table in Fig. 7.5-6b. The excitation function, $E = CD + C'y$, is also the characteristic function of a D latch: $Y = CD + C'y$.

TABLE 7.5-1 Tables for the circuit of Fig. 7.5-5:
(a) Excitation and transition table; (b) State table;
(c) Output table

(a)

x_1x_2

y_1y_2	00	01	11	10
00	00	00	10	01
01	01	00	11	01
11	01	10	11	11
10	00	10	10	11

E_1E_2
Y_1Y_2

(b)

x_1x_2

S	00	01	11	10
1	(1)	(1)	4	2
2	(2)	1	3	(2)
3	2	4	(3)	(3)
4	1	(4)	(4)	3

S

(c)

x_1x_2

S	00	01	11	10
1	01	00	00	01
2	10	10	00	00
3	11	10	10	11
4	11	11	01	01

Z_1Z_2

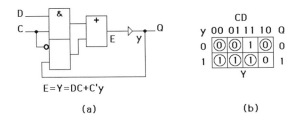

$E = Y = DC + C'y$

(a)

$$
\begin{array}{c}
\qquad\qquad CD \\
y \quad 00 \ \ 01 \ \ 11 \ \ 10 \quad Q
\end{array}
$$

y	00	01	11	10	Q
0	0	0	1	0	0
1	1	1	1	0	1

Y

(b)

Figure 7.5-6 *D* latch analysis: (a) latch circuit; (b) transition table.

7.5-3 Transmission Gate Memory Loops

CMOS bistable elements are often constructed using transmission gates. Figure 7.5-7 shows a logic diagram of a *D* latch that incorporates transmission gates in the way they are used in CMOS. When this circuit is analyzed by breaking the feedback loop, the resulting excitation function is $E = CD + C'y$. Since this is the same function as was obtained for the *D* latch of Fig. 7.5-6, the analysis shows that the same type of latch operation is obtained by the transmission gate circuit as by the circuit using only AND and OR gates.

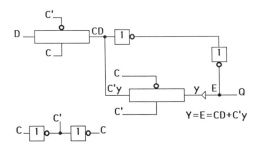

$Y = E = CD + C'y$

Figure 7.5-7 Analysis of transmission gate *D* latch.

7.6 RACES IN SEQUENTIAL CIRCUITS

In Chap. 2 a mathematical model for digital circuits was developed, and a switching algebra was formulated. To obtain a simple model and an algebra that could be easily used, several idealizing assumptions were made. One of the most serious of these was the assumption that no delay is involved in changing a signal from one of its values to its other value. A very important aspect of sequential circuits involves the delay in the feedback loops, and it seems appropriate to consider some of the effects of this delay now.

A sequential circuit is shown in Fig. 7.6-1, and the tables for the analysis of this circuit are shown in Table 7.6-1. When the inputs are both equal to 1 and $y_1 = 0$, $y_2 = 1$, the transition table shows that $Y_1 = 1$ and $Y_2 = 0$ (indicated by the * in Table 7.6-1). This means that both the gates *A* and *B* are unstable. The outputs of both gates should change. If these two events occur simultaneously, the transition specified in the transition table will actually take place. However, it is extremely unlikely that both outputs will change simultaneously and that the new values will propagate through the circuit at the same time. Thus, instead of going directly to the $y_1 = 1$, $y_2 = 0$ state, the circuit will go either to the $y_1 = 1$,

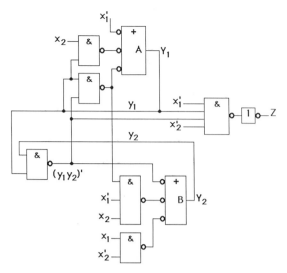

$Y_1 = X_1 + X_2 y_1 + y_1(y_1 y_2)' = X_1 + X_2 y_1 + y_1 y_2'$

$Y_2 = y_1 y_2 + (y_1' + y_1 y_2) x_1' x_2 + x_1 x_2' = y_1 y_2 + x_1' x_2 y_1 + x_1 x_2'$

$z = x_1' x_2 y_1 (y_1' + y_2') = x_1' x_2 y_1 y_2'$

Figure 7.6-1 Sequential circuit illustrating races.

$y_2 = 1$ state or to the $y_1 = 0$, $y_2 = 0$ state. If the circuit goes to the $y_1 = 0$, $y_2 = 0$ state, the A gate will still be unstable (since in this state $Y_1 = 1$ and $Y_2 = 0$) and the circuit will now go to the $y_1 = 1$, $y_2 = 0$ state. In this case the desired operation is achieved. On the other hand, if the circuit goes to the $y_1 = 1$, $y_2 = 1$ state, it will remain there, since this state is stable and the circuit operation will be incorrect. This situation where more than one of the internal variables are unstable is called a **race**. If the final stable state to which the circuit goes depends on the order in which the internal variables change, then a **critical race** is said to be present.

To obtain reliable circuit operation, critical races must be avoided. One approach to eliminating these is to "fix" the races, that is, choose gates so that the order in which they change is controlled by their electrical characteristics. For the circuit of Fig. 7.6-1, this would mean using an A gate whose propagation delay was definitely longer than the propagation delay of the B gate. There are two difficulties with this technique for handling critical races. First, the electrical characteristics of the gates will change with time. What was a reliable circuit when first constructed may no longer be a reliable circuit after it has been in operation for some time. Also, there are tables in which it is impossible to fix the critical races. For example, if the entry in the $y_1 = 0$, $y_2 = 0$ row of the $x_1 = 1$, $x_2 = 1$ column of Table 7.6-1a were 00 instead of 10, the critical race could not be avoided by controlling the electrical properties of the internal gates. A more generally satisfactory technique for avoiding critical races is to arrange the transition table so that they never occur. A technique for doing this will be presented in Chap. 9. Avoiding the situation where more than one of the internal variables are unstable at one time is one method for eliminating critical races. The critical race can be removed from Table 7.6-1 without changing the circuit behavior by

TABLE 7.6-1 Tables for Fig. 7.6-1: (a) Excitation and transition table; (b) Output table; (c) Transition diagram

(a)

x_1x_2

y_1y_2	00	01	11	10
00	⓪⓪	01	10	11
01	00	⑪	10*	11
11	01	⑪	⑪	⑪
10	⑩	⑩	⑩	11

Y_1Y_2

(b)

x_1x_2

y_1y_2	00	01	11	10
00	0	0	0	0
01	0	0	0	0
11	0	0	0	0
10	1	0	0	0

Z

(c)

replacing the 10 entry for $x_1 = 1$, $x_2 = 1$, $y_1 = 0$, $y_2 = 1$ by a 00 entry. The resulting tables are shown in Table 7.6-2.

There is still a race present in the $x_1 = 1$, $x_2 = 0$ column, but this is not a critical race, since the final stable state must be 11, independent of the order in which the internal variables change.

7.6-1 The Flow Table

A state table such as Table 7.6-2d describes some of the internal behavior of the corresponding circuit, since for $x_1 = x_2 = 1$ it specifies the multiple transition from state 2 to state 4 via state 1. As far as the external circuit performance is concerned, this multiple transition is usually not important.[4] It is customary to describe the circuit performance by means of a **flow table**, which is identical with the state table except that multiple transitions are not shown; when the circuit goes from one unstable state to another unstable state, the entry specifying the first unstable state is replaced by an entry specifying the final stable state which is reached. Table 7.6-2e is the flow table corresponding to the state table of Table 7.6-2d. The 1 entry corresponding to $x_1 = x_2 = 1$, $s_j = 2$ has been replaced by a 4 entry, since the final stable state reached is 4.

The major importance of the flow table is in synthesis, since in specifying the desired performance of a circuit no information is available about internal multiple transitions. It may be necessary to introduce multiple transitions in the design

---

[4] Unless a transient output is developed in the intermediate state.

Sec. 7.6   Races in Sequential Circuits

TABLE 7.6-2 (a) Excitation table and transition table: (b) Output table; (c) Transition diagram; (d) State table; (e) Flow table

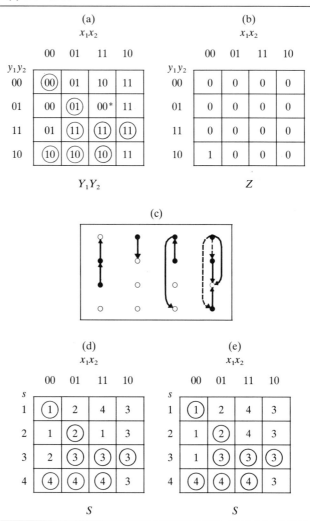

procedure for economy or to avoid critical races. In summary, a flow table specifies the final stable state which is reached, and a state table specifies the next state, whether this state is stable or unstable.

7.7 FUNDAMENTAL-MODE FLIP-FLOPS

A **flip-flop** is a gated bistable element that does not have the transparency property of a latch. Thus, a change in a flip-flop output is never a direct response to a change in a synchronous input. A flip-flop output changes only in response to a

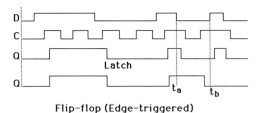

Flip-flop (Edge-triggered)

Figure 7.7-1 Waveforms for D latch and D flip-flop.

transition on a control input or a change in an asynchronous input. Figure 7.7-1 shows waveforms for both a D latch and a D flip-flop. The latch and flip-flop outputs are the same until t_a, when the D input changes while $C = 1$. The latch responds to the t_a change and the flip-flop doesn't. In general, flip-flop and latch response is the same except when the synchronous inputs change while $C = 1$.

A flip-flop is a more complex and costly element than a latch. The flip-flop has a very important advantage over a latch: It is possible to "read in" a new state at the same time that the old state is being "read out." Because of the transparency property, this is not in general possible in a latch. In a latch the state being read in replaces the original state immediately. There is thus a danger that the new state replaces the old state as the state being read out.

Registers will be defined next since they provide the most direct illustration of the difference between a flip-flop and a latch. A **register** is a circuit that is capable of storing several bits of information. It consists of several bistable elements that are associated with one another in a fixed sequence. There are common control signals that cause information to be entered into all bits of the register. Figure 7.7-2a shows a 4-bit register. While Load = 1 the values of the A_i signals are entered into the corresponding latches, which retain their last value when Load changes to 0. The standard symbol for the Fig. 7.7-2a circuit is shown in Fig. 7.7-2b. The topmost block of this symbol is the "common-control" block and any inputs to this block represent inputs that are connected in the same fashion to all of the elements below the common-control block. By means of the common-control block notation it is possible to avoid showing in detail all of the interconnections of signals that are common to all elements of a register or similar circuit.

A facility often associated with a register is the ability to shift its contents. A register with this capability is called a **shift register**. Shifting the contents of a

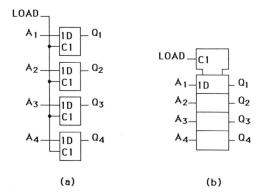

(a) (b)

Figure 7.7-2 Four-bit latch register: (a) logic diagram; (b) standard symbol.

Sec. 7.7   Fundamental-Mode Flip-Flops   **303**

register is an operation in which the contents of the register are replaced by the same contents displaced one position to either the right or left. Thus if the contents of the register are given by

$$X_1 \quad X_2 \quad X_3 \quad X_4$$

$$a \quad b \quad c \quad d$$

after a (1-bit) right shift they will become

$$X_1 \quad X_2 \quad X_3 \quad X_4$$

$$0 \quad a \quad b \quad c$$

Since the X_1 latch has no element to its left, a 0 is shifted into X_1. [A closely related operation is the Rotate operation, in which the contents of the last stage of the register (X_4) are entered into X_1.]

A direct approach to providing a shift-right capability for the register of Fig. 7.7-2a is shown in Fig. 7.7-3a: the Q output of latch X_1 is connected to the D input of latch X_2, the Q output of latch X_2 is connected to the D input of latch X_3, etc. There is a difficulty with this circuit. Suppose that the initial contents of the register are

$$X_1 \quad X_2 \quad X_3 \quad X_4$$

$$0 \quad 1 \quad 0 \quad 1$$

When the shift signal equals 1, the contents will change to

$$X_1 \quad X_2 \quad X_3 \quad X_4$$

$$0 \quad 0 \quad 1 \quad 0$$

The X_3 latch now has a 1 stored, but a 0 is being gated in so that the contents will change again to become

$$X_1 \quad X_2 \quad X_3 \quad X_4$$

$$0 \quad 0 \quad 0 \quad 1$$

Finally, X_4 will change to 0 so that all four latches will have 0's stored. One way to prevent the 0 of X_1 being shifted into the other three latches is to remove the shift signal after the hold time of the latches so that only one new value is shifted into a latch. This requires very precise timing of the shift signal. This scheme can be made more practical by using the circuit of Fig. 7.7-3b in which a delay is placed at the output of each latch. The delay value is chosen so that there is time to remove the shift signal before the new latch value is propagated to the input of the next latch. In effect, the old latch value is being stored temporarily in the delay.

Another approach is shown in Fig. 7.7-3c. Here the old latch values are stored in additional latches placed between the original latches. This circuit structure, sometimes called a **double-rank** structure, requires the use of two shifting signals. It is possible to use shift and (shift)' for this purpose. When shift is

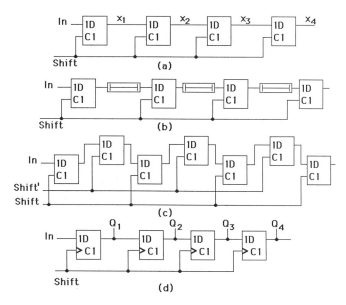

Figure 7.7-3 Shift register designs: (a) *D* latches interconnected directly; (b) use of delays; (c) double-rank design; (d) use of *D* flip-flops.

inactive the value in each latch is copied into its successor latch in the upper rank. Then when shift becomes active, this connection is broken and the upper rank values are shifted down into the following stages. The upper rank latches are being used in place of the delays of Fig. 7.7-3b to store the old latch values. The double-rank scheme has the advantage of less critical timing constraints, but can be more expensive than the scheme using delays.

The use of *D* flip-flops to form a shift register is shown in Fig. 7.7-3d. Since the flip-flops do not respond to changes on *D* after the control input has changed to 1, the values in the flip-flops will only be shifted one position for each pulse on the shift input. The symbol for a *D* flip-flop is formed by adding a dynamic input symbol ($>$) to the control input of the *D* latch symbol. A **dynamic input** responds only to a 0-to-1 transition of the input.

The standard symbol for the flip-flop shift register of Fig. 7.7-3d is shown in Fig. 7.7-4a. The SRG 4 label in the common-control block indicates that the device is a four-stage shift register. The $>C1$ input label indicates a dynamic input that controls the $1D$ input of the first stage. The $> \rightarrow$ input label denotes a

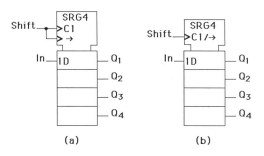

Figure 7.7-4 Standard symbol for *D* flip-flop shift register of Fig. 7.7-3d: (a) one form of symbol; (b) preferred form of symbol.

dynamic input that causes the contents of the stages to shift up one position. A more common version of the standard symbol is shown in Fig. 7.7-4b. In this symbol the two input connections to the common control block are combined; the solidus (/) is used to separate symbols showing the different functional effects of an input.

There can be a problem with the circuits of Fig. 7.7-3 if the shift signal does not arrive at each of the bistable elements at the same time. This phenomenon is called **clock skew**.

The necessity of concurrent read in and read out of bistable elements is very common in digital systems. Because of this, flip-flops have become standard circuit elements and are available in a variety of forms. Most of the modern IC flip-flop circuits operate in fundamental mode. The important fundamental-mode flip-flops are discussed in this section. It is also possible to base the design of a flip-flop on the use of delays as in Fig. 7.7-3b. While this was done in early designs, it is not as reliable as the use of fundamental-mode flip-flops and is no longer used.

7.7-1 The D Flip-Flop

A logic diagram for a D flip-flop is shown in Fig. 7.7-5a and its analysis given in Figs. 7.7-5d–f. Study of the flow table (Fig. 7.7-5f) shows that when the C input changes from 0 to 1, the flip-flop output changes to become equal to the signal on the D input. Any changes in D while C is 1 have no effect on the circuit. The waveforms of Fig. 7.7-1 are repeated as Fig. 7.7-5c to illustrate the difference

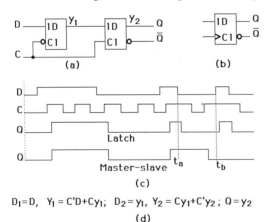

$$D_1 = D, \quad Y_1 = C'D + Cy_1; \quad D_2 = y_1, \quad Y_2 = Cy_1 + C'y_2; \quad Q = y_2$$

(d)

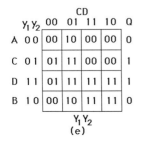

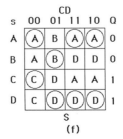

Figure 7.7-5 Edge-triggered D flip-flop: (a) logic diagram for a master-slave circuit; (b) logic symbol; (c) waveforms; (d) excitation functions; (e) transition table; (f) flow table.

between the D latch and the D flip-flop. The operation of the circuit of Fig. 7.7-5a is similar to that of the double-rank circuit of Fig. 7.7-3c. When the control input is at 0, the D value is copied into the first latch of the circuit. This is often called the **master latch**. When the control input changes to 1, the master latch is decoupled from the D input and the second latch, called the **slave latch**, has the value of the master latch copied into it. The output value changes when a new value is copied into the slave latch from the master latch, that is, when the control input goes from 0 to 1. A circuit having a structure with two latches, one a master and the other a slave, such as Fig. 7.7-5a is called a **master-slave circuit**.

The function implemented by the circuit of Fig. 7.7-5a is that of an **edge-triggered** or **E-T** D flip-flop. The logic symbol for such a flip-flop is shown in Fig. 7.7-5b. The symbol placed at the C input is used to indicate that the device has a dynamic control input and is thus edge triggered. It is called edge triggered because the state of the flip-flop is determined by the signal present at D when the control input changes from 0 to 1. The D value is sampled by the leading edge of the control signal. Further, the output changes value only immediately following this edge of the control signal. The circuit of Fig. 7.7-5a is one structure that is used (typically in CMOS) to realize this function. There are a variety of other implementations for the D flip-flop that are in use. Rather than list them here, their properties will be studied via the problems at the chapter end.

There is one realization that deserves special attention because it is so different from the others. This is the MOS **dynamic** D flip-flop as shown in Fig. 7.7-6. The switches in this circuit are realized by pass transistors in NMOS circuits and by transmission gates in CMOS circuits. There is no bipolar equivalent to this circuit in current use. This circuit relies on the capacitance associated with an inverter input to store a signal. It will function correctly only if the control input switches at a minimum frequency that depends on the particular circuit parameters. If the control input is held fixed for too long, the charge will leak off the input nodes and the stored signal will be lost. Flip-flop designs such as that of Fig. 7.7-5 are called **static** to emphasize their property of operating correctly even when the control inputs are held fixed for long periods of time.

A word of caution is in order here. The terminology and symbology for flip-flops has been in a confused state for many years. The new IEEE standard provides a consistent terminology and will be followed in this book. The manufacturers are slowly adopting this standard. Older manufacturers' literature and textbooks use a varied collection of terms and symbols which may conflict with the standard definitions. Comparing the material presented here with earlier publications can be confusing due to apparent inconsistencies caused by the lack of agreement on terms and symbols. Every effort will be made to use only IEEE standard terms and symbols here. When a nonstandard term or symbol is used, the deviation will be pointed out. In addition, an attempt will be made to point out nonstandard terms and symbols that are in common use.

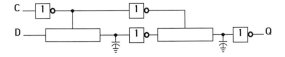

Figure 7.7-6 Logic diagram for MOS dynamic D flip-flop.

7.7-2 *The* J-K *Flip-Flop*

The *D* flip-flop is derived from the *D* latch by removing the transparency property. The other type of latch, the *S-R* latch, can also be transformed into a flip-flop. *S-R* flip-flops used to be available as catalog parts, but they have been almost completely replaced by the *J-K* flip-flop. The two synchronous inputs—*J* and *K*—to this flip-flop act as set and reset inputs. The difference between the *S-R* and the *J-K* flip-flop is that the *J* and *K* inputs are permitted to both be equal to 1 at the same time. If $J = K = 1$ when the control input is activated, the state of the flip-flop changes or "toggles." Figure 7.7-7 shows the *J-K* flip-flop.

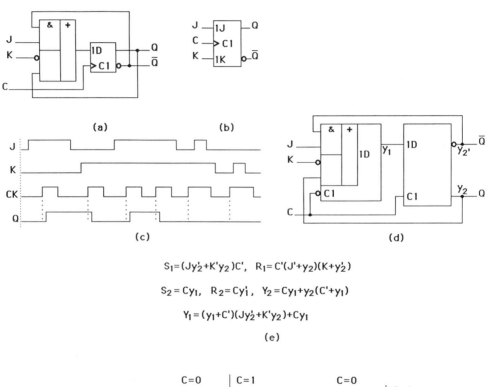

$$S_1 = (Jy_2' + K'y_2)C', \quad R_1 = C'(J'+y_2)(K+y_2')$$

$$S_2 = Cy_1, \quad R_2 = Cy_1', \quad Y_2 = Cy_1 + y_2(C'+y_1)$$

$$Y_1 = (y_1+C')(Jy_2'+K'y_2) + Cy_1$$

(e)

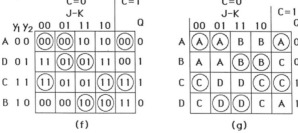

(f) (g)

Figure 7.7-7 Edge-triggered *J-K* flip-flop: (a) derivation from edge-triggered *D* flip-flop; (b) IEEE standard symbol; (c) typical waveforms; (d) latch-level diagram; (e) excitation functions; (f) transition table; (g) flow table.

TABLE 7.7-1 Flip-flop state just after C input changes from 0 to 1

J-K	Before	After
00	Q	Q
01	Q	0
11	Q	Q'
10	Q	1

The *J-K* flip-flop has replaced the *S-R* device as a catalog part since the *J-K* can be used whenever the *S-R* could be used. Furthermore, the use of the *J-K* can lead to simplifications in the rest of the network because of the simple toggle input.

Figure 7.7-7a shows the derivation of the edge-triggered *J-K* flip-flop from the *D* flip-flop. The IEEE standard symbol for this device is shown in Fig. 7.7-7b, and part (c) of the figure shows typical waveforms. An implementation using *D* latches is shown in Fig. 7.7-7d and is analyzed in Fig. 7.7-7f. Whenever the *C* input changes from 0 to 1, the *Q* output becomes (or remains) equal to the value as given in Table 7.7-1. There is no change in the flip-flop output when *C* returns to 0.

Older versions of the *J-K* flip-flop—the master-slave or pulse-triggered flip-flop, and the data-lockout flip-flop—operate a little differently than the edge-triggered design just described. Since these forms of the *J-K* flip-flop are no longer used for new designs they will not be discussed here. The IEEE standard does provide symbols as shown in Fig. 7.7-8, and [Peatman 80] and [Wakerly 76] describe and compare the different *J-K* flip-flop implementations.

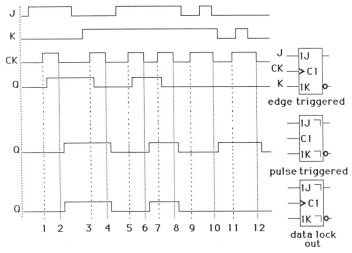

Figure 7.7-8 Different types of *J-K* flip-flops.

7.7-3 The T Flip-Flop

There is one other standard flip-flop, the *T* **flip-flop**, which is also sometimes called a **toggle** or a **change flip-flop**. The standard symbol for an edge-triggered *T* flip-flop is shown in Fig. 7.7-9a and typical waveforms are shown in Fig. 7.7-9d. The operation of this flip-flop is described in Table 7.7-2. If $T = 0$ when the control input changes from 0 to 1, there is no change in the flip-flop state. If $T = 1$ when the control input changes from 0 to 1, the flip-flop state changes (becomes 0 if previously 1, becomes 1 if 0 when the control input change occurs). Figure 7.7-9b shows the derivation of a *T* flip-flop from a *J-K* flip-flop, and the connections to a *D* flip-flop to obtain a *T* flip-flop are shown in Fig. 7.7-9c. In the *J-K* design, whenever a *C*-pulse arrives the flip-flop will toggle if $T = 1$ since this will cause *J* and *K* to both be 1. Nothing happens if $T = 0$ since then both *J* and *K* are 0. For the design using a *D* flip-flop, *Q* is applied to *D* when $T = 0$, and when $T = 1$ the signal at *D* is Q'.

The *T* flip-flop is not available as a catalog part and is not common in cell libraries or standard cells. It is easily obtained from a *J-K* or *D* flip-flop. The *T* flip-flop is often used in the early design stages since it can be very convenient as a conceptual device. Binary counters are one example of a class of circuits that benefit from design using *T* flip-flops. In the final design the *T* flip-flops are replaced by their equivalent *D* or *J-K* based designs.

TABLE 7.7-2 Edge-triggered *T* flip-flop state after control input changes from 0 to 1

T	Before	After
0	Q	Q
1	Q	Q'

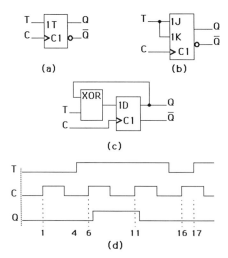

(a)

(b)

(c)

(d)

Figure 7.7-9 Edge-triggered *T* flip-flop: (a) IEEE standard symbol; (b) derivation from edge-triggered *J-K* flip-flop; (c) derivation from edge-triggered *D* flip-flop; (d) typical waveforms.

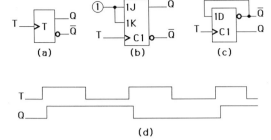

(a) (b) (c)

Figure 7.7-10 Nongated T flip-flop: (a) IEEE standard symbol; (b) derivation from J-K flip-flop; (c) derivation from D flip-flop; (d) Typical waveforms.

(d)

7.7-4 Non-gated Flip-Flops

All of the flip-flops just described are **gated flip-flops**: Their state after a control pulse arrives is determined or gated by the values of other inputs such as D, J, K, T. There are two non-gated flip-flops which can be very useful in design even though they are not offered as standard parts or cells.

The **non-gated T flip-flop** is fairly common, particularly in connection with binary counter design. This type of T flip-flop has only one input and changes state whenever a pulse occurs on the input. It has the same action as a gated T flip-flop with a permanent 1 signal connected to the T input. The symbol for this version of the T flip-flop is shown in Fig. 7.7-10 along with typical waveforms and realizations using J-K or D flip-flops.

The **non-gated S-R flip-flop** is not at all common, but can be very convenient for some designs, particularly when the circuit has more than one pulse input. This flip-flop has two inputs—S and R. A pulse on the S input causes the flip-flop to go to its 1 state. The state change occurs after the **trailing** edge of the pulse. The effect of the R input is to cause the flip-flop to go to the 0 state. Usually, both inputs are never both equal to 1 at the same time. If this does happen, the input that changes back to 0 last will determine the flip-flop state. The symbol for a non-gated S-R flip-flop is shown in Fig. 7.7-11b. The delayed output symbol placed at the Q and $\overline{Q}$ outputs indicates that the state change doesn't happen until the trailing edge of the activating pulse. A logic diagram for an implementation is shown in Fig. 7.7-11a and typical waveforms are given in part (c).

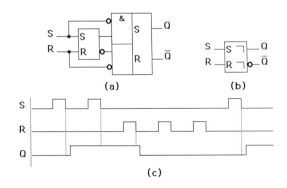

(a) (b)

(c)

Figure 7.7-11 Nongated S-R flip-flop: (a) logic diagram; (b) IEEE standard symbol; (c) waveforms.

7.7-5 Flip-Flop Conversions

A number of flip-flops have been described in the preceding sections. The most important of these are the edge-triggered D flip-flop and the edge-triggered J-K flip-flop. The S-R and T flip-flops are not commonly available as either catalog parts or as standard cells. These two flip-flops are used mainly in full custom designs or internally in catalog parts or standard cells.

Figures 7.7-9 and 7.7-10 present circuits for converting J-K and D flip-flops into T flip-flops, and the conversion of a D flip-flop into a J-K flip-flop is shown in Fig. 7.7-7. It is possible in a similar fashion to derive any type of flip-flop from any other type. Design of sequential circuits using flip-flops as memory elements is discussed in Chap. 9. The process of converting one flip-flop type into another flip-flop type is a special case of the general synthesis problem considered in Chap. 9.

7.8 ESSENTIAL HAZARDS

As discussed in Sec. 7.2-3 the presence of a logic hazard in a sequential circuit can cause the circuit to malfunction. On the other hand, elimination of all combinational hazards doesn't guarantee correct operation independent of circuit delays. Almost all fundamental-mode sequential circuits and in particular all fundamental-mode flip-flops contain a hazard called an **essential hazard**. It differs from the combinational hazards discussed in Chap. 3 in two ways: Essential hazards are present only in sequential circuits, and they cannot be eliminated without controlling the delays in the circuit.

An essential hazard results from a signal that travels through two paths, one of them having only combinational logic and the other passing through a latch or other memory element. This is illustrated in Fig. 7.8-1, which shows an S-R flip-flop with $S = 1$, $R = 0$, $y_1 = 0$, $y_2 = 0$, and C changing from 0 to 1. There are two paths along which the effect of the C change is propagated to gate B: Path 1 passes through gate A and latch 1; path 2 goes through the inverter I directly to gate B. By looking at the logic diagram it may appear that path 1 will always have less delay than path 2. This is not the case since the actual electrical circuit may not correspond directly to the logic diagram. For example, the AND gate A may be incorporated in the latch so that there is only one gate delay between C and y_1. Depending on the relative delay in these two paths, three possibilities exist for the signal generated at the output of gate B:

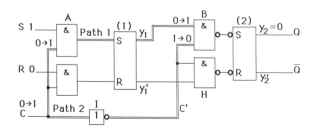

Figure 7.8-1 Logic diagram of an S-R flip-flop.

1. The output of B remains at 1 and the flip-flop operates correctly. This will happen if the path 1 delay is longer than the path 2 delay.

2. A short 0-pulse is generated at the output of gate B. This will happen if the path 1 delay is a little shorter than the path 2 delay. In this case latch 2 can become metastable.

3. A long 0-pulse is generated at the output of gate B. This will happen if the path 1 delay is substantially shorter than the path 2 delay. In this case, latch 2 will be set and the final circuit state will have both y_1 and y_2 equal to 1. The Q output will incorrectly change to 1 while the C input is 1. (The flip-flop is transparent and is thus operating like a latch rather than a flip-flop.)

To guarantee correct operation the circuit must be designed to ensure that only possibility 1 can actually occur. This is done in the 74L71 by replacing gates B and H (a similar problem is possible involving propagation through gate H) with transistors as shown in Fig. 7.8-2. This modification makes the delay through path 2 definitely shorter than the path 1 delay. The C input is connected directly to the emitters of transistors B and H. As soon as the C input rises, the collectors of the two transistors are held at a high signal independent of the signals on the bases. Since the base signals must pass through latches and the emitter signals are connected directly, a very substantial delay in the interconnect would be required to permit the base signal to arrive first. This circuit is also discussed on p. 112 of [Kohonen 72].

Logic diagrams are not sufficient for estimating delays when studying hazards. Accurate delay estimates require study of the electrical circuits. In some situations even the electrical circuit diagram may not be sufficient to estimate delays. It is possible for the placement of the devices on the chip and the routing of the interconnect to produce path delays significantly longer than would be expected from the electrical circuit. This is most likely when automatic placement and routing programs are used.

7.8-1 Techniques for Controlling Essential Hazards

While the approach of avoiding essential hazards by careful electrical design is used in other bipolar catalog flip-flops besides the 74L71, it does not provide a general solution to the problem of essential hazards. It is not always possible to speed up all input paths that are involved in essential hazards. One technique that is always applicable is to delay the outputs of all bistable elements (latches or feedback loops) by a sufficient time so that paths through these elements are always longer

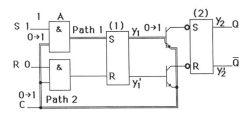

Figure 7.8-2 74L71 S-R flip-flop. Input gates of latch 2 are replaced by transistors to speed-up gating into latch 2.

than paths passing through only combinational logic. (Detailed proofs of this statement and other theory about essential hazards can be found in [Unger 69].) The delay of the bistable outputs can be implemented by careful electrical design or by explicit delay elements. This approach has the disadvantage of slowing down the system operation. Another variation of this approach requires a careful analysis of the delays in all appropriate paths and the insertion of delays only in paths likely to activate essential hazards.

As will be explained in the following chapter, many systems do not operate in fundamental-mode at the system level. The internal state variables are implemented with flip-flops that operate internally in fundamental-mode, but the system operation is pulse-mode (discussed in Chap. 8). Since essential hazards are a problem only for fundamental-mode, they need be controlled only in the design of the flip-flops. This can be done, as discussed in the preceding paragraph, by careful electrical design of the flip-flops.

Another approach is based on the fact that it is usually sufficient to control the essential hazards caused by changes in the clock input to the flip-flops. Most flip-flops use a master-slave structure in which the latch inputs are gated by C or C'. Essential hazards can be avoided by replacing C and C' with a **nonoverlapping two-phase clock**—a pair of signals, $C1$ and $C0$, related to C as shown in Fig. 7.8-3b. $C1$ changes from 0 to 1 at the same time that C changes from 0 to 1, but $C1$ changes back to 0 before C does. $C0$ has a similar relation to C'. This creates a time interval, t_0, during which both $C1$ and $C0$ are equal to 0. Use of $C1$ and $C0$ in a master-slave structure such as Fig. 7.8-3a has the same effect as placing a delay of t_0 at the latch 1 outputs: a change to 1 of the ($C1$) enable signal for latch 1 is delayed until t_0 after the ($C0$) enable signal for latch 2 changes to 0. The advantage of the structure of Fig. 7.8-3 comes from the fact that the signals $C0$ and $C1$ can be used for all the flip-flops. This means that it isn't necessary to control the delays in each flip-flop. Instead, the critical timing circuitry is concentrated in the common circuitry that generates and distributes the $C1$ and $C0$ signals. The relation between the $C1$ and $C0$ signals must be preserved by the

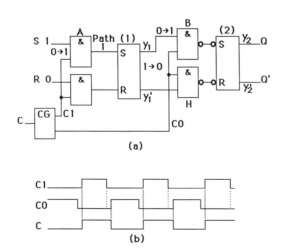

Figure 7.8-3 *S-R* flip-flop with two-phase nonoverlapping clock: (a) circuit; (b) waveforms.

circuitry that distributes these signals throughout the system. A circuit for generating a two-phase nonoverlapping clock is given in Sec. 7.9.

Control of essential hazards is vital to ensure correct operation of a flip-flop, but they are not often included in textbook discussions of flip-flops. As an example of the level of treatment of this subject the reader is referred to page 290 of [Taub 77]. This book has a generally good presentation of flip-flops, but the discussion of essential hazards indicates a lack of appreciation of their importance. Better coverage is provided in [Maley 63]. The definitive theoretical consideration of essential hazards is to be found in [Unger 69]. The major results of this treatment of essential hazards are summarized in the following subsection.

7.8-2 Theoretical Considerations

An interesting and important challenge is how to design sequential circuits so that they work properly even when the propagation delays of their components vary from their nominal values. Of course, it is obvious from the start that it must be possible to put some maximum bound on the magnitude of the delays; without this bound, fundamental-mode operation wouldn't be possible since there would be no way of bounding the time for the circuit to stabilize internally aftcr an input change. If a maximum value for internal propagation delays can be assumed, it is then possible to design an arbitrary fundamental-mode circuit so that its output sequence will not depend on the internal component delay values [Unger 69]. The requirements on the design are:

1. No internal variable races
2. The combinational circuitry is hazard-free
3. Only one input signal is changed at a time
4. There is a lower bound on the propagation delay of the outputs of the bistable elements

The last condition is necessary to guarantee that the input variable changes propagate throughout the circuit before any of the internal variable changes are propagated.

It is always possible to guarantee proper operation by satisfying these conditions. For some circuits it may be necessary to introduce extra delays at the latch outputs. However, delays are often not needed for all of the bistable elements. In designing sequential circuits to operate correctly for realistic delay parameter variations, it can be very helpful to identify those transitions that are possible timing problems. In other words, it can be important to discover any essential hazards that are present. Testing a flow table for essential hazards will be studied with the help of Fig. 7.8-4, which shows the possible responses to a change in one input variable.

An essential hazard is present when an input change causes a bistable element to change state and that state change is propagated to another bistable before the original input change arrives at the second bistable element. The hazard shown in Fig. 7.8-1 has latch 1 as the first bistable and the hazard occurs when the y_1

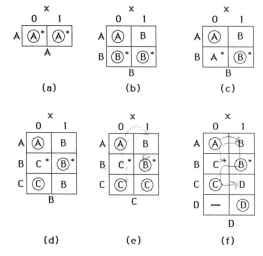

Figure 7.8-4 Possible sequential-circuit responses to a single change in input (fundamental mode).

input to latch 2 changes before the C change arrives. Another way of saying the same thing is that the second bistable receives an internal state change before the input state change arrives. Thus the second bistable goes to a next internal state determined by the new internal state and the old input state. This does not always make a difference. Consider the flow table fragment of Fig. 7.8-4a. If the internal state is A, changing x doesn't cause any change of state and thus the final internal state will be A no matter what the internal delays are. On the other hand, for the table of Fig. 7.8-4f if the initial state is A and x is changed from 0 to 1, any bistable that gets the state change to B and not the x change will itself change to state C. The input change will eventually arrive and cause a further state change to D. The final circuit state will be D rather than B and an essential hazard is present. A similar analysis shows that improper delays can cause the final state of Fig. 7.8-4e to be C rather than the correct B state. The two flow table fragments of Fig. 7.8-4e and f thus correspond to essential hazards and any flow table having either of these patterns will contain an essential hazard. Study of the other parts of Fig. 7.8-4 shows that they do not correspond to essential hazards. An easy way to test a flow table for essential hazards is given in the following definition, which is a restatement of the conclusions just arrived at from Fig. 7.8-4.

DEFINITION. A total state S_j and an input variable x_i represent an **essential hazard** for a flow table T if and only if when the table is initially in state S_j, the state reached after one change in x_i is different from the state reached after three changes in x_i when fundamental-mode operation is assumed.

Figure 7.8-5 shows the flow table for the S-R flip-flop of Fig. 7.8-1. Study of this table shows that there are two essential hazards (three if the $S = R = 1$ input state is allowed). For the total state with $C = 0$, $S = 1$, $R = 0$, and internal state 1, a single change of C leads to state 2 and two more changes of C leave the circuit in state 3. Since states 2 and 3 are different, this corresponds to an essential

$y_1 y_2$	C=0	C=1, S-R: 00	01	11	10	Q
(00) 1	①	①	①	①	2	0
(10) 2	3	②	1	1	②	0
(11) 3	③	③	4	4	③	1
(01) 4	1	④	④	④	3	1

Figure 7.8-5 Flow table for the *S-R* flip-flop of Fig. 7.8-1.

hazard. Similarly, with the circuit in internal state 3, if $S = 0$, $R = 1$, and C changes from 0 to 1, an essential hazard is present.

The importance of essential hazards is indicated by the following theorem. By identifying the essential hazards present in a flow table it is possible to determine what steps must be taken to protect the circuit operation from false operation due to delay parameter variation.

THEOREM 7.8-1. A sequential circuit for fundamental-mode operation that is not affected by stray delays in the combinational circuitry can be constructed without delays in the y_i leads if and only if the corresponding flow table docs not contain any essential hazards [Unger 69].

It follows from the theorem that only tables with at least three internal states can have essential hazards. Unger also showed that if essential hazards are present, it is always possible to construct a sequential circuit with only one delay element. This is done by using a combinational circuit to switch the single delay element into the appropriate y_i branch during each input change.

7.9 GENERAL PROPERTIES

Fundamental-mode sequential circuit operation is very general. A circuit operating in fundamental-mode can be designed (using the techniques to be presented in Chap. 9) to implement any deterministic input-output behavior that is not specified in terms of analog quantities. Precise discussions of formal realizability theory are not of interest here; however, it is important to characterize informally the properties of realizable sequential circuit behavior. Any input-output specification that has the five properties listed below will be called a **sequential function**. Any sequential function can be realized with a sequential circuit operating in fundamental-mode.

DEFINITION. Any sequential circuit input-output behavior satisfying the following five properties will be called a **sequential function**.

Sequential Circuit Property 1. No future dependence: The output at any specific time depends only on the present and past inputs.

Sequential Circuit Property 2. Finite memory requirement: The amount of information required to determine the output is finite.

Sequential Circuit Property 3. No analog dependence: The sequence of values of the input signals completely determines the output. There may be timing bounds on the signals in order to permit the circuit components to respond properly to input changes. These timing considerations must be bounds rather than exact values. They depend on the circuit realization and can be changed by using a different circuit implementation.

Sequential Circuit Property 4. Deterministic operation: The output may not depend on any internal random variables; it is determined completely by the sequence of values of the input signals.

Sequential Circuit Property 5. Single input changes: The output must not depend on simultaneous changes in more than one input signal.

Examples of input-output specifications that violate properties 1 and 2 are given in Chap. 9. Property 5 is necessary since it is not possible to guarantee that simultaneous input changes will be propagated in synchronism through the sequential circuit. Properties 3 and 4 are illustrated by the following example.

Example 7.9-1: Circuit with a Random Output Obtained by Explicit Signal-Length Dependence

Figure 7.9-1a shows a sequential circuit that cannot be operated in fundamental-mode. When the input $x = 1$, the circuit never stabilizes but rather continues to cycle through all four states as shown in the analysis of Table 7.9-1. Since fundamental-mode operation prohibits an input change while the circuit is unstable internally, no further changes in the input would be allowed in fundamental-mode operation. In spite of the inability to operate this circuit in fundamental-mode, a useful function is realized by the circuit. If x is returned to 0, the final state will be stable and will depend on the state the circuit happened to be in when the transition to 0 occurred. If the input x is manually generated, since the speed of internal cycling of the circuit is much faster than human response time the final state when x is returned to 0 will be essentially random. The probability of getting output $Z_1 = 1$ will be 1/2 and the probabilities of the other two outputs are both 1/4. (This assumes that the circuit is realized so that the cycling while $x = 1$ is such that the circuit remains in each of the states for equal amounts of time.) Thus the circuit is an electronic version of the spinner shown in Fig. 7.9-1b, which is often used to generate random moves for board games. If it were possible to generate very accurate durations for the x input, it would be possible to obtain deterministic operation from this circuit, but the more usual application for this type of circuit is in connection with generating random outputs with fixed probabilities.

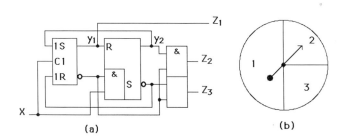

Figure 7.9-1 Non-fundamental-mode circuit: (a) logic diagram; (b) board game spinner.

TABLE 7.9-1 Analysis of Fig. 7.9-1: (a) Excitation functions; (b) Transition table; (c) State table

(a)

$$Y_1 = xy_2 + (xy_2')'y_1 = xy_2 + x'y_1 + y_1y_2$$

$$Y_2 = xy_1' + y_1'y_2; \qquad Z_1 = y_1; \qquad Z_2 = y_1'y_2; \qquad Z_3 = y_1'y_2'$$

(b)

$y_1 y_2$	$x=0$	$x=1$	$z_1z_2z_3$
0 0	0 0	0 1	0 0 1
0 1	0 1	1 1	0 1 0
1 1	1 0	1 0	1 0 0
1 0	1 0	0 0	1 0 0
	Y_1Y_2		

(c)

s	$x=0$	$x=1$	$z_1z_2z_3$
1	1	2	0 0 1
1	2	3	0 1 0
1	4	4	1 0 0
1	4	1	1 0 0
	S		

Figure 7.9-2a shows a circuit for deriving a pair of two-phase nonoverlapping pulse trains from a single pulse train. The output waveforms are given in Fig. 7.9-2b assuming the same propagation delay for each of the three logic elements in the circuit (zero interconnect delay). This circuit is a borderline case of fundamental-mode operation; the shape of the output waveforms does not depend on the precise values of the element delays but does depend on their existence. Also, it is the only circuit seen thus far in which the output waveform depends directly on the unstable state outputs. Table 7.9-2 gives the analysis of this circuit.

Any sequential circuit behavior that satisfies the previous five properties can be realized by a circuit operated in fundamental mode. Techniques for doing this will be presented in Chap. 9. Fundamental-mode is a way to operate a circuit: The input changes are subject to the requirement that no input may be changed until all of the internal signals in the circuit have become stable. There are some circuit designs that result in deterministic behavior only when operated in fundamental-mode. Such circuits are often called fundamental-mode circuits, even

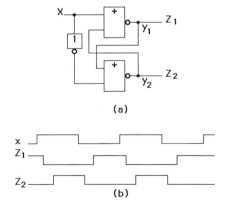

(a)

(b)

Figure 7.9-2 Two-phase nonoverlapping pulse generator: (a) logic diagram; (b) waveforms.

TABLE 7.9-2 Analysis of Fig. 7.9-2: (a) Excitation functions; (b) Transition table; (c) State table

(a)

$$Y_1 = x'y_2', \qquad Y_2 = xy_1'$$

(b)

$y_1 y_2$	X = 0	X = 1	$Z_1 Z_2$
0 1	0 0	0 1	0 1
0 0	1 0	0 1	0 0
1 0	1 0	0 0	1 0
1 1	0 0	0 0	1 1

$Y_1 Y_2$

(c)

s	X = 0	X = 1	$Z_1 Z_2$
A	B	A	0 1
B	C	A	0 0
C	C	B	1 0
D	B	B	1 1

S

though the term *fundamental-mode* applies strictly to an operating method rather than a circuit design.

Any fundamental-mode sequential circuit constructed of combinational circuits and feedback loops or latches can be analyzed using the techniques of this chapter. By placing further restrictions on the allowed input-output behavior it is possible to define modes of operation that permit simpler analysis. There is one important restricted operating mode—**pulse-mode**—which is the subject of the following chapter. Most sequential circuits are intended to be operated in pulse-mode. They often use flip-flops as internal memory elements. The analysis procedures presented in this chapter must be modified to handle pulse-mode operation. This is discussed in Chap. 8.

7.R REFERENCES

[CHANEY 72] Chaney, T. J., S. M. Ornstein, and W. M. Littlefield, "Beware the Synchronizer," *Dig. COMPCON '72*, San Francisco, pp. 317–319, Sept. 12–14, 1972.

[CHANEY 73] Chaney, T. J., and C. E. Molnar, "Anomalous Behavior of Synchronizer and Arbiter Circuits," *IEEE Trans. Comput.*, C-22, No. 4, pp. 421–425, 1973.

[CHANEY 79] Chaney, T. J., "Comments on 'A Note on Synchronizer or Interlock Maloperation'," *IEEE Trans. Comput.*, C-28, No. 10, pp. 802–805, 1979.

[COURANZ 75] Couranz, G. R., and D. F. Wann, "Theoretical and Experimental Behavior of Synchronizers Operating in the Metastable Region," *IEEE Trans. Comput.*, C-24, No. 6, pp. 604–616, 1975.

[EICHELBERGER 77] Eichelberger, E. B., and T. W. Williams, "Logic Design Structure for LSI Testability," *Proc. 14th Des. Autom. Conf.*, New Orleans, La., pp. 462–468, June 20–22, 1977.

[EICHELBERGER 83] Eichelberger, E. B., "Latch Design Using 'Level Sensitive Scan Design'," *Dig. COMPCON Spring '83*, San Francisco, pp. 380–383, Feb. 28–Mar. 3, 1983.

[FAIRCHILD 73]   Fairchild Semiconductor, *The TTL Applications Handbook*, Aug. 1973.

[HILL 68]   Hill, F. J., and G. R. Peterson, *Introduction to Switching Theory and Logical Design*, John Wiley & Sons, Inc., New York, 1968.

[HOLT 78]   Holt, C. A., *Electronic Circuits: Digital and Analog*, John Wiley & Sons, Inc., New York, 1978.

[HUFFMAN 54]   Huffman, D. A., "The Synthesis of Sequential Switching Circuits," *J. Franklin Inst.*, Vol. 257, No. 3, pp. 161–190; No. 4, pp. 275–303, 1954.

[IEEE 84]   *IEEE Standard Dictionary of Electrical and Electronics Terms*, 3rd ed., IEEE, New York, 1984.

[KINNIMENT 76]   Kinniment, D. J., and J. V. Woods, "Synchronisation and Arbitration Circuits in Digital Systems," *Proc. IEE*, Vol. 123, No. 10, pp. 961–966, 1976.

[KOHONEN 72]   Kohonen, T., *Digital Circuits and Devices*, Prentice-Hall, Inc., Englewood Cliffs, N.J., 1972.

[LACROIX 82]   Lacroix, G., P. Marchegay, and G. Piel, "Comments on 'The Anomalous Behavior of Flip-Flops in Synchronizer Circuits'," *IEEE Trans. Comput.*, C-31, No. 1, p. 77, 1982.

[MALEY 63]   Maley, G. A., and J. Earle, *The Logic Design of Transistor Digital Computers*, Prentice-Hall, Inc., Englewood Cliffs, N.J., 1963.

[MARINO 81]   Marino, L. R., "General Theory of Metastable Operation," *IEEE Trans. Comput.*, C-30, No. 2, pp. 107–115, 1981.

[McCLUSKEY 63]   McCluskey, E. J., "Fundamental-Mode and Pulse-Mode Sequential Circuits," *Proc. IFIP Congr. 1962, Int. Conf. Inf. Process.*, Munich, Aug. 27–Sept. 1, 1962, pp. 725–730, ed. Cicely M. Popplewell, North-Holland Publishing Company, Amsterdam, 1963.

[McCLUSKEY 65]   McCluskey, E. J., *Introduction to the Theory of Switching Circuits*, McGraw-Hill Book Company, New York, 1965.

[PEARCE 75]   Pearce, R. C., J. A. Field, and W. D. Little, "Asynchronous Arbiter Mode," *IEEE Trans. Comput.*, C-24, No. 9, pp. 931–932, 1975.

[PEATMAN 80]   Peatman, J. B., *Digital Hardware Design*, McGraw-Hill Book Company, New York, 1980.

[PECHOUCEK 76]   Pechoucek, M., "Anomalous Response Times of Input Synchronizers," *IEEE Trans. Comput.*, C-25, No. 2, pp. 133–139, 1976.

[PLUMMER 72]   Plummer, W. W., "Asynchronous Arbiters," *IEEE Trans. Comput.*, C-21, No. 1, pp. 37–42, 1972.

[ROSENBERGER 82]   Rosenberger, F., and T. J. Chaney, "Flip-Flop Resolving Time Test Circuit," *IEEE J. Solid-State Circuits*, SC-17, No. 4, pp. 731–738, 1982.

[STOLL 82]   Stoll, P. A., "How to Avoid Synchronization Problems," *VLSI Des.*, pp. 56–59, Nov.–Dec. 1982.

[STROM 78]   Strom, B. I., "Proof of the Equivalent Realizability of the Time-Bounded Arbiter and a Runt-Free Inertial Delay," Bell Laboratories, Holmdel, N.J., 1978.

[TAUB 77]   Taub, H., and D. Schilling, *Digital Integrated Electronics*, McGraw-Hill Book Company, New York, 1977.

[TI 81]   Texas Instruments, *1981 Supplement to the TTL Data Book*, 2nd ed., Texas Instruments, Inc., Dallas, 1981.

[UNGER 57]   Unger, W. H., "A Study of Asynchronous Logical Feedback Networks," Research Lab. Electronics, *MIT, Tech. Rep. 320*, Apr. 26, 1957.

[UNGER 69]   Unger, S. H., *Asynchronous Sequential Switching Circuits*, Wiley-Interscience, New York, 1969.

[VEENDRICK 80]   Veendrick, H. J. M., "The Behavior of Flip-Flops Used as Synchronizers and Prediction of Their Failure Rate," *IEEE J. Solid-State Circuits*, SC-15, No. 2, pp. 169–176, 1980.

[WAGNER 83]   Wagner, K. D., "Design for Testability in the Amdahl 580," *Dig. COMPCON Spring '83*, San Francisco, pp. 384–388, Feb. 28–Mar. 3, 1983.

[WAKERLY 76]   Wakerly, J. F., *Logic Design Projects Using Standard Integrated Circuits*, John Wiley & Sons, Inc., New York, 1976.

7.P PROBLEMS

7.1   Write the IEEE standard symbol for a latch having the logic design shown in Fig. P7.1.

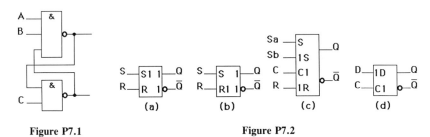

Figure P7.1   **Figure P7.2**

7.2   Derive the characteristic functions for the latches shown in Fig. P7.2.

7.3   Analyze Fig. P7.3.   Note the set and reset dependencies.

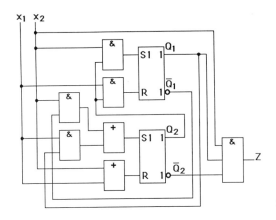

Figure P7.3

7.4   Analyze the circuit shown in Fig. P7.4.

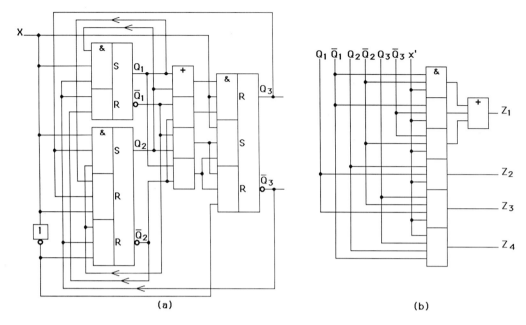

Figure P7.4

7.5 You are to analyze the circuit of Fig. P7.5.

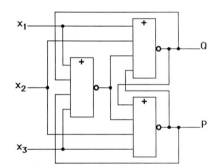

Figure P7.5

(a) Insert fictional amplifiers to break all feedback loops. Use as few amplifiers as possible.

(b) Write excitation functions.

(c) Form transition and output tables assuming that at most one of the input variables is equal to 1 at any time.

(d) Form the flow table.

(e) Convert the circuit to one constructed of NAND gates with the same behavior. Use as few additional gates as possible.

7.6 In the circuit of Fig. 7.5-5 the feedback loops are to be broken (fictional amplifiers inserted) in a place other than that shown in the figure. Choose another location to break the loops, and analyze the circuit, forming the excitation table, transition table, output table, and state table. Explain any discrepancies between this analysis and the analysis given in Sec. 7.3.

7.7 You are to analyze the circuit of Fig. P7.7.
   (a) Insert fictional amplifiers to break feedback loops.
   (b) Write excitation functions.
   (c) Form the transition and output tables.

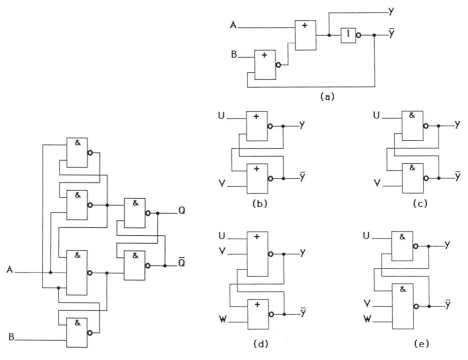

Figure P7.7   Figure P7.8

7.8 **(a)** For each of the circuits in Fig. P7.8, write the standard latch symbol showing set and reset dependencies. (Do not use any gate symbols.)
   (b) When the circuit of Fig. P7.8a is stable, $\bar{y} = y'$. In general, for stable latch conditions, $\bar{y}$ can be a function of y, S, and R. You are to write a functional expression for $\bar{y}$ for each of the circuits in Fig. P7.8b–e.
   (c) Write the characteristic function for each of the latches in Fig. P7.8.
   (d) Redraw the circuit diagram for the 54/7474 D flip-flop (Fig. P7.7), replacing each of the pairs of cross-coupled NAND gates with a single latch symbol [use the result of part (a)].
   (e) Derive the next-state functions (Y_1, Y_2, Y_3) from the diagram of part (d) [use the results of parts (c) and (d)].

7.9 An oscillator generating a continuous train of pulses is to be gated ON and OFF. An ordinary gate cannot be used, because if the gate ON or OFF signal occurs during the pulse, a shortened pulse is not to be allowed. A circuit to perform this function

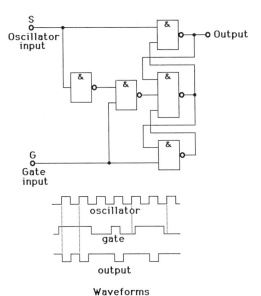

oscillator

gate

Waveforms

Figure P7.9

is shown in Fig. P7.9. Analyze this circuit obtaining state and output tables and a state diagram.

7.10 This problem involves circuits to convert from one flip-flop type to another flip-flop type.

(a) Draw circuits using only combinational circuit elements and S-R flip-flops to realize a J-K flip-flop, a D flip-flop, and a T flip-flop.

(b) Draw circuits using only combinational circuit elements and D flip-flops to realize an S-R flip-flop, a J-K flip-flop, and a T flip-flop.

(c) Draw circuits using only combinational circuit elements and T flip-flops to realize an S-R flip-flop, a D flip-flop, and a J-K flip-flop.

(d) Draw circuits using only combinational circuit elements and J-K flip-flops to realize an S-R flip-flop, a D flip-flop, and a T flip-flop.

7.11 Inspect the flow tables of Table P7.11 for essential hazards. If any exist, indicate them by specifying the single and triple transitions fulfilling the hazard condition.

TABLE P7.11

	x_2x_1					x_2x_1		
00	01	11	10		00	01	11	10
ⓐ	b	—	ⓐ		ⓐ	—	b	ⓐ
ⓑ	ⓑ	c	a		—	c	ⓑ	d
—	—	ⓒ	d		d	ⓒ	b	—
b	—	—	ⓓ		ⓓ	—	f	ⓓ
					—	ⓔ	f	ⓔ
					—	c	ⓕ	e

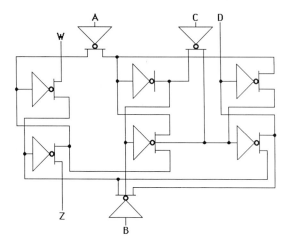

Figure P7.12

7.12 Analyze the circuit of Fig. P7.12. The technology is I²L Leads A, B, C, and D are inputs. Leads W and Z are outputs.
(a) Excitation table.
(b) Transition table.
(c) Flow table.
(d) State diagram.
(e) Word statement.

7.13 *Flip-flop timing parameters:* The circuit for a CMOS D flip-flop is shown in Fig. P7.13a. The setup time can be calculated as follows: When C changes from 0 to 1, transmission gate $TG1$ becomes active and its input signal W is passed into the feedback loop. Since W is determined by the signal at D, this W signal must be correct before the C change arrives at $TG1$. The delay for a change of D to propagate to W is the sum of the propagation delays of the gate $TG2$ plus that of the inverters $I3$ and $I4$. The delay for a change of C to propagate to the control input of $TG1$ is the sum of the propagation delays of $I1$ and $I2$. Since the D change must arrive before the C change, the setup time is

$$T_{su} = T_{pd}(TG2 + I3 + I4) - T_{pd}(I1 + I2)$$

The hold-time requirement is that the signal at D must not change until $TG2$ becomes inactive. Since the change in C passes through $I1$ and $I2$, the hold time is thus

$$T_{hold} = T_{pd}(I1 + I2)$$

Control pulse width: When C is 0 the D signal propagates through $TG2$, $I3$ and $I4$ to the $TG1$ input. Thus, C must remain in the 0 state at least long enough to allow this propagation:

$$\text{minimum 0-state } C \text{ pulse width} = T_{pd}(TG2 + I3 + I4)$$

When the control pulse is 1, data are gated from the master latch into the slave latch via $TG3$ and propagate through $I5$ and $I6$ to the input of $TG4$. The pulse C must be 1 long enough to permit this propagation so that

$$\text{minimum 1-state } C \text{ pulse width} = T_{pd}(TG3 + I5 + I6)$$

(a) Which, if any, of these parameter values depend on the load driven by the flip-flop?

(b) Write expressions for the setup, hold, and pulse-width parameters for Fig. P7.13b in terms of the delays of the individual gates.

(c) Repeat part (b) for the 5474 flip-flop (Fig. P7.13c).

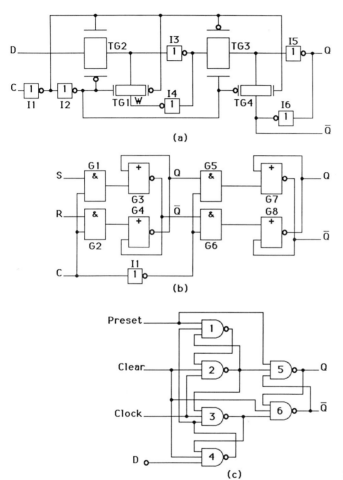

(a)

(b)

(c)

Figure P7.13

8

ANALYSIS OF PULSE-MODE SEQUENTIAL CIRCUITS

8.1 INTRODUCTION

Chapter 7 presented fundamental-mode analysis, a technique for determining the effect of any stable input transition on all feedback loops of the circuit. Sequential circuits must be studied at this very detailed level in order to understand their basic operation and the effects of delays on them.

Armed with this understanding it is then possible to analyze most sequential circuits in less detail (thus less work). Design can also usually be done in less detail, but there are some sequential functions for which fundamental-mode design produces the best circuit (the $1/3f$ circuit of Sec. 8.4, for example).

The design of fundamental-mode circuits is not easy. In particular, the necessity of avoiding critical races makes the process of assigning internal variables to internal states rather complex. Also, the initial determination of the flow table and the process of minimizing the number of internal states require care. Fortunately, most sequential circuits correspond to a special class of circuits called **pulse-mode circuits**, which can be analyzed and designed more easily than the general fundamental-mode circuits. Shift registers (Secs. 7.7 and 11.4) and counters (Sec. 11.5) are examples of pulse-mode circuits.

A *pulse-mode circuit* has one or more inputs that are treated as pulses. The pulse inputs can be characterized by the property that the other circuit inputs are not expected to change while a pulse input is in its active state. Also, at most one pulse is in its active state at any given time; the pulses are nonoverlapping. The concept of a pulse is discussed in detail in the following subsection. The remaining sections of this chapter discuss various implementations of pulse-mode sequential circuits. Design techniques for both pulse-mode and fundamental-mode sequential circuits are presented in Chap. 9.

Any pulse-mode circuit can be implemented using flip-flops as the internal state elements. (This is shown in Chap. 9.) When a flip-flop is used as an internal state element, only the two states of the Q output are important. A fundamental-mode flip-flop has at least four internal states, but only two states are available at the flip-flop outputs. A flip-flop implementation of a pulse-mode circuit can be analyzed by replacing each flip-flop by its equivalent latch circuit, and then using the fundamental-mode analysis techniques of Chap. 7. By using pulse-mode analysis techniques the same circuit can be analyzed with two states per flip-flop rather than the four states per flip-flop of the fundamental-mode analysis. One of the benefits of pulse-mode operation is that fewer internal states must be treated. However, don't forget that some sequential functions cannot be implemented with a pulse-mode circuit.

In pulse-mode analysis the internal state changes *only* in response to the arrival of a pulse, and the state *changes only once* for each pulse occurrence. Fundamental-mode analysis will typically require two internal state changes for each occurrence of an input pulse. A fundamental-mode circuit can be characterized as potentially responding with an internal state change to every level change of an input. A pulse-mode circuit changes state only once for both level changes of a pulse input.

Pulse-mode circuits can be analyzed and designed more simply than fundamental-mode circuits. This design simplicity is obtained by (1) using more complex internal state elements than the simple feedback loops or latches of fundamental-mode circuits, and (2) restricting the sequential functions that can be implemented.

It was pointed out in Sec. 7.7 that three different shift register structures are possible. These three structures, shown in Fig. 8.1-1, represent the three general

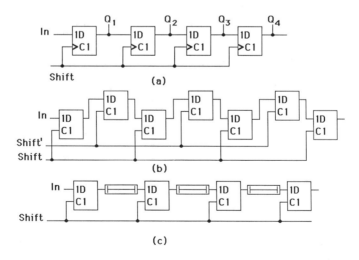

Figure 8.1-1 Shift registers illustrating the pulse-mode structures: (a) flip-flop structure; (b) two-phase latch structure; (c) one-phase latch structure.

implementations of pulse-mode circuits. Just as the shift register can be realized with flip-flops, pairs of latches, or latches and delays, so can any arbitrary pulse-mode circuit.

By far the most common pulse-mode circuits have only one pulse input, just as the shift registers have only one shift input signal. Such circuits are called **finite-state machines**. Analysis of flip-flop finite-state machines is described in Sec. 8.2-1. This analysis is extended to latch structures in Secs. 8.2-2 and 8.2-3. Circuits with more than one pulse input are treated in Sec. 8.3 and more general types of circuits are presented in Sec. 8.4.

8.1-1 The Concept of a Pulse

The concept of a "pulse" occurs very often in engineering and has great intuitive appeal. Figure 8.1-2a shows a single positive rectangular pulse. It consists of two transitions—one from 0 to 1 and the other from 1 to 0. The 0-to-1 transition is often called the **leading** or **rising edge** and the 1-to-0 transition is called the **trailing** or **falling edge**. The time interval from the rising to the falling edge is called the **pulse width**.

It is sometimes convenient to treat signals that are normally 1 or whose active state is a 0. For such signals the concept of a **negative pulse** is appropriate (see

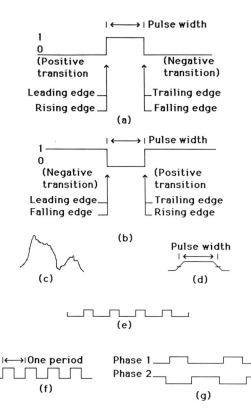

Figure 8.1-2 The pulse concept: (a) a positive rectangular pulse; (b) a negative rectangular pulse; (c) a realistic pulse waveform; (d) a trapezoidal pulse; (e) a pulse train; (f) a square wave; (g) two-phase nonoverlapping clocks.

Fig. 8.1-2b). Note that for a negative pulse the leading edge corresponds to a falling edge and the trailing edge is a rising edge. Pulses will be assumed to be positive unless specifically stated to be negative.

This rectangular pulse is a very simplified representation for the actual waveforms that occur in digital integrated circuits. A more realistic waveform is shown in Fig. 8.1-2c. Some of the characteristics of actual pulses are discussed in Sec. 4.4. The most serious inaccuracy in the rectangular pulse approximation is its failure to show the transition times. A trapezoidal pulse such as shown in Fig. 8.1-2d is a better representation than a rectangular pulse since the transition times are shown explicitly. When only the relative ordering of signals is important, rectangular pulses are sufficient. Trapezoidal pulses are used when the transition times are important. Since in this chapter the order of arrival of the signals is usually the main issue, rectangular pulses can be used.

The length of time that the pulse remains equal to 1 is called the **pulse width**. The minimum permissible pulse width is usually specified; a physical system will fail to respond to any pulse having a width below some minimum time determined by the technology of the system. Unless stated otherwise, it will be assumed that pulses are of sufficient length to meet the system pulse-width requirements. In most situations it will not be necessary to restrict the maximum pulse width. When such a restriction is appropriate (such as when single latches are used to implement a finite-state machine), the term **bounded pulse** will be used. Otherwise, any 0-to-1 transition followed by a 1-to-0 transition of the same signal will be considered a pulse.

Figure 8.1-2e shows a waveform consisting of a sequence or "train" of pulses. The most common usage of the term pulse is in connection with a periodic signal that is equal to 0 for most of each period and takes on the value 1 for only a small fraction of the period. The clock input to a finite-state machine is often such a signal. The periodicity of such a signal is not necessary; in this book a pulse train will not be assumed to be periodic unless this condition is explicitly stated.

A concept closely related to that of a pulse is a **square wave** such as is shown in Fig. 8.1-2f. A square wave is a periodic signal that is 1 for half of each period and 0 for the other half of the period. It is sometimes useful to consider a square wave to be a pulse train.

Another important related concept is that of **two-phase nonoverlapping clock signals**. This is illustrated in Fig. 8.1-2g. It consists of a pair of periodic pulse trains with the property that at least one of the two signals is 0 at any given time. In other words, pulses are never present on both signals. This concept was introduced in Sec. 7.8-1 in connection with controlling essential hazards.

8.1-2 Transition Variables

It is sometimes convenient to have a notation for specifying the transitions of a signal. For this purpose a **transition variable** $\langle X \rangle \uparrow$ associated with a signal X will be defined. Transition variables are illustrated in Fig. 8.1-3 and are defined formally as follows.

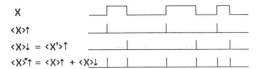

X
$\langle X \rangle \uparrow$
$\langle X \rangle \downarrow = \langle X' \rangle \uparrow$
$\langle X \rangle^* \uparrow = \langle X \rangle \uparrow + \langle X \rangle \downarrow$

Figure 8.1-3 Transition variables.

DEFINITION.   The transition variable $\langle X \rangle \uparrow$ is equal to 1 at time t if and only if the variable X makes a transition from 0 to 1 at time t.   The transition variable $\langle X \rangle \downarrow$ is equal to 1 at time t if and only if the variable X makes a transition from 1 to 0.   The symbol $\langle X' \rangle \uparrow$ can also be used for the X transition from 1 to 0 since X' makes a transition from 0 to 1 when X changes from 1 to 0.   The transition variable $\langle X \rangle^* \uparrow$ is equal to 1 at time t if and only if the variable X makes a transition (from 0 to 1 or from 1 to 0) at time t.

It follows from this definition that $\langle X \rangle^* \uparrow = \langle X \rangle \uparrow + \langle X \rangle \downarrow$.

For primary input signals the associated transition variables can be easily determined directly from the input waveforms.   The transitions of combinational network output signals can be related to the input signals by means of the network function.   For example, the transition variables of the outputs of AND gates, OR gates, and XOR gates are given by the expressions

$$\langle XY \rangle \uparrow = Y\langle X \rangle \uparrow + X\langle Y \rangle \uparrow \tag{8.1-1}$$

$$\langle X + Y \rangle \uparrow = Y'\langle X \rangle \uparrow + X'\langle Y \rangle \uparrow \tag{8.1-2}$$

$$\langle X \oplus Y \rangle \uparrow = Y\langle X \rangle \downarrow + X\langle Y \rangle \downarrow + Y'\langle X \rangle \uparrow + X'\langle Y \rangle \uparrow \tag{8.1-3}$$

The output of an AND gate will make a positive transition when input Y makes a positive transition while input X equals 1 or when input X makes a positive transition while input Y equals 1.   The general expression for the transition of an output in terms of the inputs is given by

$$\langle f(x_1, x_2, \ldots , x_n) \rangle \uparrow = \sum_{i=1}^{n} \{ f_{x_i} f'_{x_i'} \langle x_i \rangle \uparrow + f'_{x_i} f_{x_i'} \langle x_i \rangle \downarrow \} \tag{8.1-4}$$

The symbols f_{x_i} and $f_{x_i'}$ refer to the residues of f.   Residues are defined and discussed in Sec. 5.3.   The use of this expression is illustrated in the following examples.

Example 8.1-1

$f = x + y'z$: $f_x = 1$, $f_{x'} = y'z$, $f_y = x$, $f_{y'} = x + z$, $f_z = x + y'$, $f_{z'} = x$

$\langle f \rangle \uparrow = (y + z')\langle x \rangle \uparrow + x(x'z')\langle y \rangle \uparrow + x'(x + z)\langle y \rangle \downarrow + (x + y')x'\langle z \rangle \uparrow + (x'y)x\langle z \rangle \downarrow$

$\langle f \rangle \uparrow = (y + z')\langle x \rangle \uparrow + x'z\langle y \rangle \downarrow + x'y'\langle z \rangle \uparrow$

	xy			
z	0 0	0 1	1 1	1 0
0	0	0	1	1
1	1 ←	0	1	1

f

The last term of the expression for $\langle f \rangle \uparrow$ indicates that when $x = y = 0$ and z makes a 0-to-1 transition, f will have a 0-to-1 transition. That this is correct is shown by the first column of the map. The second term shows that when $x = 0$, $z = 1$ and y changes from 1 to 0, the function f will change from 0 to 1. This transition is marked on the map with an arrow. It is also possible to determine $\langle f \rangle \uparrow$ by using equations 8.1-1,2,3 as illustrated in part (b) of the following example.

Example 8.1-2

$$f = wx + yz$$

(a) Using equation (8.1-4),

$$f_w = x + yz \qquad f_{w'} = yz \qquad f_y = wx + z \qquad f_{y'} = wx$$

$$f_x = w + yz \qquad f_{x'} = yz \qquad f_z = wx + y \qquad f_{z'} = wx$$

$$\langle f \rangle \uparrow = (x + yz)(y' + z')\langle w \rangle \uparrow + x'(y' + z')yz\langle w \rangle \downarrow$$
$$+ (w + yz)(y' + z')\langle x \rangle \uparrow + w'(y' + z')yz\langle x \rangle \downarrow$$
$$+ (wx + z)(w' + x')\langle y \rangle \uparrow + z'(w' + x')wx\langle y \rangle \downarrow$$
$$+ (wx + y)(w' + x')\langle z \rangle \uparrow + y'(w' + x')wx\langle z \rangle \downarrow$$
$$= x(y' + z')\langle w \rangle \uparrow + w(y' + z')\langle x \rangle \uparrow + z(w' + x')\langle y \rangle \uparrow + y(w' + x')\langle z \rangle \uparrow$$
$$\langle f \rangle \uparrow = (y' + z')(x\langle w \rangle \uparrow + w\langle x \rangle \uparrow) + (w' + x')(z\langle y \rangle \uparrow + y\langle z \rangle \uparrow)$$

(b) Using equations (8.1-2) and (8.1-1)

$$f = wx + yz$$

$$\langle f \rangle \uparrow = \langle wx + yz \rangle \uparrow = (wx)'\langle yz \rangle \uparrow + (yz)'\langle wx \rangle \uparrow$$
$$= (w' + x')(y\langle z \rangle \uparrow + z\langle y \rangle \uparrow) + (y' + z')(w\langle x \rangle \uparrow + x\langle w \rangle \uparrow)$$

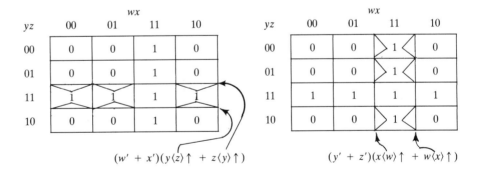

$$(w' + x')(y\langle z \rangle \uparrow + z\langle y \rangle \uparrow) \qquad\qquad (y' + z')(x\langle w \rangle \uparrow + w\langle x \rangle \uparrow)$$

8.2 FINITE-STATE MACHINES

The most common sequential circuits belong to a special class of pulse-mode sequential circuits called **finite-state machines**. They are easier to design and analyze than general fundamental-mode circuits, but cannot realize all sequential functions.

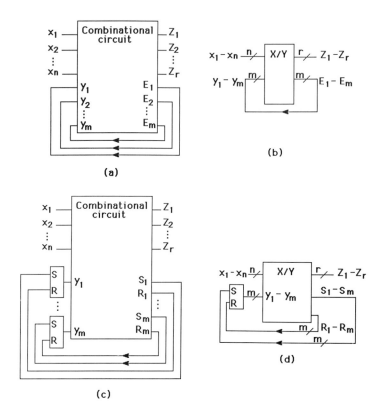

Figure 8.2-1 Fundamental-mode sequential-circuit structures: (a) feedback loops used for internal variables; (b) concise form of part (a); (c) latches used for internal variables; (d) concise form of part (c).

Fundamental-mode circuit structures are shown in Fig. 8.2-1. Part (a) shows the structure when feedback loops are used to store the internal variables and part (b) is a more concise representation of the same structure with i signal lines represented by one line labeled $i/$. The box with X/Y represents an arbitrary combinational circuit. Parts (c) and (d) show the structure with latches used for the internal variables.

Any finite-state machine can be implemented by the general circuit structure shown in Fig. 8.2-2. This structure contains (loop-free) combinational circuits and edge-triggered D flip-flops. A specific circuit using this structure is shown in Fig. 8.2-4. Other implementations are possible: the D flip-flops can be replaced by other types of flip-flops, such as J-K, S-R, or T, and can be pulse-triggered or data lockout rather than edge triggered. The combinational circuits can be implemented with a PLA. In fact PLAs that include D flip-flops are available as standard catalog parts called "programmable logic sequencers" or "registered PLAs." With such a part an entire finite-state machine can be realized with one integrated circuit.

Finite-state machines with flip-flops as the internal state elements will be called **flip-flop machines**. They are discussed in Sec. 8.2-1. Latches can be used

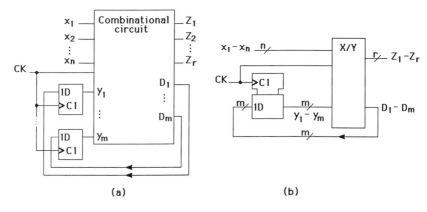

Figure 8.2-2 Flip-flop finite-state machine structure: (a) D flip-flop used for internal variables; (b) concise form of part (a).

instead of flip-flops as internal state elements. Such implementations will be called **latch machines**. The two latch machine structures are shown in Fig. 8.2-3. They are discussed in Secs. 8.2-2 and 8.2-3.

All finite-state machines satisfy the following three properties—single edge, external trigger, and single clock—in addition to the five general properties given in Sec. 7.9.

SINGLE-EDGE PROPERTY. All internal state changes occur in response to an input variable changing from 0 to 1. A change of an input from 1 to 0 never causes an internal state change.

Since the naming of input variables is somewhat arbitrary it is clear that it is possible to have an input variable that causes state changes when the variable makes a 1-to-0 transition, but for such a variable no internal state changes can be caused by a 0-to-1 transition.

This property is guaranteed in the Fig. 8.2-2 flip-flop structure by the use of flip-flops and the fact that no input is connected in uncomplemented form to one flip-flop control input and in complemented form to another flip-flop control input.

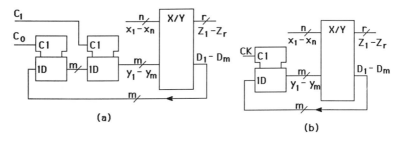

Figure 8.2-3 Latch finite-state machine structures: (a) two-phase latch machine structure; (b) one-phase latch machine structure.

Because state changes in a finite-state machine occur only in response to a 0-to-1 transition of the clock signal and a pulse consists of one 0-to-1 transition followed by a 1-to-0 transition, it is sometimes useful to consider the state changes as responses to the occurrence of clock pulses. The single-edge property can be restated using this terminology as: All internal state changes occur in response to the arrival of a pulse at a circuit input.

EXTERNAL-TRIGGER PROPERTY. An internal-state transition never causes a subsequent internal-state transition.

For a flip-flop implementation such as in Fig. 8.2-2, this property means that no flip-flop output is connected to the control input of a flip-flop. Circuits with such connections are sometimes used and will be discussed in Sec. 8.4; however, they are not finite-state machines.

The external-trigger property follows from the single-edge property. It would have been possible to rely on the single-edge property and not list the external-trigger condition as a separate item. In the interest of clarity it was decided to accept some overlap between the properties rather than to attempt to minimize their number.

In circuits with the external-trigger property, internal variable races are not a problem. Several internal variables (bistable elements) can be changed simultaneously without introducing the possibility of an incorrect state being entered. The first internal variable change cannot itself cause another internal variable change. The final internal state is independent of the order in which the internal variables change; thus, internal variable races don't cause problems.

It is because of the external-trigger property that critical races are not a problem in choosing internal variable assignments for finite-state machines (and pulse-mode circuits in general). This is one of the reasons that pulse-mode circuits are easier to design than fundamental-mode circuits.

SINGLE-CLOCK PROPERTY. There is one distinguished input, usually called the **clock input**. Output changes occur only in synchronism with this clock input.

Although the word "clock" suggests regular, periodic operation, this is not essential. However, the spacing is usually regular. The output cannot change in response to a change in one of the nonclock inputs to the circuit. The values of the nonclock inputs affect whether a clock transition causes an output change, but the nonclock inputs do not affect the output directly.

The single-clock property is a restriction on the class of sequential functions that can be realized with finite-state machines. The single-edge and external-trigger properties are restrictions on the internal structure of finite-state machines. However, any single-clock sequential function can be realized with a finite-state machine; the two trigger properties do not induce a further restriction on the class of sequential functions realizable with finite-state machines. The trigger properties are used because of the simplifications in design and analysis that they permit. Of course, any single-clock sequential function can also be realized with a fundamental-mode circuit. Circuits that satisfy the two trigger properties but not the single-clock property are discussed in Sec. 8.3.

8.2-1 Flip-Flop Machines

Figure 8.2-4 shows an example of a finite-state machine that implements an "up-down Gray code counter." Three versions of the logic diagram are shown in Fig. 8.2-4a,b,c. The first shows each flip-flop separately with the common CK control input connection shown explicitly. The second version uses a common control block to show the CK control input. The third version uses the **N (negate)(EXCLUSIVE-OR) dependency** notation instead of the detailed connection of the F input to each flip-flop. The N dependency is defined so that when the Nm input $= 0$ the dependent input, m, is unaffected and when $Nm = 1$ the dependent input is complemented. Comparison of the excitation functions of Fig. 8.2-4d with the logic diagrams of parts (b) and (c) of the figure shows that they both specify the same excitation functions. The diagram of part (c) is more

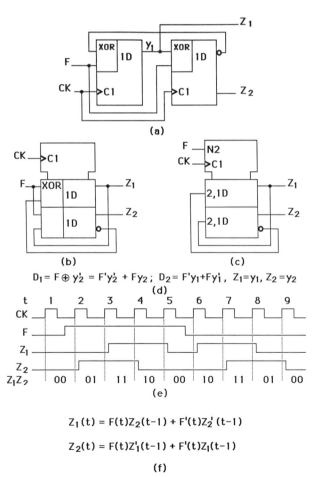

(a)

(b)   (c)

$$D_1 = F \oplus y_2' = F'y_2' + Fy_2 ; \quad D_2 = F'y_1 + Fy_1' , \quad Z_1 = y_1, \ Z_2 = y_2$$

(d)

(e)

$$Z_1(t) = F(t)Z_2(t-1) + F'(t)Z_2'(t-1)$$

$$Z_2(t) = F(t)Z_1'(t-1) + F'(t)Z_1(t-1)$$

(f)

Figure 8.2-4 Finite-state machine circuit for a Gray code up-down counter: (a) logic diagram; (b) standard symbol diagram; (c) standard symbol diagram using N dependency; (d) excitation functions; (e) input-output waveforms; (f) t-expressions.

TABLE 8.2-1 Operation of Gray code up-down counter of Fig. 8.2-4a

F	
1	Counts forward through number of input clock pulses in Gray code modulo 4
0	Counts backward through number of input clock pulses in Gray code modulo 4

compact than the other logic diagrams since the signals that are connected to all of the flip-flops are not shown explicitly. On the other hand, it may be more difficult to understand the more concise diagram without a good familiarity with the standard symbols. To ease the transition to the standard symbols, many logic diagrams will be shown in both the common control block and the detached flip-flop forms. This circuit has two inputs: F and CK (the clock). Its operation is summarized in Table 8.2-1. When $F = 1$, the circuit displays on Z_1, Z_2 the Gray code number representing the count modulo 4 of the number of positive clock transitions (or pulses) received. When $F = 0$, the circuit counts backward (modulo 4) through the Gray code numbers representing the number of pulses (positive clock transitions) received. This circuit operation is similar to that of the 54/74LS169A up-down counter. The differences are that the 54/74LS169A counts modulo 16 in binary rather than modulo 4 in Gray.

It would be possible to analyze this circuit using the fundamental-mode techniques of Chap. 7. This could be done by replacing each of the flip-flops by an equivalent circuit such as that shown in Fig. 7.7-3a. The resulting circuit would consist of gates and latches; it could be analyzed as a fundamental-mode circuit. The use of a fundamental-mode circuit representation for the flip-flops is valid even if the actual circuit uses ac coupled flip-flops: Both types of flip-flop have the same input-output characteristics, so they have the same effect on the rest of the circuit. Using fundamental-mode techniques to analyze sequential machines requires a lot of unnecessary work. Formal techniques for analyzing finite-state machines directly will be developed next.

The internal state of a finite-state machine built with E-T flip-flops changes only when a positive transition occurs at the clock input. For an E-T D flip-flop, if a positive clock transition occurs at time t, the value of the output Q at time $t + t_{pd}$ is equal to the value of the D input at time t. The output remains at this value until the arrival of the next positive transition of the clock. This operation is illustrated in Fig. 8.2-5.

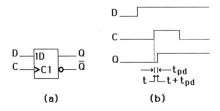

Figure 8.2-5 Operation of a E-T D flip-flop: (a) symbol; (b) waveforms.

The present total state of a finite-state machine is given by the states of the flip-flops, the values of the input variables, and the value of CK. The next state depends on the states of the flip-flops, the values of the input variables, and on whether CK is changing. Thus, unlike fundamental-mode operation, for finite-state machines the next state is not a simple switching function of the present total state. The next state depends on the **static present total state** of the nonclock variables, and on the **dynamic state** of the clock input. The internal state (values of the flip-flops) does not change unless the clock has a positive transition. When the clock does make a positive transition, the internal state becomes equal to the next state determined from the static present state by the next-state functions. Thus, the next state is determined by the static present total state and the presence or absence of a positive clock transition. Since the internal state changes only for positive clock transitions, it is sufficient to show the next-state values that occur after such a transition. The transition table for a finite-state machine lists the values of the next internal state after a positive clock transition as a function of the static present total state.

The operation of the circuit of Fig. 8.2-4 is described by the transition table of Table 8.2-2b. In this table the values of y_1, y_2, and F represent values at some time t. The $Y_1^+ Y_2^+$ entries in the table give the values of y_1 and y_2 at time $t + t_{pd}$ under the assumption that a positive clock transition occurs at time t. The table entries are equal to $D_1(y_1, y_2, F) = F' \oplus y_2$ and $D_2(y_1, y_2, F) = F \oplus y_1$.

The symbol Y^+ is used for the next-state function of finite machines (and pulse-mode circuits) instead of the Y symbol used in analyzing fundamental-mode circuits. This change of notation is introduced to emphasize the dependence of the Y^+ function on a transition of the clock pulse input.

The Z_1 and Z_2 values are derived from the flip-flop outputs. They are thus functions of the internal state of the circuit ($Z_1 = y_1$, $Z_2 = y_2$) and are shown in separate columns.

TABLE 8.2-2   Formal analysis of Gray code up-down counter of Fig. 8.2-4a: (a) Excitation functions; (b) Transition table; (c) State table

(a)

$$D_1 = F' \oplus y_2; \quad D_2 = F \oplus y_1; \quad Z_1 = y_1; \quad Z_2 = y_2$$

(b)

$y_1 y_2$	$\langle CK \rangle \uparrow$ F 0	1	$Z_1 Z_2$
0 0	10	01	0 0
0 1	00	11	0 1
1 1	01	10	1 1
1 0	11	00	1 0
	$Y_1^+ Y_2^+$		

(c)

$(y_1 y_2)$	s	$\langle CK \rangle \uparrow$ F 0	1	$Z_1 Z_2$
(0 0)	A	D	B	0 0
(0 1)	B	A	C	0 1
(1 1)	C	B	D	1 1
(1 0)	D	C	A	1 0
		S		

DEFINITION. The symbols Y_i^+ represent the values of the flip-flop outputs at time $t + t_{pd}$ under the assumption that, at time t, for E-T flip-flops a positive clock transition occurs.

State Tables. The state table of Table 8.2-2c is derived from the transition table of Table 8.2-2b in the same manner as for fundamental-mode tables. Each combination of values for $y_1 y_2$ is replaced by a decimal number or letter throughout the table.

The concept of an "operating point" was introduced in Sec. 7.4-2 in connection with the use of transition and state tables for analysis of fundamental-mode operation. This concept is not as relevant for finite-state machine analysis. In analyzing finite-state machines it is possible to suppress some of the details of the internal operation of the circuit without losing the ability to predict input-output behavior. Because of this, the transition table does not include all total states of the circuit. For example, there are not separate entries for the two clock values. The table shows only the next states immediately after a positive clock transition. The transition and state tables for finite-state machines are used by simply reading off the next-state values from the tables. There is no necessity to trace successive state changes (as in fundamental-mode) since such changes are not allowed in finite-state machines.

State Diagram. A **state diagram** is often used to describe the action of a finite-state machine. The state diagram for the circuit of Fig. 8.2-4 is shown in Fig. 8.2-6. Each state of the circuit is represented by a circle (node) of the diagram and the output values corresponding to the state are entered within the circle. Lines connecting the circles are used to indicate the state transitions that occur when a clock pulse arrives at the circuit. The input values corresponding to the transitions are used as labels on the edges connecting nodes. The state diagram contains exactly the same information as the state table. The state table is usually

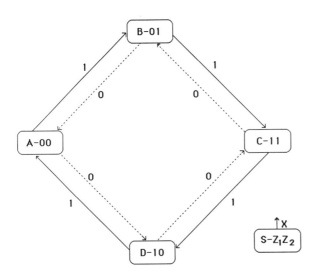

Figure 8.2-6 State diagram for the circuit of Figure 8.2-4.

easier to use for carrying out the circuit design. The state diagram may be more convenient for visualizing the circuit operation. The state diagram is sometimes useful in analyzing a circuit or in determining the initial circuit specification.

Flip-flop Characteristic Equations. Figure 8.2-7 shows a circuit that has J-K flip-flops as the internal state elements. The procedure for obtaining the transition

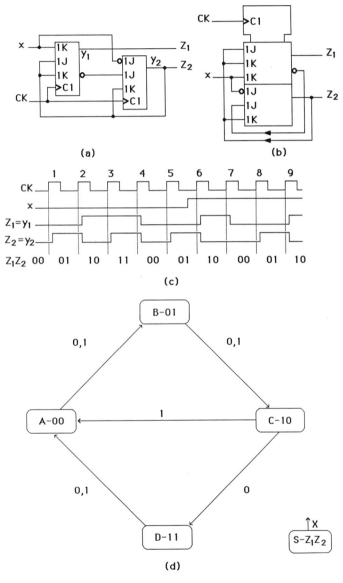

(a)

(b)

(c)

(d)

Figure 8.2-7 Example of a circuit using J-K flip-flops. The circuit counts up in binary, modulo 4 if $x = 0$ and modulo 3 if $x = 1$: (a) logic design; (b) logic design with common internal clock; (c) waveforms; (d) state diagram.

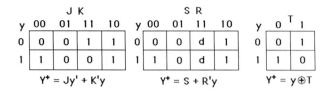

$$Y^+ = Jy' + K'y \qquad Y^+ = S + R'y \qquad Y^+ = y \oplus T$$

Figure 8.2-8 Characteristic equations for flip-flops.

table for a circuit that uses other than D flip-flops is analogous to the technique used for analyzing fundamental-mode circuits with S-R latches. The transition table is derived from the excitation functions by means of the **characteristic equation** for the particular types of flip-flops used in the circuit. The derivation of the J-K flip-flop characteristic equation is shown in Fig. 8.2-8 along with the derivations for the S-R and T flip-flops.

J-K Flip-flops. The characteristic equation for a J-K flip-flop is: $Y^+ = Jy' + K'y$. This equation gives the value of the flip-flop state just after a positive clock transition in terms of the values of the flip-flop state and the J and K inputs just before the transition. Table 8.2-3 shows the analysis of the Fig. 8.2-7 circuit. By inspection of the transition table it is seen that the circuit counts the number of clock pulses modulo 4 when $x = 0$ and counts modulo 3 when $x = 1$.

Pulse Outputs. Figure 8.2-9a shows the Fig. 8.2-7 circuit augmented with three additional outputs: Z_3, z_4, and z_5. Lowercase z's are used for z_4 and z_5 since they are pulse rather than level outputs. Part (c) of this figure shows some typical

TABLE 8.2-3 Analysis of the circuit of Fig. 8.2-7: (a) Excitation functions; (b) Next-state functions; (c) Transition table; (c) State table

(a)

$$J_1 = y_2; \quad K_1 = y_2 + x, \quad J_2 = y_1' + x', \quad K_2 = y_2, \quad Z_1 = y_1 \quad Z_2 = y_2$$

(b)

$$Y_1^+ = J_1 y_1' + K_1' y_1 = y_1' y_2 + x' y_1 y_2'$$

$$Y_2^+ = J_2 y_2' + K_2' y_2 = y_2'(x' + y_1')$$

(c)

$\langle CK \rangle \uparrow$

$y_1 y_2$	x=0	x=1	$Z_1 Z_2$
0 0	0 1	0 1	0 0
0 1	1 0	1 0	0 1
1 1	0 0	0 0	1 1
1 0	1 1	0 0	1 0

Y_1^+, Y_2^+

(d)

$\langle CK \rangle \uparrow$

$y_1 y_2$	s	x=0	x=1	$Z_1 Z_2$
(0 0)	A	B	B	0 0
(0 1)	B	C	C	0 1
(1 0)	C	D	A	1 0
(1 1)	D	A	A	1 1

S

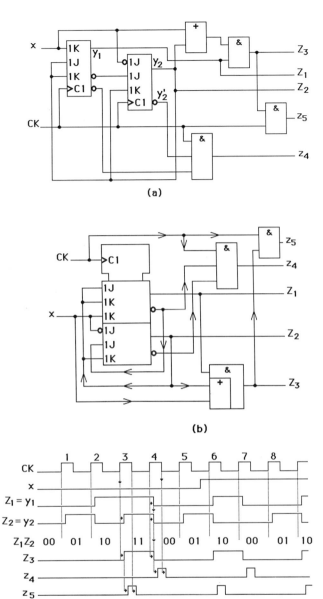

Figure 8.2-9 Modulo-3 or 4 counter of Fig. 8.2-7 with added outputs: (a) logic diagram; (b) standard diagram; (c) waveforms.

waveforms for the circuit inputs and outputs. The output Z_3, $y_1(x + y_2)$, depends on the input x as well as the flip-flop outputs in contrast with the Z_1 and Z_2 outputs, which depend only on the flip-flop outputs. The Z_3 output is equal to 1 while the circuit holds a maximum count for its present direction of counting ($y_1 y_2 = 1\ 1$ for $x = 0$ and $y_1 y_2 = 1\ 0$ for $x = 1$).

The z_4 output, $y_1'y_2'CK$, depends on the clock input as well as the flip-flop outputs. The clock pulse that causes the circuit to enter the $y_1y_2 = 00$ state is gated out on z_4.

The z_5 output, $y_1(x + y_2)CK$, depends on both the input x and the clock input as well as the flip-flop outputs. The clock pulse that causes the circuit to enter its maximum count is gated out on z_5.

The transition and output tables are shown in Table 8.2-4a. The outputs Z_1, Z_2, and Z_3 depend only on the static present total state. These functions are shown in the output table of Table 8.2-4b which is just another representation of the Z_1, Z_2, and Z_3 excitation functions given in Table 8.2-4d. The next-state variables and the z_4 and z_5 outputs depend on the clock pulse in addition. These relations are shown in Table 8.2-4a, the transition table. The interpretation of the transition table is: When a rising transition of the clock input occurs, the flip-flop states change to the new values given in the transition table for the appropriate current values and x input value. The clock pulse is gated to a z_i output if the **new state** values correspond to the z_i function. Thus the clock pulse is gated to z_4 if the

TABLE 8.2-4 Tables for the circuit of Fig. 8.2-9: (a) Transition table; (b) Output table; (c) State output tables; (d) Next-state and output functions

(a)

$\langle CK \rangle \uparrow$

$y_1\,y_2$	x 0	1
0 0	0 1, 0 0	0 1, 0 0
0 1	1 0, 0 0	1 0, 0 1
1 1	0 0, 1 0	0 0, 1 0
1 0	1 1, 0 1	0 0, 1 0

$Y_1^+ Y_2^+ , z_4 z_5$

(b)

$\langle CK \rangle \uparrow$

$y_1\,y_2$	x 0	1
0 0	0 0 0	0 0 0
0 1	0 1 0	0 1 0
1 1	1 1 1	1 1 1
1 0	1 0 0	1 0 1

$Z_1 Z_2 Z_3$

(c)

$\langle CK \rangle \uparrow$

$y_1\,y_2$	s	x 0	1
(0 0)	A	B, 0 0	B, 0 0
(0 1)	B	C, 0 0	C, 0 1
(1 0)	C	D, 0 1	A, 1 0
(1 1)	D	A, 1 0	A, 1 0

$S, z_4 z_5$

s	x 0	1
A	0 0 0	0 0 0
B	0 1 0	0 1 0
C	1 0 0	1 0 1
D	1 1 1	1 1 1

$Z_1 Z_2 Z_3$

(d)

$$Y_1^+ = y_1'y_2 + x'y_1y_2' \qquad Y_2^+ = y_2'(x' + y_1')$$

$$z_4 = y_1'y_2'CK \qquad z_5 = y_1(x + y_2)CK$$

$$Z_1 = y_1, \qquad Z_2 = y_2 \qquad Z_3 = y_1(x + y_2)$$

new state $y_1 y_2 = 0\ 0$ is caused by the clock pulse.[1] In terms of filling in the transition table, the values used for the z_4 and z_5 entries are determined by the Y^+ entries rather than the static total state values. The state table is derived from the transition table as described previously for Table 8.2-2.

Inspection of the waveforms of Fig. 8.2-9c shows that clock pulse 4 is gated onto the z_4 output by an AND gate that has y_1' and y_2' as its other inputs. The same clock pulse that is gated onto z_4 causes y_1 and y_2 to change from 11 to 00. Since there is a delay in propagating these changes to the z_4 AND gate, the pulse that appears on z_4 will have its rising edge delayed. The net effect is that the rising edge of the z_4 pulse will be delayed by the maximum propagation delay of the circuit flip-flops plus the propagation delay of the AND gate, while the falling edge will be delayed only by the propagation delay of the AND gate. The z_4 pulse will be shorter than the clock pulse by the maximum flip-flop propagation delay. This will happen for all of the z_4 pulses. The z_5 pulses will be shortened even more because the gating signal to the z_5 AND gate is propagated through the OR gate and AND gate driving the Z_3 output as well as the y_2 flip-flop.

It is possible to avoid this shortening of the output pulses at the expense of delaying the change of the Z_1, Z_2, and Z_3 values until the falling edge of the clock pulse. This is done by using the falling rather than the rising edge of the clock pulse to control the flip-flops as shown in Fig. 8.2-10. Note that in this circuit the z_4 and z_5 functions are changed to $z_4 = y_1(x + y_2)CK$, $z_5 = (x'y_1y_2' + xy_1'y_2)CK$. They now must depend on the static present state when the clock pulse arrives rather than the next state. The next state is not entered into the flip-flops until the trailing edge of the clock pulse. The transition, output and state tables are the same for Fig. 8.2-10 as for Fig. 8.2-9. A finite-state machine whose outputs depend only on the flip-flop outputs is often called a **Moore machine**. If the outputs are pulses such as z_4 and z_5, the machine is called a **Mealy machine**. The circuit of Fig. 8.2-7 would thus be called a Moore machine. The circuits of Figs. 8.2-9,10 fall into neither category since they have both types of outputs.

T **Flip-flops.** Figure 8.2-11a shows an up-down modulo-4 Gray counter that uses T flip-flops as the bistable elements. The corresponding waveforms are shown in Fig. 8.2-11b and the formal analysis is given in Table 8.2-5. The state and transition tables in Table 8.2-5 are identical to those of Table 8.2-2, showing that the circuits of Figs. 8.2-4 and 8.2-11c have the same functionality.

Non-gated Flip-flops. Non-gated T flip-flops (Fig. 7.7-10) can also be used to realize finite-state machines. A circuit that uses non-gated T flip-flops and has the same functionality as that of Fig. 8.2-11 is shown in Fig. 8.2-12a. A non-gated T flip-flop will change state whenever there is a positive transition at the T input. For the circuit of Fig. 8.2-12a, the expressions for T_1 and T_2 are:

---

[1] This is the condition for E-T flip-flops. For pulse-triggered flip-flops the gating of the clock pulse is conditioned by the **old state** since the state does not change until the falling edge of the clock pulse. Because E-T flip-flops are by far the most common, the discussion will concentrate on the use of E-T flip-flops.

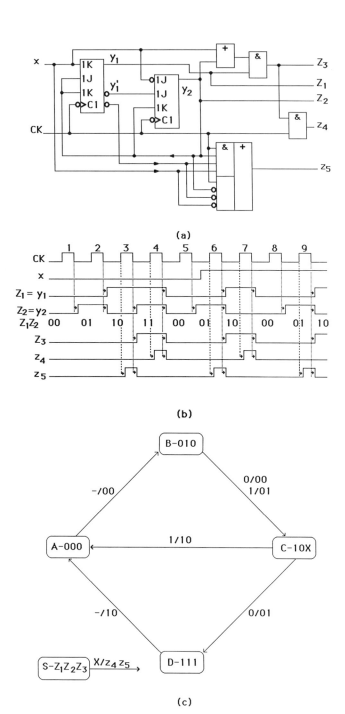

Figure 8.2-10 Circuit of Figure 8.2-9 modified to use inverted clock inputs to the flip-flops: (a) logic diagram; (b) waveforms; (c) state diagram.

Analysis of Pulse-Mode Sequential Circuits   Chap. 8

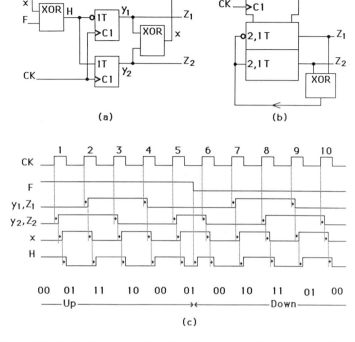

(a)

(b)

(c)

Figure 8.2-11 Finite-state machine for a Gray code up-down counter using T flip-flops as bistable elements; (a) logic diagram; (b) concise logic diagram; (c) waveforms.

TABLE 8.2-5 Formal analysis of Gray code up-down counter of Fig. 8.2-11: (a) Equations; (b) Transition table; (c) State table

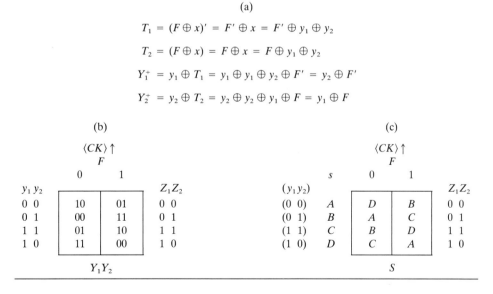

(a)

$$T_1 = (F \oplus x)' = F' \oplus x = F' \oplus y_1 \oplus y_2$$

$$T_2 = (F \oplus x) = F \oplus x = F \oplus y_1 \oplus y_2$$

$$Y_1^+ = y_1 \oplus T_1 = y_1 \oplus y_1 \oplus y_2 \oplus F' = y_2 \oplus F'$$

$$Y_2^+ = y_2 \oplus T_2 = y_2 \oplus y_2 \oplus y_1 \oplus F = y_1 \oplus F$$

(b)

$\langle CK \rangle \uparrow$

	F		
	0	1	$Z_1 Z_2$
$y_1 y_2$			
0 0	10	01	0 0
0 1	00	11	0 1
1 1	01	10	1 1
1 0	11	00	1 0
	$Y_1 Y_2$		

(c)

$\langle CK \rangle \uparrow$

		F		
$(y_1 y_2)$	s	0	1	$Z_1 Z_2$
(0 0)	A	D	B	0 0
(0 1)	B	A	C	0 1
(1 1)	C	B	D	1 1
(1 0)	D	C	A	1 0
		S		

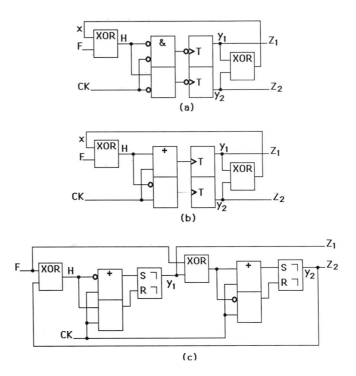

Figure 8.2-12 Finite-state machine Gray code up-down counter: (a) using non-gated T flip-flops; (b) same as part (a) with AND gates replaced by OR gates; (c) using nongated S-R flip-flops.

$T_1 = (H'CK')' = H + CK$ and $T_2 = (HCK')' = H' + CK$. In order to determine the conditions for y_i to change state it is necessary to determine $\langle T_i \rangle \uparrow$, which can be done as follows:

$$\langle T_1 \rangle \uparrow \ = \ \langle H + CK \rangle \uparrow \ = \ H'\langle CK \rangle \uparrow \ + \ CK'\langle H \rangle \uparrow \qquad H = F \oplus y_1 \oplus y_2$$

$$\langle T_2 \rangle \uparrow \ = \ \langle H' + CK \rangle \uparrow \ = \ H\langle CK \rangle \uparrow \ + \ CK'\langle H \rangle \downarrow \qquad H' = F' \oplus y_1 \oplus y_2$$

The first term in the expression for $\langle T_1 \rangle \uparrow$ is $H'\langle CK \rangle \uparrow$, which is equal to $(F' \oplus y_1 \oplus y_2)\langle CK \rangle \uparrow$. This represents the same condition for a change in y_1 as that derived in Table 8.2-5 for the gated T-flip-flop circuit of Fig. 8.2-11. A similar correspondence exists for the first term in the expression for T_2. Thus if the second terms in the expressions for $\langle T_1 \rangle \uparrow$ and $\langle Y_2 \rangle \uparrow$ are always 0, the two circuits will have the same behavior. The second term in the $\langle T_1 \rangle \uparrow$ expression is $CK'\langle H \rangle \uparrow \ = \ CK'\langle F \oplus y_1 \oplus y_2 \rangle \uparrow$. The values of y_1 and y_2 should never change while $CK = 0$ since y changes are caused by a positive transition of CK. This could fail to be true for very short CK pulses or in the presence of a large clock skew, but these possibilities are typical timing issues that are present in all designs. The other possibility for a nonzero contribution from the second term is for F to change while $CK = 0$. This can be avoided by synchronizing the changes in F with the presence of a positive CK value. Thus, by control of the F transitions

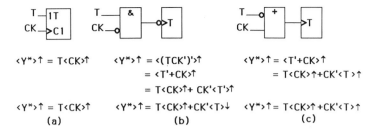

$\langle Y^* \rangle \uparrow = T\langle CK \rangle \uparrow$　　$\langle Y^* \rangle \uparrow = \langle (TCK')' \rangle \uparrow$　　$\langle Y^* \rangle \uparrow = \langle T' + CK \rangle \uparrow$

$= \langle T' + CK \rangle \uparrow$　　$= T\langle CK \rangle \uparrow + CK'\langle T \rangle \uparrow$

$= T\langle CK \rangle \uparrow + CK'\langle T' \rangle \uparrow$

$\langle Y^* \rangle \uparrow = T\langle CK \rangle \uparrow$　　$\langle Y^* \rangle \uparrow = T\langle CK \rangle \uparrow + CK'\langle T \rangle \downarrow$　　$\langle Y^* \rangle \uparrow = T\langle CK \rangle \uparrow + CK'\langle T \rangle \uparrow$

(a)　　　　　　　　　(b)　　　　　　　　　(c)

Figure 8.2-13 *T* flip-flop conversions: (a) gated *T* flip-flop; (b) nongated *T* flip-flop with inverted control input; (c) nongated *T* flip-flop with noninverted control input.

and proper design of the circuit, the non-gated *T* circuit will have the same behavior as the gated *T* circuit.

Another form of a Gray code up-down counter with non-gated *T* flip-flops is shown in Fig. 8.2-12b. This circuit uses OR gates rather than AND gates to realize the *T* input functions. Figure 8.2-13 shows the general equivalences among *T* flip-flop input structures. The non-gated flip-flops have no advantage for finite-state machines in general. They are convenient for some types of counters. For specific technologies and functions they could be the best implementation.

Finite-state machines can also be realized using non-gated pulse-triggered *S-R* flip-flops. A circuit using these elements to realize the Gray up-down counter is shown in Fig. 8.2-12c. The flip-flops in this circuit are set on the trailing edge of a pulse at the *S* input and are reset on the trailing edge of a pulse at the *R* input. The analysis of this circuit is done using the same general approach as for the circuits with non-gated *T* flip-flops. Neither of the non-gated flip-flops are used often for finite-state machines. They are more important for more general pulse-mode circuits having more than one pulse input. This application is discussed in Sec. 8.3.

Asynchronous Inputs. Some FSM functions are best implemented without using the state table formalism. One is the **Reset function** that resets (puts in the 0 state) all of the circuit flip-flops. Figure 8.2-14 shows the general FSM structure of Fig. 8.2-1 with circuitry added to implement the Reset function. The Reset function is used to place the circuit in a fixed initial state when starting up its operation and also to control its state during testing.

One reason for designing the reset function circuitry without using the state table is that since circuit reset is such a common function, standard designs for reset circuitry are available. Another reason is that the reset function can be added to a circuit without modifying the circuitry designed for the specific circuit behavior. The circuit Reset function is usually implemented by means of a separate **asynchronous** Reset input on each of the circuit flip-flops, as shown in Fig. 8.2-14 (see also Fig. 8.2-17).

Another standard FSM function that is often implemented with asynchronous flip-flop inputs is the **Parallel Load**, **PL**, **function**. The PL function causes the states of the circuit flip-flops to become equal to a set of level circuit inputs. In

Sec. 8.2　Finite-State Machines

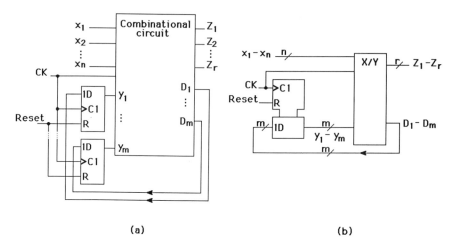

(a)   **(b)**

Figure 8.2-14   General FSM structure with D flip-flops and a circuit reset function: (a) logic diagram; (b) using common control block.

the implementation shown in Fig. 8.2-15a,b the gating of the $W_1, \ldots, W_m$ values into the circuit flip-flops is accomplished in two steps: First, the circuit reset signal is applied to place all the flip-flops in the 0 state; next, the PL signal is pulsed to set those flip-flops that correspond to $W_i = 1$. The parallel load function can be accomplished in one step by means of the structure shown in Fig. 8.2-15c,d. In this structure both the 0- and 1-values are gated into the flip-flops by means of asynchronous flip-flop inputs. This technique is faster than the two-step method but requires more circuit elements.

The use of asynchronous flip-flop inputs to implement the parallel load function can cause testing difficulties. A PL structure that does not use asynchronous flip-flop inputs is shown in Fig. 8.2-16. In this structure the parallel data are loaded into the circuit flip-flops on a *CK* transition if the (level) *PL* signal is 1. When $PL = 0$ the circuit operates normally. The Gray code up-down counter of Fig. 8.2-4 with the additional circuitry to implement the circuit reset and synchronous PL function is shown in Fig. 8.2-17a.

The G (AND dependency) notation is used in Figs. 8.2-16b and 8.2-17. The correspondence between this notation and the earlier notation is shown in Fig. 8.2-16c. The $G1$ notation on the b input of this figure means that any other inputs labeled 1 are 0 unless $b = 1$ and any other inputs labeled $\bar{1}$ are 0 unless $b = 0$.

The other common use of asynchronous flip-flop inputs, besides the circuit reset and parallel load functions, applies specifically to counter circuits. The asynchronous flip-flop inputs are sometimes used in counters to shorten the normal counter cycle so as to obtain a reduced modulus. This technique is considered in Chap. 11 in connection with the general discussion of counter circuits.

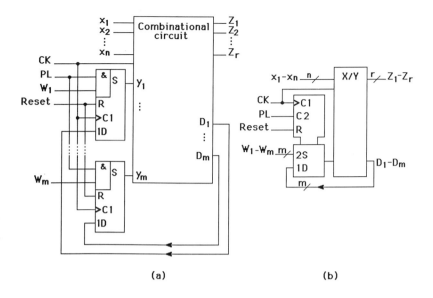

(a)   (b)

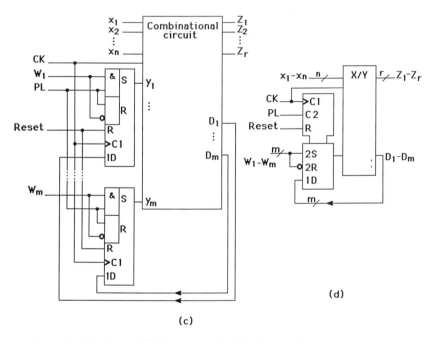

(c)   (d)

Figure 8.2-15 General FSM structure with D flip-flops, a PL function, and a circuit reset function: (a) two-step load logic diagram; (b) common control block version of (a); (c) one-step load logic diagram; (d) common control block version of part (c).

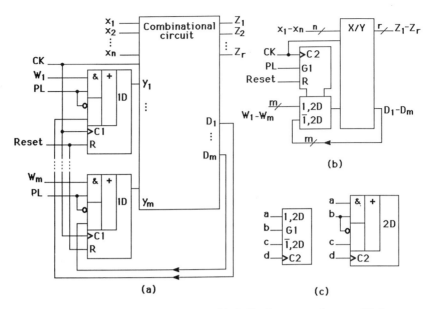

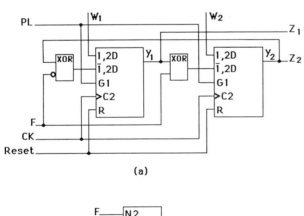

Figure 8.2-16 General FSM structure with D flip-flops, a synchronous PL function, and a circuit reset function: (a) logic diagram; (b) common control block and G dependency; (c) explanation of G (AND) dependency.

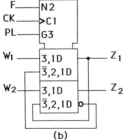

Figure 8.2-17 Gray code up-down FSM counter with a synchronous PL function and a circuit reset function: (a) logic diagram; (b) standard diagram.

8.2-2 Two-Phase Latch Machines

Finite-state machines are often realized using latches rather than flip-flops as the internal state elements. In fact, there are two latch-based structures in common use for finite-state machines. One of these structures uses a two-phase (non-overlapping) clock. It will be described in this subsection. The other structure uses a single-phase clock. It is discussed in Sec. 8.2-3.

Double Latch Design. Figure 8.2-18 shows the general structure of a finite-state machine in which the E-T D flip-flops of Fig. 8.2-1c have been replaced by two latches in a master-slave connection. The master latches (those with inputs from the combinational logic block) are called **L1 latches**, and the slave latches (whose inputs come from the master latches) are called **L2 latches**. The $L2$ latches in Fig. 8.2-18a are shown as S-R latches, and as D latches in part (b). A clock skew driver such as that discussed in connection with Fig. 7.2-16 is used to derive the control signals to the latches. The $C1$ signal plays the same role as the control input in a master-slave flip-flop and the $C0$ signal replaces the C' flip-flop signal. Typically, the $C1$ and $C0$ signals do not overlap (they are never both equal to 1 at the same time). This is to reduce hazards as discussed in Chap. 7. The $C0$ and $C1$ signals are usually periodic with a fixed period.

A machine having the structure of Fig. 8.2-18 will be called a **two-phase latch machine**. This structure is used in various IBM systems and is called a **double latch design** by IBM [Eichelberger 78]. Figure 8.2-19 shows a double latch design for the circuit of Fig. 8.2-4. The formal analysis procedure for a double latch

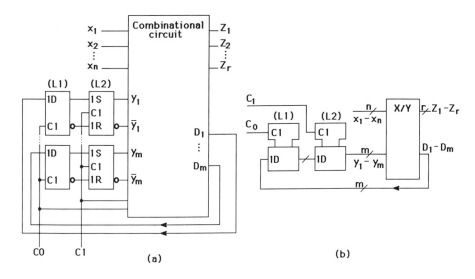

Figure 8.2-18 Double latch design for a two-phase latch finite-state machine: (a) logic diagram; (b) standard diagram.

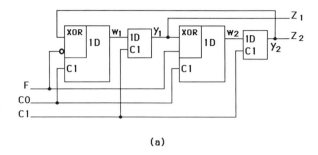

(a)

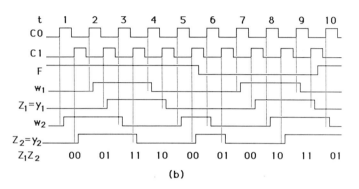

(b)

Figure 8.2-19 Double latch design for the Gray code up-down counter of Fig. 8.2-4. (a) logic diagram; (b) input-output waveforms.

design is the same as for a flip-flop machine. The circuit of Fig. 8.2-19 has the same transition and state tables as the circuit of Fig. 8.2-2 and Table 8.2-2.

Single Latch Design. Another form of two-phase finite-state machine structure, called a **single latch design**, is shown in Fig. 8.2-20a. This structure is a generalization of the double latch design. It is derived from the double latch structure of Fig. 8.2-18 by inserting a combinational network between the $L1$ and $L2$ latches (in addition to the combinational network already between the $L2$ and $L1$ latches). A modulo-8 binary counter using the single latch structure is shown in Fig. 8.2-20c. Use of the single latch structure permits a reduction in the number of $L1$ latches from three to two. Single latch structures are analyzed by calculating the Y^+ functions for the $L1$ latches and then using these functions in the calculation of the Y^+ functions for the $L2$ latches. The transition table is formed from the Y^+ functions of the $L2$ latches. Table 8.2-6 shows the calculation of the next-state functions and the transition table for the Fig. 8.2-20c circuit.

Both the single and the double latch designs are two-phase finite-state machines.

DEFINITION. A **two-phase finite-state machine** is a finite-state machine that has latches as internal state elements and two-phase clock signals. No latch has

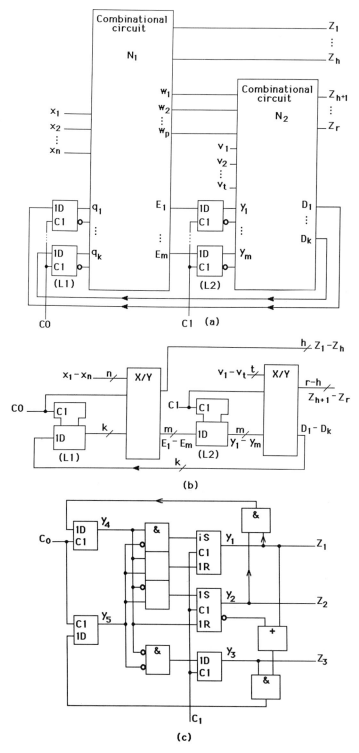

Figure 8.2-20 Single latch design for a two-phase latch finite-state machine: (a) general structure; (b) concise structure; (c) modulo-8 binary counter circuit.

TABLE 8.2-6 Analysis of Fig. 8.2-20c circuit: (a) Calculation of excitation and next-state functions; (b) Transition table

(a)

$$Y_4^+ = y_2 y_3 \qquad\qquad Y_5^+ = y_3(y_1 + y_2')$$

$$S_1 = y_4 y_5' = y_1' y_2 y_3 \qquad R_1 = y_4 y_5 = y_1 y_2 y_3$$

$$Y_1^+ = y_1 \oplus y_2 y_3$$

$$S_2 = y_4' y_5 = y_2' y_3 \qquad R_2 = y_4 = y_2 y_3$$

$$Y_2^+ = y_2 \oplus y_3 \qquad\qquad Y_3^+ = D_3 = y_4' y_5' = y_3'$$

(b)

$y_1 y_2 y_3$	C1			$Z_1 Z_2 Z_3$
0 0 0	0	0	1	0 0 0
0 0 1	0	1	0	0 0 1
0 1 0	0	1	1	0 1 0
0 1 1	1	0	0	0 1 1
1 0 0	1	0	1	1 0 0
1 0 1	1	1	0	1 0 1
1 1 0	1	1	1	1 1 0
1 1 1	0	0	0	1 1 1
	$Y_1^+ Y_2^+ Y_3^+$			

its output connected to the input of any latch controlled by the same phase clock signal.

8.2-3 One-Phase Latch Machines

The two-phase latch machine has two ranks of latches: The $L1$ latches and the $L2$ latches. It is also possible to realize finite-state machines with structures having only one rank of latches as shown in Fig. 8.2-21. Such a structure is called a **one-phase latch machine**. It has fewer elements than the two-phase structure, but requires more careful control of delays and clock pulse width.

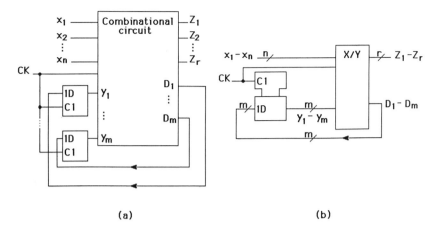

(a)   (b)

Figure 8.2-21 General structure of a one-phase latch machine: (a) detached latches; (b) concise form.

A one-phase latch machine realization of the Gray code up-down counter of Figs. 8.2-4 and 8.2-19 is shown in Fig. 8.2-22. Figures 8.2-4 and 8.2-22 are identical except that Fig. 8.2-22 has D latches in place of the D flip-flops of Fig. 8.2-4. The analysis procedure for a one-phase latch machine is the same procedure as for an E-T flip-flop machine.[2] In both structures the new internal state is entered directly after the arrival of the positive clock transition. In the flip-flop machine the external trigger property is taken care of by the fact that the flip-flops respond only to positive control input transitions. In the one-phase latch machine the values of the circuit delays and clock pulse width determine whether the external trigger property holds. The restrictions on these parameters that are necessary to ensure the external trigger property will be discussed next.

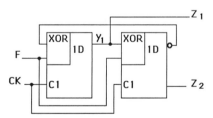

Figure 8.2-22 One-phase latch realization of Gray code up-down counter.

[2] Care must be taken in determining the precise timing of any outputs such as z_4 and z_5 in Fig. 8.2-7 that involve gating out of the clock pulses.

Timing Constraints. To prevent multistepping in the one-phase latch machine design, it is necessary to ensure that the clock pulse has returned to 0 before the new values of the latch inputs propagate to the latches. (It will be shown that the time from when the CK pulse returns to 0 until the new latch input values arrive must be at least equal to the hold time of the latches.) This is the purpose of the interstage delays in the shift register circuit of Fig. 8.1-1c. It is also possible to insert delays at the latch outputs in the general one-phase latch machine of Fig. 8.2-21. A more common technique is to rely on the propagation delay through the combinational network to prevent multistepping. This requires control of the maximum clock pulse width. The timing as related to multistepping is illustrated in Fig. 8.2-23. Part (a) of this figure shows the general structure of Fig. 8.2-21 redrawn with only two latches and their related circuitry shown. Part (b) shows

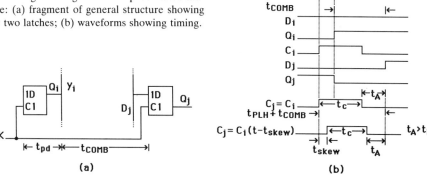

Figure 8.2-23 Representation of multistep-related timing in the general one-phase latch machine: (a) fragment of general structure showing only two latches; (b) waveforms showing timing.

the waveforms that result when a clock pulse arrives, causing Q_i to change from 0 to 1, with the new Q_i value propagating through the combinational circuitry and causing D_j to change from 0 to 1. Two different waveforms for C_j, the clock input to latch j, are shown at the bottom of Fig. 8.2-23b: The upper C_j waveform shows the situation where the positive CK edge arrives at latch j at the same time as it arrives at latch i, the lower C_j waveform is for the case where C_j is delayed by t_{skew} from C_i. The symbols used in this discussion are defined in Table 8.2-7.

The time interval from the arrival of the trailing edge of the clock pulse at latch j until the arrival of the new value of the data input D_j is t_A. If the clock pulses arrive at both latches at the same time, the value of t_A can be seen from the figure to be equal to

$$t_A = t_{PLH} + t_{COMB} - t_C \qquad (8.2\text{-}1)$$

To ensure that the D_j value at time t (positive edge of CK) is properly latched, it is necessary to hold this value fixed for at least t_h after the negative edge of CK. In other words, D_j should not be allowed to change until at least t_h after the falling edge of CK, which means that $t_A > t_h$. Using (8.2-1) for t_A, the following condition is obtained:

$$t_h < m(t_p) + m(t_{COMB}) - t_C \qquad (8.2\text{-}2)$$

TABLE 8.2-7 Definition of symbols

t_{PLH}	Latch propagation delay when changing state from 0 to 1, defined in Section 7.2-3
$m(t_p)$	Minimum value of t_{PHL} and t_{PLH}
t_{COMB}	Propagation delay from y_i to D_j through combinational circuits
$m(t_{COMB})$	Minimum value of t_{COMB}
t_C	Width of clock pulse
t_w	Required control pulse width for proper latch operation, defined in Section 7.2-3
t_h	Hold time, defined in Section 7.2-3
t_{skew}	The maximum time interval between the arrival of a transition of CK at two different latches
t_A	The time interval from the falling edge of CK until the arrival of a new value of D_j at the j latch input, defined on Fig. 8.2-23b

It is more useful to state this as a condition on t_C, the clock pulse width:

$$t_C < m(t_p) + m(t_{COMB}) - t_h \qquad (8.2\text{-}3)$$

or as a condition on $m(t_{COMB})$, the minimum delay through the combinational circuitry:

$$m(t_{COMB}) > t_C - m(t_p) + t_h \qquad (8.2\text{-}4)$$

Clock Skew. In most systems it is not possible to guarantee that the clock signal will arrive at all latches at the same time. The phenomenon of the clock arriving at different latches at different times is called **clock skew** [Morris 71], [Fairchild 73]. To ensure correct operation it is necessary to bound the largest variation in arrival times. This upper bound on the clock skew is represented by t_{skew}. When clock skew is taken into account the value of t_A becomes

$$t_A = m(t_p) + m(t_{COMB}) - t_C - t_{skew} \qquad (8.2\text{-}5)$$

With clock skew included, the bounds on t_C and $m(t_{COMB})$ given by (8.2-3) and (8.2-4) become

$$t_C < m(t_p) + m(t_{COMB}) - t_h - t_{skew} \qquad (8.2\text{-}6)$$

and:

$$m(t_{COMB}) > t_C - m(t_p) + t_h + t_{skew} \qquad (8.2\text{-}7)$$

The latch minimum propagation delay, $m(t_p)$, and hold time, t_h, are properties of the latches used in the circuit implementation. The latches also have a requirement on the width of the control pulse, t_w. The clock skew, t_{skew} is a property of the particular physical implementation. For proper operation of a one-phase latch circuit the values of $m(t_{COMB})$ and t_C must be controlled to satisfy (8.2-7). The clock pulse width, t_C, must also satisfy the latch control pulse requirement

$$t_C > t_w \qquad (8.2\text{-}8)$$

Combining (8.2-8) and (8.2-6) yields the following condition on t_C:

$$t_w < t_C < m(t_p) + m(t_{COMB}) - t_h - t_{skew} \qquad (8.2-9)$$

At first glance it appears that the one-phase latch machine would be a less expensive circuit than either the flip-flop machine or the two-phase latch machine since it uses a single latch in place of either a flip-flop or a pair of latches. However, the more severe timing constraints of the one-phase latch machine design can require a more expensive physical implementation than either of the other two structures. It is not possible to give a general rule about the comparative economy of the three finite-state machine structures. All of them are used extensively in present-day computers. The one-phase latch structure is used in the Amdahl 580 series computers. The implementation is described in [Grant 74]. The one-phase latch structure forms the basis for many pipelined structures ([Kogge 81] and [Waser 82]).

8.3 MULTIPLE-PULSE MODE CIRCUITS

Finite-state machines are a subclass of a more general class of circuits designed to operate in pulse-mode. These **pulse-mode circuits** satisfy the single-edge and external-trigger properties but not necessarily the single-clock property.

DEFINITION. A sequential circuit is said to be operating in **pulse-mode** if and only if the single-edge and the external-trigger properties are satisfied.

In a general pulse-mode circuit there can be more than one input signal that directly initiates internal state changes. Such inputs are called **pulse inputs**, while the remaining inputs are called **level inputs**. Because of the single-edge property, a pair of transitions is treated as a single entity with respect to causing state changes. The circuit can thus be thought of as responding to pulses on the pulse inputs. The remaining inputs condition the effect that the pulse inputs have on the circuit. Since it is the level of the signals present at these other inputs that is important, they are called level inputs.

DEFINITION. In a sequential circuit designed to operate in pulse-mode there are two classes of inputs: **Pulse inputs** and **level inputs**. Internal state changes in the sequential circuit always occur in response to a transition of one of the pulse inputs and never in response to a level-variable transition or value.

A finite-state machine is a pulse-mode circuit with one pulse input, the clock input. The emphasis in this section is on pulse-mode circuits that are not finite-state machines, that is, pulse-mode circuits that have more than one pulse input.

DEFINITION. A pulse-mode circuit with more than one pulse input will be called a **multiple-pulse mode circuit**. Such a circuit operates in pulse mode (single-edge and external-trigger properties hold) and has more than one input pulse signal.

Multiple-pulse mode circuits are usually designed under the assumption that the input pulses never overlap and are separated by intervals sufficient to allow the circuit to respond to each pulse input individually. This assumption will be made throughout this book unless explicitly stated otherwise. In some applications it is possible to have independent pulse sources that are not guaranteed to be nonoverlapping. For such a situation it may be necessary to construct a circuit to filter the pulse inputs to remove overlap. Such circuits are discussed on p. 299 of [Tietze 78].

The requirement of handling more than one input pulse makes it necessary to use different structures than those used for finite-state machines. The remainder of this section describes the multiple-pulse mode structures in current use. There are three such structures. Section 8.3-1 describes a structure based on multiport bistable elements. Such structures are used in design-for-testability scan path designs which are described in Chap. 10. The structures used in standard circuits that count up and down two pulse trains are described in Secs. 8.3-2 and 8.3-3. The Sec. 8.3-2 structures use a latch to convert the input pulses into a level up-down signal so that the finite-state machine structures described in Sec. 8.2 can be used. Nongated flip-flops are used in the structures of Sec. 8.3-3.

8.3-1 Multiport D Flip-Flop Realizations

Figure 8.3-1 shows the general structure of a pulse-mode circuit with two pulse inputs and two-port flip-flops; a specific example of such a circuit is given in Fig. 8.3-2a. This circuit is similar to the the up-down counters of Sec. 8.2 in that it is a Gray code up-down counter. It differs from the previous examples in having two pulse inputs: FP and BP. The operation of the circuit is illustrated in the waveforms of Fig. 8.3-2b: A pulse on FP causes the count to be increased by one and a pulse on BP causes the count to be decreased by one. The analysis of the Fig. 8.3-2a circuit is shown in Table 8.3-1.

The notation for Y_i^+ is an extension of the finite-state machine notation. Since there is more than one pulse input, it is necessary to indicate separately the new y values caused by each pulse input positive transition.

DEFINITION. In a pulse-mode circuit, the next-state values after a positive pulse input transition will be represented by

$$Y^+ = D_1 \langle P_1 \rangle \uparrow + D_2 \langle P_2 \rangle \uparrow + \cdots$$

where D_i is the new value of Y^+ after a positive transition of P_i.

For multiport D flip-flops, the next-state values are given directly by the inputs to the individual D inputs. The analysis procedure consists of determining the next-state functions for each flip-flop. The transition table has a separate column for each pulse input. The entries in the column corresponding to $\langle P_i \rangle \uparrow$ are determined directly from the D_i values for each flip-flop. This analysis technique treats the pulse-mode circuit as a combination of a number of finite-state machines (one for each pulse input).

Sec. 8.3   Multiple-Pulse Mode Circuits   **361**

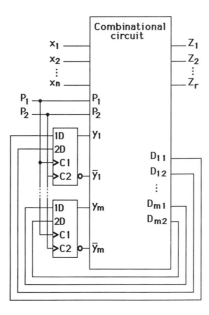

Figure 8.3-1 General pulse-mode structure with multiport flip-flops.

The multiport D flip-flops can be replaced with other types of multiport flip-flops: J-K, S-R, or T. This extension is straightforward and will not be discussed further here. It is also possible to use multiport latches instead of flip-flops. This is often done in design-for-testability scan path structures. These structures are discussed in detail in Chap. 10.

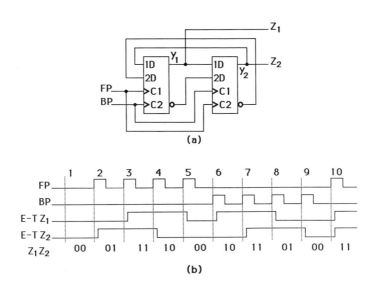

Figure 8.3-2 Pulse-mode Gray code up-down counter with two pulse inputs using two-port flip-flops: (a) circuit; (b) waveforms.

TABLE 8.3-1 Analysis of Fig. 8.3-2a circuit: (a) Excitation functions; (b) Transition table; (c) State table

(a)

$$Y_1^+ = D_1 = y_2\langle FP\rangle\uparrow + y_2'\langle BP\rangle\uparrow \qquad Z_1 = y_1$$
$$Y_2^+ = D_2 = y_1'\langle FP\rangle\uparrow + y_1\langle BP\rangle\uparrow \qquad Z_2 = y_2$$

(b)

$y_1 y_2$	$\langle FP\rangle\uparrow$	$\langle BP\rangle\uparrow$	$Z_1 Z_2$
1 0 0	0 1	1 0	0 0
2 0 1	1 1	0 0	0 1
3 1 1	1 0	0 1	1 1
4 1 0	0 0	1 1	1 0

$$Y_1^+ Y_2^+$$

(c)

s	$\langle FP\rangle\uparrow$	$\langle BP\rangle\uparrow$	$Z_1 Z_2$
1	2	4	0 0
2	3	1	0 1
3	4	2	1 1
4	1	3	1 0

$$S$$

8.3-2 Function-Select Signal Structures

Figure 8.3-3 shows a circuit that realizes the same sequential function as Fig. 8.3-2, but uses an *S-R* latch to develop a level function-select signal, *F*. An AND gate is used to combine the two pulse trains, *FP* and *BP*, into a single *CK* pulse train. The remainder of the circuit (shown enclosed by a dotted line box) is a finite-state machine (FSM) identical to the circuit of Fig. 8.2-4a. Table 8.3-2 shows the state table for the two-pulse mode circuit of Fig. 8.3-3 in part (a) and the state table for the FSM portion of the circuit in part (b). The only difference between the two state tables is in the column headings. In the table of part (b) the headings

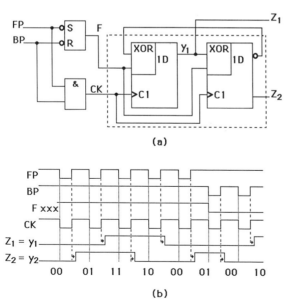

(a)

(b)

Figure 8.3-3 Pulse-mode Gray code up-down counter with two pulse inputs and a function-select signal: (a) circuit; (b) waveforms.

Sec. 8.3   Multiple-Pulse Mode Circuits

363

TABLE 8.3-2 State tables for the circuit of Fig. 8.3-3: (a) State table for two-pulse mode circuit; (b) State table for FSM portion of the circuit

(a)					(b)				
s	$\langle FP \rangle \uparrow$	$\langle BP \rangle \uparrow$	Z_1	Z_2	s	$F\langle CK \rangle \uparrow$	$F'\langle CK \rangle \uparrow$	Z_1	Z_2
A	B	D	0	0	A	B	D	0	0
B	C	A	0	1	B	C	A	0	1
C	D	B	1	1	C	D	B	1	1
D	A	C	1	0	D	A	C	1	0
		S					S		

$F\langle CK \rangle \uparrow$ and $F'\langle CK \rangle \uparrow$ occur in place of the headings $\langle FP \rangle \uparrow$ and $\langle BP \rangle \uparrow$ of part (a).

In the Fig. 8.2-4 circuit, the level signal F controls whether the circuit counts up or down when a pulse arrives. The F signal in the Fig. 8.3-3 circuit is set to 0 or 1 on the falling edge of the input pulse. The rising edge of the pulse then causes the circuit to count in the proper direction. For correct operation of the Fig. 8.3-3 circuit it is necessary to have the inactive pulse state be 1 rather than 0 as in the finite-state machine circuit of Fig. 8.2-4. The normal condition of the FP and BP inputs is thus 1. A negative pulse causes the circuit count to change.

The general structure of a two-pulse mode circuit realized by means of a derived function-select signal and a finite-state machine is shown in Fig. 8.3-4. The FSM (finite-state machine) shown in the figure has the same state table as the two-pulse mode circuit with the following replacements of the column headings: All $\langle P_1 \rangle \uparrow$ entries in column headings for the two-pulse mode circuit are replaced by $M\langle CK \rangle \uparrow$ in the FSM state table and $\langle P_2 \rangle \uparrow$ entries are replaced by $M'\langle CK \rangle \uparrow$. The FSM portion of the circuit is usually realized using the flip-flop based designs described in Sec. 8.2-1.

The structure just described is used in the SN54/74ALS192 and SN54/74ALS193 up-down counters. The F, LS, L, and standard TTL versions of these counters use the structure to be described in the following subsection.

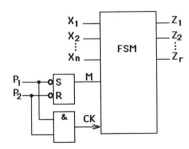

Figure 8.3-4 General structure of two-pulse-mode circuit realized with a function-select signal and a FSM.

The structure described here for two-pulse mode circuits is easily extended to circuits having more than two pulse inputs. More than one mode latch is required when there are three or more pulse inputs. The circuit structure is a direct extension of the structure just described for two-pulse inputs.

8.3-3 Non-gated Flip-Flop Structures

Non-gated flip-flops are often used to implement multiple-pulse mode circuits. Figure 8.3-5 shows a circuit that uses non-gated T flip-flops to realize the same Gray code up-down counter function as Figs. 8.3-3 and 8.3-2. The analysis of this circuit is shown in Table 8.3-3. In this analysis it is assumed that the input pulses are active low as in Fig. 8.3-3. Active-low input pulses ensure that multistepping will not occur in violation of the single transition property of pulse-mode operation.

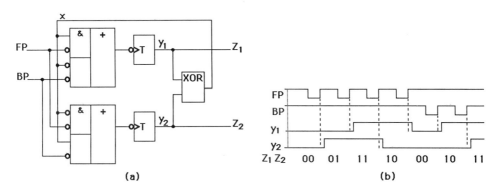

Figure 8.3-5 Two-pulse-mode Gray code up-down counter using nongated T flip-flops: (a) circuit diagram; (b) waveforms.

TABLE 8.3-3 Formal analysis of Fig. 8.3-5a: (a) Equations assuming that FP and BP are active-low pulses; (b) Tables

(a)

$$T_1 = (XFP' + X'BP')' \qquad T_2 = (X'FP' + XBP)'$$

$$\langle Y_1^* \rangle \uparrow = X \langle FP \rangle \uparrow + X' \langle BP \rangle \uparrow \qquad \langle Y_2^* \rangle \uparrow = X' \langle FP \rangle \uparrow + X \langle BP \rangle \uparrow$$

$$X = y_1 \oplus y_2$$

(b)

y_1 y_2	$\langle FP \rangle \uparrow$	$\langle BP \rangle \uparrow$	Z_1 Z_2		y_1 y_2		$\langle FP \rangle \uparrow$	$\langle BP \rangle \uparrow$
0 0	0 1	1 0	0 0		(0 0)	A	B	D
0 1	1 1	0 0	0 1		(0 1)	B	C	A
1 1	1 0	0 1	1 1		(1 1)	C	D	B
1 0	0 0	1 1	1 0		(1 0)	D	A	C

The equivalence between two-port T flip-flops and non-gated T flip-flops is shown in Fig. 8.3-6. Table 8.3-4 gives the formal analysis of the circuits of Fig. 8.3-6. In the analysis of part (b) it is assumed that the terms $P_1'\langle T_1'\rangle \uparrow$ and $P_2'\langle T_2'\rangle \uparrow$ are equal to 0. This assumption is based on P_1 and P_2 being active-low pulses. Thus when P_i is inactive, $P_i' = 0$. When a P_i pulse occurs, P_i' changes to 1, but the flip-flop states don't toggle until the trailing edge of the pulse. Thus any transition of T_i will not happen until P_i' has returned to 0.

The non-gated T flip-flop structures described here are the basis for the F, LS, L, and standard TTL SN54/74192 and 193 up-down counters. The non-gated S-R flip-flops discussed in Sec. 8.2-1 can also be used for multiple-pulse mode circuits.

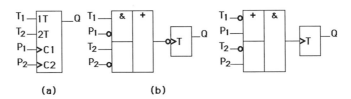

(a) **(b)**

Figure 8.3-6 Equivalent two-pulse T flip-flop circuits: (a) two-port flip-flop; (b) nongated negative edge-triggered flip-flop; (c) nongated positive edge-triggered flip-flop.

TABLE 8.3-4 Formal analysis of Fig. 8.3-6: (a) Two-port flip-flop; (b) Non-gated negative edge-triggered flip-flop; (c) Non-gated positive edge-triggered flip-flop

---

(a)

$$\langle Y^*\rangle \uparrow = T_1\langle P_1\rangle \uparrow + T_2\langle P_2\rangle \uparrow$$

(b)

$$\langle Y^*\rangle \uparrow = \langle (T_1P_1' + T_2P_2')'\rangle \uparrow = \langle (T_1' + P_1)(T_2' + P_2)\rangle \uparrow$$

$$= (T_2' + P_2)\langle T_1' + P_1\rangle \uparrow + (T_1' + P_1)\langle T_2' + P_2\rangle \uparrow$$

$$= (T_2' + P_2)(T_1\langle P_1\rangle \uparrow + \underbrace{P_1'\langle T_1'\rangle \uparrow}_{0}) + (T_1' + P_1)(T_2\langle P_2\rangle \uparrow + \underbrace{P_2'\langle T_2'\rangle \uparrow}_{0})$$

$$= (T_2' + P_2)(T_1\langle P_1\rangle \uparrow) + (T_1' + P_1)(T_2\langle P_2\rangle \uparrow)$$

$$= T_1\langle P_1\rangle \uparrow + T_2\langle P_2\rangle \uparrow \qquad \text{if } P_1 + P_2 = 1$$

(c)

$$\langle Y^*\rangle \uparrow = \langle (T_1' + P_1)(T_2' + P_2)\rangle \uparrow$$

8.4 NON-PULSE-MODE CIRCUITS

Most sequential circuits are designed to operate in pulse mode. In fact, the concept of pulse-mode operation was formulated to describe the common class of circuits. However, there are some instances when circuits are designed so that they specifically violate the pulse-mode conditions. The most common example of such circuits are the "ripple counters," which are discussed in Chap. 11. This class of counter violates the external-trigger property of pulse-mode operation. Their design is based on "multistepping"—the situation in which a state change of one flip-flop directly causes a change in another flip-flop. This is implemented by connecting the output of one flip-flop to the control input of another flip-flop.

Since non-pulse-mode operation is rare and more complex than pulse-mode operation, there are no good general design techniques for such circuits. The purpose of this section is to present some examples of circuits that do not operate in pulse mode. This will be done by discussing a number of different circuits to implement the same function. The function to be realized is illustrated in Fig. 8.4-1.

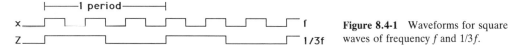

Figure 8.4-1 Waveforms for square waves of frequency f and $1/3f$.

The circuit has a single input, x, that is assumed to be a square wave of frequency f. The circuit output, Z, is to be another square wave of frequency $1/3f$. It is important that the output be a square wave rather than some other signal with frequency $1/3f$. Both types of circuit (square and nonsquare wave) are used, but the square-wave requirement is an important design feature for the circuits to be presented here.

Finite-state Machine Circuit. Figure 8.4-2a shows a finite-state machine that realizes the divide-by-3 function. The waveforms for this circuit are shown in part (b) of the figure. The analysis of this circuit is shown in Table 8.4-1. One undesirable feature of this circuit is the possibility of spurious spikes on the output as illustrated at times 1 and 7 of the waveforms. These are caused by the fact that at these times, y_1' changes from 1 to 0 at the same time that x changes from 0 to 1. This gives rise to the possibility that the xy_1' term in the output function will cause a temporary incorrect 1 output. This output function has a function hazard.

There is no simple way to avoid this function hazard in an FSM realization of the $1/3f$ function. As the Fig. 8.4-1 waveforms show, the output must change at both a rising and a falling edge of the input square wave. Because of the single-edge property, it is not possible to have an FSM that changes state at both of these edges. Thus the output must be formed by adding the input x to a state variable at the appropriate times. It is this combination of x with a function of the y_i's that causes the hazard pulse.

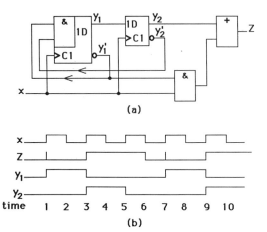

(a)

(b)

Figure 8.4-2 FSM for the $1/3f$ function: (a) logic diagram; (b) waveforms.

Circuit Without the Single-edge Property. Figure 8.4-3 shows a circuit that realizes the 1/3 function but does not satisfy the single-edge property. The analysis of this circuit is shown in Table 8.4-2. The difficulty of the output changing with both edges of the input signal is solved in this circuit by adding a flip-flop that is controlled by the falling edge of the input pulse. The analysis is straightforward and is shown in Table 8.4-2. There is no output function hazard because only one of the signals (y_2 and y_3) changes at a time. Note that this circuit requires an additional flip-flop.

Circuit With Multistepping. Multistepping is used in the circuit of Figure 8.4-4 to realize the $1/3f$ function. The analysis is shown in Table 8.4-3. Formation of the transition table is more complicated than in the previous examples. Changes in Y_1 are caused by input transitions due to the terms $y_2\langle x'\rangle \uparrow$ and $y_2'\langle x\rangle \uparrow$. First the entries for Y_1 due to these terms are placed in the transition table. There are

TABLE 8.4-1 Analysis of the circuit of Fig. 8.4-2: (a) Excitation functions; (b) Transition table; (c) State table; (d) Output table

(a)

$$D_1 = y_1'y_2' \qquad D_2 = y_1 \qquad Z = y_2 + xy_1'$$

(b)

$y_1 y_2$	$\langle x\rangle \uparrow$
0 0	1 0
0 1	0 0
1 1	0 1
1 0	0 1
	$Y_1^+ Y_2^+$

(c)

$y_1 y_2$	s	$\langle x\rangle \uparrow$
(0 0)	A	B
(1 0)	B	C
(0 1)	C	A
(1 1)	D	C
		S

(d)

$y_1 y_2$	s	x 0	1
(0 0)	A	0	1
(1 0)	B	0	0
(0 1)	C	1	1
(1 1)	D	1	1
			Z

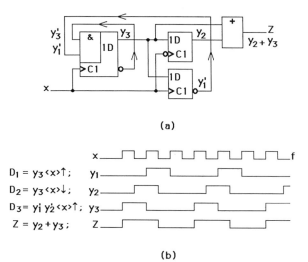

$D_1 = y_3\langle x\rangle\uparrow;$ y_1

$D_2 = y_3\langle x\rangle\downarrow;$ y_2

$D_3 = y_1' y_2'\langle x\rangle\uparrow;$ y_3

$Z = y_2 + y_3;$ Z

(b)

Figure 8.4-3 Circuit for the $1/3f$ function that does not have the single-edge property: (a) logic diagram; (b) waveforms.

four such entries (Table 8.4-3b). Wherever one of these entries corresponds to $\langle y_1'\rangle$, the appropriate entry is placed in the table for Y_2. There are two such entries (Table 8.4-3c). It is then necessary to check that none of these Y_2 entries cause a subsequent change in Y_1 due to the terms $x\langle y_2'\rangle\uparrow$ and $x'\langle y_2\rangle\uparrow$ of the $\langle Y_1^*\rangle\uparrow$ expression. They do not. The entry of the table corresponding to $\langle y_2'\rangle\uparrow$ is caused by $\langle x'\rangle\uparrow$ and thus x is equal to 0 making the term $x\langle y_2'\rangle\uparrow$ equal to zero. Thus, the remaining entries for Y are filled in as being equal to the corresponding y values (Table 8.4-3d).

TABLE 8.4-2 Analysis of the circuit of Fig. 8.4-3: (a) Excitation functions; (b) Transition table; (c) State table with lowercase letters for states not used in normal operation

(a)

$$D_1 = y_3\langle x\rangle\uparrow \qquad D_2 = y_3\langle x'\rangle\uparrow \qquad D_3 = y_1' y_3'\langle x\rangle\uparrow \qquad z = y_2 + y_3$$

(b)

$y_1 y_2 y_3$	$\langle x\rangle\uparrow$	$\langle x'\rangle\uparrow$	Z
0 0 0	001	000	0
0 0 1	001	011	1
0 1 1	110	011	1
0 1 0	011	000	1
1 0 0	000	100	0
1 0 1	100	111	1
1 1 1	110	111	1
1 1 0	010	100	1

$Y_1 Y_2 Y_3$

(c)

$(y_1 y_2 y_3)$	s	$\langle x\rangle\uparrow$	$\langle x'\rangle\uparrow$	Z
(0 0 0)	A	B	A	0
(0 0 1)	B	B	C	1
(0 1 1)	C	D	C	1
(1 1 0)	D	f	E	1
(1 0 0)	E	A	E	0
(0 1 0)	f	C	A	1
(1 0 1)	g	E	h	1
(1 1 1)	h	D	h	1

S

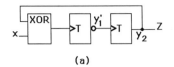

(a)

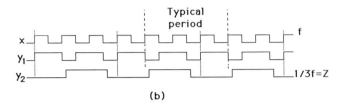

(b)

Figure 8.4-4 Circuit for the $1/3f$ function that does not have the external-trigger property: (a) logic diagram; (b) waveforms.

TABLE 8.4-3 Analysis of the circuit of Fig. 8.4-4: (a) Excitation functions; (b) Transition table entries due to $y_2'\langle x\rangle\uparrow + y_2\langle x'\rangle\uparrow$; (c) Transition table entries due to $\langle y_1\rangle\uparrow$; (d) Complete transition table; (e) State table

(a)

$$\langle Y_1^*\rangle\uparrow = \langle x\oplus y_2\rangle\uparrow = x'\langle y_2\rangle\uparrow + x\langle y_2'\rangle\uparrow + y_2'\langle x\rangle\uparrow + y_2\langle x'\rangle\uparrow$$

$$\langle Y_2^*\rangle\uparrow = \langle y_1'\rangle\uparrow$$

$$Z = y_2$$

(b)

$y_1 y_2$	$\langle x\rangle\uparrow$	$\langle x'\rangle\uparrow$
0 0	1	
0 1		1
1 1		0
1 0	0	

$Y_1 Y_2$

(c)

$y_1 y_2$	$\langle x\rangle\uparrow$	$\langle x'\rangle\uparrow$
0 0	1	
0 1		1
1 1		0 0
1 0	0 1	

$Y_1 Y_2$

(d)

$y_1 y_2$	$\langle x\rangle\uparrow$	$\langle x'\rangle\uparrow$	Z
0 0	1 0	0 0	0
0 1	0 1	1 1	1
1 1	1 1	0 0	1
1 0	0 1	1 0	0

$Y_1 Y_2$

(e)

$(y_1 y_2)$	s	$\langle x\rangle\uparrow$	$\langle x'\rangle\uparrow$	Z
(0 0)	A	B	A	0
(1 0)	B	C	B	0
(0 1)	C	C	D	1
(1 1)	D	D	A	1

S

Circuits with multistepping may operate more slowly than pulse-mode circuits due to the necessity to propagate the input through a flip-flop to the control input of another flip-flop. However, they can require fewer gates or less area than the equivalent pulse-mode circuit.

Fundamental-mode Circuit. The final example of a $1/3f$ circuit is the fundamental-mode circuit shown in Fig. 8.4-5. This is a straightforward imple-

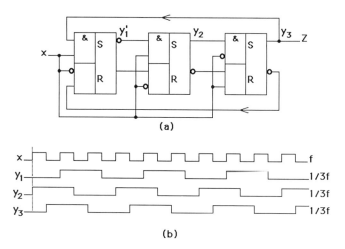

(a)

(b)

Figure 8.4-5 Fundamental-mode circuit for the $1/3f$ function: (a) logic diagram; (b) waveforms.

TABLE 8.4-4 Analysis of the fundamental-mode circuit of Fig. 8.4-5: (a) Excitation functions; (b) Transition table; (c) State table with lowercase letters used for states not used in normal operation

(a)

$$S_1 = xy_3, R_1 = x'y_3' \qquad S_2 = x'y_2, R_2 = xy_2' \qquad S_3 = xy_1', R_3 = x'y_1$$

(b)

$y_1 y_2 y_3$	$x=0$	$x=1$
A 0 0 0	0 0 0	0 1 0
g 0 0 1	0 0 1	1 1 0
C 0 1 1	0 1 1	1 1 1
B 0 1 0	0 1 1	0 1 0
F 1 0 0	0 0 0	1 0 0
E 1 0 1	1 0 1	1 0 0
D 1 1 1	1 0 1	1 1 1
h 1 1 0	0 0 1	1 1 0

$$Y_1 Y_2 Y_3$$

s	$x=0$	$x=1$	Z
A	Ⓐ	B	0
B	C	Ⓑ	0
C	Ⓒ	D	1
D	E	Ⓓ	1
E	Ⓔ	F	1
F	A	Ⓕ	0
g	g	h	1
h	g	h	0

S

mentation of this function in fundamental-mode operation. While this circuit uses three bistable elements, these are latches rather than flip-flops. In most technologies this circuit would be the least expensive of all of the designs for the $1/3f$ function shown in this section.

8.R REFERENCES

[EICHELBERGER 78] Eichelberger, E. B., and T. W. Williams, "A Logic Design Structure for LSI Testability," *J. Des. Autom. Fault-Tolerant Comput.*, 2, No. 2, pp. 165–178, 1978.

[FAIRCHILD 73] Fairchild Semiconductor, *The TTL Applications Handbook*, Aug. 1983.

[GRANT 74] Grant, G. D., "Clock Apparatus and Data Processing System," U.S. Patent 3,792,362, Amdahl Corp., 1974.

[KOGGE 81] Kogge, P. M., *The Architecture of Pipelined Computers*, McGraw-Hill Book Company, New York, 1981.

[MORRIS 71] Morris, R. L., and J. R. Miller, eds., *Designing with TTL Integrated Circuits*, Texas Instruments Electronics Series, McGraw-Hill Book Company, New York, 1971.

[TIETZE 78] Tietze, U., and C. H. Schenk, *Advanced Electronic Circuits*, Springer-Verlag Inc., New York, 1978.

[WASER 82] Waser, S., and M. J. Flynn, *Introduction to Arithmetic for Digital Systems*, Holt, Rinehart and Winston, New York, 1982.

8.P PROBLEMS

8.1 Analyze the finite-state machines shown in Fig. P8.1. Write the excitation equations, transition table, state/output table, and state/output diagram.

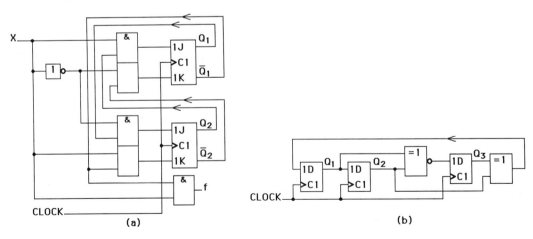

Figure P8.1

8.2 Repeat Problem 8.1 for Fig. P8.2.

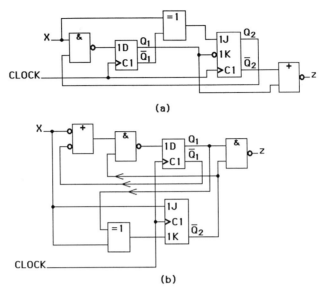

(a)

(b)

Figure P8.2

8.3 **(a)** Analyze the circuit in Fig. P8.3a. Write the excitation functions, transition table, and state table.

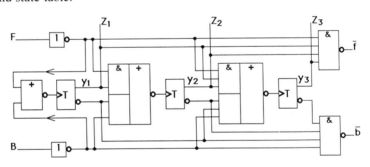

Figure P8.3a

(b) Complete the waveforms in Fig. P8.3b.

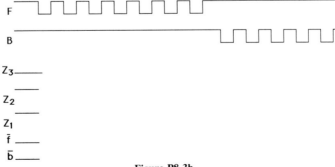

Figure P8.3b

8.4 Analyze the circuit of Fig. P8.4. Write the:
  (a) Excitation table
  (b) Transition table
  (c) Flow table
  (d) State diagram
  (e) Word statement

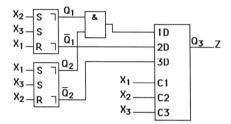

X_1, X_2, and X_3 are non-overlapping pulses.   **Figure P8.4**

8.5 **(a)** You are to redesign the circuit of Problem 8.1a to provide a parallel load capability. Show both asynchronous and synchronous implementations.
  (b) Repeat part (a) for Problem 8.1b.
  (c) Repeat part (a) for Problem 8.2a.
  (d) Repeat part (a) for Problem 8.2b.

8.6 (*Two-Phase Latch FSM*) You are to analyze the FSM circuits of Fig. P8.6. Write excitation functions, form transition and flow tables, and specify for each circuit the sequential function realized.

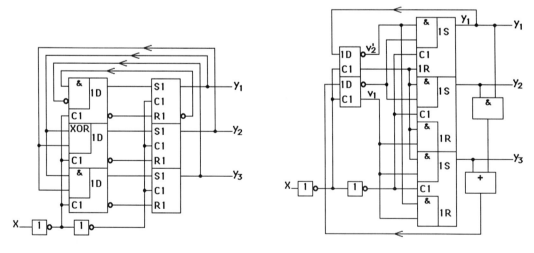

Figure P8.6 (a) Double-latch circuit; (b) single-latch circuit.

8.7 Section 8.4 has four different circuits for the $1/3f$ function. You are to draw implementations of each of these circuits using LSI logic macrocells and give the equivalent gate count for each circuit.

8.8 Figure P8.8 shows part of a sequential circuit with D flip-flops having the following timing parameters:

$$t_{PCQ} = \text{propagation delay from clock to } Q$$

$$t_{su} = \text{setup time of } D \text{ input before clock}$$

$$t_h = \text{hold time of } D \text{ input after clock}$$

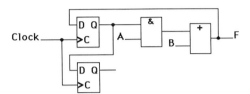

Figure P8.8

The propagation delay through the AND and OR gates is T_{PDAO}.
(a) What is the maximum clock frequency at which the circuit will still operate reliably, assuming that the clock pulse width is sufficiently low and high?
(b) If t_{PCQ} can vary between t_{PCQmin} and t_{PCQmax}, and t_h can vary between t_{hmin} and t_{hmax}, what should be the relationship between t_{PCQ} and t_h so that the circuit of Fig. P8.8 will satisfy the worst-case timing variations?

9

SEQUENTIAL-CIRCUIT SYNTHESIS

Sequential circuit operating modes and formal analysis techniques were discussed in the preceding two chapters. Design techniques are presented in this chapter. The approach to be followed is to reverse the steps that were used in the analysis procedure. Thus, the first step in the design process is to form a flow table describing the desired circuit behavior. This table must then be checked to determine whether it includes more states than are necessary. The transition table is obtained from the simplified flow table by assigning combinations of internal variables to the internal states. An excitation table is derived from the transition table, and finally the circuit diagram is drawn. Each of these steps in the synthesis procedure will be considered in order.

9.1 WRITING FLOW TABLES

Sequential circuit operation is typically described by a word statement which is often augmented with timing diagrams, t-expressions, or flow charts. This specification must be converted into a flow table by the logic designer. This conversion is a skill that the designer must develop through experience. No formal procedure is possible due to the informal nature of the initial description. In fact, it is the flow table that is the precise specification of the desired circuit operation. Once the flow table is obtained, formal procedures can be used to complete the synthesis for the final circuit.

Writing flow table specifications is a skill that is best learned by example. This aspect of the design process will be covered by writing flow tables for a number of illustrative designs. Pulse mode circuits will be covered first since they are easier than fundamental mode circuits to specify.

Some designers find it helpful to convert the word statement into some other representation of the circuit specification before writing the flow table. A popular intermediate representation, particularly when there are many input variables, is the flow chart [Comer 84], [Trendiak 81]. Special forms of flow charts, called ASM (algorithmic state machine) charts, have been developed for sequential circuits, ([Wiatrowski 80] and [Clare 73]). The state diagram (Sec. 8.2) is also used to represent sequential circuit behavior.

At first glance, it might seem that forming *exactly* the correct flow table for the desired circuit performance would be very difficult. In a sense this is true; but in actual fact, there are *very many* flow tables that correspond to the same circuit performance. All that is really necessary is to form one of the many flow tables which are suitable. Formal procedures exist for removing superfluous internal states or for transforming one flow table into another flow table without changing the corresponding circuit performance. Thus one needn't worry about using the fewest possible states when writing a flow table.

9.1-1 A Finite-State-Machine Example with a Level Output (FSM-L)

The first example is a finite-state machine (FSM-L) with one level (dc) input X, one clock-pulse input CK, and one level output, Z, as shown in Fig. 9.1-1a. When a clock pulse arrives, if the present value of X is:

(a) The same as the value of X at the last previous clock, the output becomes or remains equal to 1

(b) Opposite to the value of X at the last previous clock, the output becomes or remains equal to 0

The t-expression for this operation is: $Z(t) = X'(t) \oplus X(t - 1)$.

The flow table can be formed as follows:

1. In Fig. 9.1-1b, the input X is the same (0) at times $t = 2$ and 4, but the output Z is different—$Z(2) = 1$, $Z(4) = 0$. This means that the function can't be

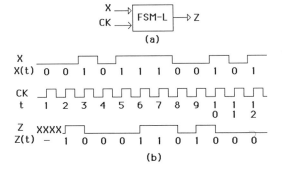

(a)

(b)

Figure 9.1-1 FSM-L Circuit: (a) block diagram; (b) waveforms.

realized with a combinational circuit—a sequential circuit with at least two internal states is required.

2. Assume that there are only two internal states—A and B—and let the output equal 0 ($Z = 0$) when the circuit is in state A and the output equal 1 ($Z = 1$) when the circuit is in state B. Table 9.1-1a shows the form of the corresponding flow table.

3. The next-state entries corresponding to each total state must now be determined. Assume that $X = 0$ and the circuit is in state A (with $Z = 0$). In order to know whether A or B is the appropriate next-state entry, the value of X at the last clock input is needed. This information is not available since it is possible to have $Z = 0$ with either $X(t - 1) = 0$ ($X(t - 2) - 1$) or $X(t - 1) = 1$ ($X(t - 2) = 0$). Two additional states must be added as shown in Table 9.1-1b. With four states the circuit can "remember" the value of X at the last clock pulse.

4. It is now possible to fill in the next-state entries. For example, when $X = 0$ and the circuit is in state A (with $Z = 0$), the next state entry must be B. Since $X = 0$, only states A and B are possible next states. With the circuit in state A, the previous value of X is known to have been 0. Thus there have been two clock pulses with $X = 0$ and the output must become $Z = 1$. This means that B rather than A is the correct next-state entry. Similar reasoning leads to the other next-state entries shown in the table.

5. The state diagram corresponding to the flow table is shown in Fig. 9.1-2. The darkened edges show that the output stays at 0 as long as X changes value at each clock pulse.

TABLE 9.1-1 Flow tables for FSM-L Example: (a) Attempt using two states; (b) Correct flow table

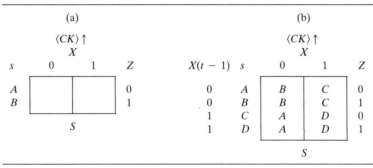

9.1-2 A Finite-State-Machine Example with a Pulse Output (FSM-P)

Figure 9.1-3 shows waveforms for an FSM that differs from the previous example only by having a pulse output rather than a level output. The CK pulse is gated onto the output, z, whenever the value of X is the same as it was when the last CK pulse occurred. A lowercase z is used for the output to indicate that it is a pulse rather than a level signal. The output waveform for the level-output circuit

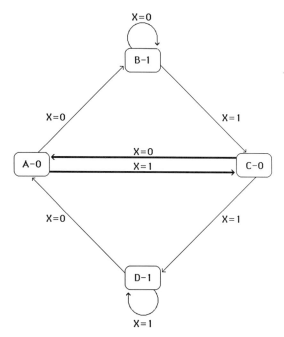

X=0

B-1

X=0   X=1

X=0
A-0 ←————————→ C-0
X=1

X=0   X=1

D-1

X=1

Figure 9.1-2 State diagram corresponding to Table 9.1-1b.

is included as part (c) of the figure to show the correspondence between the pulse and the level output signals. The *t*-expression for the pulse output is $z(t) = CK[X'(t) \oplus X(t - 1)]$.

Since the flow table for the level-output circuit has already been written, it seems that the easiest way to get the pulse-output table is to just modify the level output table. Table 9.1-2a shows the result of adding pulse-output entries to the flow table of Table 9.1-1b. For states A and B, the output is 1 in the $X = 0$ column since these states correspond to a previous X value of 0. The other entries are found by similar reasoning.

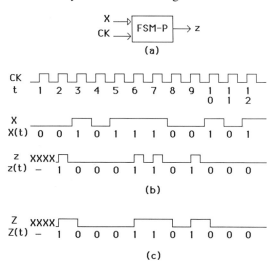

$$X \longrightarrow \boxed{\begin{array}{c} \text{FSM-P} \\ \text{(a)} \end{array}} \longrightarrow z$$

CK ⊓⊔⊓⊔⊓⊔⊓⊔⊓⊔⊓⊔⊓⊔⊓⊔
t   1 2 3 4 5 6 7 8 9 1 1 1
                                  0 1 2

X
X(t) 0 0 1 0 1 1 1 0 0 1 0 1

z   XXXX⊓_____⊓⊓_⊓___⊓_____
z(t) –   1 0 0 0 1 1 0 1 0 0 0

(b)

Z   XXXX⊓_____⊓___⊓_⊓___⊓_____
Z(t) –   1 0 0 0 1 1 0 1 0 0 0

(c)

Figure 9.1-3 Finite-state machine with one input and one pulse output: (a) block diagram; (b) typical waveforms; (c) output waveform for previous example.

TABLE 9.1-2 Flow tables for FSM-P Example: (a) Modified FSM-L table; (b) Minimum-state table

		(a)				(b)	
		$\langle CK \rangle \downarrow$				$\langle CK \rangle \downarrow$	
		X				X	
$X(t-1)$	s	0	1	$X(t-1)$	s	0	1
0	A	B, 1	C, 0	0	E	E, 1	F, 0
0	B	B, 1	C, 0	1	F	E, 0	F, 1
1	C	A, 0	D, 1			S, z	
1	D	A, 0	D, 1				

S, z

Note that the heading for the table has been changed from $\langle CK \rangle \uparrow$ to $\langle CK \rangle \downarrow$ in order to indicate that the internal state should change at the CK trailing edge rather than the leading edge as in the FSM-L circuit. This is done to avoid shortening the output pulses as discussed in Sec. 8.2.

The first two rows (A and B) of Table 9.1-2a have identical entries. This means that they can be replaced by a single row. The same is true for the last two rows (C and D). The theory justifying this will be given in Sec. 9.2. The table that results from combining these pairs of rows is shown in Table 9.1-2b, in which state E replaces the A and B pair and F replaces the C and D pair. The reason that two states are sufficient for the pulse-output circuit is that it is not necessary to maintain the output signal between CK pulses. The corresponding state diagram is shown in Fig. 9.1-4. This is an example of a general situation in which it is often true that fewer states are required for pulse outputs than for level outputs [Cadden 59].

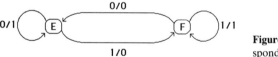

Figure 9.1-4 State diagram corresponding to Table 9.1-2b.

9.1-3 Pulse-Mode Circuits with Two Pulse Inputs (2P-L and 2P-P)

Flow tables for circuits with multiple pulse inputs are considered next. Figure 9.1-5b describes a circuit with two pulse inputs and one level output. The output is 0 as long as the pulses alternate. The second successive pulse on the same input causes the output to become and remain equal to 1 until a pulse arrives on the other input. The flow table for this circuit is shown in Table 9.1-3. When the circuit is in state A, the last input pulse must have been X_1. Thus, the appropriate entry in the $\langle X_1 \rangle \uparrow$ column is state B since the output must become 1 and the last input pulse will still be X_1. The $\langle X_2 \rangle \uparrow$ column entry for state A must be C since the output should remain 0, but the last input now becomes X_2. Similar reasoning leads to the other table entries. Note that the Table 9.1-3a entries are the same as the

TABLE 9.1-3 Flow tables for 2P-L and 2P-P Examples: (a) Table for level-output circuit, 2P-L; (b) Table for pulse-output circuit, 2P-P

(a)						(b)		
Last input	s	$\langle X_1 \rangle \uparrow$	$\langle X_2 \rangle \uparrow$	Z		Last input	s	$\langle X_1' \rangle \uparrow$	$\langle X_2' \rangle \uparrow$

Last input	s	$\langle X_1 \rangle \uparrow$	$\langle X_2 \rangle \uparrow$	Z
X_1	A	B	C	0
X_1	B	B	C	1
X_2	C	A	D	0
X_2	D	A	D	1

S

Last input	s	$\langle X_1' \rangle \uparrow$	$\langle X_2' \rangle \uparrow$
X_1	E	E, 1	F, 0
X_2	F	E, 0	F, 1

S, z

entries in Table 9.1-1b; the arrival of an X_1 pulse in this circuit has the same effect as the arrival of a clock pulse with $X = 0$ in the circuit of Fig. 9.1-1.

The output waveform for the corresponding pulse-output circuit is shown in Fig. 9.1-5c. Table 9.1-3b shows the flow table. State diagrams for both circuits are shown in Fig. 9.1-6.

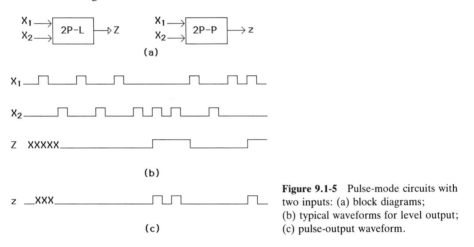

Figure 9.1-5 Pulse-mode circuits with two inputs: (a) block diagrams; (b) typical waveforms for level output; (c) pulse-output waveform.

9.1-4 Fundamental-Mode Flow Tables (FM-P)

The flow tables just written assume that the circuits operate in pulse mode. The same behavior can be realized with circuits operating in fundamental mode. This will be demonstrated by writing a fundamental-mode flow table for the 2P-P circuit of Fig. 9.1-5a.

Primitive Form. Fundamental-mode flow tables are harder to write than pulse-mode tables. Usually, fundamental-mode tables are written in a special format, called **primitive form**. A primitive-form flow table is allowed to have only one stable state in each row. This leads to extra states in the table, but reduces the difficulty of writing the table. Formal methods for transforming a flow table

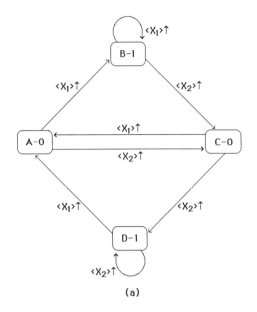

(a)

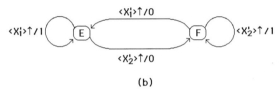

(b)

Figure 9.1-6 State diagrams corresponding to Table 9.1-3: (a) level-output circuit; (b) pulse-output circuit.

to another flow table that specifies the same circuit operation but has the minimum number of required internal states are presented in the following sections. The procedure for designing a fundamental-mode circuit starts by writing a primitive-form flow table and then reducing the table to one having as few states as possible. Even with pulse-mode tables it is necessary to use the state reduction technique to ensure that no extra states are included in the table.

A fundamental-mode circuit, **FM-P**, with two pulse inputs and one pulse output is to be designed.

1. The input pulses do not overlap or occur simultaneously.
2. An output pulse occurs with an input pulse iff the last previous input pulse occurred on the same input lead as the present input pulse. Otherwise, there are no output pulses.

The table is formed as follows:

1. When no pulses are present ($X_1 = X_2 = 0$), there must be two stable states— one for the condition where the last input was X_1 and one for the condition where the last input was X_2. This is necessary because the output when an input pulse arrives is determined by the previous input pulse. The output for each of these states is 0 (see Table 9.1-4a).

2. The next-state entries in the 01 column of rows A and B will be considered next. Since a primitive-form flow table (one stable state per row) is being written, neither of these entries can be A or B. (The entry in row A cannot be A, for this would be stable. The entry in row B cannot be A, for in this flow table each unstable state must go directly to a stable state.)

TABLE 9.1-4 Flow table for Example 9.1-4

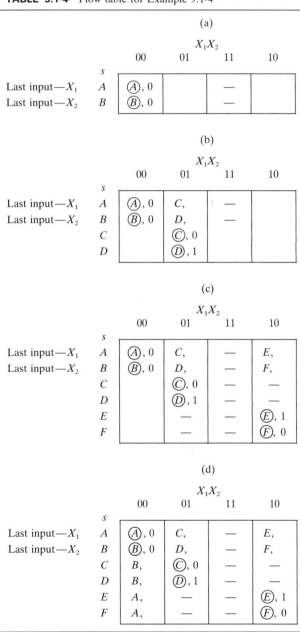

Without loss of generality the entry in row A can be chosen to be C, an arbitrary new state. This means that there must be a stable C entry in the C row of column 01 (since this is a flow table). The output associated with this stable C entry must be 0 since the present input is X_2 (01 column) and the previous input was X_1 (state A). The entry in row B can only be C or a new state D. If the C entry is chosen, a 0 output will be developed. This is incorrect, for the present input is X_2 (01 column) and the previous input was X_2 (state B). Thus the row B entry must be D, and there must be a stable D entry in the 01 column. The output for this stable D entry must be 1 because this state will occur when two successive X_2 pulses have been received (Table 9.1-4b).

3. The same reasoning applied to the 10 column shows that two additional internal states must be introduced. The outputs associated with these states are determined in the same fashion as the C and D outputs were determined (Table 9.1-4c).

4. A dash ($—$) is placed in each of the cells of the 11 column, since it is assumed that the pulses do not overlap. A dash can also be placed in the 10 column of row C: It is impossible to enter this state, for this would require a double change of input (from 01 to 10). The stable entry in row C represents the presence of an X_2 pulse; this must be followed by a transition to the 00 column (no pulse present). For similar reasons, dashes can be placed in the 10 column of row D and in the 01 column of rows E and F.

5. Four entries, in the 00 column and rows C, D, E, and F, remain to be specified. The entries in rows C and D must be B, since they are reached from the 01 column and therefore must lead to the state corresponding to a previous X_2 input. For analogous reasons, the entries in rows E and F must be A. All the next states have now been entered (Table 9.1-4d), and only the outputs corresponding to the unstable states remain unspecified.

6. One possibility is to make the unstable state output the same as the output of the stable state to which the unstable state goes. Thus, the output entry in row A of the 01 column would be 0, since the next-state entry is C and the output associated with the stable C entry in this column is 0 (see Table 9.1-5). This output specification is satisfactory, for the output associated with a stable state will occur when the stable state is entered. Associating the same output with the preceding unstable state can only speed the appearance of output changes.

Output Specifications—Fundamental-Mode. There are other output specifications which are also possible. To determine the precise constraints on these outputs, one entry will be considered in detail. If the output for an unstable state is made the same as the output for the next stable state, a 0 output must be specified in the A row of the 01 column. The question that naturally arises is whether or not the circuit will still perform correctly if a 1 output is specified instead.

There is only one way in which the circuit can enter the total state s-X_1X_2 = A-01: the circuit must initially be in the state A-00, and the X_2 input must change from 0 to 1. If this happens, the circuit will start in state A-00, change

TABLE 9.1-5 Different output specifications for Table 9.1-4: (a) Unstable entries same as stable entries; (b) Unstable entries same as stable entries only when necessary

	(a) X_1X_2					(b) X_1X_2			
s	00	01	11	10	s	00	01	11	10
A	Ⓐ, 0	C, 0	—	E, 1	A	Ⓐ, 0	C, 0	—	E, d
B	Ⓑ, 0	D, 1	—.	F, 0	B	Ⓑ, 0	D, d	—	F, 0
C	B, 0	Ⓒ, 0	—	—	C	B, 0	Ⓒ, 0	—	—
D	B, 0	Ⓓ, 1	—	—	D	B, d	Ⓓ, 1	—	—
E	A, 0	—	—	Ⓔ, 1	E	A, d	—	—	Ⓔ, 1
F	A, 0	—	—	Ⓕ, 0	F	A, 0	—	—	Ⓕ, 0
		S, z					S, z		

to state A-01 because of the X_2 change, and finally change to state C-01 because of the unstable next state associated with state A-01.

In a primitive flow table, each unstable total state can be entered from only one stable state (there is only one stable state per row), and each unstable total state is followed directly by a unique stable state (by definition of flow table). It is thus possible to associate with each unstable total state of a flow table a **predecessor state** and a **successor state**.[1] For state A-01, the predecessor is A-00, and the successor is C-01.

The output is 0 for total states A-00 and C-01. If the output is 1 for state A-01, an output sequence 0-1-0 will result when X_2 changes from 0 to 1 with the circuit initially in state A. In this output sequence the 0 outputs will be levels that remain indefinitely until an input is changed. On the other hand, the 1 output will be a transient "spike" whose duration is determined by the circuit parameters. Moreover, this spike is a spurious output since the inputs are alternating. Thus, a 1 entry for the output in the A-01 state is incorrect because it produces a spurious output.[2]

In general, *the output associated with an unstable state must be the same as the output associated with the successor state whenever the successor state and the predecessor state have the same output.* The entries of Table 9.1-5 in rows C and F of the 00 column, row A of the 01 column, and row B of the 10 column fall into this category.

The other type of unstable entry is one in which the predecessor and successor outputs differ, for example the B-01 state of Table 9.1-5. In this case the output associated with the unstable state is unimportant. If the unstable-state output is the same as the predecessor output, no change in the output will take place until the stable state is reached. At worst, this situation can introduce a slight delay in

---

[1] These are stable total states, but since there is only one stable total state for each internal state, it is sufficient to specify the internal state only.

[2] If the output is being used to light an incandescent lamp or energize some other device which does not respond to short pulses, the spurious spike output may be unimportant. This should be stated in the specifications of the circuit and will not be assumed unless explicitly mentioned.

the formation of the new output value. No spurious transient outputs are developed. Thus, *the output associated with an unstable state is unspecified (d) whenever the output of the successor state and the output of the predecessor state differ.* Table 9.1-5b shows the output specification with *d* entries for Table 9.1-4d. Usually, the *d* entries will be used rather than having the unstable-state outputs always agree with the successor-state outputs. The small amount of output delay is usually compensated for by the economy that results from using the *d* entries.

Because Table 9.1-5 was written in primitive form it contains more internal states than are actually necessary. A technique for reducing the number of internal states without changing the circuit performance will be given in the Sec. 9.4.

9.1-5 Initial States

Thus far nothing has been said about the performance of a circuit when it is first put into operation (i.e., when the "power is turned on"). For all the circuits that have been presented previously, the stable state in which the circuit will be when power is applied, the **initial state**, will depend on the specific electrical properties of the circuit elements. Nothing is included in these circuits to constrain the initial state.

For the circuits of this section it isn't necessary to control the initial state in order to get correct operation. Each of these circuits is placed in the correct state by the arrival of the second pulse, and the output is undefined until this pulse occurs. These circuits are examples of a class of sequential circuit that has its output determined by a fixed number of past input values. For example, a circuit whose output is detemined by at most k past inputs has a t-expression of the form $Z(t) = f(X(t), X(t - 1), X(t - 2), \ldots, X(t - k))$. Such circuits are sometimes called **fixed-memory-span circuits**. Even if the initial state isn't controlled, they will produce correct output values after the kth input is received.

The counter circuits presented in Chap. 8 are examples of circuits for which the output will always depend on the initial state. For such circuits to operate correctly they must be started in an initial state corresponding to zero pulses having occurred. The class of circuits for which the output can depend on an unbounded number of previous inputs are sometimes called **unbounded memory span circuits**. For such circuits it is necessary to use an additional input, usually called the **reset input**, to place the circuit in a fixed initial state. Implementation of reset inputs is discussed in Sec. 8.2 under the heading "Asynchronous Inputs." This discussion assumes that all the flip-flops are to be put into the 0-state; (i.e., reset). For some circuits the all-0 state is not the desired initial state. In this case the reset input must be connected to the asynchronous set input for those devices that should be 1 for the initial state.

Even fixed-memory-span circuits should be designed with some mechanism for controlling the internal state. Such circuits may function properly without this mechanism, but the lack of such a facility can cause the circuit to be very difficult to test. This aspect of circuit design is discussed in Chap. 10.

During the initial design stages the reset circuitry is often omitted from the logic diagram since there is a standard form for such circuitry. Of course, the final diagram must show all of the circuitry that is to be included in the actual implementation.

9.1-6 Impossible Specifications

It is not always possible to write down a flow table corresponding to a sequential-circuit specification, because the corresponding circuit may not be physically realizable. The following is an example of such a specification.

Example 9.1-1: Specification for a Nonrealizable Sequential Circuit

> A FSM is to be designed. There are two inputs: A clock pulse and a level input, which represents the bits of a binary number ($b_n b_{n-1} \ldots b_1 b_0$). The order of appearance of signals on the level input is such that less significant bits precede more significant bits in time. Thus, at the first clock pulse a signal representing b_0 will occur, at the next clock-pulse time a signal representing b_1 will occur, etc. There is to be one output lead on which pulses representing the bits of the corresponding Gray-code number ($g_n g_{n-1} \ldots g_1 g_0$) are to occur. Specifically, at the clock-pulse time when a signal representing b_i occurs at the input, a pulse representing g_i is to occur at the output.

It is impossible to design a circuit to satisfy these specifications. The reason is that the rule for translating from binary to Gray code is given by $g_i = b_i \oplus b_{i+1}$. Since the ith Gray bit depends on both the ith and the $(i + 1)$st binary bits, the output of the specified circuit at one clock time depends on the input at the same clock time and on the input at the *next* clock time.

In general, any circuit whose output at a given time depends on some future input cannot be realized physically. In order to realize a circuit for the specifications of Example 9.1-1, it would be necessary to modify the specifications so that either the ith Gray bit appears at the output when the $(i + 1)$st binary bit appears on the input or the binary bits appear at the input in reverse order, with the more significant bits preceding less significant bits.

Even if the circuit specifications do not require the present output to depend on future inputs, it may not be possible to design a realizable circuit.

Example 9.1-2: Specification for a Nonrealizable Sequential Circuit That Does Not Involve Future Dependence

> The circuit is to operate in pulse mode with inputs X_1 and X_2 and a reset input r. There is one level output, Z, that is set equal to 0 by the occurrence of a pulse on the reset lead. The output becomes (and remains) equal to 1 when a pulse arrives on the X_1 input lead provided that (1) there has been exactly one X_2 pulse since the last reset pulse, and (2) there have been an equal number of X_1 pulses occurring after the X_2 pulse and before the X_2 pulse (but after the reset pulse). Thus, the output will equal 1 after the sequences $rX_1X_2X_1$, $rX_1X_1X_1X_2X_1X_1X_1$, whereas the output will be 0 after the sequences rX_1, $rX_1X_1X_2X_2X_1X_1$, $rX_1X_1X_2X_1$. In order to satisfy these specifications, the circuit would have to be capable of counting the number of X_1 pulses that occur after the last r pulse and before the first X_2 pulse. Since there is no limit on the number of such X_1 pulses that can occur, the circuit must be able to store an unbounded count. The circuit can contain only a finite number of flip-flops,

say m, and can count at most up to 2^m. Any circuit built to satisfy these specifications could always be forced to operate incorrectly by applying a sequence of X_1 pulses containing more than 2^m pulses.

A sequential-circuit specification can be nonrealizable either because the output depends on a future input or because an unbounded number of internal states are required by the specification. A more formal discussion of realizability is given in [Rabin 59] and [Kleene 56].

9.2 SIMPLIFICATION OF COMPLETELY SPECIFIED FLOW TABLES

Any specific sequential-circuit behavior can be described by many different flow tables. (Table 9.1-2 shows two flow tables for the same sequential function.) A designer is thus forced to choose which table to use; the final circuit will depend on which table is chosen. No method exists for selecting the particular flow table that will lead to the best circuit. The usual practice is to use the flow table that has the fewest rows (i.e., the fewest internal states). A *unique* minimum-state flow table exists for any fully specified flow table, that is, for any flow table that has no don't-care entries. A procedure for deriving the minimum-state flow table corresponding to any fully specified flow table is presented in this section.

There are a variety of reasons why a flow table may have more than the fewest possible states. In formulating the flow table the designer may inadvertently introduce more states than are needed. Sometimes a flow table is most easily formed by modifying another flow table. This technique is illustrated in Sec. 9.1-2 by means of an example that also shows how extra states may occur in the new table. The primitive-form flow tables used for fundamental-mode circuits typically contain many more states than the corresponding minimum-state tables.

While state reduction is usually discussed in connection with sequential-circuit synthesis, this technique can also be useful for analysis. Any circuit with s bistable elements can have 2^s internal states; thus a flow table derived from the circuit will have 2^s rows. However, it may be possible to describe the circuit operation with fewer internal states. It is usually easier to understand a table with fewer rows.

If two flow tables both describe the same sequential function they are said to be **indistinguishable**. Table 9.1-2 shows a pair of indistinguishable flow tables.

DEFINITION. Two flow tables are said to be **indistinguishable** iff for the same input sequence both tables always specify identical output sequences.

In general, the output sequence depends on the initial internal state. For flow tables with specified initial states, this definition assumes that the output sequences are derived assuming that each table is initialized correctly. When no initial states are specified, there must be a correspondence between states of the two tables: for each possible choice of a starting state for one table, there is a corresponding starting state of the other table that leads to identical outputs.

Corresponding to each fully specified flow table T there is a flow table that is both indistinguishable from T and has fewer states than any other table indistinguishable from T. This section will present a method for deriving this minimum-state table for any given fully specified table.

Use of a minimum-state flow table leads to a circuit that has the fewest possible memory elements. Such a circuit is usually the minimum-cost realization of the sequential function; however, there are examples where this is not the case. The best-known example of a circuit that uses extra internal states to realize the minimum-cost implementation of the function is the bipolar version of the D flip-flop. A logic diagram for this circuit is shown in Fig. 7.7-4. Three sets of cross-coupled NAND gate latches are used in this circuit. The circuit thus has three internal variables and eight internal states even though the flow table realized (Table 7.7-1c) requires only four internal states. A circuit for this flip-flop with only two memory elements is shown in Fig. 7.7-3a. A TTL implementation of this circuit requires more circuit elements than the version with three internal variables. No systematic method is known for designing circuits that use extra memory elements to get optimum realizations. The techniques described here use minimum-state flow tables to obtain efficient circuits.

9.2-1 Inaccessible States

Sometimes a flow table has states that are never used during normal operation. This is illustrated in Table 9.2-1: States 3 and 4 will never occur since there is no input sequence that leads from the initial state (state 1) to either state 3 or 4. States such as 3 and 4 are called **inaccessible states**. They can be removed from the flow table without changing the sequential function described by the table.

Even if there were no initial state specified in Table 9.2-1, states 3 and 4 would be considered inaccessible and could be removed. This is because there is no way to guarantee that these states would ever be entered. The only way for one of these states to occur would be for the circuit to go to either state 3 or 4 when power is first applied. Even if state 4 occurred when power was applied, the circuit would go to state 1 or 2 after the second clock pulse and would always be in state 1 or 2 for all succeeding clocks pulses. It is not possible to predict the exact response of a circuit built according to Table 9.2-1 with no initial state required. After the circuit is first powered there can be a transient output that will depend on the electrical details of the circuit implementation. The table with no initial state is an acceptable specification only if the first few outputs are un-

TABLE 9.2-1 Flow table with inaccessible states

	$\langle CK \rangle \uparrow$		
	X		
s	0	1	Z
Initial 1	1	2	0
2	2	1	1
3	1	2	0
4	2	3	1
		S	

important. Elimination of states 3 and 4 reduces the number of possible output sequences but still allows the desired patterns to occur.

DEFINITION. An internal state J is called **inaccessible** iff either (1) there is no input sequence that leads from the initial state to state J, or (2) if no initial state is specified, there is at least one state from which no input sequence leads to state J.

Part 2 of this definition describes the situation in which, with no initial state specification, there is at least one state which could occur when power is applied that would cause state J never to be entered.

Inaccessible states are more important for analysis than for manually generated flow tables. While an inaccessible state is not entered in normal operation, it is possible for such a state to occur as a result of a temporary fault. This must be taken into account in forming the state table.

In the remainder of this section it will be assumed that any inaccessible states have been removed from the flow tables considered. More precisely, the assumptions will be made that:

1. For flow tables in which an initial state is specified, there are no states in the table which cannot be "reached" from the initial state by the application of an appropriate input sequence.

2. For flow tables with no initial-state specification, it is assumed that a corresponding circuit can be started in any one of the states and therefore that for any ordered pair of states there is an input sequence which will cause the circuit to reach the second state of the pair if started initially in the first state of the pair.

9.2-2 Indistinguishability

The problem to be considered here is that of finding, for any given flow table T, the flow table T^* that is indistinguishable from the original table and that also has the fewest internal states of any such table. Before giving the general procedure, some specific examples will be considered to illustrate the concepts involved. Table 9.1-2 is repeated below as Table 9.2-2. In Sec. 9.1-2 it was concluded on an informal basis that the two flow tables in Table 9.1-2 both represent the same sequential function. Inspection of these tables shows that both states A and B of table T have been replaced by state E of table T^*. Also, states C and D are replaced by state F. The key to deriving a minimum-state table T^* from an arbitrary table T is determining which pairs of states of T can be replaced by a single state in T^*.

Figure 9.2-1 represents the situation in which the same input sequence $\mathbf{X}$ is applied to table T in state A, table T in state B, and table T^* in state E. The corresponding output sequences are represented as $\mathbf{z}(T, A)$, $\mathbf{z}(T, B)$, and $\mathbf{z}(T^*, E)$. If T^* is indistinguishable from T, and E corresponds to both states A and B; then it must be true that $\mathbf{z}(T^*, E) = \mathbf{z}(T, A)$ and $\mathbf{z}(T^*, E) = \mathbf{z}(T, B)$. It follows from this that $\mathbf{z}(T, A) = \mathbf{z}(T, B)$.

TABLE 9.2-2 Flow tables for FSM-P Example: (a) Table T, Table 9.1-1b modified for pulse outputs; (b) Table T^*, minimum-state table

		(a) $\langle CK' \rangle \uparrow$ X					(b) $\langle CK' \rangle \uparrow$ X	
$X(t-1)$	s	0	1		$X(t-1)$	s	0	1
0	A	$B,\,1$	$C,\,0$		0	E	$E,\,1$	$F,\,0$
0	B	$B,\,1$	$C,\,0$		1	F	$E,\,0$	$F,\,1$
1	C	$A,\,0$	$D,\,1$					
1	D	$A,\,0$	$D,\,1$				$S,\,z$	
		$S,\,z$						

A convenient way to discuss this situation is to define indistinguishability between states.

DEFINITION. An internal state p_i of a sequential circuit flow table P is **indistinguishable** from a state q_j of a flow table Q (P and Q can be the same table) if and only if, when table P is placed in state p_i, table Q is placed in state q_j, and the same input sequence is applied to both tables, the same output sequence results from both tables. This must be true for all possible input sequences. The fact that states p_i and q_j are indistinguishable will be written symbolically as $p_i \sim q_j$.

It is now possible to restate the definitions of table indistinguishability in terms of indistinguishability of states.

DEFINITION: INITIAL STATES SPECIFIED. Two flow tables P and Q are indistinguishable if and only if the initial states of P and Q are indistinguishable.

DEFINITION: NO INITIAL STATE SPECIFICATION. Two flow tables P and Q are indistinguishable if and only if for each state p_i of P there exists at least one state of Q which is indistinguishable from p_i and for each state q_j of Q there exists at least one state of P which is indistinguishable from q_j.

If two states are indistinguishable, they must both have the same output for each possible input. If this were not true, there would be some input that would produce different outputs and would thus violate the indistinguishability condition. Having identical outputs is not a sufficient condition for two states A and B to be indistinguishable: The next states that the states go to could have different outputs

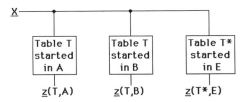

Figure 9.2-1 One X input sequence being applied to flow table T started in states A or B and at the same time being applied to table T^* started in state E.

so that $z(T, A) \neq z(T, B)$. This is illustrated by Table 9.2-3a. States A and B have identical outputs, but with $X = 1$ state A goes to state C while state B goes to state D. Since states C and D have different outputs when $X = 0$, the input sequence consisting of a 1 followed by a 0 will produce different outputs for starting states A and B. Thus states A and B are not indistinguishable, i.e., they are **distinguishable**. States A and B of Table 9.2-2a are indistinguishable since they have both identical outputs and also the same next states.

Table 9.2-3b shows a table in which two states, A and B, are indistinguishable even though they have different next-state entries. In this table it is clear that states C and D are indistinguishable since their output and next-state entries are identical. States A and B have identical outputs but different next-state entries. When $X = 1$ the next states for A and B are C and D. Since C is indistinguishable from D, the C next-state entry for state A can be replaced by D without changing the sequential function specified by the table. If this is done, states A and B have the same next-state entries when $X = 1$. Thus states A and B would be indistinguishable if they had the same next-states for $X = 0$. When $X = 0$ state A goes to state B and state B goes to state A. These transitions can never cause different outputs to be produced, so the conclusion is that states A and B are indistinguishable.

If the preceding discussion is formalized, the following theorem is easily proved.

THEOREM 9.2-1.   Two states A and B of a flow table T are indistinguishable if and only if: (a) they have identical outputs, and
(b) Their next-state entries are indistinguishable.

Methods for getting the minimum-state table T^* that is indistinguishable from a given (completely specified) table T will be presented next. The strategy is to partition the states of T into subsets such that each pair of states in the same subset are indistinguishable. The subsets are called the **indistinguishability classes** of T. For each indistinguishability class, there is one state in T^* that is indistinguishable from each state of the class. This is illustrated in Table 9.2-4. Part (a) shows a

TABLE 9.2-3   Flow tables illustrating indistinguishability: (a) A table with no indistinguishable states; (b) A table with two pairs of indistinguishable states

	(a)			(b)	
	$\langle CK' \rangle \uparrow$			$\langle CK' \rangle \uparrow$	
	X			X	
s	0	1	s	0	1
A	$B, 1$	$C, 0$	A	$B, 1$	$C, 0$
B	$B, 1$	$D, 0$	B	$A, 1$	$D, 0$
C	$A, 0$	$D, 1$	C	$A, 0$	$D, 1$
D	$A, 1$	$D, 1$	D	$A, 0$	$D, 1$
	S, z			S, z	

TABLE 9.2-4 Indistinguishable flow tables: (a) Example table T; (b) T^*, minimum-state table indistinguishable from T

	(a)				(b)	
	$\langle CK' \rangle \uparrow$				$\langle CK' \rangle \uparrow$	
	X				X	
s	0	1	s		0	1
1	1, 1	5, 0	[1]	A	A, 1	C, 0
2	1, 0	5, 0	[2]	B	A, 0	C, 0
3	2, 0	6, 0	[5, 6, 7, 8]	C	D, 0	C, 1
4	2, 0	6, 0	[3, 4]	D	B, 0	C, 0
5	3, 0	7, 1			S, z	
6	3, 0	7, 1				
7	4, 0	8, 1				
8	4, 0	8, 1				
	S, z					

flow table T and part (b) shows the corresponding table T^*. The indistinguishability classes of T are: [1], [2], [3, 4], and [5, 6, 7, 8]. Thus T^* has four states.

There are two approaches to finding the indistinguishability classes: The matrix or pair chart techniques check each pair of states to determine whether they are indistinguishable; the partition methods start with a partition that places all states with identical outputs in the same class and then adds additional classes as necessary. The partition method will be discussed next.

Testing for Indistinguishable States. Two states cannot be indistinguishable unless they have identical outputs, thus there must be at least as many indistinguishablity classes as there are different output specifications. Table 9.2-4a has three different output specifications. There must be at least three different indistinguishablity classes—[1], [2, 3, 4], [5, 6, 7, 8]—corresponding to these outputs. To find out whether these are actually indistinguishablity classes, it is necessary to check the next states to see whether they correspond to indistinguishable states. With $X = 1$, states 2 and 3 have next-state entries of 5 and 6, respectively. Since 5 and 6 are both in the same trial indistinguishablity class this test is passed. However, when $X = 0$ states 1 and 2 are the next states for states 2 and 3. Since states 1 and 2 are in different classes, this means that states 2 and 3 are not indistinguishable even though they have the same outputs. A new set of trial indistinguishability classes is formed by putting state 2 in a new class: [1], [2], [3, 4], [5, 6, 7, 8]. States 3 and 4 have identical next-state entries. States 5, 6, 7, and 8 have next-state entries that are either identical or are in the same class. Thus, this set of four classes does represent a set of indistinguishablity classes and corresponds to the minimum-state table T^* of Table 9.2-4b.

A technique for carrying out the computations required by this method is illustrated in Table 9.2-5, which shows the table T of Table 9.2-4 with each state symbol followed by a letter corresponding to an indistinguishability class. Part (a) corresponds to using the three classes A [1], B [2, 3, 4], and C [5, 6, 7, 8], based only on the outputs. Inspection of this table shows that rows 2 and 3 have

TABLE 9.2-5 Partition test for indistinguishability of Table 9.2-4a: (a) First step; (b) Second step

	(a) $\langle CK' \rangle \uparrow$			(b) $\langle CK' \rangle \uparrow$	
	X			X	
s	0	1	s	0	1
1 A	1 A, 1	5 C, 0	1 A	1 A, 1	5 C, 0
2 B	1 A, 0	5 C, 0	2 B	1 A, 0	5 C, 0
3 B	2 B, 0	6 C, 0	3 B D	2 B, 0	6 C, 0
4 B	2 B, 0	6 C, 0	4 B D	2 B, 0	6 C, 0
5 C	3 B, 0	7 C, 1	5 C	3 B D, 0	7 C, 1
6 C	3 B, 0	7 C, 1	6 C	3 B D, 0	7 C, 1
7 C	4 B, 0	8 C, 1	7 C	4 B D, 0	8 C, 1
8 C	4 B, 0	8 C, 1	8 C	4 B D, 0	8 C, 1
	S, z			S, z	

the same letter for the present state, but different next-state letters (A and B) for $X = 0$. This means that 2 and 3 must be in different indistinguishability classes. A new indistinguishability class D [3, 4] is introduced in part (b) in order to separate state 2 from state 3. Class B is changed to [2]. Both states 3 and 4 are placed in class D since they have identical next-state entries. In part (b) all present states with the same class letter have the same next-state entries. This table thus corresponds to a partition of the original states into indistinguishability classes. Since it also contains the fewest such classes it corresponds directly to the minimum-state table T^*. T^* is formed by selecting one row for each of the present-state indistinguishability classes (e.g. rows 1, 2, 5, 3) and removing all state labels except the last letter in each column. A more complex example of this process is shown in Table 9.2-6. The output entries in this table are associated with present states rather than total states to illustrate the fact that this procedure works for either type of output function.

The other approach to finding the indistinguishability classes tests each pair of states to determine whether they are indistinguishable. Methods using this approach will be called array techniques since they use an array or pair chart such as shown in Table 9.2-7 to record the results of the state-pair tests. An array of $(1/2)(s)(s - 1)$ entries rather than a full s by s matrix is sufficient for an s-state table because of the reflexive and symmetric properties of indistinguishability. The reflexive property just states that a state is always indistinguishable from itself. Since state A is always indistinguishable from state B if state B is indistinguishable from state A, the indistinguishability relation is said to be symmetric. Because of the reflexive property it isn't necessary to compare a state with itself, thus the main diagonal entries of the matrix for state pairs aren't needed. The symmetric property means that the order in which a pair of states are compared is unimportant. This means that none of the matrix entries above the main diagonal are necessary. This means that only $(1/2)(s)(s - 1)$ state pair comparisons are required rather than $(s)(s)$.

TABLE 9.2-6 Partition test for indistinguishability example: (a) Flow table; (b) Partition test; (c) Minimum-state table

(a)

$\langle CK' \rangle \uparrow$
X

	0	1	Z_1	Z_2
1	5	3	0	0
2	3	1	0	0
3	2	7	0	0
4	7	1	0	0
5	6	2	1	0
6	5	4	0	0
7	4	7	0	0

(b)

$\langle CK' \rangle \uparrow$
X

		0		1
1 A		5 B		3 A CD
2 A C		3 ACD		1 A
3 A CD		2 AC		7 A CD
4 A C		7 ACD		1 A
5 B		6 A	E	2 A C
6 A	E	5 B		4 A C
7 A CD		4 AC		7 A CD

A[1], B[5], C[2, 4], D[3, 7], E[6]

(c)

$\langle CK' \rangle \uparrow$
X

		0	1	Z_1	Z_2
[1]	A	B	D	0	0
[5]	B	E	C	1	0
[2, 4]	C	C	A	0	0
[3, 7]	D	C	D	0	0
[6]	E	B	C	0	0

Indistinguishability has another important property: transitivity, by which is meant that if state A is indistinguishable from state B and state B is indistinguishable from state C, then states A and C must be indistinguishable. Any relation defined on a set of objects that has these three properties is called an **equivalence relation**. An equivalence relation has the important characteristic of partitioning the set into nonoverlapping subsets. Each member of a subset is said to be equivalent to all the other elements in the subset. The reason that incompletely specified flow tables are more difficult to simplify than completely specified flow tables is because the relation among states that can be combined is not an equivalence relation since it isn't transitive.

Table 9.2-7 shows an array technique used to determine the indistinguishability classes of Table 9.2-4a. The array has one cell for each pair of states. The first step of this technique is to place an X in all cells that correspond to state pairs having different outputs. Each remaining pair of states is then examined. If a pair of states has identical next-state entries, an asterisk is placed in the corresponding cell to show that the pair is indistinguishable. The entries of the remaining cells are the pairs of states that must be indistinguishable in order for the pair represented by the cell to be indistinguishable. For example, in Table 9.2-7a the cell for the pair 2, 3 (row 3 of column 2) has two entries, 12 and 56. The 12 entry is present because when $X = 0$ state 2 has 1 for the next state entry while state 3 has state 2 as its next state. Thus in order for states 2 and 3 to be indis-

TABLE 9.2-7 Arrays for determining indistinguishability classes for the flow table of Table 9.2-4a: (a) First step of procedure; (b) Final array

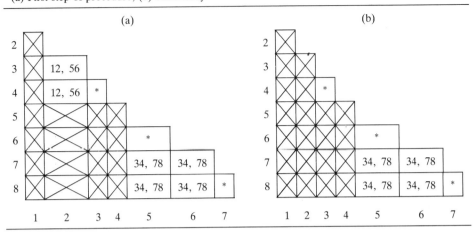

tinguishable it is necessary that states 1 and 2 are indistinguishable. The 56 entry comes from the next states when $X = 1$.

Table 9.2-7b shows the result of a second pass through the array. An X is placed in any cell that contains an entry corresponding to another cell containing an X. For example, the 2-3 cell of Table 9.2-7b has an X because it contains a 12 entry and the 1-2 cell of Table 9.2-7a has an X. The X in the 1-2 cell means that states 1 and 2 are distinguishable. Since states 2 and 3 have a pair of next-state entries (1 and 2) that are distinguishable, states 2 and 3 must be distinguishable. This process is continued until no additional X entries are generated. The remaining cells that do not contain X's are indistinguishable. Table 9.2-7b shows the result of this procedure and indicates that the indistinguishability classes for Table 9.2-4a are [1], [2], [3, 4], and [5, 6, 7, 8].

TABLE 9.2-8 Arrays for determining indistinguishability classes for the flow table of Table 9.2-6a: (a) After second step of procedure; (b) Final array

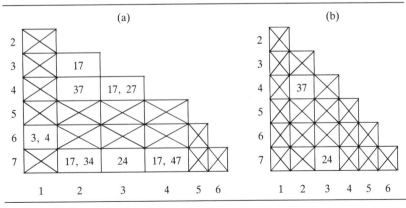

The arrays for the flow table of Table 9.2-6a are shown in Table 9.2-8. Note that the 2-3 cell does not have a 23 entry corresponding to the next-state entries in the flow table since an entry that is the same as the pair represented by the cell can never cause the cell pair to be distinguishable. A variation of the array technique described here in which several arrays are formed—one for each output specification—is sometimes useful. The choice of which method to use to solve a particular problem is a matter of personal choice. Both the array and the partition techniques will produce the same answer.

Unspecified entries are typically present in fundamental-mode flow tables and can also occur in pulse-mode flow tables. Incompletely specified flow tables are considerably more complex to simplify than completely specified tables. The discussion of forming minimum-state tables for incompletely specified flow tables is not discussed until a later section so as not to postpone the design of actual circuits any further. The next step after finding the minimum-state flow table is the formation of the transition table by assigning internal variable states to the flow-table states. This is discussed in the following section.

9.3 TRANSITION AND EXCITATION TABLES FOR PULSE-MODE CIRCUITS

Going from a pulse-mode flow table to a circuit requires converting the flow table into a transition table and then forming an excitation table. Forming the transition table requires the assignment of a unique combination of internal variable values to each state of the flow table. If the flow table has r internal states, at least $S_0 = \lceil \log_2 r \rceil$ internal variables are necessary, since the number of different combinations of values that can be assigned to m variables is 2^m. (The symbol $\lceil v \rceil$ stands for the smallest integer that is greater than or equal to v.) The formation of the transition table is straightforward since it involves a direct substitution of the same binary number for each appearance of a state symbol of the flow table. It is always possible to realize a pulse-mode circuit that uses only S_0 internal variables; for a fundamental-mode circuit it may be necessary to use more than S_0 internal variables in order to avoid critical races. The formation of transition and excitation tables for pulse-mode circuits is discussed in this section. The problems peculiar to fundamental-mode operation are considered in Sec. 9.5.

The FSM-P circuit flow table (Table 9.1-2b) is repeated as Table 9.3-1b. Since there are two states, only one internal variable is required. If $y = 0$ is used for state E and $y = 1$ is used for state F, the transition table of Table 9.3-1c results. The excitation table for D flip-flops is identical to the transition table. Part (d) of the table shows the excitation functions derived from part (c), and the resulting circuit is given in Fig. 9.3-1.

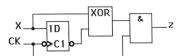

Figure 9.3-1 Logic diagram for FSM-P circuit.

TABLE 9.3-1 Design of FSM-P circuit: (a) t-expression; (b) Flow table from Table 9.1-2b; (c) Transition table; (d) Excitation functions

(a)

$$z(t) = CK[X'(t) \oplus X(t - 1)]$$

(b)

$\langle CK' \rangle \uparrow$

s	X 0	1
E	$E, 1$	$F, 0$
F	$E, 0$	$F, 1$

S, z

(c)

$\langle CK' \rangle \uparrow$

y	X 0	1
0	0, 1	1, 0
1	0, 0	1, 1

Y, z
D, z

$$D = X\langle CK' \rangle \uparrow, \qquad z = (X \oplus y')CK$$

In a sense this illustrates the entire design process. However, the question of whether a "better" circuit can be designed remains. There are two major issues: (1) would a different assignment of internal variables lead to a better circuit, and (2) whether the D flip-flop is the best type of flip-flop to use? These two questions will be considered next.

9.3-1 Internal Variable Assignments—Symmetries

For pulse-mode operation, any internal variable assignment for which a unique combination of values of the internal variables is assigned to each internal state will lead to a legitimate sequential circuit. However, the choice of a particular assignment can have a considerable effect on the economy of the final circuit. It would therefore be desirable to have a method of choosing that assignment which would result in the most economical circuit. Of course, this would depend on the criteria of economy that are used, and different assignments could result for different criteria. One possiblity would be to form the excitation table for each possible assignment and then to choose the most economical of the corresponding circuits. Before advocating such a procedure it would be wise to determine the number of such assignments that would have to be considered.

It is not true that the most economical sequential circuit for a given flow table will always contain only S_0 internal variables. It may be possible to decrease the total number of elements in the circuit by using more than the minimum number of flip-flops or feedback loops. In counting the number of assignments, only those involving S_0 internal variables will be considered. This results in a conservative estimate of the amount of work involved in enumeration but simplifies the discussion. It will not affect the final conclusions. For a flow table with r rows, the number of different assignments of S_0 variables is

$$\frac{2^{S_0}!}{(2^{S_0} - r)!}$$

This is a rapidly growing function, equaling 24 for $r = 3$ and 6270 for $r = 5$. However, it is not necessary to consider each of these assignments individually in order to determine the most economical circuit.

If a circuit were designed for a flow table using assignment I of Table 9.3-2a, a circuit corresponding to assignment II could be obtained merely by relabeling the appropriate leads in the circuit for assignment I. Since assignment II involves a permutation of the variables of assignment I, there can be no gain in economy by using assignment II rather than assignment I. Thus, assignments that are permutations of the variables of other assignments need not be considered explicitly, and only one representative from each permutation need be studied.

Assignment III of Table 9.3-2a is obtained from assignment I by complementing y_2. It is possible to obtain the excitation functions for assignment III directly from those for assignment I, as shown in Table 9.3-2b. In a flip-flop circuit the change from assignment I to assignment III might involve some rewiring (depending on the type of flip-flop) but would not involve the addition of any components. In a circuit using feedback loops there is a possibility of a change in the number of required inverters. In any case, it is not necessary to construct new excitation tables for assignments that differ from an already studied assignment

TABLE 9.3-2 Permutation and complementation of internal variables:
(a) Assignments; (b) Excitation functions

(a)

Internal states	Assignment I		Assignment II		Assignment III	
	y_1	y_2	y_1	y_2	y_1	y_2
A	0	0	0	0	0	1
B	0	1	1	0	0	0
C	1	1	1	1	1	0
D	1	0	0	1	1	1

(b)

Assignment I	Assignment III
$Y_1 = f_1(y_1, y_2, X_1, X_2)$	$Y_1 = f_1(y_1, y_2', X_1, X_2)$
$Y_2 = f_2(y_1, y_2, X_1, X_2)$	$Y_2 = [f_2(y_1, y_2', X_1, X_2)]'$
$Z = g(y_1, y_2, X_1, X_2)$	$Z = g(y_1, y_2', X_1, X_2)$
$S_1 = h_1(y_1, y_2, X_1, X_2)$	$S_1 = h_1(y_1, y_2', X_1, X_2)$
$R_1 = h_2(y_1, y_2, X_1, X_2)$	$R_1 = h_2(y_1, y_2', X_1, X_2)$
$S_2 = k_1(y_1, y_2, X_1, X_2)$	$S_2 = k_2(y_1, y_2', X_1, X_2)$
$R_2 = k_2(y_1, y_2, X_1, X_2)$	$R_2 = k_1(y_1, y_2', X_1, X_2)$

TABLE 9.3-3 Number of distinct assignments of S_0 variables to r states

r	S_0	Number of distinct assignments
1	0	1
2	1	1
3	2	3
4	2	3
5	3	140
6	3	420
7	3	840
8	3	840
9	4	10,810,800

only in some complemented variables. Two assignments are said to be distinct if it is not possible to obtain one assignment from the other by complementing and permuting variables; the number of distinct assignments of S_0 variables to r states is:

$$\frac{(2^{S_0} - 1)!}{(2^{S_0} - r)! S_0!}$$

The derivation of this formula is given in [McCluskey 59] and will not be discussed here. Table 9.3-3 lists the values given by this formula for values of r from 1 to 9. It is clear from these values that enumeration by hand is feasible for values of r up to 4 and that for values of r greater than 8 even use of a high-speed digital computer would be highly questionable. Three distinct assignments for four states are shown in Table 9.3-4. A complete study of the possible assignments of two internal variables to a four-row flow table can be made by using these assignments to form transition tables.

Table 9.3-5 shows the formation of the D flip-flop excitation functions for the FSM-L circuit of Sec. 9.1-1. Parts (b)–(d) of this table show the transition tables for the three distinct assignments listed in Table 9.3-4. In most technologies, the functions of part (d) (corresponding to assignment III) would be more expensive to implement than the functions from the other two assignments. The assignment I functions [part (b)] would probably lead to the simplest circuit.

TABLE 9.3-4 Three distinct assignments of two variables to four states

State	Assignment I		Assignment II		Assignment III	
s	y_1	y_2	y_1	y_2	y_1	y_2
A	0	0	0	0	0	0
B	0	1	0	1	1	1
C	1	1	1	0	0	1
D	1	0	1	1	1	0

TABLE 9.3-5 Design of the FSM-L circuit using D flip-flops and all three distinct internal variable assignments: (a) Flow table; (b) Transition table for Assignment I; (c) Transition table for Assignment II; (d) Transition table for Assignment III

(a)

I $y_1\ y_2$	II $y_1\ y_2$	III $y_1\ y_2$	s	$\langle CK\rangle\uparrow$ X 0	1	Z
0 0	0 0	0 0	A	B	C	0
0 1	0 1	1 1	B	B	C	1
1 1	1 0	0 1	C	A	D	0
1 0	1 1	1 0	D	A	D	1

S

(b)

$y_1\ y_2$	$\langle CK\rangle\uparrow$ X 0	1	Z
A 0 0	01	11	0
B 0 1	01	11	1
C 1 1	00	10	0
D 1 0	00	10	1

$Y_1 Y_2$
$D_1 D_2$

$D_1 = X,\qquad D_2 = y_1'$
$Z = y_1 \oplus y_2$

(c)

$y_1\ y_2$	$\langle CK\rangle\uparrow$ X 0	1	Z
A 0 0	01	10	0
B 0 1	01	10	1
D 1 1	00	11	1
C 1 0	00	11	0

$Y_1 Y_2$
$D_1 D_2$

$D_1 = X,\qquad D_2 = X \oplus y_1'$
$Z = y_2$

(d)

$y_1\ y_2$	$\langle CK\rangle\uparrow$ X 0	1	Z
A 0 0	11	01	0
C 0 1	00	10	0
B 1 1	11	01	1
D 1 0	00	10	1

$Y_1 Y_2$
$D_1 D_2$

$D_1 = X' \oplus y_1 \oplus y_2$
$D_2 = y_1 \oplus y_2$
$Z = y_1$

It should be emphasized that it may be worthwhile to complement one of the internal variables in the final circuit, but this possibility can be determined without explicitly forming any additional transition tables. Use of Table 9.3-2b is sufficient. For example, in the circuit of Table 9.3-1 there is only one other possible assignment: setting $y = 1$ to represent state E. If this is done, $D = X'\langle CK'\rangle\uparrow$ and $z = (X \oplus y)CK$. These could be more expensive to implement than the functions of Table 9.3-1d if the X' signal is not available and requires use of an Inverter. These issues are discussed in more detail in [Rhyne 77].

The cost of a sequential circuit can vary widely depending on the particular internal variable assignment used. Enumeration of all assignments is possible only for very small tables. Larger tables require the use of heuristic techniques to obtain good assignments. One such approach is presented in [Dolotta 64] and extensions are discussed in [Tumbush 74] and [DeMicheli 84]. Since the choice of a good assignment is an important component of a computer-aided-design (CAD) system, it is to be expected that improved programs will be developed. The details of these techniques are beyond the scope of this book and will not be discussed further.

9.3-2 Flip-Flop Excitation Tables

For D flip-flops the excitation table is the same as the transition table. The D excitation functions can be obtained directly from the transition table by the appropriate minimization procedure. For other types of flip-flops the transition table must be changed into an excitation table. For any flip-flop, the values of y and Y determine which signals must be applied at the inputs.

Table 9.3-6 shows the rules for the flip-flop inputs required to cause each y-Y transition. For the S-R and J-K flip-flops there are some y-Y transitions in which the value on one of the inputs can be either a 0 or a 1. Since these situations represent "don't-care" conditions, they are indicated by a d entry in the table. Thus, if an S-R flip-flop is in the 0, or reset state ($y = 0$), and is to remain in this state ($Y = 0$), it is permissible to apply either a 0 or a 1 to the R input. The S input must have a 0 applied. A table such as Table 9.3-6 which shows the relations among y, Y, and the flip-flop inputs is called a **flip-flop application table**.

Table 9.3-7 illustrates the derivation of the S and R functions for the transition table of Table 9.3-5b (assignment I for the FSM-L circuit). Part (a) of this table repeats the transition table. Part (b) shows the excitation table for S-R flip-flops and the corresponding Karnaugh map for S_1 is shown in part (c). The excitation functions are listed in part (d).

For S-R and J-K flip-flops it is possible to obtain a more compact excitation table by making use of the special codes shown in Table 9.3-6. This possibility arises because only four of the nine possible combinations of entries for S and R (or J and K) are used. An excitation table using the S-R codes is shown in Table 9.3-7e. The minimal sums for S and R (or J and K) can be determined directly from maps of the coded values. This is illustrated in Table 9.3-7f. The minimal sum for S is formed by including all fundamental products encoded with an S and as many fundamental products encoded with s or d as are helpful. In the minimal sum for R it is necessary to include all fundamental products encoded with an R and as many fundamental products encoded with r or d as are helpful.

Table 9.3-8 shows the FSM-L circuit excitation functions for D, S-R, J-K and T flip-flops for all three internal variable assignments. Assignment I yields functions that are easiest to implement in most technologies. Figure 9.3-2 shows three circuits for this circuit. Part (a) uses D flip-flops. Part (b) uses a D flip-flop for Y_1, an S-R flip-flop for Y_2, and implements Z without using an XOR gate. If both D and S-R flip-flops are available, the S-R device may be less costly than the D

TABLE 9.3-6 Flip-flop application table

y	Y	S	R	Code	J	K	Code	T
0	0	0	d	r	0	d	k	0
0	1	1	0	S	1	d	J	1
1	0	0	1	R	d	1	K	1
1	1	d	0	s	d	0	j	0

TABLE 9.3-7 Excitation functions for the FSM-L circuit using *S-R* flip-flops: (a) Transition table; (b) Excitation table; (c) Karnaugh map for S_1; (d) Excitation functions; (e) Excitation table using coded entries; (f) Map for S_1 and R_1 codes

(a)

$\langle CK \rangle \uparrow$
X

$y_1\ y_2$	0	1	Z
A 0 0	01	11	0
B 0 1	01	11	1
C 1 1	00	10	0
D 1 0	00	10	1

$Y_1 Y_2$

(b)

$\langle CK \rangle \uparrow$
X

$y_1\ y_2$	0	1	Z
0 0	0d, 10	10, 10	0
0 1	0d, d0	10, d0	1
1 1	01, 01	d0, 01	0
1 0	01, 0d	d0, 0d	1

$S_1 R_1,\ S_2 R_2$

(c)

$\langle CK \rangle \uparrow$
X

$y_1\ y_2$	0	1	Z
0 0	0	1	0
0 1	0	1	1
1 1	0	d	0
1 0	0	d	1

$S_1 = X$

(d)

$S_1 = X, \qquad R_1 = X'$

$S_2 = y_1', \qquad R_2 = y_1$

$Z - y_1 \oplus y_2$

(e)

$\langle CK \rangle \uparrow$
X

$y_1\ y_2$	0	1
0 0	r, S	S, S
0 1	r, s	S, s
1 1	R, R	s, R
1 0	R, r	s, r

SR

(f)

$\langle CK \rangle \uparrow$
X

$y_1\ y_2$	0	1
0 0	r	S
0 1	r	S
1 1	R	s
1 0	R	s

$S_1 R_1$

flip-flop. An XOR gate must contain internal inversion while the AND-NOR connection shown in part (b) for Z does not. If flip-flops that provide both Q and Q' outputs are used, it may be more efficient to use the AND-NOR network than the XOR gate. Part (c) of the figure shows a circuit that might be preferred if

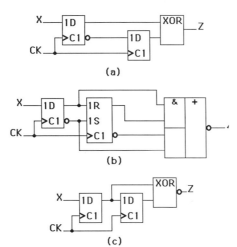

(a)

(b)

(c)

Figure 9.3-2 Three designs for FSM-L circuit using assignment I: (a) *D* flip-flops used; (b) *D* flip-flop used for y_1 and *S-R* flip-flop used for y_2; (c) circuit that does not require Q'.

TABLE 9.3-8 Excitation functions for FSM-L circuit using all three internal variable assignments for four types of flip-flops

	I	II	III
$D_1 =$	X	X	$X \oplus y_1 \oplus y_2$
$D_2 =$	y_1'	$X \oplus y_1'$	$y_1 \oplus y_2'$
$S_1 =$	X	X	$y_1'(X \oplus y_2')$
$R_1 =$	X'	X'	$y_1(X \oplus y_2')$
$S_2 =$	y_1'	$X \oplus y_1'$	$y_1'y_2'$
$R_2 =$	y_1	S_2'	$y_1'y_2$
$J_1 =$	X	X	$X \oplus y_2'$
$K_1 =$	X'	X'	J_1
$J_2 =$	y_1'	$X \oplus y_1'$	y_1'
$K_2 =$	y_1	J_2'	J_2
$T_1 =$	$X \oplus y_1$	$X \oplus y_1$	$X \oplus y_2'$
$T_2 =$	$y_1 \oplus y_2'$	$X' \oplus y_1 \oplus y_2$	y_1'
$Z =$	$y_1 \oplus y_2$	y_2	y_1

TABLE 9.3-9 Derivation of excitation functions for 2P-P Circuit; (a) Flow table; (b) Transition table; (c) S-R flip-flop excitation table; (d) T flip-flop excitation table; (e) Excitation functions

(a)

s	$\langle X_1 \rangle \downarrow$	$\langle X_2 \rangle \downarrow$
E	$E, 1$	$F, 0$
F	$E, 0$	$F, 1$

S, z

(b)

y	$\langle X_1 \rangle \downarrow$	$\langle X_2 \rangle \downarrow$
0	$0, 1$	$1, 0$
1	$0, 0$	$1, 1$

Y, z

(c)

y	$\langle X_1 \rangle \downarrow$	$\langle X_2 \rangle \downarrow$
0	r	s
1	R	S

SR

(d)

y	$\langle X_1 \rangle \downarrow$	$\langle X_2 \rangle \downarrow$
0	0	1
1	1	0

T

(e)

$$D = 0\langle X_1 \rangle \downarrow + 1\langle X_2 \rangle \downarrow$$

$$S = 1\langle X_2 \rangle \downarrow ; \qquad R = 1\langle X_1 \rangle \downarrow$$

$$T = y\langle X_1 \rangle \downarrow + y'\langle X_2 \rangle \downarrow$$

$$z = y'X_1 + yX_2$$

the flip-flops used don't have double-rail outputs (Q and Q'). If y_2 is complemented in Assignment I, the excitation function for D_2 is changed from y_1' to y_1. The circuit of part (c) which doesn't require Q' is obtained by this change of assignment. Note that it wasn't necessary to form another excitation table to obtain this circuit.

Multiple-pulse Mode Circuits. The excitation functions for the 2P-P circuit of Sec. 9.1-3 are shown in Table 9.3-9 and the corresponding logic diagrams are given in Fig. 9.3-3. Part (a) is a direct implementation of the D flip-flop functions; part (b) makes use of the non-gated S-R flip-flop discussed in Sec. 8.2-1 to realize the set-reset functions. The part (b) circuit is reset on the trailing edge of an X_1 pulse and set on the trailing edge of an X_2 pulse. Circuits using T flip-flops are shown in parts (c) and (d).

The design of the 2P-L circuit is shown in Table 9.3-10 and Fig. 9.3-4. The table shows the derivation of the excitation functions when assignment II is used. The figure shows the logic diagram of a circuit using the non-gated S-R flip-flop for y_1 and a two-port D flip-flop for y_2.

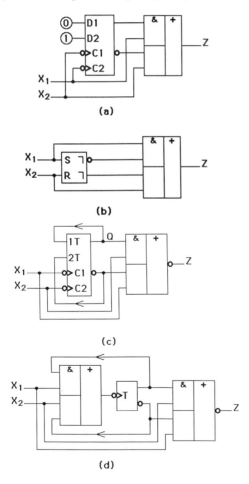

(a)

(b)

(c)

(d)

Figure 9.3-3 Logic designs for 2P-P circuit: (a) two-port D flip-flop circuit; (b) nongated S-R flip-flop circuit; (c) two-port T flip-flop circuit; (d) nongated T flip-flop circuit.

TABLE 9.3-10 Formation of excitation functions for 2P-L Circuit: (a) Flow Table; (b) Transition table using Assignment II; (c) S-R Flip-flop excitation table; (d) Excitation functions

(a)

s	$\langle X_1 \rangle \uparrow$	$\langle X_2 \rangle \uparrow$	Z
A	B	C	0
B	B	C	1
C	A	D	0
D	A	D	1

S

(b)

$y_1\ y_2$	$\langle X_1 \rangle \uparrow$	$\langle X_2 \rangle \uparrow$	Z
A	0 0	0 1	1 0	0
B	0 1	0 1	1 0	1
D	1 1	0 0	1 1	1
C	1 0	0 0	1 1	0

Y_1Y_2

(c)

$y_1\ y_2$	$\langle X_1 \rangle \uparrow$	$\langle X_2 \rangle \uparrow$
0 0	$r\ S$	$S\ r$
0 1	$r\ s$	$S\ R$
1 1	$R\ R$	$s\ s$
1 0	$R\ r$	$s\ S$

SR

(d)

$$D_1 = (0)\langle X_1 \rangle \uparrow + (1)\langle X_2 \rangle \uparrow$$

$$D_2 = y_1'\langle X_1 \rangle \uparrow + y_1\langle X_2 \rangle \uparrow$$

$$S_1 = \langle X_2 \rangle \uparrow, \qquad R_1 = \langle X_1 \rangle \uparrow$$

$$S_2 = y_1'\langle X_1 \rangle \uparrow + y_1\langle X_2 \rangle \uparrow$$

$$R_2 = y_1\langle X_1 \rangle \uparrow + y_1'\langle X_2 \rangle \uparrow$$

$$Z = y_2$$

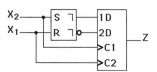

Figure 9.3-4 Logic diagram for 2P-L circuit.

9.4 STATE REDUCTION FOR INCOMPLETELY SPECIFIED FLOW TABLES

The two preceding sections show how to design a pulse-mode sequential circuit from a completely specified flow table. To design efficient circuits for incompletely specified flow tables, state reduction of such tables is necessary. Most pulse-mode circuit designs come from completely specified flow tables, but it is possible for a pulse mode circuit design to be incompletely specified. For example, some input sequences may not be possible due to the external source of the inputs. Such a situation causes unspecified entries in the flow table. Since fundamental-mode tables are written in primitive form and usually assume single input changes, they almost always have many entries unspecified. In summary, state reduction of incompletely specified flow tables is needed for almost all fundamental-mode tables and for some pulse-mode tables. This section presents a method to reduce the states in an incompletely specified flow table.

9.4-1 I-Equivalence

The first step in reducing the states in an incompletely specified table is to combine all pairs of indistinguishable states. A modified definition of indistinguishibility is needed since the definition given in Sec. 9.2 doesn't take unspecified entries into account. The term "*I*-equivalence" is often used for state indistinguishability in incompletely specified tables. For two states to be *I*-equivalent they must produce identical outputs when the outputs are specified, and they must both produce *d*-outputs when either of the states has an unspecified output (*d*). Further, if either state has an unspecified next state, both states must have the next state unspecified. In other words, for the purposes of *I*-equivalence, an unspecified output is treated as a specific output value and an unspecified next state is handled as if the dash referred to a specific state. Thus, two states are *I*-equivalent unless (1) they have different output entries for some input state, or (2) one state's next-state entry is unspecified for the same input state for which the other state's entry is specified, or (3) for some input state the next-state entries are not *I*-equivalent.

I-equivalence is illustrated by Table 9.4-1 in which part (a) shows a flow table in which the state pairs [1, 6] and [2, 3] are *I*-equivalent. Part (b) shows the reduced flow table in which each *I*-equivalent pair is replaced by a single state. Any of the techniques of Sec. 9.2 can be used to determine *I*-equivalence.

For incompletely specified flow tables, a reduced table such as Table 9.4-1b, in which all *I*-equivalent states have been combined does not necessarily represent a minimum-state flow table. For example, Table 9.4-1a can be replaced by a Table 9.4-1f which has only two states while Table 9.4-1b has four states. State reduction for flow tables having no pairs of *I*-equivalent states is considered next.

9.4-2 Compatibility

Consider states 2 and 4 of Table 9.3-1b and state *C* in Table 9.3-1c. State *C* agrees with states 2 and 4 wherever either or both are specified. Thus, a new table that has state *C* instead of states 2 and 4 will have the same specifications as Table 9.3-1b. States such as 2 and 4 whose outputs and next states agree whenever either or both are specified are said to be **compatible**. More formally, two states *A* and *B* are compatible iff:

1. The outputs are the same whenever both are specified, and
2. The next-state entries are compatible whenever both are specified.

The array techniques described in Sec. 9.2 are used to find compatible states as shown in Table 9.4-1d. If the state pair has conflicting outputs specified, they are incompatible. The other reason for the state pair to be incompatible is that their next-state entries are incompatible. A set of states for which every pair of states is compatible is called a **compatibility class**. The compatibility classes for Table 9.4-1b are listed in Table 9.4-1e. Table 9.4-2 shows an example where there are three states in one compatibility class. In general there can be many states in a compatibility class.

TABLE 9.4-1 State reduction example: (a) Flow table; (b) *I*-equivalent states removed; (c) Compatible state; (d) Pair chart; (e) Maximal compatibility classes; (f) Minimum-state table

(a)

	$\langle v \rangle \uparrow$ X		$\langle w \rangle \uparrow$ X	
s	0	1	0	1
1	6, 0	1, 0	2, 0	4, 0
2	-, d	6, 0	2, 0	4, 0
3	-, d	1, 0	3, 0	4, 0
4	5, 1	-, d	2, 0	4, 0
5	5, 1	5, 0	3, 0	4, 0
6	1, 0	6, 0	3, 0	4, 0

S, z

(b)

		$\langle v \rangle \uparrow$ X		$\langle w \rangle \uparrow$ X	
	s	0	1	0	1
(6)	1	1, 0	1, 0	2, 0	4, 0
(3)	2	-, d	1, 0	2, 0	4, 0
	4	5, 1	-, d	2, 0	4, 0
	5	5, 1	5, 0	2, 0	4, 0

S, z

(c)

[2, 4]	C	5, 1	1, 0	C, 0	C, 0

(d)

(e)

[4, 5], [2, 4], [1, 2]

(f)

		$\langle v \rangle \uparrow$ X		$\langle w \rangle \uparrow$ X	
	s	0	1	0	1
[1, 2, 3, 6]	A	A, 0	A, 0	A, 0	B, 0
[4, 5]	B	B, 0	B, 0	A, 0	B, 0

S

Maximal Compatibility Classes. Those classes that are not subsets of any other compatibility class are called **maximal compatibility classes**. For example, in Table 9.4-2 states 3 and 4 are compatible so that [3, 4] is a compatibility class. It is not a maximal compatibility class since it is a subset of the compatibility class [3, 4, 5]. There are many procedures possible for obtaining the maximal compatibility classes from the compatibility table. One of these involves considering each of the columns separately, starting at the rightmost column. This procedure is as follows:

1. List those pairs of states which are shown to be compatible in the rightmost column of the table for which any such pairs exist. For Table 9.4-2 this means that the pair 4, 5 is listed.

2. Proceed to the next column to the left. If the state to which this column corresponds is compatible with all members of a previously determined com-

patibility class, add this state to the class. If the state is not compatible with all members of a class but is compatible with a subset of the class, form a new class, including the current state and the subclass. Finally, list any compatible pairs that are not included in any already determined class. Do not retain any classes which are subsets of other classes. Repeat this step until all columns of the compatibility table have been considered. The classes remaining are the maximal compatibility classes.

For Table 9.4-2, this process will result in the following sequence of classes:

[4, 5]

[3, 4, 5]

[3, 4, 5], [2, 3]

[3, 4, 5], [2, 3], [1, 2], [1, 4]

Reduced Flow Tables. The next step after finding the maximal compatibility classes is to form a flow table in which each state corresponds to a maximal compatibility class and each state of the original table is in at least one of the maximal compatibility classes used. This new table is the reduced table. It is said to **cover**

TABLE 9.4-2 Flow table to illustrate closure: (a) Flow table; (b) Pair table; (c) Maximal compatibility classes; (d) Attempt at a two-state reduced table; (e) Minimal-state reduced table

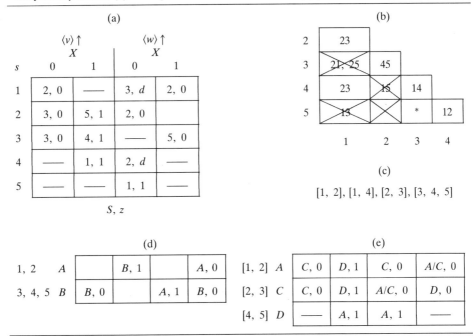

the original table since it specifies the same function as the original table whenever the function is specified. The reduced table for Table 9.4-1a is shown in Table 9.4-1f. Note that the reduced table has only two states even though there are three maximal compatibility classes. Only as many classes need be used in forming the reduced table to satisfy the requirement that each state of the original table appears in at least one of the maximal compatibility classes used in forming the reduced table.

The reduced table is filled in by entering the outputs that are specified for the states in the maximal compatibility class. These outputs must agree whenever specified since the states are compatible. For each state, P, of the reduced table, the next-state entry is a state of the reduced table that corresponds to a maximal compatibility class that includes **all** the next states specified for any of the states of the original table corresponding to the states in the maximal compatibility class represented by state P. For example, in Table 9.4-1f the next state for state B in the third column of the table must be A since states 4 and 5 have next-state entries of 2 and 3 in this column of the original table.

Compatibility is not an equivalence relation since it is not transitive. It is possible for state P to be compatible with state Q and state Q to be compatible with state R without states P and R being compatible. This is illustrated by compatibility classes [1, 2] and [2, 4] of Table 9.4-1. Because of this lack of transitivity the compatibility classes can overlap; one state can be in more than one compatibility class. This means that there can be many reduced tables that correspond to the same incompletely specified flow table. More than one of the reduced tables can have the minimum number of states. Usually, the sets of maximal compatibility classes that can be used to form the reduced table can be determined by inspection. For very complex situations, a prime implicant table approach can be used to select the sets of maximal compatibility classes that include all states of the original table.

The method just described works for *almost all* incompletely specified tables. There are some tables such as that of Table 9.4-2 for which the method breaks down. Using the method just described for this table leads to a reduced table with two states as in Table 9.4-2d. A difficulty arises when trying to fill in the next-state entries for the three total states encircled in the table. The next states corresponding to states 1 and 2 in the first column of the original table are states 2 and 3. Unfortunately, there is no state in Table 9.4-2d that corresponds to both states 2 and 3. A two-state reduced table covering the original table does not exist. It is said that the property of **closure** is not satisfied by Table 9.4-2d. When this happens the minimal state table may have states that correspond to nonmaximal compatibility classes. This is illustrated by Table 9.4-2e. The entries A/C in this table mean that either state A or state C can be used as the next state. Since tables that have a difficulty with closure are so very rare they will not be discussed any further here. The theory is presented in [Unger 69].

The derivation of the reduced table for the fundamental-mode flow table (FM-P) of Sec. 9.1 is shown in Table 9.4-3.

TABLE 9.4-3 Formation of minimal-state reduced flow table for FM-P circuit of Sec. 9.1:
(a) Primitive flow table from Table 9.1-5b; (b) Pair table; (c) Maximal compatibility classes;
(d) Reduced flow table

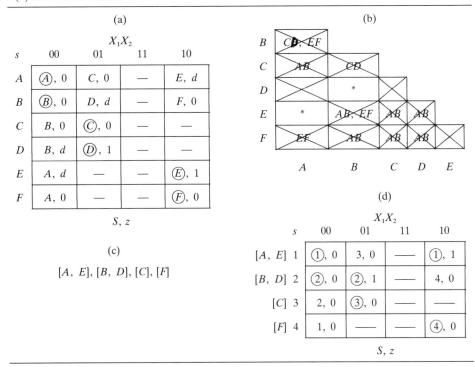

(a)

X_1X_2

s	00	01	11	10
A	⒜, 0	C, 0	—	E, d
B	⒝, 0	D, d	—	F, 0
C	B, 0	⒞, 0	—	—
D	B, d	⒟, 1	—	—
E	A, d	—	—	⒠, 1
F	A, 0	—	—	⒡, 0

S, z

(b)

(c)

[A, E], [B, D], [C], [F]

(d)

X_1X_2

s		00	01	11	10
[A, E]	1	①, 0	3, 0	—	①, 1
[B, D]	2	②, 0	②, 1	—	4, 0
[C]	3	2, 0	③, 0	—	—
[F]	4	1, 0	—	—	④, 0

S, z

9.5 INTERNAL VARIABLE ASSIGNMENTS FOR FUNDAMENTAL-MODE TABLES

It is usually more difficult to design a fundamental-mode circuit than a pulse-mode circuit for the same sequential function. There are several reasons for the increased complexity of the fundamental-mode design: (1) The fundamental-mode circuit usually has more internal states than the pulse-mode circuit. For example, the fundamental-mode FM-P circuit has four states in the reduced flow table (Table 9.4-3d), while the same function is realized in pulse-mode circuit (2P-P) with only two states. (2) The assignment of variables to the internal states must be done so as to avoid critical races. This section discusses techniques for obtaining internal variable assignments that are free of critical races.

One reason that internal variable assignments for fundamental-mode operation is difficult comes from the fact that more than S_0, the minimum number of internal variables, may be required. For example, the four-row fundamental mode flow table of Table 9.5-1a requires three internal variables. While it is always possible to find a critical-race-free assignment for an arbitrary fundamental-mode flow table, there is no simple way to find the minimum number of required internal variables.

A fundamental-mode flow table is shown in Table 9.5-1a, and a transition table for this flow table is shown in Table 9.5-1b. The three entries of Table 9.5-1b which are marked with an asterisk correspond to races, for both the internal variables are required to change. The race in the $X_1X_2 = 11$ column is noncritical because the stable 11 state will eventually be reached independently of the order in which the internal variables change. Both the races in the $X_1X_2 = 10$ column are critical; this particular internal variable assignment is not free of critical races. Permuting or complementing internal variables has no effect on races. Thus it is only necessary to check the other two distinct assignments of two variables for the presence of critical races. It is easily verified that each of the two resulting transition tables will also contain critical races. No circuit with two internal variables that is free of critical races exists for this table.

A state table that corresponds to the flow table of Table 9.5-1a is shown in Table 9.5-1c. For this state table it is possible to form a transition table that does not involve any critical races. Such a table is shown in Table 9.5-1d. The introduction of two additional states into the state table and the specification of multiple transitions permit this elimination of critical races. Of course, one additional internal variable is required.

Row A of the flow table of Table 9.5-1a shows that it must be possible to move from state A to state B by changing one internal variable and also that it must be possible to go from state A to state C by changing only one internal

TABLE 9.5-1 Elimination of critical races: (a) Flow table; (b) Transition table for part (a); (c) State table with added states; (d) Transition table for part (c)

(a)

s	X_1X_2 00	01	11	10
A	Ⓐ	B	C	C
B	Ⓑ	Ⓑ	C	D
C	Ⓒ	D	Ⓒ	Ⓒ
D	A	Ⓓ	C	Ⓓ

S

(b)

y_1y_2	X_1X_2 00	01	11	10
00	⓪⓪	01	11*	11*
01	⓪①	⓪①	11	10*
11	①①	10	①①	①①
10	00	①⓪	11	①⓪

Y_1Y_2

(c)

s	X_1X_2 00	01	11	10
A	Ⓐ	B	C	C
B	Ⓑ	Ⓑ	C	E
C	Ⓒ	F	Ⓒ	Ⓒ
D	A	Ⓓ	C	Ⓓ
E	—	—	—	D
F	—	D	—	—

S

(d)

$y_1y_2y_3$	X_1X_2 00	01	11	10
0 0 0	⓪⓪⓪	001	010	010
0 0 1	⓪⓪①	⓪⓪①	010	101
0 1 0	⓪①⓪	110	⓪①⓪	⓪①⓪
1 0 0	000	①⓪⓪	010	①⓪⓪
1 0 1	—	—	—	100
1 1 0	—	100	—	—

$Y_1Y_2Y_3$

variable. Thus state A must differ from state B in only one internal variable and must also differ from state C in some other single variable. Row D of the table shows that states A and D must also differ in only one variable. Clearly, with only two internal variables it is not possible for state A to differ from each of the remaining states in a different single variable. These relations are illustrated in Fig. 9.5-1. In this figure each internal state is represented by a node, and two nodes are joined by an edge only if the corresponding states must differ in a single internal variable. A diagram like this will be called a **state adjacency diagram**. Such a diagram is similar to the n-cubes discussed in Chap. 1 in that each edge represents a change in a single variable (two nodes connected directly by an edge must differ in only one variable). It is possible to obtain a transition table that corresponds directly to a given flow table (not to some equivalent state table) and is free of critical races if and only if it is possible to label the nodes of an n-cube with the states of the flow table so that every pair of states which are connected by an edge on the state adjacency diagram are also connected by an edge on the n-cube. Clearly, this is not possible for Fig. 9.5-1 since no n-cube can ever contain a closed path consisting of three edges or of any odd number of edges.

The failure of a state adjacency diagram to satisfy the conditions just given does not necessarily mean that a state table with additional states must be formed. The flow table shown in Table 9.5-2a has the same state adjacency diagram (Fig. 9.5-1). However, it is possible to obtain a circuit that has only two internal variables and is free of critical races by transforming this flow table into the state table of Table 9.5-2b. This can be done because it is possible to replace the transition from state A to state D by successive transitions from A to B and thence to D. A possibility such as this exists whenever the same state occurs as an unstable next-state entry more than once in a single column of a flow table or when there are some unspecified next-states in the table. In such cases it is possible to replace the state adjacency diagram with one or more weak state adjacency diagrams, each of which represents a state table having the same number of states and corresponding to the same flow table. There is only one weak state adjacency diagram for Table 9.5-2a, and it is shown in Fig. 9.5-2.

General conditions can be given for assignments leading to circuits free of critical races in terms of the weak adjacency diagrams and n-cubes. Any assignment that corresponds to a circuit having no critical races can be represented by

TABLE 9.5-2 Weak adjacency: (a) Flow table; (b) State table for part (a)

		(a) X_1X_2					(b) X_1X_2		
s	00	01	11	10	s	00	01	11	10
A	D	$Ⓐ$	—	$Ⓐ$	A	B	$Ⓐ$	—	$Ⓐ$
B	D	A	—	$Ⓑ$	B	D	A	—	$Ⓑ$
C	$Ⓒ$	$Ⓒ$	—	A	C	$Ⓒ$	$Ⓒ$	—	A
D	$Ⓓ$	C	—	B	D	$Ⓓ$	C	—	B
		S					S		

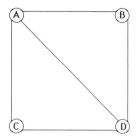

Figure 9.5-1 State adjacency diagram for Table 9.5-1a.

Figure 9.5-2 Weak adjacency diagram for Table 9.5-2b.

a labeling of an n-cube such that corresponding to each edge of the weak adjacency diagram there is a path between the appropriate nodes of the n-cube which does not pass through any other nodes of the n-cube with different labels. This is a necessary but not a sufficient condition, for it is possible to have the paths "interfere" so that some of the intermediate unlabeled nodes would have to satisfy conflicting requirements.

For Table 9.5-1a, the weak state adjacency diagram is the same as the state adjacency diagram. A 3-cube labeling that corresponds to Table 9.5-1c and satisfies Fig. 9.5-1 is shown in Fig. 9.5-3.

It is possible to show that any four-row flow table can be realized with a circuit free of critical races with at most three internal variables. This is done by considering a "worst case" in which all pairs of states are required to be adjacent, as in the state adjacency diagram of Fig. 9.5-4. There are several labelings of the 3-cube which satisfy the requirements of this diagram and therefore of all other diagrams involving four states. One such labeling of particular interest is shown in Fig. 9.5-5. This scheme is peculiar in that there are two nodes for each state. It is always possible to go from any node to a node labeled with any arbitrary other state either directly or by passing through a node with the same label as the first node. Thus, nodes B_1 and C_1 can be reached directly from node A_1, and node D_1 can be reached from node A_1 by passing through node A_2. Table 9.5-3 shows

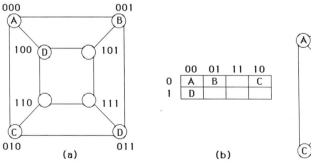

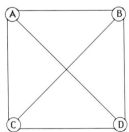

Figure 9.5-3 Labeling of the 3-cube for the diagram of Fig. 9.5-1: (a) 3-cube; (b) 3-cube map.

Figure 9.5-4 State adjacency diagram for worst-case situation involving four states.

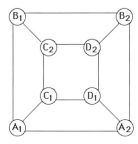

Figure 9.5-5 Labeling of a 3-cube to satisfy worst-case requirements for a 4-state table.

how this labeling of the 3-cube would be used to form a state table corresponding to the flow table of Table 9.5-1a. In Table 9.5-3b, the stable A_1 entry in the total state for $X_1X_2 = 00$, $s = A_1$ is marked with an asterisk. This entry could be replaced by a dash since there is no way for the circuit to enter this total state: There are no other stable states in the row and there is no other A_1 entry in the column.

Any four-state flow table can be realized by a circuit requiring at most three internal variables. A question still remains as to how many internal variables are required to realize any flow table having r states. Indeed, it is not obvious that an arbitrary flow table can always be realized by means of any circuit that is free of critical races. Any flow table with r states, and thus requiring a minimum of S_0 internal variables, can always be realized by a circuit that has at most $2S_0 - 1$ internal variables and does not contain any critical races. Moreover, for any value of S_0 there will be some flow tables which require exactly $2S_0 - 1$ variables. The details of this demonstration are somewhat involved and specialized. They will not be presented here. Most circuits that are designed to operate in fundamental mode do not have many states. Circuits with lots of states are designed in pulse mode. The complexity of the fundamental-mode design process makes it im-

TABLE 9.5-3 State table corresponding to Table 9.5-1a and using the labeling of Fig. 9.5-5: (a) Flow table; (b) Transition table for part (a)

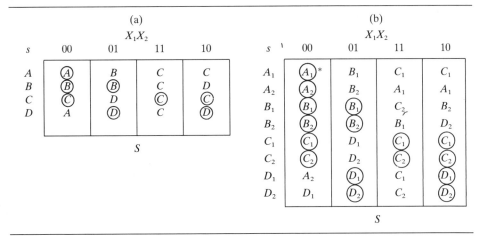

TABLE 9.5-4 Formation of transition tables and excitation functions for FM-P circuit: (a) Reduced flow table from Table 9.4-3d; (b) Transition table using Assignment III; (c) Excitation table for *S-R* latches; (d) Excitation functions; (e) Transition table for Fig. 9.5-7

(a)

X_1X_2

s	00	01	11	10
A	①, 0	3, 0	—	①, 1
B	②, 0	②, 1	—	4, 0
C	2, 0	③, 0	—	—
D	1, 0	—	—	④, 0

S, z

(b)

X_1X_2

s	y_1y_2	00	01	11	10
A	0 0	00, 0	01, 0	—	00, 1
C	0 1	11, 0	01, 0	—	—
B	1 1	11, 0	11, 1	—	10, 0
D	1 0	00, 0	—	—	10, 0

Y_1Y_2, z

(c)

X_1X_2

s	y_1y_2	00		01		11	10	
A	0 0	r	r	r	S	—	r	r
C	0 1	S	s	r	s	—	—	
B	1 1	s	s	s	s	—	s	R
D	1 0	R	r	—		—	s	r

(d)

$$S_1 = X_2'y_2, \quad R_1 = X_1'y_2'$$
$$S_2 = X_2, \quad R_2 = X_1$$
$$z = X_2y_1 + X_1y_1'$$

(e)

X_1X_2

s	y_1y_2	00	01	11	10
A	0 0	00, 0	10, 0	—	00, 1
C	0 1	01, 0	01, 1	—	11, 0
B	1 1	01, 0	11, 0	—	10, 0
D	1 0	00, 0	11, 0	—	10, 0

Y_1Y_2, z

practical to design large fundamental-mode circuits. Small circuits operating in fundamental mode can be designed with the techniques already presented here.

The questions involved in obtaining internal variable assignments for fundamental-mode circuits have been much beloved by switching theorists. As a result there is a large literature devoted to these and related topics. A very good introduction to this subject matter is [Unger 69].

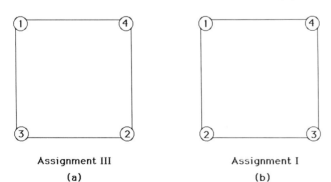

Assignment III

(a)

Assignment I

(b)

Figure 9.5-6 Adjacency diagrams for Table 9.5-4a: (a) state adjacency diagram; (b) weak state adjacency diagram.

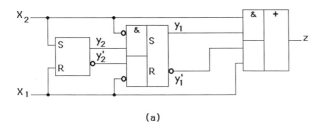

(a)

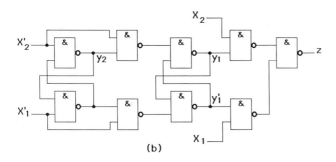

(b)

Figure 9.5-7 Logic diagrams for Table 9.5-4d: (a) using latches; (b) using NAND gates.

Table 9.5-4a shows the flow table for the FM-P circuit of Sec. 9.1-4. The corresponding state adjacency diagram is given in Fig. 9.5-6a. This diagram requires that assignment III be used to obtain a critical-race-free transition table. The resulting transition table is shown in Table 9.5-4b and the corresponding excitation table for *S-R* latches in Table 9.5-4c. Rows *B* and *C* are interchanged in the transition and excitation tables to keep adjacent rows unit distance apart in $y_1 y_2$ values. Figure 9.5-7 shows the logic diagrams that implement the excitation functions of Table 9.5-4d. The weak adjacency diagram that results from making use of the unspecified next-state entries in the flow table is shown in Fig. 9.5-6b and the corresponding transition table in Table 9.5-4e. The excitation functions derived from this table are more complex than those used to get Fig. 9.5-7. (The reader should check this statement!)

9.R REFERENCES

[CADDEN 59]   Cadden, W. J., "Equivalent Sequential Circuits," *IEEE Trans. Circuit Theory*, CT-6, No. 1, pp. 30–34, 1959.

[CLARE 73]   Clare, C. R., *Designing Logic Systems Using State Machines*, McGraw-Hill Book Company, New York, 1973.

[COMER 84]   Comer, D. J., *Digital Logic and State Machine Design*, Holt, Rinehart and Winston, New York, 1984.

[DeMICHELI 84]   DeMicheli, G., R. Brayton, and A. Sangiovanni-Vincentelli, "KISS: A Program for Optimal State Assignment of Finite State Machines," Dig. ICCAD 84, Santa Clara, Calif., pp. 209–211, Nov. 12–15, 1984.

[DOLOTTA 64]   Dolotta, T. A., and E. J. McCluskey, "The Coding of Internal States of Sequential Circuits," *IEEE Trans. Comput.*, EC-13, pp. 549–562, Oct. 1964.

[KLEENE 56] Kleene, S. C., "Representation of Events in Nerve Nets and Finite Automata," in *Automata Studies*, ed. C. E. Shannon and J. McCarthy, Princeton University Press, Princeton, N.J., 1956.

[MCCLUSKEY 59] McCluskey, E. J., and S. H. Unger, "A Note on the Number of Internal Variable Assignments for Sequential Switching Circuits," *IRE Trans. Electron. Comput.*, EC-8, pp. 439–440, Dec. 1959.

[RABIN 59] Rabin, M. O., and D. Scott, "Finite Automata and Their Decision Problems," *IBM J. Res. Dev.*, Vol. 3, No. 2, pp. 114–125, 1959.

[RHYNE 77] Rhyne, V. T., and P. S. Noe, "On the Number of Distinct State Assignments for a Sequential Machine," *IEEE Trans. Comput.*, pp. 73–75, Jan. 1977.

[TRENDIAK 81] Trendiak, N., "How to Flowchart for Hardware," *Computer*, pp. 87–102, Dec. 1981.

[TUMBUSH 74] Tumbush, G. L., and J. E. Brandeberry, "A State Assignment Technique for Sequential Machines Using J-K Flip-Flops," *IEEE Trans. Comput.*, pp. 85–86, Jan. 1974.

[UNGER 69] Unger, S. H., *Asynchronous Sequential Switching Circuits*, Wiley-Interscience, New York, 1969.

[WIATROWSKI 80] Wiatrowski, C. A., and C. H. House, *Logic Circuits and Microcomputer Systems*, McGraw-Hill Book Company, New York, 1980.

9.P PROBLEMS

9.1 A circuit is to be designed having two pulse inputs X_1 and X_2 and one dc output z. Whenever an X_1 pulse is received, the output is to become equal to 1, provided that there been exactly two X_2 pulses after the last previous X_1 pulse. Otherwise, the output is to remain equal to 0. Once the output becomes equal to 1, it is to remain equal to 1 until the next X_2 pulse. Whenever an X_2 pulse is received, the output is to become equal to 0. Write a (pulse-mode) flow table for this circuit.

9.2 A circuit is to be designed having two pulse inputs X_1 and X_2 and two dc outputs Z_1 and Z_2. The inputs are restricted so that X_1 and X_2 are never simultaneously equal to 1. When either X_1 or X_2 is equal to 1, the corresponding output Z_1 or Z_2 is to be equal to 1. When X_1 and X_2 are both equal to 0, Z_1 is to be equal to 1 if X_1 was the last input equal to 1 and Z_2 is to be equal to 1 if X_2 was the last input equal to 1. Z_1 and Z_2 are never both equal to 1.

(a) Write the fundamental-mode primitive flow table and output table for this circuit.

(b) Write the fundamental-mode flow table and output table for the same circuit *without* the restriction that X_1 and X_2 are never both equal to 1, but *with* the restriction that the X_1 pulses and X_2 pulses both have the same fixed duration when $X_1 = X_2 = 1$, $Z_1 = Z_2 = 1$.

(c) Simplify the tables of parts (a) and (b) to tables having a minimum number of states.

9.3 Find state tables that specify the same external behavior as Table P9.3a and b and which also have the minimum possible number of internal states.

(a) Let A be –, B be –.

(b) Let A be 6, B be –.

(c) Let A be 6, B be 1.

TABLE P9.3

(a)

s	X_1X_2 00	01	11	10		s	X_1X_2 00	01	11	10
1	2	5	4	1		1	0	1	1	0
2	1	8	3	5		2	1	0	1	1
3	6	5	4	1		3	0	1	1	0
4	2	5	3	4		4	0	1	1	0
5	2	5	3	7		5	1	1	0	0
6	3	8	1	5		6	1	0	1	1
7	1	6	4	5		7	1	0	1	1
8	4	2	1	4		8	1	0	1	1
		S						Z		

(b)

s	X_1X_2 00	01	11	10	$Z_1 Z_2$
1	1	–	7	4	0 0
2	2	3	8	–	0 0
3	6	–	2	3	0 1
4	6	6	1	–	0 1
5	–	A	–	4	0 0
6	2	6	8	4	0 1
7	8	4	B	–	1 0
8	7	3	5	2	1 0
		S			

9.4 A circuit is to be designed in which two pushbuttons, A and B, control the lighting of two lamps, G and R. Whenever both pushbuttons are released, neither lamp is to be lit. Starting with both buttons released, the operation of either button causes lamp G to light. Operation of the other button, with the first button still held down, causes lamp R to light. Henceforth, as long as either button remains operated, the button that first caused lamp R to light controls lamp R—causing it to extinguish when the button is released and to light when the button is operated. The other button controls lamp G in the same fashion. It is not possible to operate or release both buttons simultaneously.

(a) Form the primitive state table for the circuit just described.

(b) Reduce the number of states if possible.

(c) Assign secondary variables so that no critical races occur.

9.5 Table P9.5 specifies the behavior of a circuit in which the duration of the input pulse is controlled so as not to exceed a fixed time interval t. Draw a primitive flow table for a circuit that has the same behavior when the restriction on the length of the pulses is removed. Assume that no double changes of input occur and that X_1 and X_2 are never both equal to 1.

TABLE P9.5

s	X_1X_2 00	01	11	10		s	X_1X_2 00	01	11	10
1	1	2	–	1		1	10	10	10	10
2	2	3	–	1		2	00	00	00	00
3	3	4	–	2		3	00	00	00	00
4	4	4	–	3		4	01	01	01	01
		S						Z		

9.6 For the flow table in Table P9.6:

TABLE P9.6

	(a) $\langle C \rangle \uparrow$ $X_1 X_2$					(b)		
s	00	01	11	10		s	y_1	y_2
1	2	3	4	3		1	0	0
2	3	4	1	4		2	0	1
3	4	1	2	1		3	1	1
4	1	2	3	2		4	1	0
			S					

(a) Write the transition table when the assignment of internal variables from Table P9.6b is used.

(b) Write the excitation table when S-R flip-flops are used for memory devices, and derive the expressions for S_1, R_1, S_2, and R_2.

(c) Write the excitation table when J-K flip-flops are used.

9.7 Simplify the flow table of Table P9.7 if possible.

TABLE P9.7

	$X_1 X_2$					$X_1 X_2$			
s	00	01	11	10	s	00	01	11	10
1	①	4	4	2	1	0	0	0	1
2	1	4	3	②	2	0	0	0	1
3	1	4	③	④	3	0	0	1	1
4	1	④	④	4	4	0	0	0	0
		S					Z		

9.8 An electronic sequential circuit is to be designed using S-R flip-flops and gates. The two circuit inputs X and C are pulses which never occur simultaneously. The C pulse occurs periodically, as shown below in Fig. P9.8. The X pulse can appear (if it does appear) only singly and midway between two successive C pulses. The single level output Z is high in the interval between two successive C pulses if and only if the preceding interval contained an X pulse.

(a) Derive a minimum-row flow table and output table for the circuit specified above.

(b) Derive an excitation table.

(c) Derive an economical circuit using flip-flops and gates.

Figure P9.8

9.9 A sequential circuit is controlled by two keys, K_1 and K_2, and has a single output, Z. Either key, when depressed, remains depressed for a fixed interval of time, d. (You may assume that no double changes of input state occur.) The output Z changes state only when either K_1 or K_2 is depressed (no output change occurs when a key is released). The closing of K_1 assures that Z changes to (or remains at) the 0 state. The closing of K_2 assures that Z changes to (or remains at) the 1 state.

(a) Draw a primitive flow table for this circuit

(b) Draw a minimum-row flow table—two rows are sufficient.

(c) Design an economical circuit.

9.10 For the primitive flow table shown in Table P9.10, draw a diagram showing compatible states. Write all possible reduced flow tables that require no more than two internal variables.

TABLE P9.10

	X_1X_2				
s	00	01	11	10	Z
1	①	2	3	–	0
2	1	②	–	5	0
3	1	–	③	4	0
4	–	2	6	④	1
5	–	2	6	⑤	0
6	1	–	⑥	5	0

S

9.11 A sequential circuit is designed using the assignment of internal variables shown in Table P9.11a, and the resulting equations are

$$Y_1 = f_1(y_1, y_2, y_3, X_1, X_2, \ldots, X_r)$$

$$Y_2 = f_2(y_1, y_2, y_3, X_1, X_2, \ldots, X_r)$$

$$Y_3 = f_3(y_1, y_2, y_3, X_1, X_2, \ldots, X_r)$$

$$Z_1 = g_1(y_1, y_2, y_3, X_1, X_2, \ldots, X_r)$$

$$Z_2 = g_2(y_1, y_2, y_3, X_1, X_2, \ldots, X_r)$$

If the assignment of Table P9.11b is used for the same flow table, write expressions for Y_1, Y_2, Y_3, Z_1, and Z_2 in terms of f_1, f_2, f_3, g_1, and g_2.

TABLE P9.11

	(a)				(b)		
s	y_1	y_2	y_3	s	y_1	y_2	y_3
1	0	0	0	1	1	0	0
2	0	0	1	2	1	0	1
3	0	1	0	3	1	1	0
4	0	1	1	4	1	1	1
5	1	0	0	5	0	0	0
6	1	0	1	6	0	0	1
7	1	1	0	7	0	1	0
8	1	1	1	8	0	1	1

9.12 A sequential circuit (serial adder) having four inputs—c, v, w, X—is to be designed. The input c represents a clock pulse, and the inputs v, w, and X represent three binary numbers. There is to be a single output z, which represents the arithmetic sum of the three inputs.

One bit of the sum is to occur as an output pulse on either the z or the z' leads whenever a pulse occurs on the input lead.

(a) Draw a pulse-mode flow table for this circuit—include only those columns of the flow table that correspond to $c = 1$.

(b) Draw a flow table for a circuit which has the same performance as part (a) except that the output is a level which remains on the z lead until the next clock pulse occurs.

9.13 The flow tables in Table P9.13a and b describe fundamental-mode sequential circuits. You are to assign combinations of internal variables $(y_1 y_2 \cdots y_m)$ to the internal states, so as to avoid critical races, and form an excitation table for $Y_1 Y_2 \cdots Y_m$. Assign the all-0 combination to state 1. Do not reorder the rows of the table. Additional rows may be added if necessary. Use as few internal varibles as possible.

TABLE P9.13

(a)

s	$X_1 X_2$ 00	01	11	10
1	2	3	–	(1)
2	(2)	5	–	(2)
3	6	(3)	–	5
4	(4)	6	–	2
5	4	(5)	–	(5)
6	(6)	(6)	–	1

S

(b)

s	$X_1 X_2$ 00	01	11	10
1	3	(1)	(1)	4
2	4	(2)	(2)	(2)
3	(3)	2	1	(3)
4	(4)	1	2	(4)

S

9.14 A device has been designed as part of a coin changer. It is intended to differentiate between quarters, nickels, and dimes by means of their size. It consists of a chute through which a coin rolls, a light source, and three strategically placed light-sensitive diodes, as shown in Fig. P9.14a.

The light detectors are amplified such that three TTL level outputs are produced. These signals are to be processed by a three-input three-output *asynchronous* circuit that detects the coin's passing and then outputs a 1 on one of three lines (according to the type of coin) *until the next coin arrives*. The operation of the circuit is summarized in Fig. P9.14b; IQ, IN, and ID are the three inputs, and Q, N, and D are the outputs.

Design a fundamental-mode circuit, using only NAND gates, that will realize the specified function. Sketch the actual waveform produced by your circuit in response to the inputs shown in Fig. P9.14b.

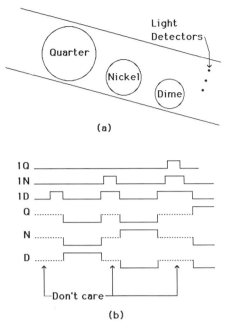

(a)

1Q
1N
1D
Q
N
D

Don't care

(b)

Figure P9.14

9.15 A modulo-5 binary counter circuit is to be designed. The circuit outputs are formed directly from the state elements. Use as few devices as possible.

(a) Design a one-phase FSM using D latches.

(b) Design a two-phase FSM using S-R latches.

(c) Design a FSM using J-K flip-flops.

(d) Design a FSM using T flip-flops.

9.16 A *fundamental-mode* sequential circuit is to be designed with two inputs and one output (Fig. P9.16). Input I is an initializing input that places the circuit in its initial state with output $z = 1$. After the circuit is initialized, the first negative transition of input X causes the output to become 0 and remain 0 until the next negative transition, when the output becomes and remains 1.

(a) Write a minimum-state flow table (show the initial state, but the R input need not be included in the table).

(b) Show all minimum-state variable assignments (types only) that are critical-race-free.

(c) Choose one assignment and derive a circuit using S-R latches (include both X and I inputs).

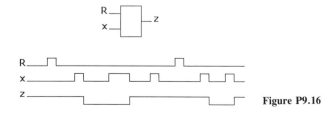

Figure P9.16

DESIGN
FOR TESTABILITY

10.1 INTRODUCTION

Integrated circuits are produced by manufacturing a wafer (a disk of silicon) having many copies, called die, of the integrated circuit. Possible sizes might be a 75-mm diameter wafer, 5-mm square die, and 100 die per wafer. Typically, only a minority, perhaps 30%, of the die work properly. Thus, the first thing that must be done after the wafer is processed is to discover which die are good. Each die on the wafer must be tested to determine whether it works properly. This testing activity is called **wafer sort**. Only the die that pass wafer sort are packaged.

Parameters such as propagation delay and drive currents are checked, a process called **parametric testing**. Whether or not the chip carries out the function it was designed for is also checked, a process called **functional testing**. The chip must also be tested after it is packaged, after it is mounted on a board, and perhaps periodically after it is placed in a system. This testing is done to ensure that the chip has not failed since the last test.

The cost of doing functional testing of a chip is increasing rapidly. This is due to the fact that the ratio between the number of devices on a chip to the number of chip I/O pins is rising. In fact, functional testing could be the most expensive part of IC manufacturing. The automatic test equipment has become very expensive (one million dollars for a tester is not uncommon) and the computing time required to calculate the input patterns to be applied to the chip has become very costly [Bardell 81]. It appears that the only economical method to reduce functional testing cost is to include circuitry on each chip to facilitate testing. The design of such circuitry is the subject of this chapter.

There are actually two types of functional testing that are important for computer systems:

1. **Implicit** or **concurrent testing**. This is sometimes called *checking*. It refers to on-line testing to detect errors that occur during normal system operation. Parity codes or duplication techniques are used. The relevant theoretical techniques deal with self-checking circuits, [Wakerly 78].

2. **Explicit testing**. This is the testing that is carried out while the tested circuit is not in use. It includes the tests done on chips while still on a wafer, production tests on packaged chips and on boards, acceptance tests, maintenance tests, and repair tests.

The present discussion will be restricted to explicit testing and the terms *testing* and *test* will be used to refer only to explicit testing and tests.

The term "design for testability (DFT)" describes those design techniques that are used to make testing of the resulting product economical. This chapter presents current DFT practice as well as proposed improvements.

Testability tends to be used somewhat imprecisely since there are various factors that contribute to test or maintenance cost. Testing cost is determined mainly by the cost of test pattern generation and by the cost of test application. Test pattern generation cost depends on either the computer time required to run the test pattern generation program plus the (prorated) capital cost of developing the program or on the number of man hours required for a person to write the test patterns plus the increase in system development time caused by the time taken to develop tests. Test application cost is determined by the cost of the test equipment plus the tester time required to apply the test (sometimes called **socket time**). There is a trade-off between test cost and repair cost. The cost of testing can be reduced by using tests that either fail to detect many faults or cannot locate many of the detected faults. This can cause a substantial increase in system production or maintenance costs. It is much more expensive to repair a faulty pc board than to discard a faulty chip, and it is much more expensive to repair a faulty system than to repair a faulty pc board.

No attempt will be made to give a precise definition of testability. Instead, it will be assumed that testability is increased whenever the costs of test generation or of test application are decreased, or the fault coverage or fault diagnosability is increased. Of course, testability will be decreased by any increase in test cost or by any decrease in fault coverage or diagnosability.

Most DFT techniques increase testability by both decreasing test cost and increasing coverage and diagnosability. The exceptions to this will be pointed out when the corresponding techniques are presented.

Attempts to understand circuit attributes that influence testability have produced the two concepts of observability (visibility) and controllability (control). **Observability** refers to the ease with which the state of internal signals can be determined at the circuit output leads. **Controllability** refers to the ease of producing a specific internal signal value by applying signals to the circuit input leads. Attempts to assign specific values to these attributes will be described in a later section. Many of the DFT techniques to be described are attempts to increase the observability or controllability of a circuit design. The most direct way to do this is to introduce **test points**, that is, additional circuit inputs and outputs to be used during testing. There is always a cost associated with adding test points. For circuit boards the cost of test points is often well justified. On the other hand, for ICs the cost of test points can be prohibitive because of IC pin limitations. Some of the techniques to be described are aimed at obtaining the benefits of test points without incurring the full cost of additional board connectors or IC pins.

The new DFT techniques are general; they involve the overall circuit structure, or they are implemented by general design rules. Older techniques are more ad hoc and typically consist of a set of guidelines listing features that enhance or detract from "ease of testing" or testability. They are aimed at the circuit designer and depend on his or her insight and willingness to worry about testability. Ad hoc techniques will be presented first, followed by presentations of more systematic DFT methods.

10.2 AD HOC TECHNIQUES

This approach to testability enhancement is aimed at the designer. It typically consists of a list of design features that create testing problems together with suggestions of preferred implementations. Table 10.2-1 lists ad hoc techniques for testability enhancement.

Initialization refers to the ability to control the initial state of registers and sequential circuits. The **initial state** of a circuit describes the contents of the memory elements right after power is first applied. Many designs do not require a specified initial state for correct functioning: they will work properly for any arbitrary initial state. There is no need to include circuitry to control the state in order to obtain correct functionality.

TABLE 10.2-1 Ad Hoc logic techniques for testability enhancement

Feature	Ad hoc technique
Unknown initial state	Initialization circuitry
Internal clock	Circuitry to disconnect internal clock and substitute tester clock
Feedback loops	Circuitry to permit tester to break feedback loop
Deep sequential circuits (counters and divider chains)	Circuitry to segment circuits into more easily controlled portions
Wired logic	Avoid
Fanin and fanout points	Add test access to these points

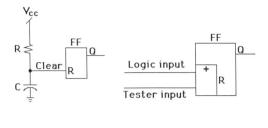

Figure 10.2-1 Initialization techniques: (a) power-up reset; (b) tester reset.

(a)   (b)

In order to test the circuitry it is necessary to place it in a known state.[1] This can be done by applying an initialization sequence as the first portion of the test input. However, such an initialization sequence can be very lengthy (particularly if long counter chains are contained in the circuit). It can also require a large amount of computation time in order to discover such a sequence. These expenses of initialization can be drastically reduced by incorporating initialization circuitry in the design. The initialization circuitry can take two forms: the circuit can be designed to be self-initializing as in Fig. 10.2-1a, or additional control inputs can be provided as in Fig. 10.2-1b to allow the tester to set the circuit state. By connecting circuits such as those of Fig. 10.2-1 to all of the flip-flop asynchronous reset (clear) inputs the initial state is fixed with all of the flip-flops cleared. If it is desired to have some of the flip-flops initially set, it is only necessary to connect the initialization circuits to the flip-flop preset inputs (asynchronous set) rather than the clear inputs.

Circuits for the other techniques listed in Table 10.2-1 are straightforward and will not be shown here. Detailed diagrams can be found in Chap. 5 of [Bennetts 84]. Table 10.2-1 deals with the logic aspects of a product to be tested. The electrical and mechanical characteristics of the product are also important to its testability. These are not discussed here because they are outside the planned scope of this book, not because they are felt to be unimportant. A discussion of DFT techniques relating to electrical and mechanical properties can be found in [Writer 75].

10.3 TESTABILITY MEASURES

The techniques listed in Table 10.2-1 require the addition of extra logic or extra connections. These additions add to the cost of the design. Thus it is desirable to limit the additions to those necessary to assure adequate testability of the design. To do this, a method of estimating the design's testability is required.

---

[1] It may seem paradoxical that the state must be controlled for testing when it needn't be controlled for correct operation. A simple resolution of the paradox can be seen by remembering that standard commercial testers do not alter the input sequence on the basis of the outputs received while the system in which a circuit is embedded does typically determine the inputs sent to the circuit on the basis of the outputs received from the circuit.

A straightforward method for determining the testability of a circuit is to use an automatic test pattern generation (ATPG) program to generate the tests and the fault coverage. The running time of the program, the number of test patterns generated, and the fault coverage then provide a measure of the testability of the circuit. The difficulty with this approach is mainly the large expense involved in running the ATPG program. Also, the ATPG program may not provide sufficient information about how to improve the testability of a circuit with poor testability. To overcome these difficulties, a number of programs have been written to calculate estimates of the testability of a design without actually running an ATPG program: TMEAS (Testability Measure Program), [Stephenson 76] and [Grason 79]; SCOAP (Sandia Controllability/Observability Analysis Program), [Goldstein 78], [Goldstein 79a], [Goldstein 79b], and [Goldstein 80]; TESTSCREEN, [Kovijanic 79a] and [Kovijanic 79b]; CAMELOT (Computer Aided Measure for Logic Testability), [Bennetts 84]; VICTOR (VLSI Identifier of Controllability, Testability, Observability, and Redundancy), [Ratiu 82].

These **testability measure programs** (TM programs) implement algorithms that attempt to predict, for a specific circuit, the cost (running time) of generating test patterns. In the process of calculating the testability measure, information is developed identifying those portions of the circuit that are difficult to test. This information can be used as a guide to circuit modifications that improve testability.

No accurate relationship between circuit characteristics and testability has yet been demonstrated. Thus the circuit parameters calculated by the TM programs are heuristic and have been chosen on the basis of experience and study of existing ATPG programs. It is not surprising that the different authors of TM programs have chosen different circuit characteristics for their estimates of testability. The technique used to demonstrate that a given TM program does indeed give an indication of circuit testability is to run both the TM program and also an ATPG program on a number of different circuits. A monotonic relation between the TM and the ATPG run time is offered as "proof" that the TM program produces a good estimate of circuit testability. The difficulty with this validation technique is the high cost of running enough examples to be meaningful. Some interesting results obtained by using statistical methods to evaluate the testability measure program approach are presented in [Agrawal 82].

All the TM programs base their estimates of testability on "controllability" and "observability" values for each circuit component. They differ in the precise definitions used for obtaining these estimates. The concepts of controllability and observability are derived from the techniques used for ATPG. They are defined in [Stephenson 76] as:

Controllability: "the ease of producing an arbitrary valid signal at the inputs of a component by exercising the primary inputs of the circuit"

Observability: "the ease of determining at the primary outputs of the circuit what happened at the outputs of a component"

The **components** referred to in the definitions are standard ICs (SSI and MSI) for board level circuits and are standard cell library modules for LSI or VLSI circuits. It is assumed that the components are interconnected by unidirectional **links**.

10.3-1 TMEAS

In TMEAS an observability value, OY, and a controllability value, CY, is assigned to each link. These values are normalized to be between 0 and 1, with 1 being the best possible value. For primary inputs, $CY = 1$ since they are assumed to have perfect controllability. Primary outputs have $OY = 1$ since perfect observability is assumed for them. Internal link values are calculated by associating with each component a **controllability transfer factor**, CTF, and an **observability transfer factor**, OTF. Two systems of N (N equals the number of components) simultaneous equations are used to determine the link CY and OY values.

Sequential components are handled by introducing implicit feedback links to represent the state transitions. No other modifications are required in TMEAS to handle sequential circuits.

The input controllability of a component is defined as the average of the input link controllabilities, and the same controllability value is assigned to all of the component output links. The component output observability is the average of the output link observabilities, and the component input links are all assigned a common observability.

In defining the controllability transfer factor it is assumed that all valid input signal values can be achieved with equal ease and that all valid output signal values are equally important. Based on these assumptions the CTF is defined as a measure of the uniformity of the input-output mapping produced by the component. For a single-output component with output = 0 for half of the possible input patterns, the value of CTF would be 1. (Thus CTF for an XOR gate is 1.) For an n-input, single-output component (such as an OR gate or a NAND gate) that has output = 0 for only one input pattern, the value of CTF is 2^{1-n}. This is also the CTF for a gate whose output is 1 for only one input pattern (AND, NOR gates). The CTF measures only the uniformity of the component input-output mapping. (Thus CTF is 1/2 for a two-input OR gate and CTF is 1/4 for a three-input NOR gate.) The controllability of the output links of a component is calculated by multiplying the component input controllability by the CTF.

The observability transfer factor is specified to approximate the probability that observation of the component outputs will permit the determination of whether an input fault has occurred. The observability of the input links of a component is calculated by multiplying the output observability by the OTF.

The overall observability of the circuit is defined as the average of the component output observabilites, and the overall controllability is the average of the component input controllabilities. The overall circuit testability is defined as the geometric mean of the overall observability and overall controllability.

In TMEAS and CAMELOT two values (one for controllability and one for observability) are determined for each node. SCOAP and TESTSCREEN each calculate a vector of six values for each node. TESTSCREEN and SCOAP differ in the methods used to calculate the values.

10.3-2 SCOAP

In SCOAP the circuit nodes are characterized as sequential or combinational according to the following definitions:

A **combinational node** is a primary circuit input or a combinational standard cell output node.

A **sequential node** is an output node of a sequential standard cell.

The controllability/observability properties of each node are represented by a vector with six elements representing the following measures:

CC0(N), combinational 0-controllability, representing the minimum number of combinational node assignments required to set node N value to 0.

CC1(N), combinational 1-controllability, representing the minimum number of combinational node assignments required to set node N value to 1

SC0(N), sequential 0-controllability, representing the minimum number of sequential nodes that must be set to specified values in order to justify a 0 on the node N.

SC1(N), sequential 1-controllability, representing the minimum number of sequential nodes that must be set to specified values in order to justify a 1 on the node N.

CO(N), combinational observability, representing both the number of combinational standard cells between node N and a primary output terminal and the minimum number of combinational node assignments required to propagate the value of node N to a primary circuit output.

SO(N), sequential observability, representing both the number of sequential standard cells between node N and a primary output terminal and the minimum number of sequential standard cells that must be controlled in order to propagate the value of node N to a primary circuit output.

The controllability/observability measures of SCOAP are not normalized like those in TMEAS. In SCOAP higher values for the measures correspond to nodes that are more difficult to test. The sequential controllabilities and observability are related to the number of time frames necessary to observe or control the value of an internal node.

In calculating the parameter values for SCOAP, all the internal node parameters are initially set to infinity. The initial settings for primary input and output nodes are given in Table 10.3-1.

TABLE 10.3-1 SCOAP initial parameter values for primary inputs and outputs

	CC0(X)	CC1(X)	SC0(X)	SC1(X)	CO(X)	SO(X)
Input	1	1	0	0	∞	∞
Output	∞	∞	∞	∞	0	0

TABLE 10.3-2 Parameter transformation rules for some typical cells

	Buffer $Y = X$	Inverter $Y = X'$	AND Gate: $Y = X1*X2$
$CC0(Y)$	$CC0(X) + 1$	$CC1(X) + 1$	min $[CC0(X1), CC0(X2)] + 1$
$CC1(Y)$	$CC1(X) + 1$	$CC0(X) + 1$	$CC1(X1) + CC1(X2) + 1$
$SC0(Y)$	$SC0(X)$	$SC1(X)$	min $[SC0(X1), SC0(X2)]$
$SC1(Y)$	$SC1(X)$	$SC0(X)$	$SC1(X1) + SC1(X2)$
$CO(X)$	$CO(Y) + 1$	$CO(Y) + 1$	See below
$SO(X)$	$SO(Y)$	$SO(Y)$	See below
$CO(X1)$	See above	See above	$CO(Y) + CC1(X2) + 1$
$SO(X1)$	See above	See above	$S0(Y) + SC1(X2)$

Each standard cell must have a set of rules determined for obtaining its output controllability parameters from the input controllability parameter values, and for obtaining the input observability parameter values from the output observability parameter values. The rules for some combinational cells are given in Table 10.3-2. Table 10.3-3 gives the rules for the D flip-flop shown in Fig. 10.3-1 (negative edge triggered with asynchronous reset). A detailed discussion of the formation of these rules is given in [Goldstein 78] and [Goldstein 79b].

The controllability parameters are calculated by starting at the primary inputs and using the transformation rules to determine the internal and primary output controllabilities. Several iterations can be required if there are feedback loops present. The observability parameter calculations start with the primary output node values. The internal and primary input observability parameters are determined by means of the cell transformation rules. The observability of a fanout node is defined to be the minimum of the observabilities of the nodes to which it fans out. There can be some parameter values that remain equal to infinity. This is an indication that the corresponding nodes are uncontrollable or unobservable, demonstrating a redundancy in the circuit. This is not a complete test for redundancy since it is possible to have a redundant node that does not lead to an infinite parameter value. This phenomenon is discussed in [Goldstein 79b].

No single measure of the circuit testability is defined in SCOAP. Instead, controllability and observability profiles (density plots) are used in which the number of nodes having a given controllability or observability value are plotted against the corresponding values. There are, in general, six such profiles for each circuit

TABLE 10.3-3 Transformation rules for D flip-flop of Fig. 10.3-1

$CC0(Q)$	min $[CC1(R) + CC0(C), CC0(D) + CC1(C) + CC0(C) + CC0(R)]$
$CC1(Q)$	$CC1(D) + CC1(C) + CC0(C) + CC0(R)$
$SC0(Q)$	min $[SC1(R) + SC0(C), SC0(D) + SC1(C) + SC0(G) + SC0(R)] + 1$
$SC1(Q)$	$SC1(D) + SC1(C) + SC0(C) + SCO(R) + 1$
$CO(D)$	$C0(Q) + CC1(C) + CC0(C) + CC0(R)$
$SO(D)$	$SO(Q) + SC1(C) + SC0(C) + SC0(R) + 1$

Figure 10.3-1 *D* flip-flop corresponding to Table 10.3-3.

analyzed. Figure 10.3-2 shows the sequential controllability profiles generated by SCOAP for the circuit of Fig. 10.3-3. The data for these profiles, shown in Table 10.3-4, is taken from [Goldstein 80]. The highest value occurs for the 1-controllability of node FB, reflecting the difficulty of placing a 1 on this node. This is an indication that some modification such as adding an asynchronous reset to flip-flop FF3 should be considered.

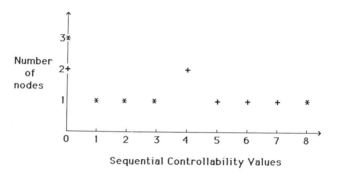

Sequential Controllability Values

(∗sequential 1-controllability, + sequential 0-controllability)

Figure 10.3-2 Profiles for the circuit of Fig. 10.3-3.

TABLE 10.3-4 Sequential controllability parameter values for Fig. 10.3-3.

Sequential	CLK	I	DIN	FB	OUT1	OUT2	OUT3
0-Controllability	0	0	4	4	5	6	7
1-Controllability	0	0	0	8	1	2	3

10.3-3 TESTSCREEN, CAMELOT, and VICTOR

TESTSCREEN is similar to SCOAP in that a six-element vector is associated with each node. The same six parameters are represented, but a different technique is used to compute their values. In TESTSCREEN the number of primary inputs that must be fixed in order to control a node value is used as the value of the node combinational controllability. Combinational observability is based on the number of primary inputs that must be fixed in order to sensitize a fault from the node to a primary output. Thus the major change from the SCOAP program is the use

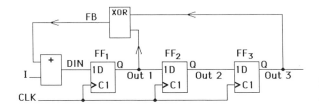

Figure 10.3-3 Circuit to illustrate SCOAP.

of primary inputs rather than the total number of nodes which need to be controlled. The use of primary inputs is justified as a measure of the logic conflicts that occur in trying to control or observe a node value. The sequential measures in TESTSCREEN are defined as the number of clock changes needed to control or observe the node's logic signal.

CAMELOT, like TMEAS, derives a controllability value and an observability value for each node. Unlike TMEAS, CAMELOT makes use of controllability values in determining the node observabilities. This is done to account for the necessity of placing values on internal nodes to sensitize a path to the output. There are other differences in the details of how the controllability and observability calculations are specified.

VICTOR is restricted to combinational circuits. It differs from the other programs in its emphasis on detecting redundant faults. It is typical in VICTOR to identify many nodes as "potentially redundant" even if few or no redundant faults are present. The potentially redundant nodes may represent nodes that are difficult to test rather than nodes that can be removed without altering the circuit function. As discussed above, SCOAP identifies some but not all redundant faults. In a sense, all the TM programs give some indication of potentially redundant faults. However, some redundant faults may be missed: It is possible for a node to be easy to control and easy to observe, but impossible to both control and observe simultaneously. Such nodes correspond to redundant faults that could be missed by the TM programs. For a discussion of redundancy, see [Floutier 79].

10.4 SCAN TECHNIQUES

A major difficulty with the **ad hoc** techniques is the requirement of adding extra control inputs or observation outputs. Testability measures help by allowing the use of only those additional external connections that are important for satisfying the testability requirements. The techniques described in this section permit access to internal nodes of a circuit without requiring a separate external connection for each node accessed. This is made possible at the cost of additional internal logic circuitry used primarily for testing. The discussion of this section assumes that the system is organized as a finite state machine—there is only one system clock. This is the preferred organization for a testable system, but systems with several clocks or internally generated clocks are in use. It is possible to introduce scan-path test methods into such systems, but the details of such applications are omitted due to space limitations.

Very few (from 1 to 4) additional external connections are used to access many internal nodes—typically all of the system bistable elements. A common feature of all of the scan methods is the serialization of the test data. Since there are more test points than external connections, the data must be transferred serially or *scanned* in and out of the circuit being tested. There are a variety of design-for-testability scan methods in use. The technique used to serialize the test data depends on the system clocking strategy. The change from normal system operation to test mode can be controlled by a level test-mode signal or by a separate test clock signal.

Besides increased accessibility the scan-path techniques have another very important benefit: sequential circuit test pattern generation is not required. Test pattern generation need only be done for the combinational circuits since the bistable elements can be accessed and tested directly.

Two approaches are used for converting between parallel and serial data: one uses a shift register and the other a multiplexer. The scan methods based on shift register techniques are often called **scan-path** methods since during testing the system bistables are connected as a shift register or scan path. The scan-path methods will be discussed next. Then the scan methods that use the multiplexer approach will be presented.

In the scan-path methods, the circuit is designed so that it has two modes of operation: one that is the normal functional mode, and another that is a test mode in which the circuit bistables are interconnected into a shift register. With the circuit in test mode it is possible to shift an arbitrary test pattern into the bistables. By returning the circuit to normal mode for one clock period, the combinational circuitry acts upon the bistable contents and primary input signals and stores the results in the bistables. If the circuit is then placed into test mode, it is possible to shift out the contents for the bistables and compare these contents with the correct response.

10.4-1 Scan Path Methods for Flip-flop Machines

The first published description of a scan-path design-for-testability structure was [Williams 73], a paper based on the Stanford Ph.D. research of Michael Williams. In this technique each of the circuit flip-flops is replaced by the flip-flop structure shown in Fig. 10.4-1.

MD Flip-flop Architectures. A multiplexer is placed at the data input to permit a selection of two different data inputs—d_0 (normal system operation) and d_1 (test mode). The choice of data input is based on the value of the control input, T. When $T = 0$, data are gated from the d_0 input on an active clock transition. Data are taken from d_1 if T is equal to 1. A D flip-flop with multiplexed data inputs as in Fig. 10.4-1 is often called a **Multiplexed Data flip-flop** or **MD flip-flop**.

It should be noted that the design of Fig. 10.4-1 has the undesirable feature of increasing the propagation delay of the flip-flop. This is not inherent in a multiplexed data flip-flop. The additional delay can be eliminated (except possibly

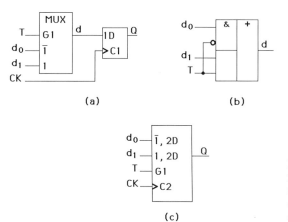

Figure 10.4-1 Multiplexed data flip-flop (MD flip-flop); (a) flip-flop with multiplexer (MUX); (b) multiplexer circuit diagram; (c) symbol for multiplexed data flip-flop (MD flip-flop).

for the effect of additional gate fanin) by redesigning the flip-flop to incorporate the multiplexer into the flip-flop circuitry.

The modification of the basic flip-flop finite state machine structure of Fig. 8.2-2 to obtain a scan-path architecture using MD flip-flops is shown in Fig. 10.4-2.

One additional input, the T input, has been added. For normal operation, T is equal to 0 and the circuit is connected as in Fig. 8.2-2. The upper data inputs $(y_1 \ldots y_s)$ act as the flip-flop D inputs. To test the circuit, T is set equal to 1. The lower data inputs become the flip-flop D inputs. Thus $D_i = Q_{i-1}$ for i from 2 to s, and a shift register is formed. The primary input X_n is connected to D_1 becoming the shift register input and Q_s, the shift register output, appears at the primary output Z_m.

Testing of the combinational logic is accomplished by:

1. Setting $T = 1$ (scan mode).
2. Shifting the test pattern y_j values into the flip-flops.
3. Setting the corresponding test values on the X_i inputs.
4. Setting $T = 0$ and, after a sufficient time for the combinational logic to settle, checking the output Z_k values.
5. Applying a clock signal to CK.
6. Setting $T = 1$ and shifting out the flip-flop contents via Z_m. The next y_j test pattern can be shifted in at the same time. The y_j values shifted out are compared with the good response values for y_j.

The flip-flops must also be tested. This is accomplished by shifting a string of 1's and then a string of 0's through the shift register to verify the possibility of shifting both a 1 and a 0 into each flip-flop. For some technologies, a more complex pattern such as 01100 may be necessary to verify that all possible data transitions are possible.

Two-port Flip-flop Architectures. A basic requirement of the scan-path technique is that it be possible to gate data into the system flip-flops from two different

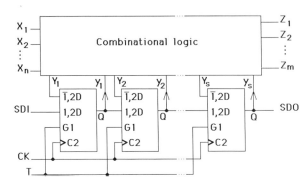

SDI is scan data input   SDO is scan data output

(a)

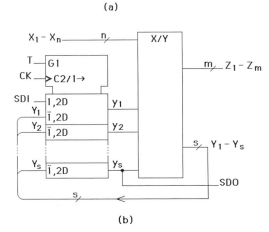

(b)

Figure 10.4-2 MD flip-flop scan-path architecture: (a) detailed diagram; (b) concise form of (a).

sources. One method of doing this is to add multiplexers to the system flip-flops as just discussed. Another possibility is to replace each system flip-flop by a **two-port flip-flop**, a flip-flop having two control inputs with the data source determined by which of the control inputs is pulsed, Sec. 8.3-1. A circuit for a two-port flip-flop is shown in Fig. 10.4-3. When a pulse is applied to $C1$, data are entered from $D1$; and when a pulse occurs at $C2$, data are entered from $D2$.

Figure 10.4-4 shows the structure of a network with two-port flip-flops used to provide the scan path. The testing procedure must be modified slightly and becomes:

1. Scan in the test vector y_j values via X_n using the test clock *TCK*.

2. Set the corresponding test values on the X_i inputs.

3. After sufficient time for the signals to propagate through the combinational network, check the output Z_k values.

4. Apply one clock pulse to the system clock *SCK* to enter the new values of Y_j into the corresponding flip-flops.

5. Scan out and check the Y_j values by pulsing the test clock *TCK*.

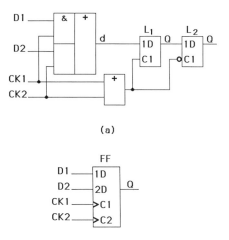

(a)

FF

(b)

Figure 10.4-3 Two-port D flip-flop:
(a) circuit; (b) symbol.

10.4-2 Two-phase Latch Machines and LSSD

The most popular technique for introducing scan-path testability into latch-based systems is IBM's LSSD (Level Sensitive Scan Design), [Eichelberger 77]. It is the standard design technique in current use at IBM. Figure 10.4-5 shows the general form of a double-latch design for a two-phase latch machine (Sec. 8.2-2) that has been converted to an LSSD structure by replacing each L1 latch by a two-port (dual-port) latch, (Sec. 7.2-2).

Examples of some specific designs using this structure are presented in [Das Gupta 78]. Other possible structures are discussed in [Eichelberger 77]. During normal operation the system is clocked with two interleaved nonoverlapping pulse trains applied to the $CK1$ and $CK2$ inputs. The way a system designed using this technique is tested is very similar to testing a system using two-port flip-flops:

1. Scan in the test vector y_j values via SDI by applying pulses alternately to the test clock input TCK (called A clock in some LSSD papers) and the system clock input $CK2$ (also called B clock).

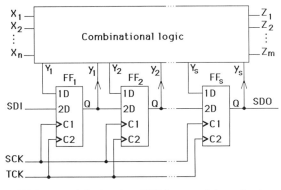

SDI is scan data input   SDO is scan data output

Figure 10.4-4 General structure of circuit using two-port flip-flops to provide scan path.

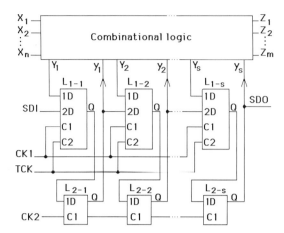

Figure 10.4-5 General structure of circuit using two-port latches to provide scan path—LSSD double-latch design. *SDI*, scanned-in test data; *SDO*, scanned-out test data; *TCK*, test clock.

2. Set the corresponding test values on the X_i inputs.

3. After sufficient time for the signals to propagate through the combinational network, check the output Z_k values.

4. Apply one clock pulse to the system clock *CK*1 to enter the new values of y_j into the corresponding *L*1 latches.

5. Scan out and check the y_j values by applying clock pulses alternately to *CK*2 and *TCK*.

LSSD refers to a design technique that provides a scan-path capability and also produces a system in which the steady-state response to allowed input changes is independent of circuit and wire delays. A system whose operation does not depend on internal delays is called **level sensitive**. The LSSD rules are given in [Eichelberger 77]. They are more detailed, but very similar to the requirements that:

1. Hazard-free D latches be used for all system bistables, (Sec. 7.2-3).

2. A two-phase latch FSM structure be used.

3. The L1 and L2 latches be interconnected in a scan-path structure such as shown in Fig. 10.4-5.

It is, in principle, possible to use *MD L*1 latches rather than dual-port *L*1 latches. The author is not aware of any systems using this structure. So many variations on the basic scan-path structures are in use that it is not possible to keep track of all of them.

10.4-3 One-phase Latch Machines

As discussed in Sec. 7.7, it is not possible in a one-phase latch machine structure to form a shift register by directly interconnecting the system latches. Either additional latches or delay elements are needed. This difficulty of forming a shift register has led to a variety of approaches to obtain a test scan capability in one-phase latch systems. One approach adds a separate test data shift register in parallel with the system latches. Two other approaches use multiplexing techniques. Each of these approaches will be described in the following subsections.

Scan-set Structures. Each of the previous methods uses the functional system flip-flops or latches to scan test data into and out of the circuit. It is also possible to add to the functional circuitry a shift register whose sole purpose is the shifting in and out of test data. A design technique based on the introduction of such a shift register is proposed in [Stewart 77] and [Stewart 78]. (*Caution:* Stewart uses the term "flip-flop" to mean either a latch or a flip-flop. When it is necessary to distinguish, he calls a latch a "latch flip-flop" and a flip-flop as defined in Sec. 10.4-1 an "edge-triggered flip-flop.") The resulting structure is shown in Fig. 10.4-6.

Test data are shifted into the flip-flop register (FF_1-FF_s) from the SDI (scan data in) connection by clocking TCK. The test data are transferred to the system latches in parallel through their $2D$ inputs by applying a pulse to UCK. Scanning out the latch data is the reverse process: The latch contents are loaded in parallel into the shift register by pulsing DCK. Shifting out the register contents is accomplished by clocking TCK. The data are shifted to the SDO (shift data out) terminal.

To implement the structure of Fig. 10.4-6, the system latches must be converted into two-port latches. There is more hardware overhead in this technique than for LSSD: two latches per system latch for scan-set versus one latch per system

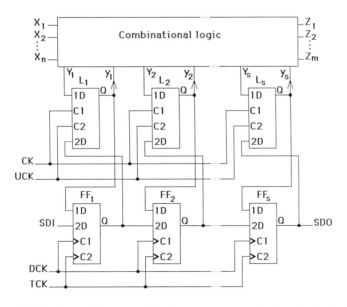

Figure 10.4-6 General structure of circuit using scan-set technique. FF_1-FF_s make up a shift register added for test purposes. L_1-L_s are system latches converted to two-port latches.

latch for LSSD. (Both techniques require the conversion of the system latches into two-port latches. Scan-set requires one shift register stage per system latch and each such stage requires the equivalent of two latches.)

Scan-set does have an important advantage compared to the techniques described above: With scan-set it is possible to gate the latch contents into the test shift register during normal system operation. This provides a means for getting a "snapshot" of system status. A technique for augmenting the LSSD structure to obtain a similar facility is discussed in [Das Gupta 81].

Another important feature of scan-set is the ability to scan circuit nodes other than latch outputs into the test shift register. Thus, it has the ability to introduce observation test points at nonlatch nodes.

Multiplexer Scan Structures. Parallel data can be serialized with a multiplexer rather than a shift register. A circuit structure that uses a multiplexer to scan out the system latches is shown in Fig. 10.4-7. This type of structure is discussed in [Stewart 78] in which the use of a 4-bit wide multiplexer is suggested. Use of more than one scan-out point increases the speed of scanning, but does increase the number of I/O connections required. One possibility for avoiding this increase is to place multiplexers on output pins to permit some of the output pins to be used both for system output and for scanning out test data, [McCluskey 81].

With a multiplexer scan structure, nodes other than latch outputs can be accessed. The scanning operation can take place while the system is operating. Complete scan out of all scan points is simplest if the scan data address register can be configured as a counter that steps through all addresses when clocked.

This multiplexer structure improves the observability of a design, but does nothing for the controllability. Setting of the system latches can be accomplished with a demultiplexer. The use of a demultiplexer for setting the system latches and a multiplexer for scan out forms the basis for the random access structure to be described next.

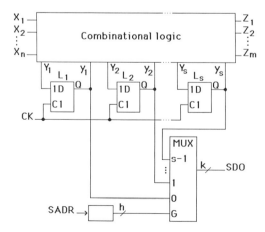

Figure 10.4-7 General structure of circuit using multiplexer to scan latch contents out. SADR is address of point(s) to be scanned out. SDO is a k-bit-wide bus with scanned-out latch values.

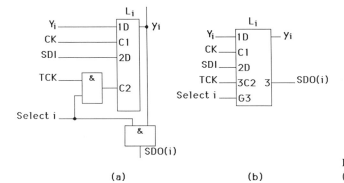

(a)   (b)

Figure 10.4-8 Addressable latch:
(a) circuit diagram; (b) symbol.

Random Access Scan Design. Fujitsu and Amdahl use the principles of multiplexing and demultiplexing to implement a scan technique for latch-based systems, [Ando 80] and [Wagner 83]. A simplified version of the latch design used is shown in Fig. 10.4-8. This is called an **addressable latch**. Inputs $1D(Y_i)$ and $C1(CK)$ are used during normal system operation.

In order to access Latch i for test purposes, the signal "Select i" must be set to 1. With Select $i = 1$, the latch content is placed on $SDO(i)$, and SDI is clocked into the latch if TCK is pulsed. The structure of a system using these latches is shown in Fig. 10.4-9.

There is associated with the circuit an address register whose contents are decoded to produce the "Select i" signals. At most one of these signals is equal to 1 at a time. Data is scanned into the latches by placing the latch i data value on SDI, the i address in the address register, and then pulsing TCK. The address register is implemented as a counter. Thus a sequence of data can be scanned into the latches by placing the sequence on SDI and pulsing the address register

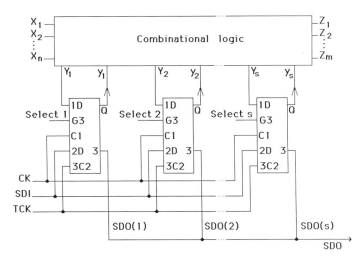

Figure 10.4-9 General structure of circuit using random-access scan.

counter and TCK in the proper time relationship. The latch contents are scanned out via SDO by pulsing the address register to select the latches in turn.

An important feature of this structure is the ability to scan out the latches during normal system operation.

The actual implementations of this technique using addressable latches have two or three select signals per latch. These signals are decoded at each latch using the circuit shown in Fig. 10.4-10 for the case of two select signals. Somewhat more complex latches are used in the actual systems in order to take advantage of the technology (ECL) and minimize the penalties due to addressability. These are described in [Ando 80] and [Wagner 83].

10.4-4 I/O Scan-path Structures

The scan-path techniques described in Secs. 10.4-1 through 10.4-3 improve testability by increasing controllability and observability (because of better internal access), and by eliminating the necessity of sequential circuit test pattern generation. The technique of this section improves testability by reducing the requirements placed on the physical test equipment.

The general I/O scan-path structure is shown in Fig. 10.4-11. The system latches are implemented in an LSSD type design so that they form a scan path (called internal scan path or ring) for test purposes. A pair of scan-path latches are introduced for each I/O bonding pad. These I/O latches are configured as another LSSD type scan path (called **external scan path** or ring). The details of the circuitry for Input bonding pads are shown in Fig. 10.4-12. The Output bonding pad latches are connected in an analogous fashion. More complete circuits are given in [Zasio 83].

The test procedure is very similar to that described in Section 10.4-2 for LSSD

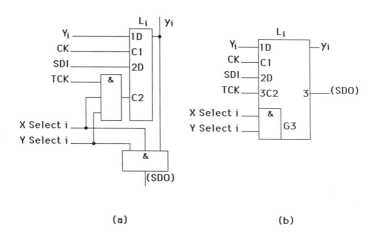

(a)   (b)

Figure 10.4-10   Addressable latch with coincident selection: (a) circuit; (b) symbol.

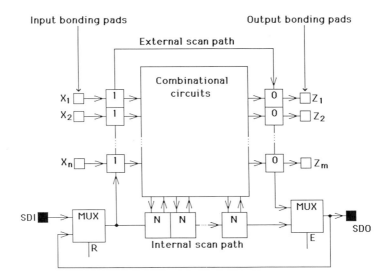

Figure 10.4-11 General structure of circuit using scan latches on input pins and output pins.

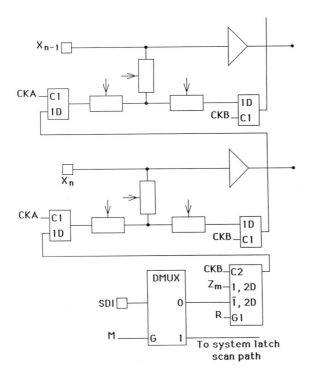

Figure 10.4-12 Details of input scan-path latches.

structures. The necessary modifications are that the X_i values are scanned in via the SDI pin (the DMUX control must be set to direct its inputs to the external ring). The Z outputs from the combinational logic must be clocked into the external ring latches which are then shifted out via the SDO pin.

The presence of the external scan path allows the chip to be tested through a small number of probe pins: 7 control pins plus 2 pins for power and ground for the design described in [Zasio 83]. This design demonstrates the testing of a 256-pin chip.

Another feature of this structure is the ability to qualify chips for speed at wafer probe by configuring the external ring as a ring oscillator. This is done by connecting the last latch in the external ring back as the input to the first latch in the ring.

Finally, this structure can easily be modified for use in a built-in self test configuration. This application will be discussed in the section on built-in self test.

10.4-5 Scan Path Economics

The costs associated with the scan-path designs are:

1. Additional circuitry is added to each flip-flop or latch. Thus, the flip-flops used for scan-path designs are more expensive than standard flip-flops.
2. One or more additional circuit pins are required. (If this is a critical design parameter, it is possible to use voltage multiplexing of the pins for test purposes.)
3. Testing time is increased by the need to shift the test patterns into the flip-flops serially. This may not be a net increase in test time: The modified circuit requires shorter test sets than the original circuit because only combinational logic test patterns are used.
4. There can be a performance penalty. The speed of normal operation may be decreased due to increased propagation delay in the scan-path latches or flip-flops.
5. Available functional area can be reduced due to the increased interconnect. This additional interconnect can also introduce a performance penalty.

Most of the overhead associated with the scan-path designs results from the modifications of the bistable elements: Flip-flops or latches. Since the bistables make up only a small portion of an entire system, the scan-path system overhead is probably at least an order of magnitude less than the overhead associated with a single bistable. The overhead can be minimized by optimizing the design of the scan-path bistables. Efficient LSSD latch designs are discussed in [Eichelberger 83a].

The performance penalty can be minimized by designing the bistables so that no additional gate delays are introduced in series with the data inputs. A design for the LSSD latches is shown in Fig. 10.4-13. Since the two data inputs are effectively in parallel, no additional gate delay is introduced by the inclusion of a

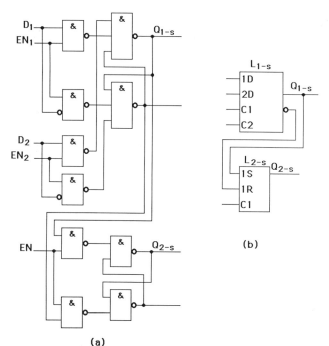

(b)

(a)

Figure 10.4-13 Design of LSSD latches to eliminate data delay and hazards; (a) NAND gate circuit; (b) corresponding logic symbol.

second data port. (There may be some decrease in speed due to increased loading.) Another feature of this design is that the latches are hazard-free: No spurious signals (glitches or spikes) are produced on the outputs when the state is changed. It is this feature that is important for level-sensitive operation. A detailed discussion of the hazard-free aspect of the design is given in [Eichelberger 77]. Elimination of hazards in a random-access scan design is discussed in [Wagner 83].

The pairs (L_1 and L_2) of LSSD latches can be converted into master-slave flip-flops by the modification shown in Fig. 10.4-14. If the resulting two-port flip-flops are used in the structure of Fig. 10.4-4, a design is obtained in which there is no delay penalty due to the use of two-port flip-flops and static hazards are avoided. However, the use of master-slave flip-flops does introduce an essential hazard which is inherent in all flip-flops.

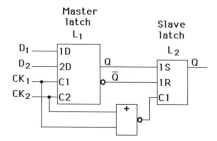

Figure 10.4-14 Master-slave flip-flop using LSSD latches.

10.4-6 Extensions

A number of testing problems can still arise in systems designed using scan path techniques. Extensions to the basic scan-path technique have been proposed to overcome these problems.

Test Pattern Generation Cost. The cost of automatic test pattern generation for the combinational portion of a large circuit can be excessive. The computation time for test generation increases rapidly with network size. (The growth in test generation time is demonstrated in [Goel 80] to be proportional to G^2 where G is the number of gates in the circuit. While this result is not universally accepted, there is general agreement that the growth is faster than linear.) The test generation cost can be substantially reduced by generating tests for subcircuits and then combining the subcircuit tests to obtain the complete network test. In [Bottorff 77] an algorithm for preprocessing an LSSD circuit description to obtain subcircuit descriptions for an automatic test pattern program is described:

1. A backtrace is performed from each primary output and from each latch. The backtrace is stopped when a primary input or latch is reached. This identifies a "cone" of all logic elements and interconnections (nets) which control the value of the starting point of the backtrace.

2. The cones are combined into subcircuits for test generation. The size and number of the subcircuits is determined by the circuit structure and the characteristics of the test generation program to be used. An attempt is made to minimize the logic that appears in more than one subcircuit by choosing cones with common logic for combination.

Sometimes this procedure fails to obtain subcircuits that are small enough for efficient test pattern generation. For such cases it has been proposed in [Hsu 78] to incorporate selective control circuitry at the subassembly (module, dip) outputs. Division of a circuit into subcircuits for test generation is also discussed in [Yamada 78]. Both of these papers call the subcircuits "partitions," although they are not partitions in a strict sense since the subcircuits will typically not be disjoint.

Imbedded Memory. It is becoming increasingly common to have memory (ROM or RAM) included as part of a circuit. Testing of such designs using scan-path techniques is not straightforward. Four specific problems arise:

1. Tests for some of the faults in the combinational logic may require that the memory outputs be set to specified values.

2. Tests for some of the faults in the combinational logic may require that the effect of the fault be propagated through the memory in order for the effect to appear at a latch or primary output.

3. To fully test a RAM it is necessary to write and read both a 1 and a 0 for each cell. For a ROM test, each cell must be read.

4. The combinational logic in that part of the "cone" driving the RAM tends to be rather large.

A modification of the basic LSSD design method to permit efficient testing of circuits with embedded memory is presented in [Eichelberger 78]. Different methods for testing such circuits are discussed in [Funatsu 78] and [Ando 80]. In these papers the embedded memories are called "arrays," although the techniques described are not intended to apply either to programmed logic arrays or to gate arrays.

Miscellaneous Extensions. The use of a random test pattern generator to obtain tests for an LSSD design is described in [Williams 77]. Modifications to the basic LSSD latch design for a variety of applications, including those in which an LSSD design is interfaced with non-LSSD circuitry, are presented in [Das Gupta 81].

10.5 EASILY TESTABLE NETWORKS AND FUNCTION-INDEPENDENT TESTING

Most of the recent work on DFT has assumed that standard design techniques would be used to implement the functional logic. These techniques aim at producing circuits that represent some compromise between maximizing the performance and minimizing the cost. The DFT techniques are design modifications that attempt to limit their impact on cost and performance while improving testability. There is an older DFT approach called **easily testable network design** which is aimed at developing design techniques that start with a functional specification and result in networks that are easy to test. In this approach there are no constraints on the cost or performance of the resulting design. The easily testable network design techniques will be described in this section. Desirable properties for **ET networks**, "easily testable" networks, were specified in [Reddy 72] as:

1. Small test sets.
2. No redundancy.
3. The test set can be found without much extra work.
4. The test set can be easily generated.
5. The test set outputs should be easily interpreted.
6. The faults should be locatable to the desired degree.

The requirement of no redundancy is present because it is not possible to test for a fault on a redundant lead, but the presence of such a fault can prevent a test set from detecting a fault on a nonredundant lead [Friedman 67]. This requirement does not create any particular difficulties; any testing scheme will be more efficient if redundancy is not present.

Test application cost is made low both by keeping socket time short and by using a simple tester. The short socket time results from the small test set (property 1). A simple tester can be used because of the requirement (4) that the test set be easily generated (by a simple logic network) so that it is not necessary to have a large memory to store precalculated test patterns, and the requirement (5) that outputs be easily interpreted, which avoids the necessity of storing output response patterns.

Low maintenance cost is the aim of the requirement (6) on fault locatability. Test pattern generation cost is small because of the requirement (3) that the test set be found without much extra work. Some of the techniques result in test sets that do not depend on the function realized by the network. They are said to allow **function independent testing**.

10.5-1 RM Networks

The design procedure presented in [Reddy 72] responds to properties 1 and 3 by constraining the final form of the network. An example of a network designed using this procedure is shown in Fig. 10.5-1a. (The function is available at the output marked f. The e output is only used during testing.) Such networks will be called **RM networks**. Their design is based on the Reed-Muller canonical form for switching functions [Muller 54], in which the switching function is expressed as the EXCLUSIVE-OR (sum modulo 2) of products of the independent variables.

The network form is such that it can be tested for all single stuck-at faults on the inputs of the AND gates as well as any combinational fault of the XOR gates with a set of $n + 4$ test inputs (n is the number of primary network inputs)

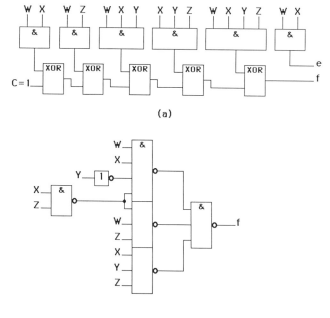

(a)

(b)

Figure 10.5-1 Networks for function $f = WXY'Z' + WX'Z + XYZ$:
(a) "easily testable" realization;
(b) NAND realization.

Design for Testability   Chap. 10

that does not depend on the function realized by the network. For an arbitrary network structure the number of patterns required to test for all single stuck-at faults is proportional to the number of gates in the network, [Goel 80]. There are usually many more gates than network inputs. Thus it seems reasonable to accept $n + 4$ as a small number of test inputs. Since the test set is independent of the function realized by the network, a tester circuit can be designed that will test any n-input design. The block diagram for such a test circuit is given in [Reddy 72]. The generalization to a test circuit that can test for any number of inputs up to some maximum seems straightforward. No extra work is required to get the test set for a specific function, so property 3 is surely satisfied. The test circuit is not costly to implement, hence property 4 is taken care of. Ease of interpretation of the test outputs (property 5) is also direct. A simple circuit is given in [Reddy 72] that produces the same output as the network being tested *for each of the test inputs*. Since this circuit need only have its outputs specified for the test pattern inputs, it is much simpler than the circuit under test. In fact, this test-output circuit can be realized in a general form which permits it to be "programmed" for a specific function.

A number of extensions to the original scheme of [Reddy 72] have been proposed: [Kodandapani 74], [Kodandapani 77], [Pradhan 78], [Page 80], and [Saluja 75]. These all preserve the RM network structure and do not change the fundamental nature of the technique.

A RM network is made up of two parts: a cascade connection of XOR gates and a number of AND gates. The XOR cascade part can be tested for any faulty gate with just four tests [Kautz 71]. This is the basic property that makes the RM network testable with a small test set. The AND gate portion can be tested for any stuck fault with an additional n tests providing an extra output (e in Fig. 10.5-1a) is used. The extra output is derived from an AND gate that has as inputs all those primary inputs that are connected to an even number of AND gates in the circuit for f. (In Fig. 10.5-1a, W is connected to four AND gates in the f network; thus W is connected to the e AND gate. Y is connected to three AND gates in the f network and is thus missing from the e gate.)[2]

The RM network technique has three very serious flaws: (1) It can require many more gates than necessary to implement the function. Figure 10.5-1b shows a NAND gate realization for the same function as the RM network of Fig. 10.5-1a. The NAND network uses five NAND gates and one inverter. The RM network has six AND gates and five XOR gates. For this simple function of only four variables the RM network has about twice as many gates as an efficient network. In many technologies the XOR gates are much more expensive than NAND gates. (2) There is a long delay in producing the output from the RM network because of the necessity to propagate signals through the XOR cascade (six gate maximum delay for Fig. 10.5-1a versus three-gate delay for Fig. 10.5-1b). There is usually a longer propagation delay for an XOR gate than for a NAND gate. (3) The RM network must be designed from a Boolean specification.

---

[2] The additional output can be avoided at the cost of adding $2E$ tests to the test set, where E equals the number of inputs connected to an even number of AND gates. In this case the test set depends on the function realized.

Thus, efficient techniques of combining known modules such as adders, multiplexers, etc., can't be used.

Several other techniques have been proposed for designing ET networks. These techniques avoid the third flaw mentioned in connection with RM networks by starting with an efficient network design obtained by standard design techniques and then modifying the network to make it possible to use a small test set. In [Hayes 74] the network is converted to a network of two-input NAND gates and inverters. The inverters are replaced by XOR gates and XOR gates are inserted into all gate inputs not driven by inverters. The second inputs to the XOR gates all become additional primary control inputs and all the XOR gate outputs become additional primary test outputs. The modified network can be tested with five test inputs. The objective of having a small test set is clearly satisfied. The extra XOR gates can easily double the total number of gates in the network and also the delay in forming the output. A related technique is described in [Saluja 74], in which each original gate is replaced by a network of gates and the test set consists of three test inputs. It suffers from the same problems of many extra gates and long propagation delays.

Rather than modifying the functional network, the technique proposed in [Das Gupta 80] embeds it in a larger network in order to obtain the ET network properties. The assumption is made that it is only necessary to test for faults at input–output terminals. Four extra inputs are added for test purposes, and only two test input patterns are required. While the number of added gates and delay is modest, the restriction to input–output faults is probably acceptable only in very special situations.

10.5-2 FITPLA

To my knowledge none of the techniques described in Sec. 10.5-1 has ever been used in an actual system design. Methods that are more promising for practical application involve modifying the PLA structure to make it easily testable. Since the PLA structure is one that is frequently used in real systems, a modification to this structure which makes it easy to test has the possibility of wide usage.

A modified PLA structure has been proposed that can be tested with a fixed test set that depends only on the size of the PLA and not on the functions realized. Further, the output response can be checked by the structure itself, so that storage of test responses is not necessary. Thus, this structure realizes a PLA for which function independent testing is possible. The number of input vectors in the test set is of the order of $n + w$, where n is the number of input variables and w is the number of word lines (product terms). The following description of the FITPLA, a modified PLA that can be tested by a function-independent test set, is based on [Hong 80], [Fujiwara 81] and [Fujiwara 84].

The basic PLA structure is shown in Fig. 10.5-2a and an example of a specific implementation given in Fig. 10.5-2b. In the following discussion it will be assumed that the signal on a word line is the logical product of the signals on the bit lines connected to the word line with crosspoints and that the signal on an output line is the logical sum of the signals on the word lines connected to the output line

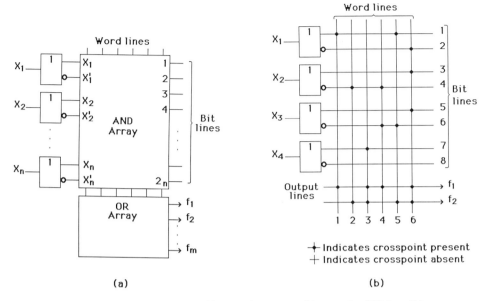

Figure 10.5-2 PLA networks: (a) general structure; (b) example of PLA realizing
$f_1 = X_1 + X_4 + X_2'X_3' + X_1'X_2X_3, f_2 = X_2' + X_4 + X_1X_3' + X_1'X_2X_3$.

with crosspoints.   Thus, in Fig. 10.5-2b the signal on word line 4 is given by
$X_2'X_3'$.   For MOS PLAs some of the signal polarities should be modified to reflect
the fact that NOR functions are realized by the arrays rather than AND and OR
functions, Sec. 6.9-1.

The strategy used in deriving the FITPLA is to provide mechanisms whereby
the selection of either a single bit line or a single word line can be forced.   Selection
of a single bit line is made possible by replacing the input decoders (that provide
X_i and X_i') with modified decoders (that provide $X_i + y_1$ and $X_i' + y_2$).   Circuits
for the decoders are shown in Fig. 10.5-3 and their operation is illustrated in Table
10.5-1.   During normal operation of the PLA both y_1 and y_2 are set equal to 0.
With $y_1 = 0$ and $y_2 = 1$, all of the bit lines driven by complemented variables are
forced to 1.   All those variables that are equal to 1 will have the corresponding
bit lines equal to 1.   Thus, by setting only one of the input variables to 0 and
$y_1y_2 = 0\ 1$, a single bit line will be equal to 0.   Similarly, setting only one of the
input variables (X_i) equal to 1 and $y_1y_2 = 1\ 0$ will cause only one of the bit lines
corresponding to X_i' to equal 0.[3]

The next modification is the addition of one word line, the **parity word line**,
to the AND ARRAY.   The connections to the parity word line are made to ensure
that there are an odd number of crosspoints on each bit line.   A circuit that checks
the parity of the signals on the word lines is also added to the PLA.   The PLA of
Fig. 10.5-2b with these modifications is shown in Fig. 10.5-4.

[3] If the input variables are decoded two at a time, a similar modification can be used to permit
selection of a single bit line.   In this situation, four y control variables are required rather than two.

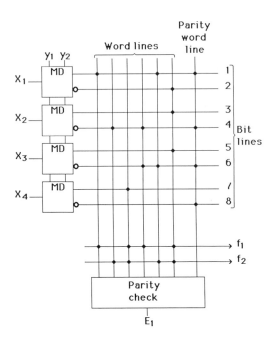

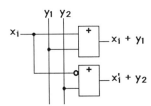

Figure 10.5-3 Design of modified input decoders.

Figure 10.5-4 PLA of Fig. 10.5-2b with AND array modifications.

TABLE 10.5-1 Operation of modified input decoders for $n = 4$.

						Bit lines							
X_1	X_2	X_3	X_4	y_1	y_2	1	2	3	4	5	6	7	8
X_1	X_2	X_3	X_4	0	0	X_1	X_1'	X_2	X_2'	X_3	X_3'	X_4	X_4'
X_1	X_2	X_3	X_4	0	1	X_1	1	X_2	1	X_3	1	X_4	1
X_1	X_2	X_3	X_4	1	0	1	X_1'	1	X_2'	1	X_3'	1	X_4
1	1	1	1	0	1	1	1	1	1	1	1	1	1
0	0	0	0	1	0	1	1	1	1	1	1	1	1
0	1	1	1	0	1	0	1	1	1	1	1	1	1
1	0	0	0	1	0	1	0	1	1	1	1	1	1

By selecting each of the bit lines individually and observing the signal on E_1, it is possible to detect any single stuck-at-1 fault on a bit line and any single crosspoint fault (a crosspoint missing or an extra crosspoint) in the AND array. This requires $2n$ test inputs since there are $2n$ bit lines. These $2n$ test inputs will be called the *A* test set (the AND array is being tested). The eight vectors of the *A* test set for the four-input example of Fig. 10.5-4 are shown in Table 10.5-2.

Testing of the OR array is done by selecting the word lines one at a time. This is made possible by an extra bit line, called the **word select line**, in the AND

Design for Testability   Chap. 10

TABLE 10.5-2 A test set for the PLA of Fig. 10.5-4.

Test set A						Bit lines							
X_1	X_2	X_3	X_4	y_1	y_2	1	2	3	4	5	6	7	8
0	1	1	1	0	1	0	1	1	1	1	1	1	1
1	0	0	0	1	0	1	0	1	1	1	1	1	1
1	0	1	1	0	1	1	1	0	1	1	1	1	1
0	1	0	0	1	0	1	1	1	0	1	1	1	1
1	1	0	1	0	1	1	1	1	1	0	1	1	1
0	0	1	0	1	0	1	1	1	1	1	0	1	1
1	1	1	0	0	1	1	1	1	1	1	1	0	1
0	0	0	1	1	0	1	1	1	1	1	1	1	0

array. The word select line has crosspoints connected to each of the word lines. Along with the word select line, a shift register, **SHR**, is added to the PLA. This shift register has one stage per word line and each stage output is connected to one of the word select line crosspoints. During normal operation an all-1 pattern is held in SHR. These modifications are shown in Fig. 10.5-5.

Detection of faults in the OR array is based on the addition of an output line, the **OR parity line**, which has crosspoints to ensure that there is an odd total number of crosspoints on each word line in the OR array. Verification of this

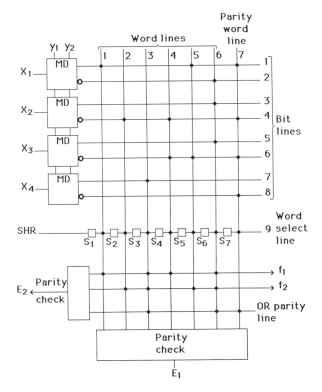

Figure 10.5-5 PLA of Fig. 5-4 with OR array modifications added.

odd parity is done by means of a parity checker, the E_2 **checker**, that is connected to all the output lines.

Selection of a single word line is accomplished by shifting into SHR a pattern having 0's in all stages except that corresponding to the selected word, and setting 1's on all bit lines by placing appropriate signals on the X_i and y_j lines. These are shown in Table 10.5-3. Any single crosspoint fault in the OR array or stuck fault on a single (output) line in the OR array will be indicated by a change in the E_2 signal. Single stuck faults on the word lines are indicated by an incorrect E_1 signal. (A stuck-at-0 fault will be discovered when the faulty word line is selected. Single stuck-at-1 faults will be indicated by more than one word line having a 1 on it.) A single stuck-at-0 on a bit line will be detected at E_1 by the failure to select the word line having a crosspoint on the stuck bit line.

A summary of the fault detection in the FITPLA is given in Table 10.5-4. During the application of the A test set, an all-1 pattern should be present in SHR. In addition to testing for faults in the PLA proper it is also necessary to test the two parity check circuits. This is discussed in [Hong 80]. Subsequent research has resulted in techniques for designing the parity checkers so that they are self-checking ([Khakbaz 84], [Khakbaz 83a], and [Khakbaz 82]). Extension of the FITPLA design so that multiple as well as single faults are detected is discussed in [Saluja 81].

A number of other techniques for designing testable PLAs have been proposed. Some of them such as [Bozorgui-Nesbatt 84] are aimed at designs that require specific test patterns but generate patterns that detect extra and missing

TABLE 10.5-3 Test set B for the PLA of Fig. 10.5-4

X_1	X_2	X_3	X_4	y_1	y_2	S_1	S_2	S_3	S_4	S_5	S_6	S_7	Bit line 12345678	Word line 1234567	E_1	E_2
1	1	1	1	0	1	1	0	0	0	0	0	0	11111111	1000000	1	1
0	0	0	0	1	0	1	0	0	0	0	0	0	11111111	1000000	1	1
1	1	1	1	0	1	0	1	0	0	0	0	0	11111111	0100000	1	1
0	0	0	0	1	0	0	1	0	0	0	0	0	11111111	0100000	1	1
1	1	1	1	0	1	0	0	1	0	0	0	0	11111111	0010000	1	1
0	0	0	0	1	0	0	0	1	0	0	0	0	11111111	0010000	1	1
1	1	1	1	0	1	0	0	0	1	0	0	0	11111111	0001000	1	1
0	0	0	0	1	0	0	0	0	1	0	0	0	11111111	0001000	1	1
1	1	1	1	0	1	1	0	0	0	1	0	0	11111111	0000100	1	1
0	0	0	0	1	0	1	0	0	0	1	0	0	11111111	0000100	1	1
1	1	1	1	0	1	0	0	0	0	0	1	0	11111111	0000010	1	1
0	0	0	0	1	0	0	0	0	0	0	1	0	11111111	0000010	1	1
1	1	1	1	0	1	0	0	0	0	0	0	1	11111111	0000001	1	1
0	0	0	0	1	0	0	0	0	0	0	0	1	11111111	0000001	1	1

TABLE 10.5-4 Fault detection summary

	Single stuck faults			Crosspoint faults		
Value	Location	Test set	Checker	Location	Test set	Checker
0	Bit line	B	E_1	AND array	A	E_1
1	Bit line	A	E_1	OR array	B	E_2
0, 1	Output line	B	E_2			
0, 1	Word line	B	E_1			
0	X_i, y_j input	B	E_1			
1	X_i, y_j input	A	E_1			
0	OR gate input	B	E_1			
1	OR gate input	A	E_1			

crosspoints as well as single-stuck faults. Other papers such as [Treuer 85] present self-testing PLA structures.

10.6 BUILT-IN SELF TEST

Testing of a circuit requires the application of an appropriate set of test vectors and the comparison of the actual circuit response with the correct response. The techniques presented in the previous sections are aimed at facilitating the application of the test vectors (controllability) and the observation of the circuit response (observability). It is assumed that the test vectors will be applied to the circuit by a tester that is capable of storing the test patterns and the corresponding correct responses. Such testers are expensive.

Several techniques have been proposed for reducing the complexity of the external tester by moving some or all of the tester functions onto the chip itself. These techniques will be presented in this section.

Tester cost is not the only difficulty encountered in using an external tester. As discussed in the introduction, there are also problems with:

1. Generating the test patterns: The turnaround time to obtain the test patterns and the computation cost are becoming too large.
2. The number of test patterns becoming too large to be handled efficiently by the tester hardware.
3. The time taken to apply the test patterns.

The techniques of this section are intended to solve these problems as well as to reduce the tester cost.

The inclusion of on-chip circuitry to provide test vectors or to analyze output reponses is called **built-in self test** (BIST), **built-in test** (BIT), **self-test**, **autonomous test**, or **self-verification**. There is some ambiguity in the use of these terms. In particular, BIT and self-test are sometimes used to mean implicit testing (concurrent checking) or system level periodic testing [Clary 79]. The discussion in this chapter is restricted to explicit testing techniques.

Any test method must consist of (1) a strategy for generating the inputs to be applied, (2) a strategy for evaluating the output responses, and (3) the implementation mechanisms. Each of these topics will be considered in turn. The various options for strategies and implementations suitable for BIST will be presented.

10.6-1 Input Test Stimulus Generation

Test vectors can be generated (manually or by a test pattern generation program) and stored, **off-line test pattern generation**; or they can be calculated while they are being applied, **concurrent test pattern generation**. In theory it would be possible to generate test vectors off line and store them in an on-chip ROM. This has not been an attractive scheme; it does nothing to reduce the cost of test pattern generation and it requires a very large ROM. All of the BIST methods to be described here rely on concurrent test pattern generation.

A number of techniques have been proposed for concurrent test pattern generation. If the chip includes a processor and memory it is possible to use a test program to generate appropriate signals to stimulate the circuitry.[4] It has been suggested that it is sufficient that this program be written to force state changes or "wiggle" the circuit nodes [Gordon 77]. The difficulty with this approach is that such a test may fail to detect many faults [Hughes 85]. More systematic approaches to writing test programs are described in [Hayes 80]. The test programs usually rely on a **functional test approach**: They typically are written to exercise the functionality of the various system components. They can be based on the system diagnostic programs. Some reconfiguration of the circuit during test mode (to permit initialization and perhaps to break feedback loops) may be necessary to ensure good fault coverage [Gordon 77].

Two concurrent test pattern generation approaches that do not depend on the availability of an instruction processor have been proposed. Since these can be used with or without an instruction processor they are more general than the test program approach. One of these—**random testing**—uses a set of randomly generated patterns as test patterns. The other—**exhaustive testing**—uses all possible input combinations as test patterns. The random technique has the advantage of being applicable to sequential as well as combinational circuits; however, there are difficulties in determining the required test sequence length and fault coverage. Some circuits may require modification to obtain adequate coverage with reasonable test lengths, [Eichelberger 83b]. Exhaustive testing eliminates the need for a fault model and fault simulation. For large numbers of inputs this technique may require too much time. Some form of circuit partitioning is required to reduce the number of inputs in this case.

An important problem connected with concurrent random test pattern generation is the determination of the length of the random sequence that is required to obtain a satisfactory fault coverage. One straightforward technique uses fault

---

[4] This test program may be stored in ROM. This should not be confused with the technique of storing the actual test patterns in ROM.

simulation to determine fault coverage. The difficulty with simulation is its high cost. An analytical method of estimating fault coverage would be preferable. A number of approaches have been suggested, see [Chin 85]. None of the techniques yet developed is capable of getting accurate fault coverage estimates without a great deal of computation.

Another approach is aimed at discovering those faults that are hard to detect with random patterns. Two schemes for coping with these "random-pattern resistant" faults have been proposed. One would generate test patterns for these faults (using a deterministic technique such as the D algorithm) and store these patterns in a ROM. Thus some few patterns would be obtained from the ROM and the remaining patterns would be randomly generated. The other scheme modifies the network being tested so that none of its faults are "random-pattern resistant" ([Eichelberger 83b] and [Savir 83]).

Random Testing. If an instruction processor is available, the random test patterns can be generated by a program. A thorough discussion of random number programs is given in [Knuth 69]. For random test pattern generation it is not so important that the numbers used be strictly random since they are not being used for statistical purposes. A simple program for random test pattern generation is presented in [Brack 79]. Random test patterns can also be generated by means of a simple circuit called an **autonomous linear feedback shift register** or **ALFSR**. An autonomous linear feedback shift register, is a series connection of delay elements (D flip-flops) with no external inputs and with all feedback provided by means of EXCLUSIVE-OR gates (XORs). A four-stage ALFSR is shown in Fig. 10.6-1a and the general standard form of ALFSR is shown in Fig. 10.6-1b. The symbol h_i in Fig. 10.6-1b indicates the possible presence of a feedback connection from the output of each stage. If $h_i = 1$, there is feedback from stage i; and if $h_i = 0$, the stage i output is not connected to the XOR feedback network. The ALFSR can be specified by just listing the values of the h_i or by specifying the generating function as shown in Fig. 10.6-1.

Another possible realization of an ALFSR, called a **modular realization** is shown in Fig. 10.6-2. There are as many XOR gates in the modular realization as there are feedback taps in the standard circuit. The gates are placed in the "reverse" positions from the locations of the feedback taps. If in the standard LFSR there are m "taps," inputs to the XOR network generating the feedback signal, $m - 1$ two-input XOR gates are required if an iterative structure is used to realize the XOR network. This is the minimum-gate realization. It is slower than a tree network, which also requires $m - 1$ gates but has a delay of log m gate propagations rather than $m - 1$ gate delays. The modular circuit also requires $m - 1$ XOR gates. It has a delay of only one gate propagation. For circuits with more than two feedback signals, faster operation always results with the modular rather than the standard LFSR.

The sequence of states for the ALFSR of Fig. 10.6-1 is shown in Table 10.6-1. Note that the sequence repeats after 15 ($2^n - 1$) clocks. This is the maximum period for a four-stage ALFSR; the all-0 state of the register cannot occur in the maximum length cycle since an all-0 state always has a next state that

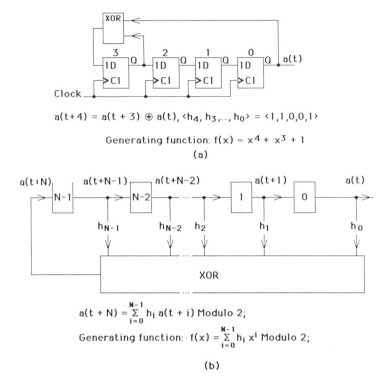

$$a(t+4) = a(t + 3) \oplus a(t), \langle h_4, h_3, ..., h_0 \rangle = \langle 1,1,0,0,1 \rangle$$

Generating function: $f(x) = x^4 + x^3 + 1$

(a)

$$a(t + N) = \sum_{i=0}^{N-1} h_i \, a(t + i) \text{ Modulo } 2;$$

Generating function: $f(x) = \sum_{i=0}^{N-1} h_i \, x^i \text{ Modulo } 2;$

(b)

Figure 10.6-1 Standard form of autonomous linear feedback shift register, AFLSR: (a) four-stage circuit; (b) *N*-stage circuit.

is also all 0's due to the use of XORs to form the feedback signal. In general, the maximum period for an *n*-stage ALFSR is $2^n - 1$. There are maximum-length realizations for all values of *n*. The generating function corresponding to a maximum-length ALFSR is called a **primitive polynomial**. Tables of primitive polynomials can be found in [Golumb 82], [Peterson 72], and many other publications. Table 10.6-2 lists one primitive polynomial for each value of *n* from 1 to 32.

Of course, the signals produced by an ALFSR are not really random since they are produced by a fixed circuit. Truly random signals are not required for test pattern generation. What is necessary is signals that produce the same types

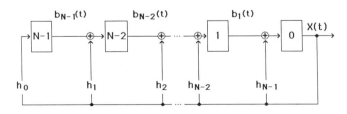

Figure 10.6-2 General modular realization of an ALFSR.

TABLE 10.6-1 State sequence for Fig. 10.6-1a

State	Q_1	Q_2	Q_3	Q_4	State	Q_1	Q_2	Q_3	Q_4
0	1	0	0	0	8	1	1	0	1
1	1	1	0	0	9	0	1	1	0
2	1	1	1	0	10	0	0	1	1
3	1	1	1	1	11	1	0	0	1
4	0	1	1	1	12	0	1	0	0
5	1	0	1	1	13	0	0	1	0
6	0	1	0	1	14	0	0	0	1
7	1	0	1	0	15 = 0	1	0	0	0

of test patterns as random signals. The output of an ALFSR can be shown to possess many of the properties of random signals. The sequences produced by maximum-length ALFSRs are called **pseudo-random (pr) sequences** or **pseudo-noise sequences** to distinguish them from truly random sequences. For test pattern generation pseudo-random sequences are better than random sequences since the

TABLE 10.6-2 One primitive polynomial for each n from 1 to 32

n	$f(X)$
1,2,3,4,6,7,15,22	$1 + X + X^n$
5,11,21,29	$1 + X^2 + X^n$
10,17,20,25,28,31	$1 + X^3 + X^n$
9	$1 + X^4 + X^n$
23	$1 + X^5 + X^n$
18	$1 + X^7 + X^n$
8	$1 + X^2 + X^3 + X^4 + X^n$
12	$1 + X + X^4 + X^6 + X^n$
13	$1 + X + X^3 + X^4 + X^n$
14,16	$1 + X^3 + X^4 + X^5 + X^n$
19,27	$1 + X + X^2 + X^5 + X^n$
24	$1 + X + X^2 + X^7 + X^n$
26	$1 + X + X^2 + X^6 + X^n$
30	$1 + X + X^2 + X^{23} + X^n$
32	$1 + X + X^2 + X^{22} + X^n$

pr-sequences can be reproduced for simulation. One period of the output sequence produced by the ALFSR of Fig. 10.6-1a is.

$$(0\ 0\ 0\ 1\ 1\ 1\ 1\ 0\ 1\ 0\ 1\ 1\ 0\ 0\ 1)$$

The five-stage ALFSR with feedback connections given by $H = \langle 5, 2, 0 \rangle$ has the following output sequence:

$$(111110001101110101010000100101100)$$

There are three properties of pr-sequences that are used to demonstrate their randomness characteristics:

PROPERTY 1.   A pr-sequence has 2^{n-1} 1's and $(2^{n-1} - 1)$ 0's.

PROPERTY 2.   There is one run of n (consecutive) 1's and one run of $n - 1$ 0's. For $n - 1 > r > 0$, there are two exp $[n - (r + 2)]$ runs of length r for 1's and the same number of runs of 0's. Thus for the $\langle 5, 2, 0 \rangle$ sequence given above, there are one run of 5 1's, one run of 4 0's, one run each of 3 0's or 1's, two runs of 2 0's or 2 1's, and four single 1's or 0's.

PROPERTY 3.   This is the autocorrelation property that measures the similarity between a pr-sequence and a shifted version of the same sequence. Any pair of such sequences will be identical in $2^{n-1} - 1$ positions and will differ in 2^{n-1} positions. For the Fig. 10.6-1a sequence there are seven matches and eight mismatches between pairs of shifted sequences:

$$(0\ 0\ 0\ 1\ 1\ 1\ 1\ 0\ 1\ 0\ 1\ 1\ 0\ 0\ 1)0$$

$$(0\ 0\ 0\ 1\ 1\ 1\ 1\ 0\ 1\ 0\ 1\ 1\ 0\ 0\ 1)$$

The randomness characteristics of pr-sequences are discussed and proved in [Golomb 82].

For each $n > 4$ there are a number of different LFSRs that all produce maximal-length sequences. The maximal-length LFSR sequences occur in pairs. With each sequence is associated another sequence, called the **reverse sequence**, that consists of the symbols of the original sequence in reverse order. Thus, the $\langle 5, 2, 0 \rangle$ LFSR has the following sequence:

$$(111110001101110101010000100101100)$$

and the reverse sequence

$$(001101001000010101110110001111)$$

is produced by the $\langle 5, 3, 0 \rangle$ LFSR. The specification for the LFSR corresponding to the reverse sequence is obtained by replacing each entry i in the original specification by $n - i$. There is only one pr-sequence that is self-reverse, the sequence for $n = 2$. Since the characteristics of the reverse sequence are easily determined from the original sequence, it is only necessary to study half of the total number of pr-sequences in detail. Two pr-sequences will be said to be distinct if neither is the reverse of the other. The number of distinct pr-sequences (LFSRs) for n

TABLE 10.6-3 $N(n)$ = number of distinct pr-sequences for n-stage LFSRs

n	$N(n)$	n	$N(n)$
2	1	17	3,855
3	1	18	3,888
4	1	19	13,797
5	3	20	12,000
6	3	21	42,336
7	9	22	60,016
8	8	23	178,480
9	24	24	138,240
10	30	25	648,000
11	88	26	859,950
12	72	27	2,101,248
13	315	28	2,370,816
14	378	29	9,203,904
15	900	30	8,910,000
16	1,024	31	34,636,833
		32	33,554,432

from 2 to 32 is given in Table 10.6-3. It is clear that there are lots of choices of ALFSRs for n larger than 10. The best choice for any given application is not always clear and often the design requiring the simplest feedback circuitry is chosen.

Exhaustive and Pseudo-exhaustive Testing. The application of all 2^n input combinations to the (combinational) circuit being tested will be called **exhaustive testing**. Any binary counter can be used to develop these signals. Since the order of generation of the combinations is not important, it may be more efficient to use an ALFSR modified so that it cycles through all states. To do this it is necessary to modify the ALFSR so that the all-0 state is included in the state sequence ([de Visme 71] and [McCluskey 81]).

The result of modifying the four-stage ALFSR of Fig. 10.6-1a in this fashion is shown in Fig. 10.6-3a. A term equal to $Q'_1Q'_2Q'_3$ is added to the XOR gate inputs to inhibit the introduction of a 1 into the low-order stage for the state 0001. This causes the next state to become 0000 and the following state to be 1000. The general form of full-cycle ALFSR is shown in Fig. 10.6-3b. By algebraic simplification it is possible to reduce the required circuitry. The simplified version of the circuit of Fig. 10.6-3a is shown in Fig. 10.6-4.

Exhaustive testing provides a thorough test, but can require a prohibitively long test time for networks with many (20 or more) inputs. It is possible to reduce the test time to a practical value while retaining many of the advantages of exhaustive testing with the techniques to be described next. These **pseudo-exhaustive** techniques apply all possible inputs to portions of the circuit under test rather than to the entire circuit. The first technique is applicable to multi-output circuits in which none of the outputs depend on all of the inputs. It is called **verification testing**, [McCluskey 84].

Most combinational networks have more than one output. In many cases each

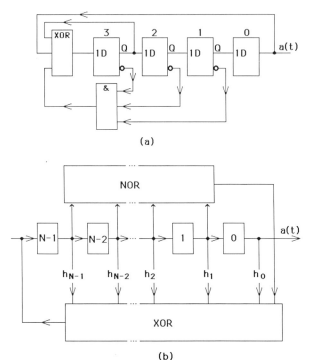

(a)

(b)

Figure 10.6-3 ALFSR modified to cycle through all states: (a) four-stage circuit; (b) N-stage circuit.

of the outputs depends on only a subset of the inputs. For example, the parity generator network of the TI SN54/74LS630 (shown in Fig. 10.6-5) has 23 inputs and 6 output functions, but each output depends on only 10 of the inputs. It may not be practical to exhaustively test the outputs by applying all combinations of the network inputs (2^{23} for the example). However, it may be possible to exhaustively test each output by applying all combinations of only those inputs on which the output depends. For the SN74LS630, each output can be exhaustively tested with $2^{10} = 1024$ input patterns and all six outputs tested one after another with $(6)(1024) = 6144$ patterns. In fact, for this circuit it is possible by an appropriate choice of input patterns to apply all possible input combinations to each output concurrently rather than serially. Thus, with only 1024 rather than $(6)(1024)$ test patterns, each output can be tested exhaustively by using verification testing techniques.

The SN74LS630 is an example of a circuit for which it is possible to test all outputs concurrently by applying (to the entire circuit) only as many patterns as

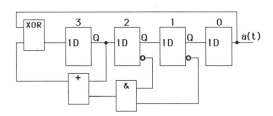

Figure 10.6-4 Simplified form of Fig. 10.6-3a circuit.

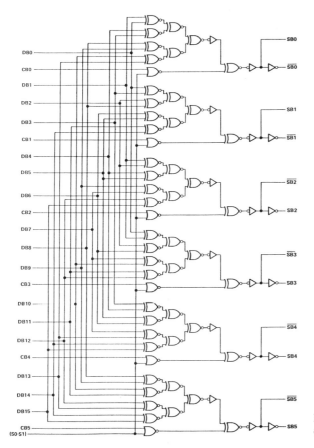

Figure 10.6-5 Parity generator network of the TI SN54/74LS630.

are necessary to exhaustively test one of the outputs. Two inputs that never appear in the same output function can have the same test signal applied to both. This fact can be used to reduce the number of required test signals. If the number of required test signals is equal to the maximum number of inputs upon which any output depends, the circuit is called a **maximal test concurrency circuit** or **MTC circuit**.

An example of a very simple MTC circuit with three inputs and two outputs is shown in Fig. 10.6-6. The f output depends only on inputs w and x while the g output depends on x and y. It is possible to apply the same test signal to both w and y since no output depends on both of these inputs. The four input patterns shown in the figure are such that all possible combinations of values are applied to w and x, and also all combinations of x and y are present. Thus both outputs f and g are tested exhaustively by only four input patterns rather than the eight patterns required for full exhaustive test.

Figure 10.6-7 shows a very simple example of a non-MTC circuit. There are three inputs and each possible pair occurs in some output function. Thus, no two inputs can have the same test signal applied to both. Three test signals are required; however, it is possible to test each of the output functions exhaustively with only

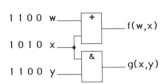

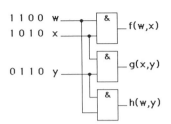

Figure 10.6-6 Simple example of an MTC circuit with verification test inputs.

Figure 10.6-7 Simple example of a three-input, three-output non-MTC circuit with verification test inputs.

four test patterns. All outputs are tested concurrently with the same number of test patterns that are necessary to test one of the outputs. This is an example of the general situation of an n-input circuit in which each output depends on at most $n - 1$ inputs. Such circuits can always have all outputs tested concurrently with at most 2^{n-1} test patterns. The appropriate patterns are all n-bit vectors having the same parity (either all even parity as in Fig. 10.6-7 or all odd parity).

A simple example of a non-MTC circuit for which it is not possible to verify (test concurrently) all outputs with the same number of patterns required for testing a single output is shown in Fig. 10.6-8. In this circuit each of the six outputs depends on two of the four inputs.

All six outputs are tested with the five input patterns shown on the figure. To test the circuit exhaustively would require $2^4 = 16$ patterns. Testing exhaustively each of the output functions in succession takes $(4)(6) = 24$ patterns. It is possible to test pairs of outputs such as $f1$ and $f6$ at the same time since they depend on disjoint sets of inputs. This strategy requires three tests of four patterns each, or 12 total patterns. The numbers of inputs and outputs used in this example are too small to be significant. However, it does serve to illustrate the percentage reduction in test length obtainable with verification test techniques.

It has been shown in [McCluskey 84] that any network for which no output depends on all inputs can be tested pseudo-exhaustively with fewer than 2^n test patterns. This paper also derives a specification for test sets that consist of constant-weight vectors. These test sets are suitable for concurrent test pattern generation since they can be generated by constant-weight counters. The constant-weight test set is shown to be a minimum-length test set for many networks. Other circuits for concurrent generation of verification test patterns are discussed in [Wang 85].

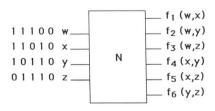

Figure 10.6-8 Simple example of a four-input, six-output non-MTC circuit with verification test inputs.

It is still possible that a verification test set, even though smaller than 2^n, is too long. Also, there are many circuits with an output that depends on all inputs. Such circuits require 2^n inputs for exhaustive test and this may be too large a set. In other words, there are circuits for which the verification test approach does not result in a satisfactory test procedure. A pseudo-exhaustive test is still possible for such circuits, but it is necessary to resort to a partitioning or segmentation technique. Such a procedure is described in [McCluskey 81]. The technique presented in this paper relies on exhaustive testing, but divides the circuit into segments or partitions to avoid excessively long input test sequences. It differs from previous attempts along these lines in that the partitions may divide the signal path through the circuit rather than just separating the signal paths from one another. While it is possible to use multiplexers to enforce the segmentation, they are not necessary. A partitioning method that does not alter the functional circuitry is described in [McCluskey 81].

To exhaustively test each subcircuit, all subcircuit inputs must be controllable at the input of the circuit and all subcircuit outputs must be observable at the circuit outputs. This can be achieved in two ways: (1) hardware partitioning and (2) sensitized partitioning.

Access to the embedded inputs and outputs of the subcircuit under test can be achieved by inserting multiplexers and connecting the embedded inputs and outputs of each subcircuit to those primary inputs and outputs that are not used by the subcircuit under test [Bozorgui-Nesbat 80]. By controlling the multiplexers, all the inputs and outputs of each subcircuit can be accessed using primary input and output lines.

Multiplexers can reduce the operating speed of the circuit and can be costly to implement. However, it is possible to achieve the same testing discipline without actually inserting any multiplexers at all.

Circuit partitioning and subcircuit isolation can be achieved by applying the appropriate input pattern to some of the input lines. The effect achieved is similar to that of hardware partitioning: Paths from the primary inputs to the subcircuit inputs and paths from the subcircuit output to the primary output can be sensitized. Using these paths each subcircuit can be tested exhaustively.

10.6-2 Output Response Analysis

Storage of a fault dictionary (all test inputs with the correct output responses [Breuer 76]) on chip requires too much memory to be a practical technique. The simplest practical method for analyzing the output response is to match the outputs of two identical circuits. Identical circuits may be available either because the function being designed naturally leads to replicated subfunctions [Sridhar 79] or because the functional circuitry is duplicated redundantly for concurrent checking [Sedmak 79]. If identical outputs are not available it is necessary to resort to some technique for compacting the response pattern. Techniques for reducing the volume of output data were originally developed in connection with portable testers. Their use is usually called **compact testing** [Losq 78], but this technique is sometimes also called **response compression**. In compact testing, the output response pattern is passed through a circuit, called a **compacter**, that has fewer output bits than input bits. The output of the compacter is called the **signature** of the test response. The aim is to reduce the number of bits that must be examined to determine whether the circuit under test is faulty.

Many portable testers use transition counting as a compaction technique. This involves counting the number of transitions (0 following a 1 or 1 following a 0) in the response sequence [Hayes 76]. Transition counting has not received serious consideration for BIST since recent research has developed better methods.

The choice of a compaction technique is influenced mainly by two factors:

1. The amount of circuitry required to implement the technique.
2. The loss of "effective fault coverage." In general, a fault will go undetected if none of the input test patterns produces an incorrect circuit output in the presence of the fault. With output response compaction it is also possible for a fault to fail to be detected even though the output response differs from the fault-free response. This will happen whenever the output reponse from a faulty circuit produces a signature that is identical to the signature of a fault-free circuit. This phenomenon is called **aliasing**.

DEFINITION. A faulty circuit test output response signature that is identical to the fault-free signature is called an **alias**.

Many compaction schemes have been studied. These techniques can be grouped into three classes:

1. Parity techniques
2. Counting techniques
3. Linear feedback shift register (LFSR) techniques

A comparison of parity techniques, LFSR techniques, and combined parity and LFSR techniques is given in [Benowitz 75] for pseudo-random test patterns. No advantages were discovered for the use of parity techniques. The use of parity techniques in connection with exhaustive testing is discussed in [Carter 82a] and [Carter 82b]. High values for stuck fault detection are demonstrated.

The only counting technique that has been seriously considered for BIST is called **syndrome analysis** [Savir 80]. This technique is applicable only to exhaustive testing and requires counting the number of 1's in the output response stream. It has been shown that it is possible to detect any single stuck fault in the circuit using this method, although some circuit modification may be required [Savir 81]. A generalization of syndrome testing that uses Walsh coefficients has been studied [Susskind 81], but has yet to have its practicality demonstrated. All the actual implementations of BIST using compaction rely on LFSR techniques; thus these will be described in more detail.

The compaction techniques all require that the fault-free signature for the circuit be known. This can be found by (fault-free) simulation of the design or by measurement on an actual circuit that has been verified to be fault-free by some other method.

Signature analysis. The most popular BIST compaction circuit is an LFSR with its input equal to the output response of the circuit under test. This circuit was called a **cyclic code checker** when it was first proposed in [Benowitz 75]. Figure 10.6-9 shows a cyclic code checker based on the circuit of Fig. 10.6-1a.

This method of output response compaction is most often called **signature analysis**, a term coined by Hewlett-Packard to describe its use in their product, the 5004A Signature Analyzer [Chan 77]. The term *signature* was coined by them to describe the LFSR contents after shifting in the response pattern of the circuit being tested.

The usefulness of signature analysis depends on the fact that the final values of the LFSR flip-flops, the signature, depends on the bit pattern that is applied at the input. If a fault causes the output bit sequence to change, this will usually result in a different signature in the LFSR. However, aliasing can occur. It is possible for a fault to cause an output bit sequence that produces the same final LFSR contents as the fault-free circuit. In this case the fault will be undetected. The output sequences that have this property depend on the structure of the LFSR used. They are characterized in [Benowitz 75] in terms of division of the Galois field polynomial representation of the LFSR and the output response sequences.

Table 10.6-4 illustrates the alias phenomenon for the LFSR of Fig. 10.6-9. Both the faulty and the fault-free sequences shown in the table will leave the same signature—1001—in the LFSR. The **error sequence** is defined as the (bitwise) sum modulo 2 of the faulty and fault-free sequences. It can be shown that aliasing will occur whenever the error sequence is equal to the LFSR feedback vector $<H>$ or to the sum (bitwise modulo 2) of shifted versions of $<H>$.

Any compaction technique can cause some loss of effective fault coverage due to aliasing. Experience with the HP product and simulation studies of BIST designs [Perkins 80] have not discovered any signature analysis applications for which aliasing is a problem. However, it has not been possible to derive any general properties of the effective fault coverage obtained by signature analysis. As discussed in connection with Table 10.6-4, it is possible to characterize the alias error sequences; but no simple relationship between the circuit faults and the resulting errors has yet been found. The problem of determining effective coverage loss for LFSR compaction is discussed in [Smith 80].

TABLE 10.6-4 Aliasing waveforms for LFSR of Fig. 10.6-9

Time:	0 1 2 3 4 5 6 7
Fault-free output sequence:	0 1 1 0 1 0 0 1
Faulty output sequence:	0 0 0 0 1 1 0 1
Error sequence:	0 1 1 0 0 1 0 0
Feedback vector $\langle H \rangle = \langle 1\ 1\ 0\ 0\ 1 \rangle$	
Signature vector $= \langle 1\ 0\ 0\ 1 \rangle$	
Other alias error sequences	
	1 1 0 0 1 0 0 0
	1 0 1 0 1 1 0 0
	0 0 0 1 1 0 0 1
	1 0 0 0 0 1 1 1

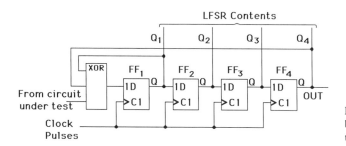

Figure 10.6-9 Four-stage linear feedback shift register used as a serial signature analyzer.

Two methods are suggested in [Benowitz 75] for signature analysis for a multioutput circuit under test. One of them, the **serial signature analyzer**, uses a multiplexer to direct each of the outputs to the LFSR in turn. A circuit for this is shown in Fig. 10.6-10a. With this scheme the input test patterns would have to be applied to the network m times for an m-output network.

The other technique, the **parallel signature analyzer**, compacts K network outputs in parallel using a K-bit parallel code checker (Fig. 10.6-10b). The parallel technique requires each test pattern to be applied only m/K times. In the parallel technique, network outputs are connected to the LFSR through XOR gates added to the shift lines between stages as well as connecting a network output to the first LFSR stage. The design of a four-stage parallel signature analyzer is detailed in Fig. 10.6-11.

In general, the parallel signature analyzer is faster but requires more added circuitry than the serial signature analyzer [Benowitz 75]. A detailed comparison of these two techniques in a particular system is presented in [Benowitz 76]. Fault coverage data, derived by hardware fault insertion, are also reported. Another study of fault coverage for a parallel signature analyzer is reported in [Konemann 80]. Physical fault insertion was carried out on an experimental microprocessor with an 8-bit parallel signature analyzer. In this paper, the term *multiple-input signature register* is used. The serial signature analyzer is not discussed.

Besides requiring more hardware than the serial analyzer, the parallel signature analyzer has an additional alias source: An error in output Z_j at time t_i

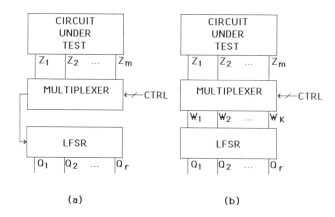

(a)   (b)

Figure 10.6-10 Connection of multi-outputs to LFSR signature analyzer: (a) serial signature analysis using a multiplexer; (b) parallel signature analysis.

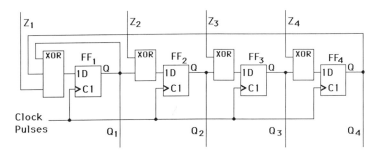

Figure 10.6-11 Four-stage LFSR configured as a parallel signature analyzer.

followed by an error in output Z_{j+1} at time t_{i+1} will have no effect on the signature. More generally, an error in output Z_j at time t_i followed by an error in output Z_{j+h} at time t_{i+h} will have no effect on the signature ([Hassan 82], [Sridhar 82], and [Hassan 83]).

10.6-3 Circuit Structures for BIST

Several schemes for incorporating BIST techniques into a design have been proposed. They fall naturally into four classes: those that assume no special structure to the circuit under test, those that make use of scan paths in the circuit under test, those that reconfigure the scan paths for test application and analysis, and those that use the concurrent checking (implicit test) circuitry of the design.

BIST Structure for Circuits without Scan Paths. Figure 10.6-12 shows the method described in [Benowitz 75]. Two LFSRs and two multiplexers are added to the circuit. One multiplexer (MUX 1) selects the inputs to the circuit—normal inputs for regular operation and the LFSR pseudo-random pattern output for testing. The other multiplexer (MUX 2) routes the circuit outputs in turn to the serial signature analyzer during test. This serial signature analyzer has circuitry to match the final signature with the known correct signature. It provides a failure indication if a different pattern results after the test phase. The only assumption

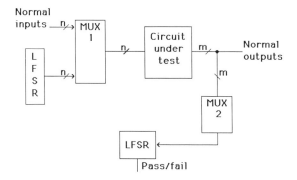

Figure 10.6-12 Circuit with LFSRs added to generate random test patterns and to compute output signature.

made about the circuit under test is that it does not contain memory. Sequential as well as combinational logic circuits can be present in the circuit under test.

A similar structure is described in [Perkins 80]. This structure makes use of a tester circuit that is external to the chip, but could be located on the same board. Pseudo-random patterns are applied in parallel to the chip inputs and a parallel signature analyzer receives both the chip outputs as well as the test inputs. A special feature of this design is its ability to be configured by means of a tester circuit register to apply input signals to the appropriate chip input pins. Testing of RAM and ROM chips is discussed. The most novel feature of the structure of [Perkins 80] is the inclusion of a source resistance detector at each logic input and an output current detector at each logic output. The main purpose of these detectors is to watch over the integrity of the interconnection system.

BIST Structure for Circuits with Scan Paths. For designs that incorporate a scan path, it is possible to make use of this feature for the BIST circuitry. A structure that does this was proposed in [Eichelberger 83b] and is shown in Fig. 10.6-13. In addition to the internal LSSD scan latches, an external scan path (Fig. 10.4-13) is required. The external scan-path input is connected to the scan-out point of the internal scan path. Pseudo-random test patterns are generated in a pattern generator circuit and are scanned into the combined scan path. The system clocks are pulsed and the scan path latches are scanned out into the serial signature analyzer circuit. The resulting signature is then compared in the analyzer with a precalculated fault-free circuit signature in order to generate a failure signal. The scan-out point is also connected to a pin so that, in case of a failure, intermediate signatures can be examined externally for diagnostic purposes.

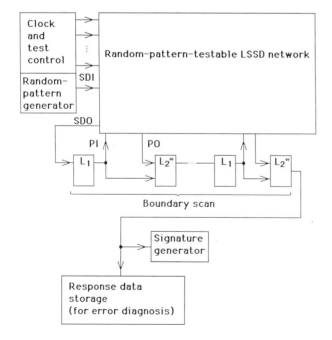

Figure 10.6-13 BIST structure using scan paths.

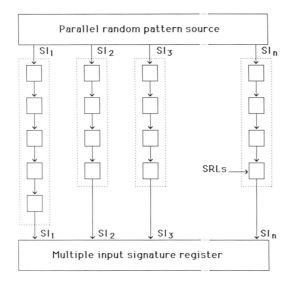

Figure 10.6-14 Multichip module BIST structure using chip scan paths.

Multiple input signature register

A similar design for a multichip module is presented in [Bardell 82]. This design, shown in Fig. 10.6-14, uses a special test chip added to the module. The test chip contains a shift register pattern generator and a parallel signature analyzer. The scan paths on each chip are loaded in parallel from the pattern generator. The system clocks are then pulsed and the test results are scanned out to the parallel signature analyzer. New test patterns can be scanned in at the same time that the test results are being scanned out.

BIST Structure Using Register or Scan-Path Reconfiguration. A concern with BIST designs is the amount of extra circuitry required. One technique for reducing the extra circuitry is to make use of the flip-flops or latches already in the design for test generation and analysis. The system registers are redesigned so that they can function as pattern generators or signature analyzers for test purposes.

The structure described in [Konemann 79] and [Konemann 80] applies to circuits that can be partitioned into independent modules. Each module is assumed to have its own input and output registers, or such registers are added to the circuit where necessary. No precise definition of a module is given, nor is the problem of identifying modules discussed. It is assumed that the circuit modularity is evident. The registers are redesigned so that for testing purposes they can act as either shift registers or parallel signature analyzers. The redesigned register is called a BILBO (built-in logic block observer).

The details of the BILBO design for a four-stage register are shown in Fig. 10.6-15. When both control inputs B_1 and B_2 are equal to 1, the circuit functions as a parallel read-in register with the inputs Z_i gated directly into the flip-flops. When both control inputs are equal to 0, the register is reconfigured into a serial read-in shift register. Test data can be scanned in via the serial input port or scanned out via the serial output port. Setting $B_1 = 1$ and $B_2 = 0$ converts the

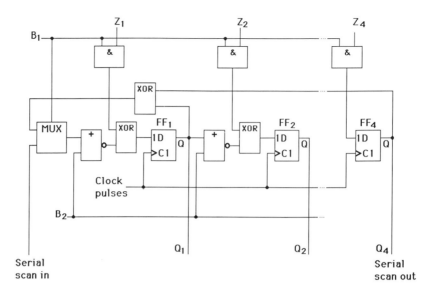

Figure 10.6-15 Four-stage BILBO; details of stages 3 and 4 are omitted.

register into a parallel signature analyzer. It can be used in this configuration as a test vector generator by holding the Z_i inputs fixed. The register is reset when $B_1 = 0$ and $B_2 = 1$.

It is possible to design reconfigurable registers using multiport flip-flops. Designs using this technique are discussed in [McCluskey 81] in connection with pseudo-exhaustive testing. The circuit that results from using this approach to convert the LFSR of Fig. 10.6-3a to a reconfigurable circuit is shown in Fig. 10.6-16. In this design, the circuit functions as a parallel read-in and read-out

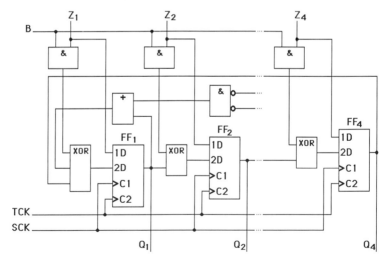

Figure 10.6-16 Reconfigurable circuit resulting from conversion of the circuit of Fig. 10.6-3a.

register under control of the system clock input, SCK. When a clock pulse is applied to SCK it is routed to the CI terminals of the flip-flops, causing the Z_i data to be entered into the flip-flops via the D_1 inputs. For testing use, the test clock, TCK, is pulsed. If control input B is held at 1, the register functions as a parallel signature analyzer. If $B = 0$, the register functions as a counter to generate the input test vectors. The B control input has been added to avoid the necessity of holding the Z_i inputs fixed when using the register to generate test vectors (as is required in the BILBO design of Fig. 10.6-15). If this feature is not desired, the B input and all of the AND gates to which it is connected can be removed and replaced with a straight-through connection of the Z_i. Serial shifting is not accommodated with this design, although the modification to add it is simple. In [McCluskey 81], the use of this type of reconfigurable register is described in connection with pseudo-exhaustive testing.

The two techniques just described are most suitable for circuits that can be partitioned so that the input and output registers of the resulting modules can be reconfigured separately. They can be used for scan path designs, but the existence of scan paths is not a requirement. There are other reconfiguration techniques that are suitable for scan-path designs.

A very good technique is that used by Storage Technology Corporation, (STC) as described in [Komonytsky 82] and [Komonytsky 83]. The basic design of the STC circuits incorporates both an internal LSSD scan path and an external scan path. The BIST modification provides for the reconfiguration of the input scan-path latches into an ALSFR for use as a pseudo-random pattern generator and the reconfiguration of the output scan-path latches into a signature analyzer. A test pattern is generated in the ALFSR, scanned into the internal latches, the system clock is pulsed, and the resulting latch contents are scanned out to the signature analyzer. The details of the design are presented in the two references cited. Another scheme that uses the external scan path as a test pattern generator and response analyzer is described in [Resnick 83]. This designs forms the basis for the National Semiconductor SCX6360 CMOS Gate Array.

Other BIST designs using LFSRs for test vector generation and signature analysis are described in [Eiki 80], [Heckelman 81], and [Fasang 80].

BIST structure using concurrent checking circuits. For systems that include concurrent checking circuits, it is possible to use this circuitry to verify the response during explicit (off-line) testing. Thus the necessity of implementing a separate response analysis circuit such as a signature analyzer is avoided. This approach to BIST is described in [Sedmak 79] and [Sedmak 80]. Since the checking circuitry recommended involves duplication of the functional circuitry and comparison of the outputs of the two implementations, this technique avoids the alias problem and consequent loss of effective fault coverage of a signature analyzer. Figure 10.6-17 shows a suggested BIST implementation using this scheme. (The duplicate circuitry is actually realized in complementary form to reduce design and common-mode faults.) The test patterns are shifted serially into the input registers from the ISG (input stimulus generator) circuits which are added for test pattern generation. The ISG cycles through all input patterns thus generating exhaustive test

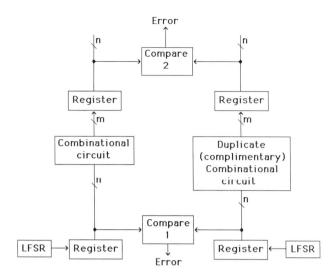

Figure 10.6-17 BIST using concurrent checking compare circuits for output response analysis.

patterns. The contents of the two input registers are checked by the compare 1 circuit. The output response of the combinational circuitry is checked by the compare 2 circuit. Another design that uses the concurrent check circuits for BIST is described in [Lu 83].

10.R REFERENCES

[AGRAWAL 82]   Agrawal, V. D., and M. R. Mercer, "Testability Measures—What Do They Tell Us?" *Dig. 1982 IEEE Test Conf.,* Philadelphia, pp. 391–396, Nov. 11–13, 1982.

[ANDO 80]   Ando, H., "Testing VLSI with Random Access Scan," *Dig. COMPCON Spring '80,* San Francisco, pp. 50–52, Feb. 25–28, 1980.

[BARDELL 81]   Bardell, P. H., and W. H. McAnney, "A View from the Trenches: Production Testing of a Family of VLSI Multichip Modules," *Dig. 11th Annu. Int. Symp. Fault-Tolerant Comput.* (FTCS-11), Portland, Maine, pp. 281–283, June 24–26, 1981.

[BARDELL 82]   Bardell, P. H., and W. H. McAnney, "Self-Testing of Multichip Logic Modules," *Dig., 1982 IEEE Test Conf.,* Philadelphia, pp. 200–204, Nov. 11–13, 1982. (Reprinted in *Test & Measurement World,* pp. 26–29, March 1983.)

[BARZILAI 81]   Barzilai, Z., et.al., "The Weighted Syndrome Sums Approach to VLSI Testing," *IEEE Trans. Comput.,* pp. 996–1000, Dec. 1981.

[BENNETTS 84]   Bennetts, R. G., *Design of Testable Logic Circuits,* Addison-Wesley Publishing Co., Reading, Mass., 1984.

[BENOWITZ 75]   Benowitz, N., D. F. Calhoun, G. E. Alderson, J. E. Bauer, and C. T. Joeckel, "An Advanced Fault Isolation System for Digital Logic," *IEEE Trans. Comput.,* C–24, No. 5, pp. 489–497, 1975.

[BENOWITZ 76]   Benowitz, N., D. F. Calhoun, and G. W. K. Lee, "Fault Detection/

Isolation Results from AAFIS Hardware Built-In Test," *NAECON '76 Rec.,* pp. 215–222, 1976.

[Bottorff 77] Bottorff, P. S., R. E. France, N. H. Garges, and E. J. Orosz, "Test Generation for Large Logic Networks," *Dig. 14th Des. Autom. Conf.,* New Orleans, La., pp. 479–485, June 20–22, 1977.

[Bozorgui-Nesbat 80] Bozorgui-Nesbat, S., and E. J. McCluskey, "Structured Design for Testability to Eliminate Test Pattern Generation," *Dig. 10th Annu. Int. Symp. Fault-Tolerant Comp.* (FTCS–10), Kyoto, Japan, pp. 158–163, Oct. 1–3, 1980.

[Bozorgui-Nesbat 84] Bozorgui-Nesbat, S. and E. J. McCluskey, "Lower Overhead Design for Testability of Programmable Logic Arrays," *Dig., 1984 IEEE Test Conf.,* Phila., pp. 856–865, Oct. 15–18, 1984.

[Brack 79] Brack, J. W., "Random Numbers with Software," *Mach. Des.,* pp. 76–77, Feb. 8, 1979.

[Breuer 76] Breuer, M. A., and A. Friedman, "Design to Simplify Testing," in *Diagnosis and Reliability of Digital Systems,* Computer Science Press, Inc., Woodland Hills, Calif., pp. 291–303, 1976.

[Carter 64] Carter, W. C., H. C. Montgomery, R. J. Preiss, and H. J. Reinheimer, "Design of Serviceability Features for the IBM System/360," *IBM J. Res. Dev.,* pp. 115–126, Apr. 1964.

[Carter 82a] Carter, W. C., "The Ubiquitous Parity Bit," *Dig. 12th Annu. Int. Symp. Fault-Tolerant Comput.* (FTCS–12), Santa Monica, Calif., pp. 289–296, June 22–24, 1982.

[Carter 82b] Carter W. C., "Signature Testing with Guaranteed Bounds for Fault Coverage," *Dig. 1982 IEEE Test Conf.,* Philadelphia, pp. 75–82, Nov. 11–13, 1982.

[Chan 77] Chan, A. Y., "Easy-to-Use Signature Analyzer Accurately Troubleshoots Complex Logic Circuits," *Hewlett-Packard J.,* pp. 9–14, May 1977.

[Chin 85] Chin, C. K. and E. J. McCluskey, "Test Length for Pseudo Random Testing," *Dig. 1985 IEEE Test Conf.,* Philadelphia, pp. 94–99, Nov. 19–21, 1985.

[Clary 79] Clary, J. B., and R. A. Sacane, "Self-Testing Computers," *Computer,* Vol. 12, No. 10, pp. 49–59, 1979.

[Daehn 81] Daehn, W., and J. Mucha, "A Hardware Approach to Self-Testing of Large Programmable Logic Arrays," *IEEE Trans. Comput.,* C–30, No. 11, pp. 829–833, Nov. 1981.

[Das Gupta 78] Das Gupta, S., E. B. Eichelberger, and T. W. Williams, "LSI Chip Design for Testability," *Dig. 1978 IEEE Int. Solid-State Circuits Conf.,* San Francisco, pp. 216–217, Feb. 15–17, 1978.

[Das Gupta 80] Das Gupta, S., C. R. P. Hartmann, and L. D. Rudolph,, "Dual-Mode Logic for Function-Independant Fault Testing," *IEEE Trans. Comput.,* C-29, No. 11, pp. 1025–1029, 1980.

[Das Gupta 81] Das Gupta, S., R. G. Walther, and T. W. Williams, "An Enhancement to LSSD and Some Applications of LSSD in Reliability, Availability, and Serviceability," *Dig. 11th Annu. Int. Symp. Fault-Tolerant Comput.* (FTCS–11), Portland, Maine, pp. 32–34, June 24–26, 1981.

[deVisme 71] deVisme, G. H., *Binary Sequences,* The English Universities Press Ltd., London, 1971.

[Eichelberger 77] Eichelberger, E. B., and T. W. Williams, "A Logic Design Structure for LSI Testability," *Proc. 14th Des. Autom. Conf.,* New Orleans, La., pp. 462–468, June 20–22, 1977.

[EICHELBERGER 78] Eichelberger, E. B., T. W. Williams, E. I. Muehldorf, and R. G. Walther, "A Logic Design Structure for Testing Internal Array," *Dig. 3rd USA–Japan Comput. Conf.,* San Francisco, pp. 266–272, Oct. 10–12, 1978.

[EICHELBERGER 83a] Eichelberger, E. B., "Latch Design Using 'Level Sensitive Scan Design'," *Dig. COMPCON Spring '83,* San Francisco, pp. 380–383, Feb. 28–Mar. 3, 1983.

[EICHELBERGER 83b] Eichelberger, E. B., and E. Lindbloom, "Random-Pattern Coverage Enhancement and Diagnosis for LSSD Logic Self-Test," *IBM J. Res. Dev.,* Vol. 27, No. 3, pp. 265–272, 1983.

[EIKI 80] Eiki, H., K. Inagaki, and S. Yajima, "Autonomous Testing and its Application to Testable Design of Logic Circuits," *Dig. 10th Annu. Int. Symp. Fault-Tolerant Comput.,* (FTCS–10), Kyoto, Japan, pp. 173–178, Oct. 1–3, 1980.

[FASANG 80] Fasang, P. P., "BIDCO, Built-in Digital Circuit Observer," *Dig. 1980 IEEE Test Conf.,* Philadelphia, pp. 261–266, Nov. 11–13, 1980.

[FLOUTIER 79] Floutier, D., "Some Basic Properties of Redundancy in Combinational Logic Networks," unpublished.

[FRIEDMAN 67] Friedman, A. D., "Fault Detection in Redundant Circuits," *IEEE Trans. Electron. Comput.,* pp. 99–100, Feb. 1967.

[FUJIWARA 81] Fujiwara, H., and K. Kinoshita, "A Design of Programmable Logic Arrays with Universal Tests," *IEEE Trans. Comput.,* C–30, No. 11, pp. 823–828, Nov. 1981.

[FUJIWARA 84] Fujiwara, J., "A New PLA Design for Universal Testability," *IEEE Trans. Comput.,* Vol. C-33, Aug. 1984, pp. 745–750.

[FUNATSU 75] Funatsu, S., N. Wakatsuki, and T. Arima, "Test Generation Systems in Japan," *Dig. 12th Annu. Des. Autom. Conf.,* Boston, pp. 114–122, June 23–25, 1975.

[FUNATSU 78] Funatsu, S., N. Wakatsuki, and A. Yamada, "Designing Digital Circuits with Easily Testable Consideration," *Dig. 1978 IEEE Semiconductor Test Conf.,* Cherry Hill, N.J., pp. 98–102, Oct. 31–Nov. 2, 1978.

[GOEL 80] Goel, P., "Test Generation Costs Analysis and Projections," *Dig. 17th Annu. Des. Autom. Conf.,* Minneapolis, Minn., pp. 77–84, June 23–25, 1980.

[GOLDSTEIN 78] Goldstein, L. H., "Controlability/Observability Analysis of Digital Circuits," *SAND78-1895,* Sandia Laboratories, Albuquerque, N. Mex., Nov. 1978.

[GOLDSTEIN 79a] Goldstein, L. H., "Controlability/Observability Analysis of Digital Circuits," *Design for Testability Workshop,* Boulder, Colo., Apr. 1979.

[GOLDSTEIN 79b] Goldstein, L. H., "Controlability/Observability Analysis of Digital Circuits," *IEEE Trans. Circuits Syst.,* CAS-26, No. 9, pp. 685–693, 1979.

[GOLDSTEIN 80] Goldstein, L. H., and E. L. Thigpen, "SCOAP: Sandia Controlability/Observability Analysis Program," *Dig. 17th Des. Autom. Conf.,* Minneapolis, Minn., pp. 190–196, June 23–25, 1980.

[GOLUMB 82] Golumb, S. W., *Shift Register Sequences,* Aegean Park Press, Laguna Hills, Calif., 1982.

[GORDON 77] Gordon, G., and H. Nadig, "Hexadecimal Signatures Identify Troublespots in Microprocessor Systems," *Electronics,* pp. 89–96, Mar. 3, 1977.

[GRASON 79] Grason, J., "TMEAS, A Testability Measure Program," Bell Laboratories, Murray Hill, N.J., 1979.

[GRASSL 82] Grassl, and H.-J. Pfleiderer, "A Self-Testing PLA," *Dig. 1982 IEEE Int. Solid-State Circuits Conf.,* pp. 60–61, Feb. 10, 1982.

[HASSAN 82] Hassan, S. Z., "Algebraic Analysis of Parallel Signature Analyzers," *Center for Reliable Computing Tech. Rep. 82-5,* Computer Systems Laboratory, Stanford University, Stanford, Calif., June 1982.

[HASSAN 83] Hassan, S. Z., D. J. Lu, and E. J. McCluskey, "Parallel Signature Analyzers—Detection Capability and Extensions," *Dig. COMPCON Spring '83,* San Francisco, Feb. 28–Mar. 3, 1983.

[HAYES 74] Hayes, J. P., "On Modifying Logic Networks to Improve Their Diagnosability," *IEEE Trans. Comput.,* C-23, No. 1, pp. 56–62, 1974.

[HAYES 76] Hayes, J. P., "Transition Count Testing of Combinational Logic Circuits," *IEEE Trans. Comput.,* C-27, No. 6, pp. 613–620, 1976.

[HAYES 80] Hayes, J. P., and E. J. McCluskey, "Testability Considerations in Microprocessor-Based Design," *Computer,* pp. 17–26, Mar. 1980. Reprinted in *Tutorial: Microcomputer System Software and Languages,* B. E. Allen, Ed., IEEE Catalog EHO 174–3, pp. 198–206. An expanded version was issued as Stanford Computer Systems Laboratory Tech. Report No. 179, Nov. 1979.

[HECKELMAN 81] Heckelman, R. W., and D. K. Bhavsar, "Self-Testing VLSI," *Dig. 1981 IEEE Solid State Circuits Conf.,* pp. 174–175, Feb. 19, 1981.

[HONG 80] Hong, S. J., and D. L. Ostapko, "FITPLA: A Programmable Logic Array for Function Independent Testing," *Dig. 10th Int. Symp. Fault-Tolerant Comput.* (FTCS–10), Kyoto, Japan, pp. 131–136, Oct. 1–3, 1980.

[HSU 78] Hsu, F., P. Lolechy, and L. Zobniw, "Selective Controllability: A Proposal for Testing and Diagnosis," *Dig. 1978 IEEE Semiconductor Test Conf.,* Cherry Hill, N.J., pp. 170–175, Oct. 31–Nov. 2, 1978.

[HUGHES 85] Hughes, J. L. A., S. Mourad, and E. J. McCluskey, "An Experimental Study Comparing 74LS181 Test Sets," *Dig. COMPCON Spring '85,* San Francisco, pp. 384–387, Feb. 25–28, 1985.

[KAUTZ 71] Kautz, W. H., "Testing Faults in Combinational Cellular Logic Arrays," *Proc., 8th Annu. IEEE Symp. Switching and Automata Theory,* pp. 161–174, Oct. 1971.

[KHAKBAZ 82] Khakbaz, J., "Self-testing Embedded Parity Trees," *Dig. 12th Annu. Int. Symp. Fault-Tolerant Comput.* (FTCS–12), Santa Monica, Calif., June 22–24, 1982.

[KHAKBAZ 83a] Khakbaz, J., and E. J. McCluskey, "Self-Testing Embedded Code Checkers," *Dig. COMPCON Spring '83,* San Francisco, pp. 452–457, Feb. 28–Mar. 3, 1983.

[KHAKBAZ 83b] Khakbaz, J., "A Testable PLA Design with Low Overhead and High Fault Coverage," *Dig. 13th Annu. Int. Symp., Fault-Tolerant Comput.* (FTCS–13), Milan, Italy, pp. 426–429, June 28–30, 1983. See also *Stanford CRC Tech.* Reps. 83–3 and 82–17.

[KHAKBAZ 84] Khakbaz, J., and E. J. McCluskey, "Self-Testing Embedded Parity Checkers," *IEEE Trans. Comput.,* C-33, No. 8, pp. 753–756, Aug. 1984.

[KNUTH 69] Knuth, D. E., *The Art of Computer Programming,* Vol. 2: *Seminumerical Algorithms,* Addison-Wesley Publishing Company, Inc., Reading, Mass., 1969.

[KODANDAPANI 74] Kodandapani, K. L., "A Note on Easily Testable Realizations for Logic Functions," *IEEE Trans. Comput.,* C–23, No. 3, pp. 332–333, 1974.

[KODANDAPANI 77] Kodandapani, K. L., and R. V. Setlur, "A Note on Minimal Reed-Muller Canonical Forms of Switching Functions," *IEEE Trans. Comput.,* C–26, No. 3, pp. 310–313, 1977.

[KOMONYTSKY 82] Komonytsky, D., "LSI Self-Test Using Level Sensitive Scan Design and Signature Analysis," *Dig. 1982 IEEE Test Conf.,* Philadelphia, pp. 414–424, Nov. 15–18, 1982.

[Komonytsky 83]   Komonytsky, D., "Synthesis of Techniques Creates Complete System Self-Test," *Electronics,* pp. 110–115, Mar. 10, 1983.

[Konemann 79]   Konemann, B., J. Mucha, and G. Zwiehoff, "Built-in Logic Block Observation Technique," *Dig. 1979 IEEE Test Conf.,* Cherry Hill, N.J., pp. 37–41, Oct. 23–25, 1979.

[Konemann 80]   Konemann, B., J. Mucha, and G. Zwiehoff, "Built-in Test for Complex Digital Integrated Circuits," *IEEE J. Solid-State Circuits,* SC–15, No. 3, pp. 315–318, 1980.

[Kovijanic 79a]   Kovijanic, P. G., "Computer-Aided Testability Analysis," *AUTOTEST-CON,* pp. 292–294, Sept. 1979.

[Kovijanic 79b]   Kovijanic, P. G., "Testability Analysis," *Dig. 1979 IEEE Test Conf.,* Cherry Hill, N.J., pp. 310–316, Oct. 23–25, 1979.

[Losq 78]   Losq, J., "Efficiency of Random Compact Testing," *IEEE Trans. Comput.,* C–27, No. 6, pp. 516–525, 1978.

[Lu 83]   Lu, D. J., and E. J. McCluskey "Recurrent Test Patterns," *Proc. 1983 Int. Test Conf.,* Philadelphia, pp. 76–82, Oct. 18–20, 1983.

[Mann 81]   Mann, F. A., "Explanation of New Logic Symbols," Chap. 5 in *1981 Supplement to the TTL Data Book for Design Engineers,* 2nd ed., Texas Instruments, Inc., Dallas, 1981.

[McCluskey 81]   McCluskey, E. J., and S. Bozorgui-Nesbat, "Design for Autonomous Test," *IEEE Trans. Comput.,* C–30, No. 11, pp. 866–875, Nov. 1981.

[McCluskey 84]   McCluskey, E. J., "Verification Testing—A Pseudoexhaustive Test Technique," *IEEE Trans. Comput.,* C–33, No. 6, pp. 541–546, June 1984.

[Muller 54]   Muller, D. E., "Application of Boolean Algebra to Switching Circuit Design and Error Detection," *IRE Trans. Electron. Comput.,* pp. 132–140, Sept. 1954.

[Page 80]   Page, E. W., "Minimally Testable Reed-Muller Canonical Forms," *IEEE Trans. Comput.,* C–29, No. 8, pp. 746–750, Aug. 1980.

[Perkins 80]   Perkins, C. C., S. Sangani, H. Stopper, and W. Valitski, "Design for In-Situ Chip Testing with a Compact Tester."

[Peterson 72]   Peterson, W. W., and E. J. Weldon, *Error-Correcting Codes,* 2nd ed., The Colonial Press, Inc., 1972.

[Pradhan 78]   Pradhan, D. K., "Universal Test Sets for Multiple Fault Detection in AND-EXOR Arrays," *IEEE Trans. Comput.,* C-27, No. 2, pp. 181–187, 1978.

[Pradhan 80]   Pradhan, D. K., and K. Son, "The Effect of Untestable Faults in PLAs and a Design for Testability," *Dig. 1980 IEEE Test Conf.,* Philadelphia, pp. 359–367, Nov. 11–13, 1980.

[Ramanatha 82]   Ramanatha, K. S., "A Design for Complete Testability of Programmable Logic Arrays," *Dig. 1982 IEEE Test Conf.,* Philadelphia, pp. 67–74, Nov. 11–13, 1982.

[Ratiu 82]   Ratiu, I. M., A. Sangiovanni-Vincentelli, and D. O. Pederson, "VICTOR: A Fast VLSI Testability Analysis Program," *Dig. 1982 IEEE Test Conf.,* Philadelphia, pp. 397–401, Nov. 11–13, 1982.

[Rault 71]   Rault, J. -C., "A Graph Theoretical and Probabilistic Approach to the Fault Detection of Digital Circuits," *Dig. 1971 Int. Symp. Fault-tolerant Comput.,* (FTC–1), Pasadena, Calif., pp. 26–29, Mar. 1971.

[Reddy 72]   Reddy, S. M., "Easily Testable Realizations for Logic Functions," *IEEE Trans. Comput.,* C–21, No. 11, pp. 1183–1188, Nov. 1972.

[SALUJA 74]   Saluja, K. K., and S. M., Reddy, "On Minimally Testable Logic Networks," *IEEE Trans. Comput.,* C-23, No. 5, pp. 552–554, 1974.

[SALUJA 75]   Saluja, K. K., and S. M. Reddy, "Fault Detecting Test Sets for Reed-Muller Canonic Networks," *IEEE Trans. Comput.,* C-24, No. 10, pp. 995–998, 1975.

[SALUJA 81]   Saluja, K. K., K. Kinoshita, and H. Fujiwara, "A Multiple Fault Testable Design of Programmable Logic Arrays," *Dig. 11th Annu. Int. Symp. Fault-Tolerant Comput.* (FTCS–11), Portland Maine, pp. 44–46, June 24–26, 1981.

[SAVIR 80]   Savir, J., "Syndrome-Testable Design of Combinational Circuits," *IEEE Trans. Comput.,* C-29, No. 6, pp. 442–451, 1980.

[SAVIR 81]   Savir, J., "Syndrome-Testing of 'Syndrome-Untestable' Combinational Circuits," *IEEE Trans. Comput.,* C-30, No. 8, pp. 606–608, 1981.

[SAVIR 83]   Savir, J., G. Ditlow, and P. H. Bardell, "Random Pattern Testability," *Dig. 13th Annu. Int. Symp. Fault-Tolerant Comput.,* (FTCS–13), Milan, Italy, pp. 80–89, June 28–30, 1983.

[SEDMAK 79]   Sedmak, R. M., "Design for Self-Verification: An Approach for Dealing with Testability Problems in VLSI-Based Designs," *Dig. 1979 IEEE Test Conf.,* Cherry Hill, N.J., pp. 112–124, Oct. 23–25, 1979.

[SEDMAK 80]   Sedmak, R. M., "Implementation Techniques for Self-Verification," *Dig. 1980 IEEE Test Conf.,* Philadelphia, pp. 267–278, Nov. 11–13, 1980.

[SHEDLETSKY 77]   Shedletsky, J. J., "Random Testing: Practicality vs. Verified Effectiveness," *Dig. 7th Annu. Int. Conf. Fault-Tolerant Comput.* (FTCS–7), Los Angeles, pp. 175–179, June 28–30, 1977.

[SMITH 80]   Smith, J. E., "Measure of the Effectiveness of Fault Signature Analysis," *IEEE Trans. Comput.,* C–29, No. 6, pp. 510–514, 1980.

[SON 80]   Son, K., and D. K. Pradhan, "Design of Programmable Logic Arrays For Testability," *Dig. 1980 IEEE Test Conf.,* Philadelphia, pp. 163–166, Nov. 11–13, 1980.

[SRIDHAR 79]   Sridhar, T., and J. P. Hayes, "Testing Bit-Sliced Microprocessors," *Dig. 9th Annu. Int. Symp. Fault-Tolerant Comput.* (FTCS–9), Madison, Wisc., pp. 211–218, June 20–22, 1979.

[SRIDHAR 82]   Sridhar, R., D. S. Ho, T. J. Powell, and S. M. Thatte, "Analysis and Simulation of Parallel Signature Analyzers," *Dig. 1982 IEEE Test Symp.,* Philadelphia, pp. 656–661, Nov. 11–13, 1982.

[STEPHENSON 76]   Stephenson, J. E., and J. Grason, "A Testability Measure for Register Transfer Level Digital Circuits," *Dig. 6th Int. Symp. Fault-Tolerant Comput.* (FTCS–6), Pittsburgh, pp. 101–107, June 21–23, 1976.

[STEWART 77]   Stewart, J. H., "Future Testing of Large LSI Circuit Cards," *Dig. 1977 IEEE Semiconductor Test Conf.,* Cherry Hill, N.J., pp. 6–15, Oct. 25–27, 1977.

[STEWART 78]   Stewart, J. H., "Application of Scan/Set for Error Detection and Diagnostics," *Dig. 1978 IEEE Semiconductor Test Conf.,* Cherry Hill, N.J., pp. 152–158, Oct. 31–Nov. 2, 1978.

[SUSSKIND 81]   Susskind, A., "Testability and Reliability of LSI," RADC Rep. RADC-TR–80–384, Rome Air Development Center, Griffiss Air Force Base, N.Y., Jan. 1981.

[TREUER 85]   Treuer, R., H. Fujiwara and V. K. Agarwal, "Implementing a Built-In Self-Test PLA Design, *IEEE Design and Test of Computers*, Vol. 2, No. 2, pp. 37–48, April 1985.

[WAGNER 83]   Wagner, K. D., "Design for Testability in the Amdahl 580," *Dig. COMPCON Spring '83,* San Francisco, pp. 384–388, Feb. 28–Mar. 3, 1983.

[WAKERLY 78]   Wakerly, J. F., *Error-Detecting Codes, Self-Checking Circuits, and Applications,* Elsevier North-Holland, Inc., New York, 1978.

[WANG 85]   Wang, L. T., and E. J. McCluskey, "Built-in Self Test for Random Logic," *Proc. ISCAS 85* (1985 Int'l. Symp. Circuits and Systems, Vol. 3), Kyoto, Japan, pp. 1305–1308, June 5–7, 1985.

[WILLIAMS 73]   Williams, M. J. Y., and J. B. Angel, "Enhancing Testability of Large Scale Integrated Circuits via Test Points and Additional Logic," *IEEE Trans. Comput.,* C–22, No. 1, pp. 46–60, Jan. 1973.

[WILLIAMS 77]   Williams, T. W., and E. B. Eichelberger, "Random Patterns within a Structured Sequential Logic Design," *Dig. 1977 IEEE Semiconductor Test Conf.,* Cherry Hill, N.J., pp. 19–27, Oct. 25–27, 1977.

[WRITER 75]   Writer, P. L., "Design for Testability," *'75 ASSC Conf. Rec.* (Automatic Support Systems Symposium for Advanced Maintainability), pp. 84–87, Oct. 1975.

[YAJIMA 81]   Yajima, S., and T. Aramaki, "Autonomously Testable Programmable Logic Arrays," *Dig. 11th Annu. Int. Symp. Fault-Tolerant Comput.* (FTCS–11), Portland, Maine, pp. 41–43, June 24–26, 1981.

[YAMADA 78]   Yamada, A., N. Wakatsuki, T. Fukui, and S. Funatsu, "Automatic System Level Test Generation and Fault Location for Large Digital Systems," *Dig. 15th Des. Autom. Conf.,* Las Vegas, Nev., pp. 347–352, June 19–21, 1978.

[ZASIO 83]   Zasio, J. J., "Shifting Away from Probes for Wafer Test," *Dig. COMPCON Spring '83,* San Francisco, pp. 395–398, Feb. 28–Mar. 3, 1983.

10.P PROBLEMS

10.1   (Use SCOAP testability analysis rules for the following problem.)

(a) Function $F(A, B, C, D) = ABCD$ can be realized in two forms using three AND gates. These are shown in Fig. P10.1a. For each implementation determine the combinational observabilities and controllabilities of all the nets in the circuit. Which one of these two implementations, in your opinion, is a more testable circuit?

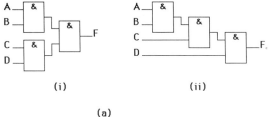

(a)

Figure P10.1a

(b) Function $F(A, B, C, D) = A + B + C + D$ can be realized in two forms, using three two input OR gates, as shown in Fig. P10.1b. For each implementation determine the combinational observabilities and controllabilities of the nets in the circuit. Make comments similar to part (a) about the relative testability of these two implementations.

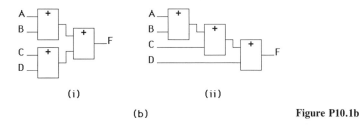

(i)   (ii)

(b)   **Figure P10.1b**

10.2 A measure of the testability of a fault, or how easy it is to test for a particular fault, can be defined as follows:

$$\text{testability of Fault } F_i = \frac{\text{no. of input patterns that detect } F_i}{2^{\text{no. of inputs}}}$$

Using this definition and the combinational circuit shown in Fig. P10.2 calculate the testability of the following faults:

(a) $b/0$

(b) $h/1$

(c) $h/0$

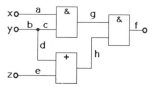

Figure P10.2

10.3 Design a two-input multiplexed data latch that does not have the extra propagation delay of the structure of Fig. 10.4–3.

10.4 64 ICs are to be interconnected to form a circuit that will be tested using scan techniques (Fig. P10.4). The ICs will be packaged on four PC boards, each containing 16 ICs. Each IC has 1024 internal latches connected into a scan path. Assume that the scan data out (SDO) is driven by a tri-state driver which is enabled by the scan clock.

Consider the three following options for interconnecting the scan path of the individual ICs into the circuit scan path.

1. Connect the 64 ICs serially into a single scan path.
2. Connect the 16 ICs on each PC board into a single scan path and add control logic to select the board to be scanned.
3. Use control logic to select the specific IC to be scanned.

Do the following:

(a) For each option, draw a block diagram of the circuit showing scan-path connections and any control logic. How many control signals are needed? How much control logic must be added?

(b) For each option, compute the number of bits of data that must be scanned in and out to load a test pattern into the entire circuit and scan out the test result.

(c) For each option, compute the average number of bits of data that must be scanned in and out to load a test pattern into a single IC and scan out the test result.

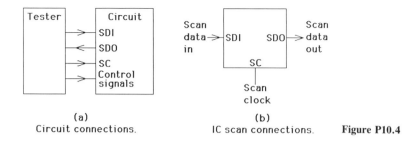

(a)
Circuit connections.

(b)
IC scan connections.   **Figure P10.4**

(d) Briefly (in one paragraph) describe appropriate criteria for choosing which of these options should be selected.

10.5   Eight identical ICs are connected as shown in Fig. P10.5a. Each IC has 64 internal latches in the scan path. The output DO is a tri-state output whose enable signal is driven by the first latch in the scan chain and whose data value is driven by the second latch in the scan chain (see Fig. P10.5b). To test this circuit of eight ICs, it is desired to scan in the following data string (reading from left to right):

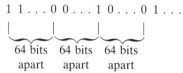

(a) Why is this not a suitable test pattern to scan-in to this circuit?

(b) Describe three methods for solving this problem.

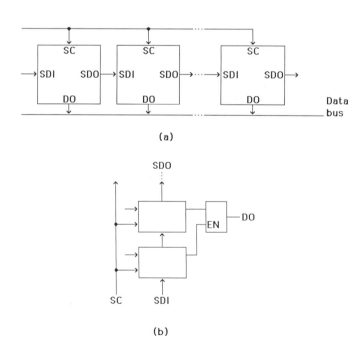

(a)

(b)

Figure P10.5

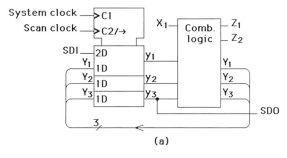

(a)

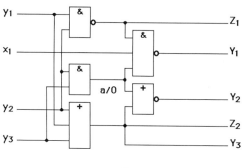

(b)   **Figure P10.6**

10.6 Consider the circuit shown in Fig. P10.6a. The flip-flops have two clocked ports and are connected to form a scan path. The combinational logic for this circuit is shown in Fig. P10.6b. It is desired to test for the fault $a/0$ shown in the combinational logic.

(a) Use path sensitization to find a test for $a/0$. Show the sensitized path on the combinational logic diagram in Fig. P10.6b.

(b) In what order are the values for the bits y_1, y_2, and y_3 scanned in and out

	In	Out
First bit		
Second bit		
Third bit		

(c) Complete the testing sequence information below.

  (i) Scan in the following test vector y values.

  $y_1 =$
  $y_2 =$
  $y_3 =$

  (ii) Set the test value on input X_1.

  $X_1 =$

  (iii) After signal propagation is complete, check the circuit outputs.

	Good circuit	Faulty circuit
Z_1		
Z_2		

  (iv) Apply one pulse to the system clock.

(v) Scan out and check the new y values.

	Good circuit	Faulty circuit
y_1		
y_2		
y_3		

10.7 Figure P10.7 shows the structure of an (AND-OR) PLA. A FIT (function independent testing) Hong/Fujiwara design is to be used to realize the functions given by the maps in Table P10.7a.

TABLE P10.7a

x_3	x_1x_2 00	01	11	10
0	0	0	1	1
1	0	0	1	0

f_1

x_3	x_1x_2 00	01	11	10
0	0	0	0	0
1	1	1	1	0

f_2

(a) Determine the product terms needed to realize these functions and indicate them on the Karnaugh maps in Table P10.7a. Use a minimum number of product lines. On Fig. P10.7, place $\times$'s at all intersections that should have crosspoints connected.

(b) Write expressions for the product terms realized and label the terms on the Karnaugh maps in Table P10.7a.

(c) Fill in Table P10.7b with the appropriate set of test patterns (assume that the shift register has been tested):

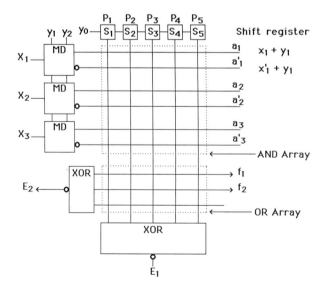

Figure P10.7

TABLE P10.7b

	S_1	S_2	S_3	S_4	S_5	X_1	X_2	X_3	Y_1	Y_2	Check all tests that detect: $a_1/0$	$a'_1/1$
1												
2												
3												
4												
5												
6												
7												
8												
9												
10												
11												
12												
13												
14												
15												
16												

10.8 It is desired to test the multiplexer shown in Fig. P10.8 for stuck-at faults on the inputs and output.

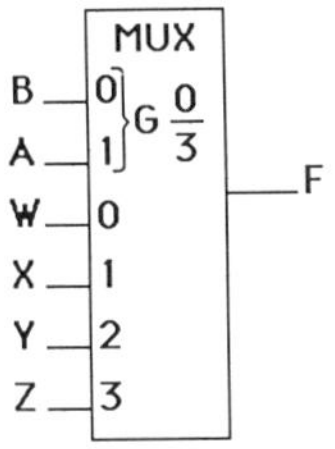

```
W X Y Z A B | F
0 x x x 0 0 | 0
1 x x x 0 0 | 1
x 0 x x 0 1 | 0
x 1 x x 0 1 | 1
x x 0 x 1 0 | 0
x x 1 x 1 0 | 0
x x x 0 1 1 | 0
x x x 1 1 1 | 1
```

Figure P10.8

(a) How many test patterns are needed for exhaustive testing?

(b) Assume that random test patterns are generated with equal probability of a "1" or "0" for each bit.

For each fault in Table P10.8, list the conditions under which it will be detected (for

TABLE P10.8

Fault	Conditions for detection	Probability
$F/1$		
$X/0$		
$A/0$		
$A/0$ $X/0$		

example, $X = Y = 0$) and the probability that the conditions will be satisfied by a single random test pattern.

10.9 For the circuit in Fig. P10.9 generate the dependency list for each output (i.e., the set of inputs each output depends on). From this list determine a suitable partitioning of the gates. The goal is to test each partition independently.

  (a) How many input patterns are needed to test the function realized by each output if we were to do these tests in sequence (i.e., test W first, then X, etc.)?

  (b) Write down 16 input patterns (each pattern is a binary vector of 10 bits) that exhaustively test the function realized by each output line; this time all four output lines are tested in parallel.

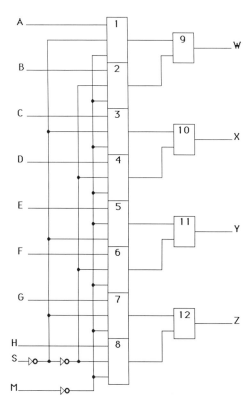

Figure P10.9

10.10 For the parity generator circuit in Fig. P10.10, determine how many inputs are needed to test the function generated by each output line. How many tests are needed to test output the line marked EVEN exhaustively?

Rather than exhaustively testing the whole circuit, determine a set of partitions that can be exhausted with fewer test patterns than 20 input patterns each (keep the number of partitions under six).

Write down the necessary number of (9-bit vector) test patterns needed to exhaustively test all your partitions.

10.11 The circuit for a dual four-input multiplexer is shown in Fig. P10.11. A pseudo-exhaustive test set is to be developed.

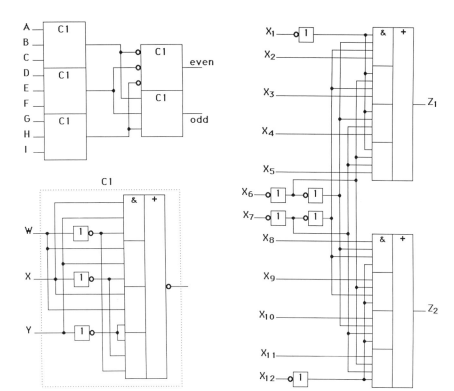

Figure P10.10

Figure P10.11

(a) Write down the dependence matrix and the partitioned dependence matrix for this circuit.

(b) Write down the RVTS for this circuit.

(c) List any stuck-at faults that are not detected by the set of part (b).

(d) List any bridging faults that are not detected by the set of part (b).

(e) Use partitioning techniques (autonomous test) to obtain a minimum-length pseudo-exhaustive test set. (Show the partitions used.)

(f) List any stuck-at faults not detected in part (e).

(g) List any bridging faults not detected in part (e).

(h) Repeat parts (e), (f), and (g) with the restriction of not more than three partitions for each output.

10.12 The circuit in Fig. P10.12 is used to compact a stream of input data to produce a signature; this signature is used to distinguish between error-free patterns (P_c) and erroneous patterns (P_e).

$$8 \quad 7 \quad 6 \quad 5 \quad 4 \quad 3 \quad 2 \quad 1 \quad 0 \quad \longleftarrow \text{ time}$$

$$\text{Assume that } P_c = 1 \quad 0 \quad 1 \quad 0 \quad 1 \quad 1 \quad 0 \quad 0 \quad 1$$

(a) Determine which of the patterns in Table P10.12a will be indistinguishable from P_c. *Hint:* You do not have to calculate the actual signature.

TABLE P10.12a

Time	P_e		Distinguished	Not distinguished
	8 7 6 5 4 3 2 1 0			
a	1 1 0 1 1 1 0 0 1			
b	1 0 0 0 0 0 0 0 1			
c	1 1 1 1 0 1 0 0 1			
d	1 1 0 0 0 1 0 0 1			

(b) There are only two P_e's with fewer than 3 bits in error that cannot be distinguished from P_c. Write down these two patterns in Table P10.12b.

TABLE P10.12b

	8	7	6	5	4	3	2	1	0	← time
P_1:										
P_2:										

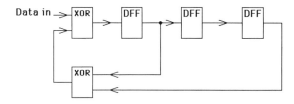

Figure P10.12

11

SEMICUSTOM AND MSI DESIGN

11.1 INTRODUCTION

The first digital electronic design was done by specifying interconnections of individual gates. This is the design approach described in the previous chapters of this book. However, it quickly became clear that there are some digital functions that are useful in many designs. Each individual designer made of a file of good circuits for these common functions and used an already designed circuit whenever needing a function for which there was a suitable circuit in his or her design file. Implicit in this procedure is the use of what is now called a hierarchical design approach whereby the desired circuit is split up into high-level functions—counters, adders, shifters, etc.—and then the circuit is realized as an interconnection of implementations for these functions.

By the mid-sixties it was possible to integrate more than ten gates on a single chip. The term **Medium Scale Integration (MSI)** was coined to describe chips having from 10 to 100 gates. Chips with fewer gates are called **Small-Scale Integration (SSI).** Typical SSI chips are listed in Table 11.1-1.

TABLE 11.1-1 Typical SSI chips

6 Inverters	4 2-input gates
3 3-input gates	2 4-input gates
1 or 2 AND-OR-Invert gates	1 or 2 flip-flops

Some of the MSI parts consist of individual gates. These differ from their SSI counterparts by having more gates or larger fanin gates. It quickly became apparent that it wasn't economical to provide sufficient pins on an IC package to permit access to all of the gates that could be integrated on a single chip. Thus MSI parts implementing more complex functions than gates or flip-flops were introduced. The availability of these complex MSI functions required a change in design style; a designer had to use the standard functions rather than personal circuits. The ability to use the MSI functions efficiently became an important design skill. Design using MSI parts is described in this chapter.

Chips having from 100 to approximately 10,000 gates or memory bits are called **Large Scale Integration, (LSI),** and the term **Very Large Scale Integration (VLSI)** is used for chips having more than 10,000 gates or bits. The distinction between LSI and VLSI is less important than the other classifications. Both LSI and VLSI are used to realize standard catalog parts such as memories and large arithmetic circuits. VLSI is used both for catalog parts such as microprocessors as well as custom and semicustom parts. Section 4.1 has a discussion of custom and semicustom parts. For the purposes of this chapter, the important distinction is that custom design uses single gates or circuit elements, while semicustom design uses more complex building blocks. The previous chapters apply directly to custom design. Since the complex building blocks used for semicustom design are very similar to the MSI parts, this chapter applies to semicustom as well as MSI design.

The most important MSI parts are those of the 54/74 series and the 4000 series. The 54/74 series is available in TTL chips [TI 84] and also in CMOS chips (called 54C/74C or 54HC/74HC for CMOS) [National 84]. The 4000 series is a CMOS family [RCA 83]. There are ECL families such as ECL 10K, ECL III, and ECL 100K, but these are used only for very high speed applications. Table 11.1-2 lists the types of complex functions available in MSI parts. Semicustom products—gate arrays and standard cell designs—typically offer building blocks called **macrofunctions** that realize complex functions. In fact, many such products offer macrofunction implementations of standard TTL or CMOS MSI chips. Most of the examples in this chapter use the TTL MSI functions since these are the most complex functions in current use, for semicustom as well as catalog parts.

TABLE 11.1-2 MSI complex function categories

Arithmetic circuits	Shift registers
Comparators	Counters
Multiplexers/Demultiplexers	Decoders/Encoders
Parity Circuits	

11.2 DECODING AND ENCODING

There are a large number of different ways of using binary signals to represent information. Numerical information can be specified by binary numbers or binary-coded-decimal numbers and many different BCD schemes are used. Each representation has its advantages and disadvantages. Several different representations or encodings may be used for the same information in different parts of a system in order to match the representation to the function being carried out. The use of different encodings means that there must be circuitry to convert from one code to another. Thus there is a whole class of combinational circuits whose function is to convert from one code to another—**code converters** or **coders.** There is no mystery about how to design these circuits; they are multiple-output combinational circuits and as such can be designed using the techniques of the preceding chapters. Some code conversions are very common, so common that they have received special attention; catalog part or macrofunction implementations are available and standard symbols are defined for them.

Most of the codes used in systems have the property that almost all combinations of values of the code word bits are used.[1] In the most common BCD schemes four code bits are used to represent 10 decimal digits and thus 10 out of the 16 combinations of code bit values are used. Another very important code uses n bits to represent n items of information. Each code word has exactly one bit equal to 1 and all others 0. Such a code is called a *one-out-of-n* or *one-hot* code. Obviously, this code is not used because of its economy—10 bits instead of four are required in a one-hot code for a decimal digit. However, many situations arise when only one signal of a group should be energized because only one event should occur. In such situations the one-hot code must be used.

A circuit that has n inputs and $m = 2^n$ outputs such that for each input combination at most one of the outputs is energized is called a **decoder.** If exactly one of the outputs is active for each input combination, the circuit is called a **complete decoder.** An example of such a circuit for the case of $n = 3$ is shown in Fig. 11.2-1, and the corresponding table of combinations is shown in Table 11.2-1. The Standard symbol of Fig. 11.2-1b is a general symbol for a coder element with the label BIN/OCT, specifying that the input code is binary and the output code is 1-out-of-8.

The circuit to carry out the inverse transformation from 2^n to n leads is called an **encoder** and is shown in Fig. 11.2-2 for $n = 3$. Table 11.2-2 shows the corresponding table of combinations. Since encoders from a one-out-of-n code require just n OR gates, they are so simple as to be seldom discussed.

TABLE 11.2-1 Truth table of binary-to-octal decoder

Input			Output							
x	y	z	D_0	D_1	D_2	D_3	D_4	D_5	D_6	D_7
0	0	0	1	0	0	0	0	0	0	0
0	0	1	0	1	0	0	0	0	0	0
0	1	0	0	0	1	0	0	0	0	0
0	1	1	0	0	0	1	0	0	0	0
1	0	0	0	0	0	0	1	0	0	0
1	0	1	0	0	0	0	0	1	0	0
1	1	0	0	0	0	0	0	0	1	0
1	1	1	0	0	0	0	0	0	0	1

[1] Of course additional bits may be added for reliability purposes.

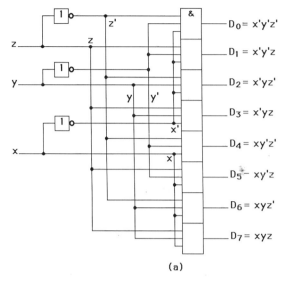

(a)

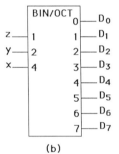

(b)

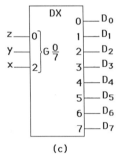

(c)

Figure 11.2-1 Binary-to-octal (3-line-to-8-line) decoder: (a) logic diagram; (b) standard symbol; (c) alternative standard symbol.

TABLE 11.2-2 Truth table of octal-to-binary encoder

Input								Output		
D_0	D_1	D_2	D_3	D_4	D_5	D_6	D_7	x	y	z
1	0	0	0	0	0	0	0	0	0	0
0	1	0	0	0	0	0	0	0	0	1
0	0	1	0	0	0	0	0	0	1	0
0	0	0	1	0	0	0	0	0	1	1
0	0	0	0	1	0	0	0	1	0	0
0	0	0	0	0	1	0	0	1	0	1
0	0	0	0	0	0	1	0	1	1	0
0	0	0	0	0	0	0	1	1	1	1

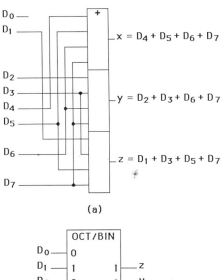

$$x = D_4 + D_5 + D_6 + D_7$$

$$y = D_2 + D_3 + D_6 + D_7$$

$$z = D_1 + D_3 + D_5 + D_7$$

(a)

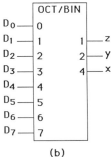

(b)

Figure 11.2-2 Octal-to-binary encoder: (a) logic diagram; (b) standard symbol.

Decoders are more complex than encoders and have received a great deal of attention. Circuits that have n inputs but fewer than 2^n outputs because not all 2^n input combinations occur are still called decoders. Actually, more precise terminology calls the circuits with all 2^n outputs present **complete decoders.** An example of a decoder with fewer than 2^n outputs is a circuit to convert an 8421 BCD digit to the corresponding decimal digit. Two versions of such a decoder are shown in Fig. 11.2-3. Part (a) of this figure shows a circuit that will not have any output energized in case one of the six noncode inputs is present—a decoder with **false data rejection.** The circuit of part (b) has fewer gate inputs, but this circuit will have an output if a noncode input is present—a decoder without false data rejection. Part (c) shows the Standard symbol for a decimal-to-binary code converter. This is a simple form of the Standard symbol that does not indicate whether or not false data are rejected.

11.2-1 Decoder Structures

The circuits of Figs. 11.2-1 and 11.2-3 are examples of **one-stage decoders**—each input passes through exactly one gate before reaching the output. Such decoders are easily designed for any number, n, of input variables; there are 2^n outputs, each derived from an n-input AND gate. For any value of n, the one-stage decoder

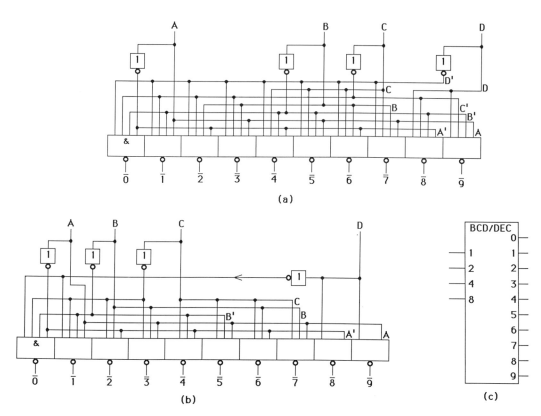

Figure 11.2-3 BCD-to-decimal decoder (logic diagrams): (a) with false-data rejection; (b) without false-data rejection; (c) standard symbol.

is the decoding circuit that uses the fewest gates if AND gates with n inputs can be realized. For large values of n, it may not be practical to obtain the AND function with a single gate and several gates may be required to realize the n-input AND.

In custom and semicustom design, low propagation delay and small area are typical design objectives. The delay is related to the number of logic levels. Area is correlated to the number of transistors, which is in turn determined by the number of gate inputs. It is often necessary to compromise between these two objectives since circuits with few stages sometimes use many more than the minimum number of gate inputs. For example, a one-stage decoder for six variables requires 384 gate inputs, but it is possible to decode six variables with a circuit containing only 176 gate inputs.

Much is known about the design of efficient decoding networks. The complete decoding network realization that requires fewest gate inputs is the **balanced complete decoding network** [Burks 54]. The minimum-gate network is not always the best design choice. Besides the one-stage decoders, other important classes of decoding networks are the **tree decoder** and the **matrix decoder.**

Both the balanced and the tree networks are made up of networks that are

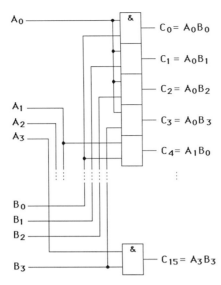

$C_0 = A_0 B_0$

$C_1 = A_0 B_1$

$C_2 = A_0 B_2$

$C_3 = A_0 B_3$

$C_4 = A_1 B_0$

$C_{15} = A_3 B_3$

Figure 11.2-4 Basic decoding unit with two four-lead input groups.

called **basic decoding units.** A basic decoding unit is a one-stage network of two-input AND gates. An example of a basic decoding unit is shown in Fig. 11.2-4 with the corresponding table of combinations shown in Table 11.2-3. The inputs to a basic decoding unit are divided into two groups; each group carries one-hot signals. The outputs of a basic decoding unit carry the one-hot signals that correspond to all possible combinations of signals on the input leads. The Fig. 11.2-4 circuit has two groups of four input leads, each group carrying 1-out-of-4

TABLE 11.2-3 Table of combinations for basic decoding unit of Fig. 11.2-4

A_1 A_2 A_3 A_4	B_0 B_1 B_2 B_3	C_0 C_1 C_2 C_3 C_4 C_5 C_6 C_7 C_8 C_9 C_{10} C_{11} C_{12} C_{13} C_{14} C_{15}
1 0 0 0	1 0 0 0	1 0 0 0 0 0 0 0 0 0 0 0 0 0 0 0
1 0 0 0	0 1 0 0	0 1 0 0 0 0 0 0 0 0 0 0 0 0 0 0
1 0 0 0	0 0 1 0	0 0 1 0 0 0 0 0 0 0 0 0 0 0 0 0
1 0 0 0	0 0 0 1	0 0 0 1 0 0 0 0 0 0 0 0 0 0 0 0
0 1 0 0	1 0 0 0	0 0 0 0 1 0 0 0 0 0 0 0 0 0 0 0
0 1 0 0	0 1 0 0	0 0 0 0 0 1 0 0 0 0 0 0 0 0 0 0
0 1 0 0	0 0 1 0	0 0 0 0 0 0 1 0 0 0 0 0 0 0 0 0
0 1 0 0	0 0 0 1	0 0 0 0 0 0 0 1 0 0 0 0 0 0 0 0
0 0 1 0	1 0 0 0	0 0 0 0 0 0 0 0 1 0 0 0 0 0 0 0
0 0 1 0	0 1 0 0	0 0 0 0 0 0 0 0 0 1 0 0 0 0 0 0
0 0 1 0	0 0 1 0	0 0 0 0 0 0 0 0 0 0 1 0 0 0 0 0
0 0 1 0	0 0 0 1	0 0 0 0 0 0 0 0 0 0 0 1 0 0 0 0
0 0 0 1	1 0 0 0	0 0 0 0 0 0 0 0 0 0 0 0 1 0 0 0
0 0 0 1	0 1 0 0	0 0 0 0 0 0 0 0 0 0 0 0 0 1 0 0
0 0 0 1	0 0 1 0	0 0 0 0 0 0 0 0 0 0 0 0 0 0 1 0
0 0 0 1	0 0 0 1	0 0 0 0 0 0 0 0 0 0 0 0 0 0 0 1

Figure 11.2-5 Symbol for basic decoding unit.

$$A = 2^a, B = 2^b, C = 2^{a+b}$$

signals. (These input signals might be derived from two two-variable complete decoding networks.) The circuit has 16 outputs, only one of which is 1 for any input combination. Figure 11.2-5 shows the symbol for a basic decoding network with input groups having 2^a and 2^b leads and thus 2^{a+b} output leads.

Figure 11.2-6 shows examples of balanced and tree networks using the symbol of Fig. 11.2-5. Note that in these figures a lead with a "2" label corresponds to a lead carrying a 1-out-of-2 signal and thus represents a binary variable—one of the input variables. A basic decoding unit with two input groups both having "2" labels is thus a two-variable one-stage complete decoding network. The tree network is a cascade of basic decoding units with one of the input binary variables introduced in each unit. The balanced decoding network is designed so that each of its component basic decoding units has an equal number of leads in its two input groups whenever possible. When this is not possible, the number of leads in the two groups differs by one power of two.

In many designs such as memories a minimum-gate-input network is not desirable, but it is worthwhile to use a **matrix decoder** to reduce the number of inputs required on the AND gates. In this circuit, shown in Fig. 11.2-7, two networks are used to each decode half of the input variables and then a bank of 2^n two-input AND gates is used to combine the outputs of those two networks to obtain the final 2^n outputs.

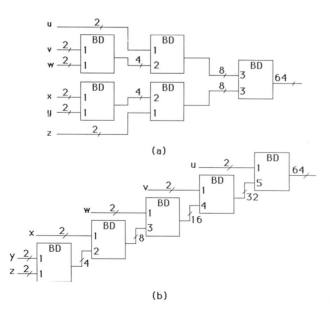

Figure 11.2-6 Examples of balanced and tree decoding networks: (a) balanced decoding network for six variables—$uvwxyz$; (b) tree decoding network for six variables—$uvwxyz$.

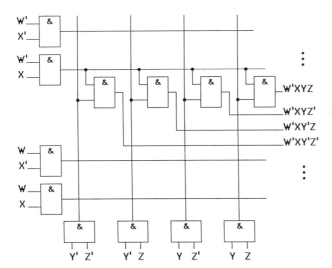

Figure 11.2-7 Matrix decoder for four variables—$WXYZ$.

11.2-2 MSI Decoder Structures

Decoding networks can be realized by interconnecting AND gates, but decoders are so useful that MSI implementations exist. Figure 11.2-8 shows the logic diagram for the 5442/7442 4-line-to-10-line decoder (1-out-of-10) [TI 84]. LSI Logic offers the same function as Macrofunction M42C with a slightly different circuit, [LSI 85]. This circuit is almost the same as the BCD-to-decimal decoder with false data rejection shown in Fig. 11.2-3a. The two differences are that the MSI circuit has (1) all but one of its outputs equal to 1 rather than 0, and (2) an additional n inverters connected to the inputs. The extra inverters are included so that each input will present a load of only one TTL element rather than requiring that the inputs be capable of driving eight elements. The fact that the element outputs are inverted is usually not a problem since they will be connected to inverting drivers or other logic circuits that can accept this type of input.

The 5442/7442 is not only useful for converting BCD to decimal but is also used to convert three binary variables to octal (a three-variable complete decoder) as shown in Fig. 11.2-9. For this application the D input is used to "strobe" or control the time when the output signals are enabled, and the 8 and 9 outputs are not used. Figure 11.2-10a shows two 5442/7442 elements interconnected to completely decode 4 bits to 1-out-of-16. Six bits can be completely decoded with nine MSI devices as shown in Fig. 11.2-10b.

Even though it is possible to obtain a 4-bit to 1-out-of-16 decoder by interconnecting two 5442/7442 elements, this function is so important that it is provided in a single MSI device—the 54154/74154 element shown in Fig. 11.2-11. This element is similar to the 5442/7442 except that 16 rather than 10 outputs are provided and the 54154/74154 includes two control inputs—$1G$ and $2G$. Only when both of these inputs are 0 will the decoding take place. A 1-signal on either or both controls forces all of the outputs to 1. Thus, two strobe or enable inputs are available.

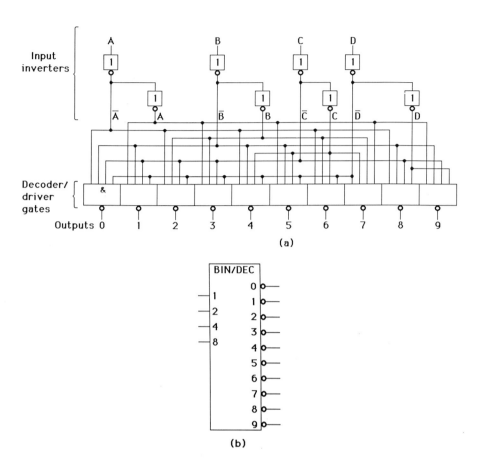

(a)

(b)

Figure 11.2-8 The 5442/7442 4-line-to-10-line decoder: (a) logic diagram; (b) symbol.

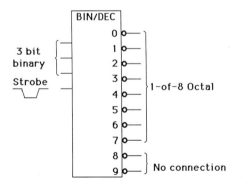

Figure 11.2-9 A 5442/7442 device connected as a binary-to-octal decoder.

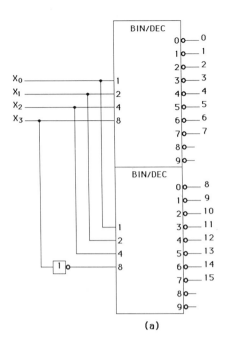

(a)

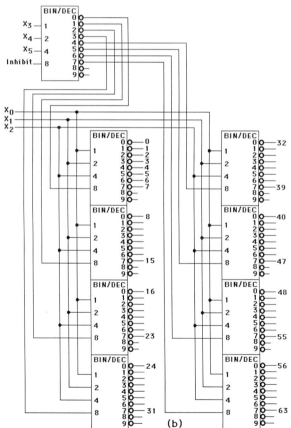

(b)

Figure 11.2-10 Interconnections of 5442/7442 elements to decode more than four variables: (a) 1-out-of-16 decoder; (b) 1-out-of-64 decoder using 4-line-to-10-line decoders.

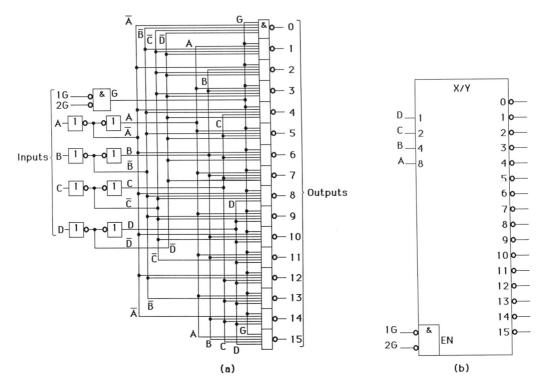

Figure 11.2-11 The 54154/74154 4-line-to-16-line decoder: (a) logic diagram; (b) symbol.

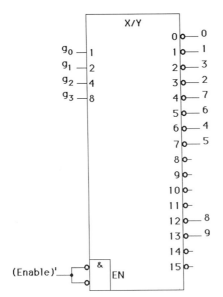

Figure 11.2-12 Connections to 54154/74154 to translate Gray to decimal.

TABLE 11.2-4 Gray-to-decimal conversion

G_3	G_2	G_1	G_0	Decimal digit
0	0	0	0	0
0	0	0	1	1
0	0	1	1	2
0	0	1	0	3
0	1	1	0	4
0	1	1	1	5
0	1	0	1	6
0	1	0	0	7
1	1	0	0	8
1	1	0	1	9

Any 4-bit encoding of the decimal digits can be decoded to decimal (1-out-of-10) code by using the appropriate output terminals of the 54154/74154 element.[2] Figure 11.2-12 shows the connections to translate from Gray code to decimal and the corresponding table is shown in Table 11.2-4.

11.2-3 MSI Decoder Implementations of Arbitrary Functions

Since a complete decoding network generates all of the fundamental products of the input variables, any arbitrary function can be realized by connecting the outputs corresponding to terms of the canonical sum to an output OR gate. Table 11.2-5 shows the table of combinations for two four-variable functions, one of which is 1 when exactly one of the input variables equals 1 and the other which is 1 when exactly three input variables are 1. The corresponding realization using a 54154/74154 element and two four-input NAND gates[3] is shown in Fig. 11.2-13.

11.2-4 General Code Conversions

The binary, BCD, and one-hot codes are most common, but there are other codes that are used often enough so that it is worthwhile having special conversion circuits and corresponding symbols. Table 11.2-6 shows the table of combinations for one such code—the seven-segment display code. The is the code used to drive a seven segment display, as shown in Fig. 11.2-14. The standard symbol for a circuit to convert from a 4-bit binary code to the seven-segment display code is shown in part (b) of the figure. The active-low BL input is a blanking signal: since the outputs have a G dependency on BL, they are all 0 when BL is 0.

---

[2] Specific MSI elements are available for decoding certain 4-bit codes to decimal (e.g., the 5443/7443 element decodes the excess-3 code).

[3] Available in a single integrated-circuit package, 5420/7420, having two four-input NAND gates.

TABLE 11.2-5 Table of combinations for f_1 which is 1 when exactly one input is 1, and f_3 which is 1 when exactly three inputs are 1

	w	x	y	z	f_1	f_3
(0)	0	0	0	0	0	0
(1)	0	0	0	1	1	0
(2)	0	0	1	0	1	0
(3)	0	0	1	1	0	0
(4)	0	1	0	0	1	0
(5)	0	1	0	1	0	0
(6)	0	1	1	0	0	0
(7)	0	1	1	1	0	1
(8)	1	0	0	0	1	0
(9)	1	0	0	1	0	0
(10)	1	0	1	0	0	0
(11)	1	0	1	1	0	1
(12)	1	1	0	0	0	0
(13)	1	1	0	1	0	1
(14)	1	1	1	0	0	1
(15)	1	1	1	1	0	0

$$f_1 = w'x'y'z + w'x'yz' + w'xy'z' + wx'y'z' = S_1(w, x, y, z)$$
$$f_3 = w'xyz + wx'yz + wxy'z + wxyz' \quad\quad = S_3(w, x, y, z)$$

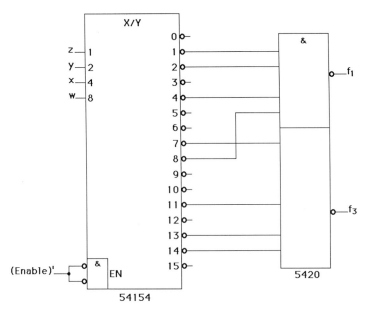

Figure 11.2-13 Circuit to realize f_1 and f_3 of Table 11.2-5.

TABLE 11.2-6 Table of combinations for conversion from binary to seven-segment display code

	D C B A	BL	a	b	c	d	e	f	g
0	0 0 0 0	1	1	1	1	1	1	1	0
1	0 0 0 1	1	0	1	1	0	0	0	0
2	0 0 1 0	1	1	1	0	1	1	0	1
3	0 0 1 1	1	1	1	1	1	0	0	1
4	0 1 0 0	1	0	1	1	0	0	1	1
5	0 1 0 1	1	1	0	1	1	0	1	1
6	0 1 1 0	1	0	0	1	1	1	1	1
7	0 1 1 1	1	1	1	1	0	0	0	0
8	1 0 0 0	1	1	1	1	1	1	1	1
9	1 0 0 1	1	1	1	1	0	0	1	1
10	1 0 1 0	1	0	0	0	1	1	0	1
11	1 0 1 1	1	0	0	1	1	0	0	1
12	1 1 0 0	1	0	1	0	0	0	1	1
13	1 1 0 1	1	1	0	0	1	0	1	1
14	1 1 1 0	1	0	0	0	1	1	1	1
15	1 1 1 1	1	0	0	0	0	0	0	0

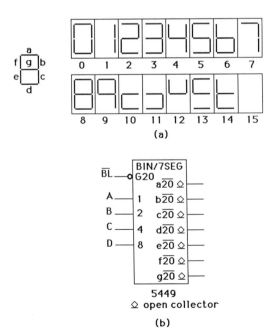

Figure 11.2-14 Seven-segment display: (a) number representation; (b) standard symbol.

Table 11.2-7 shows another example of a standard code converter—a **highest-priority encoder.** The table gives the table of combinations for a circuit that has an arbitrary 10-bit ordered input and an output that is the BCD encoding of the number of the position of the most significant 1 bit. The Standard symbol for this circuit is shown in Fig. 11.2-15. The 74147 MSI part realizes this function but has active-low inputs and outputs.

TABLE 11.2-7 Table of combinations for highest-priority encoder with BCD output

Inputs									Outputs			
1	2	3	4	5	6	7	8	9	8	4	2	1
0	0	0	0	0	0	0	0	0	0	0	0	0
d	d	d	d	d	d	d	d	1	1	0	0	1
d	d	d	d	d	d	d	1	0	1	0	0	0
d	d	d	d	d	d	1	0	0	0	1	1	1
d	d	d	d	d	1	0	0	0	0	1	1	0
d	d	d	d	1	0	0	0	0	0	1	0	1
d	d	d	1	0	0	0	0	0	0	1	0	0
d	d	1	0	0	0	0	0	0	0	0	1	1
d	1	0	0	0	0	0	0	0	0	0	1	0
1	0	0	0	0	0	0	0	0	0	0	0	1

Figure 11.2-15 Standard symbol for highest-priority encoder.

Often a code conversion that is not common enough to have a special symbol must be represented. Two Standard symbols for this situation are shown in Fig. 11.2-16. The symbol of part (a) numbers each of the inputs with a weight so that an input value is determined by summing the weights that correspond to 1 inputs. The input value is 3 if $a = 1$, $b = 1$ and $c = 0$. For each such input value, all outputs with that label will equal 1 and all other outputs will be 0. For $a = 1$, $b = 1$, $c = 0$; outputs e and f will be 1. The part (b) symbol refers to a table [T1] for the definition of the correspondence between input and output. The appropriate table for the part (b) symbol to represent the same conversion as the part (a) symbol is shown in part (c).

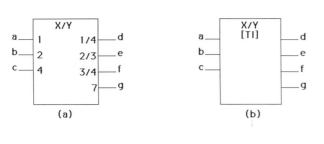

Table T1

Inputs			Outputs			
c	b	a	g	f	e	d
0	0	0	0	0	0	0
0	0	1	0	0	0	1
0	1	0	0	0	1	0
0	1	1	0	1	1	0
1	0	0	0	1	0	1
1	0	1	0	0	0	0
1	1	0	0	0	0	0
1	1	1	1	0	0	0

(c)

Figure 11.2-16 Standard symbols for arbitrary code conversion: (a) using input weights; (b) using a table; (c) table for the weights of part (a).

11.3 DEMULTIPLEXING AND MULTIPLEXING

Two functions that are very closely related to decoding are demultiplexing and multiplexing. A **demultiplexer** is a circuit that routes information from a single input to one of several outputs. The output to which the information is transferred is determined by an encoded address supplied to the circuit. An example of a demultiplexer with four outputs and two address bits is shown in Fig. 11.3-1. Clearly, the demultiplexer of Fig. 11.3-1a could be realized by making use of a 2-line-to-4-line decoder as shown in Fig. 11.3-1b. However, it is more economical to combine

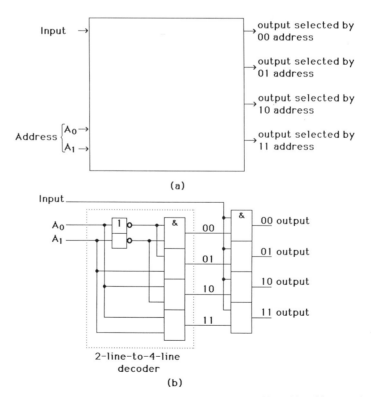

Figure 11.3-1 Demultiplexer with four outputs and two address bits: (a) general form; (b) realization using 2-line-to-4-line decoder.

the demultiplexer output AND gates with the decoder AND gates. The 54154/74154 4-line-to-16-line decoder (Fig. 11.2-11) can be used as a demultiplexer to route one input bit to one of 16 outputs. This is done by connecting the input bit to $G1$, using $G2$ as an enable or strobe input, and using A, B, C, and D as address inputs. By appropriate interconnections of 54154/74154 elements it is possible to route one bit to more than 16 destinations or to route more than one input bit. If more than one input bit is to be routed to fewer than 16 destinations it is possible to make use of the 54155/74155 element, shown in Fig. 11.3-2, that permits two input bits to be routed to one of four destinations or one input bit to be routed to one of eight destinations.[4] Figure 11.3-3 shows the connections for these two applications.

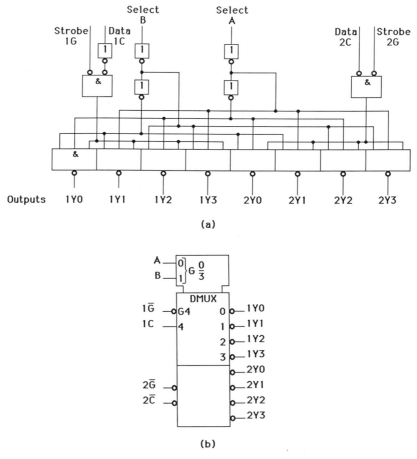

(a)

(b)

Figure 11.3-2 Logic diagram for a demultiplexer with two input bits and four pairs of outputs (54155/74155).

[4] The advantage of using the 54155/74155 to route one bit to eight destinations rather than using the 54154/74154 is that the former is a 16-pin package while the latter is a 24-pin package.

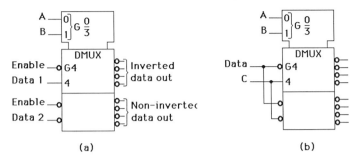

Figure 11.3-3 Connections for using 54155/74155 demultiplexer to (a) route two input bits to one of four destinations; (b) route one input bit to one of eight destinations.

A **multiplexer** is a circuit that can select information from one of several input terminals and route that input to a single output lead. The input terminal selected is determined by an encoded address supplied to the circuit. Figure 11.3-4 shows an example of a multiplexer with four inputs and two address bits. A realization of this multiplexer using a 2-line-to-4-line decoder is shown in Fig. 11.3-4b. Since

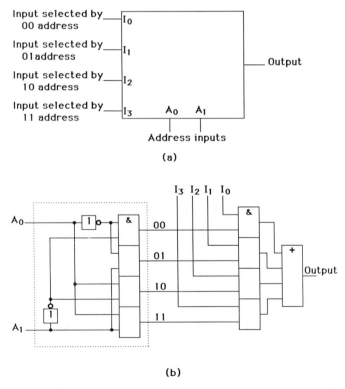

Figure 11.3-4 Multiplexer with four inputs and two address bits: (a) general form; (b) realization using 2-line-to-4-line decoder.

multiplexing is a very frequently used operation, MSI multiplexers exist. An MSI 16-input multiplexer, the 54150/74150, is shown in Fig. 11.3-5. Figure 11.3-6 shows two eight-input multiplexers: The 54151/74151, which includes a strobe input and complementary outputs, and the 54152/74152, which has only the eight data and three address inputs and a single output. A multiplexer for two outputs and four pairs of inputs, the 54153/74153, is shown in Fig. 11.3-7. These devices can be interconnected to handle more outputs and inputs using techniques similar to those used for decoders.

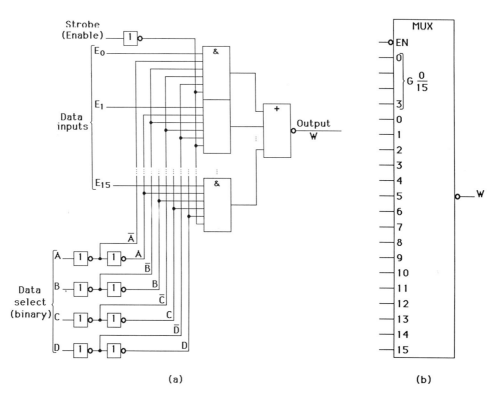

(a)   (b)

Figure 11.3-5 Logic diagram of the 54150/74150 16-input multiplexer: (a) logic diagram; (b) standard symbol.

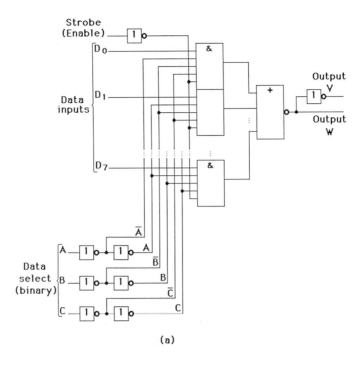

(a)

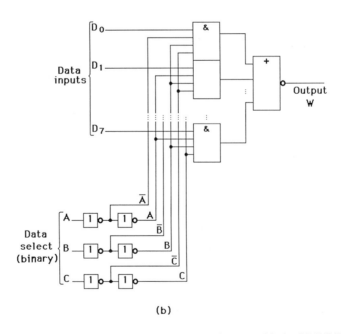

(b)

Figure 11.3-6 Logic diagrams for eight-input multiplexers: (a) the 54151/74151, which includes a strobe input and complementary outputs; (b) the 54152/74152, which has only eight data and three address inputs and a single output; (c) standard symbols.

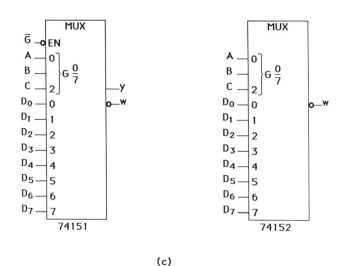

(c)

Figure 11.3-6 (Continued)

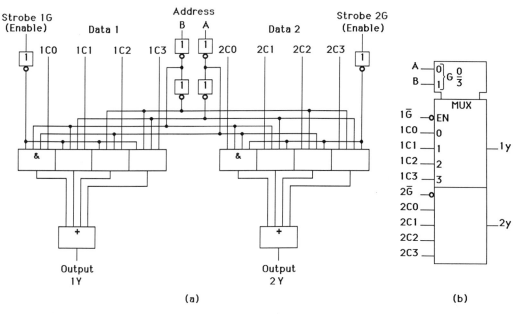

(a)

(b)

Figure 11.3-7 The 54153/74153 multiplexer which has two outputs and four pairs of inputs: (a) logic diagram; (b) standard symbol.

11.3-1 Arbitrary Function Realizations Using Multiplexers

By connecting either a fixed 1 or fixed 0 signal to each of the multiplexer inputs, the multiplexer can be made to realize any arbitrary switching function. Thus the multiplexer can be used as a *universal logic element*. In Sec. 2.4 it was shown that any function could be represented by the expression

$$f(x_1, x_2, \ldots, x_n) = f_0 p_0 + f_1 p_1 + \cdots + f_{2^n-1} p_{2^n-1}$$

where the subscripts refer to rows of the table of combinations for $f(x_1, x_2, \ldots, x_n)$ and the f_i and p_i represent the corresponding values of the function (f_i) and fundamental products (p_i). The logic expression for the output of a multiplexer such as the 54151/74151 is

$$Y = D_0 A'B'C' + D_1 A'B'C + \cdots + D_7 ABC \quad \text{or}$$

$$Y = D_0 p_0(ABC) + D_1 p_1(ABC) + \cdots + D_7 p_7(ABC).$$

Since the expressions for $f(x_1, x_2, \ldots, x_n)$ and Y have the same form, it is possible to make Y realize any $f(A, B, C)$ by setting $D_0 = f_0(A, B, C)$, $D_1 = f_1(A, B, C)$, $\ldots, D_7 = f_7(A, B, C)$. Figure 11.3-8 shows an example of the use of this technique to realize the function of Table 11.3-1.

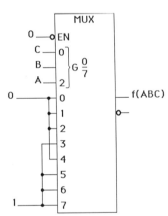

Figure 11.3-8 Realization of the function of Table 11.3-1 using a 541511/74151 multiplexer.

TABLE 11.3-1 Table of combinations for a function that is 1 if two or more inputs are equal to 1, $ST_2(A, B, C)$

	A	B	C	f
(0)	0	0	0	$0 = f_0$
(1)	0	0	1	$0 = f_1$
(2)	0	1	0	$0 = f_2$
(3)	0	1	1	$1 = f_3$
(4)	1	0	0	$0 = f_4$
(5)	1	0	1	$1 = f_5$
(6)	1	1	0	$1 = f_6$
(7)	1	1	1	$1 = f_7$

In fact, it is possible to realize an arbitrary **four**-variable function with an eight-input multiplexer by making use of the general functional expression:

$$f(x_1, x_2, \ldots, x_n) = f(x_1, 0, 0, \ldots, 0, 0)x_2'x_3' \cdots x_{n-1}'x_n'$$

$$+ f(x_1, 0, 0, \ldots, 0, 1)x_2'x_3' \cdots x_{n-1}'x_n + \cdots$$

$$+ f(x_1, 1, 1, \ldots, 1, 1)x_2x_3 \cdots x_{n-1}x_n$$

In this expression each of the $f(x_1, c_1, c_2, \ldots, c_{n-1})$ represents the quantity that the function will equal with x_i set equal to c_i ($2 \leq i \leq n$) and thus will have a value of $0, 1, x_1$, or x_1'. Table 11.3-2 shows the function f_1 of Table 11.2-5 represented in a fashion to facilitate expressing the function in this form and placing the values of $f(w, x = c_1, y = c_2, z = c_3)$ in evidence. Table 11.3-2a is just a chart for the function that separates w from x, y, z. Whenever both entries in a single column of this chart have the same value (0 in column 011) this value is the value of the corresponding $f(w, x = c_1, y = c_2, z = c_3)$. When the two different values in the column are the same as the row labels, the value of the corresponding $f(w, x = c_1, y = c_2, z = c_3)$ is w and if the values are opposite from the row labels, then $f(w, x = c_1, y = c_2, z = c_3)$ is w'. These values are shown in Table 11.3-2b, and Table 11.3-2c gives the resulting functional expression.

By setting $D_0 = f(x_1, 0, 0, \ldots, 0, 0)$, $D_1 = f(x_1, 0, 0, \ldots, 0, 1)$, $\ldots$, $D_{2^{n-1}-1} = f(x_1, 1, 1, \ldots, 1, 1)$, the expressions for the function and the multiplexer become identical and thus the multiplexer can be used to realize the function. To

TABLE 11.3-2 Specifications for a function $f(w, x, y, z)$ that equals 1 when exactly one of the independent variables is equal to 1, $S_1(w, x, y, z)$: (a) Chart that separates out w variable; (b) chart showing coefficients in expansion about all variables except w; (c) Expansion of $f(w, x, y, z)$ about all variables except w

(a)

$x\ y\ z$

w	000	001	010	011	100	101	110	111
0	0	1	1	0	1	0	0	0
1	1	0	0	0	0	0	0	0

$f(w, x, y, z)$

(b)

$x\ y\ z$

000	001	010	011	100	101	110	111
w	w'	w'	0	w'	0	0	0

$f(w, c_1, c_2, c_3)$

(c)

$$f(w, x, y, z) = wp_0(x, y, z) + w'p_1(x, y, z) + w'p_2(x, y, z) + w'p_4(x, y, z)$$

realize a four-variable function such as that of Table 11.3-2 using an eight-input multiplexer, three of the variables (x, y, z) are connected to the address inputs (A, B, C) and each of the data inputs has connected to it either 0, 1, or the remaining variable (either directly or complemented). Figure 11.3-9 shows a 54151/74151 with the appropriate connections to realize the function of Table 11.3-2.

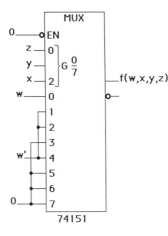

Figure 11.3-9 Realization of the function of Table 11.3-2 using a 54151/74151 multiplexer.

11.4 SHIFT REGISTERS

This section and the next present sequential macrofunctions. Registers and shift registers are discussed here and counters in the following section.

Registers and shift registers were introduced in Sec. 7.7. This section discusses shift registers in more detail since they are important elements for hierarchical design. A register is a circuit capable of storing several bits of information. Figure 11.4-1 shows a four-bit register.

Shift registers differ in whether data can be entered or read out in parallel or serially, and in their shift capability. For simplicity, only flip-flop implementations are described; two-phase structures are also used but are easily derived

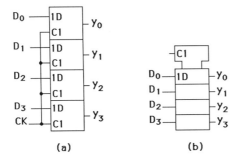

Figure 11.4-1 Four-bit latch register: (a) logic diagram; (b) standard symbol.

from the flip-flop designs. The simplest form of shift register is shown in Fig. 11.4-2. Data can be entered only serially and can be read out only in parallel. The "SRG 4" label in the common control block of the Standard symbol indicates that a four-stage shift register is represented. The label C1/→ on the dynamic control input shows that this input has two effects: All other inputs with a 1 label are controlled by this input, and the right arrow means that the register contents are shifted once from top to bottom (or left to right) for each control pulse. If there is a number after the arrow (→ m), this means that the contents are shifted m rather than one stage for each control pulse.

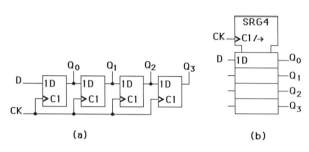

Figure 11.4-2 Four-bit serial-in, parallel-out shift register: (a) logic diagram; (b) standard symbol.

A parallel read in capability can be added to a shift register using the general techniques described in Sec. 8.2-1. A serial-in, parallel-in, serial-out shift register is shown in Fig. 11.4-3. The common control block of part (b) has a **mode** input labeled M1 [Shift]: The M1 means that when that input is active, all items conditioned with a 1 are activated. In this symbol there are two such items: The serial input to the first stage and the shift arrow associated with the dynamic control input. The bracketed item [Shift] is simply a comment to make the symbol easier to interpret. The mode input M2 [Load] activates the data inputs to each stage of the register.

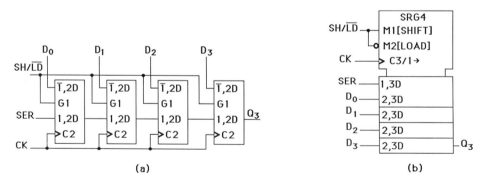

Figure 11.4-3 Four-bit serial-in, parallel-in, serial-out shift register: (a) logic diagram; (b) standard symbol.

The most general shift register is called a **universal shift register**. It can shift in either direction in addition to having both parallel and serial input and output capabilities. A universal 4-bit shift register is shown in Fig. 11.4-4. Its operation is summarized in Table 11.4-1.

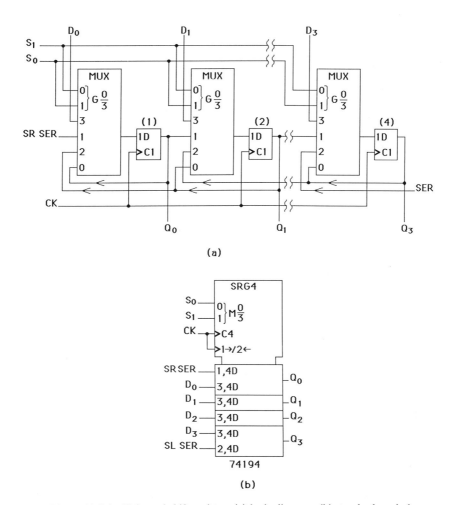

Figure 11.4-4 Universal shift register: (a) logic diagram; (b) standard symbol.

TABLE 11.4-1 Operation of the universal shift register of Fig. 11.4-4

$S_1 S_0$	
0 0	No operation
0 1	Shift right Serial data enters SR SER
1 0	Shift left Serial data enters SL SER
1 1	Parallel load

Scan-path compatibility. The general scan-path design-for-testability techniques of Sec. 10.4 require that all system bistables have a test data input in addition to the normal system data input. For a shift register it is not necessary to provide

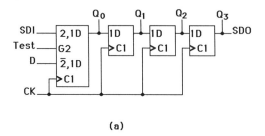

(a)

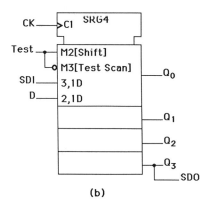

(b)

Figure 11.4-5 Shift register of Fig. 11.4-1 with scan-path capability added: (a) logic diagram; (b) standard symbol.

these two inputs for all stages of the register. If the first register stage has a test data input, the normal shift operation can be used to transfer the test data from the first stage to the other stages. A serial-out capability permits test data to be scanned out of the register. The overhead due to the provision of DFT scan path is thus lower for designs with lots of shift registers than for general designs. Figure 11.4-5 shows the shift register of Fig. 11.4-1 modified to have a scan-path test mode capability.

11.5 COUNTERS

A counter is a sequential circuit that implements one (or more) of the following functions:

1. Counts the number of input pulses received and stores a number representing this count.

2. Provides an output pulse train that is derived from the input pulses but is at a lower frequency. If the ratio between the input and output frequencies is fixed, the circuit is called a **frequency divider** or **scaler**. The name **binary rate multiplier** is used for circuits having a variable frequency ratio [Wakerly 76].

3. Provides a sequence of binary patterns for applications such as addressing memory.

Since the same basic logic designs are used for all three purposes, the generic name *counter* is used to describe these structures. A variety of standard structures are used to implement counters: binary counters, shift counters, and interconnected counters. These structures are described in this section. Binary counters are commonly used when a numerical count of the arriving pulses is required. They are also used often for frequency division. When scan techniques are used to enhance testability there is a penalty for using the binary counters. With binary counters each stage must be capable of accepting test data inputs as well as normal count inputs. Shift counters can be made "scannable" by adding an extra input only to the first stage, as described at the end of the previous section. This can reduce the scan overhead substantially as compared to that associated with a binary counter realization.

11.5-1 Binary Ripple Counters

The simplest form of counter is the **binary ripple counter**. A circuit for such a counter is shown in Fig. 11.5-1 along with the corresponding waveforms. Table 11.5-1 lists the states of the three flip-flops in this counter. It shows that these

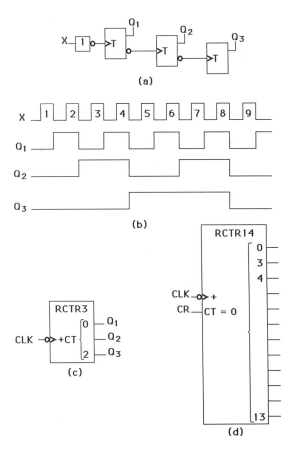

Figure 11.5-1 Three-stage (modulo-8) binary ripple counter: (a) using nongated T flip-flops; (b) waveforms; (c) standard symbol; (d) standard symbol for 4020 CMOS MSI part.

TABLE 11.5-1 States of flip-flops in counter of Fig. 11.5-1

Q_3	Q_2	Q_1	
0	0	0	At start
0	0	1	After pulse 1
0	1	0	After pulse 2
0	1	1	After pulse 3
1	0	0	After pulse 4
1	0	1	After pulse 5
1	1	0	After pulse 6
1	1	1	After pulse 7
0	0	0	After pulse 8

states correspond to the sequence of binary numbers. The lowest order bit—Q_1—changes state with each input pulse. This action is achieved in the circuit by connecting X_1' to the T input of the first flip-flop. The second bit Q_2 changes whenever Q_1 changes from 1 to 0. This action is obtained by connecting Q' to the control input of the next flip-flop to cause triggering on the falling transition of Q. The relationship between Q_i and Q_{i+1} is the same as that between Q_1 and Q_2, so the same interconnections can be used. The Standard symbol is shown in part (c) of the figure. The general qualifying symbol "RCTR 3" indicates that the part is a three-stage ripple counter. The " + " after the dynamic input symbol > means that an input pulse causes an up-count (a "-" would indicate a down count). The output grouping bracket preceded by CT shows that the output values represent the count value. The Standard symbol for a 14-stage MSI ripple counter, the 4020, is shown in Fig. 11.5-1d. The "$CT = 0$" label on the CR input shows that the contents of the counter are set to 0 when a CR signal is applied. The fact that 1 and 2 are missing from the output labels indicates that the second- and third-stage outputs are not available as output signals.

The circuit of Fig. 11.5-1 is called a **binary counter** because its sequence of states is the same as the sequence of binary numbers. It is a **modulo-8 counter** because it sequences through eight distinct states. Since it has three flip-flops that are used to provide circuit outputs, it is a **three-stage counter**. The term **ripple counter** is used since the input pulses are not connected directly to all the flip-flops—the input pulse can directly cause a change only in Q_1. This change can then cause a change in Q_2, which may cause Q_3 to change, etc. Thus, an input pulse may initiate a sequence of changes which "ripple" through the stage at the counter. Ripple counters are sometimes called **asynchronous counters** since the different stages of the counter do not all change state at the same time.

In many situations the output desired from a counter is not the binary number representing the state but a signal on one of 2^m lines, where m is the number of states in the counter. This form of output can be obtained by connecting a decoding network to the counter as shown in Fig. 11.5-2.

A ripple counter has a serious disadvantage when decoded outputs are desired: Spurious output pulses called decoding spikes may occur. Fig. 11.5-3 shows wave-

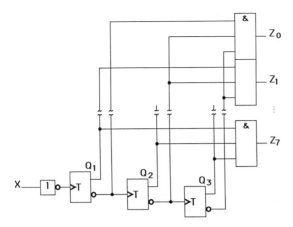

Figure 11.5-2 Binary ripple counter with decoded outputs.

forms for the circuit of Fig. 11.5-2 in which an explicit delay t_{pd} is shown between the trailing edge of the clocking signal and the corresponding change in the flip-flop outputs. Input pulse 2 causes Q_1 to change to 0, which causes Q_2 to become 1. There is a time interval during which both Q_1 and Q_2 are 0. Since Q_3 is 0 throughout this period the Z_0 gate will have all of its inputs (Q_1', Q_2', Q_3') equal to 1 and will produce a momentary 1 output. This spurious output pulse is called a *decoding spike*. It is caused by the functional hazard due to the change of more than one input to the AND gate. Table 11.5-2 shows the complete sequence of states (both stable and unstable) that occur in a three-stage binary ripple counter.

The possibility of decoding spikes exists in any counter unless all flip-flops change simultaneously or each input pulse causes only one flip-flop to change state. One way to avoid these spikes is thus to design the counter so that it has one of these characteristics. Such counters will be discussed later. It is also possible to avoid the effects of decoding spikes by using a **strobe pulse** to ensure that the decoded counter state is not read out until after the counter stable state has been

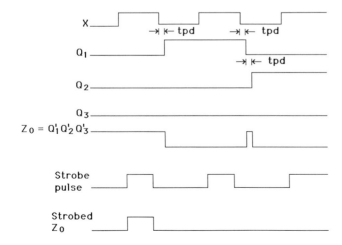

Figure 11.5-3 Waveforms for decoded outputs from binary ripple counters (Figs. 11.5-2 and 11.5-4).

TABLE 11.5-2 Complete sequence of states for three-stage binary ripple counter

| Input pulse | Decimal Output | | Binary state |
	Spurious	Stable	
			⟨0 0 0⟩
1		1	⟨0 0 1⟩
2	0		0 0 0
		2	⟨0 1 0⟩
3		3	⟨0 1 1⟩
4	2		0 1 0
	0		0 0 0
		4	⟨1 0 0⟩
5		5	1 0 1
6	4		1 0 0
		6	⟨0 1 0⟩
7		7	⟨1 1 1⟩
8	6		1 1 0
	4		1 0 0
		0	⟨0 0 0⟩

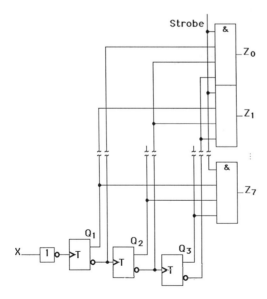

Figure 11.5-4 Decoding network for a three-stage ripple counter with strobe input.

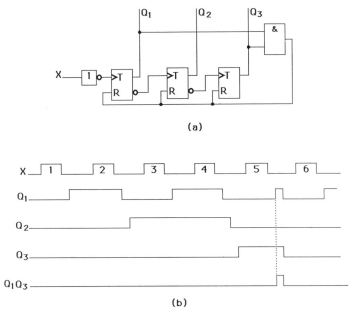

(a)

(b)

Figure 11.5-5 Modulo-5 three-stage binary ripple counter: (a) logic diagram; (b) waveforms.

reached. A decoding network with strobe pulse connections is shown in Fig. 11.5-4. The timing of the strobe pulse is shown in Fig. 11.5-3.

Nonbinary-modulus counters. It is a simple matter to design an m-stage binary ripple counter. This will be a modulo-2^m counter. Often a counter with a modulus that is not of power of 2 is desired. By a simple modification it is possible to convert a modulo-2^m counter to a counter with fewer states. What is done is to use the clear inputs to the counter flip-flops to place the counter in the all-0 state once the maximum desired count is reached. Figure 11.5-5 shows a modulo-5 counter designed using this approach and the corresponding waveforms. As soon as state 5 is reached, the CR signal becomes equal to 1 and immediately clears all the flip-flops via their CR inputs. The counter is thus prevented from becoming stable in state 5. The general procedure for obtaining a modulo N counter (for N not a binary power) is to:

1. Design a counter with modulus equal to the smallest binary power greater than N.
2. Connect to an AND gate all flip-flop outputs that are equal to 1 for state N.[5]

---

[5] This gate is to equal 1 only for state N. It is not necessary to connect the Q_i' inputs from those stages which are 0 for the Nth state because of the sequence in which the states occur in a binary counter.

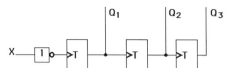

Figure 11.5-6 Three-stage binary ripple down counter.

3. Connect the AND gate output to the asynchronous reset input of all flip-flops of the counter.

The timing of the signals in such a counter must be carefully controlled, particularly the relationship between the reset timing and the input pulse frequency. A more reliable design results from using a finite-state machine design for the desired modulus.

Down and up-down counters. It is sometimes useful to have a binary counter that will cycle through the binary numbers in decreasing rather than increasing order. The design of such a counter, called a **binary down counter**, is shown in Fig. 11.5-6. Table 11.5-3 shows the sequence of stable states for such a counter. To count down it is desired to have Q_i toggle whenever Q_{i-1} changes from 0 to 1. Since these flip-flops change for the 0-to-1 input transition, this action can be easily obtained by connecting Q_{i-1} to the input of the Q_i flip-flop. A counter that will count either up or down depending on the condition of a control signal input, a **reversible**, or **up-down binary counter**, is shown in Fig. 11.5-7. Setting the count-up signal equal to 1 has the effect of connecting Q_i' to T_{i+1}, and Q_i is connected to T_{i+1} when countdown is 1. Clearly only one of the count-up, count-down signals should equal 1 at any time.

Ripple counters are not finite-state machines since they do not have the external-trigger property. Ripple counters are used because of their simplicity, but they have many undesirable features. One disadvantage of ripple counters is the presence of decoding spikes. Another drawback is the long time taken for the state changes to ripple through the flip-flops. In a modulo-2^m, m-stage counter, the time required by the transition from the all-1 state to the all-0 state will be equal to $(m)(t_{pd})$, where t_{pd} is the time required for one flip-flop to toggle. This *settling delay* limits the rate at which the counter can be changed and read out.

TABLE 11.5-3 Sequence of stable states for counter of Fig. 11.5-6

State	Q_3	Q_2	Q_1	
0	0	0	0	At start
7	1	1	1	After pulse 1
6	1	1	0	After pulse 2
5	1	0	1	After pulse 3
4	1	0	0	After pulse 4
5	0	1	1	After pulse 5
6	0	1	0	After pulse 6
7	0	0	1	After pulse 7
0	0	0	0	After pulse 8

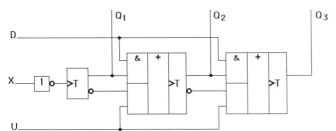

Figure 11.5-7 Reversible or up-down three-stage binary ripple counter.

11.5-2 Synchronous Counters

The ripple counter decoding spikes and long delays are avoided in a **synchronous counter** in which all flip-flops are changed simultaneously. The general form of a synchronous counter is shown in Fig. 11.5-8. The input pulses are connected directly to the clocking input of each of the flip-flops. For each state of the counter, the appropriate J and K signals to cause the correct next state are determined by the logic network and supplied to each of the flip-flops.

The logic diagram for a synchronous binary counter is shown in Fig. 11.5-9a. Examination of Table 11.5-1 shows that flip-flop Q_i should change state whenever flip-flops $Q_{i-1}, Q_{i-2}, \ldots, Q_1$ are all equal to 1 and an input pulse arrives. In Fig. 11.5-9a the condition that all lower-order flip-flops be in the 1 state is detected by the AND gate connected to the T input of each flip-flop. Since the input pulses are connected to the C input of the flip-flops they toggle when $T = 1$, indicating that all previous flip-flops are 1. The time required to change the state of this counter is t_{pd} (the propagation delay of a flip-flop) plus t_g (the delay through one gate). Thus the maximum pulse rate that such a counter can handle is $f = 1/(t_{pd} + t_g)$. For an m-stage counter of the type shown in Fig. 11.5-9a, the output of the lowest-order flip-flop (Q_1) is connected to ($m - 2$) AND gates. The T input to the highest-order flip-flop requires an $m - 1$ input AND gate. For large values of m these requirements for a flip-flop to drive many AND gates and for an m-input gate may be difficult to satisfy. These difficulties can be avoided by using a **series carry synchronous counter** such as that shown in Fig. 11.5-9b. This counter makes use of the fact that T_i can be realized as $T_i = T_{i-1}Q_{i-1}$, so that only two-input AND gates are required and each flip-flop output is only connected to one AND gate. This circuit can operate at a maximum frequency $f = 1/[t_{pd} + (m - 2)t_g]$ and thus is slower than the **parallel carry synchronous counter** of Fig. 11.5-9a.

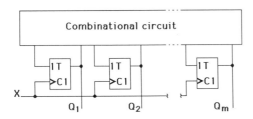

Figure 11.5-8 General form of a synchronous counter.

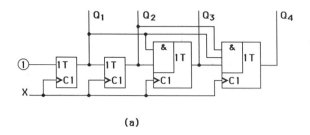

(a)

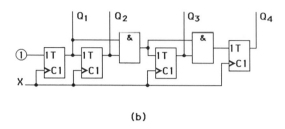

(b)

Figure 11.5-9 Four-stage synchronous binary counters: (a) parallel carry; (b) series carry.

Synchronous counters usually do not require strobe pulses since decoding spikes can occur only if the flip-flop propagation delays (t_{pd}) vary significantly.

Situations arise in which a counter that sequences through a series of states different from the binary numbers is required. One approach to designing such a circuit is to use a binary counter with a combinational circuit that translates from the binary flip-flop values to the desired sequence of outputs. It is more usual to design a counter that produces the desired sequence directly at its flip-flop outputs. The synthesis techniques given in Chap. 9 for finite-state machines provide a straightforward method for the design of such a counter.

Table 11.5-4 illustrates this design process for the case of a counter to sequence through the states of one binary-coded-decimal digit. The first step in such a design is to list the desired sequence of states as in Table 11.5-4a. Next to each state is listed the state to which the counter should change after one input pulse. The entries that represent changes are shown in boldface. Table 11.5-4a corresponds to the transition table of Chap. 9 and Table 11.5-4b is the appropriate excitation table. The resulting excitation functions are given in Table 11.5-4c, and Fig. 11.5-10 shows the circuit.

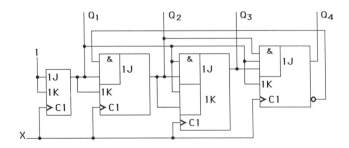

Figure 11.5-10 BCD synchronous counter.

TABLE 11.5-4 Tables for designing BCD synchronous counter: (a) Transition table; (b) Excitation table; (c) Excitation functions

(a)

Present State					Next State			
Q_4	Q_3	Q_2	Q_1		Q_4	Q_3	Q_2	Q_1
0	0	0	0		0	0	0	**1**
0	0	0	1		0	0	**1**	**0**
0	0	1	0		0	0	1	**1**
0	0	1	1		0	**1**	**0**	**0**
0	1	0	0		0	1	0	**1**
0	1	0	1		0	1	**1**	**0**
0	1	1	0		0	1	1	**1**
0	1	1	1		**1**	**0**	**0**	**0**
1	0	0	0		1	0	0	**1**
1	0	0	1		**0**	0	0	**0**

(b)

J_4	K_4	J_3	K_3	J_2	K_2	J_1	K_1
0	d	0	d	0	d	1	d
0	d	0	d	1	d	d	1
0	d	0	d	d	0	1	d
0	d	1	d	d	1	d	1
0	d	d	0	0	d	1	d
0	d	d	0	1	d	d	1
0	d	d	0	d	0	1	d
1	d	d	1	d	1	d	1
d	0	0	d	0	d	1	d
d	1	0	d	0	d	d	1

(c)

Q_4Q_3				
Q_2Q_1	00	01	11	10
0 0	0	0	d	d
0 1	0	0	d	d
1 1	0	(1	d)	d
1 0	0	0	d	d

$$J_4 = Q_3Q_2Q_1$$

Q_4Q_3				
Q_2Q_1	00	01	11	10
0 0	d	d	d	0
0 1	d	d	d	1
1 1	d	d	d	d
1 0	d	d	d	d

$$K_4 = Q_1$$

$J_1 = K_1 = 1$

$J_2 = Q_1Q_4'$
$K_2 = Q_1$

$J_3 = Q_1Q_2$
$K_3 = Q_1Q_2$

$J_4 = Q_1Q_2Q_3$
$K_4 = Q_1$

11.5-3 Shift Counters

The counters described in Secs. 11.5-1 and 11.5-2 all have the property that they require the fewest possible flip-flops. For a modulus M counter, m stages are used, where m is the smallest integer such that $2^m \geq M$. Such counters are sometimes given the generic name of *binary counters* even though they are not restricted to counting sequences of binary numbers. To avoid possible confusion, we will coin the term **minimum-stage counter** to describe counters having this property.

When decoded states are required as outputs, or when a scan path is required for testability, it is often most economical to use a modified shift register as a counter. Such a counter has more stages than a minimum-stage counter, but has very simple circuitry for forming the decoded outputs. Counters based on shift registers are called **shift counters**. The **ring counter** is the simplest type of shift counter.

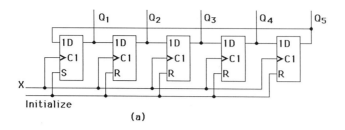

(a)

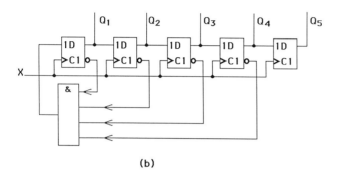

(b)

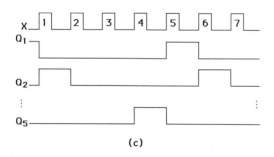

(c)

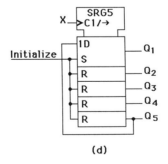

(d)

Figure 11.5-11 Five-stage ring counter: (a) without self-correction; (b) with self-correction; (c) waveforms; (d) standard symbol for (a).

TABLE 11.5-5 Sequence of states for ring counter of Fig. 11.5-11

Input pulse	Q_5	Q_4	Q_3	Q_2	Q_1	
	0	0	0	0	1	Initial state
1	0	0	0	1	0	
2	0	0	1	0	0	
3	0	1	0	0	0	
4	1	0	0	0	0	
5	0	0	0	0	1	
6	0	0	0	1	0	

Ring Counters. A five-stage ring counter is shown in Fig. 11.5-11a. It consists of a five-stage shift register with the output of the last stage connected to the input of the first stage. In the initial state the first stage is 1 and all other stages are 0. Table 11.5-5 lists the sequence of states for this counter, which uses five flip-flops to obtain five states. A minimum-stage counter requires only three stages for five states. However, the ring counter provides spike-free decoded outputs directly, while the minimum-stage counter requires a separate decoding network.

One possible drawback of the ring counter is the fact that if one of the unused states, say 01010, is entered due to noise, the counter will sequence indefinitely through nonvalid states and provide false outputs. This problem can be eliminated by modifying the counter as in Fig. 11.5-11b. This form of the counter requires an additional AND gate which realizes $Q'_{m-1}Q'_{m-2} \cdots Q'_1$ and is used for the input to the low-order stage. This stage will be set to one only when all stages but the highest order are equal to zero (condition $d000 \ldots 0$). Thus, even if a false state is entered, the counter will automatically return to a valid state after at most $m-1$ pulses. Thus such a counter is **self-correcting**. If the possibility of a few incorrect outputs after the circuit is first started is acceptable, it is possible to omit the initializing input and rely on the self-correcting feature of the circuit for initialization. The circuit is then **self-initializing**.

Johnson Counters. The number of states in a ring counter can be doubled ($2m$ states for m stages) by using Q'_m instead of Q_m as the first stage input. Such a counter is called a **twisted-ring counter**, **switch-tail counter**, **Johnson counter**, or **Mobius counter**. The logic diagram for such a counter is shown in Fig. 11.5-12a and its sequence of states is listed in Table 11.5-6.

An output network is required in order to obtain decoded outputs from a twisted-ring counter. However, only a single two-input AND gate is needed for each decoded output. Table 11.5-6 identifies the AND gate inputs for each state of the counter. In the list of binary states, the two flip-flop conditions used to identify the state are underlined. Inspection of these entries shows that they identify the states uniquely.

The possibility of entering false states and the need for initialization are present in twisted-ring counters just as in ring counters. Modifications to provide self-synchronization are possible. Figure 11.5-12b shows a five-stage twisted-ring

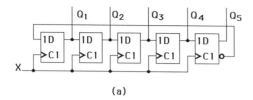

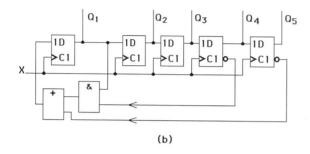

Figure 11.5-12 Five-stage, modulo-10 twisted-ring counter: (a) basic counter; (b) counter with self-correction.

counter that is self-correcting due to the fact that $D_1 = D'_5 + Q'_4Q_1$ rather than $D_1 = D'_5$ as in Fig. 11.5-12a. The additional term, Q'_4Q_1, ensures that if the counter ever enters an incorrect state, it will return to the correct sequence. Table 11.5-7 lists all of the spurious states for the five-stage twisted-ring counter. The sequence in which these states occur is shown by placing the immediate successor state directly below each state where possible. Arrows are used to indicate other state transitions, with dashed lines showing the transitions for a counter without self-correction (Fig. 11.5-12a) and the solid lines indicating the transitions for a self-correcting counter (Fig. 11.5-12b).

TABLE 11.5-6 Sequence of states for five-stage twisted-ring counter

State	Q_5	Q_4	Q_3	Q_2	Q_1	Decoder
0	0	0	0	0	0	$Q'_5Q'_1$
1	0	0	0	0	1	Q'_2Q_1
2	0	0	0	1	1	Q'_3Q_2
3	0	0	1	1	1	Q'_4Q_3
4	0	1	1	1	1	Q'_5Q_4
5	1	1	1	1	1	Q_5Q_1
6	1	1	1	1	0	$Q_2Q'_1$
7	1	1	1	0	0	$Q_3Q'_2$
8	1	1	0	0	0	$Q_4Q'_3$
9	1	0	0	0	0	$Q_5Q'_4$
0	0	0	0	0	0	

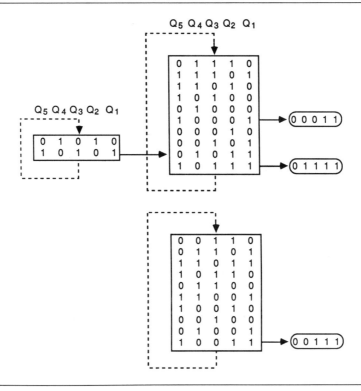

The general design for an m-stage twisted-ring counter has $D_i = Q_{i-1}$, for $i = 2, 3, \ldots, m$ and $D_1 = Q'_m + Q_1 Q'_{m-1} \cdots Q'_{m-p}$. The value of p must be chosen so that $p = m/3$ if $m/3$ is an integer and $p = \lfloor m/3 \rfloor$ if $m/3$ is not an integer.[6] Thus, for $m = 7$, $D_1 = Q'_7 + Q_1 Q'_6 Q'_5$ and for $m = 9$, $D_1 = Q'_9 + Q_1 Q'_8 Q'_7 Q'_6$. For a derivation of this design, see [Bleickhardt 68] and [Morris 71].

The twisted-ring counter as presented only provides even $(2m)$ moduli. An odd cycle length can be obtained by connecting $Q'_m Q'_{m-1}$ to the low-order stage input, thus eliminating the all-1 state. A five-stage, modulus-nine twisted-ring counter is shown in Fig. 11.5-13 and the corresponding state sequence is listed in Table 11.5-8.

Interconnected Counters. For large moduli (greater than 12) ring counters become uneconomical. However, it is possible to retain some of their advantages by combining several ring counters of smaller moduli to obtain the desired modulus. Two techniques of combining counters are useful: **series** or **cascade**, and **parallel**. In both cases the desired modulus is factored and then a counter for each factor is implemented. In the series technique one counter is cycled directly by the input

---

[6] The symbol $\lfloor f \rfloor$ stands for the floor of f and is the greatest integer not greater than f, $\lfloor 7/3 \rfloor = 2$.

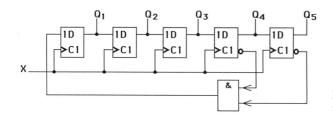

Figure 11.5-13 Five-stage modulo-9 twisted-ring counter.

pulses but the next counter is cycled by an input pulse only when the first counter is in a specific one of its possible states. Figure 11.5-14a shows a logic diagram for a modulus-24 counter made up of a series connection of modulus-4 and modulus-6 twisted-ring counters. The modulus-6 counter is advanced only when the modulus-4 counter is in the 1-state when an input pulse arrives. The sequence of states assumed by this counter is illustrated in Table 11.5-9.

In the parallel technique of combining counters, all component counters are cycled directly by the input pulses. The higher modulus is obtained by decoding the outputs of the counters together. Figure 11.5-15b shows a modulus-24 counter obtained by connecting a modulus-3 counter and a modulus-8 counter in parallel. The sequence of states entered by this counter is illustrated in Table 11.5-10. Since the two moduli (3 and 8) are relatively prime—no number divides both of them— they will reenter the same pair of states only after 24 input pulses have been received. If a nonprime pair of numbers such as four and six were used as moduli for a parallel counter, a counter of modulus 12 rather than 24 would be obtained. Since $4 = 2 \cdot 2$ and $6 = 2 \cdot 3$, the same state would be reentered after $4 \cdot 3 = 12$ pulses, as illustrated in Table 11.5-11. This restriction to relatively prime moduli is a constraint on parallel counter designs that is not present for series counters.

Scan-path Implementations. Shift counters are easily modified to permit scan-path testing, particularly when a level test-mode signal is used to place the system in test mode. The technique illustrated in Fig. 11.4-5 can be simply ex-

TABLE 11.5-8 Table of states for a five-stage, modulus-9 twisted-ring counter

State	Q_5	Q_4	Q_3	Q_2	Q_1	Decoder
0	0	0	0	0	0	$Q_5'Q_1'$
1	0	0	0	0	1	$Q_2'Q_1$
2	0	0	0	1	1	$Q_3'Q_2$
3	0	0	1	1	1	$Q_4'Q_3$
4	0	1	1	1	1	$Q_5'Q_4$
5	1	1	1	1	0	Q_2Q_1'
6	1	1	1	0	0	Q_3Q_2'
7	1	1	0	0	0	Q_4Q_3'
8	1	0	0	0	0	Q_5Q_4'
0						

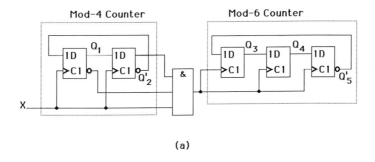

(a)

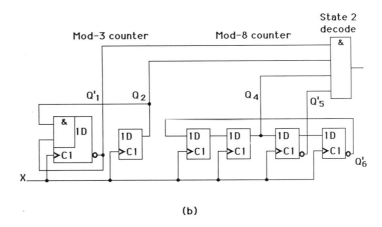

(b)

Figure 11.5-14 Modulus-24 composite counters: (a) series connection of Mod-4 and Mod-6 counters; (b) parallel connection of Mod-3 and Mod-8 counters.

TABLE 11.5-9 Sequence of states for the counter of Fig. 11.5-14 (Series combination of modulus-4 and modulus-6 twisted-ring counters)

State	Modulus-6 counter			Modulus-4 counter		State	Modulus-6 counter			Modulus-4 counter	
	Q_5	Q_4	Q_3	Q_2	Q_1		Q_5	Q_4	Q_3	Q_2	Q_1
0	0	0	0	0	0	12	1	1	1	0	0
1	0	0	0	0	1	13	1	1	1	0	1
2	0	0	0	1	1	14	1	1	1	1	1
3	0	0	0	1	0	15	1	1	1	1	0
4	0	0	1	0	0	16	1	1	0	0	0
5	0	0	1	0	1	17	1	1	0	0	1
6	0	0	1	1	1	18	1	1	0	1	1
7	0	0	1	1	0	19	1	1	0	1	0
8	0	1	1	0	0	20	1	0	0	0	0
9	0	1	1	0	1	21	1	0	0	0	1
10	0	1	1	1	1	22	1	0	0	1	1
11	0	1	1	1	0	23	1	0	0	1	0

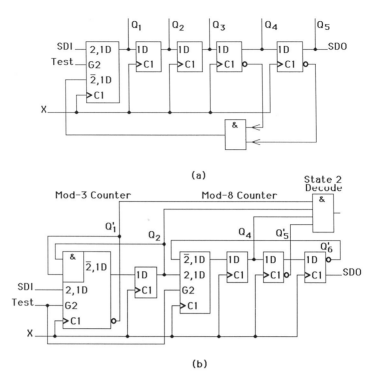

Figure 11.5-15 Shift counters with scan-paths: (a) Mod-9, 5-stage twisted ring counter; (b) parallel Mod-3 and Mod-8 counters.

TABLE 11.5-10 Sequence of states for the counter of Fig. 11.5-14b parallel modulus-3 and modulus-8 twisted-ring counters

State	Modulus-8 Counter				Modulus-3 Counter		State	Modulus-8 Counter				Modulus-3 Counter	
	Q_6	Q_5	Q_4	Q_3	Q_2	Q_1		Q_6	Q_5	Q_4	Q_3	Q_2	Q_1
0	0	0	0	0	0	0	12	1	1	1	1	0	0
1	0	0	0	1	0	1	13	1	1	1	0	0	1
2	0	0	1	1	1	0	14	1	1	0	0	1	0
3	0	1	1	1	0	0	15	1	0	0	0	0	0
4	1	1	1	1	0	1	16	0	0	0	0	0	1
5	1	1	1	0	1	0	17	0	0	0	1	1	0
6	1	1	0	0	0	0	18	0	0	1	1	0	0
7	1	0	0	0	0	1	19	0	1	1	1	0	1
8	0	0	0	0	1	0	20	1	1	1	1	1	0
9	0	0	0	1	0	0	21	1	1	1	0	0	0
10	0	0	1	1	0	1	22	1	1	0	0	0	1
11	0	1	1	1	1	0	23	1	0	0	0	1	0

TABLE 11.5-11 Sequence of states for parallel modulo-4 and modulo-6 counters

State	Modulo-6 Counter			Modulo-4 Counter	
	Q_5	Q_4	Q_3	Q_2	Q_1
0	0	0	0	0	0
1	0	0	1	0	1
2	0	1	1	1	1
3	1	1	1	1	0
4	1	1	0	0	0
5	1	0	0	0	1
6	0	0	0	1	1
7	0	0	1	1	0
8	0	1	1	0	0
9	1	1	1	0	1
10	1	1	0	1	1
11	1	0	0	1	0
12	0	0	0	0	0

tended to shift counters. The first stage must be changed to an MD flip-flop with one of the D inputs being the counter feedback and the other the test scan data. Figure 11.5-15a shows the twisted ring counter of Fig. 11.5-13 with an added scan-path input. Parallel counters must have each of their component counters modified individually. This is demonstrated in Fig. 11.5-15b for the parallel counter of Fig. 11.5-14b.

11.5-4 Linear Feedback Shift Registers

For applications where the binary patterns which the flip-flops of the circuit represent are important—as in counters or sequencers—the designs of Secs. 11.5-1 and 11.5-2 are most useful. When decoded signals on many leads are desired, as in a time pulse distributor, the designs of Sec. 11.5-3 are usually most efficient.

For situations in which the specific output patterns are not important, the most efficient circuit is often a **linear feedback shift register (LFSR)** or **linear sequence generator**. This circuit is also very important for encoding and decoding error control codes. Another use is generating pseudo-random numbers. This is an important feature of many test schemes, Sec. 10.6-1.

The general form of the basic linear shift register counter is shown in Fig. 11.5-16. The specific circuit for a three-stage linear shift register counter is shown in Fig. 11.5-17 and the corresponding sequence of states is given in Table 11.5-12.

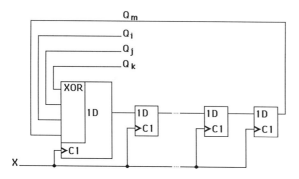

Figure 11.5-16 General form of basic linear shift register counter.

The linear shift register counter is similar to the ring and twisted-ring counters of the previous section in that it is basically a shift register counter. In the counters of Sec. 11.5-3, the state of the low-order stage depends only on the state of the highest-order stage. In the LFSR, the low-order stage depends on the state of intermediate stages as well as the high-order stage. However, the new state is not some arbitrary function of the flip-flop states—it is always the sum-modulo-2 or EXCLUSIVE OR function.

The circuit of Fig. 11.5-17 has three stages, $m = 3$, and cycles through $2^m - 1 = 7$ states. It is possible to obtain a $(2^m - 1)$ state counter for any m by choosing the appropriate Q_i to connect to the EXCLUSIVE OR gate driving the D_1 input. This is proved in [Elspas 59]. An m-stage linear shift register counter that cycles through $2^m - 1$ distinct states is said to be of **maximum length**. Such a counter will cycle through all of its 2^m possible states except the all-0 state. If it were to enter the all-0 state, it would remain in this state since the EXCLUSIVE OR of any number of zero inputs is zero. Thus zeros would be continually entered into the low-order flip-flop. Some technique is necessary to ensure that such a counter does not start off in this all-0 condition. It is also possible to add some circuits to the basic LFSR structure to cause it to cycle through all 2^n states. This technique is presented in Sec. 10.6-1, which discusses LFSR design in detail.

LFSR up-down counters can be designed by placing multiplexers at the input to each flip-flop. This is illustrated in Fig. 11.5-18. Since the LFSR is a shift counter, a scan path can be added as described at the end of Sec. 11.5-4. This feature is included in the Fig. 11.5-18 counter.

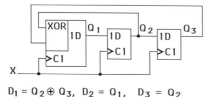

$D_1 = Q_2 \oplus Q_3, \quad D_2 = Q_1, \quad D_3 = Q_2$

Figure 11.5-17 Three-stage linear shift-register counter.

TABLE 11.5-12 Sequence of
states for three-stage linear shift
register counter $D_1 = Q_2 \oplus Q_3$,
$D_2 = Q_1$, $D_3 = Q_2$

State	Q_1	Q_2	Q_3
0	0	0	1
1	1	0	0
2	0	1	0
3	1	0	1
4	1	1	0
5	1	1	1
6	0	1	1
0	0	0	1

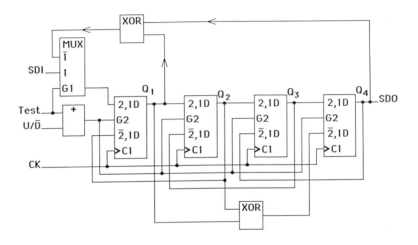

Up $D_1 = Q_1 \oplus Q_4$, $D_2 = Q_1$, $D_3 = Q_2$, $D_4 = Q_3$,

Down $D_1 = Q_2$, $D_2 = Q_3$, $D_3 = Q_4$, $D_4 = Q_2 \oplus Q_1$,

Figure 11.5-18 Four-stage LFSR up-down counter with scan-path test capability.

11.R REFERENCES

[BLEICKHARDT 68] Bleickhardt, W., "Multimoding and Its Suppression in Twisted Ring Counters," *Bell Syst. Tech. J.*, Vol. 47, No. 9, pp. 2029–2050, Nov. 1968.

[BURKS 54] Burks, A. W., R. McNaughton, C. H. Ollmar, D. W. Warren, and J. B. Wright, "Complete Decoding Nets: General Theory and Minimality," *J. Soc. Ind. Appl. Math.*, Vol. 2, No. 4, pp. 201–243, 1954.

[LSI 85] LSI Logic Corporation, *CMOS Macrocell Manual*, LSI Logic Corporation, Milpitas, CA, 1985.

[MORRIS 71] Morris, R. L., and J. R. Miller, eds., *Designing with TTL Integrated Circuits*, Texas Instruments Electronics Series, McGraw-Hill Book Company, New York, 1971.

[NATIONAL 84] National Semiconductor, *CMOS Databook*, National Semiconductor Corp., Santa Clara, Calif., 1984.

[RCA 83] RCA, "RCA CMOS Integrated Circuits," RCA Solid State Division, Somerville, N.J., 1983.

[TI 84] Texas Instruments, *The TTL Data Book*, Vol. 3, Texas Instruments, Inc., Dallas, 1984.

[WAKERLY 76] Wakerly, J. F., *Logic Design Projects Using Standard Integrated Circuits*, John Wiley & Sons, Inc., New York, 1976.

11.P PROBLEMS

11.1 Given $f_1(w, x, y, z) = \Sigma(0, 5, 7, 12, 13, 14, 15)$ and $f_2(w, x, y, z) = \Sigma(0, 2, 5, 8, 10, 12, 14)$:

    (a) Show the connections on the two 16-input multiplexers in Fig. P11.1a that will cause them to realize these two functions (no additional logic elements are necessary; assume that voltages representing logic 1 and logic 0 are available). *Note:* When $A = B = 1$ and $C = D = 0$, input 3 is connected to the output; when $A = 0$ and $B = C = D = 1$, input 14 is connected to the output, etc.

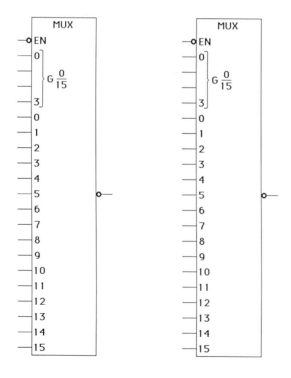

(a)

Figure P11.1a

(b) Repeat part (a) using the two eight-input multiplexers in Fig. P11.1b. (Additional circuit elements may be necessary; use only inverters, NAND gates, or NOR gates—as few as possible.) *Note:* When $A = 0$, $B = 1$, $C = 1$, input 6 is connected to the output.

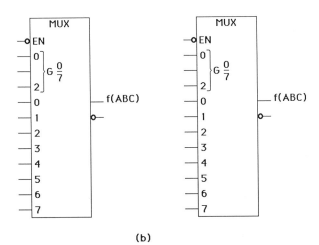

(b)

Figure P11.1b

(c) Repeat part (a) using the dual four-input multiplexer in Fig. P11.1c. (Additional circuit elements may be necessary; use inverters, NAND gates, or NOR gates—as few as possible.) *Note:* When $A = 0$, $B = 1$, inputs 2 are connected to the outputs. You are to realize both f_1 and f_2 using only one multiplexer.

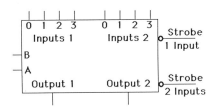

(c)

Figure P11.1c

11.2 You are to design a network that has 11 data bits as inputs and 16 output bits which represent the corresponding Hamming single-error-correcting, double-error-detecting code words. Use the 54180/74180 MSI device and clearly label each bit. Use odd parity.

11.3 Design a network to decode states 1, 2, 5, 6, and 21 in the circuit of Fig. 11.5-14a.

11.4 Design a series counter for modulus 96:
(a) Use component counters of moduli 4, 4, and 6.
(b) Use component counters of moduli 8 and 12.
(c) What set of moduli for the component counter requires the fewest flip-flops?
(d) Compare the complexities of complete decoding networks for the counters of parts (a) and (b).

11.5 A combinational circuit C is to be designed that has four inputs—w, x, y, z—and two outputs—F and G. In normal operation the inputs represent a word in the Gray code corresponding to a number from 0 to 9. The output F is to be 1 iff the input represents a value that is less than or equal to 4. If a noncode word is applied to the inputs, the output F is to equal 0 and the output G is to equal 1 (G is 0 for valid code word inputs). Assume that double-rail inputs are available.

(a) Assume that you are to design the circuit C in a semicustom chip using only one type of cell: a cell implementing the 54153 multiplexer. C can be realized with a single multiplexer cell by connecting two input variables to the common control inputs of the multiplexer cell. The other variables are connected to the individual multiplexer blocks, one of whose outputs realizes F and the other G. Show *all* possible implementations that satisfy the design specifications. Use the 54153 symbol in Fig. P11.6.

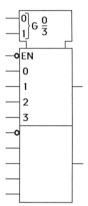

Figure P11.6

For parts (b)–(d), assume that you are to design the circuit C using a PLA.

(b) Design a nonfolded PLA using single-bit phase splitters. Use as few word lines as possible. Assume that a word line (horizontal) carries a signal to the AND of all bit lines having crosspoints on the word line. Label each of the word lines with the product realized.

(c) Design a minimum-area folded version of the PLA of part (b).

(d) Design a minimum-area nonfolded version of the PLA of part (b) using 2-bit decoders. Label each line clearly with an identification of the signal that it carries.

(e) Design a network using only NOR gates for the circuit C. Use as few gates as possible. Assume double-rail inputs are available.

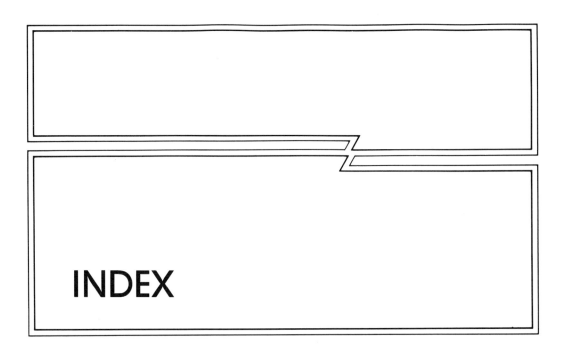

INDEX

Primitive polynomial, 458
Product:
    canonical, 38
    fundamental, 37
    lines, 238
    minimal, 204
Programmable array, 236
Propagation delay time, 101, 283
Property:
    single-clock, 336
    single-edge, 335
    external-trigger, 336
Propositional logic, 53
P-set, 89
Pseudo-exhaustive testing, 461, 472
Pseudo-noise, 459
Pseudorandom, 459
Pulse, 330
    bounded, 331
    input, 360
    mode, 328, 360
    negative, 330, 331
    outputs, 342
    positive, 330, 331
    rectangular, 331
    strobe, 519
    train, 331
    trapezoidal, 331
    width, 331

R

Races, 299, 366
Radix, 1
Radix complement, 8
RAM, 446
Random access scan design, 441
Random-pattern resistant faults, 457
Random testing, 457
Ratio, aspect, 123
Ratioed logic, 122
Ratioless circuits, 123
Reconfigurable register, 473
Reconfiguration techniques, 473
Rectangular pulse, 331
Rectifier, 125
Redundancy, 433, 447
Reed–Muller canonical expansion, 50
Reed–Muller canonical form, 448

Register, 303
    shift, 303
Reset input, 386
Residue, 169, 181
Response compression, 465
Reverse-biased diode, 125
Ring, Boolean, 57
Ring counter, 525–527
    self-initializing, 527
    self-correcting, 527
Ripple counter, 517
Rise time, t_r, 136
Rising edge, 330
RM networks, 448
ROM, 446
ROM-based design, 192
Row splitting, 245
Runt pulse, 82

S

Saturated switching, 135
Saturation region, 134
Scan, 433
Scan path, 514
Scan path counters, 530
Scan-set structures, 439
SCOAP, 430
Segmentation, 465
Self-test, 455
Self-verification, 455
Sensitized partitioning, 465
Sequential circuit, 273
    output specifications, 384
Sequential function, 317
Sequential network, 33
Serial signature analyzer, 468
Series-carry counter, 523
Series-parallel network, 78
Series switches, 32
Set:
    active, 87
    inactive, 87
    stable, 86
    unstable, 86
Set algebra, 56
Set and reset dependencies, 276, 277
Set-reset latch, 275
Setup time, 281, 326

Two-port flip-flop, 435
Two-stage circuit, 194
Type, function, 42

U

Unate, 173
Unbounded memory span circuit, 386
Union, 56
Unit-distance code, 17, 36
Universal set, 57
Universal shift register, 514
Unstable set, 86
Unstable variable, 86
Unused crosspoint, 240
Up/down counter, 522
Used crosspoint, 240

V

Vacuous variable, 169
Variable:
    internal, 289
    next-state, 289
    present-state, 289
    stable, 86
    transition, 331
    unstable, 86
Venn diagram, 57
Verification testing, 461
Very large scale integration, 490

VICTOR, 432
VLSI, 490
Voltage, threshold, 114

W

Wafer sort, 424
Walsh coefficients, 466
Wave, square, 331
Weight, binary pattern, 16
Width, pulse, 331
Wired AND, 104
Wired logic, 142, 426
Wired OR, 104
Word lines, 238

X

x_i-residue, 169
XOR gate, 48

Y

Y^+, 340

Z

0-set, 85

IEEE Standard Logic Symbols

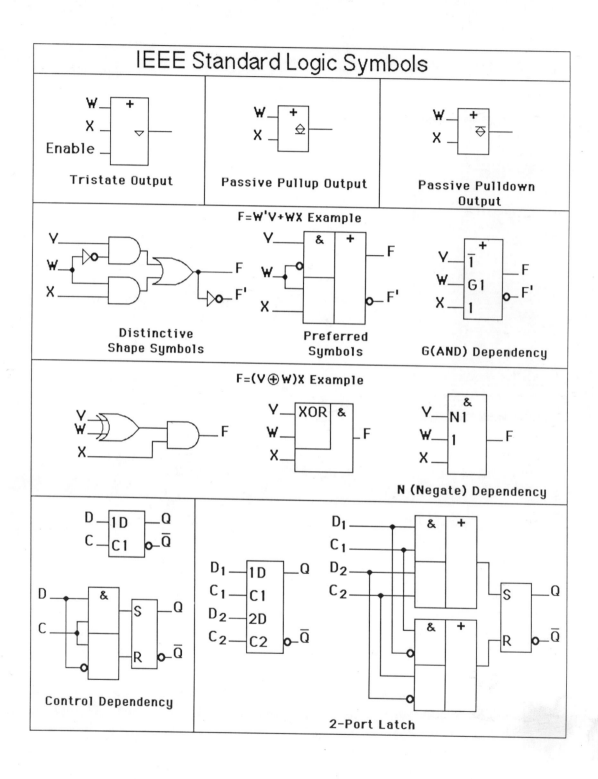

Tristate Output

Passive Pullup Output

Passive Pulldown Output

F=W'V+WX Example

Distinctive Shape Symbols

Preferred Symbols

G(AND) Dependency

F=(V⊕W)X Example

N (Negate) Dependency

Control Dependency

2-Port Latch